WORLDVIEW TRAINING

TEACHER MANUAL

UNDERSTANDING THE TIMES

A Summit Ministries Curriculum

Understanding the Times Curriculum
4TH EDITION, 2006

AUTHORS

David Noebel, Kevin Bywater, Jeff Myers, Connie Willems, Jeff Baldwin, Jr.,
Micah Wierenga, Todd Cothran, Jason Graham,
Mike Sligh, and Paul Ryle

EDITORS

Michael Bauman
Sharon Berry
James Bowers
Joel Brown
Jay Butler
Angela Bywater
Renee Cothran
John Dunham
Tom Eckblad
Chuck Edwards
Suzanne Florentine
Trudy Friesema
Ken Gasper
Holly Gooden
Sandi Gooden

Nancy Hay
Charissa Imken
Bill Jack
Abraham Lee
Amanda Lewis
Kara Linden
George Martin
Joel Putnam
Blake Roeber
David Rogers
Sarah Schultz
Jae Stellema
Sarah Tozlian
Sonnie Wierenga

Summit is an educational Christian ministry whose very existence is a response to our current post-Christian culture. Today, countless Christian youth have fallen victim to the popular ideas of our modern world. Most have adopted these ideas into their own worldview, while still others go on to renounce their Christian faith altogether.

Summit views its role in God's kingdom as a catalyst to counteract this alarming trend. However, our ultimate goal supersedes simply training. As Christians are challenged to stand strong in their faith and defend truth, they will also be equipped to have a positive influence on the society in which they live.

Fourth printing (2013), Printed by Bang Printing, Brainered, MN USA

SPECIAL CONTRIBUTORS

Kerby Anderson is National Director of Probe Ministries International. He holds degrees from Oregon State University, Yale University, and Georgetown University. He is the author of several books, including *Genetic Engineering*; *Origin Science*; *Living Ethically in the 90s*; *Signs of Warning, Signs of Hope*; and *Moral Dilemmas*. He also served as general editor for *Marriage, Family and Sexuality*. Kerby is a nationally syndicated columnist whose editorials have appeared in the *Dallas Morning News*, the *Miami Herald*, the *San Jose Mercury*, and the *Houston Post*. He is the host of "Probe," and serves as host of "Point of View" (USA Radio Network).

Dr. Michael Bauman is Professor of Theology and Culture, and Director of Christian Studies at Hillsdale College, Hillsdale, Michigan. He also is a former president of the Evangelical Philosophical Society, and was once a member of the editorial department of *Newsweek* magazine. Dr. Bauman has published numerous books, articles and political editorials; his books include *God and Man in the Twentieth Century*, *Man and Creation*, and *Are You Politically Correct?* He is a contributing editor for *Ultra Cycling* magazine and co-editor of *The Schwarz Report*. His latest books are *90 Days in the Christian Classics* and *Christianity A to Z*.

Dr. Francis J. Beckwith is Associate Professor of Church-State Studies and Associate Director of the J. M. Dawson Institute for Church-State Studies at Baylor University. Among his books are *Do the Right Thing: Readings in Applied Ethics & Social Philosophy*, *Relativism: Feet Firmly Planted in Mid-Air*, and *Politically Correct Death: Answering the Arguments for Abortion Rights*. He and his wife Frankie currently reside in Woodway, TX.

Dr. E. Calvin Beisner is Associate Professor of Historical Theology and Social Ethics at Knox Seminary. He holds degrees from the University of Southern California, International College, and University of St. Andrews (Scotland). Prior to coming to Knox, Cal taught at Covenant College and has for many years been an author and lecturer on issues of Christian faith and practice. He is a CAPO (Center for the Advancement of Paleo-Orthodoxy) Fellow and has been a contributing editor for such publications as *World Magazine*, *Christian Research Journal*, and *Crosswinds*. He also has written a number of books including: *Where Garden Meets Wilderness*; *Man, Economy, and the Environment in Biblical Perspective*; and *Answers for Atheists, Agnostics, and Other Thoughtful Skeptics*.

Dr. John C. Bergstrom is the Richard B. Russell, Jr. Distinguished Professor of Public Policy at the University of Georgia, Athens, Georgia. He teaches and conducts research related to natural resource, environmental, and agricultural issues and policy. As a Christian professor, he is interested in the integration of biblical teaching on stewardship and our responsibilities as stewards and managers of God's creation. He lives in Watkinsville, Georgia with his wife and four children and is a member of Faith Presbyterian Church (PCA) in Watkinsville.

Dr. Craig Blomberg is currently a Distinguished Professor of New Testament at Denver Seminary. Craig completed his Ph.D. in New Testament, specializing in the parables and the writings of Luke through Acts, at Aberdeen University in Scotland. In addition to writing numerous articles in professional journals, multi-author works, and dictionaries or encyclopedias, he has authored or edited 15 books, including *The Historical Reliability of the Gospels*, *Interpreting the Parables*, *Matthew* for the New American Commentary series, *1 Corinthians* for the NIV Application Commentary series, *Jesus and the Gospels*, *Neither Poverty nor Riches*, *Making Sense of the New Testament*, *Preaching the Parables*, and *Contagious Holiness*.

Dr. Raymond G. Bohlin is President of Probe Ministries. He received his Ph.D. in molecular biology from the University of Texas at Dallas. Raymond is the co-author of the book *The Natural Limits to Biological Change*, served as general editor of *Creation, Evolution and Modern Science*, and has published numerous journal articles. Raymond was also named a 1997–98 and 2000 Research Fellow of the Discovery Institute's Center for the Renewal of Science and Culture.

Kevin Bywater is a researcher, author, and lecturer for Summit Ministries and a current Ph.D. candidate in New Testament at the University of Durham, England. He holds a bachelor's degree in philosophy and a master's degree in theology. As a former member of the Church of Jesus Christ of Latter-day Saints, Kevin is dedicated to helping Christians understand and effectively reach members of pseudo-Christian religions. He has published articles on cults, worldviews, and Islam, and has co-authored (with David A. Noebel and J. F. Baldwin) *Clergy in the Classroom: The Religion of Secular Humanism*. Kevin, his wife, Angela, and their five children currently live in both Colorado Springs, Colorado, and Oxford, England, where Kevin is the Resident-Scholar for the Summit Oxford Program.

J. Todd Cothran served as Director of Curriculum and Resource at Summit Ministries. He holds a B.A. in communications from the University of South Carolina as well as an M.A. in Christian Apologetics from Biola University. Todd, his wife Renee (whom he met here on summer staff in 1993), and their four children love and cherish their community of friends here at the Summit as well as the vibrant and committed body of believers at their local church where Todd serves as a shepherding elder, Bible study leader, and Sunday school teacher.

Gary DeMar is Founder and President of American Vision, a worldview and apologetics ministry in Atlanta, Georgia. He has published a number of articles and books including *The Reduction of Christianity*, *Surviving College Successfully*, *America's Christian History: The Untold Story*, and *War of the Worldviews*. Gary lives in Atlanta, Georgia with his wife Carol. They have two grown sons.

F. Carolyn Graglia served from 1954 through 1959 as Attorney, General Litigation Section, Civil Division, Department of Justice, Washington, D. C.; Law Clerk, Judge Warren E. Burger, Court of Appeals, District of Columbia Circuit; Special Counsel for Federal Housing Administration litigation, Department of Justice, Washington, D. C.; Attorney, Covington & Burling, Washington, D. C. She retired from legal practice in 1959 to become a homemaker and mother of three daughters. When the children were grown, she consulted for several years on constitutional law and antitrust litigation and then began to write and lecture on family issues. She has published articles in *The Harvard Journal of Law and Public Policy*, *The Texas Law Review*, *The Weekly Standard*, *The Wall Street Journal*, *The Women's Quarterly*, *Claremont Review of Books*, and *The Brigham Young University Law Review*. She is also author of the book *Domestic Tranquility: A Brief Against Feminism*. Mrs. Graglia has been married for over fifty years to Lino A. Graglia, Professor of Law, University of Texas Law School.

George Grant is Director of the King's Meadow Study Center, Teaching Pastor at Christ Community Church (PCA), coordinator of the Gileskirk Curriculum Project, and instructor at Franklin Classical School. He is the author of dozens of books in the areas of history, biography, politics, literature, and social criticism, and he has written hundreds of essays, articles, and columns. His work on behalf of the homeless, for international relief and development, for racial reconciliation, and for the sanctity of life has been profiled in such varied media outlets as *The Wall Street Journal*, *The Washington Post*, Focus on the Family, The 700 Club, The Coral Ridge Hour, Point of View, Crossfire, *World Magazine*, and *Christianity Today*. His books include *The Micah Mandate: Balancing the Christian Life*, *Shelf Life: How Books Have Changed the Destinies of Men and Nations*, and *Going Somewhere: A Novel*.

Joseph P. Gudel is a long-time contributing writer for the *Christian Research Journal*, an ordained pastor in the Lutheran Church—Missouri Synod and a Ph.D. candidate at Concordia Theological Seminary in Fort Wayne, IN.

Dr. Phillip E. Johnson is the Jefferson E. Peyser Professor of Law, Emeritus, at the University of California at Berkley, where he taught for thirty years. Known as a founding father of the Intelligent Design movement, he is the author of *Darwin on Trial*, *Reason in the Balance*, *Defeating Darwinism by Opening Minds*, and *Wedge of Truth*, among others. He is also a regular columnist for Touchstone and is active in scientific debate. Phillip has two children and currently lives with his wife, Kathie, in Berkeley, California.

Scott Klusendorf is Founder and President of Life Training Institute. He travels throughout the United States and Canada training pro-life advocates to graciously and incisively make a defense of the lives of the unborn. He also addresses students and other groups on key bioethical issues, training staff and students at pro-family organizations such as Focus on the Family, New Jersey Right to Life, Ohio Right to Life, and Southern California Right to Life, to name a few. He has participated in 23 debates on abortion at the collegiate and graduate level. As a guest lecturer in bioethics, Scott has taught pro-life apologetics at both the graduate and undergraduate level at Orange Coast College and Trinity International University Law School. Scott is a Magna Cum Laude graduate of UCLA.

Greg Koukl is Founder and President of Stand to Reason, a ministry dedicated to training Christians to think more clearly about their faith and to make an even-handed, incisive, yet gracious defense for Christianity and Christian values in the public square. An award-winning writer, Greg has published the book *Relativism: Feet Firmly Planted in Mid-Air* with Dr. Francis J. Beckwith, and is also the author of *Precious Unborn Human Persons*. Greg received his B.A. in Bible from Azusa Pacific University; his master's in Christian Apologetics from Simon Greenleaf University and is working on his master's in Philosophy of Religion and Ethics at Talbot School of Theology. He hosts his own radio talk show advocating clear-thinking Christianity and defending the Christian worldview.

Charles Moore grew up in California. At age seventeen, under the influence of Young Life, he decided to follow Christ. After college, he went on to seminary and graduate school, where he received degrees in Philosophy of Religion and Ethics. After ten years of teaching at Denver Seminary, he and his wife moved to New York to become members of the Bruderhof Community. Since then, he has been an assistant editor at Plough Publishing. Charles has written numerous articles for various publications and compiled and edited a variety of books, including *Provocations: The Spiritual Writings of Kierkegaard* and *Tolstoy: Essential Writings*.

Dr. J. P. Moreland is a Professor of philosophy at Talbot School of Theology, Biola University in La Mirada, California. Dr. Moreland has 4 earned degrees: a B.S. in chemistry from the University of Missouri, a Th.M. in theology from Dallas Theological Seminary, an M.A. in philosophy from the University of California-Riverside, and a Ph.D. in philosophy from the University of Southern California. He has been involved in planting churches, debating on over 200 college campuses around the country, and serving with Campus Crusade for Christ for over 10 years, as well as authoring and co-authoring numerous books, including *Scaling the Secular City*, *Does God Exist?*, *Immortality: The Other Side of Death*, and *Love Your God With All Your Mind*. He has also published in over 40 articles and journals which include *Philosophy and Phenomenological Research*, *American Philosophical Quarterly*, *Australian Journal of Philosophy*, *Metaphilosophy*, and *Faith and Philosophy*. He, his wife Hope, and daughters Allison and Ashley live in Yorba Linda, California.

Dr. Jeff Myers is Associate Professor of Communication Arts at Bryan College, Dayton, Tennessee. He's also President of the Myers Institute for Communication and Leadership. He speaks to more than 50,000 people each year in corporations, schools, homeschool conferences, parent groups and youth-serving organizations. Over the last decade, Dr. Myers has worked with Summit Ministries to develop cutting-edge leadership experiences in Colorado, Tennessee, North Carolina, and Alberta, Canada. He is the author of six books and three video coaching systems including *Understanding the Times*, the curriculum that introduced worldview training to America's Christian schools, and *Secrets of Great Communicators*. Dr. Myers earned a Doctor of Philosophy degree from the University of Denver. He and his wife Danielle have four children—Graham, Emma, Cate, and Stuart—and live in Tennessee.

Nancy Pearcey is the Francis A. Schaeffer scholar at the World Journalism Institute, where her book *Total Truth* serves as the basis for a worldview curriculum. After earning an M.A. from Covenant Theological Seminary, she pursued further graduate work in philosophy at the Institute for Christian Studies in Toronto. Currently she serves as a Visiting Scholar at the Torrey Honors Institute at Biola University, and a Senior Fellow at the Discovery Institute. Pearcey has authored or contributed to several works, including the ECPA Gold Medallion winner *How Now Shall We Live?* and *The Soul of Science*.

Dr. Walt Russell is Professor of New Testament at Talbot School of Theology. Walt is the author of numerous articles and books, including *Playing With Fire: How the Bible Ignites Change in Your Soul*. Walt lives in Southern California with his wife of over 30 years and their two children Elizabeth and Jonathan. He's "bonkers" about saltwater fishing, jazz, and classical music, and rabidly follows the Kansas City Chiefs and Royals with J. P. Moreland, his best friend for over 30 years.

Dr. Leland Ryken is the Clyde S. Kilby Professor of English at Wheaton College, where he has taught for over 40 years. He has published over 25 books on such varied topics as literature and the arts from a Christian perspective, the Bible as literature, work and leisure, the Puritans, and Bible translation.

John Stonestreet is Executive Director of Summit Ministries. Mr. Stonestreet holds a M.A. in Christian Thought from Trinity Evangelical Divinity School and is on the Biblical Studies faculty at Bryan College. A popular speaker at camps, conventions, and conferences, he works annually with thousands of parents, teachers, and students on developing a biblical worldview, understanding comparative worldviews, defending the Christian faith, applying a biblical worldview to education, and engaging important cultural issues. He is a Fellow of the Wilberforce Fellows, a division of Breakpoint, and is the co-author with W. Gary Phillips and William E. Brown of *Making Sense of Your World: A Biblical Worldview*, 2nd. ed., as well as numerous web and journal articles. John joined the Summit team in 1999, and has served numerous roles including directing the eastern Summit programs in Tennessee and Virginia. He, his wife Sarah, and three daughters live in Colorado Springs, Colorado.

Table of Contents

UNDERSTANDING THE TIMES

Preparation

A Summit Ministries Curriculum

THE AIM OF THIS CURRICULUM

Many people think that those in the military, high government offices or important financial positions control the world. In this they are mistaken; our world revolves around *ideas*. Militaries exude power and authority, yet they are prisoners to the ideologies of their representative nations. Politicians and those in positions of governmental authority may think they rule the world, but they are held captive by the ideas they have embraced about government. Executives in large corporations may think they have the world by the tail, but they too are indebted to their ideas/beliefs about business practices/values and economic trends. Ideas lie behind every historical event and social policy. Ideas are the guiding force behind every twist and turn in public opinion; they determine what we accept or reject in the arts, media, business, medicine, education, government, church, family, etc.

We will never fully understand our world unless we understand the ideas that form its structure. Issues like stem-cell research, abortion, the homosexual rights movement, and political correctness will bewilder us if we divorce these issues from the ideas on which they are based. The reasons behind the cruelty of Ted Bundy, Joseph Stalin, or Adolf Hitler will elude us unless we understand their ideas. Without a thorough understanding of ideas, we will watch with feelings of helplessness and uncertainty as our world constantly tries to persuade us of the validity of its beliefs and practices.

Understanding the Times is about ideas. This curriculum will help you understand that everyone has a "worldview," a way of interpreting everything that happens in the world. The Bible has an explanation for the universe, but so does Islam, Secular Humanism, Marxism, Postmodernism, and the New Age movement. Each of these worldviews is founded upon ideas. A worldview will dictate (consciously or unconsciously) how we should interpret and respond to the world around us. If we can understand the prominent worldviews in our world, we will better understand the underlying framework of many issues that Christians face. We will learn how to anticipate the response of a Muslim, Secular Humanist, Marxist, Postmodernist, or New Ager. Where once you saw thousands of confusing issues, you will see a big picture. Moreover, as you journey through the complex yet enlightening information this curriculum contains, you will learn to see ideas from a biblical Christian perspective.

The goal of this curriculum is to help open your eyes to the war of ideas competing for your heart and mind. You will begin to realize that the worldly problems we call "issues" are symptoms, not the disease. The disease is found in Romans when Paul declares, "all have sinned and fall short of the glory of God" (3:23). Because all human beings are sinners (the *disease*), we will naturally produce and indulge in sin (the *symptoms*)—"For the wages of sin is death" (6:23a). We must start addressing the disease if we want to be effective in dealing with the symptoms.

Another way to look at this is to say that *ideas have consequences*. Since our world is utterly opposed to God, it produces bad ideas which, in turn, lead to bad consequences. Yet there is hope in the midst of this sinful world. Those who understand the ideas that rule the world will have the opportunity to influence the world of ideas. First Chronicles 12:32 tells the story of one small tribe in Israel that was chosen to lead because it "understood the times, and knew what Israel ought to do." It is our hope that you too will understand the times and thus know what God would have you do.

THE NEED FOR THIS CURRICULUM

Our goals for this curriculum are twofold. The first goal is defensive: we want to help protect Christian youth from being deceived by anti-Christian worldviews. The second goal is offensive: we want to train up Christian leaders who can actively champion the truth of Christianity in a culture of relativism, paganism, hedonism, and confusion.

> Nothing short of a great Civil War of Values rages today throughout North America. Two sides with vastly differing and incompatible world-views are locked in a bitter conflict that permeates every level of society... the struggle now is for the hearts and minds of the people. It is a war over ideas. And someday soon, I believe, a winner will emerge and the loser will fade from memory. For now, the outcome is very much in doubt.[1]

What James Dobson and Gary Bauer describe is the current struggle among worldviews as Christians, Muslims, Secular Humanists, Marxists, New Agers, and Postmodernists vie for the hearts and minds of

[1] James C. Dobson and Gary L. Bauer, *Children at Risk* (Dallas: Word, 1990), 19–20.

individuals. Many Christian students, parents, and teachers falsely assume that Christian youth are immune to false ideas simply because they have been raised in a Christian environment. However, even students raised in Christian homes, who attend church regularly, and are enrolled in Christian schools are vulnerable to non-Christian ways of thinking. Christian youth in large numbers are rejecting certain biblical truths or even turning away from Christianity altogether. Without proper worldview training, the trends outlined below will likely continue:

CHRISTIANS RENOUNCING THEIR FAITH IN COLLEGE: According to findings published in a UCLA dissertation, Dr. Gary Railsback notes that up to 59% of Christians renounce their faith before graduating from college (this is up from 51% in 1989). Shockingly, there is little statistical difference between Christian students enrolled at secular and Christian institutions.[2]

CHRISTIANS THINKING MORE LIKE HUMANISTS: Each year, thousands of Christian school students take the Nehemiah Institute worldview assessment test. Students are presented with a series of relevant questions, and then asked to pick the multiple-choice answer that best expresses their beliefs. Based on their answers, students are scored along a spectrum from "Biblical Christian" (100–70) to "Moderate Christian" (69–30) to "Secular Humanist" (29–0) to "Marxist" (anything below a '0' score). From 1988 until 2000, it was found that students enrolled in Christian schools moved from an average in the low 50s (meaning they scored at the lower end of "Moderate Christian") to an average of about 20 in the year 2000 (meaning they responded to key social, political, and religious issues like a Secular Humanist).[3]

REJECTION OF MORAL ABSOLUTES AMONG CHRISTIAN TEENS AND ADULTS: The well known Christian statistician George Barna reports that among teenagers, a mere 9% of Christian teens believe in moral absolutes versus 4% of non-Christian teens.[4]

While these trends are alarming, we must remember that God's truth is more powerful than the false ideas capturing the minds of our culture. For years, the Christian community has drawn a line between the *sacred* and the *secular*. Christians have been encouraged to focus only on "sacred" activities and avoid involvement with "secular" activities such as politics, culture, science, or philosophy. In reality, no such distinction exists. *Understanding the Times* is a call to understand the spiritual nature of the struggle between good and evil, and the way in which it impacts every area of life and culture—the distorted sexual mores, the rewriting of history to exclude God, and the attempt to impose a humanistic utopian vision on the world. This curriculum operates on the premise that *this* generation must be prepared to undertake a *pro-active* Christianity—one that seeks to *redeem* culture and all of God's creation, rather than *reject* it.

This curriculum does not teach that Christians are victims of some global conspiracy. It holds firmly, however, to the biblical description of evil as persuasive and in direct rebellion against God's will.

Years ago, Francis Schaeffer astutely noted that Christians were beginning to view the world in "bits and pieces instead of totals." In the twentieth century, Christians rather abruptly lost sight of their responsibilities in society, and gradually lost the ability to discern good from evil. Christianity entered a downward spiral in which we quickly lost the capacity to stand for righteousness and justice. Before long, complicated "issues" seemed so overwhelming that most Christians numbly retreated from their societal responsibilities into the comfort zone of *self*. Generally speaking, Christianity ceased to reflect God's love and character to the unbelieving world. Today, many Christians are more concerned with their personal faith, personal growth, and personal church than with the world at large that they are called to love and serve.

However, the current generation of Christians has started to notice the previous generation's shirking of cultural responsibilities, though they are perhaps unsure of what needs to change, how to take action, or even where they should begin. Assuming responsibility used be the mark of adulthood, but this timeless "rite of passage" between childhood and adulthood has become blurry. In its absence, young people often feel compelled to prove their adulthood by engaging in premarital sex, declaring independence, and so on.

[2] This study was done in 1989 by Gary Lyle Railsback, "An Exploratory Study of the Religiosity and Related Outcomes Among College Students," University of California at Los Angeles, 1994. The greatest losses were at Catholic universities, reporting 59% of Christian freshmen renounced their faith by their senior year. Protestant universities showed a 31% loss.
[3] In addition, Christian students in public schools scored considerably lower, with an average of 8.2 in 2004. Source: http://www.nehemiahinstitute.com/index.php
[4] Source: http://www.barna.org/cgi-bin/PagePressRelease.asp?PressReleaseID=106&Reference=C

Understanding the Times provides a constructive "rite of passage." Through it, we want to pass the torch to you, the next generation, by explaining the mistakes of the past and endowing you with the responsibility for shaping the future of the world.

USING THIS MANUAL

Before beginning this curriculum, it will be helpful to understand its structure and layout.

> *Teacher notes and discussion helps will be found throughout this curriculum in boxes just like this; where necessary, Student Manual page references will be provided in the following format:* SM p. 3

> Scope: Study the scope of this course, its layout, and activities, and plan the use of the curriculum according to your calendar. You have been given both a 180- and 90-day syllabus.

ICONS: The following icons are used throughout this manual in order to indicate the primary purpose and medium of the activity by which they appear.

Reading Assignment	Video Outline	Discussion Questions	Writing Assignment	Class Activity

> *Activities will appear in boxes just like this.*
>
> Corresponding activity handouts are found on the *Teacher's CD-ROM* in the "Handouts" folder.

UNITS: There are 10 units to this curriculum plus an Introduction and Conclusion section. The following elements are found within each unit:

1. **Table of contents:** At the beginning of each unit is a table of contents or section outline that lists the components and their corresponding page numbers. All textbook readings will be underlined, essays *italicized*, and videos "quoted."

2. **180-day and 90-day Syllabus:** Also at the beginning of each unit is both a two- and one-semester syllabus outlining your daily classroom and homework assignments.

> Both a one-semester and two-semester syllabus has been provided. Those doing one-semester could also choose to complete only the first half of the two-semester syllabus. Overall this would be less aggressive while still giving the students a solid foundation in five core disciplines.
>
> To prepare for each unit, look over the corresponding syllabus carefully and plan your classroom activities accordingly. You may also need to remind your students of what materials to bring to class (for example: Bibles, manuals, and/or textbooks). *Note*: Make-up days have been provided.

You can also use some discussion time to take a field trip (e.g. a creation tour of the zoo), or as an opportunity to bring in a special speaker (e.g. an expert in some worldview area or perhaps even an advocate of a non-Christian worldview like Mormonism or Islam).

3. **Video outlines:** Each unit has corresponding video presentations and outlines. Videos may be divided into multiple parts, and average between 20 to 40 minutes in length. Each presentation has a set of video outlines with fill-in-the-blank notes.

Remember to make arrangements for a TV/DVD player on these days. Also, it is wise to direct your students not to fill in their blank notes while watching the presentations. It is more important for your students to pay attention to the content than it is for them to fill in blanks. After each presentation, you should have ample time as a class to review and complete each outline. Since your students do not have direct access to each video, these outlines will serve as notes for the video subject content. Also, do not feel confined to the video lessons if you are capable of presenting the materials yourself.

4. **Video discussion questions:** Each video (with the exception of the intro videos for each unit) has an accompanying set of discussion questions. These questions should be completed individually after watching each presentation, and then reviewed the following day with the entire class.

Please review the questions and the provided responses before each classroom discussion period. Be prepared to examine these questions with your students, get them to disagree, play devil's advocate, etc. We cannot stress enough how important these in-class discussions are to this curriculum. The more involved your students are in the discussion, the better they will understand the materials.

5. **Textbook reading assignments:** Each unit has a corresponding textbook reading assignment. These assignments are found within the book titled *Understanding the Times*.

6. **Textbook discussion questions:** Each textbook reading assignment has an accompanying set of discussion questions. These questions should be completed individually after reading, and then reviewed the following day with the entire class.

Please review the questions and the provided responses before each classroom discussion period. Be prepared to examine these questions with your students, get them to disagree, play devil's advocate, etc. We cannot stress enough how important these in-class discussions are to this curriculum. The more involved your students are in the discussion, the better they will understand the materials.

7. **Essay reading assignments:** Each unit has corresponding essay reading assignments.

8. **Essay discussion questions:** Each essay reading assignment has an accompanying set of discussion questions. These questions should be completed individually after reading, and then reviewed the following day with the entire class.

Please review the questions and the provided responses before each classroom discussion period. Be prepared to examine these questions with your students, get them to disagree, play devil's advocate, etc. We cannot stress enough how important these in-class discussions are to this curriculum. The more involved your students are in the discussion, the better they will understand the materials.

9. **Dear Doug essay assignment (180-day syllabus only):** Each unit (except Unit Five and Conclusion) has a corresponding essay assignment. These essays will be 1–2 page written responses to problems addressed in letters from Doug, a friend who has just begun college.

> These assignments are found near the end of each section (except Unit Five and Conclusion). This assignment will be more difficult than most; thus you should grade accordingly. A rough outline of possible responses has been provided.

10. **Unit Test:** At the end of each unit (except Unit Five) is a corresponding unit test. The questions for these tests may be matching, multiple choice, true/false, fill-in-the-blank, or short answer. Each test is based on the video, textbook, and essay discussion questions as well as the Fact Sheets.

> If your students need help, study guides for this test are available on the *Teacher's CD-ROM* in the "Study Guides" folder. The masters for the unit tests are found on the *Teacher's CD-ROM* in the "Tests" folder. Print off the appropriate test and make one copy for each student.

11. **Worldview Paper:** At the end of Unit Five there will be a 4–6 page paper defining and comparing the Christian, Islamic, Secular Humanist, Marxist, New Age, and Postmodernist worldviews.

12. **Comprehensive Exam:** At the end of the Conclusion Unit, there will be a comprehensive multiple choice exam covering all the materials from the course. Questions for the comprehensive exam are found in the video, textbook, and essay discussion questions as well as the Fact Sheets.

> The masters for this exam are found on the *Teacher's CD-ROM* in the "Tests" folder. Print off the exam and make one copy for each student.

13. **Extra Credit:** At the end of each unit, we suggest giving your students an opportunity for extra credit by helping them to put their faith in action. A number of potential ideas are listed below.

> - Adopt a child (e.g. with Compassion International or World Missions)
> - Serve in a soup kitchen
> - Work in a local downtown mission
> - Go street witnessing
> - Volunteer in churches for a variety of jobs
> - Send Christmas cards to shut-ins
> - Host children's birthday parties at a rehabilitation center
> - Begin a senior citizen outreach program (e.g. reading, painting, or writing letters)
> - Start a recycling project
> - Volunteer at a local ministry, charity, or non-profit business
> - Offer free childcare for children of young parents
> - Prepare a meal for a struggling family
> - Do a community service project (e.g. pick up trash, clean a park, etc.)
> - Many other possibilities exist
>
> We cannot emphasize enough the importance of providing opportunities for action in this course. Without action, students may relegate what they are hearing to dry academic philosophies and not realize that these ideas can directly impact their lives on a daily basis. Therefore, while we did not want to overload your syllabus, we do think it is important for you to offer some of the previous ideas for

extra credit. These opportunities will help students to move beyond in-class performance to true assimilation. Also, the list is by no means exhaustive. Encourage creativity and allow students to submit proposals for extra credit activities.

FACT SHEETS: A number of fact sheets are provided with the manual. They are categorized according to various worldview subjects, and provide helpful resources for college research and writing assignments.

TRANSLATION: For this curriculum, we have chosen to use the New King James Version of the Bible unless otherwise noted.

GRADING: There are 2000 points possible for this course (1500 for the one-semester):

180-Day

Assignments	Number	Points	Total Points	Points Earned
Dear Doug Letters	10	50	500	
Unit Tests	10	100	1000	
Worldview Paper	1	200	200	
Final Exam	1	300	300	

90-Day

Assignments	Number	Points	Total Points	Points Earned
Unit Tests	10	100	1000	
Worldview Paper	1	200	200	
Final Exam	1	300	300	

An Excel spreadsheet for grading is located on the Teacher's CD-ROM in the "Grading" folder. Because of varying circumstances, you may not be able cover all the material provided. Therefore, grading may need to be adjusted accordingly.

COLLEGE CREDIT: Bryan College (a nationally accredited university in Dayton, Tennessee) has teamed up with Summit Ministries to offer college credit to students taking the Understanding the Times course. For those following the 180-day syllabus, three credit hours are offered; for those following the 90-day syllabus, two credit hours are offered. You can earn college credit now!

Requirements:
1. Submit application and tuition to **Summit Ministries** by May 1st (halfway through the year)
2. Complete the *Understanding the Times* syllabus requirements (180- or 90-day) with at least a C:
    a. Read the revised 2nd edition textbook and all assigned supplemental essays
    b. Write the 4–6 page research paper
    c. Write 10 responsive Essays (3 credit hours only)
    d. Take 10 unit Tests and the Final Exam
3. Submit copies of your Unit Tests and Final Exam to **Summit Ministries** by June 1st

For more information, please visit the High School Curriculum page at www.summit.org. If you are interested in pursuing this option, ask your teacher for an application.

This is an excellent opportunity for students to earn college credit while still in high school. The tuition cost is nominal (roughly equivalent to a community college course) and there is little extra work for student or teacher. Download the application from the Summit website (High School Curriculum).

If you have further questions, please email (utt@summit.org) or call 719-685-9103.

ADDITIONAL SUMMIT RESOURCES

SUMMIT HOMEPAGE: The online hub for Summit's conferences, curriculum, and resources. www.summit.org

SUMMIT TRUTH & CONSEQUENCES: A free monthly e-news article that reviews current issues from a worldview perspective. To sign up, visit the RESOURCES page at www.summit.org.

SUMMIT JOURNAL: A free monthly review of the news and cultural events, edited by Dr. David Noebel. To sign up, visit the RESOURCES page at www.summit.org.

SUMMIT WEBSTORE: For the most up-to-date selection of worldview-oriented books, videos, and CDs covering such topics as apologetics, Darwinism, Relativism, Pluralism, Skepticism, and many others, click on the STORE tab at www.summit.org.

SUMMIT JAT (JUST A THOUGHT): A Summit Ministries community discussion project aimed at thinking through issues of faith and worldview. To join in, visit the RESOURCES page at www.summit.org.

SUMMIT CONFERENCES: To learn more about our intensive two-week educational conferences that analyze the major worldviews of our day and contrast them with the Christian Worldview, please visit the CONFERENCES page at www.summit.org.

Educators can attend our Spring Conference, which is held each year in Colorado Springs. For more information, please visit the CONFERENCES page at www.summit.org.

ADDITIONAL RESOURCES
Included below is a list of organizations and publications that can provide you with valuable information. To explore some of the topics you will be studying, we've provided you with places to begin your own research. Please note that this list is not intended to be comprehensive and that the inclusion of an organization on this list does not constitute an implicit endorsement of that organization by Summit Ministries.

PUBLICATIONS:
Note: Many organizations give free subscriptions to students.

Areopagus Journal | **Apologetics Resource Center** | www.arcapologetics.org | 205.408.0136 |

Biblical Worldview | **American Vision** | www.americanvision.org | 770.222.7266 |

Christian Research Journal | **Christian Research Institute** | www.equip.org | 888.700.0274 |

Citizen Magazine | **Focus on the Family** | www.fotf.org | 800.232.6459 |

First Things | **Institute of Religion and Public Life** | www.firstthings.com | 712.627.1985 |

Freeman Journal | **Foundation for Economic Education** | www.fee.org | 800.960.4333 |

Human Events | www.humanevents.org | 800.787.7557 |

Imprimis | **Hillsdale College** | www.hillsdale.edu | 517.437.7341 |

Intercollegiate Review | **Intercollegiate Studies Institute** | www.isi.org | 800.526.7022 |

Journal of the Evangelical Theological Society | **Evangelical Theological Society** | www.etsjets.org |

Philosophia Christi | **Evangelical Philosophical Society** | www.epsociety.org |

Southern Baptist Journal of Theology | **Southern Baptist Theological Seminary** | www.sbts.edu |

Summit Journal | **Summit Ministries** | www.summit.org | 719.685.9103 |

World Magazine | www.worldmag.com | 800.951.6397 |

ONLINE RESOURCES:
Access Research Network | www.arn.org | 719.633.1772 |

American Vision | www.americanvision.org | 770.222.7266 |

Christian Answers | www.christiananswers.net |

Christian Apologetics & Research Ministry | www.carm.org |

Christian Research Institute | www.equip.org | 888.700.0274 |

Discovery Institute | www.discovery.org | 206.292.0401 |

Leadership University | www.leaderu.com | 972.516.0516 |

Probe Ministries | www.probe.org | 972.480.0240 |

Stand to Reason | www.str.org | 719.685.9103 |800.273.2766

Summit Ministries | www.summit.org | 719.685.9103 |

Veritas Forum | www.veritas.org | 617.491.2055 |

THINK TANKS:
Cato Institute | www.cato.org | 202.842.0200 |

Concerned Women for America | www.cwfa.org | 202.488.7000 |

Eagle Forum | www.eagleforum.org | 618.462.5415 |

Family Policy Network | www.familypolicy.net | 202.657.5384 |

Family Research Council | www.frc.org | 800.225.4008 |

Federalist Society | www.fed-soc.org | 202.822.8138 |

Foundation for Thought and Ethics | www.fteonline.com |

Heritage Foundation | www.heritage.org | 202.546.4400 |

CAMPUS MINISTRIES:
Campus Crusade for Christ | www.campuscrusadeforchrist.com | 407.826.2000 |

Intercollegiate Studies Institute | www.isi.org | 800.526.7022 |

Probe Ministries | www.probe.org | 972.480.0240 |

Ravi Zacharias International Ministries | www.rzim.org | 770.449.6766 |

Reformed University Fellowship | www.ruf.org |

We *highly recommend* that you take advantage of this list and begin a resource library for your class. The time investment at the beginning of the school year will be greatly outweighed by the worthwhile results. To begin your library, e-mail or call any of the organizations in which you are interested, asking them to send available resources. When the information arrives, organize it in a topical filing system in your classroom. Make this filing system available to students as they research term papers or take action on issues. Your students will also benefit simply by knowing that these organizations and resources exist. In fact, you may want to photocopy the list of resources for them, encouraging them to take it with them to college. Many of these organizations will be happy to help when your students are researching college papers.

Everything following this box is included only in the Teacher Manual.

TEACHING HELPS

Keys to Successful Video Presentations:
Preview *at least* the first 15 minutes of each presentation with the class notes in front of you in order to gain a basic understanding of the speaker and message. Also, make sure video presentations can be easily seen and heard by the entire class. This may mean rearranging your classroom, putting your TV on a stand, or getting external speakers.

Leading a Group Discussion:
Understanding the Times is a course that will spark discussion and debate. In fact, this is one of the main purposes of the class. Students need to experience exchanging ideas with one another. Keep in mind that there are at least three different purposes for discussion questions.

One purpose is *review*. Students are asked a general question to reinforce a point the text or the video presentation made, and to make sure that they understood the information they encountered.

Another purpose is *reflection and observation*. Students will be asked, "What did you think of what the speaker said? Do you agree? Why or why not?" or "What have you seen that might reinforce what the speaker said?" You may want to "warm up" a discussion with these types of questions, even when they aren't specifically listed.

A third purpose is *connection*. This is the most common type of question, particularly for discussion days. These questions will also be the hardest to answer! Students are asked to connect what they just heard with something else they know. The purpose of these questions is to move students past simply parroting what they have heard to actually *thinking* about a new idea. As the teacher and discussion leader, you may need to ask a question, such as "If the Bible is historically accurate, how should Christians respond to scientific discoveries that seem to contradict it?" and then ask several more questions to guide students to the correct answer. This requires learning to help students tie thoughts together. Build on the answers they give you so they can see the continuity between ideas as they reason to conclusions.

Please note that there is a distinct difference between a question/answer time and a discussion. In a strict question/answer session, you ask a question and one person answers it. Then you ask another question and another person answers. In a discussion, one person responds to your question and then others respond to the first person's comments. Both types of discussion can be very profitable.

As the teacher, you are responsible for creating an atmosphere that is conducive to discussion. Make it clear to the class that everyone's response matters, not just two or three eager students. Listen to the students, and interact in a way that encourages them to speak up again, even if their response was not previously correct. Encouraging the entire class to participate may also mean taming the enthusiasm of some of your more vocal students while encouraging the quieter ones to share. (One idea is to give a particularly vocal student the job of leading the discussion in an evenhanded way.)

A key to leading discussion is learning how to ask questions and make comments. By using good facilitating skills, you can 1) connect with the group, 2) include quieter students, 3) clarify responses, and 4) help students evaluate responses. A few examples of each follow:

1. Connecting with the group:
   - "I know this question seems a little detailed/confusing/involved at first, but let's think through it."
   - "I can really see it coming together by what you're saying!"
   - "Is this starting to make sense?"

2. Including quiet participants:
   - "Kevin, you look like you don't agree with what Todd said. Why?"
   - "Micah, we haven't heard from you in a while. What do you think about that?"
   - "Jason, you're smiling/look puzzled/etc…what are you thinking?"

3. Clarifying responses:
   - "What do you mean by _____?"
   - "So, what you are saying is that _____ (restating the response)?"
   - "Why do you think that?"
   - "How do you know that to be true?"
   - "On what are you basing that conclusion?"

4. Helping students evaluate responses:
   - "We've basically been hearing _____. Does anybody disagree with that? Why?"
   - "I think that's a great response, but let's pretend I'm a skeptic. Why should I believe that?"
   - "Can anybody think of a different angle than what Charissa just said? Why?"
   - "I'm going to 'thicken the plot' by throwing this in: _____. How does this change what we've been saying?"

Another key to leading a discussion is having a balance of interaction and guidance. Students should be allowed to interact with each other and with you, but you *will* need to guide the discussion. Don't be afraid to challenge students. Discussions are a great time to help students move beyond sloppy thinking. Do this by using questions that help to clarify and evaluate responses. You can also play the devil's advocate role. Consistently challenge students to base their replies on Scripture rather than conjecture (keep a couple of concordances on hand for looking up verses). There will be times when you will need to bring the discussion back on track, or step in with truth when the students have slipped into speculation.

Above all, a discussion doesn't have to follow the same format every day. Consider some of the following ideas for adding variety to your discussions:

1. If your class is large, divide into smaller groups (4–6 students) for a preliminary discussion, then have the groups come back together to present their conclusions. Or, have each of the smaller groups research only part of the issue at hand.
2. Leave the room for five minutes, letting the students conduct a discussion on a specific question, then have them report on their conclusion and reasoning process when you return.
3. Brainstorm all the possible answers to a question. Write them on the board or overhead as they are introduced. Which worldviews are represented? Which answers reflect the biblical Christian worldview?
4. Ask how a person from each of the worldviews discussed in the textbook would answer a question.
5. Ask students to write down their answers to a question, then gather them up and read them anonymously.
6. Let a student lead the discussion.
7. Divide the class into two groups, with each group taking one side of the issue.
8. When you're going to carry a discussion over to the next day, take the opportunity to have your students survey parents, siblings, and friends on the issues.[5]

TEACHING STUDENTS TO BE READERS:

It is not enough to hand a book or an article to a student and tell him, "Here, read this." Today, many students have to be taught *how* to read. They may know how to take the words off the page, but we want them to go beyond that and take the *ideas* off the page. For this class, the readings are useless if they are not understood.

Students should learn to "pre-read" a book by knowing who the author is, when it was published, the key points it will cover (table of contents), and who and what the author thinks is important (index and bibliography). Key points for each chapter may be gleaned by reading the sub-headings and last few paragraphs.

Encourage students to begin marking their books (if they own them). Key points, phrases, people, dates, words, and definitions should be highlighted, underlined, or annotated. In the margins, they can jot questions, comments, or connections with other passages in the book. (When reading books that they don't own, students can use a piece of paper as a bookmark, using it to record their comments.) Also, encourage them to create their own index. As they read and note key points or quotes, they can record the page numbers and topics on a blank page in the back of the book. They will find this incredibly useful when they are going back to research a topic or find a particular quote. When the students have finished the reading, they should be able to summarize it, listing the author, the targeted audience, and the key points.[6]

---

[5] For more information on leading discussions, consult one of the many books available on the subject, especially Neal McBride's *How to Lead Small Groups* (Colorado Springs, CO: NavPress, 1990).

[6] For more resources on teaching reading skills, read one of these or other available books: Mortimer J. Adler and Charles Van Doren, *How to Read a Book* (New York: Touchstone, 1972); James W. Sire, *How to Read Slowly* (Downers Grove, IL: InterVarsity, 1978); Gene Edward Veith, *Reading Between the Lines* (Wheaton, IL: Crossway, 1990); and Neil Postman, *Amusing Ourselves to Death* (New York: Penguin, 1985).

TEACHER MANUAL

UNDERSTANDING THE TIMES

Introduction

Topics:
Apologetics
Hermeneutics
Leadership
Worldviews

A Summit Ministries Curriculum

SECTION OUTLINE

180-DAY SYLLABUS

DAY	IN CLASS	HOMEWORK	
1	READ Student Manual 'Preparation'	READ <u>UTT</u> Textbook 'Introduction 0.1'	
2	WATCH "Introduction to Worldviews" video		
3	REVIEW "Introduction to Worldviews" video questions	READ <u>UTT</u> Textbook 'Introduction 0.2'	
4	REVIEW <u>UTT</u> Textbook 'Introduction 0.2' questions	READ <u>UTT</u> Textbook 'Introduction 0.3'	
5	REVIEW <u>UTT</u> Textbook 'Introduction 0.3' questions		
6	READ *Playing with Fire* essay	ASSIGN Dear Doug Letter	
7	REVIEW *Playing with Fire* essay questions		
8	WATCH "Loving God with Your Mind" video P1		
9	WATCH "Loving God with Your Mind" video P2		
10	REVIEW "Loving God with Your Mind" video questions		
11	WATCH "Ambassadors for Christ" video		
12	REVIEW "Ambassadors for Christ" video questions		
13	READ *Total Truth* essay		
14	REVIEW *Total Truth* essay questions	Dear Doug Letter assignment DUE	
15	TAKE Introduction Test		

90-DAY SYLLABUS

DAY	IN CLASS	HOMEWORK	
1	READ Student Manual 'Preparation'	READ <u>UTT</u> Textbook 'Introduction 0.1'	
2	WATCH "Introduction to Worldviews" video	READ <u>UTT</u> Textbook 'Introduction 0.2-0.3'	
3	REVIEW "Introduction to Worldviews" video questions		
4	REVIEW <u>UTT</u> Textbook 'Introduction 0.2-0.3' questions		
5	TAKE Introduction Test		

"INTRODUCTION TO WORLDVIEWS"
WITH KEVIN BYWATER

I. We Are in a _____Battle_____

    A. Two kinds of people: _____captors_____ and _____captives_____

    B. **Colossians 2:8:** to not be taken _____captive_____

    C. **2 Corinthians 10:3–5:** to take every thought _____captive_____

    D. **2 Timothy 2:22–26:** to set the _____captives_____ free

II. What is a Worldview?

"A world view is a way one views the whole world. And since people have vastly different views of the world, depending on the perspective from which they view the world, it is clear that one's world view makes a world of difference. A world view is a way of viewing or interpreting all of reality. It is an interpretive framework through which or by which one makes sense out of the data of life and the world." — Norman L. Geisler and William D. Watkins, *Worlds Apart*, 11.

"A worldview is the perspective through which you understand and approach life and the world."

III. Illustrating Worldviews

    A. _____Glasses_____

    B. _____Filter_____

    C. Optical illusions

IV. Questions Every Worldview Must Answer

    A. What is _____God_____?

    B. What is _____human_____ ?V. The Worldview Triangle

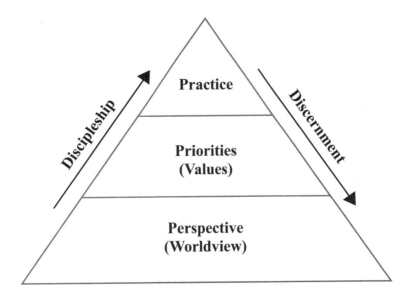

V. The Worldview Triangle

One key worldview principle: _____ideas_____ have consequences

VI. Developing Your Own Worldview

A. Don't _____read_____ your Bibles… _____study_____ them!

B. Read other worldview materials.

C. Put yourself in challenging situations.

D. Stretch your intellectual boundaries.

E. Engage in _____cultural_____ analysis.

F. Watch your time closely.

VII. The Goals of Developing a Christian Worldview

A. Be a faithful disciple of Christ.

B. Know _____why_____ we believe _____what_____ we believe.

C. Learn to think consistently.

D. Learn to engage our culture without compromise.

E. Be faithful _____ambassadors_____ of Christ.

"INTRODUCTION TO WORLDVIEWS"
VIDEO QUESTIONS

Answer the questions below on a separate sheet of paper and be prepared to review your answers in class. Reflection Questions will not be found in the text. These are merely designed to help you start thinking about issues from a worldview perspective.

1. What are three key verses used in the discussion of worldviews?

[Read each of these passages and try to supply some context.]

In Colossians 2:8, Paul warns the Colossians not to be taken captive by vain or deceptive philosophies. But what constitutes a vain or deceptive philosophy? Would we recognize one if we saw it? The point of worldview analysis is to analyze the elements of the Christian worldview, and to compare the Christian worldview to other worldviews. If one does not know what is Christian and what is not, then he or she may unknowingly or unquestioningly adopt an idea contrary to the teachings of Christ.

In 2 Corinthians 10:3–5, Paul informs the Corinthians that Christians should demolish strongholds (i.e. arguments and pretensions) set up against the knowledge of God. This is to say that Christians don't just avoid adopting false worldviews; they also spread truth and correct the falsehoods that others believe.

In 2 Timothy 2:22–26, Paul instructs Timothy to teach truth to others that have been taken captive. The hope is that they will be set free. It is important to note that Paul requests that Timothy "not quarrel; instead, you must be kind to everyone, able to teach, not resentful." Notice the attitude that Christians are to have when talking with others.

2. What is a worldview? What are some illustrations?

A worldview is a way of viewing or interpreting the whole world. It is an interpretive framework or something you look through when interpreting reality. A worldview is the perspective through which you understand and approach life and the world. All people have a worldview—a way in which they see and interpret the world.

First, a worldview is much like a pair of glasses. If one has a correct prescription, then he or she can see the world as it truly is. With an incorrect prescription, the world can become distorted.

Second, a worldview is like a filter. It enables one to filter out impurities.

Third, a worldview is like an optical illusion. Just as one can see different things in an optical illusion, different individuals can interpret reality differently. This does not mean, though, that there are different ways the world truly exists and works.

3. **What questions must every worldview answer? Why are these questions relevant?**

First, every worldview must answer the question, "What is God?" How one answers this question can greatly impact the way one perceives the world and how he or she chooses to live within it. Here is how some positions address this question:

- Atheism—there is no God
- Agnosticism—no one can know if there is a God
- Polytheism—there are many Gods
- Pantheism—everything is God
- Monotheism—there is only one God
- Deism—there is a God, but he has nothing to do with the world today

Second, every worldview must answer the question, "What is humanity?" This leads to subsequent questions:

- Do we have a sinful nature?
- Are we basically good?
- Are we perfectible?

[Other questions to discuss: 1) What is moral? 2) From where did humanity originate?]

4. **What is the purpose of the worldview triangle? Why is it important to develop a Christian worldview?**

The worldview triangle is a pictorial illustration used to demonstrate how our worldview ultimately affects our behavior. Our worldview is the foundation upon which our priorities and practices are built. As we develop our own worldview, we are engaged in discipleship. As we encounter the world around us and seek to understand other people's worldviews we are involved in discernment.

If we develop our worldview according to the Bible, our behavior will begin to look like that of Christ. Likewise, we can compare our practices with our worldview assumptions and see if we are living out what we claim to believe.

5. **Reflection Question: What does the dictum "ideas have consequences" mean?**

[Answers will vary, but discuss the consequences that could follow these ideas: there is no God; miracles cannot happen; and God did not create the world.]

UNDERSTANDING THE TIMES
INTRODUCTION QUESTIONS

Answer the questions below on a separate sheet of paper and be prepared to review your answers in class. Answers to the Reflection Questions will not be found in the text, but are designed to help you start thinking about issues from a worldview perspective.

INTRODUCTION 0.2

1. **What is a worldview and what are some of the fundamental questions a worldview answers?**

Essentially, a worldview is the way we view our world and our place in it. A worldview answers fundamental questions such as *Why are we here? What is the meaning or purpose of life? Is there a difference between right and wrong? Is there a God? Are humans just highly evolved animals?* [UTT 0.2.2]

2. **How do Norman Geisler and William Watkins define a worldview? What are two illustrations that demonstrate how a worldview works?**

"A worldview is a way of viewing or interpreting all of reality. It is an interpretive framework through which or by which one makes sense of the data of life and the world."

- **Eyeglasses**—If your prescription is not correct, what you see through your glasses will be distorted. Without the proper prescription, glasses will not help you see the world; rather, they will keep you from seeing the world as it truly is.

- **Tree**—Like the roots of a tree, a worldview is essential to life and stability. Just like the roots of a tree, we do not see someone's worldview, we only see the exposed part of the tree—their actions. [UTT 0.2.3]

3. **How is the term "worldview" defined in Understanding the Times?**

A worldview refers to any bundle of ideas, beliefs, convictions, or values that provides a framework or map to help you understand God, the world, and your relationship to God and the world. Specifically, a worldview should contain a particular perspective regarding each of the following ten creational disciplines: theology, philosophy, ethics, biology, psychology, sociology, law, politics, economics, and history. [UTT 0.2.3]

4. **Reflection Question: Does a person's belief in the existence of God affect his or her life? If yes, give an example of how that belief may affect his or her ideas about life.**

[Answers will vary greatly, but there should be a logical conclusion from the students' beginning premise.]

SM
6

UNDERSTANDING THE TIMES

7

If people believe in God, then they believe that there is a supernatural realm above and beyond matter. This would lead to the possibility of standards for truth and morality. If a person does not believe in the existence of God, humanity is just matter in motion. Man has no intrinsic worth, and morals are not independent from human beings.

5. **Reflection Question: Francis Schaeffer said, "The basic problem of the Christians in this country in the last eighty years or so, in regard to society and in regard to government, is that they have seen things in bits and pieces instead of totals." What does Schaeffer mean by "bits and pieces?"**

[Answers will vary. However, in the discussion time, try to guide them using this answer.]

We have compartmentalized our lives. We see our relationship with Christ as something that is completely separate from what we do at work, play, in the ballot box, etc. We need to understand that God's Word is relevant to every area of our lives, not just church-related activities. He has something to say about economics, politics, law, philosophy, and social relationships. We need to see all of the world and our activities within this world as being under the lordship of Christ.

ARTICLE ACTIVITY

Look through the newspaper and different magazines to find short articles that deal with various topics that can be categorized under the different worldview disciplines (have at least one article per student if possible). You do not need an article for every discipline, and some articles may fit under two or three disciplines.

Write the ten disciplines on the board. Have the students read the articles and then ask the class which disciplines that article would fit under. You may want to highlight parts of the article to make it easier for your students.

INTRODUCTION 0.3

6. **Which verses from Genesis fit with the worldview disciplines listed in the *Understanding the Times* textbook?**

Genesis 1:1	"In the beginning God created the heavens and the earth"	Theology and Philosophy
Genesis 2:9	"knowledge of good and evil"	Ethics
Genesis 1:21	"after their kind"	Biology
Genesis 2:7	"man became a living soul"	Psychology

Genesis 1:28	"Be fruitful and multiply"	Sociology and Ecology
Genesis 3:11	"I commanded you"	Law
Genesis 9:6	"Whoever sheds man's blood"	Politics and Law
Genesis 1:29	"it shall be for food"	Economics
Genesis 3:15	"enmity between you and the woman"	History [UTT 0.3.2]

7. In what way does the person of Jesus Christ underline the significance of each discipline?

Colossians 2:9	"fullness of the Godhead"	Theology
John 1:1	Christ is the Logos of God	Philosophy
John 1:9; 3:19–20	"the true light"	Ethics
John 1:4; 11:25	"the life"	Biology
Luke 1:46–47; Titus 2:13	"Savior"	Psychology
Luke 1:30–31; Isaiah 9:6	"Son"	Sociology
Genesis 49:10; Isaiah 9:7	Christ is lawgiver	Law
Revelation 19:16; 1 Timothy 6:15; Isaiah 9:6; Luke 1:33	"King of kings and Lord of lords"	Politics
Psalm 24:1; 50:10–12; 1 Corinthians 10:26	Christ is owner of all things	Economics [UTT 0.3.2]

8. According to 2 Corinthians 10:4–5, once we understand the world, what are we to do?

"Demolish arguments and every pretension that sets itself up against the knowledge of God." [UTT 0.3.3]

9. **What evidence supports the claim that Secular Humanism is "religious" in nature?**

- *Humanist Manifestoes I, II*, "no deity will save us, we must save ourselves…"
- John Dewey's book titled *A Common Faith*
- *Torcaso vs. Watkins*
- Humanist counselors in religious listings
- *American Humanist Association*'s religious tax-exempt status
- Car ornament—Fish with Darwin's name inscribed
- Archie J. Bahm's *The World's Living Religions* lists Humanism as a religion
- *Humanist Sermons* edited by Curtis W. Reese
- Ian S. Markham's *A World Religions Reader* lists Secular Humanism as a religion. [UTT 0.3.5–6]

---

10. **What legal and constitutional problem should result from classifying Secular Humanism as a religion? Can humanist teaching be considered *neutral*? Why or why not?**

- Using the humanistic interpretation of the First Amendment, religion in public schools (be it humanistic or otherwise) is a First Amendment violation.
- No educational approach is neutral. To leave God out is a theological decision. It implies that God is irrelevant and unimportant to life. [UTT 0.3.6]

PLAYING WITH FIRE
BY WALT RUSSELL

THE HAZARDS OF READING ON A BATTLEFIELD

As she worked her way toward the front of the room, I could tell the young woman was really angry with me. Her eyes were blazing and her jaw was set. This was surprising because the setting was fairly benign: speaking to a large evangelical church's singles group on "How to Interpret the Bible." At the beginning of my two times with them, however, I was already offending the troops! I braced myself.

Twenty-four year-old "Janet" (not her real name) was angry at my emphasis on seeking to discover authors' intentions when we read their texts. She was an evangelical Christian and a second grade teacher in a public school. She prided herself in helping her 20 students learn to love literature. She would read them a story as they gathered around her, and then ask each child, "What does the story mean to you?"

She prodded them to come up with their own unique meanings. With such strong encouragement, the class of 20 would eventually have 20 different meanings for the one story. Janet sensed that I was opposed to such "love of literature." Pouring a little emotional gasoline on the fire, I said, "Janet, you're certainly doing your part to insure that these 7 year-olds will never recover from a radically relativistic view of meaning!" Now I had her full attention.

Actually, Janet's and my little story about where a text's meaning resides is really part of a larger, more tangled story that's over a hundred years old. It started with some American literary critics early in the 20th century who shifted the focus from the author to the text. This literary perspective, later called "New Criticism," banished the author and focused instead on a "close reading" or "explication" of the text. When created, a text supposedly becomes an independent creation, like a newborn set free on its own. The autonomous text's meaning is discovered by studying the way it naturally goes together as a whole. New Criticism triumphed in the United States from about 1930 to 1960. As the text moved into the spotlight, authors were shuffled to the periphery.

But to understand Janet's and my little discussion we need to know the story from 1960 to the present. This is because the movement away from authors did not stop at the text. Rather, it continued its movement all the way to us as readers. In the last 40 years, reading and interpreting has been redefined from *seeking the intentions of authors* through reading their texts to *continually recreating the text through the presuppositions of readers*. Since the 1960s the emphasis has shifted to the astonishing assumption that readers not only create the meaning, but also in some sense *create the text itself* through the contouring of their presuppositions! With this view none of us can really share the same text!

The classical view of meaning is that a text is *a window* into an author's intentions. For example, we peer through the window of the biblical text to interpret what the Divine and human authors intend to say. By contrast, the postmodern sense is that a text is *a mirror* by which readers generate meaning. Janet was holding up a mirror to her second graders and encouraging them to generate their own meanings in light of their own images. The irony is that this does not teach a "love of literature," but rather fosters a self-centered fascination with one's own thoughts! If this is how Christians interpret the meaning of the Bible, then we are trapped within our own mirrors—our own set of presuppositions. We are not hearing God's voice, only our own. We are trapped inside our own heads.

The first problem with this view of meaning is that any positive presentation of it is self-refuting. In order to communicate "readers create meaning," relativistic authors have to scab off of the real world and the way meaning actually works to communicate their relativistic ideas. In other words, they expect us to interpret accurately their authorial intention that readers can't get to authorial intention! Or approach it from another perspective: If you're a student, ask your professor who expounds this view of meaning to reread your paper on which she gave you a D until she creates a meaning for it worthy of an A. Say that it's unfair that she graded *you* harshly for *her* poor reader-generated meaning! No one can live in a world where readers generate meaning because it doesn't exist.

Another problem with the present relativism in meaning in the West is the very fact that it is *in the West*. The 30 percent of the world that lives in the West has reaped the bitter fruit of a 500-year march toward extreme individualism. Those of us born right after World War II have reached the lunatic fringe in living out a radical and narcissistic self-absorption. It has destroyed our marriages, families, churches, national cohesion, and meaningful sense of community.

The good news is that our children have sensed the futility of this radical perspective and are saying, "We can't take it anymore! We don't want to deny the group dimension of ourselves anymore. We want to have meaningful connections with one another. We want to have stable community and long-lasting relationships."

Good move. Now simply stop denying the universal dimension of language too! Recognize that words, ideas, and genres are public, sharable things that we use in order to communicate with one another. While an individual intersects with them, the components of language are essentially group oriented things. They make individual communication possible. While we complicate the interpretive process with our individual presuppositions, they are not an insurmountable barrier. We simply recognize the "fuzzing" that our presuppositions can cause and seek to use good interpretive methods to transcend any clouding they may bring.

The Church in the West has been deeply impacted by this misunderstanding of meaning. We need go no further than the main question we ask when interpreting the Bible: "What does this verse mean to you?" The trickle-down of a century of bad interpretive theories has led to our widespread relativistic interpretation of the Bible. We have been profoundly wounded in the midst of the spiritual warfare that has surrounded the issue of meaning. Our anti-intellectualism has actually increased the casualty list.

Another culprit is our naiveté about the setting in which we read. We read right in the middle of a remarkable spiritual battlefield. While the casualties are initially subtler, they are ultimately more obvious. The spiritual warfare is blazing around us. It has effectively neutralized the greatest wealth of Bible study resources available in the history of the Church. Not by preventing their publication, but by undercutting their usefulness with a relativistic view of meaning! Why do I need a Bible dictionary to help determine Paul's meaning in Philippians 1:6 if the ultimate trump card is what it means to me? How brilliantly diabolical and strategic such a view of meaning is. It effectively cuts us off from God's voice and imprisons us within our own voice. It is Satan's ancient question, "Indeed, has God said?…" in postmodern dress.

Perhaps it is no overstatement to imagine that when you pick up your Bible and start reading it, you are instantly transported to the field of spiritual battle. Perhaps that funny odor is not burning pizza but flaming arrows; perhaps you need to avoid being a casualty! Probably not a bad idea also to be fighting for the right army! These are just some of the hazards of reading on a battlefield.

'INDIANS SLAY TIGERS' AND BRAKING FOR GENRES

"INDIANS SLAY TIGERS!"—the newspaper headline virtually screams out at you. The thought of something being slain is repulsive. You're gripped by a mental image of southern India's Bengal tiger. You imagine its beautiful face, its stripes and piercing eyes. Then your image is shattered by the sudden blast of a high-powered rifle. You see the exquisite creature writhe in pain, fall gracelessly in its tracks and die. Having read no further than the headline, you feel sick, as if you've witnessed something tragic.

But *should* you feel this way? The slaughter of an endangered species—especially one as magnificent as the Bengal tiger—is horrifying, no doubt. But suppose you failed to notice that the headline "INDIANS SLAY TIGERS!" appeared in the *sports page* of the morning paper. Clearly enough, it now refers to different Indians, different Tigers, and a different manner of slaying than you originally thought. And is it really that tragic that the Cleveland Indians badly beat the Detroit Tigers in a major league baseball game last night? Not unless you're a long-suffering Detroit Tigers' baseball fan. But how do you now know that the headline is about baseball and not tiger-slaying in India? You look at the words "INDIANS SLAY TIGERS" and you know exactly what each word means. When you combine these words, how can they not mean exactly what you first thought they did—that *Indians slay tigers*? Answer: because their meanings are communicated (as the meanings of *all* words are) through *genres*!

Whether we recognize that we are doing so or not, we interpret all things in life, from casual conversations to scholarly articles, in terms of their perceived genres or types of communication. When we develop an ability to discern cues within a text that indicate what kind of literature we're working with and what to expect (or not to expect) from it, we have achieved what some call "literary competence." We develop literary competence by growing up in a culture and learning its various genres—its various styles of communication. If we have literary competence, after reading "INDIANS SLAY TIGERS!" in the sports page, we would never picture tigers in India because we would instantly know that correct interpretation within *this* genre requires assuming that "TIGERS" and "INDIANS" refer to *teams* rather than people from India and large striped cats. Our interpretation of any section in the newspaper begins instantaneously when we recognize the genre and adjust our expectations accordingly. The beauty of genres is that they are public, sharable forms of communication that immediately enable the understanding of meaning. Genres are one of God's enduring gifts of common grace that help us communicate to one another with accurate understanding.

The *words* of the Bible are God-breathed, by the Holy Spirit, into the human-crafted *genres* exhibited in the Bible. We find every God-breathed word of Scripture within a genre. Because genres set limits on our possible interpretations of words, if God had *not* placed the words of Scripture within genres, we wouldn't understand one word of the Bible. So God has spoken to us "in many portions and many ways" (Hebrews 1:1) through particular biblical genres such as historical narrative, law, poetry, wisdom literature, apocalyptic literature, prophecy, gospels, letters, parables, and on and on. If our literary competence with the Bible approaches the literary competence we have with the morning newspaper, we should be able to jump into any part of the Scriptures and interpret its words accurately. But sadly, much of our Bible-reading parallels our weeping for Bengal tigers after reading a headline in the sports section of the newspaper!

In front of a large adult fellowship in an evangelical church, I recently spoke on the topic of being genre-sensitive in reading the Bible. To illustrate, I turned to Proverbs 22:6, "Train up a child in the way he should go, even when he is old he will not depart from it." I asked, "Can we claim this as a promise for parents?" Not wanting to appear a fool, no one ventured an answer. Most assumed that we could claim it as a promise and had, in fact, done so many times! To provoke them a bit further, I shared a proverb from American history—*early to bed, early to rise, makes a man healthy, wealthy, and wise.* "Anyone want to claim that as a promise?" I asked, rhetorically. "No. Why not?…Because it's a proverb," I said, answering my own question. "Then why do you think that you can change a *biblical* proverb into a promise?" I anticipated the answer that eventually emerged from the fog: "Because this proverb about child-raising is *in the Bible*!" I deadpanned, "So what?" Their response: "God can supernaturally do whatever He wants in the Bible."

True, God *can* do whatever He wants, in the Bible and elsewhere. If He *wants*, God can tell us how to make lasagna through the gospel of John, tell us that Christ died for our sins through a cookbook and, of course, promise the salvation of our kids through Proverbs 22:6. But how is this relevant? If their answer is correct and *we* can change *God's* proverbs into promises, then we really have no idea what God is saying in Proverbs, do we? If Proverbs 22:6 isn't a proverb (or *is* a proverb, but doesn't need to be *interpreted* as a proverb), then we don't know *what* it is or *how* to interpret it. Having no limit for its possible interpretation, it can morph into whatever *we* want it to be. It really has no genre except what we choose to give it, based on our present needs. One person can make it a promise, another can make it a riddle, and the cynical, burnt out parent can make it an ironic joke. Without genre, it is vague and meaningless, and we really don't know what God intended to say. What it does provide, however, is an occasion for us to craft God's words into whatever words we want to hear!

Hopefully, those of you familiar with such methods of interpretation get the idea of how foolish and dangerous much of our Bible reading has become. It is another example of the tragic shift in interpretive focus from seeking authors' intentions to unpacking readers' presuppositions. When we ignore genres in the interpretive process, we are ignoring one of the most important aids to understanding. Why? Because genres are one of those *community things* that authors and readers must share if they want to communicate clearly and efficiently with one another. When I ignore the chosen genre of a biblical passage, I effectively *individualize and privatize* the interpretive process and jerk the Bible out of everybody else's hands. Whether I'm teaching the passage or reading it, I have taken it out of the public arena where we can share and discuss its meaning.

The personal cost of ignoring biblical genres may also be great. I can still picture a distinguished, older gentleman I conversed with two decades ago. We were studying Proverbs that Saturday and I had just claimed that proverbs are not promises but instances of wisdom literature that emphasize wise choices. I used the example of Proverbs 22:6 and the earnest but erroneous claiming of that proverb by parents as a promise in child-rearing. The dear fellow literally stood up from his chair, red-faced and flustered. He and his wife had two boys who appeared to trust Christ as children but wandered from the faith as teenagers and had not returned as adults. As faithful parents, he and his wife had gotten on their knees and prayed for their wayward sons several times each week, claiming the "promise" of their return in Proverbs 22:6 for over 20 years! In the midst of their parental pain over the eternal well-being of their sons, they took comfort in the "promise" of Proverbs 22:6. Imagine the disillusionment in God and His "promises" that would inevitably accompany their years of false hope if their sons never returned to the Lord. What's worse, the pain and disillusionment were due to some well-intentioned but genre-ignoring saint who made a proverb into a promise—somewhere in the process of interpreting Proverbs 22:6, God's words became his words and God's intended meaning was distorted.

Such, however, does not have to be the case if we will brake for the genres of the Bible. As the diversity of biblical literature testifies, God seems to.

OVERCOMING VERSE-BITE CHRISTIAN CULTURE

"Never Read a Bible Verse!" That's the title of a little booklet my friend and Christian radio personality, Gregory Koukl, has written to help people read the Bible well. What great advice. "That's right, never read a Bible verse. Instead, always read a paragraph—at least." But the current is flowing the other way in our popular sound-bite culture. Not to be left out (or left behind!), the Church has its own version of sound-bite culture: *verse-bite culture*. In verse-bite culture we take a sentence or sentence-fragment from a biblical paragraph, memorize it out of context, write it on a little card, put it on a billboard, a plaque, a rock, etc. Somehow we think that just because this little chunk of Scripture has a verse number in front of it, it was meant to be a freestanding unit of thought. Nothing could be further from the truth.

Apart from the fact that chapter and verse divisions weren't added to the New Testament text until 1560—long after the New Testament's inspired authorship—there is a more important reason for never reading just a Bible verse, and instead reading at least the paragraph that contains it.

By nature, meaning comes from the top down, from a text's larger units to its smaller ones. The paragraph is there because of the *whole text's* thesis. The sentence (or "verse") is there because of the *paragraph's* thesis. The word is there because of the *sentence's* thesis. You get the idea. The contours of the larger units of a text determine the meaning of its smaller units. This is also the way our minds work—from the big idea down to its smaller parts. The same is true of the Bible. A biblical sentence (verse) is simply a part of a paragraph and develops some aspect of the *paragraph's* big idea. Therefore, the *minimal* unit of thought to read is the paragraph. A wise Bible reader will learn to think in terms of paragraphs and will regularly ask, "What's the big idea of this paragraph?"

Let's test this approach to reading the Bible by looking at a well-known verse of Scripture, 1 Thessalonians 5:22—"Abstain from all appearance of evil." I confess that whenever I encounter this verse, I picture old, withered saints shaking their bony fingers in younger believers' faces and exhorting them about some questionable behavior. In this recurring scenario, the godly, mature Christians find it necessary to exhort the younger saints not because they have done something that *actually is* evil, but simply because they behaved in a manner that could have the *appearance* of being evil.

This understanding of the teaching of 1 Thessalonians 5:22 can be traced back to the King James Version of 1611. The KJV chose the word "appearance" for the Greek word *eidos*, which means *visible form, outward appearance, kind or sort*. Since this translation emerged, well-intentioned Christians have focused only on the "outward appearance" aspect and concluded that we are not only to avoid evil, but we are also to avoid anything that could *outwardly appear* to be evil. Hence, the genesis of the widely used ethical dictum, "Avoid every appearance of evil." However, there are multiple problems with this interpretation.

One is that it doesn't fit into the big idea of the paragraph containing it. In fact, this understanding is totally secondary to the paragraph's big idea. Let me briefly explain.

1 Thessalonians is the Apostle Paul's letter to a group of new Christians being persecuted by their fellow citizens in northern Greece. It's an adversarial context for the church, so Paul spends much of his time defending his church-planting team's integrity and actions in chapters 1–3. In chapters 4–5 ("the moral

exhortation" section), he addresses five successive threats to the life of this church body. 1 Thessalonians 5:12–22 addresses the fifth and final significant issue facing this new band of Christians.

Verses 12–22 deal broadly with the concerns that arise when the church gathers for her weekly assembly. Paul gives instructions about fostering healthy church body life in this context by rightly esteeming leaders (verses 12–13), dealing sensitively with the saints' varying needs (verses 14–15), establishing a joyful assembly (verses 16–18), and not squelching the ministry of the Holy Spirit in prophetic utterances in the assembly (verses 19–22). Note that verse 22 helps develop the exhortation about prophecy in the church. While the paragraph covers a broad range of issues, these issues coherently develop the big idea of "what our body life should look like when the church gathers."

By briefly working our way down from the broader context of the whole letter to the paragraph (5:12–22), we're now ready to look at the immediate context for verse 22. Notice the logical flow of the argument about prophetic utterances in verses 19–22:

"**19 Do not quench the Spirit;**"—*This is the general exhortation of the argument.*

"**20 do not despise prophetic utterances.**"—*A specific NEGATIVE aspect of the exhortation.*

"**21 BUT examine everything carefully;**"—*A contrasting POSITIVE aspect of the exhortation.*

"**hold fast to that which is good;**"—*What we should do with GOOD prophecies after examining them.*

"**22 abstain from every form of evil.**"—*Or "abstain from every evil form of utterance."—This is what we should do with EVIL prophetic utterances.*

Note that the topic is *very specific*. It is about the specific topic of prophetic utterances when the church officially gathers. As is generally the case with Scripture, God and the human authors are very specific in their discussions. They seldom sprinkle broad moral sayings like "avoid every appearance of evil" in free-standing fashion. Rather, they usually speak in a closely argued style developing a big idea, especially in the New Testament letters. Such is the case with 1 Thessalonians 5:22. Paul is exhorting the young Christians at Thessalonica to stay away from every evil prophetic utterance. However, by removing verse 22 from its very specific paragraph development, we abstract the language from its anchor and create a much more general, vague concept—*a verse-bite*. (Yes, in a nice tone, I've just said that *we distort God's words and thoughts!*) This seems to be an enormous price to pay for not taking a few extra seconds to read the unit of thought—at least the paragraph—containing the verse in question. The Bible's big ideas are expressed in the big ideas of its paragraphs and we should attend to them.

Moreover, if 1 Thessalonians 5:22 is a broad, moral dictum, did Jesus avoid every appearance of evil? I think not! One of His constant criticisms at the hands of religious people was that He spent time with "defiling people" like tax gatherers, swindlers, irreligious people ("sinners"), and probably even prostitutes. Though He was perfect, sinless—though He never did anything that was *actually* evil—by the standards of the religious, Jesus seemed regularly to have the *appearance* of evil. But perhaps this is the accusation we must bear along with Jesus rather than inappropriately withdrawing from the sin-scarred people in our lives. Perhaps this is also part of our rebuke at the hands of those who don't read 1 Thessalonians 5:22 in context. Perhaps this is part of the bitter fruit of a verse-bite Christian culture.

GRAVE LESSONS ABOUT APPLICATION

I was staring into the open grave of my son Christopher. It was an unspeakably painful moment. The nightmare all parents dread had become my life. Had I been physically able to muster more tears, I would have been weeping uncontrollably. As I watched four men struggle to lower a steel lid over the grave vault holding Christopher's miniature white casket, I realized I would see his little smiling face no more, and run my fingers through his beautiful blond hair never again. We would never snuggle together or touch one another again. Our time together was *over*. As I stood there, looking into what felt like an abyss, I realized that I was in the most despairing, skeptical, and faithless state I had ever been in. I felt like cursing God for the rest of my life. I was on the edge of the dark, bottomless pit of hell.

The excruciating pain of my son's death was a defining moment for me, profoundly shaping my view of God's Word. Previous to that moment, while God's Word had been central to my life, I thought its primary purpose was to give me guidance and doctrinal stability. While I knew His Word was about real human experiences (like suffering and death), it had seemed flat, two-dimensional, like a blueprint or a map. To me, it had been little more than a divinely inspired collection of *information*. I had experienced no great loss or defeat in life up to that point, and I even thought that 1 Thessalonians 4:13–18 (which deals with the death of loved ones) was about nothing more than the timing of Christ's return. Sure, a few Christians in Thessalonica died, but that was simply an occasion for Paul to teach about the end-times.

Over the years, I had logged quite a bit of time studying 1 Thessalonians 4:13–18, trying to understand it. I sought to comprehend the Apostle Paul's teaching about the relationship between death and Christ's coming for His church. I struggled to know the *facts* about Jesus' raising the dead at the rapture of the church, and once I knew these facts, I even meditated upon them. In other words, I laid a *basis of knowledge* about this part of God's Word. And part of my knowledge was the correct application of the passage: "Therefore encourage one another with these words" (verse 18).

In a culture that is rapidly moving into emotivism, the above paragraph is terribly out of step. How dare I use words like "study," "understand," "comprehend," "facts" and "knowledge" when talking about death?

I used these strong, cognitive words intentionally, because one of the purposes of the Word of God is to give us *knowledge*; we are instructed to *learn* about the things Scripture recounts. While this isn't the ultimate end of God's Word, it is certainly the essential beginning. The Bible has a very real cognitive dimension; *knowledge* of certain things is absolutely necessary for meaningful living on planet earth. Quite simply, we must know what biblical passages mean before we can apply their meaning to our lives.

As I pondered the fact that my son's little body was being covered by a steel lid and several feet of dirt, I wondered how God could possibly resurrect his body through such obstacles. It was at this curious, yet horrifying moment that God graciously reminded me of my study of 1 Thessalonians 4:13–18. I began to ponder with new tear-clouded eyes Paul's graveside theology for the grieving Thessalonians:

> [13]But we do not want you to be uninformed, brothers, about those who are asleep, that you may not grieve as others do who have no hope. [14]For since we believe that Jesus died and rose again, even so, through Jesus, God will bring with him those who have fallen asleep. [15]For this we declare to you by a word from the Lord, that we who are alive, who are left until the coming of the Lord, will not precede those who have fallen asleep. [16]For the Lord himself will descend from heaven with a cry of command, with the voice of an archangel, and with the sound of the trumpet of God. And the dead in Christ will rise first. [17]Then we who are alive, who are left, will be caught up together with them in the clouds to meet the Lord in the air, and so we will always be with the Lord. [18]Therefore encourage one another with these words. (ESV)

While these verses contained rich truths about the end times, this passage suddenly seemed far more oriented toward families and friends grieving the death of loved ones. It was theology wrapped in real, gritty, painful, emotion-filled experience. It was shaped to address not an abstract and mechanical interest in the end-times, but the tear-stained eyes of believers who had lost their friends and family members, even their children. It was addressed, at that moment, *to me*. It was God's Word to me, pulling me back from the abyss of despair and unbelief. It was God's Word to me, giving me emotional comfort and a hope that could overcome unspeakable tragedy. It was God's Word to me in my grief, so that I could grieve my heart out, yet "not grieve as others do who have no hope." In that graveside realization, I learned to apply God's Word in a very different way. Perhaps I began to apply it in the way God intended, with both my mind and heart, with *both* my intellect and my emotions. At that moment I learned how desperately I needed to apply God's Word to my life.

Although it has been almost 22 years since my graveside pondering of 1 Thessalonians 4:13–18, I continue to unpack the significance of this experience. It was pivotal in helping me wed the *informing* dimension of the Bible with its *transforming* one. My scales had been tipped toward the information/knowledge end and needed to be balanced with the corresponding transformational intention of the Scriptures. It is always a both/and. While my generation has emphasized the Bible's informing dimension, younger generations are hungering for its transforming dimension. Perhaps my generation's imbalanced emphasis on knowledge has fueled your generation's imbalanced emphasis on experience. Neither is complete by itself. We must know the Bible's *information* before we can experience the Bible's *transformation*. I could never have been comforted by the remarkable truths of Christ's uniting of loved ones at the "catching-up" of the church without first *knowing* those truths. More bluntly, I could never have experienced this timely application of God's Word in the midst of the darkest moment of my life if I hadn't first mastered the information about it. It was a grave lesson, but a life-changing one, about application.

---

*This essay originally appeared as a four-part series on the *Boundless* website:

Walter Russell, "The Hazards of Reading on a Battlefield," [article online] http://www.boundless.org/features/a0000825.html
Walter Russell, "Indians Slay Tigers," [article online] http://www.boundless.org/features/a0000842.html
Walter Russell, "Overcoming Verse-Bite Culture," [article online] http://www.boundless.org/features/a0000853.html
Walter Russell, "Grave Lessons about Application," [article online] http://www.boundless.org/features/a0000864.html

**Reproduction rights granted by *Boundless* and Walt Russell.

PLAYING WITH FIRE
ESSAY QUESTIONS

Answer the questions below on a separate sheet of paper and be prepared to review your answers in class.

1. **Based on the context of 1 Corinthians 8:1, what does Paul mean when he states "knowledge puffs up, but love builds up?"**

Paul is certainly not advocating ignorance. He is emphasizing that we need to use our knowledge and understanding for the benefit of others, not simply to demonstrate how smart we may be. In other words, truth should be used to build others up, not to beat others up.

Using the principles that you have learned from this essay, answer the following questions regarding Matthew 18:19–20.

2. **How are these verses typically understood?**

These verses are typically understood in one of two ways:
- That prayer is answered through agreement of multiple prayers.
- That Jesus' presence is promised at any gathering of two or three of his children, whether it is a prayer meeting, worship time, or just about anything else.

3. **To which paragraph do verses 19–20 belong?**

Verses 19–20 belong to the paragraph enveloped by 15–20.

4. **What theme is presented in the verses 21–35?**

The theme of verses 21–35 is forgiving a brother who sins against you.

5. **What phrase is repeated in verses 15 and 21?**

The repeated phrase is "sins against you."

6. **The first reference to "two or three witnesses" occurs in Deuteronomy 19:15. How is this phrase understood in the context of verses 15-21?**

This phrase was used to explain the procedure for establishing an accusation against someone. Two or three witnesses were required to testify to prevent one person from bringing an unverifiable charge.

SM
14

INTRODUCTION

7. In what three places in the New Testament do we find the phrase "two or three witnesses?"

> 2 Corinthians 13:1, 1 Timothy 5:19, Hebrews 10:28
>
> - **2 Corinthians 13:1**—There are two traditional understandings of this passage. First, the Apostle Paul could be referring to the fact that he has already taken two trips to Corinth and will be taking a third, thus equating each trip with a "witness." The second is that he will set up a full judicial inquiry and discipline will be carried out after a just trial with sufficient witnesses.
>
> - **1 Timothy 5:19**—In discussing the elders of Timothy's church, Paul warns him that he should not receive accusations against an elder unless they are verified by two or three witnesses.
>
> - **Hebrews 10:28**—The writer is using this phrase to compare desecrating Christ with ignoring the law of Moses. In making this comparison, he is saying that desecrating Christ is far worse than setting aside the law. The punishment for ignoring the Mosaic Law was being condemned to death on the testimony of two or three witnesses…how much worse will be the punishment of those who desecrate Christ!

8. Because of the way this phrase is typically understood in the rest of the Bible, how should we understand it in the context of Matthew 18?

> In reference to accusations brought against a brother, such charges should not stand unless brought by two or three witnesses. If multiple witnesses truthfully testify against a brother, then he is judged as guilty.

9. How do verses 19–20 contribute to our understanding of the rest of the paragraph?

> Verses 19–20 give a promise to those witnesses that when they stand in judgment over their brother, they will have Jesus' presence as a sign of his approval.

10. How then should this passage be applied today?

> In verses 15–17, four stages of confrontation are laid out: 1) go alone, 2) go with one or two other believers, 3) bring it before the whole church, and 4) refuse fellowship with the person. Verse 18 then declares that God honors in heaven what believers decide on earth in regards to church discipline. Finally, verses 19–20 repeat the promise of heavenly authorization through a special sense of Jesus' presence when two or three witnesses testify.

"LOVING GOD WITH YOUR MIND"

WITH J. P. MORELAND

PART ONE

I. Being a Teenager Today

A. There were no "_____teenagers_____" until after World War II.

"Teenagers today have their own values and their own heroes—and many times those heroes and values are communicated through television commercials and through pop culture like music and movies. And they really end up being contrary—not all the time, but sometimes—to the cause of Jesus Christ."

B. Teenagers often don't have good adult role models.

II. How Did We Get Here?

A. The church

"Up until about the time of the Civil War… Christians worked really hard at thinking and learning how to understand what they believed and why."

"Around the middle to the late 1800s Christians became anti-intellectual. They began to emphasize feelings and private devotions. They began to devalue and lose their interest in knowing how to study and think and read the Bible, and to learn to really be learned about one's faith. The Church became kind of illiterate about its own faith."

1. The awakenings in the middle 1800s

"The problem was that the evangelistic preaching that took place in these awakenings tended to be very, very anti-intellectual and tended to address people's emotions and feelings only."

2. Secular attacks

"Right when the church had a whole bunch of new converts that didn't know very much about the Christian faith, a tremendous assault was launched against Christianity in the centers of higher learning."

"The Christian community was not prepared to address those assaults by argument against argument, and instead, they withdrew and retreated from culture."

B. Philosophy and science

    1. Immanuel Kant and David Hume (late 1700s)

"Their ideas were, largely, that we can only know things if we can sense them with our five senses. And if you can see it, touch it, taste it, smell it, or hear it, you can know it's real. If you can't, you can't know it, even though you might believe in it."

"The great truths of God, the soul, immortality, and right and wrong were banished from the realm of knowledge. That means that they are only matters of private faith and blind belief."

    2. Charles Darwin's *On The Origin of Species* (1859)

    3. The Scopes Trial (1926)

        i. Christians were unprepared in their thinking and were made to look ignorant.

        ii. Winning the trial, but losing the battle

"We lost the battle in that trial because we communicated to the people watching the trial that the only reason we won was that we were still popular. We did not win because our arguments were better than our opponents' arguments."

III. Anti-intellectualism in the Church

A. The separation of <u>faith</u> and reason

"In order to cope with a culture that was beginning to turn secular, the church began to separate faith and reason… Many people said that faith is one thing and reason is another thing… that evidence is a bad thing."

"The Bible teaches that faith is trusting what we have evidence to believe is true."

"If faith and reason aren't relevant to one another, then youth directors and pastors who preach and teach will try to address people's feelings, and will not argue their case before their people. The result is that we don't learn anything over a long period of time."

B. The separation of the <u>sacred</u> and the secular

"Centuries ago, when a person fell in love with Jesus Christ, he or she thought that to be a disciple meant that 'everything in my life should be dedicated to Christ.' That meant that if I am a lawyer or a businessman or an educator, I should think as a Christian in what I do for a living. I had better learn about what Christ thinks about that subject matter."

"Today, there is a separation of the sacred and the secular. What I mean is that 95% of the church's teaching is directed to private, personal morality and holiness, and to my personal feelings of warmth and tenderness toward Jesus Christ… But we almost never hear of a Sunday school class that studies business or environmentalism or economic theory from a Christian point of view."

IV. The Gospel and Our Culture

"Because Christians have stopped emphasizing what we believe and why, we have changed how we present the gospel to non-Christians… We used to emphasize that the gospel is really true and makes sense, and you should believe it because it is true and makes sense."

"When you present Christ to people today, if people don't want to accept it, they don't reject it because they think it is false. Today, people don't view the gospel as relevant to their lives… They respond that way because we present the gospel as something to meet their personal needs rather than that it is simply true and real and makes sense."

V. What about World Missions?

"Missions have been hurt because we have spent all of our money in evangelism (which is important), but we haven't spent enough money in training thoughtful leadership for the churches in these cultures we have evangelized."

"There is sometimes a confusion in thinking that the Great Commission is fulfilled simply in evangelism, yet we lose sight of full-fledged discipleship [i.e. learning]."

VI. The Lack of Courage

"We have courage to speak about things we know something about… Now if a person doesn't really understand a whole lot about their own Christian faith… and they don't know how to defend their faith, they are not going to be really courageous about speaking out on behalf of their faith and when they do speak out they will come across as defensive and uninformed."

"We have not valued an informed commitment to Jesus Christ. We have not produced enough Christians who really have thought through the issues carefully and have a real intelligent view of the subject."

"What we need is for Christians to not only care about these issues, but to have more courage to speak about them… to be calm and confident because they have paid the price to study these issues and to know why they believe what they believe."

VII. The Empty Self

A. _____Individualistic_____: a person who thinks about himself or herself, and not about his or her role in the community

B. _____Self-Centered_____: a person who believes everything exists to make him or her happy

My wife, my husband, my parents, my parents' car, my coach, my youth pastor, and even Jesus Christ himself exists to make me happy. If they don't make me happy, then I will turn to something else.

C. _____Infantile_____: a person that is very preoccupied with his or her body and/or appearance and with pleasure

D. ___Passive___: a person who is a consumer of entertainment and incapable of creating

"Teenagers fight being individualistic, being self-centered, being infantile, and being passive. And if they don't overcome that, they're never going to grow up and become functional, healthy adults—and they will never be disciples of Jesus Christ who will change the world and fulfill the Great Commission."

PART TWO

VIII. Overcoming the Empty Self

A. Denying ourselves for Jesus' sake

    1. Learn to ___serve___ other people

    2. It takes ___practice___

B. Learn to understand why we believe what we believe

"It is only if we really know what and why we believe what we believe that we will have a standpoint to step back from our culture and be able to separate what is good and bad, and not get sucked into our culture. If they can do that, then people can resist the messages in their culture that encourage the empty self, and have the strength to resist those messages."

C. Knowledge is not bad

"Childlike faith is a heart that is ready to trust. But when Jesus is talking about a childlike faith, he is not talking about a faith that doesn't mature and become informed and learned."

    1. It is the abuse of knowledge that is bad, not knowledge itself.

    2. The solution to knowledge "puffing up" is not ignorance, but humility.

IX. The Biblical View of the Mind

A. The God of the Bible is pictured as a rational, intelligent, thoughtful God.

B. In certain Eastern religions you have to abandon your mind.

The God of the Bible does not say 'empty your mind and get rid of it'… He tells us, through the apostle Paul, that we are changed and transformed by having our minds renewed. — Romans 12:2

C. If you want to learn how to share your faith, read the book of Acts.

"When the apostles went to unbelievers, they reasoned and argued and gave evidence for the Christian religion. They learned and read non-Christian literature [see Acts 17]."

D. A specific command regarding our minds

You shall love the Lord your God with all your heart, with all your soul, with all your mind, and with all your strength. And you shall love your neighbor as yourself. — Matthew 22:37–39

"Our love for others grows deeper as we gain a greater knowledge and understanding of them... It's important, if we are going to have a real and full love for God, that we learn to think the way he thinks."

X. Developing a Christian Mind

A. Ask questions

1. Don't act as if you understand something that you do not.

2. Don't be obnoxious in asking your questions.

3. Unbelief is sin, but doubt and questions are not sin.

B. _____Study_____ the Bible

"The Bible for many people has become a rabbit's foot; we rub it for a short period of time in the morning and then hope that it will give us good luck throughout our day."

"Stop asking the question, 'What does this passage mean to you?' Start asking, 'What does this passage mean?' And 'Why do you think it means that?'"

"Get into the habit of reading entire books of the Bible in one sitting... Learn how to study a book rather than just read it."

C. Take your studies seriously.

D. Learn to think logically.

XI. As You Prepare for College

"Be prepared for the fact that there are going to be professors that are dead set on undermining your faith in Jesus Christ... Now when that happens you need to relax. You need to realize that you are eighteen and nineteen years old and if you can't answer your professors questions that it doesn't mean that there aren't Christians who can."

A. Ask questions, but be respectful.

B. Ask your professor if he or she has read contrary Christian opinions.

C. Find Christian resources relevant to your major area of study.

XII. Stretching Your Intellectual Boundaries

   A. Band together in small study groups (apart from church).

      1. Pick a hot-button issue, not a self-help book.

      2. Act on your study (e.g. letters to the editor).

   B. We need to change Sunday school in our churches.

XIII. Concluding Remarks

"Many of the important world-changing movements in history were started by teenagers and young people... and that is because they're still fresh enough and idealistic enough to believe the world can be changed."

"If you're going to change the world, you had better be informed about the issues before you change it... and have an informed commitment to changing the world, and not just a youthful zeal that is without knowledge."

"LOVING GOD WITH YOUR MIND"
VIDEO QUESTIONS

Answer the questions below on a separate sheet of paper and be prepared to review your answers in class.

1. What is it like being a teenager today?

It is difficult to grow up because the culture no longer expects children to mature. Instead, teenagers are allowed—and at times even expected—to act like children. It is interesting to note that until World War II, there was no term for "teenager." Until that period of time, an individual was considered either a child or an adult. In our culture today we have teenagers—basically young adults that are allowed to continue acting like children.

The problem exists in part because of societal expectations—our culture no longer expects or encourages young adults to mature. Also, there are few adults today that would qualify as good role models for teenagers. Many teenagers have created and withdrawn into their own subculture. Teenagers now have their own heroes, values, music, and the like. This leads to another difficulty with being a teenager today: sometimes this subculture promotes ideas contrary to the cause of Jesus Christ.

[There are many other difficulties with being a teenager today, so ask your students about their own struggles with being a Christian teenager.]

2. What is the intellectual state of the church today? How did we get here?

Up until the Civil War, Christians worked hard to understand what they believed and why they believed it. In fact, Christians founded the vast majority of the first hundred colleges in the United States for the purpose of learning about truth and God. Most of the early scientists and intellectual elites were Christians. However, sometime around the mid to late 1800s, Christianity underwent a change. The emphasis on a faith that relied on heart and head shifted to an emphasis upon emotions. This shift is the result of a number of forces, some outside the church, but also some from within.

Beginning in the early 1800s, there were a number of secular intellectual attacks on Christianity. Charles Darwin's book *On the Origin of the Species* made evolution a popular theory. Likewise, David Hume and other philosophers popularized the idea that the physical world was all that there is. Following these attacks, a number of critics arose challenging the validity of the Bible.

Around the time that these secular theories were becoming popular, Christianity saw the emergence of a number of revivals often referred to as the "Great Awakenings." From these revivals many individuals came to Christ. However, the major emphasis was not on the mind, but rather on the heart. Consequently, a large number of new believers that were not learned in Christian thought or doctrine were born. Christians were no longer intellectually equipped to combat these types of ideas. Therefore, the church began to withdraw from the intellectual arena altogether.

Today many within the church draw a line between faith and reason. Many modern Christians paradoxically accept the "truths" of Darwin in their science classes while at the same time affirming within the church the claims of Genesis. Likewise, Christians no longer apply Christianity to their

SM
21

entire lives. They divide their lives between sacred and secular, acting one way in the world and another in church. Christians no longer see a link between their faith and the totality of their actions.

3. How is the gospel often presented in our culture today? How have world missions been affected by the dumbing down of Christianity?

Because Christians have stopped emphasizing the mind, we have changed how we present Christ to the culture at large. Christians used to present Christianity as something that was true and that made sense. Today, we present Christianity as a means to feel better about one's self. Therefore, when people reject Christ, they are usually not rejecting a message that they believe is either true or false. They are rejecting a message that doesn't seem relevant to their lives.

World missions have also suffered from Christianity's recent turn away from the mind. Since Christians are no longer educated or encouraged to think, many missionaries have fallen for dangerous anti-Christian ideas (e.g. Marxism). Likewise, many missionaries have not been trained or educated about Christianity. They in turn fail to effectively educate those they convert. The result is a culture of converts that know little about Christianity—Christians that have been evangelized but not discipled.

[Discuss the requirement of the Great Commission. How does evangelism differ from discipleship?]

4. What are some characteristics of the empty self? How do we overcome the empty self?

Today Christian teenagers must overcome the characteristics of the empty self, that is, they must fight the current accepted trend of being individualistic, self-centered, infantile, and passive. More specifically, the empty self is:

- Individualistic—a person who thinks about himself or herself and not about his or her role in the community
- Self-centered—a person who believes everything exists to make him or her happy
- Infantile—a person who is very preoccupied with his or her body and/or appearance and with pleasure
- Passive—a person who is a consumer of entertainment and incapable of creating

To overcome these current cultural characteristics, Christian teenagers must accept that Christianity is a call to deny one's self. A Christian is a servant of God commanded to live for his Savior, serve others, and ultimately expand God's kingdom. Therefore, it is important to learn to serve other people—to give time and resources to friends, family, and the less fortunate. Christians must engage their minds and seek to understand why they believe what they believe. Only then will Christians be able to recognize counter-Christian attitudes like the empty self.

5. What is the biblical view of the mind? How does one develop a Christian mind?

In certain Eastern religions, one is asked to abandon the mind. However, this is not the case with Christianity. The Bible presents God as rational, intelligent, and thoughtful. Christ studied the Scriptures, taught his followers, and was able to interact with and respond to the critics of his day. Paul, following this example, reasoned from the Torah when witnessing to the Jews and used logic and reason when interacting with pagan philosophers (see Acts 17). Moreover, the first of the two greatest commands in Scripture is to "love the Lord with all your heart, soul, mind, and strength."

To develop a Christian mind, it is important for Christians to ask many questions. We should not act as if we understand something when we do not, nor should we be embarrassed to ask for an explanation. We must also learn to study our Bibles. Today, many Christians merely read small sections of the Bible out of context and consider this activity to be study. Instead, we need to read entire books at a time and seek to learn what the author was saying. Sadly, our modern Bible studies today most often begin by asking what a text means to the reader, rather than what God intended it to mean.

"AMBASSADORS FOR CHRIST"
WITH GREG KOUKL

I. An Ambassador

Therefore, we are ambassadors for Christ, as though God were speaking through us; we beg of you on behalf of Christ, be reconciled to God. — 2 Corinthians 5:20

A. As believers, we are already ambassadors.

B. People draw conclusions about the Sovereign based on _____us_____.

"People are drawing conclusions about your God and about your gospel and about your Savior and about your Bible and about your way of life based on you."

"As a Christian, you may be the only 'living Bible' that some people ever read."

C. We can be good ambassadors or bad ambassadors.

II. _____Knowledge_____: An accurately informed mind

A. We are to be offensive and defensive.

Do not be taken captive by philosophy and empty deception, according to the tradition of men, and not according to Christ. — Colossians 2:8 (paraphrased)

We have weapons that are divinely powerful for the destruction of fortresses. We are tearing down speculations and every lofty thing raised up against the knowledge of God, and we are taking every thought captive to the obedience of Christ. — 2 Corinthians 10:3–5 (paraphrased)

1. Truth is our spiritual weapon.

2. We are in a battle for minds.

3. Jesus and Paul addressed ideas with _____truth_____.

4. We are not to be taken captive; we are to defend the truth against false philosophies.

B. We need knowledge of the _____answers_____.

1. The answers come from the Bible, but…

"Evangelicals have developed a dangerous habit: reading a passage looking for private messages from the Spirit instead of learning what the Spirit is teaching through the inspired writers."

2. We practice relativism (a false philosophy of our time).

"There is no Biblical justification for receiving private messages from text originally intended by God to teach something else. This is not Christianity… this is superstition. Bible verses do not change meaning. A text can never mean what it never meant."

3. Never read a Bible verse; always read a paragraph or more.

4. You can only get the answers by reading the Bible in ___context___.

C. We need knowledge of the ___questions___.

1. Questions are in the context of culture.

2. Two mistakes Christians often make:

   i. Ridicule

   ii. Throwing Bible verses

3. We need to know definitions.

4. We need to know the reasons for people's beliefs.

III. ___Wisdom___: An artful method

A. Tactics: Maneuvering in conversation—ask questions

B. Clarity

1. Present the truth in a compelling way, i.e. get rid of Christian lingo.

2. Adapt your message to the specific person or circumstances.

IV. ___Character___: An attractive manner

A. Two extremes

1. We are so nice we would never offend ___anybody___.

2. We don't care what anybody thinks, so we offend ___everybody___.

B. We are not to be bullies

1. Gentle and reverent (1 Peter 3:15)

2. Patient and not quarrelsome (2 Timothy 2:24–25)

C. Be ordinary

    1. Get rid of tired, worn-out words and phrases that have ceased to communicate something specific.

    2. Be a genuine, healthy, balanced, winsome, attractive, likeable human being.

D. Learn to say, "I could be wrong."

E. Learn to say, "That is a good point."

"Christianity is offensive enough. Don't add any more offense to it. But we dare not remove the offense inherent to the Gospel."

"AMBASSADORS FOR CHRIST"
VIDEO QUESTIONS

Answer the questions below on a separate sheet of paper and be prepared to review your answers in class.

1. What does it mean to be an ambassador for Christ?

> An ambassador is a representative between two parties. Christians are God's diplomats to the world. Our actions and attitudes reflect our Savior. When we are argumentative, lazy, ignorant, selfish, or just outright sinful, these actions and attitudes reflect badly on God. We are communicating to the world the perceived character of God in us. Every Christian is an ambassador for Christ right now. The question we need to ask ourselves is what kind of an ambassador are we?

2. What does it mean to reconcile and be reconciled? What can we learn from 2 Corinthians 5:20? What are three key elements for being an effective ambassador for Christ?

> As Christians, we have been reconciled to God through Christ. This means our separation from God by sin has been restored. We are now a new creature with new attitudes and actions, loyal subjects to our God and Savior. Now that we have been reconciled, we are to go out and tell others of reconciliation with God. As his ambassadors, we should exhibit his qualities and demonstrate his ability to transform human beings.
>
> Second Corinthians 5:20 states that "we are ambassadors for Christ, as though God were speaking through us; we beg of you on behalf of Christ, be reconciled to God." Within the larger context of verses 18–20 the world "reconcile" is used five times:
>
> - God reconciled us to himself through Christ.
> - We have been given the ministry of reconciliation.
> - God was in Christ reconciling the world to himself.
> - God has committed to us the word of reconciliation.
> - We are ambassadors for Christ begging others to be reconciled to Christ.
>
> Three key elements for being an effective ambassador: 1) knowledge, 2) wisdom, and 3) character.

3. What does it mean to have knowledge while being an ambassador for Christ? Is the purpose offensive or defensive? How do we get knowledge of the answers?

> Having knowledge means having an accurately informed mind. If we are to be ambassadors for Christ and to reconcile the world to him, we must know something about both God and the world. Without knowledge, we have no means to communicate to the world and no means with which to distinguish the ideas of the world from those of God. Therefore, Paul informs Christians that they are to use knowledge both defensively and offensively. Defensively, we are not to be "taken captive" by the ideas of men. Offensively, we are to inform others of the truth (Colossians 2:8 and 2 Corinthians 10:5 respectively). This is a battle for hearts and minds, and our spiritual weapon is truth.

SM
25

The knowledge of the answers is found within the Bible. The best way to learn these answers is to study the Bible. However, Christians today make at least two mistakes in the way they study the Scriptures. The first mistake is treating the Bible like a Ouija board. Christians take passages written at a specific time, to specific persons, for a specific message and re-apply the words (devoid of their original meaning) to themselves, claiming God gave them this passage. This practice is relativism, an idea prevalent in our society. This is just the type of false philosophy that Paul warned the Corinthians against. The second mistake, which is much more easily committed, is merely taking a verse out of context and misapplying its message. The best way to avoid this mistake is to read a verse within its larger context. It is sad, but while Christians know many Bible verses, they have no idea what the Bible actually says.

The knowledge of the questions comes from the world. Just as the Bible was written within a context, today people have questions and explanations about reality that come from their own context—issues relating to Postmodernism, Islam, Christianity, evolution, homosexuality, abortion, etc. To discover these questions, Christians must engage others within their culture in an understandable way.

4. **What does it mean to have *wisdom* while being an ambassador for Christ?**

Wisdom is having the ability to present truth in an artful manner. This is done in at least two ways. First, find a creative way to communicate. For example, rather than telling someone they are sinner, you can ask him or her questions to reveal this truth. By asking questions, we avoid seeming judgmental. By asking questions, you force the other person to think through the issues and come up with the truth on their own.

A second component to wisdom is being able to present a clear message. In our culture, this means not speaking in Christianese, but rather presenting truth in words that the average unbeliever is capable of understanding.

5. **What does it mean to have *character* while being an ambassador for Christ?**

Character is the balance between two extremes. Some Christians are so nice that they offend no one. Others are so aggressive and uncaring that they offend everyone. As Christians, we should not shy away from the truth (which can be offensive), but we do want to be as kind and considerate as possible. In fact, the Bible instructs us to be gentle and reverent (1 Peter 3:15) and to be patient and not quarrelsome (2 Timothy 2:24–25).

It is also a good idea to abandon trite and culturally ambiguous Christian language. Within Christianity we have developed our own lingo that many unbelievers cannot comprehend. Moreover, some Christians come across as being "overly-Christian" or "annoyingly-Christian." These Christians don't seem normal to the world at large, and unbelievers can't take their Christianity seriously. Another good character trait to learn is humility, specifically being able to admit that you may be wrong. If you are trying to convince someone else that they are wrong, then you must be equally willing to admit that you might be wrong. Obviously, Christians believe Christianity is true, but pure dogmatism will get us nowhere with others. Likewise, we should be willing to admit that those we disagree with at times have good points and valid concerns. Being able to connect and identify honestly with others makes a better Christian ambassador than hardheaded stubbornness.

WITNESSING ACTIVITY
Pair off your students and challenge them to present the Gospel to each other without using theologically-laden terms like *atonement, baptism, born again, depravity, glorify, justification, Messiah, repentance, propitiation, salvation, sovereignty*, etc.

TOTAL TRUTH
BY NANCY PEARCEY

INTRODUCTION

"Your earlier book says Christians are called to redeem entire cultures, not just individuals," a schoolteacher commented, joining me for lunch at a conference where I had just spoken. Then he added thoughtfully, "I'd never heard that before."

The teacher was talking about *How Now Shall We Live?*[1] and at his words I looked up from my plate in surprise. Was he really saying he'd never even heard the idea of being a redemptive force in every area of culture? He shook his head: "No, I've always thought of salvation strictly in terms of individual souls."

That conversation helped confirm my decision to write a follow-up book dealing with the worldview themes in *How Now Shall We Live?* Just a few years ago, when I began my work on that earlier volume, using the term *worldview* was not on anyone's list of good conversation openers. To tell people that you were writing a book on *worldview* was to risk glazed stares and a quick change in subject. But today as I travel around the country, I sense an eagerness among evangelicals to move beyond a purely privatized faith, applying biblical principles to areas like work, business, and politics. Flip open any number of Christian publications and you're likely to find half a dozen advertisements for *worldview* conferences, *worldview* institutes, and *worldview* programs. Clearly the term itself has strong marketing cachet these days, which signals a deep hunger among Christians for an overarching framework to bring unity to their lives.

This book addresses that hunger and offers new direction for advancing the worldview movement. It will help you identify the secular/sacred divide that keeps your faith locked into the private sphere of "religious truth." It will walk you through practical, workable steps for crafting a Christian worldview in your own life and work. And it will teach you how to apply a worldview grid to cut through the bewildering maze of ideas and ideologies we encounter in a postmodern world. The purpose of worldview studies is nothing less than to liberate Christianity from its cultural captivity, unleashing its power to transform the world.

"The gospel is like a caged lion," said the great Baptist preacher Charles Spurgeon. "It does not need to be defended, it just needs to be let out of its cage." Today the cage is our accommodation to the secular/sacred split that reduces Christianity to a matter of private personal belief. To unlock the cage, we need to become utterly convinced that, as Francis Schaeffer said, Christianity is not merely religious truth, it is total truth—truth about the whole of reality.

POLITICS IN NOT ENOUGH

The reason a worldview message is so compelling today is that we are still emerging from the fundamentalist era of the early twentieth century. Up until that time, evangelicals had enjoyed a position of cultural dominance in America. But after the Scopes trial and the rise of theological modernism, religious conservatives turned in on themselves: They circled the wagons, developed a fortress mentality, and championed "separatism" as a positive strategy. Then, in the 1940s and 50s, a movement began that aimed at breaking out of the fortress. Calling themselves *neo-evangelicals*, this group argued that we are called not to escape the surrounding culture but to engage it. They sought to construct a redemptive vision that would embrace not only individuals but also social structures and institutions.

Yet many evangelicals lacked the conceptual tools needed for the task, which has seriously limited their success. For example, in recent decades many Christians have responded to the moral and social decline in American society by embracing political activism. Believers are running for office in growing numbers; churches are organizing voter registration; public policy groups are proliferating; scores of Christian publications and radio programs offer commentary on public affairs. This heightened activism has yielded good results in many areas of public life, yet the impact remains far less than most had hoped.

---

[1] *How Now Shall We Live?* was coauthored by Charles Colson (Wheaton, IL: Tyndale, 1991) and is hereafter cited as *How Now?* I would also like to recognize the contribution of Harold Fickett, an outstanding writer and storyteller, who wrote the chapter in *How Now?* consisting of extended stories. In offering the current book in part as an advance on themes developed in *How Now?* I'd like to clarify that all citations of that earlier volume refer solely to chapters that I authored.

Why? Because evangelicals often put all their eggs in one basket: They leaped into political activism as the quickest, surest way to make a difference in the public arena—failing to realize that politics tends to reflect culture, not the other way around.

Nothing illustrates evangelicals' infatuation with politics more clearly than a story related by a Christian lawyer. Considering whether to take a job in the nation's capital, he consulted with the leader of a Washington-area ministry, who told him, "You can either stay where you are and keep practicing law, or you can come to Washington and *change the culture*." The implication was that the only way to effect cultural change was through national politics. Today, battle-weary political warriors have grown more realistic about the limits of that strategy. We have learned that "politics is downstream from culture, not the other way around," says Bill Wichterman, policy advisor to Senate Majority Leader Bill Frist. "Real change has to start with the culture. All we can do on Capitol Hill is try to find ways government can nurture healthy cultural trends."[2]

On a similar note, a member of Congress once told me, "I got involved in politics after the 1973 abortion decision because I thought that was the fastest route to moral reform. Well, we've won some legislative victories, but *we've lost the culture*." The most effective work, he had come to realize, is done by ordinary Christians fulfilling God's calling to reform culture within their local spheres of influence—their families, churches, schools, neighborhoods, workplaces, professional organizations, and civic institutions. In order to effect lasting change, the congressman concluded, "we need to develop a Christian worldview."

LOSING OUR CHILDREN

Not only have we "lost the culture," but we continue losing even our own children. It's a familiar but tragic story that devout young people, raised in Christian homes, head off to college and abandon their faith. Why is this pattern so common? Largely because young believers have not been taught how to develop a biblical worldview. Instead, Christianity has been restricted to a specialized area of religious belief and personal devotion.

I recently read a striking example. At a Christian high school, a theology teacher strode to the front of the classroom, where he drew a heart on one side of the blackboard and a brain on the other. The two are as divided as the two sides of the blackboard, he told the class: The heart is what we use for religion, while the brain is what we use for science. An apocryphal story? A caricature of Christian anti-intellectualism? No, the story was told by a young woman who was in the class that day. Worse, out of some two hundred students, she was the only one who objected. The rest apparently found nothing unusual about restricting religion to the domain of the "heart."[3]

As Christian parents, pastors, teachers, and youth group leaders, we constantly see young people pulled down by the undertow of powerful cultural trends. If all we give them is a "heart" religion, it will not be strong enough to counter the lure of attractive but dangerous ideas. Young believers also need a "brain" religion—training in worldview and apologetics—to equip them to analyze and critique the competing worldviews they will encounter when they leave home. If forewarned and forearmed, young people at least have a fighting chance when they find themselves a minority of one among their classmates or work colleagues. Training young people to develop a Christian mind is no longer an option; it is part of their necessary survival equipment.

HEART VERSUS BRAIN

The first step in forming a Christian worldview is to overcome this sharp divide between "heart" and "brain." We have to reject the division of life into a sacred realm, limited to things like worship and personal morality, over against a secular realm that includes science, politics, economics, and the rest of the public arena. This dichotomy in our own minds is the greatest barrier to liberating the power of the gospel across the whole of culture today.

---

[2] Bill Wichterman, in discussion with the author. Wichterman develops his thesis in greater detail in "The Culture: Upstream from Politics," *Building a Healthy Culture: Strategies for an American Renaissance*, Don Eberly, ed. (Grand Rapids, MI: Eerdmans, 2001), 76–101. "While cultural conservatives bemoan judicial activism that reinterprets the plain meaning of the written Constitution, they forget that the courts are only finishing on parchment a job already begun in the hearts of the American people… Politics is largely an expression of culture."
[3] Cited in Mary Passantino, "The Little Engine That Can," a review of Phillip Johnson's *The Right Questions*, *Christian Research Journal* (April 2003).

Moreover, it is reinforced by a much broader division rending the entire fabric of modern society—what sociologists call the public/private split. "Modernization brings about a novel dichotomization of social life," writes Peter Berger. "The dichotomy is between the huge and immensely powerful institutions of the public sphere [by this he means the state, academia, large corporations]…and the private sphere"—the realm of family, church, and personal relationships.

The large public institutions claim to be "scientific" and "value-free," which means that values are relegated to the private sphere of personal choice. As Berger explains: "The individual is left to his own devices in a wide range of activities that are crucial to the formation of a meaningful identity, from expressing his religious preference to settling on a sexual life style."[4] We might diagram the dichotomy like this:

Modern societies are sharply divided:

PRIVATE SPHERE
Personal Preferences

PUBLIC SPHERE
Scientific Knowledge

In short, the private sphere is awash in moral relativism. Notice Berger's telling phrase "religious preference." Religion is not considered an objective truth to which we *submit*, but only a matter of personal taste which we *choose*. Because of this, the dichotomy is sometimes called the fact/value split.

Values have been reduced to arbitrary, existential decisions:

VALUES
Individual Choice

FACTS
Binding on Everyone

As Schaeffer explains, the concept of truth itself has been divided—a process he illustrates with the imagery of a two-story building: In the lower story are science and reason, which are considered public truth, binding on everyone. Over against it is an upper story of noncognitive experience, which is the locus of personal meaning. This is the realm of private truth, where we hear people say, "That may be true for you but it's not true for me."[5]

The two-realm theory of truth:

UPPER STORY
Nonrational, Noncognitive

LOWER STORY
Rational, Verifiable

When Schaeffer was writing, the term *postmodernism* had not yet been coined, but clearly that is what he was talking about. Today we might say that in the lower story is modernism, which still claims to have universal, objective truth—while in the upper story is postmodernism.

---

[4] Peter Berger, *Facing Up to Modernity: Excursions in Society, Politics, and Religion* (New York: Basic, 1977), 133.
[5] Francis Schaeffer deals with the divided concept of truth in *Escape from Reason* and *The God Who Is There*, which can be found in *The Complete Works of Francis Schaeffer* (Wheaton, IL: Crossway, 1982).

Today's two-story truth:

POSTMODERNISM
Subjective, Relative to Particular Groups

MODERNISM
Objective, Universally Valid

The reason it's so important for us to learn how to recognize this division is that it is the single most potent weapon for delegitimizing the biblical perspective in the public square today. Here's how it works: Most secularists are too politically savvy to attack religion directly or to debunk it as false. So what do they do? They consign religion to the value sphere—which takes it out of the realm of true and false altogether. Secularists can then assure us that of course they "respect" religion, while at the same time denying that it has any relevance to the public realm.

As Phillip Johnson puts it, the fact/value split "allows the metaphysical naturalists to mollify the potentially troublesome religious people by assuring them that science does not rule out 'religious *belief*' (so long as it does not pretend to be *knowledge*)."[6] In other words, so long as everyone understands that it is merely a matter of private feelings. The two-story grid functions as a gatekeeper that defines what is to be taken seriously as genuine knowledge, and what can be dismissed as mere wish-fulfillment.

JUST A POWER GRAB?

This same division also explains why Christians have such difficulty communicating in the public arena. It's crucial for us to realize that nonbelievers are constantly filtering what we say through a mental fact/value grid. For example, when we state a position on an issue like abortion or bioethics or homosexuality, *we* intend to assert an objective moral truth important to the health of society—but *they* think we're merely expressing our subjective bias. When we say there's scientific evidence for design in the universe, *we* intend to stake out a testable truth claim—but *they* say, "Uh oh, the Religious Right is making a political power grab." The fact/value grid instantly dissolves away the objective content of anything we say, and we will not be successful in introducing the *content* of our belief into the public discussion unless we first find ways to get past this gatekeeper.

That's why Lesslie Newbigin warned that the divided concept of truth is the primary factor in "the cultural captivity of the gospel." It traps Christianity in the upper story of privatized values, and prevents it from having any effect on public culture.[7] Having worked as a missionary in India for forty years, Newbigin was able to discern what is distinctive about Western thought more clearly than most of us, who have been immersed in it all our lives. On his return to the West, Newbigin was struck by the way Christian truth has been marginalized. He saw that any position labeled *religion* is placed in the upper story of values, where it is no longer regarded as objective knowledge. To give just one recent example, in the debate over embryonic stem cell research, actor Christopher Reeve told a student group at Yale University, "When matters of public policy are debated, *no religions should have a seat at the table.*"[8]

To recover a place at the table of public debate, then, Christians must find a way to overcome the dichotomy between public and private, fact and value, secular and sacred. We need to liberate the gospel from its cultural captivity, restoring it to the status of public truth. "The barred cage that forms the prison for the gospel in contemporary western culture is [the church's] accommodation…to the fact-value dichotomy," says Michael Goheen, a professor of worldview studies.[9] Only by recovering a holistic view of total truth can we set the gospel free to become a redemptive force across all of life.

---

[6] Phillip E. Johnson, *The Wedge of Truth: Splitting the Foundations of Naturalism* (Downers Grove, IL: InterVarsity, 2000), 148, emphasis added. See also my review "A New Foundation for Positive Cultural Change: Science and God in the Public Square," *Human Events* (September 15, 2000), at www.arn.org.
[7] Lesslie Newbigin, *A Word in Season: Perspectives on Christian World Missions* (Grand Rapids, MI: Eerdmans, 1994); see especially the chapter titled "The Cultural Captivity of Western Christianity as a Challenge to a Missionary Church."
[8] "Reeve: Keep Religious Groups Out of Public Policy," The Associated Press (April 3, 2003), emphasis added.
[9] Michael Goheen, *"As the Father Has Sent Me, I Am Sending You"* (Zoetermeer: Uitgeverij Boekencentrum, 2000), 377.

MENTAL MAPS

To say that Christianity is the truth about total reality means that it is a full-orbed worldview. The term means literally a *view* of the *world*, a biblically informed perspective on all reality. A worldview is like a mental map that tells us how to navigate the world effectively. It is the imprint of God's objective truth on our inner life.

We might say that each of us carries a model of the universe inside our heads that tells us what the world is like and how we should live in it. A classic book on worldviews is titled *The Universe Next Door*, suggesting that we all have a mental or conceptual universe in which we "live"—a network of principles that answer the fundamental questions of life: Who are we? Where did we come from? What is the purpose of life? The author of the book, James Sire, invites readers to examine a variety of worldviews in order to understand the mental universe held by other people—those living "next door."

A worldview is not the same thing as a formal philosophy; otherwise, it would be only for professional philosophers. Even ordinary people have a set of convictions about how reality functions and how they should live. Because we are made in God's image, we all seek to make sense of life. Some convictions are conscious, while others are unconscious, but together they form a more or less consistent picture of reality. Human beings "are incapable of holding purely arbitrary opinions or making entirely unprincipled decisions," writes Al Wolters in a book on worldview. Because we are by nature rational and responsible beings, we sense that "we need some creed to live by, some map by which to chart our course."[10]

The notion that we need such a "map" in the first place grows out of the biblical view of human nature. The Marxist may claim that human behavior is ultimately shaped by economic circumstances; the Freudian attributes everything to repressed sexual instincts; and the behavioral psychologist regards humans as stimulus-response mechanisms. But the Bible teaches that the overriding factor in the choices we make is our ultimate belief or religious commitment. Our lives are shaped by the "god" we worship—whether the God of the Bible or some substitute deity.

The term *worldview* is a translation of the German word *Weltanschauung*, which means a way of looking at the world (*Welt* = world; *schauen* = to look). German Romanticism developed the idea that cultures are complex wholes, where a certain outlook on life, or spirit of the age, is expressed across the board—in art, literature, and social institutions as well as in formal philosophy. The best way to understand the products of any culture, then, is to grasp the underlying worldview being expressed. But, of course, cultures change over the course of history, and thus the original use of the term *worldview* conveyed relativism.

The word was later introduced into Christian circles through Dutch neo-Calvinist thinkers such as Abraham Kuyper and Herman Dooyeweerd. They argued that Christians cannot counter the spirit of the age in which they live unless they develop an equally comprehensive biblical worldview—an outlook on life that gives rise to distinctively Christian forms of culture—with the important qualification that it is not merely the relativistic belief of a particular culture but is based on the very Word of God, true for all times and places.[11]

NOT JUST ACADEMIC

As the concept of *worldview* becomes common currency, it can all too easily be misunderstood. Some treat it as merely another academic subject to master—a mental exercise or "how to" strategy. Others handle worldview as if it were a weapon in the culture war, a tool for more effective activism. Still others, alas, treat it as little more than a new buzzword or marketing gimmick to dazzle the public and attract donors.

---

[10] Albert M. Wolters, *Creation Regained: Biblical Basics for a Reformational Worldview* (Grand Rapids, MI: Eerdmans, 1985), 4.
[11] For a brief history of the term *worldview* from a Christian perspective, see Albert M. Wolters, "On the Idea of Worldview and Its Relation to Philosophy," in *Stained Glass*, Paul Marshall, Sander Griffioen, and Richard J. Mouw, eds. (Lanham, MD: University Press of America, 1989), 65–80. For a more detailed account, see David K. Naugle, *Worldview: The History of a Concept* (Grand Rapids, MI: Eerdmans, 2002). For a brief history from a non-Christian perspective, see the first two sections of Eugene F. Miller, "Positivism, Historicism, and Political Inquiry," *American Political Science Review 66*, no. 3 (September 1972): 796–817. Miller writes: "All human expressions point beyond themselves to the characteristic worldview (*Weltanschauung*) of the epoch or culture to which they belong. This underlying impulse or spirit makes the culture a whole and determines the shape of all thought and evaluation within it. We grasp the documentary meaning of human objectifications by seeing them as unconscious expressions of worldview. Even theoretical philosophy is but a channel through which the spirit of the age finds expression."

Genuine worldview thinking is far more than a mental strategy or a new spin on current events. At the core, it is a deepening of our spiritual character and the character of our lives. It begins with the submission of our minds to the Lord of the universe—a willingness to be taught by Him. The driving force in worldview studies should be a commitment to "love the Lord your God with all your heart, soul, strength, and mind" (see Luke 10:27).

That's why the crucial condition for intellectual growth is *spiritual* growth, asking God for the grace to "take every thought captive to obey Christ" (2 Corinthians 10:5). God is not just the Savior of souls, He is also the Lord of creation. One way we acknowledge His Lordship is by interpreting every aspect of creation in the light of His truth. God's Word becomes a set of glasses offering a new perspective on all our thoughts and actions.

As with every aspect of sanctification, the renewal of the mind may be painful and difficult. It requires hard work and discipline, inspired by a sacrificial love for Christ and a burning desire to build up His Body, the Church. In order to have the mind of Christ, we must be willing to be crucified with Christ, following wherever He might lead—whatever the cost. "Through many tribulations we must enter the kingdom of God" (Acts 14:22). As we undergo refining in the fires of suffering, our desires are purified and we find ourselves wanting nothing more than to bend every fiber of our being, including our mental powers, to fulfill the Lord's Prayer: "Thy Kingdom come." We yearn to lay all our talents and gifts at His feet in order to advance His purposes in the world. Developing a Christian worldview means submitting our entire self to God, in an act of devotion and service to Him.

---

*This essay originally appeared as a chapter in Nancy Pearcey, *Total Truth: Liberating Christianity from Its Cultural Captivity* (Wheaton, IL: Crossway, 2004), 17–25.

**Reproduction rights granted by Crossway Books.

TOTAL TRUTH
ESSAY QUESTIONS

Answer the questions below on a separate sheet of paper and be prepared to review your answers in class.

1. **What is meant by the assertion that "politics tend to reflect culture, not the other way around?"**

It is a common misconception that the most effective place to promote change is from the seat of a public office. While laws usually reflect the general consensus of the people, they rarely change that consensus. In fact, many Christians today are unaware that they can change culture through the business of everyday life. Nancy Pearcey cites the example of a Christian lawyer who was told by a Washington–area ministry leader, "You can either stay where you are and keep practicing law, or you can come to Washington and *change the culture*." What this person and others fail to realize is that we do not cease being Christians in the world at large. This is not to say that Christian influence is not needed in government—but that it is needed in every arena of life. All of us can make an impact for Christ in our everyday lives, occupations, and relationships. [SM pp. 26–7]

[Discuss how Christians might change culture in a variety of jobs and relationships.]

2. **How has the concept of truth been divided in modern society?**

The concept of truth has been divided into two arenas—facts and values (i.e. private truth and public truth). Facts are believed to come from science, while values are derived from religion. Facts describe the world as it really is, while values simply express individual or cultural preferences. [SM pp. 27–9]

3. **According to our modern society, what are some examples of public and private truths?**

[Answers will vary, but here are a few examples.]

Public truth:
- The Earth revolves around the sun.
- Mount Everest is the highest point on our planet.
- The capital of Switzerland is Bern.
- Herbert Hoover was the president of the United States of America from 1929–33.
- Water is made up of a combination of hydrogen and oxygen.

Private truth:
- An intelligent being created the whole universe.
- Being involved in a homosexual act is wrong.
- The Christian Bible is inspired by God.
- Jesus Christ died for the sins of his people.
- Jehovah's Witnesses present a skewed view of Jesus. [SM pp. 28–9]

4. **Why is using the word "values" to describe religious claims a useful strategy for those who endorse the fact/value split?**

> If proponents of the fact/value split were to openly attack religion, they would not gain much of a hearing because of the current politically correct atmosphere. Arguing for a fact/value split allows secularists to feign tolerance for religious beliefs. Claiming that religion provides a different kind of knowledge (namely values) allows religion to maintain a voice in the private sphere, while effectively banishing it from the public sphere. [SM pp. 29]

5. **How might the fact/value split affect the way modern culture understands the nature of marriage and the abortion debate?**

> If one assumes the fact/value split, then any views regarding how marriage should be defined or restricted must be judged at the level of personal or societal values, rather than fact. For example, to say that marriage should only take place between a man and a woman becomes a subjective opinion. No view on the definition or restriction of marriage can be held up as more correct than any other. If you don't like gay marriage, then marry another heterosexual but don't act as if everyone should hold your opinion. If this were a dispute of fact (a scientific matter), then experiments could be performed to settle the question, but it is not.
>
> Similarly, when a fact/value dichotomy is applied to the abortion debate, the issue of humanness (that is, being physiologically human) may be placed within the realm of facts. Science tells us that a fetus is human, but the issue of personhood (whether or not a human fetus is a person) is often consigned to the area of values, allowing each person to determine when a fetus is human based on his or her individual beliefs. Those holding to a fact/value split believe this disagreement is about values and not facts. In their minds, this argument is merely over personal opinion, thus Christian "belief" is not taken seriously. [SM p. 29]

DEAR DOUG
WRITING ASSIGNMENT

Hey there!

Well, I'm finally settled into my dorm room. You wouldn't think that it would take so long to move into a room the size of a closet, but when you're sharing that space with a roommate you have to be creative.

My roommate's name is Nathan and we hit it off pretty early. I can't say we have a lot in common, but we both like to talk. After the first day of class we talked until four in the morning! At one point he noticed my Bible and asked if I was a Christian. When I said that I was, he asked me *why*. I've never really thought about it that deeply until that moment. Well, it wasn't that I've never shared my faith with anyone before—it was just that he was asking me for deeper reasons. I told him that I believe in the God of the Bible and that I asked Jesus into my heart when I was young. I said that I believe God has a plan for my life and that the purpose of my life is to glorify him. Nathan got very confused. He said he didn't understand what I meant by "asking Jesus into my heart" and "God having a plan for my life" and that "the purpose of my life is to glorify God." When I really thought about it, I wasn't sure myself what all those phrases mean. I was just repeating what I'd heard in church.

Nathan is a really nice and intelligent guy. I'd like to be able to discuss my faith with him, but the questions he asks make me wonder if I've thought through my faith for myself. Nathan told me he holds to a non-Christian worldview, that he's "searching for truth." He's open to talking about Christianity, but says he has a hard time understanding my "Christianese." The problem is that I don't know how else to communicate with him. I've never thought about what some of the words and phrases we use at church mean. How can I talk about my beliefs with non-Christians without using those terms?

Also, I didn't want to look ignorant, so I didn't tell Nathan that I'm not sure what he meant by "worldview." What is a worldview? He's interested in learning about my beliefs, but what does it mean to have a Christian worldview?

Well, it's already past midnight, so I'd better get some sleep. I have a class at eight tomorrow morning and can't skip breakfast if I want to have my brain awake that early!

Oh, one last thing… do you know why you are a Christian? I *know* that I am, but after my conversations with Nathan, I am not sure I know *why* I am. Just curious.

Tell everyone hi,
Doug

Doug has brought up four different subjects; below is a rough outline of possible responses:

1. How do I talk about my beliefs with non-Christians? (12.5 points)

It is important to keep in mind that many terms and phrases Christians use within the church mean nothing to individuals outside of that context. If we as Christians are going to effectively communicate God to others, we need to use a "non-cryptic" vocabulary. This means we may need to translate our Christian lingo into everyday terms to accurately present God to others.

Beyond that, Christians themselves often forget to explore what terms and phrases specific to Christianity mean, parroting "Sunday school answers" instead of taking ownership of our faith. For example, Doug told Nathan that the purpose of his life is "to glorify God." But do most Christians know what such a common statement means? How does living for God bring Him glory? How are *you* glorifying God with your life? Stating that this is our purpose is only the beginning of a discussion, not the end.

2. What is a worldview? (12.5 points)

Below are two definitions for a worldview given in this course:

- Any ideology, philosophy, theology, movement, or religion that provides an overarching approach to understanding God, the world, and man's relations to God and the world." — Noebel and Bywater

- "A worldview is a way of viewing or interpreting all of reality. It is an interpretive framework through which or by which one makes sense out of the data of life and the world." — Geisler and Watkins

Some illustrations given in this course include a triangle, an iceberg, and a tree.

3. What does it mean to have a Christian worldview? (12.5 points)

Holding to a Christian worldview is to view all of life through the perspective of Jesus Christ. As we study and adopt the perspectives of Christ as spelled out in the Scriptures, we should adjust how we perceive and live within the world.

4. Do you know why you are a Christian? (12.5 points)

Answers will vary. Students will cite either an existential rationale and/or a reasoned rationale. Various answers are acceptable.

INTRODUCTION TEST

"INTRODUCTION TO WORLDVIEWS" VIDEO QUESTIONS

Fill in the blanks: (3 points possible per answer [8 for 90-day])

1. In Colossians 2:8, Paul warns the Colossians not to be taken <u>captive</u> by vain or deceptive philosophies.

2. In 2 Corinthians 10:3-5, Paul informs the Corinthians that Christians should demolish <u>strongholds [or arguments or pretensions]</u> set up against the knowledge of God.

3. In 2 Timothy 2:22-26, Paul instructs Timothy to teach the <u>truth</u> to others that have been taken captive. The hope is that they will be set free.

Short answer: (9 points possible per answer [12 for 09-day])
4. **What is a worldview?**

> A worldview is a way of viewing or interpreting the whole world. It is an interpretive framework or something you look through when interpreting reality. A worldview is the perspective through which you understand and approach life and the world. Everyone has a worldview—a way in which they see and interpret the world.

'INTRODUCTION' TEXTBOOK QUESTIONS

Short answer: (9 points possible per answer [12 for 90-day])

5. **What are some fundamental questions a worldview answers?**

> A worldview answers such fundamental questions as: *How did we get here? Why are we here? What is the meaning or purpose of life? Is there a difference between right and wrong? Is there a God? Are humans just highly evolved animals?*

6. **How is a worldview like a pair of eyeglasses? How is a worldview like a tree?**

> • Eyeglasses—If your prescription is not correct, what you see through your glasses will be distorted. Without the proper prescription, glasses will not help you see the world; rather, they will keep you from seeing the world as it truly is.
>
> • Tree—Like the roots of a tree, a worldview is essential to life and stability. Just like the roots of a tree, we do not see people's worldview; we only see the exposed part of the tree—their actions.

CD-ROM

 UNDERSTANDING THE TIMES 45

Matching: (1 point possible per answer [4 for 90-day])
some options may be used more than once or not at all; some questions may have multiple answers

7. __a/b/d__ "God created the heavens and the earth." (Genesis 1:1)

8. __d__ "after their kind" (Genesis 1:21)

9. __f__ "Be fruitful and multiply" (Genesis 1:28)

10. __i__ "it shall be for food" (Genesis 1:29)

11. __e__ "man became a living soul" (Genesis 2:7)

12. __c__ "knowledge of good and evil" (Genesis 2:9)

13. __j__ "enmity between you and the woman" (Genesis 3:15)

14. __g__ "I commanded you" (Genesis 3:11)

15. __h/g__ "Whoever sheds man's blood" (Genesis 9:6)

16. __g__ "Christ is lawgiver" (Genesis 49:10)

a. Theology
b. Philosophy
c. Ethics
d. Biology
e. Psychology
f. Sociology
g. Law
h. Politics
i. Economics
j. History

PLAYING WITH FIRE ESSAY QUESTIONS
True or False: (3 points possible per answer)
if an answer is false, restate it to make it true

17. **"What does a text mean to me?" is the key question when reading and interpreting the Bible.**

> False: "What did the author(s) intend to communicate?" is the key question when interpreting the Bible.

18. **The classical view of meaning is that a text is a mirror by which readers generate meaning.**

> False: The postmodern view of meaning is that a text is a mirror by which readers generate meaning.

19. **Meanings are communicated through genres.**

> True

20. **If God had not placed the words of Scripture within genres, we wouldn't understand Scripture.**

> True

21. **Biblical proverbs are instances of promises from God.**

> False: Biblical proverbs are instances of <u>wisdom literature that emphasize wise choices</u>.

22. **Bible verses were meant to be freestanding units of thought.**

> False: Bible verses were <u>not</u> meant to be freestanding units of thought.

23. **A Bible verse is simply a part of a paragraph and develops some aspect of the paragraph's big idea.**

> True

24. **Within its context, 1 Thessalonians 5:22 means to abstain from all appearances of evil.**

> False: Within its context, 1 Thessalonians 5:22 means to abstain from all <u>evil utterances</u>.

25. **We must know what biblical passages mean before we can apply their meaning to our lives.**

> True

26. **We must know the Bible's information before we can experience the Bible's transformation.**

> True

"AMBASSADORS FOR CHRIST" VIDEO QUESTIONS
Short answer: (9 points possible per answer)

27. **What does it mean to be an ambassador for Christ?**

> An ambassador is a representative between two parties. Christians are God's diplomats to the world. Our actions and attitudes reflect our Savior. When we are argumentative, lazy, ignorant, selfish, or just outright sinful, these actions and attitudes reflect badly on God. We are communicating to the world the perceived character of God in us. Every Christian is an ambassador for Christ right now. The question we need to ask ourselves is what kind of an ambassador are we?

TOTAL TRUTH ESSAY QUESTIONS
True or false: (3 points possible per answer)
*if an answer is false, restate it to make it true

28. Politics tend to change culture.

> False: Politics tend to <u>reflect</u> culture.

29. The heart is for religion and the mind is used for science.

> False: We use both the <u>heart and mind</u> for religion.

30. In modern society, the concept of truth is often divided into fact and value.

> True

31. "Muhammad was God's final prophet" is an example of a fact claim.

> True

32. A worldview is like a mental map that tells us how to navigate the world effectively.

> True

WORLDVIEW TRAINING

TEACHER MANUAL

UNDERSTANDING THE TIMES

Unit One

Topics:
Cults
Proof of God
Religious Pluralism
Theology

A Summit Ministries Curriculum

180-Day Syllabus

Day	IN CLASS	HOMEWORK	
1	Watch "Theology" video		
2	Read UTT Textbook 'Theology 1.1'	Read UTT Textbook 'Theology 1.2'	
3	Review UTT Textbook 'Theology 1.1-1.2' questions	Read UTT Textbook 'Theology 1.3'	
4	Read UTT Textbook 'Theology 1.4'		
5	Review UTT Textbook 'Theology 1.3-1.4' questions	Read UTT Textbook 'Theology 1.5'	
6	Read UTT Textbook 'Theology 1.6'		
7	Review UTT Textbook 'Theology 1.5-1.6' questions	Assign Dear Doug Letter	
8	Read *Are All Religions One?* essay		
9	Review *Are All Religions One?* essay questions		
10	Watch "Existence and Nature of God" video		
11	Review "Existence and Nature of God" video questions		
12	Watch "Marks of the Cults" video P1		
13	Watch "Marks of the Cults" video P2		
14	Review "Marks of the Cults" video questions	Dear Doug Letter assignment Due	
15	Take Unit One Test		

90-Day Syllabus

Day	IN CLASS	HOMEWORK	
1	Watch "Theology" video	Read UTT Textbook 'Theology 1.1-1.2'	
2	Review UTT Textbook 'Theology 1.1-1.2' questions	Read UTT Textbook 'Theology 1.3-1.4'	
3	Review UTT Textbook 'Theology 1.3-1.4' questions	Read UTT Textbook 'Theology 1.5-1.6'	
4	Review UTT Textbook 'Theology 1.5-1.6' questions		
5	Watch "Marks of the Cults" video P1		
6	Watch "Marks of the Cults" video P2		
7	Review "Marks of the Cults" video questions		
8	Take Unit One Test		

UNDERSTANDING THE TIMES
THEOLOGY QUESTIONS

Answer the questions below on a separate sheet of paper and be prepared to review your answers in class. Reflection Questions will not be found in the text. These are merely designed to help you start thinking about issues from a worldview perspective.

THEOLOGY 1.1

1. **What are the two "foundations" upon which Christian theism rests?**

General revelation and special revelation [UTT 1.1.1]

2. **What is the difference between general and special revelation? What does it mean that general revelation is "a necessary but insufficient" means of revelation? What is God's most direct form of special revelation?**

General revelation is God's communication regarding his existence to all persons at all times, while special revelation is God's more specific communication about such elements as salvation. For example, general knowledge about God can be gained through nature or the moral law, and specific knowledge of God's saving plan for his creation can only be known through Jesus or Scripture.

General revelation is valuable for understanding God, but it is insufficient in regards to salvation—it cannot tell us all we need to know about the way of salvation. Therefore, special revelation is needed to communicate God's desired plan for creation. God's most complete revelation came in the person and work of Christ. [UTT 1.1.2]

3. **What is a linchpin? How is special revelation "the linchpin of Christianity?" How does general revelation function as a "prod?"**

A linchpin is a pin passed through the end of an axle to keep a wheel in position. Metaphorically, a linchpin is a person or thing vital to an enterprise or organization.

Special revelation is our linchpin because it holds everything together. We can define reality by understanding God's Word. The story of the Bible is the story of God's work of redemption. It is the "Grand Story" which has at its center Christ, the linchpin who holds it all together. In him true meaning is found.

Although God's revelation through nature, in and of itself, fails to bring people to a saving knowledge of God, it is capable of bringing people to a general knowledge of God. The majority of intellectuals agree that the concepts of purpose and design, for example, have validity in regard to the question of the existence of God. Therefore, general revelation merely provokes us to seek after God (Acts 17:26–27). [UTT 1.1.3]

4. **When C. S. Lewis says, "Unless I believe in God, I can't believe in thought," what does he mean?**

> It makes much more sense to think that our own rational thought processes are the product of some higher intelligence rather than billions of years of random incidents. Human reasoning must be suspect if it is not the result of a previous reasoning process. [UTT 1.1.3]

5. **What are some of the characteristics of the personal God? From which biblical references do we learn about these characteristics?**

Daniel 4:35	Sovereign
Proverbs 15:3, 21	Moral
Exodus 32:11–14	Patient
John 10:28	Faithful
Hebrews 1:10	Powerful
Isaiah 46: 8–11	Purposeful
Genesis 6:17–7:24; Genesis 19; Leviticus 10:1–7; Leviticus 18–20; 2 Kings 17; 2 Chronicles 36; Ezekiel 33:11; Jude 15	Just
John 1:12; 3:16; Romans 3:24; 5:8; 6:11; Colossians 1:20; 2 Corinthians 5:17–21; 1 Peter 1:18; Ephesians 1:7	Loving and Forgiving [UTT 1.1.5–7]

THEOLOGY 1.2

6. **What are the key beliefs of Islam? According to Islam, who is Muhammad? What roles do Jesus, Moses, and other biblical figures play in Islam?**

> First, Muslims believe there is a God and only one God (monotheism).
>
> Second, Muslims believe in angels and a hierarchy of angels. Gabriel is the highest angel. They also assert that two angels are assigned to each person to record his or her good and bad deeds. Muslims also hold to a belief in creatures know as Jinn—bad or mischievous spirits.
>
> Third, Muslims believe that God has sent at least one prophet to every nation and these prophets all taught the same message: "There is only one God. All people should submit to him. There will be a

day of judgment of deeds, both good and evil." Muslims affirm that Adam, Noah, Abraham, David, Solomon, Jonah, John the Baptist, and Jesus were all prophets. However, they see Muhammad as the quintessential and last of God's prophets.

Fourth, they believe that the prophets were given holy books: Moses was given the Torah; David, the Psalms; Jesus, the Gospels; and Muhammad, the Qur'an. However, the only uncorrupted holy book in existence today is the Qur'an, which God divinely protected. (Thus, Muslims see the Bible as a corrupted work with contradictions and historical and scientific errors.)

Fifth, there is a day of judgment. God will judge everyone, and salvation is granted to those whose good deeds outweigh their bad. However, there are teachings within Islam regarding forgiveness. Only God knows who will be saved, thus there is no assurance of salvation within Islam. The only exception to this rule is for those individuals that participate in Jihad, or holy war. As with Christianity, there are two eternal destinations: heaven and hell. [UTT 1.2.2]

7. What are the key practices (or pillars) of Islam?

The first pillar is the confession of faith (the shahada)—"There is no God but God and Muhammad is his prophet." The second pillar is prayer. Muslims pray five times a day facing Mecca and at noon on Friday gather for prayer at the mosque. The third pillar is fasting. During the daylight hours in the month of Ramadan, Muslims abstain from eating, drinking, smoking, and intimate relations. The fourth pillar is alms. Muslims give 2.5 percent of their annual income to the poor and needy. The fifth pillar is pilgrimage. All Muslims are expected to make a pilgrimage to Mecca at least once in their lifetime, if their finances and health permit. [UTT 1.2.3]

8. What are the Qur'an and the Hadith?

The Qur'an and the Hadith are the two primary sources for Islamic theology. According to Islam, the Qur'an is the incomparable, infallible, and final revelation from God (Qur'an 17:88-89), confirming all previous revelations (10:37; 46:12).The Hadith are traditions of the teachings, rulings, and actions of Muhammad and his chief companions. [UTT 1.2.4]

9. What do Muslims believe regarding the doctrine of the Trinity? Why do they hold this view?

Many Muslims are confused about the doctrine of the Trinity. This probably is due to how the Qur'an misrepresents it. The Qur'an teaches that the doctrine of the Trinity is essentially polytheistic (that is, affirming the existence of more than one true God). Because these misrepresentations are encased in the Qur'an, and Muslims attribute absolute authority to the Qur'an, despite our appeals to Scripture and our explanations of the doctrine, it is extremely difficult to persuade Muslims that Christianity is unwaveringly and unqualifiedly monotheistic. [UTT 1.2.7]

10. Muslims claim that Islam fulfills Christianity. What are the main problems with this view?

Muslims purport that Islam fulfills Christianity, just as Christianity fulfills Old Testament religion. Yet if one religion is to fulfill another, there must be significant continuity between the two. In other words, essential elements of the first must not be denied by the second; there must be continuity of essence, though not necessarily of form. Christianity builds upon Judaism, affirming the Old Testament as both true and authoritative. Over and over again in the New Testament we see Jesus, Paul, and others citing the Old Testament as truth and affirming its divine inspiration (2 Timothy 3:14–17; 1 Peter 1:24–25). Muslims, on the other hand, deny the authority and accuracy of both the Old and New Testaments. Ultimately, Islam is not the fulfillment of Christianity because it denies the validity and truth of Christianity as a whole (while Christianity affirms the truth of the Old Testament). [UTT 1.2.7]

THEOLOGY 1.3

11. What term best describes Secular Humanist theology? How do Humanists view the supernatural?

Secular Humanists are atheists. The core of their belief is that there is no God and no supernatural realm to reality. [UTT 1.3.1–2]

12. According to Corliss Lamont, from where did the idea of God or gods come?

Corliss Lamont insisted that the creation of the cosmos was not a divine act; rather it was human beings and their creative imaginations that invented the concept of the divine to explain the existence of the cosmos. [UTT 1.3.2]

13. What is the premise of the humanistic children's book *What About God?*

The underlying argument of the story *What About God?* is that God is a mythical creature similar to dragons and fairies, certainly not someone to whom human beings should look for guidance or salvation. [UTT 1.3.4]

14. Why did life-long atheist Antony Flew abandon atheism and accept theism?

At age 81, after decades of being a leading proponent for atheism, Antony Flew felt compelled to conclude that some sort of intelligent cause must have been responsible for the birth of the universe. The important point of this event is that science and reason drove Flew to this conclusion, not revelation or history. Theism does not represent mere faith in things unseen, but is a position that can be supported by both logic and evidence. [UTT 1.3.5]

[Please remember that Flew accepted a form of theism and not Christianity.]

15. **Reflection Question: According to Paul Kurtz, since there is no God, man must save himself. What does Kurtz mean by "save" himself?**

> *[Answers will vary. Help the students to understand the implications of this kind of view.]*
>
> Kurtz holds that man is the highest and most evolved being. Kurtz believes that humanity can figure out the best course for evolution, that we must create a system of morals independent from a universal standard, and that science and reason should be employed to solve the problems facing the world in which we live.
>
> Discuss how this could lead to elitism—in the end those who have the most power or who can best manipulate the process will be the ones who set the rules and define what is right and wrong.

THEOLOGY 1.4

16. **What term best describes Marxist-Leninist theology?**

> Like Secular Humanists, Marxists base their worldview on a theological belief in atheism. [UTT 1.4.1–2]

17. **How did Karl Marx view humanity and its role in history?**

> Since Karl Marx left no room for God in his worldview, he believed that it was up to mankind to perform the functions traditionally relegated to the divine. For Marx, humanity is God. We created God in our own image. We created religion in order to worship ourselves.
>
> Because Marx believed that we are God, he also believed we must seize control of reality and shape it to our specifications. Because the institutions of society rested on a foundation of theism, Marx determined to change all social institutions and re-establish them on atheistic foundations. [UTT 1.4.2]

18. **What well-known quote by Karl Marx best summarizes his sentiment toward religion?**

> "Religion," said Marx, "is the sigh of the oppressed creature, the sentiment of a heartless world, as it is the spirit of spiritless conditions. It is the opium of the people." [UTT 1.4.3]

19. **Fyodor Dostoevsky said the problem with Communism is not economic, but what?**

> Atheistic [UTT 1.4.7]

20. **Reflection Question: Why did Marx and Lenin both desire to wipe "even the flirting of the idea of God" out of existence?**

> *[Answers will vary, but should get to the heart of their materialistic attitude toward life.]*
>
> To Marx and Lenin, human beings and everything that exists are merely atoms in motion, nothing more. Those "atoms in motion" that believe in a God are weak-minded and dangerous to the establishment of a Communistic government and the future hope of utopia. For Marx and Lenin there can be nothing above the state. Therefore, those who are too weak-minded to understand the truth of atheism and cling to the supernatural must be exterminated at any cost.

THEOLOGY 1.5

21. **Why is the life of Christ important to Cosmic Humanists?**

> Focusing on the life of Christ allows the New Age theologian to postulate, as does John White, that "The Son of God… is not Jesus but our combined Christ-consciousness." The Cosmic Humanist does not regard Jesus as God, but rather as one of a few human beings to have achieved a high level of consciousness, a divine state of awareness to which every person is encouraged to aspire. [UTT 1.5.1]

22. **According to Cosmic Humanism, who is God?**

> According to New Agers, God is not something "out there." Rather, we are God—or more correctly stated, everything is God and God is everything. It is for this reason that Shirley MacLaine recommends that every person begin the day by affirming his or her own deity. Everyone should realize and become comfortable with the fact that they are God. [UTT 1.5.2]

23. **According to Cosmic Humanism, what happens when a person dies?**

> Cosmic Humanists believe that humanity's central goal is to realize divine nature and thus transcend the simplistic notion that we are either matter or spirit. Moreover, virtually every New Ager believes that the soul is both indestructible and eternal. In other words, New Agers believe that every human being has always existed. Each of us was present in some form or another since eternity past. The cycle of life and death is merely the process of reincarnation. The body may pass away, but the soul will continue its quest for godhood in other bodies. [UTT 1.5.3]

24. **What is the theological view of Cosmic Humanism?**

> Cosmic Humanism holds a pantheistic theology—everything is god and god is everything.
>
> The most blatant example of pantheistic theology occurs in a New Age children's book entitled *What is God?* "There are many ways to talk about God. Does that mean that everything that everybody

ever says about God is right? Does that mean that God is everything? Yes! God is everything great and small! God is everything far away and near! God is everything bright and dark! And God is everything in between! If everything is God, God is the last leaf on a tree; if everything is God, God is an elephant crashing through the jungle." [UTT 1.5.4]

25. **Reflection Question: How have you seen pantheism portrayed in popular culture?**

[Answers will vary.]

THEOLOGY 1.6

26. **What is the theological view of classical Postmodernism?**

Atheism [UTT 1.6.1]

27. **Why are Postmodernists such as Jacques Derrida and Michel Foucault unwilling to clearly state their theological beliefs?**

To claim to be an atheist is to make an absolute statement about reality—that there is no God. Since Derrida and Foucault claim that there is no universal reality or objective "way things are," both try to avoid making such absolute theological statements. [UTT 1.6.4]

28. **What is deconstruction? How might this theory be applied to texts such as the Bible?**

Derrida concluded that since there is no ultimate reality or eternal truth, words and sentences could not refer to anything "out there." Rather, Derrida insisted that human beings "construct" reality through their use of language. Each text finds its meaning in the reader rather than with the writer. The author's meaning is thus unavoidably "deconstructed" or altered by the reader and becomes captive to the reader's whims. [UTT 1.6.5]

Those who apply Derrida's theory of deconstruction to the Bible believe that it is merely a book constructed by human beings who were locked into their own culture, experiences, and language. The Biblical authors were writing about their own subjective experiences, not necessarily communicating objective, eternal truths about God and mankind. Therefore, when people read the Bible today, they bring their own interpretive grid to the text. A feminist will read the Bible one way, a homosexual another, and an evangelical yet another. No one can claim to be right. Moreover, no one can transcend his or her own subjectivity to get at the originally intended message. The theory of deconstruction can be used to explain how some cultures can read the Bible and proceed to slaughter another race, while other cultures reading the same Bible build hospitals, schools, orphanages, and homeless shelters. [UTT 1.6.5]

29. How has Postmodernism influenced the notion of religious pluralism?

> Although most early Postmodernists were atheists, the logical conclusion of their denial of truth has been the promotion of religious pluralism. Religious pluralism is the belief that one must be tolerant of all religious beliefs because no single religion can claim to possess universal truth.
>
> This notion harmonizes with the defining tenets of the Postmodern mood—skepticism of absolute truth, of any discernable foundation for knowledge, and in the end, of any metanarrative (an overarching story that defines reality). Many of those immersed in the present Postmodern culture deny religious truth, instead relegating religious claims to the sphere of preference. For example, you either like the idea of Jesus being the Savior or you do not. Miracles either appeal to you or they do not. This attitude accommodates and equalizes all religious preferences. [UTT 1.6.6]

30. Reflection Question: **What do you think Friedrich Nietzsche is saying in his poem *The Madman*?**

> *[Answers will vary.]*
>
> Although Nietzsche was an atheist, he clearly understood the ramifications of a society that no longer believed in the reality of God. Nietzsche realized (almost prophetically) that removing God from a culture built upon belief in the divine would inevitably lead to chaos. [UTT 1.6.3]

> ## APOLOGETICS ROLE-PLAY ACTIVITY
>
>
> Divide the students into small groups and appoint one person in each group as the "atheist" (or you may choose to play the atheist yourself). The students in the group should attempt to convince the atheist either that there is a God or that the Christian worldview is more reasonable than the atheistic/naturalistic worldview. If you conduct the role-play in groups, give the atheist a short list of challenges often presented to Christians.
>
> Possibilities include:
> * "Prove that there is a God"
> * "How can you believe in a book that is so full of errors?"
> * "All religions are the same"
> * "How can you believe in those old myths like Noah's Ark and the parting of the Red Sea?"
>
> Conduct the role-play for 10–15 minutes, then debrief. Help your students understand how they can answer the questions raised by the atheist.

Are All Religions One?

By Douglas Groothuis

We live in a culture of increasing religious diversity. Just walk around and look at bulletin boards on any university campus, and you will find advertisements for Hindu yoga, Buddhist meditation, Islamic societies, Christian fellowships, and a mind-numbing collection of assorted spiritual teachings and practices. A survey of the phone book yields the same result. There we find not only Christian churches and Jewish synagogues, but Buddhist and Hindu temples, as well as Muslim mosques. This fact is not altered by any amount of talk about America being, or having been, a "Christian nation."

Despite this increasing diversity, adherents of thee different religions routinely declare that their beliefs are both objectively true and essential for spiritual liberation. The dizzying plethora of religious options has led many to argue that religious claims to an exclusive and saving truth are persistent evidence of an unenlightened and outmoded dogmatism. Religions, therefore, must succumb to a saner and more humble estimation of themselves, in order to avert religious controversy and strife.

The Elephant and the Blind Men

According to many, a popular parable about an elephant and several blind men illustrates a vital truth about the relationship among the world's religions. The story promises that religious intolerance and even violence can be overcome through mutual understanding and humility. Can a mythical elephant and some blind men deliver the elixir for our religious struggles and confusions?

As the story goes, several blind men were feeling an elephant. (Just how the elephant became placid enough to endure this inspection is never explained.) The man who felt the tusk said the beast was smooth and hard. The one feeling the tail described the elephant as thin and wiry. The man who touched the ear believed the animal to be a soft and flexible creature. The man rubbing his hand over the hide said the elephant was hard and rough like clay. Each man had but a limited exposure and understanding of the entity he was assessing. Because of his ignorance of the whole truth, each man assumed the entire elephant matched his very limited description. Of course, the elephant is made of all the things the blind men described. The tusk is smooth, the ear is soft, the hide is rough, and the tail is wiry.

The moral of the story is that each religion has only partial knowledge, but each mistakenly thinks it has captured the essence of religious truth. From an enlightened vantage point, one sees that all religions are part of the one divine reality (the same elephant). Therefore, the squabbles, struggles and even wars that are fought over religious disagreements are pointless. All religions capture some important religious truths, and they should honor each other accordingly. Those who invoke this parable advise their audience to remember this story the next time they are tempted to make exclusive claims about their part of the religious elephant.

What is Religion?

We will return to our elephant and his friends in due time. First we need to consider the nature and function of religion in order to evaluate the claim that all religions are, in some significant sense, one.

Defining religion is notoriously difficult. We know that Buddhism, Islam, Christianity, Judaism and Hinduism are religions. What essential attribute do they share that makes them religions and not something else?

Some have argued that a sense of ultimate commitment is the defining feature of all religions. In that case, one could label Marxism a religion, although it is atheistic and advocates no methods for spiritual enlightenment, apart from understanding Marxist philosophy and fomenting revolution.

On the other hand, we know that Buddhism is a religion, yet Theravada Buddhists are either agnostic or atheistic. Theism, therefore, is not an essential aspect of religion. Furthermore, many who believe in God but adhere to no religious tradition would be called irreligious.

A loose but workable understanding of religion is that religions claim to explain the nature of the sacred and how humans can come to terms with it. All the major world religions make truth-claims about ultimate reality, the human condition, and how humans can find spiritual liberation.

A "truth-claim "is an assertion that claims to accurately represent or correspond with reality. This is the doctrinal dimension of religion, which is indispensable to its identity.[1] Religions founders, whether Buddha or Jesus or Muhammad, purport to have received knowledge of objective truth—truth that all need to know. The various truth-claims of religions have a strong experiential focus. A philosopher may speculate about the Absolute, but she will not gather a religious sect to follow her conjectures even to the death. Religions, on the other hand, pronounce truths that are viewed as momentous and life-changing.

For instance, after Siddhartha Gautama found enlightenment and became the Buddha ("enlightened one"), he preached the way to enlightenment (nirvana)—a teaching that could not be found in the Hindu systems of his time. The Buddha claimed that if one wanted release from the wheel of birth and rebirth (reincarnation), one must follow his teaching on the eightfold path to freedom from craving and suffering.

In another context, Jesus of Nazareth proclaimed that he himself was "the way the truth and the life," and that peace with God the Father could come only through him (John 14:6). These claims were not offered as idle speculations or religious opinions, but as transformational truths. Neither Buddha nor Christ were religious relativists who went around mumbling, "This is true for me, but it may not be true for you." They were far more sober than that.

Religions are embedded in cultures and serve a number of social and psychological functions. They serve to unite a community, to give hope, or to challenge or sanction secular powers. As William James pointed out in *The Varieties of Religious Experience*, despite the vast differences between religions "there is a certain uniform deliverance in which religions all appear to meet. This common element has two parts: (1) an uneasiness; and (2) its solution. (1) The uneasiness, reduced to its simplest terms, is a sense that there is something wrong about us as we naturally stand. (2) The solution is a sense that we are saved from the wrongness by making proper connection with the higher powers."[2]

However, the nature of the problem and the manner of the solution proposed have been defined in widely differing ways. Religions may be similar in form and function, but they claim contradictory things about ultimate reality, the human condition, and spiritual liberation. G. K. Chesterton made this point in his classic work Orthodoxy when he countered the idea that "the religions of the earth differ in rites and forms, but they are the same in what they teach." This idea, he maintained,

> is false; it is the opposite of the fact. The religions of the earth do not greatly differ in rites and forms; they do greatly differ in what they teach… The truth is that the difficulty of all the creeds of the earth is not as alleged in this cheap maxim: that they agree in meaning, but disagree in machinery. It is exactly the opposite. They agree in machinery; almost every great religion on earth works with the same external methods, with priests, scriptures, altars, sworn brotherhoods, special feasts. They agree in the mode of teaching; what they differ about is the thing to be taught… Creeds that exist to destroy each other both have scriptures, just as armies that exist to destroy each other both have guns.[3]

Chesterton emphasizes that the use of certain cultural forms does not imply any agreement on the actual religious teachings propounded through those forms. For instance, both socialists and capitalists have strongly held worldviews that they express in magazines and books. However, the common use of literature to promote beliefs does nothing to harmonize conflicting beliefs. When Chesterton says that creeds exist to destroy each other, he is not arguing that religions should take up arms against each other.

He means that every religion issues truth-claims about essential elements of its worldview that cannot be squared with the essential truth-claims of other religions. For instance, Hindus, Christians, and Muslims all pray; yet they differ in their idea of the God to whom they pray.

One straightforward way to test the idea that all religions are one is to compare the essential teachings of three major religious traditions. If all the major world religions were ultimately expressions of the same reality, we would expect them to agree on matters of *ultimate reality, the human condition, and spiritual liberation*. At the very least we would expect to find some strategy by which to unify their apparently

---

[1] On truth-claims and religion, see Mortimer Adler, *Truth in Religion: The Plurality of Religions and the Unity of Truth* (New York: Macmillan, 1990) and Harold Netland, *Dissonant Voices: Religious Pluralism and the Quest for Truth* (Grand Rapids, MI: Eerdmans, 1991).

[2] William James, *The Varieties of Religious Experience: The Works of William James*, ed. Frederick Burkhardt (Cambridge: Harvard University Press, 1985), 400.

[3] G. K. Chesterton, *Orthodoxy* (Garden City, NY: Doubleday, 1959), 128–29.

contradictory teachings, as with the elephant story.

A chief temptation in the study of comparative religion is to alter religious teachings in order to squeeze them into a common system. In a recent popular book, *Living Buddha, Living Christ*, the Buddhist monk Thich Nhat Hanh describes the Christian ceremony of Communion as a way in which Christians reflect on their interconnections with the earth, as represented by the wine and the bread. He says:

> If we allow ourselves to touch the bread deeply, we become reborn, because our bread is life itself. Eating it deeply, we touch the sun, the clouds, the earth, and everything in the cosmos. We touch life, and we touch the Kingdom of God.[4]

Hanh straps Christian Communion onto the Procrustean bed of Buddhism so as to describe it in a manner that denies the Christ-centered practice of remembering Jesus' broken body (the bread) and shed blood (the wine) which were offered through his death on the cross. This maneuver does nothing to bring greater understanding to religious discussion, because it does not honor the intrinsic meaning of the religion being described. The kingdom of God, biblically understood, is not a matter of oneness with the cosmos, but of God's personal reign and redeeming presence.

To test the idea that all religions are one, we will compare the teachings of Christianity, Islam, and non-dualistic Hinduism in these three basic areas; ultimate reality, the nature of humanity, and spiritual liberation. We will be careful to describe each system of belief in a way that is faithful to the different traditions—and leave the Procrustean bed to Procrustes and his erring followers.

ULTIMATE REALITY: TRINITY, ALLAH, OR BRAHMAN?

What Christianity Says:
Both the Old and the New Testaments reveal God to be the unique and supreme Creator of the universe. "In the beginning God created the heavens and the earth" (Genesis 1:1). God is the eternal Creator; he cannot be identified with the cosmos because he is transcendent, separate from creation in his essential being. Paul preached that God is a self-existent being upon whom the universe depends (Acts 17:25). God announced himself to Moses in the burning bush as "I AM WHO I AM" (Exodus 3:14). God is a self-reflective, personal being–a center of consciousness in relation to his creation. The prophet Isaiah repeatedly describes God's unmatched power and excellence in personal and sovereign terms: "Turn to me and be saved, all you ends of the earth; for I am God, and there is no other" (Isaiah 45:22). When Jesus taught his disciples to pray, he said they should address God as their "Father" (Matthew 6:9). The personal language the Bible uses to describe God refers to God's very character; it is not a poetic accommodation used to describe a being beyond personality, as in some forms of Hinduism.

Beyond being merely monotheistic, Christianity is Trinitarian, which distinguishes it from other forms of theism. There is one God (Deuteronomy 6:4), who eternally exists in three equal persons: the Father (Ephesians 1:3), the Son (John 1:1) and the Holy Spirit (Acts 5:1–5). The doctrine of the Trinity does not imply that one equals three, which would be a logical contradiction. Instead it teaches that there is one divine essence or substance that exists in three persons. So God is one in one sense and three in a different sense. This doctrine is not explicit in the Old Testament, but it is intimated and certainly not precluded.[5] The New Testament writings teach that Jesus is God Incarnate, the promised Messiah of the Old Testament. Jesus said, "I and the Father are one," which his audience identified as a claim to deity (John 10:30). The apostle Paul affirmed that Jesus suspended some of his divine prerogatives by becoming a human servant for the purpose of redeeming his erring creatures (2 Corinthians 8:9; Philippians 2:6–11).

What Islam Says:
Islam claims to be a fulfillment of Christianity, yet it denies many essential Christian teachings. The Qur'an,

---

[4] Thich Nhat Hanh, *Living Buddha, Living Christ* (New York: G.P. Putnam's Sons, 1995), 31. Hanh often redefines Christianity in Buddhist terms.
[5] On this see Millard Erickson, *God in Three Persons: A Contemporary Interpretation of the Trinity* (Grand Rapids, MI: Baker, 1995), 159–74.

Islam's holy book, teaches that God (Allah) is an absolute unity that allows for no distinctions of persons. Islam insists that Allah is the Creator and sovereign Lord of the universe and is the ultimate Judge of all people. In his passionate condemnation of idolatry, Muhammad, the prophet of Allah, rejected the idea that Jesus, a human being, could in any sense be God. Jesus was hailed as a great prophet of Allah and even as the Messiah, but not God Incarnate. Islam rejects the worship of Jesus as *shirk* (the sinful worship of the creature instead of the creator). The Qur'an affirms that

> Allah is One, the Eternal God.
> He begat none, nor was He begotten.
> None is equal to Him (Surah 112:1–4).

In claiming that "He begat none," these verses deny the biblical claim that Jesus is the "only begotten Son" (John 3:16 KJV). It is very likely that Muhammad never understood the orthodox view of the Trinity and instead rejected several heretical views common during his time, including Adoptionism, the teaching that Jesus became God after first existing as a human.[6] Nevertheless, Islam continues to reject the idea that the divine unity can include three coeternal and equal persons.

Islam and Christianity are both monotheistic: there is but one God, and he cannot be identified with his creation. God alone is worthy of worship and honor. They agree on this doctrine. However, Islam contradicts the New Testament witness that God is most fully revealed in Jesus Christ and that Jewish monotheism anticipated the fuller revelation of God as triune. When Muslims worship God without Christ, Christians remember the apostle John's statement "No one who denies the Son has the Father" (I John 2:23). When Christians worship God in three persons and Christ as the incarnation of God, Muslims pronounce them guilty of shirk and cite a passage in the Qur'an where Jesus is said to deny his deity (Surah 5:115–118). This is a titanic divide between the two faiths.

What Nondualistic Hinduism Says:

Outside the monotheistic traditions lies the worldview of nondualistic (or Advaita Vedanta) Hinduism. Hinduism is a religion of great variety, with six major schools and plenty of theological disagreements. I have chosen one school as representative of pantheistic monism, a worldview that has recently influenced the West largely through Transcendental Meditation and the New Age movement.[7] In its classic form as taught by Sankara (A.D. 788–820), nondualistic Hinduism claims that reality is ultimately one (monism). All apparent distinctions, dualities and diversities are not real but illusory (*maya*) and due to ignorance (*avidya*) of the ultimate reality. This great oneness or nonduality is Brahman, the supreme deity of Hindu scripture. Brahman is the totality of reality (pantheism); there is nothing but Brahman.

Monism cannot become a partner with monotheism. Nondualism denies the duality of the Creator-creature distinction that is affirmed by both Islam and Christianity. While Islam and Christianity teach that the creation must not be worshiped, nondualistic Hinduism teaches that there is nothing but the divine. The dualistic idea of separating Creator from creation must be dropped. The self itself is divine in essence. In one famous Hindu scripture, the Chandogya Upanishad, a son asks his father about the nature of God. He is told, "That art thou."[8] The self is identical with God.

Furthermore, the God of nondualistic Hinduism is not a personal being but an impersonal principle or essence which is beyond personality. Although nondualists may accommodate popular sentiments by allowing worship of a personal God (*saguna Brahman*), this is deemed a lower and inadequate understanding from which one should graduate to a higher knowledge of God as impersonal (*nirguna Brahman*).[9] Brahman is not a personal agent who enters into relationship with his creatures. There are no agents, no creatures, no relationships. All is one.[10]

---

[6] See Geoffrey Parrinder, *Jesus in the Qur'an* (New York: Oxford Press, 1977), 137.

7 On the relationship between pantheistic monism and New Age perspectives, see Douglas Groothuis, *Unmasking the New Age* (Downers Grove, IL: InterVarsity, 1986) and *Confronting the New Age* (Downers Grove, IL: InterVarsity, 1988).

[8] Swami Prabhavananda and Frederick Manchester, *The Upanishads: Breath of the Eternal* (New York: Mentor, 1957), 70.

[9] For an insightful discussion and critique of this distinction, see Stuart Hackett, *Oriental Philosophy: A Westerner's Guide to Eastern Thought* (Madison: University of Wisconsin Press, 1979), 145–67.

[10] For a good general treatment of pantheistic monism see James Sire, *The Universe Next Door*, 2nd ed. (Downers Grove, IL: InterVarsity, 1988), 135–55.

The notion that the teachings of all religions are essentially the same has not fared well so far in our analysis of differing views of ultimate reality. As we look at the different views of human nature and spiritual liberation, we will discover more fundamental disagreements.

THE HUMAN CONDITION: SINFUL, DEFECTIVE, OR DIVINE?

What Christianity Says:

To borrow a phrase form Blaise Pascal, Christianity sees humans as deposed royalty.[11] Man and woman were made in the image and likeness of God for the purpose of having fellowship with God and each other, and in order to cultivate and develop God's good creation (Genesis 1–2). Scripture roots humanity not in an impersonal deity but in the creative activity of God. We share a God given dignity as persons created by a personal God. However, humans disobeyed the wise will of God and fell into disobedience and sin (Genesis 3). Ever since, all people have suffered both by nature and by choice from the effects of this Fall from grace (Romans 3). We were divinely created, but we bear the marks of rebellion. According to Paul, "All have sinned and fall short of the glory of God" (Romans 3:23). The Bible views sin as a force that has corrupted every aspect of human nature and affects all areas of life. It is primarily a moral offense against a morally perfect God, and it severs the divine-human relationship (Psalm 51:4).

What Islam Says:

Islam also teaches that humans are creations of God but have lost their original innocence before God (Surah 20:116–22). Yet, as Harold Netland notes:

> Although Islam does acknowledge Adam's sin and expulsion from the Garden, it does not have anything corresponding to the Christian doctrine of original sin and the total depravity of human nature. There is, of course, a sense of sin in Islam, but it seems to signify more a weakness, defect, or flaw in human character rather than the radical corruption of human nature.[12]

Men and women are not enslaved to sin, according to Islam. With resolution of will, they are able to obey Allah and resist human and demonic temptations. This teaching opposes the Christian understanding of sin as entrenched and pervasive. As Bishop Stephen Neill put it, "At the heart of the Muslim-Christian disagreement, we shall find a deep difference in the understanding of the nature of sin."[13]

What Nondualistic Hinduism Says:

According to nondualistic Hinduism, human beings are inherently one with Brahman. The individual self (sometimes referred to as Atman) is not a creature of Brahman or distinct from Brahman in being. The sense of separation comes only from ignorance of one's ultimate identity. Since God is impersonal and all-encompassing, there is not notion of sin as a moral offense against a holy God. There is a breach in the divine-human relationship through immortality. The core problem is a lack of awareness of one's true essence as divine. As Sankara taught, "The difference between the individual self and the highest Lord is owing to wrong knowledge only, not to any reality."[14]

SPIRITUAL LIBERATION: FAITH, WORKS, OR ENLIGHTENMENT?

Lastly, we come to the vital matter of spiritual liberation. As William James observed, all religions offer purported solutions to the human condition. Just what is wrong? How can it be corrected? Again we find three entirely different sets of answers.

---

[11] Blaise Pascal, *Pensees* 116/398 (New York: Penguin, 1966), 59.
[12] Netland, *Dissonant Voices*, 89.
[13] Stephen Neill, *Crises of Belief: The Christian Dialogue with Faith and No Faith* (London: Hodder & Stoughton, 1984), 88.
[14] Quoted from *A Sourcebook in Indian Philosophy*, ed. Sarvepalli Radhkrishnan and Charles A. Moore (Princeton, NJ: Princeton University Press, 1957), 515.

What Christianity Says:

Christians hail Jesus as the Lord and Savior of humanity. Contrary to Islam, Christians esteem Jesus and God Incarnate, who lived a perfect life, died a sacrificial death on the cross so that people could be reconciled to a holy God, and rose from the dead to vindicate his mission (Romans 1:4). Jesus proclaimed that "God so loved the world that he sent his one and only Son, that whosoever believes him shall not perish but have eternal life" (John 3:16). Paul taught that there is one mediator between God and humanity, Christ Jesus, who gave himself as a ransom for all people (I Timothy 2:5–6). In Christianity, spiritual liberation bestows on the believer the complete forgiveness of sins and a righteous standing before God. This is received by faith alone in Christ alone through God's grace alone (Ephesians 2:8). The sincere believer can be assured that he or she has received eternal life because "the Spirit himself testifies with our spirit that we are God's children" (Romans 8:16).

What Islam Says:

In Islam there is no mediator between Allah and his creatures. Muhammad is a bearer of information about Allah, but not a savior.[15] He may be emulated as an example, but he is never looked to for salvation. One must stand or fall on one's merit, according to one's obedience to the commands of Allah: "no soul shall bear another's burden and… each man shall be judged by his own labours" (Surah 53:38). The Qur'an breathes the last judgment in its every chapter (*surah*). Judgment hangs heavily in the air: "On that day no soul shall suffer the least injustice. You shall be rewarded according to your deeds" (Surah 36:45; compare 82:19). Deeds will determine paradise or hell. Salvation comes through works, not by faith alone. Yet no Muslim is assured of his or her eternal fate at the judgment.[16]

What Nondualistic Hinduism Says:

Spiritual liberation (*moksha*) for nondualistic Hindus is attained through the proper yoga (spiritual practice). Sankara taught that *jnana* yoga (the yoga of knowledge) was the means to realize the self's identity as Brahman. Sankara said that "the man who has once comprehended Brahman to be the Self does not belong to this transmigratory [reincarnational] world as he did before. He, on the other hand, who still belongs to this transmigratory world as before has not comprehended Brahman to be the Self."[17] One who experiences *moksha* is released from the wheel of reincarnation and rests in the divine identity. Faith in an external being (a personal God) is excluded because there is no external being. All is one. Good works done to earn salvation are also eliminated, since salvation is not given by another being. Everyone is Brahman (whether one knows it or not). The knowledge of one's divine essence is what brings salvation.

ASSESSING THE DIFFERENCES

Let us return to the proverb of the elephant and the blind men. What can this story do to harmonize the conflicting accounts of spiritual reality? We should first realize that the elephant story puts the world's religions in the position of blind men! No world religion would accept this assessment, because they each claim to reveal ultimate and universal truths, not partial insights needing elaboration from other religions. The religious interpreter who employs the elephant story is claiming to look down on all the religions from an elevated vantage point that none of them have attained. In essence, the interpreter is creating a new supra-religion that denies the particular claims of the actual religions he or she is assessing.[18] But can the supposedly elevated view really reconcile the divergent claims we have discovered?

Although an elephant can be rough in one spot and smooth in another, it cannot be smooth all over and rough all over simultaneously. When Islam claims that God is absolutely unitary with no allowance for three persons or the Incarnation, it excludes the Christian doctrine of the Trinity. It cannot be harmonized with this doctrine by saying that part of God is absolutely unitary and part is a Trinity. God cannot possess contradictory attributes (nor can anything else). Neither can we align the nondualistic views of impersonal

[15] See Josef van Ess, "The Image of God and Islamic Mysticism, the Image of Man and Society," in *Christianity and the World's Religions*, ed. Hans Kung, Heinrich von Stietencron and Heinze Bechert (Garden City, NY: Doubleday, 1986), 71.

[16] See Netland, *Dissonant Voices*, 90–91.

[17] Quoted in Radhkrishnan and Moore, ed., *Sourcebook*, 513.

[18] On this see Lesslie Newbigin, *The Gospel in a Pluralist Society* (Grand Rapids, MI: Eerdmans, 1989), 9–10.

Brahman with the thoroughly personal notions of deity found in Islam and Christianity. God's nature cannot be both personal and impersonal because personality cancels out impersonality and vice versa. One either has personality or does not. An elephant may be partially smooth and partially rough at the same time. Neither can God be both personal and impersonal.

The same difficulties are encountered with the different religious teachings on human nature and spiritual liberation, concepts closely tied to the varying doctrines of ultimate reality. Humans cannot be both one with Brahman and distinct from their Creator. Sankara's assessment of our ignorance of our divinity is at odds with monotheism.

Neither can the disagreement between Islam and Christianity be solved through recourse to the elephant story. If we are morally incapacitated by sin (Christianity), we are not merely wounded by sin (Islam) and vice versa. It follows that if we can be saved by works (Islam), it is false to say we are saved by faith alone through the grace of God totally apart from works (Christianity). Differing descriptions of ultimate reality lead to differing descriptions of the human problem and to differing prescriptions for its solution. It seems that the elephant and its benighted observers have let us down.

Nevertheless, several modern thinkers–of whom John Hick is the most prominent—have tried to harmonize the world's religions.[19] Hick's theory of religions pluralism is too involved to be adequately criticized here.[20] However, we can inspect some important elements of his approach in order to highlight its problems.

JOHN HICK'S RELIGIOUS PLURALISM

Hick believes that all the major religions produce saintly people; therefore, salvation cannot be restricted to one religion. His strategy for reconciling conflicting truth-claims involves creating an all-encompassing category called the Real, which signifies the ultimate reality that is the source of the diverse manifestations of the major world religions. Hick knows that religions disagree on the nature of ultimate reality, humanity and spiritual liberation. Rather than siding with one religion against the others, he claims that all express "the Real" in different but equal ways.

However, this removes from the Real any meaningful intellectual content. We cannot say it is personal, because this would oppose pantheism; neither can we say it is impersonal, because this would oppose theism. We cannot even say it is divine, since Theravada Buddhism does not equate nirvana with a deity. The upshot is that Hick's idea of the Real becomes itself unreal. How can something be neither personal nor impersonal? Furthermore, why would the Real manifest itself in one religion by offering salvation only through Christ and in another religion by offering it through a mystical intuition of Brahman? The Real would be perjuring itself.

Hick tries to handle these disagreements by claiming that whenever a religion makes exclusive claims about reality (as they all do in one way or another), the religion overextends itself. The enlightened vantage point sees all religions as partial expressions of the Real–even if the religions themselves allow no such category. Again, Hicks creates a suprareligious (and ultimately irreligious) category in order to harmonize religions. In so doing, he hauls out the old Procrustean bed, this time fitted with more modern sheets.

Another problem haunts Hick's efforts. In his system, the Real is really unknowable or ineffable. He claims that it is beyond the reach of concepts. Hick is forced into this position if he is to defend the equality of mutually contradictory religious claims. This appeal to the unknowable really solves nothing and triggers an avalanche of problems. If all Hick can say of the Real is that it exists and is the source of the world's religions, he can say nothing specific about its actual nature. Hick admits that we cannot refer to the Real as having knowledge or as being powerful, good or loving. The blind men knew more about the elephant than Hick says religions know about the Real! If the Real is unknowable, it cannot adequately explain the nature of the world's religions. If our concepts about the Real never capture its essential nature, why should we trust the concept that the Real is the source of religious manifestations, especially when these traditions explicitly contradict each other on fundamental doctrines? The real becomes mute—and meaningless.

---

[19] The most developed statement of Hick's position is *An Interpretation of Religion* (New Haven, CT: Yale University Press, 1988).

[20] For more thorough critiques, see Netland, *Dissonant Voices*, especially chaps. 5–7, and Ronald Nash, *Is Jesus the Only Savior?* (Grand Rapids, MI: Zondervan, 1995), chapters. 1–6.

ACCOUNTING FOR JESUS CHRIST

The ideas of Hick and other religious pluralists finally collapse when they meet the person of Jesus Christ. They cannot accept him as he is presented in the New Testament and still claim that all religions are one.

Although many religions claim that God intervenes in or influences the world, Christianity is unique in claiming that God became a human being in history, once and for all, for the purpose of our redemption. Hinduism teaches that the impersonal Brahman sometimes takes a personal form as an avatar to help enlighten the ignorant. Avatars are often historically shadowy figures and have little in common with Christ.[21] Although the Buddha and Christ are often compared, the historical Buddha made no claims of divinity or even of being an oracle of God. Rather, he taught of way of liberation based on meditation and right action, irrespective of any deity.[22] And Islam insists that although Muhammad is Allah's prophet, Allah himself cannot be embodied.

The historical narratives of the New Testament all affirm that Jesus of Nazareth was a man–but more than a man. We find Jesus announcing that he came to seek and to save what was lost and "to give his life as a ransom for many" (Matthew 20:28). He claimed the divine "authority on earth to forgive sins" (Mark 2:10). When debating religious leaders of his day he said, "Before Abraham was, I am" (John 8:58), a clear assertion of being identified with the divine "I AM WHO I AM" of the Old Testament (Exodus 3:14).

Jesus backed up these claims with impeccable and unrepeatable credentials. He healed the sick, raised the dead, taught with unparalleled authority, associated with the lowly, and fulfilled a score of Old Testament prophecies concerning the promised Messiah, the suffering servant who was to be wounded for our transgressions but vindicated by God (Isaiah 53). The apostle Paul proclaimed that this vindication burst forth in Jesus' resurrection from the dead (Romans 1:4), a verifiable fact of history (I Corinthians 15:1–9).[23]

Are all religions one? Given their contradictory claims and the nature of truth, they cannot all be one with the truth. They offer vastly different views of spiritual reality and salvation. Yet in Christ, we are offered spiritual reality in the flesh, a reality that welcomes all to partake of his grace. As Jesus said:

> Come to me, all you who are weary, and burdened, and I will give you rest. Take my yoke upon you and learn from me, for I am gentle and humble in heart, and you will find rest for your souls. For my yoke is easy and my burden is light (Matthew 11:28–29).

Jesus himself welcomes into his family needy people from every race and religious background. All who know Christ as Lord are brothers and sisters in God's adopted family. By turning away from our sinful patterns of life and by turning toward Jesus as Savior, we also embrace a rich variety of God's multicolored and multiethnic people worldwide. The spiritual unity found in Jesus Christ (Galatians 3:26–28) is a tonic to the ethnocentrism and racism that plague the planet.

The apostle Paul taught that Jesus' death on the cross reconciles us to God and allows us to be reconciled to each other in order to create a new humanity (Ephesians 2:15). All religions are not one, but all people can find oneness at the foot of Christ's cross.

---

*This essay originally appeared as a booklet produced by InterVarsity Press
   Douglas Groothuis, *Are All Religions One?* (Downers Grove, IL: InterVarsity, 1999).
**Reproduction rights granted by InterVarsity Press.

---

[21] On the avatar doctrine in relation to the Incarnation, see Geoffrey Parrinder, *Avatar and Incarnation* (New York: Barnes and Noble, 1970).

[22] For an insightful comparison between Buddha and Jesus, see Russell Aldwinkle, *More Than a Man: A Study in Christology* (Grand Rapids, MI: Eerdmans, 1976), 211–46.

[23] See William Lane Craig, "Did Jesus Rise from the Dead?" in *Jesus Under Fire: Modern Scholarship Reinvents the Historical Jesus*, ed. Michael J. Wilkins and J. P. Moreland (Grand Rapids, MI.: Zondervan, 1995), 141–76.

ARE ALL RELIGIONS ONE?
ESSAY QUESTIONS

Answer the questions below on a separate sheet of paper and be prepared to review your answers in class.

1. **What is the moral of the elephant illustration?**

The moral of the elephant illustration is that each religion has only partial knowledge of religious truth or reality. Christianity, Islam, Hinduism, and every other religion on earth will collectively give us the totality of religious truth. Therefore, all religions should be careful not to make exclusive claims about the whole of reality because all other religions also have a portion of the truth. [SM p. 39]

2. **How is religion defined?**

A religion is a system of belief that attempts to define the nature of the divine and how humans can understand and interact with it. All religions make truth-claims about ultimate reality, the human condition, and spiritual liberation. Therefore, a religion is a way of viewing reality, i.e. a worldview. This is why some atheistic worldviews such as Marxism are labeled as religious. [SM pp. 39–41]

3. **Why weren't Buddha, Christ, or Muhammad religious relativists?**

Siddhartha Gautama rejected Hinduism's notions of truth and chose another religious system that he believed to be true. Jesus Christ claimed that he was divine and the only path to salvation, while Muhammad taught that Jesus was not God and that salvation could only be obtained through obedience to Allah. All three of these individuals were not simply offering the world their opinions or making claims about their preferences, but in fact disagreed with each other on key issues. Buddha, Jesus, and Muhammad each taught that they had the truth and that those who opposed them were wrong. [SM p. 40]

4. **According to Christianity, why can God not be identified with the cosmos?**

Christians believe that creation must have originated from something other than itself. In addition, something that is created cannot be compared to its creator. Therefore, Christians believe that God (the Creator) and the cosmos (the creation) cannot be one and the same. [SM p. 41]

5. **How is non-dualism incompatible with both Christianity and Islam?**

Non-dualism denies the separation between the Creator and his creation. Both Islam and Christianity affirm this distinction, while non-dualistic Hinduism sees God as part of creation. In fact, this branch of Hinduism sees everything as interconnected, meaning that we are all part of God (Brahman). [SM p. 41–2]

SM
47

6. **What happens when a religious pluralist tries to harmonize contrary religious beliefs?**

In order to harmonize contrary religious beliefs, the religious pluralist must alter them so drastically that the result can no longer be legitimately identified with the original source beliefs.

For example, the Buddhist monk Thich Nhat Hanh tried to redefine the Kingdom of God to reflect Buddhist principles rather than Christian definitions. Hanh taught that the Kingdom of God was basically oneness with the cosmos, whereas Christ taught that it was God's redeeming presence and personal reign. [SM p. 41]

7. **How do Christianity, Islam, and non-dualistic Hinduism view the human condition?**

Christianity sees human beings as enslaved to sin, which has corrupted every aspect of human nature and affects all areas of life. It is primarily a moral offense against a morally perfect God and it severs our relationship with him.

Islam does not see mankind as being enslaved to sin. Humanity is seen as weak, defective, or flawed in character. However, human beings do not possess a corrupted human nature. With resolution of will, human beings are able to obey Allah and resist human and demonic temptation.

Non-dualistic Hinduism sees human beings as inherently one with Brahman. Individuals (or Atman) are not distinct from Brahman, but are merely part of the divine everything. There is no sin or moral offense against a holy God because there is no personal God to offend. The only breach in the divine-human relationship has come through immorality. [SM p. 43]

8. **How does one find spiritual liberation according to Christianity? Islam? Non-Dualistic Hinduism?**

According to Christianity, spiritual liberation—the complete forgiveness of sins and a righteous standing before God—is received by faith alone in Christ alone through grace alone. Human beings do not earn salvation through works or achieve liberation through enlightenment.

According to Islam, human beings stand or fall on each individual's merit and obedience to the commands of Allah. No soul can bear another's burden—each person is judged by his or her own deeds. Therefore, humanity has no savior. Instead, human beings are granted either salvation or damnation based upon the comparative weight of their good and bad works.

According to non-dualistic Hinduism, spiritual liberation consists of release from the wheel of reincarnation and rest within the divine identity (Brahman). This can only be reached through enlightenment or knowledge of one's divine essence. Those who do not reach this state are destined to be reincarnated. [SM pp. 43–4]

9. **In the elephant illustration, who are the blind men and who is the interpreter? Why wouldn't world religions accept the elephant illustration?**

In the illustration, the blind men are the world's religions, each possessing an accurate understanding only of their portion of the elephant. For example, if one of the blind men were to claim that the entire elephant were rough because his portion were rough, he would be incorrect in making such a generalization. Similarly, if Christianity were to claim that all individuals receive salvation through Jesus Christ alone, this assertion would be an incorrect generalization about all people.

In the illustration, the interpreter of the story is the one with the bird's eye view of the elephant. He is the religious pluralist, the only individual with the privilege of possessing the entire truth.

Religions would reject such an illustration because each religion claims to reveal universal truths about reality. Most religions do not claim to have only partial insight that needs elaboration from other religions or the religious pluralist. [SM pp. 44–5]

10. **What is a truth-claim? Why does religious pluralism ultimately fail when applied to religions that are making truth-claims?**

A truth-claim is an assertion that professes to accurately represent reality. All religions make such statements, which are indispensable to every system of religious belief. In general, religions make claims about the whole of reality rather than a mere part of it. [SM p. 39]

Religious pluralism could only be viable if religions were not making truth-claims. However, most religions are making such claims. Either those religions are incorrect in making truth-claims or some of their claims are incorrect. It is logically impossible for two contradictory truth-claims to both be true in the same sense at the same time. For example, consider the following:

- Humans cannot be both one with Brahman and distinct from their Creator.
- God cannot be both personal and impersonal.
- If we are morally incapacitated by sin, we are not merely wounded by sin.
- If we are saved by faith alone, then works cannot save us. [SM pp. 44–5]

"EXISTENCE AND NATURE OF GOD"
WITH FRANK BECKWITH

"Your faith does not rest on the latest argument by the best philosopher that came out yesterday… your faith rests on what you know to be true by your commitment to Christ. The arguments and reasons are part of the puzzle; they give you reinforcement as to why you believe."

I. Attributes of God

"One of the great paradoxes of believing that everyone is part of God is that most people don't realize it… if you were God, wouldn't you know it? Being omniscient and not knowing it is a really big problem."

  A. Creator and sustainer (of all *else* that exists)

      1. "Who made God?" misses the point

      2. Acts 17:25; Colossians 1:16; Romans 11:36

  B. _____Omnipotent_____: All-powerful

      1. Nonsense question: "Can God make a rock so big that he cannot lift it?"

        "Omnipotence does not mean that God can do anything that you can string together in words. Stringing together things in words may not be anything that is actually even possible… For example, God cannot make a married bachelor… but that doesn't count against God. If it is not a thing that is conceptually possible, then God cannot do it."

      2. Things that God cannot do:

          i. Make square circles or married bachelors (nonsensical things)

          ii. Sin, lie, cease to exist (goes against his perfection)

            "Neither do we lessen God's power when we say that he cannot die or be deceived. This is the kind of inability, which, if removed, would make God less powerful than he is. It is precisely because he is omnipotent that some things are impossible." — Saint Augustine

  C. _____Omniscient_____: All-knowing

      1. Knows past, present, and future

      2. Psalm 139:17–18; Isaiah 46:10, 41:21–24

D. _____Disembodied_____: Spirit

    1. Everywhere: Aware of everything and sustains everything

    2. Nowhere: Transcends time and space

    3. John 4:24

E. _____Necessary_____: Cannot not exist

F. _____Rational Agent_____: A person or being

II. The Existence of God

A. God's existence is not dependent upon us.

    1. Our belief in him does not make God real.

    2. He exists independently of our minds.

B. We cannot observe God in his fullness.

III. Arguments for the Existence of God

"To present an argument to those who do not believe… is not saying that in order for you to believe you must have an argument. There are numerous people on this planet who are perfectly rational for believing in God who are not philosophers."

A. _____Transcendental_____ Argument

    1. Atheistic/naturalistic worldview

        i. Only physical things exist—no soul, mind, or morality

        ii. Human beings are the result of blind chance and evolution.

    2. Theistic Christian worldview

        i. Physical and non-physical things exist—morality, minds, souls, numbers

        ii. While physical things change, non-physical things do not—e.g. logic.

    3. If your mind is the result of blind chance, how can you trust your own mind?

    "If you knew that a computer had software downloaded at random, would you buy that computer? No… because you know it wouldn't give you true information. Your mind according to the naturalistic worldview is not only physical, but the result of chance and survival of the fittest… it may be that we've survived as the result of us not knowing the truth about the world. Maybe our minds lie to us and that helps us survive. How do you know that you know anything? In an atheistic worldview, you have no assurance of even knowledge itself."

    4. Evil only makes sense if there is an objective good

B. ____Kalam Cosmological____ Argument

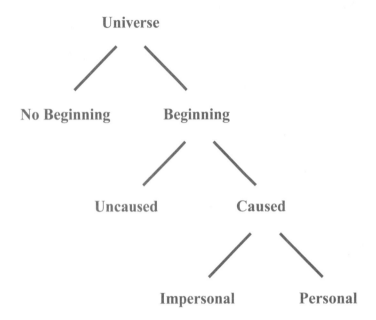

1. No beginning vs. beginning

    i. Big Bang Theory: Something came from nothing

    ii. Second Law of Thermodynamics: Universe is moving toward heat death

    iii. Actual infinite: unlimited set

        1) Logically impossible

        2) If the past were infinite, we couldn't be here today.

2. Uncaused vs. caused

    i. If the universe were uncaused, then it would have always existed.

    ii. An actual infinite is logically impossible.

3. Impersonal vs. personal

IV. Conceptually Possible vs. Logically Impossible

A. Miracles are both conceptually and logically possible.

    1. Virgin birth

    2. Prior to the 1900s, flying in an airplane

B. Nonsense is neither conceptually nor logically possible.

"EXISTENCE AND NATURE OF GOD"
VIDEO QUESTIONS

Answer the questions below on a separate sheet of paper and be prepared to review your answers in class.

1. Who made God?

Many theists will point out that something cannot come from nothing. Since the universe is a "something," it must have come from "something" as opposed to "nothing." However, this argument is often countered with the question, "Who made God?" This is a fair question. If we contend that everything comes from something else, then it seems logical to ask about God's origins.

However, theists do not argue that everything comes from something else. We believe that reason and experience demonstrates that all natural things come from something else. God, on the other hand, does not fit into this category. In fact, it was God who created, designed, and sustains everything that exists.

[Have your students review in context Acts 17:25, Colossians 1:16, and Romans 11:36.]

2. How is God omnipotent? Are there things God cannot do? How is God omniscient? How is God omnipresent?

To claim that God is omnipotent is not to say that God can do anything and everything, as some individuals assume. Rather, the quality of omnipotence means that God is the most powerful being. There are things God cannot do. God cannot perform acts that are contrary to his perfection (e.g. sin, lie, cease to exist). God also cannot perform nonsensical acts (e.g. square circles, married bachelors). He cannot make an object so heavy that he cannot lift it, name a number higher than infinity, or be more omnipotent than omnipotent.

To claim that God is omniscient is to say that God is all-knowing—that he knows all things past, present, and future.

[Have your students review in context Psalm 139:17-18 and Isaiah 46:10, 41:21-24.]

To claim that God is omnipresent is to say that God is a disembodied spirit and that he is aware of everything. As a spiritual being, God transcends both time and space, so in another sense it would be truthful to say that God is nowhere.

3. What is the Transcendental Argument for the existence of God?

The Transcendental Argument for the existence of God is a rational comparison of atheism and theism that focuses on the practical outcomes of both worldviews.

If there is no God and the cosmos is merely matter/energy, then it follows that only physical things exist. This would mean that there is no supernatural, no God, and no soul. On the other hand, if

SM
51

there is a God and if the cosmos is composed of both material and immaterial elements, then it is possible for the supernatural, God, and souls to exist.

If there is no God and nothing supernatural, then there is no explanation for things such as reason, morality, logic, and numbers. The naturalistic worldview can neither explain the existence of these entities nor allow for their existence at all in their worldview. It follows that if our brains are the result of mere chance, we would have no guarantee that our mind is telling us the truth about the world.

4. What is the Kalam Cosmological Argument for the existence of God?

The Kalam Cosmological Argument is a rational reflection of three exhaustive dilemmas regarding the origin of the cosmos.

First, either the universe has always existed or it had a beginning. If the universe has always existed, then it has existed since infinity past—a logical impossibility. To demonstrate this, consider a library composed of an infinite number of red and black books. If this scenario were possible, then the library would contain as many black books (an infinite number) as red and black books together (also an infinite number). Likewise, if you removed the infinite black books from the library, you would still have an infinite number of red books. In other words, removing books would somehow not change the total.

Moreover, most scientists are in agreement that the cosmos came into being at a particular point of time known as the big bang. This belief is rational because scientific evidence shows that the universe is exhausting its usable energy. The cosmos appears to have been wound (begun with a particular amount of usable energy), and has been winding down ever since (depleting its usable energy). If the universe is headed toward an end, it must have had a beginning.

Second, if the universe had a beginning, then it was either uncaused or caused. If the universe came into being at a particular point in history, yet was uncaused, then the question arises as to how such an event could be spontaneously born. Consider the lighting of a match—its ignition is a direct effect of some type of cause, such as striking the match. Since any effect is always the result of a cause, the universe must also have had an initial cause.

Third, if the universe had a caused beginning, then the initiating agent was either impersonal or personal. The only way for this event to be caused is through a free personal agent; non-personal agents are incapable of such spontaneous initiation. For example, experience has demonstrated that only free personal agents can initiate a spontaneous event (e.g. lifting an arm).

5. What is the difference between conceptually possible concepts and logically impossible concepts?

Logically impossible concepts are ideas, such as square circles or married bachelors, which are inherently contradictory and cannot exist. On the other hand, things that are conceptually impossible are at least imaginable. For example, the virgin birth, turning water into wine, and raising the dead are conceptually impossible actions, but since we can imagine such events, they are not logically impossible. Similarly, two hundred years ago the concept of airplanes, space shuttles, and personal computers was conceptually possible, although not physically possible.

"MARKS OF THE CULTS"
WITH KEVIN BYWATER

PART ONE

"Idolatry is idolatry, whether it is metal or mental."

"We human beings are perpetual idol factories and if we will not worship the true God who made us, then we will make gods to worship." — John Calvin

I. What is a Cult?

A. _____Psychological_____ definition: mind-control, brain-washing

B. _____Sociological_____ definition: a sub-group that deviates from the norm

C. _____Dictionary_____ definition: from *cultus* (Latin); a group of people having common beliefs and practices; a religion

D. A cult *is* a religion.

E. Pseudo-Christian religion

"A pseudo-Christian religion is a group of people gathered around an individual (or a group of individuals or an organization), who, while claiming to be the true Christian Church and teach true Christianity, actually distorts and denies the foundational and distinctive doctrines of the Christian faith."

But I am afraid that just as Eve was deceived by the serpent's cunning, your minds may somehow be led astray from your sincere and pure devotion to Christ. For if someone comes to you and preaches a Jesus other than the Jesus we preached, or if you receive a different gospel from the one you accepted, or a different Spirit from the one you received, you put up with it easily enough. — 2 Corinthians 11:3–4

1. They use our vocabulary, but not our dictionary.

For such people are false apostles, deceitful workers, masquerading as apostles of Christ. And no wonder, for Satan himself masquerades as an angel of light. It is not surprising, then, if his servants masquerade as apostles of Christ. Their end will be what their actions deserve. — 2 Corinthians 11:13–15

But even if we or an angel from heaven should preach a gospel other than the one we preached to you, let him be eternally condemned. As we have said before, so now I say again: If anybody is preaching to you a gospel other than what you accepted, let him be eternally condemned. — Galatians 1:6–9

2. How can we discern true teachers from false teachers?

   i. We must study what is true.

   and

   ii. We must study what is false.

> You, dear children, are from God and have overcome them, because the one who is in you is greater than the one who is in the world. They are from the world and therefore speak from the viewpoint of the world, and the world listens to them. We [apostles] are from God, and whoever knows God listens to us; but whoever is not from God does not listen to us. This is how we recognize the Spirit of truth and the spirit of falsehood. — 1 John 4:1–6

3. We need to know the Word of God.

PART TWO

II. Cults Add to the Word of God (John 17:17; 2 Timothy 3:15–17; 2 Peter 1:3)

They may deny…

A. The reliability of the Bible

> "The Bible is the word of God, written by men. It is basic in Mormon teaching. But the Latter-day Saints recognize that errors have crept into this sacred work because of the manner in which the book has come to us. Moreover, they regard it as not being complete as a guide… Supplementing the Bible, the Latter-day Saints have three other books: the *Book of Mormon*, the *Doctrine and Covenants*, and the *Pearl of Great Price*. These with the Bible constitute the standard works of the church." — *What of the Mormons?*, 9, 11.

  1. Missing Books

    i. Which books are missing?

    ii. How do you know these books were supposed to be Scripture?

    iii. Do we really need these books?

    iv. Do you have those books? (Isaiah 40:8)

  2. Did Jesus and the Apostles criticize the Old Testament?

B. The clarity of the Bible (2 Peter 3:15–16, Psalm 119:105)

> "Is [the Bible] too puzzling and complex to be understood? Can the average person understand it? What help is needed for one to grasp the meaning of the Scriptures?… It is obvious that we need help if we are to understand the Bible… [T]he fact is that we cannot understand the Bible on our own. We need help… Jehovah, through his organization, however, has allowed his loyal servants to understand its meaning today… You too can gain this understanding with the assistance of those who are experienced in 'handling the word of the truth aright'…

All who want to understand the Bible should appreciate that the 'greatly diversified wisdom of God' can become known only through Jehovah's channel of communication, the faithful and discreet slave [i.e. The Watchtower Bible and Tract Society]." — *The Watchtower* (1 October 1994), 4, 6, 8.

C. The sufficiency of the Bible (2 Timothy 3:15–17, Proverbs 30:5–6)

III. Cults Subtract from the Trinity

They may teach…

A. _____Unitarianism_____: The Father is God, the Son is merely a creature, and the Holy Spirit is an impersonal force (Hebrews 1–2)

"Jesus Christ further deserves honor because He is Jehovah's chief angel, or archangel." Footnote 9: "Why do we conclude that Jesus is the archangel Michael…?" — *The Watchtower* (1 February 1991), 17.

In [the] beginning the Word was, and the Word was with God, and the Word was a god. — John 1:1 *The New World Translation of the Holy Scriptures*

1. Don't argue from John 1:1, 8:58, 20:28

2. Use Isaiah 45:22–23 = Philippians 2:9–11

B. _____Modalism_____: Only one person in the godhead who appears as three persons: the Father in the Old Testament, the Son in the New Testament, and the Holy Spirit today (Matthew 3:16–17, Matthew 26)

C. _____Tritheism_____: Three separate gods (Isaiah 40–46)

"Many men say there is one God; the Father, the Son and the Holy Ghost are only one God. I say that is a strange God anyhow—three in one, and one in three! It is a curious organization… All are to be crammed into one God, according to sectarianism. It would make the biggest God in all the world. He would be a wonderfully big God—he would be a giant or a monster." — *Teachings of the Prophet Joseph Smith*, 372.

"I have always declared God to be a distinct personage, Jesus Christ a separate and distinct personage from God the Father, and that the Holy Ghost was a distinct personage and a Spirit; and these three constitute three distinct personages and three Gods." — *Teachings of the Prophet Joseph Smith*, 370.

"…for I am going to tell you how God came to be God. We have imagined and supposed that God was God from all eternity. I will refute that idea, and take away the veil, so you may see… he was once a man like us; yea, that God himself, the Father of us all, dwelt on an earth, the same as Jesus Christ himself did; and I will show it from the Bible… Here, then, is eternal life—to know the only wise and true God, and you have got to learn to be Gods yourselves, and to be kings and priests to God, the same as all Gods have done before you." — *Teachings of the Prophet Joseph Smith*, 345–46.

IV. Cults Multiply the Terms of Salvation (Ephesians 2:8–10, Titus 2:11–14; 3:4–8)

They may have…

A. A high view of human nature (Ephesians 2:1ff, Romans 5:12ff)

"The Church of Jesus Christ of Latter-day Saints discounts the notion of Original Sin and its ascribed negative impact on humanity… [W]e believe that we are not born sinners… In other words, we're born good; we learn to sin as we grow older." — M. Russell Ballard, *Our Search for Happiness*, 87.

"Indeed, we honor and respect Adam and Eve for their wisdom and foresight. Their lives in the Garden of Eden were blissful and pleasant; choosing to leave that behind so they and the entire human family could experience both the triumphs and travails of mortality must not have been easy. But we believe they did choose mortality, and in so doing made it possible for all of us to participate in the Heavenly Father's great, eternal plan." — M. Russell Ballard, *Our Search for Happiness*, 87.

"The decision of Adam and Eve to eat the forbidden fruit was not a sin, as it is sometimes considered by other Christian churches. It was a transgression—an act that was formally prohibited but not inherently wrong." — *Preparing for Exaltation*, Lesson 3

B. A low view of the atonement of Christ (Colossians 2:13, Galatians 2:21)

C. An unbiblical view of heaven

    1. Too restrictive

       or

    2. Too inclusive

D. No assurance of salvation

V. Cults Divide Their Followers' Loyalties

They may…

A. Divide families

    1. Separatistic

    2. Exclusivistic

B. Be authoritarian

    1. Demanding

    2. Controlling

C. Become the mediator (1 Timothy 2:5)

VI. Witnessing Essentials

A. Be prayerful

B. Be prepared

    1. Know what you believe.

    2. Know what others believe.

    3. Ask what others believe.

C. Be patient

D. Be persistent

"MARKS OF THE CULTS"
VIDEO QUESTIONS

Answer the questions below on a separate sheet of paper and be prepared to review your answers in class.

1. **What are the different ways of defining a cult? Ultimately, what is a cult? What is a pseudo-Christian religion? How do we discern false teaching?**

> When psychologists think of the word cult, they envision brainwashing. When sociologists speak of cults, they are usually referring to a sub-group that merely deviates (either positively or negatively) from the norm. However, the dictionary definition of a cult is more basic—a group of people having common beliefs and practices. Strictly speaking, a cult is a religion.
>
> Popular usage equates the term with dangerous brainwashing sub-groups like the Branch Davidians or Heaven's Gate. For Christians, however, the term "cult" is typically used to denote a false Christian religion.
>
> As Christians, it is necessary for us to discern true Christian beliefs from false Christian beliefs. Therefore, we will define a pseudo-Christian religion (or cult) as a group of people gathered around an individual (or a group or organization), who, while claiming to be the true Christian Church and teach true Christianity, actually distorts and denies the foundational and distinctive doctrines of the Christian faith. According to this definition, Mormons and Jehovah's Witnesses are cults.
>
> To discern the difference between true and false Christian teaching, we must understand the doctrines of both Scripture and the various cults.
>
> *[Review 2 Corinthians 11:1–15, Galatians 1:6–10, and 1 John 4:1–6 with your students.]*

2. **In what ways do cults add to the Word of God?**

> In an effort to make up for the supposed discrepancies of the Scriptures, cults will often add materials to the Word—extra books, personal revelation, or special interpretative teachings. This is usually accomplished by denying one or more of the following: the reliability, clarity, or sufficiency of the Bible.
>
> Mormons claim that the Bible has been corrupted and thus additional materials are needed for compensation. Mormons add the following works: the *Book of Mormon*, the *Doctrine and Covenants*, and the *Pearl of Great Price*. Sometimes, to prove their point regarding the Bible's corruption, they may bring up the fact that certain books mentioned in Scripture (like the book of Jasher) are not contained within the Holy Bible. It is important to realize that although Scripture mentions such books, it never asserts that these "missing books" belong within Scripture. Moreover, the Mormons do not have these "missing books" either. Beyond this point, it is instructive to remember that Jesus and the Apostles cited the Old Testament countless times as both authoritative and complete. They never characterized the Word as anything less.
>
> *[Review Isaiah 40:3–8 with your students.]*

SM
57

80

Unit One

The Watchtower Society claims that Scripture is too difficult and/or too complex for the average reader to comprehend. Therefore, their unique interpretations are offered up as truth. Their position is that a person cannot understand the Bible on his or her own. Instead, he or she needs assistance from others. They assert that only they can tell you what the Bible really says.

[Review 2 Peter 3:14–16 and Psalm 119:105 with your students.]

In the end, both Mormons and Jehovah's Witnesses deny the sufficiency of the Bible on its own. Additional books or special teaching are needed to understand God and His desires for humanity.

[Review 2 Timothy 3:12–17 and Proverbs 30:1–7 with your students.]

3. In what ways do cults subtract from the Trinity?

In an effort to explain the "true" nature of God, cults will often distort the traditional church teaching of the Trinity. Many cults teach one of the following heresies: Unitarianism, Modalism, or Tritheism. Unitarianism is the belief that the Father is God, the Son is merely a creature, and the Holy Spirit is merely an impersonal force. This means that God is composed of only one being—the Father. At some point in time, the Father created the Son just as he created earth, angels, and humanity. Jesus Christ is believed to be the Archangel Michael. Also, they believe that the Holy Spirit is not a being at all; rather he is an impersonal force, like electricity or magnetic fields. This is the view purported by Jehovah's Witnesses.

[Review Hebrews 1–2 and Isaiah 45:22–23 in relation to Philippians 2:9–11.]

Modalism is the belief that there is only one person in the godhead who appears (or pretends) to be three persons: the Father in the Old Testament, the Son in the New Testament, and the Holy Spirit today. This view of the Trinity presents a singular God as an actor performing different roles throughout history.

[Review Matthew 3:13–17 and Matthew 26 with your students.]

Tritheism is the belief that the Father, Son, and Holy Spirit are actually three separate Gods and not three separate beings comprising one singular God. This is the view held by the Mormons, who believe that Father, Son, and Holy Spirit were all once human individuals, but at some point in time became Gods. In fact, according to Mormonism, all of humanity is on its way to becoming Gods. This is how the universe works and has worked for all of eternity.

[Review Isaiah 40–46 with your students.]

4. In what ways do cults multiply the terms of salvation?

Cults will often increase the requirements of salvation. This is usually the result of a high view of human nature, a low view of the atonement of Christ, an unbiblical view of heaven, or a lack of assurance of salvation.

[Review Ephesians 2:8–10 and Titus 2:11–14, 3:4–8 with your students.]

The Mormon Church denies the notion of original sin and claims that the actions of Adam and Eve have had no effect on the human condition. In fact, the Mormons do not view Adam and Eve's disobedience as sin. Rather, they herald their actions as a choice, and a good choice at that.

[Review Ephesians 2:1ff and Romans 5:12ff.]

Some cults will also claim that the work of Christ was not sufficient for salvation. To his work we must add other works or requirements.

[Review Colossians 2:1–17 and Galatians 2:11–21.]

Similarly, some cults present heaven as either too restrictive (only a select few will be let in) or too inclusive (all but the worst will be allowed). Jehovah's Witnesses teach that only 144,000 will find their way to heaven, while Mormons say all but the worst will make it to heaven.

Lastly, some cults restrict the assurance of salvation, claiming that no one can know for sure if they will be saved.

5. **In what ways do cults divide their followers' loyalties?**

Cults divide the loyalties of their followers by either dividing families, being overly authoritarian, or appointing themselves as mediators. Well-known groups like the Branch Davidians and Heaven's Gate were both separatistic and exclusivistic. Members separated themselves from their families and from outsiders. The Branch Davidians claimed to be the "true way." Leaders of these groups are often very authoritative, demanding a great deal of their followers and controlling many of their actions. Leaders will even set themselves up as a mediator between members of the cult and outsiders.

UNIT ONE navigation label

DEAR DOUG
WRITING ASSIGNMENT

Hey!

Okay, first off… our football team is number one! Game days are crazy around here. Just wait until you're a freshman. I made it through orientation and figured out my schedule. My major classes for this semester are psychology, biology, ethics, as well as philosophy—which hits right after lunch, so I'm always falling asleep!

I think I'm getting the hang of college life. Now if only I had someone to do my laundry, everything would be perfect. My roommate Nathan and I are getting along great. We have even started hanging out regularly with a few other people from the dorm—Muhammad, Sarah, Paige, and Mark. Last night we went to a coffee shop off University Ave. to listen to this guitarist Sarah likes. I think it was the first time he'd ever played in front of a live audience!

Anyway, afterwards we all started talking about theology and religion. It was a very interesting conversation. You should have heard the questions they all were asking each other.

Nathan had a question for me—if God created all of nature, wouldn't that make everything divine? I wasn't sure what he meant, so I couldn't really respond to him. And Muhammad wanted to know more about the Trinity, but I didn't really know much about that either. I hope you can help me understand this: how can God be three and one at the same time?

Sarah believes there isn't a God at all, that we just invented the idea of him and an afterlife to make ourselves feel better, and Mark completely agreed. He said that we would never find peace until we could evolve past our need for God. He sees the idea of religion as a human invention, with God as a father figure to help us all feel safer. I guess anything's possible. Do you think God is a human invention? At the end, Paige said that since we can't know for sure which religion is true, we should just be tolerant of everyone's beliefs.

I wasn't really sure how to respond to them. I mostly just listened to what everyone else had to say. They had some good questions and I hadn't actually thought much about all this. Everyone expected me to represent the Christian side of the conversation. What is the Christian view of God?

Well, I should go. I have a date tonight… that's right, a real date! I'll tell you about it some other time. Thanks for all your help. I want you to know that I really appreciate your friendship.

I'll keep in touch,
Doug

Doug has brought up five different subjects; below is a rough outline of possible responses.

1. **If God created all of nature wouldn't that make everything divine? (10 points)**

> Just because a person creates something does not make the creator and the thing the same substance. Beyond that, such an assumption would have to include dung, empty space, and even evil as part of God as well, an end result few would be willing to support.

2. **How can God be three and one at the same time? (10 points)**

> The concept of the Trinity is not a contradiction, but it is a concept that needs some explanation. Simply put, God is made up of three persons—Father, Son, and Spirit. All three are simultaneously distinct persons and one God.

3. **Do you think that God is a human invention? (10 points)**

> Many Marxists and Secular Humanists believe that as long as humanity is relying on a deity to save them, they will not be able to save themselves. In other words, they view belief in God as a hindrance to progress because it thwarts our realization of human self-salvation. As soon as we throw away the roadblock of the divine, we will be able to move forward, working together to realize our full potential and create a better, freer, more tolerant society.

4. **What is the Christian view of God? (10 points)**

> Christianity affirms the existence of an intelligent, powerful, loving, just, and awesome God who exists in the Trinity of Father, Son, and Holy Spirit. From the Christian perspective, "In the beginning God" (Genesis 1:1; cf. Colossians 2:9) is the foundation for all meaning. God is the source of everything else that exists. Christianity further proclaims that this powerful, intelligent God who created all things is the same God who took upon himself human form in the person of Jesus Christ and died for our sins. Christianity proclaims a God who not only created the world, but also loves it so much that he sent his only Son to die for it.

5. **Should we be tolerant of all religious beliefs? (10 points)**

> While it is true that there are many different religions, most of which disagree on a number of points, it does not imply that no religion is correct. If no religion were true, then no single religion would be better than any other. Moreover, there would be no objective basis to condemn abhorrent religious practices like human sacrifice, female circumcision, and jihad. In fact, nearly every religion claims to be exclusively true, making a policy of religious tolerance difficult to maintain.

It must be kept in mind, however, that the word tolerance has lost its original meaning. To be tolerant of something automatically implies that you think that position is wrong. If you didn't think it was wrong, you would be in agreement, the concept of tolerance would not even come into play. When the term is used correctly, Christianity is the most tolerant belief system. There are many things of the world that Christianity disagrees with, but Christians are tolerant of these beliefs, meaning, Christians do not declare jihad, or throw homosexuals in jail, we are tolerant of differing beliefs but that does not mean we condone all beliefs and activities.

Unit One Test

'Theology' Textbook Questions

Matching: (2 points possible per answer [2 for 90-day])
some options may be used more than once or not at all; some questions may have multiple answers.

1. __c__ Christianity
2. __d__ Islam
3. __a__ Secular Humanism
4. __a__ Marxism-Leninism
5. __b__ Cosmic Humanism
6. __a__ Postmodernism
7. __f__ Nature
8. __f__ Moral Law
9. __e__ Jesus Christ
10. __e__ Scripture

a. Atheism
b. Pantheism
c. Trinitarian Monotheism
d. Unitarian Monotheism
e. Special Revelation
f. General Revelation
g. Tri-theism

Short answer: (4 points possible per answer [10 for 90-day])
11. What are the key beliefs of Islam?

First, there is a God and only one God (monotheism). They reject the doctrine of the Trinity and the deity of Jesus Christ.

Second, they believe in angels and a hierarchy of angels. Gabriel is the highest angel. They also assert that two angels are assigned to each person to record his or her good and bad deeds. Muslims also hold to a belief in creatures know as Jinn—bad or mischievous spirits.

Third, Muslims believe that God has sent at least one prophet to every nation and these prophets all taught the same message: "There is only one God. All people should submit to him. There will be a day of judgment of deeds, both good and evil." Muslims affirm that Adam, Noah, Abraham, David, Solomon, Jonah, John the Baptist, and Jesus were all prophets. However, they also see Muhammad as a prophet. In fact, they view Muhammad as the quintessential and last of God's prophets.

Fourth, they believe that the prophets were given holy books: Moses was given the Torah, David the Psalms, Jesus the Gospel, and Muhammad the Qur'an. However, the only uncorrupted holy book in existence today is the Qur'an. This was the only book that God divinely protected. Thus, Muslims see the Bible as a corrupted work with contradictions and historical and scientific errors.

Fifth, there is a day of judgment. God will judge everyone and salvation is granted to those whose good deeds outweigh their bad. However, there are teachings within Islam regarding forgiveness.

Only God knows who will be saved, thus there is no assurance of salvation within Islam. The only exception to this rule is for those individuals that participate in Jihad. As with Christianity, there are two eternal destinations: heaven and hell.

12. What are the key practices (or pillars) of Islam?

The first pillar is the confession of faith (the shahada)—"There is no God but God, and Muhammad is his prophet." The second pillar is prayer. Muslims pray five times a day facing Mecca and at noon on Friday all Muslims gather for prayer at the mosque. The third pillar is fasting. During the daylight hours in the month of Ramadan Muslims abstain from eating, drinking, smoking, and intimate relations. The fourth pillar is alms. Muslims give 1/40th of their net income to the poor and needy. The fifth pillar is pilgrimage. Every Muslim who is physically and financially able is to make a pilgrimage to Mecca at least once in his or her lifetime.

13. According to Cosmic Humanism, who is God?

According to New Agers, God is not something "out there," rather we are God or more correctly stated, everything is God and God is everything. It is for this reason that Shirley MacLaine recommends that every person should begin their day by affirming his or her own deity, everyone must come to realize and become comfortable with the fact that they are God.

14. According to Cosmic Humanism, what happens when a person dies?

Cosmic Humanists believe that humanity's central goal is to realize divine nature and thus transcend the simplistic notion that we are either matter or spirit. Moreover, virtually every New Ager believes that the soul is both indestructible and eternal. In other words, New Agers believe that every human being has always existed. Each of us was present in some form or another since eternity past. The cycle of life and death is merely the process of reincarnation. The body may pass away, but the soul will continue its quest for godhood in other bodies.

15. How has Postmodernism influenced the notion of religious pluralism?

Although most of the early Postmodernists were atheists, the logical conclusion of their denial of truth has been the promotion of religious pluralism. Religious pluralism is the belief that one must be tolerant of all religious beliefs because no single religion can claim to possess universal truth.

This notion harmonizes with the defining tenets of the Postmodern mood—skepticism of absolute truth, of any discernable foundation for knowledge, and, in the end, of metanarratives (any overarching story that defines reality). Many of those immersed in the present Postmodern culture deny religious truth, instead relegating religious claims to the sphere of preference. For example, you either like the idea of Jesus being the Savior or you do not. Miracles either appeal to you or they do not. This attitude accommodates and equalizes all religious preferences.

ARE ALL RELIGIONS ONE? ESSAY
True or False: (3 points possible per answer)
*if an answer is false, restate it to make it true.

16. **Atheistic worldviews like Marxism are not religious.**

   False: Atheistic worldviews like Marxism <u>are</u> religious.

17. **Religions may be similar in form and function, but they claim contradictory things about ultimate reality, the human condition, and spiritual liberation.**

   True

18. **According to Christianity, God is one divine substance that exists in three persons.**

   True

19. **According to Islam, Allah is one with his creation.**

   False: According to Islam, Allah is <u>separate</u> from his creation.

20. **Muhammad rejected the idea that Jesus was a great prophet.**

   False: Muhammad rejected the idea that Jesus was <u>God</u>.

21. **If Brahman is the totality of reality, then all apparent distinctions, dualities, and diversities are merely illusory.**

   True

22. According to non-dualistic Hinduism, there is more than Brahman.

False: According to non-dualistic Hinduism, there is <u>nothing but</u> Brahman.

23. Monism is compatible with monotheism.

False: Monism <u>cannot be connected</u> with monotheism

24. Christianity and Islam teach that creation is to be worshiped along with the Creator.

False: Christianity and Islam teach that the creation <u>must not</u> be worshiped.

25. According to Islam, men and women are not enslaved to sin.

True

26. In Islam, salvation comes through works plus faith.

False: In Islam, salvation comes through <u>works alone</u>.

27. According to non-dualistic Hinduism, spiritual liberation is not reached through an external God or good works.

True

"EXISTENCE AND NATURE OF GOD" VIDEO
Short answer: (4 points possible per answer)

28. What do Christian theologians mean when they claim that God is omnipotent?

To claim that God is omnipotent is not to say that God can do anything and everything, as some individuals assume. Rather, the quality of omnipotence means that God is the most powerful being. There are things God cannot do. God cannot perform acts that are contrary to his perfection (e.g. sin, lie, cease to exist.). God also cannot perform nonsensical acts (e.g. square circles, married bachelors). He cannot make an object so heavy that he cannot lift it, name a number higher than infinity, or be more omnipotent than omnipotent.

29. What is the Transcendental Argument for the existence of God?

> The Transcendental Argument for the existence of God is a rational comparison of atheism and theism that focuses on the practical outcomes of both worldviews.
>
> If there is no God and the cosmos is merely matter/energy, then it follows that only physical things exist. This would mean that there is no supernatural, no God, and no soul. On the other hand, if there is a God and if the cosmos is composed of both material and immaterial elements, then it is possible for the supernatural, God, and souls to exist.
>
> If there is no God and nothing supernatural, then there is no explanation for things such as reason, morality, logic, and numbers. The naturalistic worldview can neither explain the existence of these entities nor allow for their existence at all in their worldview. It follows that if our brains are the result of mere chance, we would have no guarantee that our mind is telling us the truth about the world.

"MARKS OF THE CULTS" VIDEO
Short answer: (4 points possible per answer [10 for 90-day])

30. What is a Pseudo-Christian religion?

> A pseudo-Christian religion (or cult) is a group of people gathered around an individual (or a group or organization), who, while claiming to be the true Christian Church and teach true Christianity, actually distorts and denies the foundational and distinctive doctrines of the Christian faith. According to this definition, Mormons and Jehovah's Witnesses are cults.

Fill in the Blank: (3 points possible per answer [5 for 90-day])

31. Generally speaking, cults:

- Add to the _____Word of God_____
- Subtract from the _____Trinity_____
- Multiply the _____terms of salvation_____
- Divide the _____body_____

TEACHER MANUAL

UNDERSTANDING THE TIMES

Unit Two

Topics:
Critical Thinking
Philosophy
Postmodernism
Theodicy

A Summit Ministries Curriculum

180-DAY SYLLABUS

DAY	IN CLASS	HOMEWORK	
1	WATCH "Philosophy" video		
2	READ <u>UTT</u> Textbook 'Philosophy 2.1'	READ <u>UTT</u> Textbook 'Philosophy 2.2'	
3	REVIEW <u>UTT</u> Textbook "Philosophy 2.1-2.2" questions	READ <u>UTT</u> Textbook 'Philosophy 2.3'	
4	READ <u>UTT</u> Textbook 'Philosophy 2.4'		
5	REVIEW <u>UTT</u> Textbook 'Philosophy 2.3-2.4' questions	READ <u>UTT</u> Textbook 'Philosophy 2.5-2.6'	
6	REVIEW <u>UTT</u> Textbook 'Philosophy 2.5-2.6' questions	ASSIGN Dear Doug Letter	
7	WATCH "Understanding Postmodernism" video P1		
8	WATCH "Understanding Postmodernism" video P2		
9	REVIEW "Understanding Postmodernism" video questions		
10	WATCH "Evil and Suffering" video P1		
11	WATCH "Evil and Suffering" video P2		
12	REVIEW "Evil and Suffering" video questions	READ *Critical Thinking* essay P1	
13	REVIEW *Critical Thinking* essay questions P1	READ *Critical Thinking* essay P2	
14	REVIEW *Critical Thinking* essay questions P2	Dear Doug Letter assignment DUE	
15	TAKE Unit Two Test		

90-DAY SYLLABUS

DAY	IN CLASS	HOMEWORK	
1	WATCH "Philosophy" video	READ <u>UTT</u> Textbook 'Philosophy 2.1-2.2'	
2	REVIEW <u>UTT</u> Textbook "Philosophy 2.1-2.2" questions	READ <u>UTT</u> Textbook 'Philosophy 2.3-2.4'	
3	REVIEW <u>UTT</u> Textbook "Philosophy 2.3-2.4" questions	READ <u>UTT</u> Textbook 'Philosophy 2.5-2.6'	
4	REVIEW <u>UTT</u> Textbook "Philosophy 2.5-2.6" questions		
5	WATCH "Understanding Postmodernism" video P1		
6	WATCH "Understanding Postmodernism" video P2	READ *Critical Thinking* essay P1	
7	REVIEW *Critical Thinking* essay questions P1		
8	TAKE Unit Two Test		

UNDERSTANDING THE TIMES
PHILOSOPHY QUESTIONS

Answer the questions below on a separate sheet of paper and be prepared to review your answers in class.

Unit Two

PHILOSOPHY 2.1

1. **How do some Christians use Colossians 2:8 to support their belief that faith does not need to be defended on philosophical grounds? What is wrong with this interpretation?**

   The verse speaks of "hollow and deceptive philosophy," but it goes on to describe a dangerous philosophy as one that "depends on human tradition and the basic principles of this world rather than on Christ." [UTT 2.1.1]

2. **What led former atheist C.E.M. Joad to embrace the Christian view of the universe?**

   Joad turned to Christianity because he felt that this religious view of the universe covered more of the facts of experience than any other worldview. [UTT 2.1.1]

3. **What does "faith precedes reason" mean? How does Edward T. Ramsdell explain this idea?**

   All methods of knowing ultimately rely on certain assumptions. Edward T. Ramsdell writes, "The natural man is no less certainly a man of faith than the spiritual, but his faith is in the ultimacy of something other than the Word of God. The spiritual man is no less certainly a man of reason than the natural, but his reason, like that of every man, functions within the perspective of his faith." [UTT 2.1.2]

4. **What is Christianity's basis for special revelation?**

   Special revelation is based on history, the law of the evidence, and the science of archaeology. [UTT 2.1.2]

5. **What is the Christian view of the relationship between the natural and the supernatural? How does this view differ from that of the naturalist?**

   According to Christianity, matter is not the whole of reality; there is also the supernatural. Moreover, matter is temporal and will ultimately pass away. The material universe was purposely created out of the mind of the living Logos (John 1:1–4), and all the cosmos, existing independently of God, relies on God for its very existence and explanation. In other words, the Christian explanation for nature (the world of matter) is that the supernatural created the natural.

   According to the naturalist, matter is all that exists; there is no supernatural. [UTT 2.1.5]

SM
61

---

6. **Which system of philosophy influenced Islamic philosophers? What kind of problem does this create for the Islamic view of God?**

The early Islamic philosophers were heavily influenced by the Greek philosophers. This led to a contradiction in their view of God: following Aristotle, some Muslims came to believe that the material world was eternal, yet they also affirmed that matter existed because God brought it into being. [UTT 2.2.2]

7. **Which argument did Muslims develop for the existence of God?**

Early Muslim philosophers developed the Kalam Cosmological Argument, which reasons that since every event has a cause, the beginning of the universe (an event), must also have some underlying cause. Therefore, since the universe exists, it must have come into being; and since it came into being, the universe is not eternal. [UTT 2.2.2]

8. **Are Muslims naturalists or supernaturalists? Why? Do Muslims believe in life after death?**

Islam affirms the existence of entities beyond the natural world. Their affirmation of the existence of God illustrates that Muslims are not naturalists. Beyond their theology, Muslims also uphold the existence of the human soul, as well as the existence of angels and jinn. Islam affirms supernaturalism over and against naturalism—not all things may be known through human senses, nor may we limit the field of existence to what our senses perceive. [UTT 2.2.3]

Fundamental to Islam is the belief in final judgment, implying a belief in life after death. Not only do Muslims affirm life after death and a day of final judgment, they also affirm the bodily resurrection of the dead (though they deny that Jesus died and was resurrected). [UTT 2.2.4]

9. **Do Muslims believe in miracles? Does the fact that Muhammad did not perform any miracles cause a problem for Muslims?**

Orthodox Islamic philosophy affirms the occurrence of miracles and the existence of supernatural beings. The Qur'an records Muhammad performing no miracles in support of his claim to be a prophet. This is a problem because Muhammad claimed to be the greatest prophet of all. Jesus performed numerous miracles to support His claims. As Blaise Pascal said, "Any man can do what Mahomet has done; for he performed no miracles… No man can do what Christ has done." [UTT 2.2.5–6]

10. **How do Muslims interpret Deuteronomy 18:15–18 and John 14:16? How do Christians usually interpret these verses?**

Muslims view these verses as foretelling Muhammad's coming, rather than prophesying Jesus Christ.

Deuteronomy 18:15–18

- *A prophet*—Matthew 13:57; Mark 6:4; John 4:44, and Luke 13:33 and many other texts clearly identify Jesus Christ a prophet.
- *Like Moses*—Peter proclaims that Jesus is the prophet Moses foretold.
- *From among the Israelites*—Matthew 21:11 states, "This is Jesus, the prophet from Nazareth in Galilee" and Acts 3:19–23 likewise is referencing Deuteronomy when it reads, "raise up a prophet like me from among your own people."
- *Put his words in his mouth*—John 7:16; John 8:28; and John 12:49 all speak to the fact that God gave Jesus "the words to speak."
- *He will proclaim to the Israelites everything God commands him*—John 7:16; John 8:28; and John 12:49 all speak to the fact that Jesus used God's words to teach the Israelites.

Muslims claim that Jesus did not proclaim the law, but Jesus did speak to the Law. This is seen most clearly in the Sermon on the Mount in Matthew 5:17–20. We also see Jesus giving new laws to his people in John 14:34, as well as "the law of Christ" in Galatians 6:2 and 1 Corinthians 9:21.

John 14:16

- *Another counselor*—Muslims claim that the Holy Spirit cannot be the future Comforter because he was already present helping and guiding Jesus. Muslims further claim that "*paracletos*" has been corrupted and it should read "*periclytos,*" which is an almost literal translation of *Muhammad* or *Ahmad*. But there is absolutely no manuscript evidence to support this claim. Of the over 5,000 manuscripts now available, not one uses the word *periclytos*. So, the charge of textual corruption is without historical or textual support.

Further, while Muslims assert that the identification of the Counselor with the Holy Spirit is a misinterpretation, in the very context of John 14:16 Jesus draws just this identification: "But the Counselor, the Holy Spirit, whom the Father will send in my name, will teach you all things and will remind you of everything I have said to you" (John 14:26). Although Muslims claim that this statement was made up by later Christians, such a claim would need at least *some* evidence. [UTT 2.2.8–10]

PHILOSOPHY 2.3

11. What is the essence of naturalism?

The essence of naturalism is that whatever exists can be explained by natural causes. Thus, in a Humanist's mind, the supernatural cannot exist. [UTT 2.3.1]

12. How did Roy Wood Sellars regard the Christian worldview? In his opinion, what has rendered Christianity obsolete?

According to Sellers, Christianity's supernaturalistic framework has been disproved by the growth of knowledge about nature through the naturalistic sciences. [UTT 2.3.2]

---

13. What is the cosmology of the Secular Humanist?

According to the Secular Humanist, matter has always existed (had no beginning and will have no end), even though it is ever-changing. [UTT 2.3.3]

14. For the naturalist, what is the ultimate means of perception?

Science [UTT 2.3.4]

15. How does the naturalist's *monistic* view of the mind and body differ from the Christian's *dualistic* view? What are two troubling implications of a naturalistic answer to the "mind-body" question?

For the naturalist, mind is merely the product of matter and evolution. For the Christian, the mind existed before matter and brought matter into existence. Christianity views the mind dualistically—as both physical (the brain) and spiritual (the soul).

First, a monistic view of the mind implies that mankind is not immortal and that there is nothing supernatural in our makeup that survives death (no life after death). Second, this viewpoint implies that we should not put confidence in the reasoning powers of a brain produced by evolution, since a "better mutation of mind could occur any day." [UTT 2.3.6]

PHILOSOPHY 2.4

16. How does Lenin describe matter?

[The differences between Secular Humanism and Marxism/Leninism are not so much differences in philosophy—both are naturalistic worldviews—but in attitude and agenda. Secular Humanists would see their atheistic agenda prevail through education, legislation, and other social institutions. Marxists look to outright revolution to overturn the present system and create a whole new society.]

According to Lenin, matter is primarily nature and sensations. Thoughts and consciousness are merely the highest products of matter. Lenin viewed all of reality as philosophically naturalistic—that people, plants, animals, stars, etc., are merely matter. [UTT 2.4.1]

17. What is the Marxist view of truth and knowledge (epistemology)?

According to Marxism, truth is ultimately discovered through science, a virtually infallible source of knowledge. Nothing can be considered "knowledge" until it has been scientifically tested and proven. Therefore, supernatural revelation will never produce truth. [UTT 2.4.2]

18. What is the Marxist dialectic and how does it work?

[You may want to draw a diagram on the board to visually represent how the dialectic works.]

The Marxist dialectic is the view that life is a constantly evolving process resulting from the clash of opposing forces:

- Every established idea (thesis) is eventually opposed by another idea (antithesis).
- Eventually, an entirely new entity will emerge from this opposition (synthesis), which renders both thesis and antithesis obsolete.
- This synthesis eventually becomes a thesis that is opposed by an antithesis… and so forth without end.

The result of this philosophical view is that reality is constantly changing—nothing is ever certain. [UTT 2.4.3]

19. What is the Marxist metaphysical belief?

Marxists do not believe in God or anything supernatural in the universe. They proclaim that the material universe is all that exists, that it has always existed, and that it always will. [UTT 2.4.5]

20. How does Marxism address the mind-body question? What is the problem with their explanation?

According to Marxism, thoughts are nothing more than the material world reflected by the human mind and translated into the forms of thought.

Marxism claims that consciousness is just a subjective reflection of objective reality in order to avoid labeling consciousness as supernatural. Yet this claim only results in bringing its own origins into question. [UTT 2.4.6]

PHILOSOPHY 2.5

21. Are Cosmic Humanists in agreement with the tenets of naturalism?

Cosmic Humanists reject naturalism and materialistic philosophies because such explanations ignore the all-pervasive supernatural. [UTT 2.5.1]

[Discuss how this view is different from the Christian's rejection of naturalism. Christians reject naturalism not because they believe physical reality to be non-existent or unimportant, but because they believe naturalism is short-sighted and limits reality.]

22. What is the Cosmic Humanist view of philosophy?

Cosmic Humanists hold to a philosophy of non-naturalism (that there is nothing natural) and therefore view all of reality as spiritual. [UTT 2.5.1]

[Discuss how this view is different from a Christian saying that every aspect of the Christian's life is sacred—work, pleasure, relationships, etc. For the Christian, every aspect of life is sacred when it is dedicated to God. Far from denying the importance of the physical realm, the Christian acknowledges that it is important: God himself entered that realm.]

23. How do Cosmic Humanists understand truth? Where does the Cosmic Humanist look to find truth?

According to Cosmic Humanism, we create our own truth according to the principle "if it feels like truth to you, it is." Thus, for the Cosmic Humanist all knowledge exists subjectively within ourselves and by connecting with our inner spiritual being we can tap into this knowledge. [UTT 2.5.2]

[Explore this idea and its implications further with your students. If we can create our own truth, then what can be said about the truth constructed by a racist, psychopathic killer, or schizophrenic? Is their "truth" also valid?]

24. Why do different Cosmic Humanist thinkers express different interpretations of reality?

Cosmic Humanists differ about reality because each Cosmic Humanist ultimately arrives at his or her own truth. [UTT 2.5.3]

25. According to Cosmic Humanism, what is the only substance that actually exists?

According to Cosmic Humanism, all is spiritual and all is connected. There are no dual substances or multiple entities. Rather, everything is part of one divine, non-natural substance. [UTT 2.5.4]

PHILOSOPHY 2.6

26. Why is the statement "God so loved the world" nonsensical to a Postmodernist?

For Postmodernists, since there is no universal Truth (capital "T"), there are only "truths" (small "t") that are particular to a society or group of people and limited to individual perception. There is no true "grand story," only the subjective stories of communities. Therefore, Postmodernists reject the notion of metanarratives as nonsensical. Since Christianity is a metanarrative (an explanation of reality), Postmodernists regard its "absolute" claims, such as "God so loved the world" as impossible. [UTT 2.6.2]

27. What is literary deconstruction? What does this theory mean for the Bible?

Deconstruction involves reading a text to ferret out its hidden or multiple meanings (polysemy). From a framework of deconstruction, a reader's interpretation of a text is more important than the text itself or the meaning its author is attempting to communicate. In the end, the subjectivity of the reader ultimately determines meaning, not the author. For example, a reader may feel that a particular text is racist, even if the author never intended to convey such a stance. If deconstruction is true, then the Bible can no longer convey truth. Scripture would have no more authority to speak about ultimate truths and reality than a comic book. [UTT 2.6.3]

28. What is the "correspondence theory" of truth? Why do Postmodernists reject this theory?

The "correspondence theory" of truth states that a proposition is true only if it corresponds to reality. Postmodernists claim that this kind of Truth is impossible to achieve because there is no "way things are" (a theory known as anti-realism). Therefore, there is no objective reality for propositions to correspond to, only personal, small "t" truths and their resulting constructions of reality. Our words only correspond to other words and, in the end, create our understanding of reality. Since words only signify other words, then words can never be used in the pursuit of Truth. [UTT 2.6.4]

29. What is the primary idea behind "word play?"

Postmodernists insist that all human beings are conditioned by their culture, language, experiences, and situation in life—no one is able to "break through" his or her culture or language to engage reality objectively. Therefore, when we contend that the assertion "water wets" is true, we are merely parroting what we have been taught by our community—the rules of our language. If a community did not agree with this assertion, then the phrase would no longer be true for that community. [UTT 2.6.4]

30. What four points does Kevin J. Vanhoozer use to summarize Postmodern philosophy?

- Knowledge—Postmodernism limits knowledge to local narratives.
- Reason—Postmodernism rejects the notion of universal rationality; reason is always situated within particular narratives, traditions, institutions, and practices.
- Metanarratives—Postmodernism rejects unifying, totalizing, and universal schemes in favor of new emphases on difference, plurality, fragmentation, and complexity.
- Human beings—Postmodernism rejects the notion that the person is an autonomous individual with a rational consciousness that transcends his or her particular place in culture, language, history, and gendered body. [UTT 2.6.6]

"UNDERSTANDING POSTMODERNISM"
WITH JOHN STONESTREET

I. Understanding Postmodernism

    A. Both a _____*philosophy*_____ and a _____*cultural mood*_____ that describes "our times"

    B. We are all, in a sense, postmodern

II. Historical Perspective

    A. Pre-modern Period: < to 1600

        1. Strong belief in the _____supernatural_____

        2. Authority of oral and written traditions to give the "Big Story"

        3. Truth is objective, corresponds to reality, and may be known via:

            i. Revelation

            ii. Faculties (reason and senses)

            iii. Experience

    B. Modern Period: 1600 to 1960

        1. _____Skepticism_____ of the supernatural

        2. Authority of observation, human reason, and science to give the "Big Story"

            i. Belief in progress

        3. Truth is objective, corresponds to reality, and may be known via:

            i. Revelation

            ii. Faculties (reason and senses)

            iii. Experience

    C. Postmodern Period: 1960 to ?

        1. Skeptical of all claims to knowledge

        2. Rejects all authorities claiming to give a "Big Story"

            i. Disbelief in progress

Unit Two (side tab)

3. Truth and reality are only _____subjective_____ constructs attained via:

    i. Revelation

    ii. Faculties (reason and senses)

    iii. Experience

PART TWO

III. Key Thinkers

  A. **Friedrich Nietzsche** (1844–1900)

    1. *Beyond Good and Evil* (1891)

    2. "God is dead"

    3. "Truth is an illusion"

  B. **Jacques Derrida** (1930–2004)

    1. *Of Grammatology* (1976)

    2. Deconstruction: no real meaning to any text

  C. **Michel Foucault** (1926–1984)

    1. *Madness and Civilization* (1960)

    2. Critique of the discourses of power (language is used to oppress others)

  D. **Richard Rorty** (1931– ?)

    1. *Philosophy and the Mirror of Nature* (1979)

    2. Anti-foundationalism

    3. Anti-essentialism

    4. Truth is a social construct

IV. Postmodernism: The Philosophy

  A. Rejection of "_____essentialism_____"

    1. Things do not have real qualities independent of our knowing them.

      "In the naming, the things named are called into their thinging; thinging they unfold world, and thus are abiding ones." — Martin Heidegger

    2. There are only interpretations in different ways by different people

3. What is "normal" (i.e. knowledge) is really determined by power.

4. What one believes to be true is only the product of his/her cultural situation.

5. Truth is nothing more than interpretation.

> "Truth is… a mobile army of metaphors, metonymies, anthropomorphisms, a sum, in short, of human relationships which, rhetorically and poetically intensified, ornamented and transformed, come to be thought of, after long usage by a people, as fixed, binding, and canonical. Truths are illusions, worn-out metaphors now impotent to stir the senses, coins which have lost their faces and are considered metal rather than currency." — Friedrich Nietzsche

B. Rejection of _____ universal explanations _____

1. There are no legitimate metanarratives.

2. Any universal theory rejects and suppresses something or someone.

3. All metanarratives are tools of oppression.

C. Role of the "interpretive" community

1. Meaning can only be derived from one's cultural context ("history is bunk").

2. Words create (not reflect) reality and have no normative meanings.

3. Meaning is created by one's interpretive community.

D. Rejection of _____ traditional logic _____

1. Everything is interpretation.

2. All interpretations are valid.

3. Coherence and consistency are illusions.

V. Where You Will Find It

A. **Literature**: Deconstructionism

B. **Philosophy**: Relativism, pragmatism

C. **Art**: Dada, surrealism, pop-nihilism

D. **History**: Revisionist (anti-metanarrative)

E. **Sociology**: Multiculturalism

VI. The Contradictions

A. Proposing that "there is no truth," which is a truth statement

B. Asking that we agree with the postmodern interpretation that there is nothing but interpretation

C. Announcing authoritatively that authoritative announcements are invalid

D. Offering the metanarrative that there are no metanarratives

E. Claiming it is immoral to oppress people with morality

VII. The Culture

A. Truth is not objective, but based on personal feelings.

B. There are no universal values that apply everywhere to everyone.

C. Basis for moral action is not universal rights and morals, but relationship with the other person.

D. We are the product of our culture; nothing more.

E. No one has the right to tell others that they are wrong in their interpretation.

VIII. Postmodernism and Christianity

A. Christianity IS a _____ metanarrative _____.

B. Christianity IS _____ historical _____.

C. Christianity DOES propose moral norms, authority, and objective truth.

D. What becomes of Scripture and interpretation of Scripture?

E. There are points of agreement:

   1. _____ Modernism _____ is flawed.

   2. Community is vitally important.

   3. Without God, knowledge is impossible.

> "I came to realize that the search of the philosophers for a grand scheme that would encompass everything was illusory. Only a theism that combined a God with equal measures of truth, love, and justice could do the trick. But since I could not imagine myself being religious, and had indeed become more raucously secular, I did not consider that an option for me." — Richard Rorty, *Trotsky and the Wild Orchids*

"UNDERSTANDING POSTMODERNISM"
VIDEO QUESTIONS

Answer the questions below on a separate sheet of paper and be prepared to review your answers in class.

1. How can we historically divide the pre-modern, modern, and postmodern periods? How did each period view truth?

Roughly speaking, the history of the Western world can be divided into three different time frames:

Pre-modernism (< to 1600) had a strong belief in the supernatural—God, the divine, gods, miracles, etc. Authority and knowledge rested with those in power, like the clergy and the monarchy. Truth, while found in both our faculties and experience, was predominantly discovered through revelation.

Modernism (1600 to 1960) was much more skeptical of the supernatural. Authority and knowledge rested with the educated—scholars, scientists, etc. Human knowledge was believed to be the source of progress and the means to a better understanding of reality. Truth, while found in both revelation and experience, was predominantly uncovered through human faculties (i.e. reason and the five senses).

Postmodernism (1900 to ?) is skeptical of absolute claims to knowledge, truth, and reality, believing that in the past such claims led to war and oppression (e.g. Marxism, Islam, Christianity, Crusades, World Wars 1 and 2, Vietnam, and the Cold War). Postmodern thinkers do not believe true progress can be realized. Truth, while found in both revelation and human faculties, is predominantly attained through human experience and community.

2. What four elements define the philosophy of Postmodernism?

Postmodernism rejects the notion of essentialism—the belief that things have intrinsic defining qualities. For example, according to essentialism, a human being is inherently a person regardless of his or her attributes. For a Postmodernist, there is no such thing as a human being per se. A human being becomes a person because society labels him or her a person.

It follows that if there is no truth or essence to things, there is no one metanarrative. Such "universal explanations" are believed to be oppressive. According to postmodernists, those in positions of power holding to one worldview will inevitably force that worldview on others.

In the end, truth for the Postmodernist is based on the common beliefs of one's "interpretative community." Truth and reality become matters of cultural interpretation rather than independent entities.

Postmodernists also reject traditional logic, insisting that logic is merely one community's version of truth, allowing all methodologies and interpretations relating to truth to be valid.

3. **In what five ways is Postmodernism a contradiction?**

First, Postmodernism asserts that there is universally no truth. However, this statement is presented as universally true. Second, Postmodernism asserts that all interpretations are valid, yet they insist that everyone believe their interpretation about interpretations. Third, Postmodernism authoritatively announces that authoritative announcements are invalid. Fourth, Postmodernism is a metanarrative that rejects the existence of metanarratives as a whole. Fifth, Postmodernism claims that morality, like everything else, is a social construct. Thus, we should not force our moral beliefs on others, an assertion which itself assumes a universal morality.

4. **On what areas do Christianity and Postmodernism disagree?**

First, Postmodernism asserts that there is no truth (and thus no way the world actually is), but Christianity asserts that there is truth and the world is a certain way. For example, Christians believe that sin exists regardless of community agreement. Christianity is also a metanarrative (grand story). According to Christianity, everything came from God, mankind turned from God and caused creation to fall, yet it will one day be restored.

Second, Postmodernism believes that an objective historical account is nonexistent, since history is merely the perspective of a particular community (usually the most powerful one). Thus, there are as many different histories as there are historical perspectives. Christianity, on the other hand, believes there is an actual history of the world, that God entered that history, and that there is evidence to support this claim.

Third, Postmodernism believes that morality, like truth, is relative to community and interpretation. Christianity, however, believes in universal moral standards that are mandatory for all communities and cultures.

Fourth, Postmodernism asserts that no one can decipher any text because words have no inherent meaning. They insist that we create the meaning of a text as we read it. This meaning is shaped by our culture and life experiences and is inescapable. Christians, on the other hand, believe that there is a right and wrong interpretation to Scripture and that we can get past our cultures and experiences to discern the Word of God.

5. **What do Christianity and Postmodernism have in common?**

First, both Christianity and Postmodernism agree that modernism has gone too far. According to modernism, truth is discovered primarily through reason and the five senses. However, there are truths that can neither be touched nor reasoned, e.g. issues of morality or the notion of love.

Second, both Christians and Postmodernists agree that community is a vitally important aspect of life. It is through community that we learn, grow, and discover what it means to be selfless.

"EVIL AND SUFFERING"
WITH JOHN STONESTREET

I. Defining Evil

    A.   **Moral Evil** : Evil that is the result of human choices (Sept. 11, murder, etc.)

    B.   **Natural Evil** : Evil where there is no human will involved (natural disasters, etc.)

    C.   **Maximum Evil** : Gratuitous evil, innocent suffering

II. Approaching the Problem of Evil

    A. Logical side (Focus—the existence of evil)

        1. How could an omniscient, omni-benevolent, omnipotent God allow evil?

        2. Logical syllogism

> Proposition 1: If God were all-*good*, he *would* destroy evil
>
> Proposition 2: If God were all-*powerful*, he *could* destroy evil
>
> Proposition 3: Evil has not been destroyed
>
> Conclusion: There is no all-good, all-powerful God

    B. Personal side (Focus—the existence of pain and suffering)

        1. Why did God allow that evil to happen to me?

        2. We struggle with this side most.

    C. Other worldviews and the problem of evil

        1. **Naturalism**

            i. Physical world is all there is.

            ii. There is no real evil, only bad luck.

            iii. Evil has no meaning.

        2. **Transcendentalism** [Non-naturalism]

            i. Physical world is an illusion.

SM
68

ii. Evil is an illusion.

iii. Evil is the result of karmic debt (and is deserved).

3. **Theism**

    i. God allowed evil in the world for his own purposes.

    ii. Islamic position

"The gist is that good and evil are foreordained. What is foreordained comes necessarily to be after a prior act of divine volition. No one can rebel against God's judgment; no one can appeal His decree and command. Rather, everything small and large is written and comes to be in a known and expected measure." — Al-Ghazali, *Theodicy in Islamic Thought*

III. Bad Solutions

A. **_Fideism_**: the problem should be ignored

Redefines man's ability to know God

B. **_Illusionism_**: evil does not exist

Redefines evil or the world

C. **_Finitism_**: God cannot control all evil

Redefines God's power

> Proposition 2: If God were all-powerful, he *could* destroy evil

D. **_Transmoralism_**: God is beyond moral categories

Redefines God's goodness

> Proposition 1: If God were all-good, he *would* destroy evil

PART TWO

IV. Biblical Resolution

A. A view of the past

    1. God's creation was very good (Genesis 1).

    2. Free will is an essential component of true humanity (Genesis 2).

    3. We are not good (Genesis 3).

B. A view of the future

"These are they who have come out of the great tribulation; they have washed their robes and made them white in the blood of the lamb. Therefore, they are before the throne of God and serve Him… He who sits on the throne will spread His tent over them. Never again will they hunger, never again will they thirst. For the Lamb at the center of the throne will be their Shepherd; He will lead them to springs of living water. And God will wipe away every tear from their eyes." — Revelation 7:14–17

Proposition 1: If God were all-*good*, he *would* destroy evil

Proposition 2: If God were all-*powerful*, he *could* destroy evil

Proposition 3: Evil has not **YET** been destroyed

Conclusion: Evil will one day be destroyed by an all-good, all-powerful God

---

1. All evil will be destroyed one day.

2. The end will be better than the beginning.

    i. Revelation 4 and 5

    ii. A world redeemed is better than a world that never fell.

    iii. God doesn't just forgive sins, he redeems.

C. A view of the present

1. What is the answer for personal suffering?

"But He was pierced for our transgressions, He was crushed for our iniquities; the punishment that brought us peace was upon Him, and by His wounds we are healed." — Isaiah 53:5

"Surely He took up our infirmities and carried our sorrows." — Isaiah 53:4

"It is the woman who has been raped that understands what rape is, not the rapist. It is the person who has been slandered who understands what slander is, not the slanderer. It is the one who died for our sins who understands what evil is, not the skeptics." — Ravi Zacharias

2. Our God suffers with us

"For we do not have a high priest who is unable to sympathize with our weaknesses, but we have one who has been tempted in every way, just as we are—yet without sin." — Hebrews 4:15

"EVIL AND SUFFERING"
VIDEO QUESTIONS

Unit Two

Answer the questions below on a separate sheet of paper and be prepared to review your answers in class.

1. **What are three types of evil? What are some examples? Which is the hardest type to deal with and why?**

Evil can be divided into three different categories:

- Moral Evil—Evil that is the result of human choices
- Natural Evil—Evil where there is no human will involved
- Maximum Evil—Gratuitous evil or innocent suffering

The first category consists of acts done by humans to other humans (e.g. rape, murder, torture, terrorism). The second category consists of acts of nature and are not the result of human actions (e.g. tsunamis, hurricanes, tornadoes, volcanoes). The last category includes acts from the first and second categories, but only those that affect "innocent" human beings (e.g. abortion, molestation of a child, mental retardation). Most would consider this third category the hardest to make sense of since there seems to be no logical explanation for why the innocent suffer.

2. **What are two different sides to the problem of evil and suffering? Which side do we struggle with the most?**

There are two ways to address the problem of evil and suffering. The first is the logical side; it attempts to make sense of the existence of evil. It asks how an omniscient, omni-benevolent, omnipotent God could allow evil. The second side is the personal side; it attempts to make sense of the existence of pain and suffering. It asks why God would allow evil to happen to me.

The logical side is expressed by the following logical syllogism:

- Proposition 1—If God were all-*good*, he *would* destroy evil
- Proposition 2—If God were all-*powerful*, he *could* destroy evil
- Proposition 3—Evil has not been destroyed
- Conclusion—There is no all-good, all-powerful God

The personal side is the hardest to deal with because it isn't abstract, but deals with hurt that real human beings experience, sometimes the suffering of an innocent and sometimes personal suffering in our own lives.

3. **How do differing worldviews view the existence of evil?**

Christianity is not the only worldview that must deal with existence of evil and suffering. Every worldview must explain its existence. Naturalism, which purports that only the physical world exists, sees no meaning behind evil. For the naturalist, evil is just bad luck. Another worldview that must

SM
71

deal with problem of evil is transcendentalism. This worldview purports that the physical world and everything in it is just an illusion. Thus, evil and suffering become mere illusions; some may also see it as the result of karma. Lastly, theistic worldviews purport that both the natural and supernatural exist. The theist must argue that God has allowed evil for some purpose.

4. What are some bad solutions to the problem of evil? Why are these solutions problematic?

There are at least four bad solutions to the problem of pain and suffering:

- **Fideism**—asserts that the dilemma should be ignored
  This position is problematic because it merely closes its eyes to the problem. Christians and unbelievers alike desire to understand evil and suffering. This position ultimately redefines our ability to know God.

- **Illusionism**—purports that evil does not exist
  This position is problematic because it flies in the face of what every human being knows to be true—humanity experiences evil and suffering. This position ultimately redefines either the evil or the world.

- **Finitism**—proposes that God cannot control all evil
  This position is problematic because it limits God's abilities. This position ultimately redefines God's power in relation to his creation.

- **Transmoralism**—asserts that God is beyond moral categories
  This position is problematic because it paints God as unjust. According to this position God can allow and/or commit evil and suffering and at the same time be innocent. Human beings, on the other hand, are held to a higher standard and are subject to judgment when they commit evil acts. This position ultimately redefines God's goodness.

5. What is the biblical resolution to the problem of evil and suffering?

The problem of evil and suffering is a very complicated issue. It cannot be answered in a truncated fashion. When considering the dilemma of how a good God and evil can coexist, it is helpful to consider the issue of time in three forms: past, future, and present.

Past—According to the Christian worldview, when God formed the universe he considered his creation good. However, Adam and Eve freely choose to disobey God. This disobedience resulted in a fallen world and a fallen race. That is, neither mankind nor nature exists today as God originally intended it to. Thus, we have moral evil (man-caused) and natural evil (non-man-caused).

This is the Christian explanation for the existence of the evil and suffering. However, it does not explain how evil can exist with a good God. If God could do anything and were truly good, then wouldn't he thwart all evil and suffering? Christians fully believe he could do so, but in regards to moral evil, human beings would no longer be free agents. That is, God would be directing us. Just as it is difficult to imagine a good God existing with evil, it is equally difficult to imagine a good God that allows human choice. If all our actions were determined to be good (or at least not evil), then how could human beings ever be considered good?

Future—The Bible informs us that although creation has fallen, it will someday be restored and evil will be destroyed; fallen humanity will one day be redeemed. In fact, we are told that the end will be even better than the beginning. And a world redeemed is better than a world that had never fallen.

Present—Also unique to the Christian worldview is its view of the present. According to Scripture we have a God that does not merely allow suffering; he also suffered with us and even for us.

[Review Isaiah 53:1–8 and Hebrews 4:14–16 with your students.]

CRITICAL THINKING
BY THE SUMMIT STAFF

INTRODUCTION

In the following essay, we will briefly discuss the nature of an argument, the law of non-contradiction, and a selection of informal fallacies. We will also present a helpful cache of tough questions, which can be used when engaging various worldviews. Finally, we will look at how to discern the assumptions behind the information presented in the media. This survey is designed to provide you with an introduction to the art of critical thinking.

LOGIC

Why are so many people in today's society swayed by mere emotionalism, or trapped by the most recent propaganda disseminated across our airwaves, television, or in the classroom? While there are several factors involved in answering this question, one primary reason is that people do not think critically.

What is an argument? Most people think an argument occurs when people get together, raise their voices, and call each other names. Properly speaking, this is not an argument, but an altercation. An argument, understood in a philosophical or logical context, is where we draw conclusions from various premises. There are several words that we use to indicate when we are presenting a premise and when we are presenting a conclusion. When indicating a premise, we use such words as *because, for, for this reason, as, if, based on the fact that*, etc. When demonstrating a conclusion, we typically use *therefore, thus, consequently, hence, it follows that*, etc. It's good to keep these indicators in mind so that you can detect an argument.

It is common for arguments to be confused with assertions. Assertions are the expressions of opinions without supporting premises. For example, it is common to hear someone assert that there are contradictions in the Bible, but just *saying* so doesn't *make* it so. When you hear assertions like this, the proper response is to ask questions, such as, "Can you give me some examples?"[1]

The Law of Non-Contradiction: This law is the foundation for all logical thinking. It may be defined as follows: a statement (a proposition) cannot be true and not true at the same time and in the same respect. For example: It cannot be both raining and not raining at the same time and in the same respect.

Humans did not invent the laws of logic any more than they invented the laws of nature—such as the law of gravity. In fact, throughout the Bible, the law of non-contradiction is implied. Without this law, nothing could be interpreted as true or false. Right thinking imitates God's thinking; and because God does not contradict himself (his Word cannot be broken—John 10:35; he cannot lie—Hebrews 6:18), Christians should seek to avoid contradiction. Without the law of non-contradiction we would never be able to detect a lie.[2]

In fact, if someone wants to deny the law of non-contradiction, that person immediately runs back into it, because he or she would have to presuppose that it's true in order to prove that it's false. Imagine the following conversation:

"Hey, I don't think the law of non-contradiction is really that important. In fact, I believe we don't need to follow it at all."

"Really? So you think we need to follow the law of non-contradiction. You really believe it's that important?"

"Didn't you hear me? I said just the opposite of what you said I said."

"If the law of non-contradiction really isn't important, then we are both correct."

---

[1] Of course, there are "hard passages" in the Bible (cf. 1 Peter 3:15ff. to see that even Peter could acknowledge that). If you have questions about such difficult passages, we recommend Gleason Archer, *New International Encyclopedia of Bible Difficulties*.
[2] A lie is a contradiction of the truth. It is a denial of reality.

When expressing a denial or affirmation of any claim, proposition, belief, or idea, one must presuppose the law of non-contradiction. It is fundamental to any kind of distinctions: right and wrong, good and bad, true and false.[3]

LOGICAL FALLACIES

A fallacy is simply a faulty argument. In the process of reasoning, there are two types of fallacies that occur: formal and informal. Formal fallacies deal with the actual *form* of the argument. When an argument is structured incorrectly it is fallacious. Even when an argument is *formally* correct, it may still be *informally* fallacious. The conclusion may not actually follow from the premises due to a faulty gathering of information, circular reasoning, or some other mistake. Informal fallacies are the more common of the two types of fallacies, and will be covered in this paper.

Below we provide a list of some common informal fallacies, a brief explanation of each, and an illustration or two. We have not provided an exhaustive catalogue because there seem to be an endless number of ways that people can make mistakes in their thinking, and we do not have the space to explain them all.

Fallacies of Ambiguity: Communication can be difficult. Difficulties arise from differing cultures, age groups, races, prejudices, and especially from differing worldviews. One of the most important ground rules for clear communication is clear definitions. We may be unnecessarily frustrated if others misunderstand what we say because they either don't know what a word means, or we simply have not supplied clear definitions for the words we use.

Equivocation

The fallacy of equivocation occurs when we use different definitions for the same word, or when a word is taken in a different way than intended (a different definition). Many words have different meanings depending on their context. Consider the following examples:

"All men are created equal? If that were so, then there wouldn't be so many rich people."
"If all men are created equal, then why am I so short?"

The difficulty that arises in these examples is that the statement "all men are created equal" means that all men should be equally valued as human beings. It was never intended to mean that we are all clones of one another, or that we would have equal incomes.

There is a special type of equivocation that can occur with relative terms like *tall* or *short*. These types of words must be understood in relation to something else. To claim that something or someone is tall assumes a relation to other people or things. The vagueness of these types of terms can only be clarified by context.

It should be noted that much of our humor rests in equivocations. In a humorous context, we call it a "play on words." Also, sometimes an equivocation can be intentional and witty, such as when Ben Franklin declared, "We must all hang together, or, most assuredly, we shall all hang separately." The word *hang* is intended to be understood quite differently in each usage.

When Christians are witnessing to people who are involved in pseudo-Christian religions (i.e. cults), they need to be very careful to define their words so as not to be misunderstood. For example, while Mormons and Jehovah's Witnesses both use the name of Jesus Christ, they have completely different meanings. The Jehovah's Witness believes that Jesus was the first *created* being and was, in fact, the Archangel Michael before he became the man Jesus. The Mormons, on the other hand, believe that Jesus is literally our older brother from a pre-existence. Jesus is believed to be the firstborn of the Father and one of many gods. Given these differences, we need to make sure that we dig deeper into the meanings of what people say and not stay at a superficial level of communication.[4]

---

[3] Of course, there are some people who still insist that such dichotomous thinking is incorrect. If it is not correct, however, then that means there is such a state as being correct. That then poses a dichotomy. They can't escape the nature of reality.
[4] The Apostle Paul warned the early Church about those who teach a different Jesus and a different gospel (see 2 Corinthians 11:2–4, 13–15; Galatians 1:6–9; 1 John 4:1–6). For a good survey and theological refutation of various pseudo-Christian religions, see Richard Abanes, *Defending the Faith* (Minneapolis: Bethany, 1997)

Fallacies of Relevance: This section will deal with fallacies that occur when something irrelevant to the question of truth is added to an argument in the attempt to persuade.

Appeal to Pity

This fallacy occurs when one tries to persuade by invoking the listener to feel sorry for the individual or group for whom one is arguing. Many times, pity is an appropriate reaction, but it is not always a valid means of persuasion.

For example, sometimes abortion advocates will argue that if you make poor women carry their babies to term, they may not be cared for properly, or that if you outlaw abortion, then women will have to return to the "back alley butchers" to get abortions. While these arguments may be emotionally persuasive, they are not relevant to the issue at hand. One is never justified in killing a child just because life becomes harder for the mother.

Ad Hominem

Ad hominem means "argument to the person." This fallacy is committed when, instead of dealing with what a person is arguing, someone attacks his or her character. This is fallacious because a person's character typically has no bearing on the truth or falsehood of his or her claims. Here are some examples:

"You are wrong because you are an intolerant, closed-minded, right-wing fundamentalist."
"You can't trust anything he says. He is a liberal pagan atheist and has no basis for morality."

Appeal to Ignorance

This fallacy can occur in two ways. 1) To argue that something is true because it hasn't been proven to be false; or 2) to argue that something is false because it hasn't been proven to be true. Just because there is no proof against your position does not prove your position true. Likewise, just because a position has not been proven does not mean that it is false. Here are a couple examples:

"You cannot prove God does not exist, therefore God exists."
"You cannot prove God does exist, therefore God does not exist."

Red Herring

A herring is a fish that can be used to distract and confuse bloodhounds on the scent of game. Similarly, this fallacy is the introduction of an irrelevant side issue into an argument which ultimately distracts and confuses the case being presented. Often positive (or even negative) reasons offered for a conclusion have nothing to do with conclusion. Here are a couple of examples:

"Of course she's a good doctor. She drives a great car and is really funny."
"You believe abortion is murder, yet you are in support of capital punishment?"

Fallacies of Presumption: Fallacies of presumption are those fallacies where someone holds to an unjustified conclusion. This is usually caused by overlooking, denying, evading, or distorting the facts.

Hasty Generalization

When you wish to make an argument for a certain position, you need to gather information for support. In doing this, you must be very careful to gather sufficient evidence to support your conclusion. The fallacy of hasty generalization is committed when a person gathers too little information to support the conclusion being argued.

Just because one or two taxi drivers are rude and obnoxious does not mean that you can generalize that all (or even most) taxi drivers behave this way. All that can legitimately be drawn from such a sampling is that the particular taxi drivers you have encountered were rude and obnoxious. In the same way, just because a person may encounter a couple of Christian TV evangelists who have questionable character does not mean one can conclude that all Christians have questionable character.

These examples get at the heart of the most common way this fallacy is manifest: prejudices. Our prejudices are typically built on a very small sampling, and then are generalized and applied to an entire group (or sub-group) of people or things.

Sweeping Generalization

The fallacy of sweeping generalization is committed when one takes a general rule and applies it absolutely to all instances, not recognizing that there are exceptions. The generalization might be a very fair one, but the application in particular, uncommon, or unique instances may not be valid.

For example, exercise is generally a good thing. Yet what if you have a heart condition? One could say, "Aerobics is the best way to exercise, and Jenny really needs exercise for her heart condition." The problem is that while aerobics might be "the best way to exercise," it would obviously not be the right way for Jenny. Instead of it helping her, it might kill her. Here are a couple more examples:

"I haven't met a single moral atheist. Therefore, no atheists are moral."
"All Christians hate homosexuals. At least, all the ones I know do."

Begging the Question

This fallacy occurs when one simply assumes what he or she is trying to prove. This situation can be demonstrated in the following conversation between two thieves who just stole three bars of gold:

Thief A: "So how are we going to divide the gold?"
Thief B: "I should get two bars and you can have one."
Thief A: "Why should you get two bars?"
Thief B: "Because I am the leader."
Thief A: "How did you get to be the leader?"
Thief B: "Because I have two bars."

Faulty Dilemma

This fallacy occurs when a person states that there are only a certain number of options, and you must choose between them, when in fact there are more options available. In John 9:2–3 the disciples posed a faulty dilemma when, concerning a man who had been blind from birth, they asked, "Rabbi, who sinned, this man or his parents, that he was born blind?" This is an either/or type of question. Instead of answering the question with one of the suggested responses, Jesus denies both and supplies a third. Jesus said, "Neither this man nor his parents sinned, but this happened so that the work of God might be displayed in his life."

Complex Question

One common attempt by unbelievers to stump believers is to ask the age-old question: "Can God create a rock so big that he can't lift it?" If you answer yes, then God's omnipotence (all-powerfulness) is denied due to the fact that he can't lift the rock. If you answer no, however, then God's omnipotence is denied because he can't create such a rock. Neither of these answers is satisfying to a Bible-believing Christian. How does one reason out of this dilemma?

This example can be classified as the fallacy of a complex question, or loaded question. What if I asked you, "Have you stopped beating your wife yet?" If you answer yes, that implies that you have been beating her. If you answer no, then you are still beating her. The problem lies in the question; it is one of those that is simply not fair to ask. You would have to respond that you have never beaten your wife, and that the question presupposes that you have. You can't answer with a simple yes or a no.

Now back to God and the big rock. You cannot answer this question with a simple yes or no. What you have to do is show that the question is not fair. (It might be good to provide the question about beating one's wife as an illustration of this.) You see, by definition, since God is omnipotent (and that is what the Bible teaches), he could create the largest rock possible. Also, because God is omnipotent, he could lift the largest possible rock. The problem with the question is that it is faulty; the question was loaded. You cannot set the creative expression of an omnipotent being against the abilities of an omnipotent being. That would be just as illogical as asking whether or not God could create a square circle or if God could count higher than infinity. It is not within the realm of reality to speak of such illusions, and they do not in any way illustrate any limitation in God's power and abilities.

False Analogy

An analogy is said to be fallacious or false if it compares two objects that are actually relevantly dissimilar or if the points of comparison are used to draw a conclusion that simply does not follow.[5] Consider the following example:

> "You Christians claim to have miracles to support your religion, but so do other religious traditions, such as Mormonism. Thus there is no reason to believe that Christianity is true."

The two objects being compared are Christians and Mormons. Their status as religions and their claim that miracles occur and support their validity are the points of commonalities. However, the conclusion that Christianity is false because another religion claims miracles does not follow. For example, it is possible that miracles occur within both religions traditions. It is also possible that either Christianity or Mormonism have lied or believed falsely regarding the miracles claimed by their religion.

False Cause

This fallacy is committed when a person believes that just because one thing followed another there must be a causal connection. In many ancient cultures, people believed that the gods caused all sickness. These cultures would therefore attempt to placate the wrath of their gods by means of various sacrifices. At times, the sickness would go away after the sacrifices. Because of this, their beliefs were reinforced. They believed that the gods had been placated, and the sickness was removed because of the sacrifice. Mere chronological sequence does not prove causation.

Straw Man

The straw man fallacy occurs when a person misrepresents another's view so as to easily discredit it. This can happen intentionally or unintentionally. The image this fallacy conjures up is that of a person building a straw man simply to knock it over. One might say, "You say that the New Testament teaches that we are not under law, and that we are saved by grace through faith alone. Therefore, what you teach is that we can sin all we want after we are saved." This is a straw man according to Paul in Romans 6:15ff. The person making such an argument simplified the New Testament's stance on the law, sin, and salvation in order to easily defeat a teaching they either didn't understand or with which they didn't agree.

Appeal to Majority

We see this fallacy when we appeal to a group of people to prove that something is true or false, right or wrong. Many times Americans fall into this trap. For example, some people think that certain sexual practices are justified because over 50% of the American public believes that they are permissible. We cannot determine right and wrong by majority vote. In the past, many people believed that the earth was flat. But just because they believed this, does it mean that the earth was indeed flat? Does majority vote make things true or right today? Just because a great number of Americans think that abortion is acceptable, does that make it so? In the end, we cannot determine right/wrong or true/false by majority vote. Such a thing can be decided only by legitimate reasons and evidence.

Appeal to Tradition

This fallacy occurs when one appeals either to what is old, or to what is new in the attempt to establish the truth. Someone may appeal to what is traditional. "We have always done it this way, it must be right." However, there may be a better way. More often today, we hear an appeal to the modern. "We moderns don't believe in the existence of God. That was for ages past when people believed in mythology." Merely because something is old or new does not make it right or true.

---

[5] This is not to say that the objects being compared do not share points of commonality; rather, the objects being compared are not supported by the analogy.

ASKING QUESTIONS[6]

Francis Scott Key, the man who penned the words of the *Star-Spangled Banner*, was also a great Christian apologist. He once wrote, "I do not believe there are any new objections to be raised to the truth of Christianity. Men may argue ingeniously against our faith, but what can they say in defense of their own?"

Mr. Key understood a profound, yet little known principle of defending the Christian faith: the best defense is a good offense. Both sides of an issue should be able to defend their position. We need to practice making our opponents[7] stand up for what they believe, and the best way to make them defend their position is by asking strategic questions.

The strategy of asking questions is a powerful one, but it must be done with the correct demeanor. We must always question the ideas presented, although we should be careful not to challenge the authority of the professor.

In addition, we must keep in mind that if we ask questions of others, they will likely ask questions of us. That means that while we want to challenge other people to defend their beliefs, they will challenge us as well. We need to know why we believe what we believe.

By asking questions we engage in worldview apologetics. We are able to go beyond someone's appearance or behavior in order to reveal and engage their worldview.

How you ask questions—the attitude revealed in your style of inquiry—will reveal whether you want to persuade someone of the truth or just win arguments. We hope that you will desire the former so that you can graciously demonstrate Christian living to unbelievers.

Asking questions is an excellent strategy for three reasons. First, it is low risk. If your opponent becomes angry or defensive at your questions, then you can simply stop asking questions, or change the subject.

Second, asking questions helps you to understand your opponent's train of thought—where they began their thinking, how their thinking progressed, and the exact conclusion for which they are trying to argue. In other words, asking questions helps you to understand them. And understanding is a primary step in seeking to persuade people of the truth.

Third, asking questions can help someone to have a better understanding of where they stand on an issue. In other words, instead of giving them an explanation, you can cause them to think through their position more clearly.

What sort of questions should we be asking? Start with questions that strike at the heart of your opponents' worldview. Such questions force them to back up and defend their assumptions. Along this line, we suggest a series of *tough questions*.

Question 1: What do you mean by that? Always begin by asking your opponents to define their terms. If they say something like, "There is no such thing as a traditional family left in the United States today," then ask, "What do you mean by traditional family?" If they say "God cannot exist because there is too much evil," then ask, "What do you mean by evil?"[8]

Question 2: How did you come to that conclusion? This question is especially helpful in coming to understand how people think. You can find out where their thoughts began, how they progressed, and how they arrived at their conclusion. Along the way, you can ask further questions about any of their points of reasoning.

Question 3: How do you know that to be true? Here we are seeking an understanding of why they believe what they believe. Ask them to supply some good support for what they are claiming to be true.

---

[6] Special thanks to Bill Jack and Jeff Myers for help on earlier editions of this material. Both Bill and Jeff are great examples of how to live inquisitively.

[7] By opponent, we mean the person of whom you are asking questions. It does not mean your enemy.

[8] To combat this particular argument, you can ask by which standard do they judge between good and evil. Keep in mind that atheists have no final universal standards by which to judge between good and evil. The existence of evil is actually a good argument for the existence of God. In the end, if God does not exist, then there is no such thing as evil either.

Question 4: Why do you believe that you are right? We should be ready to ask, "Why do you believe as you do?" This question forces one's opponent to admit when they are simply assuming their beliefs and when they have actually reasoned through their beliefs. It also helps to reveal any evidence they might offer for their arguments. Christians should, in turn, always be ready to give rudimentary reasons for their beliefs on any given subject.

Question 5: Where do you get your information? Students should be trained to ask, "Where do you get the information to prove that what you are saying is true?" This question can help distinguish between mere hearsay and documented data.

Question 6: What happens if you are wrong? Nobody likes to think about the consequences if what they believe is wrong. Yet there have been some outstanding examples of people who were willing to do just that. One such person was Blaise Pascal, a brilliant mathematician, known for his famous wager. It goes something like this: "If I become a Christian and live my life in the service of mankind, and then die only to find out that Christianity is not true, I will have lost nothing. But if I do not become a Christian and live my life selfishly, and then die only to discover that Christianity is true, I will have lost everything." Pascal's wager is a direct way of asking, "What do I have to lose if I am wrong?"[9]

Question 7: Can you give me two sources that disagree with you and explain why they disagree?[10] College professors often hold to one position very strongly against all others. In class, they may assert, either implicitly or explicitly, that what they believe to be true is the objective truth. Therefore, they may give little or no merit to any disagreements, or they may even ridicule their opponents. The astute Christian student will ask such professors to explain clearly the opposing viewpoints, along with good documentation, and then explain why they disagree. In this way, you can see if your professors have weighed different sides of the issues and made informed decisions. The professor has two options: give the merits of the opposing side (thus demonstrating to the class that his is not the only way to think about the issue), or admit that he has not studied the opposing viewpoints and has thus made an uninformed decision without weighing all the available information.

Question 8: Why is this significant? Many professors will fail, unless challenged by students, to provide the connection between their worldview and the point they are making. For example, if they claim "people are basically good, not sinful, by nature," you might ask why this point is significant. This might prompt them to explain that this justifies another view, maybe a socialistic view of the world, or elimination of the need for a savior.

Question 9: How do I know you are telling me the truth?[11] If the opponent has any hidden agenda, it will surface at this point. We should not trust someone simply because he has a Ph.D. after his name. People are fallible, and we all make mistakes. Remember, the Bereans were *nobler* because they checked the Apostle Paul against the Old Testament (Acts 17:11). A poor professor will respond simply by listing his or her qualifications. A good professor will say "Don't take my word for it. Go check it out for yourself."

Question 10: Can you give me an alternative explanation for this phenomenon? This is a good way to move a discussion back onto logical ground. Many individuals will emotionally assert things like, "His budget cuts are responsible for all of the economic ills in this nation." This is an absurd generalization, something that will become evident when asking this question.

---

9 Be careful with this question because it can always be thrown back at you.

10 Another way of asking this question is, "Can you give us some sources who disagree with your opinion, explain their positions, and tell us what is wrong with their views?"

11 Another way of asking this question is, "Why should I believe you?" But you really need to be careful here. It is difficult to ask this question in a way that doesn't seem snobbish.

ANALYZING MEDIA REPORTS

People need to recognize that most of their information about the world comes to them through the media. Yet, the media isn't some massive channel that simply dumps unbiased facts into our laps. As we have seen, everyone has a worldview: the *actors* in a news story, the *experts* who comment on it, the *reporters* of the story, even the *editors/executives* who decide which story to cover. Each of their worldviews has an impact on the information that eventually reaches you.

At times, the influence of a particular worldview may be subtle. However, it wouldn't take very long to discover that many of them don't just have a job; they have a mission. Their mission is to make a difference in the world through what they do. In fact, for many people, this is not an unusual goal. Students needs to be aware that we all approach information and life with a bias. It is simply unavoidable.

In the vast majority of cases, the editors and reporters are making an effort to be balanced. Yet what does *balanced* mean? It means reporting both sides of the issue with no indication that either side of the story has more merit. Is that true? As Christians, we believe that some things are right and other things are wrong.

As one learns to analyze media reports, he or she should apply the rules on logical thinking that are presented in this section. They should also keep the following factors in mind:

1. What is reported? It is easy to think that by reading your daily newspaper and watching the evening news you have received a thorough representation of anything relevant in your community. Students should realize that each media outlet has a limited amount of space and ability to deal with everything that is important. Think of a media outlet as a spotlight on a dark night. The spotlight will illuminate things that you would never see otherwise, but there is no way it can shine on everything at once.

Recognize also that each individual news form has restrictions and limitations. In order to make a story acceptable for television, it must have pictures. This may seem inconsequential until you realize that there are some things—like the arrival of a new bear at the local zoo—which are reported because they make great pictures and can be reported in two minutes. Yet perhaps the same day the bear arrived, the city council made a change in the zoning laws that will affect your school. City council meetings make horrible pictures, and zoning laws don't fit well into concise sound bites. Which story is truly important?

What makes an event newsworthy? Most events that are truly life-changing are not considered newsworthy: marriages, deaths, and births. Rarely do these events appear on the front page. Conversely, many events that make the front page are life changing for only a few people, or intriguing for the moment.

2. Which sides are presented? Is a response from each side presented? Does the news story even indicate that someone might think differently? For instance, in an article in the *Chicago Tribune* entitled "Life Gets Earlier Date of Origin,"[12] an Australian scientist is reported as having found that life evolved much earlier than was previously thought—going from chemical soup to living cells in just 500 million years, rather than 1 1/2 billion years. The article is well written, and acknowledges disagreement within the scientific community. However, it does not acknowledge that anyone might disagree with evolution altogether.

There are many reasons for this type of omission. Sometimes it is deliberate. At other times, a reporter may not be aware that another viewpoint exists or know a credible contact to represent a position. Also, there may not be time to consider another opinion due to deadlines.

Another reason for omitting a position on an issue is based on worldviews. How we think will affect what we believe to be credible, or even possible. For example, we know that the world is round, but some people still believe it to be flat. If you were going to write an article examining a change in a major ocean current and its effect on weather, would you contact the Flat Earth Society for comment?

In the same way, a reporter who firmly believes that the material world is all that exists may do a human-interest piece on a *miraculous* recovery from cancer. Although they might mention the chance that there might be a supernatural element involved, a *natural* cause of recovery will be sought and favored.

The reporter knows that there is no way God could have healed the patient, so this possibility is as absurd as the idea of a flat earth.

---

[12] "Life Gets Earlier Date of Origin," *Chicago Tribune* (May 2, 1993).

3. What is the tone of the report? Does the tone of the writing or speaking carry meaning in itself? Does the tone match the issue being reported? Consider the following example from an article concerning the ethical discussions raised by the movie *Indecent Proposal* (where a billionaire offers another man 1 million dollars for one night with his wife). The reporter spoke with a woman who is shocked by the number of women who would agree to take the money and sleep with the man. The reporter is writing in the first person.

> "I was really shocked," she said. "I think these people are telling the truth. Kidding is one thing, but this was a serious discussion. I love my husband. This would never even be cause for five minutes of deliberation. I would never do it. I can't believe they would."
>
> She talks as if this is going to go on record as the final rip in modern morality.
>
> "And what do you think?" she wanted to know.
>
> The woman is 53 years old, the grandmother of three. And by her own admission, she is 35 pounds overweight. I told her I could see how this would be a great moral challenge. But I thought she had the strength to get through it.
>
> "I think you can go back to worrying about Somalia, the economy, and whether Donald will marry Marla," I said. "I just don't think this is going to come up."
>
> "That's not the point," she said.
>
> "Yes, it is," I replied.[13]

4. What underlying assumptions does the news story hold? Students should become skilled in seeking *underlying assumptions* held in the report of a story. The *Twin Cities Star Tribune* ran an article entitled, "If every kid cared, the world would change,"[14] describing the impact of a few sixth graders concerned about the environment. The piece is inspiring, but the assumption is that it is permissible to do whatever is necessary to make your point (the children disobeyed school officials in holding a protest, and were suspended from school). This disobedience was presented in a positive light.

5. Who are the sources and how are they characterized? Does an article on environmentalism only quote extremist groups, or do they use more moderate sources? If the article quotes Christians, which groups or spokespersons are quoted? Are these the best sources? Why were these sources used? Consider also how the sources are characterized or described. Are they seen in a positive or negative light? The following quote is from an Associated Press article reporting on several Italian towns that banned bikinis on city streets.

> ROME (AP)—Limits on topless bathing or skimpy suits on city streets are not new. But this time the prudery illuminates attitudes about a political force that has arrived like an awkward adolescent shouldering his way onto the school bus.
>
> The prudish officials belong to the Northern League, a regionally based anti-corruption party backed by small businessmen and the middle class, with upright morals to match.
>
> The bans reflect the culture clash between the League and its rivals from traditional parties, particularly on the left, which regard the League as part of a conservative backlash.[15]

6. How are words used to describe people or organizations?
- To describe the incident: Was someone *taken* to jail or *thrown* into jail?
- To describe the people involved: A *local church* or a *fundamentalist religious group*?[16]
- To describe a position: Is someone *pro-life* or *anti-abortion*?
- To convey emotion: One article described citations by the Thomas Jefferson Center for the Protection of Free Expression. The organization cited the Federal Communications Commission

---

[13] "Premise of 'Indecent Proposal' Disturbing," Marilyn Schwartz, *Dallas Morning News*, in *Gazette Telegraph*, Colorado Springs, CO (April 26, 1993).

[14] "If every kid cared, the world would change," *Twin Cities Star Tribune*, Minneapolis (April 22, 1993).

[15] "Bikini ban in 2 Italian cities underlines new cultural clash," *Standard Examiner*, Ogden, UT (July 20, 1993).

[16] Be aware of the use of the word "fundamentalist." It is being applied indiscriminately to any religious group, whether a local church is protesting the location of an adult bookstore or David Koresh's Branch Davidian cult near Waco, Texas.

for censorship for "trying to gag controversial radio personality Howard Stern."[17] *Censorship* and *gag* are emotional words, and convey meaning.

- To give positive or negative connotations: "Focus on the Family, the Christian media conglomerate, should be up-front about its 'extreme and un-American' political agenda, a national civil liberties watchdog group said Wednesday."[18] Think of the words with generally positive connotations: *civil liberties* and *watchdog*. Negative connotations come from the words *agenda* and *conglomerate*.
- To simply describe a thing: A fascinating example of this comes from an article titled "Doctors try to save brain-dead mom's fetus." The baby is referred to as a fetus throughout the article, except when a hospital spokesman is quoted as saying, "The odds are very slim, but the baby's heart is beating."[19] Also consider Colorado's Amendment Two, which would prevent laws giving gays protected civil rights status such as those that protect minority groups. Contrast that description with "the amendment would ban laws that prevent discrimination against homosexuals,"[20] as it was described by the Associated Press.
- Even punctuation can be used to convey meaning. In the following examples, a prayer rally is presented as something a bit odd, if not downright unsavory.
  1. "Abortion clinics brace for Operation Rescue."
  2. "Saturday 'prayer rally' set for Robbinsdale."
  3. "Operation Rescue officials confirmed Wednesday that their national director, the Rev. Keith Tucci, will be in the Twin Cities this weekend and will lead a "prayer rally" in front of a Robbinsdale abortion clinic on Saturday."[21]

7. How are actions described? What are the outcomes or results of the event being reported? Are these accurate? Consider an article entitled, "Teaching multicultural history instills pride, sense of place, educators find."[22] The results of implementing a multicultural curriculum are presented as overwhelmingly positive. However, the writer does not examine the results of this curriculum on the students' standardized test scores. The program has raised self-esteem, but is that the only crucial criteria for evaluation?

8. What statistics are used? Statistics can prove just about anything—and they can be misleading. A prime example is the *accepted* statistic that homosexuals comprise 10% of the population.[23] Recent studies indicate that 2–3% is more appropriate,[24] yet the 10% figure continues to be used.

9. What is left out of the news story? This can include background sources, supporting materials or studies, and opposing viewpoints. Sometimes this omission is deliberate. However, in many cases it is simply irresponsible reporting. For example, consider the following news brief that was sent on the United Press International newswire:

> (TRENTON, NJ)— Some 15 million people could be getting parched if there is more global warming without an increase in rainfall. The U.S. Geological Survey says the Delaware River Basin which feeds Pennsylvania, New Jersey, and New York could be facing a serious drought if the overall temperature rises by just four degrees. That would cause stream flow to drop 27 percent and allow saltwater to back up in the Delaware into freshwater aquifers.[25]

---

[17] "Official's ban of fairy tale earns 'citation' for censorship," *The Clarion-Ledger*, Jacksonville, MS (April 14, 1993).

[18] "Watchdog says Focus hides aims," D'Arcy Fallon, *Gazette Telegraph*, Colorado Springs, CO (April 29, 1993).

[19] "Doctors try to save brain-dead mom's fetus," *The Commercial Appeal*, Memphis, TN (April 24, 1993).

[20] "Amendment 2 Boycott," Associated Press newswire (May 7, 1993).

[21] "Abortion clinics brace for Operation Rescue," Tim Nelson, *Pioneer Press*, St. Paul, MN (April 22, 1993).

[22] "Teaching multicultural history instills pride, sense of place, educators find," Sandy Kleffman, *San Francisco Chronicle*, in *Gazette Telegraph*, Colorado Springs, CO (April 19, 1993).

[23] Alfred C. Kinsey, *Sexual Behavior in the Human Male* (Philadelphia: Saunders, 1948).

[24] June M. Reinisch, *The Kinsey Institute New Report on Sex* (New York: St. Martin's Press, 1990), 147. See also Abraham Maslow and James M. Sakoda, "Volunteer Error in the Kinsey Study," *Journal of Abnormal and Social Psychology* 47 (April 1952), 259–62.

[25] *First-Pennsylvania News in Brief*, UPI Newswire (May 18, 1993).

That is the entire story! Almost every possible detail was left out—why the U.S. Geological Survey said what it did, any supporting statistics or studies, or support for the controversial idea of global warming in general. This example also begins with the faulty assumption that global warming is already occurring, and points out the inherent difficulties in reporting news. This news clip was intended for a radio broadcast which leaves very little time for in-depth information. Also notice the conditional words, like *could* and *if*.

10. Where is the reader or listener led into faulty reasoning? Consider the following example from United Press International:

> (MALDEN, MA)—The state Board of Education Tuesday approved a policy that encourages local school officials to implement programs to protect gay students from harassment and educate faculty members about gay issues.
>
> The policy, believed to be [the] first of its kind in the nation, was approved as part of an overall strategy intended to curb an increasing level of violence in schools, which in recent months has included the fatal shootings of a student and a librarian.
>
> The board, however, stopped short of recommending a gay studies curriculum to be offered in the public schools.[26]

Unless the reader is thinking critically, he or she might assume that the shootings cited in paragraph two were gay related—not so. The reader is led to assume that with increasing violence, gays will need protection.

TAKING ACTION

One of the difficulties with analyzing media reports is that the more you think critically, the more critical you become. It will become much harder to simply *absorb* the news. There are some positive actions you and your class can take to promote a more balanced approach to the news in your area. One key action is to make sure your local media outlets have access to credible sources. Gary Bauer, of the Family Research Council, is quoted often in secular media simply because he is one of the few people they know to contact for the "conservative Christian" viewpoint.

One of the best ways to do this is to distribute a media guide to all your local news sources. Find spokespeople on a variety of topics: women's issues, the family, religion, education (private schools, Christian education, home school), abortion, etc. Make sure your spokespeople are reasonable and articulate—choose carefully. Be sure to include teens from your school who are willing to be interviewed. List the topics and spokespersons—including addresses, day and evening phone numbers, and a short biography will lend credibility.

Send the media guide with a cover letter to all newspapers, and radio and television stations in your area. They may or may not use it, but it will be kept on file. A reporter always appreciates a source who can be reached when a deadline is looming, and is willing to speak up in a manner that is easily quotable.

Also, begin to think of good stories for your local media. Some of the community service projects your class is doing could make a great "warm fuzzy" story. Let them know.

If your local newspaper or television station doesn't have a "teen council" composed of students from area high schools—find a couple of interested students who would be willing to make the suggestion and serve on the council. Council members could serve as a sounding board on community issues affecting youth, be reporters, and take turns writing a weekly or daily "teen editorial."

---

[26] "Mass. Board of Education approves policy on gay students," UPI newswire (May 18, 1993).

CRITICAL THINKING
ESSAY QUESTIONS

Answer the questions below on a separate sheet of paper and be prepared to review your answers in class. The following are a list of statements/arguments that are fallacious in some way. Your teacher will guide you through this exercise.

PART ONE

1. **The end of a thing is its perfection; death is the end of life; therefore, death is the perfection of life.**

   Equivocation—The equivocation is on the word "end." In the first instance, end means the completion of a purpose—when we have a goal, we "work to that end," or toward the completion of our goal. The second use of "end" is the cessation of something's existence—when something or someone ceases to be. For instance, at the conclusion of many old movies, they would display the words "The End." It didn't mean that the movie had achieved its ultimate purpose; it simply meant that the movie had come to a stop. [SM p. 73]

2. **Marijuana can't be all that bad. Everyone knows about barroom brawls, but marijuana makes people peaceful.**

   Red Herring—This statement is a red herring because it diverts the listener's attention to a positive, but irrelevant issue. In this case, the argument against the use of marijuana is based on its abusive nature, rather than its peace-invoking side effects. Whether or not it results in peacefulness does not answer the question of whether or not it is abusive. To concentrate on this aspect is to avoid the real issue. [SM p. 74]

3. **Women are so sentimental. My mother and sisters always cry at the movies; my father and I never do.**

   Hasty Generalization—The generalization is that all women are sentimental. The problem with making this generalization, however, is that the evidence used to come to this conclusion is far too minimal. If there are billions of women in existence, describing them all based on the actions of only two or three is hasty. [SM pp. 74–5]

4. **The Senator is incorruptibly honest; no one has ever uncovered a scandal involving him.**

   Appeal to Ignorance—The fact that the Senator has never experienced scandal is not ironclad evidence that he is honest. Although no one has ever uncovered a scandal implicating the Senator, it does not automatically follow that no scandal actually exists. It could be that the Senator is incredibly effective at covering his tracks. Since no one knows of any scandal, his innocence is probable, but this does not mean that the conclusion of honesty is above suspicion. [SM p. 74]

5. **The so-called theories of Einstein are merely the ravings of a mind polluted with liberal, democratic nonsense, which is utterly unacceptable to German men of science.**

> **Ad Hominem**—Einstein's theories must be assessed according to their own merit. The rightness or wrongness of an idea does not depend on the character of the person who proposed it, whether a madman or a respected scientific scholar. Its validity must stand independently. [SM p. 74]

6. **Exercise keeps everyone healthy. Therefore, if Tim would just run more, it might help his heart condition.**

> **Sweeping Generalization**—One cannot argue that just because a principle is predominantly appropriate, it is therefore always appropriate. Ignoring exceptions can sometimes be fatal. We must treat general rules as just that—general. [SM p. 75]

7. **Those who favor gun control also favor disarming the police and disbanding the National Guard.**

> **Straw Man**—Most of those who are pro-gun control are not in favor of disarming the police or getting rid of the National Guard. It may be that a few in this camp take their ideas to a further extreme than most. However, one cannot misrepresent the stand of the majority simply to make one's refutation more plausible. [SM p. 76]

8. **"Death should be held of no account, for it brings but two alternatives: either it utterly annihilates the person and his soul, or it transports the spirit or soul to some place where it will live forever. What then should a good man fear if death would bring only nothingness or eternal life." — Cicero**

> **Faulty Dilemma**—Cicero is saying that there are only two alternatives for the consequences of death: either utter annihilation of the person or eternal life for the person's soul/spirit. There are, however, more alternatives. There is the belief that we are nothing but physical beings who will simply cease breathing and become food for worms. Or, most Evangelical Christians believe that those who reject God will suffer in his absence for eternity. An additional option is that these same rebellious ones will suffer for a period of time before God brings them forever into his presence. Finally, there are many people in the world who hold to reincarnation, the belief that when we die we will be reborn into new bodies or forms of life. Therefore, offering only two alternatives oversimplifies the issue and forces a choice between a spuriously limited set of options. [SM p. 75]

9. **I'm on probation, sir. If I don't get a good grade in this course, I won't be able to stay in school. Please, could you let me have at least a C?**

> **Appeal to Pity**—The system of letter grades was devised to reflect academic merit. This student, however, is not making an appeal based on his or her academic merit, but on his or her desire to stay in school. The basis of the appeal is a factor unrelated to the purpose of the letter grade. [SM p. 74]

10. **I join 2 presidents, 27 senators, and 83 representatives in describing this woman as a liar.**

> **Appeal to Majority**—The veracity of the woman's testimony should not be based upon how many people think that she is or is not lying. Rather, her words should be judged on whether or not they correspond with the facts of the case. [SM p. 76]

11. **Of course the Bible is true. It says that it is true.**

> **Begging the Question**—This statement sets up a vicious circle:
>
> A: The Bible is true.
> B: How do you know the Bible is true?
> A: I know it's true because it says it's true.
> B: How do you know that its self-proclaimed truthfulness is true?
> A: Because the Bible is true.
> B: How do you know the Bible is true?
>
> And so on and so on, with no resolvable end in sight. The reason this argument begs the question is that it does not go outside of itself for proof of its truthfulness. The initial argument merely uses itself to prove itself. [SM p. 75]

12. **It's the old time religion and it's good enough for me.**

> **Appeal to Tradition**—Buddhism was founded over 2.500 years ago, thus making it older than Christianity. If the age of a religion is the standard by which we deem it correct, then our allegiance should lie with Buddhism before Christianity. In fact, pagan animism is even older than Buddhism, so why not subscribe to it? The length of time that a religion has been in existence is not a reliable measure of its validity. [SM pp. 76–7]

13. **In defense of suicide, David Hume said, "It would be no crime in me to divert the Nile or Danube from its course, were I able to effect such purposes. Where is then the crime of turning a few ounces of blood from their natural channel?"**

> **False Analogy**—This analogy fails because the consequences of rerouting a river are not necessarily fatal, while rerouting blood outside the bloodstream is fatal. Thus, the two circumstances do not share the necessary common ground in order to make this analogy work. [SM p. 76]

14. **Why do you want to throw your money away like that?**

> **Complex Question**—This question is complex because it misses a crucial step by making an unwarranted assumption. The questioner is assuming that the other person wants to throw their money away. This is probably not a valid belief. In order to remedy this faulty approach, the inquirer

should ask, "Do you want to throw your money away?" If the person being questioned answers "Yes," then, at this point, our question is valid. If the person answers "No," as most people would respond, then the conversation could continue as the inquirer questions why the other person would be involved in the proposed venture. [SM pp. 75–6]

15. **I think his daughter's marriage must have worried him dreadfully, because his hair began to turn white after the wedding.**

False Cause—There could be a great many reasons why this gentleman's hair began to turn white. The timing of his daughter's marriage may be mere coincidence or just one factor among many that are responsible for the result. Without further evidence, a concrete inference cannot be drawn. [SM p. 76]

16. **I fail to see why hunting should be considered cruel when it gives me tremendous pleasure.**

Red Herring—If it is cruel to hunt animals, and it is wrong to be cruel, the pleasure that hunting provides has no legitimate weight on the issue. The dual issue is whether or not hunting is cruel and whether or not being cruel to animals is immoral. [SM p. 74]

17. **You are either a conservative or a liberal.**

Faulty Dilemma—What about the moderates? Since most people fall somewhere between conservative and liberal, offering only these two options creates a deceptive survey. The question is problematic because it forces the person being interviewed to make an unrealistic choice. [SM p. 75]

18. **Pro-lifers believe that a fetus should be protected because it is a "potential" human. Today I will prove that a "potential" human is not a human and therefore should not be protected.**

Straw Man—This statement is a misrepresentation of the pro-life position. Most pro-lifers do not state that the fetus is a potential human, but rather that it is a human, period. Therefore, if a person were to argue against the pro-life stance by citing reasons that we should believe that the fetus is not a potential human, they would be arguing against a position that has no substantial support in the pro-life camp. [SM p. 76]

19. **There must be intelligent life in outer space, because no one has been able to prove that there isn't.**

Appeal to Ignorance—No one has been able to prove that there isn't intelligent life in outer space. Likewise, no one has been able to prove that there is intelligent life in outer space. The lack of evidence does not grant one the warrant to form conclusive judgments. The lack of evidence provides for possibilities, not conclusions. [SM p. 74]

20. **All Christians hate homosexuals—at least all the ones I know do.**

> **Hasty Generalization**—The word "all" must be used very carefully when making a broad statement like this. Even though a small sampling of Christians might have a certain attitude, this does not mean that every other believer in the world reflects this same mentality. [SM pp. 74–5]

21. **You're wrong because you are an intolerant, closed-minded, right-wing fundamentalist.**

> **Ad Hominem**—Is it possible for a closed-minded, right-wing fundamentalist to be correct about anything? If so, then the unqualified statement "you're wrong because" is not a valid reason to discard the fundamentalist's idea. His or her idea must be evaluated on its own strength or weakness, not on the political or religious stature of its speaker. [SM p. 74]

22. **The Golden Rule is basic to every system of ethics ever devised. Everyone accepts it in some form or other. It is, therefore, an undeniably sound moral principle.**

> **Appeal to Majority**—If all cultures assumed some form of pantheism, would that make pantheism correct? Of course not. The fact that every system includes the Golden Rule should not be a determining factor for its soundness. [SM p. 76]

23. **The sign stated, "Fine for parking here." Since it said "fine," I parked here.**

> **Equivocation**—Here, the term of confusion is the word "fine." In the first use, it refers to a monetary penalty for the described action. In the second instance, "fine" means "it's all right" to partake in the described action. [SM p. 73]

24. **These rules were written 100 years ago and we have always followed them. Therefore, there is no need to change them.**

> **Appeal to Tradition**—Close to 3,000 years ago, the Israelites were commanded to build parapets around their roofs in order to avoid bloodguilt (Deuteronomy 22:8). It would be counterintuitive, however, to enforce this law today because our roofs no longer endure the high amount of traffic that Israelite homes did. Tradition is an inappropriate standard by which to measure the appropriateness of certain laws. [SM pp. 76–7]

25. **Of course I am right. I am always right.**

> **Begging the Question**—This statement leads one into endless self-verification:
>
> A: I am right.
> B: How do you know that you are right?

A: Well, I'm always right.

B: How do you know that you're always right?

A: Because I'm always right about everything, which means I'm right about always being right.

This argument assumes the truth of the case in point in order to provide justification for itself. In other words, the initial thesis is used as proof of its own validity. To reveal the unhelpfulness of the argument, we can phrase it this way: Why am I right? Because I'm right. [SM p. 75]

26. Everyone has a right to own property. Just because Jon has been declared insane doesn't mean that you can take his weapon away.

Sweeping Generalization—In a general principle, there are sometimes unspoken assumptions that cannot be overlooked. In this example, the principle of the universal right to property ownership is based on the fundamental capacity of the prospective owner for proper stewardship of that property. [SM p. 75]

27. If we outlaw abortion, countless women will die during back alley abortions.

Appeal to Pity—The basic issue underlying abortion concerns whether or not the fetus is a human being. If it were, aborting him or her would be murder. So, bringing up back alley abortions completely misses the point. If pro-lifers are correct about the humanity of every fetus, then this argument is basically saying that we should provide sanitary places for women to commit murder. This statement diverts attention away from the central issues of personhood and murder toward sanitation and black market abortions. [SM p. 74]

28. Are you still a heavy drinker?

Complex Question—In order for this question to avoid being fallacious, it must be true that the person in question was, at some point, a heavy drinker. This type of question forces the subject to admit to guilt that may or may not apply. [SM pp. 75–6]

29. Employees are like nails. Just as nails must be hit in the head in order to make them work, so must employees.

False Analogy—What are the similarities and differences between human beings and nails, and are the similarities significant enough to deem this analogy valid? The proposed common ground is found in the word *work*. When a nail works, it is driven through material that needs to be held together. When employees work, they are accomplishing any number of tasks assigned to them by their employer. Are these two uses of *work* the same? Since the work of an employee is not to be driven through two pieces of wood, then we can safely conclude that the two uses of *work* should be understood differently. Likewise, when a nail works, it is not typing a paper, evaluating stock market activities, milking a cow, flying a commercial airliner, or punching buttons on a cash register. Therefore, the analogy fails to make the desired connection. [SM p. 76]

30. **Immediately after walking under a ladder, my leg fell off. I haven't hobbled under a ladder since.**

False Cause—A common fault of many superstitious people is identifying causes where there are none to be found. Coincidence is often interpreted as causal rather than incidental. In this example, more information is needed about the subject's unexpected amputation before we can decidedly conclude that the sub-ladder stroll is to blame. [SM p. 76]

PART TWO

Read the following fictitious news story and answer the corresponding questions.

P.A.G.A.N. Invades Christian Town
Long time anti-Christian activist organization removes pro-God public display from government arena.

SHELBYVILLE — In a little–known, mid-sized, midwestern town, there was great outrage over the events of this past weekend. With little more than a court order, the lawsuit-happy organization known as P.A.G.A.N. (People Against God And Normalcy) arrived at the steps of Shelbyville's City Hall late Friday afternoon with a crane. Local judge Rod Snider, a staunch liberal, had signed an order that morning giving P.A.G.A.N. the authority to steal the town's symbol of religious freedom and moral guidance—a 50-foot statue of the Virgin Mary. I watched in disbelief as the statue honoring Christianity as the town's established religion was removed from the city steps and strapped to a rundown flatbed truck. Judge Snider sat idly by as a number of citizens protested the forced removal of the town's glorious icon. P.A.G.A.N. and its motley crew, seemingly unmoved by the demonstrations, pressed on with their desecration.

The statue has been taken to a nearby state-owned warehouse and veiled in retired green army blankets where it will be held hostage while the judge's decision is being appealed to a higher court.

The statue was generously donated to the town around six months ago after being commissioned by the respected religious leader Reverend Timothy Love. He noted that the statue was a token of the church's appreciation "to the good folks of Shelbyville."

The honorable reverend's wife, Helen Love, insists that P.A.G.A.N. is in her town largely because of the complaints of one irreligious man, Joe Sylack. Mr. Sylack, a local bar owner, rarely attends church and has apparently never appreciated the community's sacred stone image. Mrs. Love asserts that this is simply an example of a few atheists trying to make everyone else respect their religious beliefs. But Mrs. Love wants to know, "What about the town's religious beliefs?"

I interviewed one of Love's knowledgeable parishioners, Ned Landers, about the situation. He insists, "This is just another example of how our town is going to hell in a hand basket." Mr. Landers blames the situation on rock music, daytime television, and foreigners. After witnessing this contemptible event, I believe the majority of Shelbyville's citizens would agree with Mr. Lander's assessment. It seems clear that P.A.G.A.N. and Judge Snider have no respect for property, the will of the people, or God Himself.

Kent Beckman
The Shelbyville County Times

1. What incident is being reported?

> The story is reporting the removal of a 50-foot statue of the Virgin Mary from the Shelbyville Courthouse steps. The anti-Christian organization P.A.G.A.N. had challenged the placement of the statue, and last Friday its removal was approved by local judge Rod Snider.

2. Which sides are presented?

> Only the position of those desiring for the statue to remain are represented.

3. What is the tone of the report?

> The tone portrays a very negative reaction against P.A.G.A.N., Judge Snider, and Joe Sylack. The story seems inversely positive toward Reverend Love, his wife Helen, and Ned Landers.

4. On what underlying assumption is the news story based?

> The unchallenged assumption is that P.A.G.A.N. and Judge Snider do not have good reasons for their actions.

5. Who are the article's sources and how are they characterized?

> - Reverend Timothy Love—a generous, well-respected religious leader
> - Helen Love—the honorable reverend's wife
> - Ned Landers—knowledgeable

6. What words are used to describe people or organizations?

> - P.A.G.A.N.—lawsuit-happy organization, motley crew
> - Judge Rod Snider—staunch liberal, no respect for property, no respect for the will of the people, no respect for God
> - Joe Sylack—irreligious man, bar owner, rarely attends church

7. How are the parties' actions described throughout the article?

> - "…was great outrage over the events of this past weekend."
> - "…giving P.A.G.A.N. the authority to steal the town's symbol…"
> - "…where it will be held hostage…"
> - "Judge Snider sat idly by…"

- "…the forced removal of the town's glorious icon."
- "…pressed on with their desecration."
- "…apparently never appreciated the community's sacred stone image."
- "The statue was generously donated…"
- "After witnessing this contemptible event…"

8. What statistics are used?

No statistics are cited in this story.

9. What is left out of the news story?

There was no representation from individuals in support of the removal represented in this story, including Joe Sylack, a local bar owner who was accused of instigating the ordeal. Also, neither Judge Snider nor a representative from P.A.G.A.N. were quoted in the story.

10. What logical fallacies are used to lead the reader or listener into faulty reasoning?

Ad Hominem—P.A.G.A.N. was negatively characterized by its opponents and was not given the opportunity to present its rationale.

Straw Man—The only position presented was that of Reverend Love. The article assigns malicious motives to P.A.G.A.N., but does not give the organization the chance to make a case for its position.

DEAR DOUG
WRITING ASSIGNMENT

Hey, it's me again!

I love college! There's always something going on—games, intramurals, parties, concerts, late nights with friends—it's awesome! In fact, college life would be perfect if all those annoying classes didn't get in the way. With all the stuff to do here on campus, I can barely make time for class. Don't worry, though. So far my grades have been pretty good... well, all except for Philosophy 101. Half the time I don't have a clue what the prof is saying. She might as well be speaking Chinese!

That class is the worst. I keep waiting for her to just give us the answers, but she only asks a lot of questions. Sometimes it seems like we just focus on what a lot of dead guys thought about reality, knowledge, morality, whatever. I have an essay due next week about my own take on the stuff we've been learning, but I've got no idea where to start. Science tells us that evolution is a fact, so I guess reality is composed of things I can see and touch. Do you think reality, truth, and knowledge can be explained by naturalism? But then some people (like the guy down the hall) believe that nothing is natural at all—that the world is only a spiritual illusion. I'm just really confused. I believe that there is a God who created everything. So does that mean reality, truth, etc. can be explained by non-naturalism? It doesn't seem like both views can be right.

And if that's not enough, I'm supposed to be able to explain the differences between Karl Marx's philosophy and plain old atheistic materialism. What's the difference between naturalism and Marx's "dialectical materialism" anyway?

I've got so many questions and no one here seems able to answer them. Here's an important one we're not even dealing with in class. All this philosophy stuff is explained by other worldviews, like Marxism. But what does the Christian worldview say about philosophy? Is it even covered in the Bible? I'm sorry to keep bugging you with all these questions, but I really want to know.

Enough thinking for now. I'm dying to tell you about my date a couple of weeks ago. It was great! We caught an Indie flick and then headed over to the coffee shop to talk. Her name is Amber and she's lots of fun and very smart. When I made some comment about faith, she said she was an agnostic and changed the subject. It didn't bother me too much—I mean, we have such a good time together. Besides, it isn't serious... yet.

Hope to hear from ya soon,
Doug

Doug has brought up four different subjects; below is a rough outline of possible responses:

1. **Are reality, truth, and knowledge explained by naturalism? (12.5 points)**

Naturalism holds that everything is material and can be observed and measured by the senses. Thus, reality is monistic (*solely* composed of matter), and immaterial things such as God, the devil, angels, souls, and supernatural salvation must be discarded as fantasy (as well as morals, numbers, reason, and everything else that cannot be sensed).

For this view to be true, the naturalist must proclaim the design and purpose displayed in nature to be an illusion. Such things only *apparently* exhibit design, i.e., we are fooled into seeing an ultimate purpose where no such intention exists. Moreover, the universe's very existence is purposeless and generated by chance. It was not supernatural providence, but blind accident that eventually generated life and ultimately produced the human mind.

Of course, the human mind itself presents a problem for the naturalist. Does the mind exist solely within nature, just as the body does, or is the mind more than matter? For the naturalist, the mind must somehow be a physical extension of the brain. Our thoughts and emotions must somehow be explained in purely physical terms since there is no room for the immaterial.

2. Are reality, truth, and knowledge explained by non-naturalism? (12.5 points)

For the New Ager, the universe is not a machine, but a divine, living organism. God is the whole of ultimate reality and everything is, in essence, god.

Of course, since everything is divine, then we, as a portion of this god, can create our own subjective truth based on our divine knowledge of reality. There is no divine force superior to us. This presents a problem for those who hold differing viewpoints of truth and morality, as any disagreement within the divine essence is inherently impossible for the New Age worldview. Yet, if we are all part of a collective that is god, why is it that many of us are confused about this reality?

3. What is the difference between naturalism and dialectical materialism? (12.5 points)

As the Secular Humanist's philosophy is naturalistic, so too is the Marxist's philosophy. For the Marxist, the universe is infinite, made up solely of indestructible matter. The progression of life is Darwinian—a continuing struggle for existence in every corner of the universe. It is through this struggle that evolution gives us adapted forms of life and that the dialectic gives birth to human progress. Consequently, like naturalism, dialectical materialism believes science is the source of knowledge and truth. Likewise, religion and the supernatural are viewed as fantasy.

It is the dialectic element that separates Marxist philosophy from Secular Humanist philosophy. For the Marxist, the dialectic (or the struggle between opposing thesis and antithesis that result in a synthesis) gives rise to change, struggle, and survival. The dialectic thus views life as a constant struggle between opposing forces that result in a progressive evolution. For example, the dialectic can be seen scientifically in the clash between positive and negative charges in electricity; biologically between species struggling for survival; or socially between the ancient medieval feudal lords and the peasants. For Marxists, the key clash is economic, between the proletariat (or the lower class: those that do not own property) and the bourgeois (or the upper class: those who own the means of production). It is from this current economic clash that the Marxist looks for an eventual improved class (a synthesis).

4. **What is the Christian view of philosophy? Is it covered in the Bible? (12.5 points)**

At the heart of Christian philosophy is metaphysical dualism, which states that reality is made up of both the natural and the supernatural. Christians, therefore, believe that the whole of reality is neither completely natural (as in Secular Humanism and Marxism) nor entirely supernatural (as in New Age philosophy). Rather, the natural world and human beings were designed and created by God for a distinct purpose.

This philosophy of supernaturalism is able to address the mind-body dilemma, while simultaneously affirming that not everything God creates is supernatural.

For the Christian, knowledge can be gained through scientific investigation and special revelation. So, while the naturalist puts his or her faith solely in science, the Christian places his or her faith in God and Scripture above human reason alone.

UNIT TWO TEST

'PHILOSOPHY' TEXTBOOK QUESTIONS

Matching: (1 point possible per answer [2 for 90-day])
some options may be used more than once or not at all; some questions may have multiple answers

1. __c/g__ **Christianity**

2. __c/g__ **Islam**

3. __a__ **Secular Humanism**

4. __e__ **Marxism-Leninism**

5. __b__ **Cosmic Humanism**

6. __d/h__ **Postmodernism**

a. Naturalism
b. Non-naturalism
c. Supernaturalism
d. Anti-realism
e. Dialectical Materialism
f. Common Sense Realism
g. Faith and Reason
h. Deconstruction

Fill in the Blank: (5 points possible per answer [4 for 90-day])

7. _____**Realism**_____ is the belief that there is a "real world" independent of human subjects.

8. _____**Cosmology**_____ is the study of the structure, origin, and design of the universe.

9. _____**Epistemology**_____ is the study of knowledge.

10. _____**Metaphysics**_____ is the study of ultimate reality.

11. _____**Mind/Body Problem**_____ is the study of the relationship of the mind (e.g. mental events, mental functions, mental properties, and consciousness) to the physical body.

12. _____**Ontology**_____ is the study of existence and being.

13. _____**Deconstruction**_____ is a means of textual criticism that considers a text open to interpretation and laden with hidden bias, assumptions, and prejudices.

Short answer: (6 points possible per answer)

14. What is the Christian view of the relationship between the natural and the supernatural? How does this view differ from that of the naturalist?

> According to Christianity, matter is not the whole of reality; there is also the supernatural. Moreover, matter is temporal and will ultimately pass away. The material universe was purposely created out of the mind of the living Logos (John 1:1–4), and all the cosmos, existing independently of God, relies on God for its very existence and explanation. The Christian explanation for the world of matter or nature is that the supernatural created the natural.

CD-Rom

15. How does the naturalist's "monistic" view of the mind and body differ from the Christian's "dualistic" view?

> Christianity views the mind as more than matter. For the naturalist, mind is merely the product of matter and evolution. For the Christian, the mind existed before matter and brought matter into existence. Christianity views the mind dualistically—as both physical (the brain) and spiritual (the soul).

16. What is the Marxist dialectic and how does it work?

> The dialectic is the view that all of life is a constantly evolving process resulting from the clash of opposing forces:
>
> - Every established idea (thesis) is eventually opposed by another idea (antithesis).
> - Eventually, an entirely new entity will emerge from this opposition (synthesis) which renders the thesis and antithesis obsolete.
> - This synthesis eventually becomes a thesis which is opposed by an antithesis.

17. What is the "correspondence theory" of truth? Why do Postmodernists reject this theory?

> The "correspondence theory" of truth states that a proposition is true only if it corresponds to reality. Postmodernists claim that this kind of Truth is impossible to achieve because there is no "way things are" or a "real world," (a theory known as anti-realism). Therefore, there is no objective reality for propositions to correspond to, only personal, small "t" truths and their resulting constructions of reality. Our words only correspond to other words and in the end, create our understanding of reality. Since words only signify other words, then words can never be used in the pursuit of Truth.

"UNDERSTANDING POSTMODERNISM" VIDEO
Short answer: (7 points possible per answer [6 for 90-day])

18. How can we historically divide the pre-modern, modern, and postmodern periods? How did each period view truth?

> **Pre-modernism** (< to 1600) had a strong belief in the supernatural—God, the divine, gods, miracles, etc. Authority and knowledge rested with those in power, like the clergy and the monarchy. Truth, while found in both our faculties and experience, was predominantly discovered through divine revelation.
>
> **Modernism** (1600 to 1900) was much more skeptical of the supernatural. Authority and knowledge rested with the educated—scholars, scientists, etc. Human knowledge was believed to be the source of progress and the means to a better understanding of reality. Truth, while found in both revelation and experience, was predominantly uncovered through human faculties (i.e. reason and the five senses).

> **Postmodernism** (1900 to ?) is skeptical of absolute claims to knowledge, truth, and reality, believing that in the past such claims led to war and oppression (e.g. Marxism, Islam, Christianity, Crusades, World Wars 1 and 2, Vietnam, and the Cold War). Postmodern thinkers do not believe true progress can be realized. Truth, while found in both revelation and human faculties, is predominantly attained through human experience and community.

"EVIL AND SUFFERING" VIDEO
Short answer: (7 points possible per answer)

19. How do differing worldviews view the existence of evil?

> Christianity is not the only worldview that must deal with existence of evil and suffering. Every worldview must explain its existence. Naturalism, which purports that only the physical world exists, sees no meaning behind evil. For the naturalist, evil is just bad luck. Another worldview that must deal with the problem of evil is transcendentalism. This worldview purports that the physical world and everything in it is just an illusion. Thus, evil and suffering become mere illusions; some may also see it as the result of karma. Lastly, theistic worldviews purport that both the natural and supernatural exist. The theist must argue that God has allowed evil for some purpose.

20. What is the Biblical resolution to the problem of evil and suffering?

> The problem of evil and suffering is a very complicated issue. It cannot be answered in a truncated fashion. When considering the dilemma of how a good God and evil can coexist, it is helpful to consider the issue of time in three forms: past, future, and present.
>
> **Past**—According to the Christian worldview, when God formed the universe, he considered his creation good. However, Adam and Eve freely chose to disobey God. This disobedience resulted in a fallen world and a fallen race. Neither mankind nor nature exists today as God originally intended. Thus, we have moral evil (man-caused) and natural evil (non-man-caused).
>
> This is the Christian explanation for the existence of evil and suffering. However, it does not explain how evil can exist with a good God. If God could do anything and were truly good, then wouldn't he thwart all evil and suffering? Christians fully believe he could do so, but in regards to moral evil, human beings would no longer be free agents. That is, God would be directing us. Just as it is difficult to imagine a good God existing with evil, it is equally difficult to imagine a good God who allows human choice within the realm of his sovereignty. If all our actions were determined to be good (or at least not evil), then how could human beings ever be considered good?
>
> **Future**—The Bible informs us that although creation has fallen, it will someday be restored and evil destroyed. Fallen humanity will also be redeemed. In fact, we are told that the end will be even better than the beginning. A world redeemed is better than a world that had never fallen.
>
> **Present**—Also unique to the Christian worldview is its view of the present. According to Scripture, we have a God that does not merely allow suffering; he suffered with us and even for us.

CRITICAL THINKING ESSAY

Matching: (1 point possible per answer [2 for 90-day])
* *using the list on the right, choose the fallacy that best identifies the faulty reasoning below:*

21. __g__ I don't care if he did weigh three times as much as you. A good scout always tries to help. You should've jumped in and tried to save him.

22. __f__ This new diet plan worked for me. I know it can work for you, too.

23. __m__ Senator Jones says that we should not fund the attack submarine program. I disagree entirely. I can't understand why he wants to leave us defenseless like that.

24. __a__ I gave my reasons for doing it, but as usual you won't listen to reason, so you continue to fight me.

25. __o__ Sexual abstinence before marriage is Victorian.

26. __i__ If we're going to buy a car, we have to buy either a good one or a cheap one. We can't afford a good one, and we don't want a cheap one; so we will have to do without a car.

27. __d__ It's clear that Jones is innocent. He was tried for the crime before a jury of his peers, and the prosecution was unable to prove him guilty.

28. __j__ Did John ever give up his bad habits?

29. __e__ Television can't be harmful to children; it occupies their attention for hours, keeping them off the streets.

30. __h__ I enjoy only good books. I know this because if they're not good, I don't enjoy them.

31. __k__ An acorn is only a potential tree, just like a fetus is only a potential human.

32. __n__ Of course there is a God; almost everyone believes that.

33. __c__ Behold, a gluttonous man and a drunkard, a friend of tax-gatherers and sinners! (Matthew 11:19)

34. __l__ Over the past century, every major war has taken place while a Democrat was in office; therefore, we shouldn't vote for a Democrat.

35. __b__ I'm on probation, sir. If I don't get a good grade in this course, I won't be able to stay in school. Please, could you let me have at least a C?

a. Equivocation
b. Appeal to Pity
c. Ad Hominem
d. Appeal to Ignorance
e. Red Herring
f. Hasty Generalization
g. Sweeping Generalization
h. Begging the Question
i. Faulty Dilemma
j. Complex Question
k. False Analogy
l. False Cause
m. Straw Man
n. Appeal to Majority
o. Appeal to Tradition

TEACHER
MANUAL

UNDERSTANDING THE TIMES

Unit Three

Topics:
Bioethics
Biotechnology
Ethics
Moral Relativism

A Summit Ministries Curriculum

180-DAY SYLLABUS

DAY	IN CLASS	HOMEWORK	
1	WATCH "Ethics" video		
2	READ <u>UTT</u> Textbook 'Ethics 3.1'	READ <u>UTT</u> Textbook 'Ethics 3.2'	
3	REVIEW <u>UTT</u> Textbook 'Ethics 3.1–3.2' questions	READ <u>UTT</u> Textbook 'Ethics 3.3'	
4	READ <u>UTT</u> Textbook 'Ethics 3.4'		
5	REVIEW <u>UTT</u> Textbook 'Ethics 3.3–3.4' questions	READ <u>UTT</u> Textbook 'Ethics 3.5–3.6'	
6	REVIEW <u>UTT</u> Textbook 'Ethics 3.5–3.6' questions	READ *Living as if People Mattered* essay	
7	REVIEW *Living as if People Mattered* essay questions	ASSIGN Dear Doug Letter	
8	WATCH "Responding to Relativism" video P1		
9	WATCH "Responding to Relativism" video P2		
10	WATCH "Responding to Relativism" video P3		
11	REVIEW "Responding to Relativism" video questions		
12	WATCH "Biotechnology" video P1		
13	WATCH "Biotechnology" video P2		
14	REVIEW "Biotechnology" video questions	Dear Doug Letter assignment DUE	
15	TAKE Unit Three Test		

90-DAY SYLLABUS

DAY	IN CLASS	HOMEWORK	
1	WATCH "Ethics" video	READ <u>UTT</u> Textbook 'Ethics 3.1–3.2'	
2	REVIEW <u>UTT</u> Textbook 'Ethics 3.1–3.2' questions	READ <u>UTT</u> Textbook 'Ethics 3.3–3.4'	
3	REVIEW <u>UTT</u> Textbook 'Ethics 3.3–3.4' questions	READ <u>UTT</u> Textbook 'Ethics 3.5–3.6'	
4	REVIEW <u>UTT</u> Textbook 'Ethics 3.5–3.6' questions		
5	WATCH "Biotechnology" video P1		
6	WATCH "Biotechnology" video P2		
7	REVIEW "Biotechnology" video questions		
8	TAKE Unit Three Test		

Understanding the Times

Ethics Questions

Answer the questions below on a separate sheet of paper and be prepared to review your answers in class. Reflection Questions will not be found in the text. These are merely designed to help you start thinking about issues from a worldview perspective.

ETHICS 3.1

1. **Why are Christian ethics and theology inseparable? What did Francis Schaeffer mean when he said that not all things are the same to God?**

Christian ethics is inseparable from theology because Christian ethics is grounded in the character of God.

Francis Schaeffer meant that some things conform to the character of God and some things do not. In other words, some thoughts and actions are appropriate and reflect the holiness of God, while others deviate from God's character toward sin and rebellion. [UTT 3.1.1]

2. **What did Schaeffer conclude about a society without moral absolutes? Do we see this in society?**

"If there is no absolute beyond man's ideas, then there is no final appeal to judge between individuals and groups whose moral judgments conflict. We are merely left with conflicting opinions." [UTT 3.1.3]

[Examples will vary.]

3. **On what authority do Christians base their belief in moral absolutes? How specific is this authority?**

Absolutes are revealed to us in the Bible. While it is impossible to address every moral situation and dilemma, the Bible does contain enough specific values and guidelines to construct a basic foundation of morality. These principles can be applied more broadly to every specific situation across time and culture. [UTT 3.1.4]

[Explain to your students that since the Bible doesn't give us spelled-out answers to many of today's questions, it is up to us to do the hard work of studying God's Word to learn the principles by which we are to live. It is important that Christians do not use the world's reasoning when trying to answer questions of right and wrong—"I just feel like it's the thing I should do." Also remember that "all Scripture is inspired by God and profitable for teaching, for reproof, for correction, for training in righteousness" (2 Timothy 3:16).]

4. **Ethically speaking, what are Christians called to do?**

> Christians are called to love God with all our hearts, souls, strengths, and minds and to love our neighbors as ourselves (Luke 10:27). This command, like all of the other commands in the Bible, implies that Christians have moral responsibilities. [UTT 3.1.5]
>
> *[Spend extra time on this one. Help your students start thinking about what this means in terms of being a living sacrifice both to God and to others. Point out that many Christians merely desire to follow a collection of rules. However, God cares greatly about the attitudes of our hearts, not our ability to blindly follow rules. When we love God with all we have and truly love our neighbors as ourselves, lives and cultures are changed. Ethics isn't about just following rules and avoiding sin; rather it's about living a life that is pleasing to God, serving him and others, and exhibiting Christ's love to a lost world.]*

5. **What did Dietrich Bonhoeffer mean by the question, "Where are the responsible people?"**

> By "responsible" Bonhoeffer means individuals who try to make their whole life an answer to the question and call of God. He was not meaning those whose final standard is reason, principles, conscience, freedom, or virtue, but those who are ready to sacrifice all things and swear exclusive allegiance to God. [UTT 3.1.7]

> ## THE LINE ACTIVITY
> Bring a yardstick to class. Don't let the students see the stick until it is time for it to be used. Draw a line on the board (less than 3 ft. long). Ask various students to guess the length of the line. Invariably you will receive various answers. Ask them how you can know for sure how long the line is. Bring out the yardstick and measure.
>
>
>
> Relate this to having a standard in ethics. How do we know what is right and wrong? Do we have a standard by which to measure?

ETHICS 3.2

6. **Why do Muslims view Muhammad as morally exemplary even though the Hadith does not paint a flattering portrait of his life?**

> Muslims view the acts of Muhammad as empowered, guided, and approved by Allah. Thus, everything that Muhammad did was, by definition, good—Muhammad's actions were not guided by morality, but rather his actions redefine morality. [UTT 3.2.2]

7. **How do Christianity and Islam differ in relation to their beliefs about ethical absolutes?**

> The Bible grounds morality in God's essential character, but the Qur'an teaches that God ultimately cannot be known. For Muslims, certain actions are good not because they stem from God's character,

but because God chooses to call them good. God could have decreed a different set of moral principles. Therefore, Muslims know moral goodness by God's decree alone. [UTT 3.2.3]

8. **In what two ways is the term *jihad* used?**

Muslims use the term *jihad* in two ways. First, to describe the battle against temptation and sin for the sake of self-control and the development of virtue. Second, to define the battle against any and all who oppose Islam—the most self-sacrificing action a Muslim may undertake. [UTT 3.2.4]

9. **What motivates Muslims to behave ethically?**

- The development of personal virtue and spirituality
- The betterment of the state of others
- The strengthening of relationships
- The expectation of coming judgment [UTT 3.2.6]

10. **Which motivation is the strongest?**

Fear of the Day of Judgment [UTT 3.2.6]

ETHICS 3.3

11. **What is the ultimate ethical question for a Secular Humanist? What questions did Morris B. Storer outline in his book *Humanist Ethics*?**

The ultimate ethical question for atheistic humanists is which code of ethics to embrace.

Morris B. Storer listed the difficult questions that Secular Humanist ethics must somehow answer:

- Is personal advantage the measure of right and wrong, or the advantage of all affected?
- Is there truth in ethics?
- Are 'right' and 'wrong' expressions of heart or head?
- Do people have free wills?
- Do you measure morality by results or by principles?
- Do people have duties as well as rights? [UTT 3.3.1]

12. **Why are there such diverse views and conflicts regarding humanistic ethics?**

There is great disagreement over the foundation of morality in a world without God. [UTT 3.3.1]

13. Who proposed the "no-truth thesis" and what does it state?

Kai Nielsen proposed the "no-truth thesis," which states that there is no truth or falsity in moral values. [UTT 3.3.2]

14. How do most humanists attempt to dodge the "no-truth thesis?" How does Corliss Lamont address this issue?

Rather than looking to God for moral precepts, humanists rely on experience and reason in the context of ethical relativism. Lamont specifically elevates pleasure as the ultimate good, purporting that as long as humanity pursues activities that are healthy, socially useful, and in accordance with reason, pleasure and happiness will generally follow. [UTT 3.3.2]

[Explore with your students the problem of relying solely upon reason and pleasure as the basis for morality. For example, in relation to ethics, terms like reasonable, socially useful, and pleasurable can be rather subjective terms (especially in a world without God). For example, what is the basis of "reason?" Some individuals may reason that it is good to euthanize everyone over 75 and/or everyone with an IQ below 75. It would certainly save money, time, stress, etc. Similarly, what one person considers "pleasurable" another may consider sin.]

15. What did Arthur E. Gravatt, Joseph Fletcher, Herbert W. Schneider, and Paul Kurtz have to say about ethics?

- Arthur E. Gravatt—viewed morality and immorality as behavior changing from situation to situation. He reasoned that behavior is to be judged either moral or immoral based on the context and individual. In other words, some behavior might be moral for one person and not another or moral at one time and not another.
- Joseph Fletcher—saw rights and wrongs as things determined by various situations in which moral agents have to decide the most beneficial course.
- Herbert W. Schneider—calls morality an "experimental art" saying that it is merely required for living well with others. Moral right and wrong must therefore be conceived in terms of moral standards generated by society.
- Paul Kurtz—desires that moral principles be treated as "hypotheses"—tested and judged by their practical worth and outcomes. [UTT 3.3.3]

ETHICS 3.4

16. How did Karl Marx and Friedrich Engels view the issue of morality?

Marx and Engels denied that morals were central in human life; rather, they believed that biological and social evolution dictate and determine morality. What is moral or what is right or wrong is determined by evolution. If the bourgeois class hinders either biological or social evolution, then nature dictates the removal of that class. [UTT 3.4.1]

[Help your students make the connection between the Marxist view of biological and social evolution. Marxists view both through the lens of the dialectic. They believe punctuated evolution is true because stasis and sudden change (as well as survival of the fittest) match the dialectic. In the same way, the dialectic (thesis, antithesis, synthesis) helps society evolve to a higher form. Whatever weakens this new form (the bourgeois, religion, and anything else that holds back the formation of a classless society) must be eliminated.]

17. What is the Marxist-Leninist morality of the future? How will it be determined?

Marxism trusts that the future classless utopia will deliver a new morality determined by its perception of the dialectic. In other words morality is constantly evolving with the progression of time. [UTT 3.4.2]

[Help your students understand that the good of the communist cause is the ultimate and final basis for Marxist ethical considerations—every deed and motive must be measured in light of the ideal of the class struggle envisioned by Marx. If millions of people need to be killed to ensure that outcome, then it is ethically right to kill millions of people.]

18. What is the Marxist-Leninist view of "old morality?"

Marxist-Leninists wholeheartedly reject moral codes with foundations in religious beliefs, including traditional universal moral ideals. They reject such ideals as "old morality," as products of the bourgeoisie invented and used to oppress the propertyless proletariat. [UTT 3.4.3]

19. What is the Marxist code of ethics according to the book *Scientific Communism*?

Scientific Communism defines ethics as follows: "Devotion to the cause of the working class, collectivism, mutual aid, comradely solidarity, hatred toward the bourgeoisie and toward traitors to the common cause, internationalism, and stoicism in struggle are traits which not only define the content of proletarian ethics, but also characterize the moral image of the typical representatives of the working class." [UTT 3.4.4]

20. What means have Marxists historically believed would bring about a society without class distinctions? What have been the results of such an ethical system?

Marxists believe that revolution is unavoidable in order to overthrow the immoral bourgeoisie and lift up the proletariat. This forcible overthrow is perceived as morally just—it destroys the hindrances to a communist society. Put into practice, British journalist D. G. Stewart-Smith estimates that international communism has been responsible for 83 million deaths between 1917 and 1964. [UTT 3.4.6]

[It is important to remember that from a Marxist-Leninist perspective tens of millions of deaths are worth the price—little is immoral in the effort to abolish social classes and private property. In fact, to do nothing would be immoral in their eyes.]

21. What is the foundation for Cosmic Humanism's ethical system?

Cosmic Humanists approach ethics from their theological foundation of pantheism—they believe they are ultimately god. And since they are god; they get to write the moral rules. Thus, for the New Ager, there are no external moral precepts. [UTT 3.5.1]

22. According to Cosmic Humanist ethics, can anyone judge another's actions?

Cosmic Humanist ethics dictates that no one may decide whether another's actions are right or wrong. [UTT 3.5.2]

[Help your students understand the problems inherent within a subjective moral system, i.e. a moral system in which we each personally decide what is right and wrong free of any external or absolute standards.]

23. How is the word "tolerance" used by Cosmic Humanists?

Tolerance is used to denote acceptance of differing moral views. However, tolerance has traditionally meant a respectful attitude towards those with whom one disagrees. [UTT 3.5.2]

[Help your students to understand how the word "tolerance" has been twisted to mean an acceptance of all beliefs as valid. To tolerate, by definition, means you disagree but will be respectful toward those with whom you disagree. This means that Christians are in fact very tolerant. We may speak out about what is right and stand up against injustice and wickedness, but we will not try to kill or defame others who disagree with us. This does have limitations. We will not tolerate someone trying to hurt our family or others. We will not tolerate pornography being promoted as good literature in our public schools, etc.]

24. How is the line between good and evil blurred in Cosmic Humanist ethics?

Ethical relativism, as you would expect, has led Cosmic Humanists to a point where the distinction between good and evil has become hopelessly blurred. No absolute right or wrong exists; only what is right or wrong according to each individual's truth. If everything is one, it is difficult to distinguish between good and evil. What may appear evil in this life could be the reverse in a reincarnated existence. [UTT 3.5.3]

25. In what system of justice do Cosmic Humanists believe?

Cosmic Humanists believe karma is the universal system of judgment. [UTT 3.5.4]

26. What is the foundation of Postmodern ethics?

Most Postmodernists embrace an ethical system, but do not base it on unchanging universal principles or obedience to a non-human authority. [UTT 3.6.1]

27. According to Postmodernists, how does a community create its own ethical standards?

Lyotard claimed to be content with "little narratives." By this he means that philosophical and moral truth (small "t") reside in the local community. This could be referred to as cultural or communal moral relativism. [UTT 3.6.2]

28. Why are Postmodernists hesitant to use the term relativism?

Rorty defines cultural relativism as believing all moral claims are equal. Thus, Rorty claims that he is not a "cultural relativist" because he firmly believes that some moral views (namely his) are better than others. However, since Rorty also contends that there is no objective or universal moral standard for humanity to appeal to, he is forced to admit that he has no basis to prove his moral system is any better than that of the Nazis. In the end it all comes down to preferences or as Rorty puts it, "idiosyncrasies." [UTT 3.6.2]

29. According to Richard Rorty, how do ethics develop within a Postmodern community? Do all Postmodernists agree with his assessment?

For Postmodernists, moral standards are decided by both coercion and consensus. Since there is no absolute standard, every culture develops its own set of moral standards arising from various influences within each particular group. These standards are not stagnant; they change, adapt, and are constantly evolving according to the dictates of the group.

Left with no universal norms to discover, Rorty advocates the subjective "ethical standards" that he prefers, standards he is personally the most comfortable with. He therefore uses his words as "tools" of persuasion. Others are free to use these same "tools" of persuasion. And in the end, society naturally finds some point of agreement.

Morality and society operate like an unconscious negotiation–everyone in a community is presenting the beliefs they prefer and these ideas are considered, debated, and adapted until consensus emerges—although this consensus is in a constant state of arbitration.

Not all Postmodernists agree with Rorty. For example Adam Phillips insists that "any ethical boundaries are out of bounds." Thus, for Phillips no system is better than any other. [UTT 3.6.3]

30. Reflection Question: What are the possible consequences when a community is allowed to sever ethics from an absolute standard and negotiate its own ethical system?

[Answers will vary. Open this up for discussion. Refer back to the conversations you have already had concerning relativistic ethical systems, and specifically, the real danger of a certain group gaining power and control to the detriment of other groups. Also, discuss what happens when a community sets up an ethical system that is not in harmony with God's absolute standards. Examples: Nazi Germany, Communist Russia, abortion, homosexuality, etc.]

LIVING AS IF PEOPLE MATTERED
BY GEORGE GRANT

> One of the strangest disparities of history lies between the sense of abundance felt by older and simpler societies and the sense of scarcity felt by the ostensibly richer societies of today.
> —Richard Weaver

I remember only too well the first time I met Francis Schaeffer. In 1979 I was puttering around in one of my favorite used bookstores—on Locust Street, just a couple of blocks from the beautiful and magnificent Christ Church Cathedral in downtown St. Louis. The cathedral is a vivid reminder of the remarkable flowering of creativity and beauty that the Gospel has always provoked through the ages.

Just out of sight of the great Easter pinnacle is a little row of quirky stores and businesses. There are a couple of musty antique dealers, a disreputable-looking chili restaurant, a jaunty coffee shop, a boutique specializing in platform shoes from the seventies, and, of course, the bookstore—stocking a rather eccentric jumble of old magazines, cheap paperbacks, and fine first editions arranged in no apparent order.

I had just discovered a good hardback copy of Scott's *Ivanhoe* and a wonderful turn-of-the-century pocket edition of Ruskin's *Seven Lamps of Architecture*—both for less than the cost of new paperback copies—when I rounded a corner and bumped into Dr. Schaeffer. Literally.

I had been reading his books since the late sixties and looked to him as my spiritual and intellectual mentor. Not only did he express his orthodox Reformed faith in a clear and thoughtful fashion, his appreciation for the great heritage of Christendom's art, music, and ideas and his commitment to practical justice and true spirituality made him a beacon light of hope to me. In 1948, he had gone to live in the Swiss Alps just below Villars. There, in a little mountain chalet, he established a unique missionary outreach to all who might find their way to his door.

Over the years, thousands of students, skeptics, and searchers found their way to that door. He named the ministry L'Abri—a French word meaning shelter—an apt description for the function it served to the rootless generation of the Cold War era. It had always seemed to me that L'Abri was precisely the kind of witness that the church at the end of the twentieth century desperately needed.

I'd like to say that as I stood face-to-face with my hero, I was able to articulate my appreciation for all that he had done for my faith and my walk with Christ. I'd like to say that I was able to express my gratitude and then perhaps strike up a stimulating conversation about, say, epistemological self-consciousness. I'd like to say that as providence afforded me the opportunity I was able to think of all the questions I'd always wanted answered.

Unfortunately, that was not the case. Instead, the first thought that sprang into my mind was: "Oh my, he's short!" My second thought was: "What a haircut!" My third thought was: "And what's the deal with the knickers?"

In shock, I realized that I couldn't think of a single intelligent thing to say. I had fallen epistemologically unconscious.

Evidently, Dr. Schaeffer could read the awkward consternation in my eyes. He chuckled, introduced himself to me, and struck up a conversation. Amidst my embarrassed befuddlement he was cheerfully gracious and kind. He commended me on my selections and then showed me a couple other books he thought I might like—a fine paperback copy of Van Til's *The Calvinistic Concept Of Culture* and a rare edition of Schaeffer's *The Principle of Protestantism*.

Here was one of the brightest minds of our generation giving his time and attention to a gawky young Christian who couldn't even string together a coherent sentence. I later discovered that this was typical of him. Though he was often passionate, stubborn, and irascible, his life was suffused with a clear sense of calling—a calling to serve others. He demonstrated that calling on a daily basis—not just through heroic feats of sacrifice but through the quiet virtue of ordinary kindness. He believed that the Reformation doctrine of the priesthood of all believers was best portrayed in the beauty of caring human relationships. And so he listened. He cared. He gave. He put into motion Christ's tender mercies through the simplest acts of humble service.

Unit Three

I came away from that first brief encounter with Dr. Schaeffer with an entirely new understanding of biblical mercy. With a servant's heart, he treated me as if I mattered. He treated me the way we are all to treat one another.

SERVICE

Service is a much ballyhooed concept these days. The literature of business success and personal management tosses it about rather profligately. We are told, for instance, that our industrial economy has been almost completely transformed into a service economy by the advent of the information age. The service factor is the new by-word for success in the crowded global marketplace. Good service guarantees customer loyalty, management efficiency, and employee morale. It provides a competitive edge for companies in an increasingly cut-throat business environment. It is the means toward empowerment, flexibility, and innovation at a time when those qualities are essential for business survival. It prepares ordinary men and women to out-sell, out-manage, out-motivate, and out-negotiate their competition. It enables them to "swim with the sharks without being eaten alive."[1]

According to Jack Eckerd and Chuck Colson, service on the job and in the workplace can mean many things: "Valuing workers. Managing from the trenches. Communicating. Inspiring excellence. Training. Using profits to motivate."[2]

Virtually all the corporate prognosticators, strategic forecasters, motivational pundits, and management consultants agree—from Tom Peters, John Naisbitt, and Stephen Covey to Richard Foster, Michael Gerber, and Zig Ziglar. They all say that service is an indispensable key to success in business or success in life.

According to these analysts, service in business is essentially a complex combination of common courtesy, customer satisfaction, and the "spirit of enterprise." It is simply realizing that the customer is always right and then going the extra mile. It is a principle-centered approach to human relationships and community responsibilities. It is putting first things first.[3]

This new emphasis on service is not just confined to the corporate world. It has also suddenly reappeared as a stock-in-trade public virtue in the discourse of politics. Candidates now offer themselves for public service rather than to merely run for office. They invoke cheery images of community service, military service and civic service as evidence of their suitability to govern the affairs of state. Once in office they initiate vast federal programs for national service. They charge the lumbering government bureaucracy with the task of domestic service. And they offer special recognition for citizens who have performed exemplary volunteer service.

Again, service is defined rather broadly in a series of happy platitudes as an expansive sense of public-spiritedness, good neighborliness, community-mindedness, or big-hearted cooperativeness. All of these things are certainly admirable. They are fine and good as far as they go. But they are not at all what the Bible has in mind when it speaks of service—as Francis Schaeffer would no doubt have readily attested.

Biblical service isn't a tactic designed to boost profit margins, protect market shares, keep customers happy, or improve employee relations. It isn't a strategy designed to inculcate patriotism, strengthen community relations, or attract more investments. It is not a technique to pad resumes, garner votes, or patronize constituents. It isn't a style of leadership, a personality bent, or a habit of highly effective people.

Instead, biblical service is a priestly function of mercy. The Hebrew word often used for service in the Old Testament is *sharath*. It literally means "to minister" or "to treat with affection." Similarly, in the New Testament the Greek word *diakoneo* is often used. It literally means "to care for" or to "offer relief."

In both cases, the priestly connotations and the merciful intentions of service are quite evident. In both cases, the emphasis is on the interpersonal dimension rather than the institutional dimension, on mercy rather than management, on true righteousness rather than mere rightness. Biblical service is far more concerned about taking care of souls than about taking care of business.

[1] *Houston Chronicle*, 18 May 1986; *Forbes*, 14 September 1992; *Forbes*, 9 September 1993; *Wall Street Journal*, 16 April 1992; Harvey Mackay, *Swim with the Sharks* (New York: William Morrow, 1988), 1.

[2] Chuck Colson and Jack Eckerd, *Why America Doesn't Work* (Dallas: Word, 1991), 168.

[3] George Gilder, *The Spirit of Enterprise* (New York: Simon & Schuster, 1984); Michael Gerber, *Power Point* (New York: HarperCollins, 1991); Tom Peters, *Thriving on Chaos* (New York: Knopf, 1987); Stephen Covey, Roger Merrill, and Rebecca Merrill, *First Things First* (New York: Simon & Schuster, 1994).

This distinction between the ministry of service and the business of service is like the difference between faith in God and faith in faith.[4]

DOING UNTO OTHERS

God is merciful and just. He works righteousness and justice for all. Morning by morning, He dispenses His justice without fail and without partiality. All his ways are just, so that injustice is an abomination to Him. Thus, He is adamant about ensuring the cause of the abused, the meek, and the weak. Time after time, Scripture stresses this important attribute of God:

> The Lord abides forever; He has established His throne for judgment, and He will judge the world in righteousness; He will execute judgment for the peoples with equity. The Lord also will be a stronghold for the oppressed, a stronghold in times of trouble. (Psalm 9:7–9 NASB)

> "Because of the oppression of the weak and the groaning of the needy, I will now arise," says the Lord. I will protect them from those who malign them." (Psalm 12:5)

> A father to the fatherless, a defender of widows, is God in his holy dwelling. God sets the lonely in families, he leads forth the prisoners with singing; but the rebellious live in a sun-scorched land. (Psalm 68:5–6)

God cares for the needy. And His people are to do likewise. If God has comforted us, then we are to comfort others. If God has forgiven us, then we are to forgive others. If God has loved us, then we are to love others. If He has taught us, then we are to teach others. If He has borne witness to us, then we are to bear witness to others. If He has laid down His life for us, then we are to lay down our lives for one another.[5]

Whenever God commanded the priestly nation of Israel to imitate Him in ensuring justice for the wandering homeless, the alien, and the sojourner, He reminded them that they were once despised, rejected, and homeless themselves. It was only by the grace and mercy of God that they had been redeemed from that low estate. Thus they were to exercise compassion to the brokenhearted and the dispossessed. They were to serve.

Priestly privilege brings priestly responsibility. If Israel refused to take up that responsibility, then God would revoke their privilege. If they refused to exercise reciprocal mercy, then God would rise up in His anger to visit the land with His wrath and displeasure, expelling them into the howling wilderness once again. On the other hand, if they fulfilled their calling to live lives of merciful service, then they would ever be blessed.[6]

The principle still holds true. Those of us who have received the compassion of the Lord on High are to demonstrate tenderness in kind to all those around us. This is precisely the lesson Jesus was driving at in the parable of the unmerciful slave (Matthew 18:23–35).

The moral of the parable is clear. The needy around us are living symbols of our own former helplessness and privation. We are therefore to be living symbols of God's justice, mercy, and compassion. We are to do as He has done. God has set the pattern by His gracious working in our lives. We are to follow that pattern by serving others in the power of the indwelling Spirit.

In other words, the Gospel calls us to live daily as if people really matter. It calls us to live lives of selfless concern. We are to pay attention to the needs of others. In both word and deed, in both thought and action we are to weave ordinary kindness into the very fabric of our lives.

But this kind of ingrained mercy goes far beyond mere politeness. We are to demonstrate concern for the poor. We are to show pity toward the weak. We are to rescue the afflicted from violence. We are to familiarize ourselves with the case of the helpless, give of our wealth, and share of our sustenance. We are to put on "compassion, kindness, humility, gentleness and patience" (Colossians 3:12). We are to take up

---

[4] Faith in God is personal and objective. Faith in faith is impersonal and subjective. Faith in God transcends self-interest and self-fulfillment. Faith in faith descends into self-reliance and self-assurance. Faith in God is a belief in someone who has revealed himself to man "at many times and in various ways" (Hebrews 1:1). Faith in faith is simply "a belief" in something or any thing (James 2:19).

[5] To see these principles demonstrated in Scripture, read 2 Corinthians 1:4; Ephesians 4:32; 1 John 4:11; Matthew 28:20; John 15:26–27; 1 John 3:16.

[6] See Isaiah 1:11-17; Exodus 22:24; Psalm 41:1–2.

"the case of the stranger" (Job 29:16). We are to love our neighbors as ourselves (Mark 12:31) and "rescue those being led away to death" (Proverbs 24:11–12).

According to the Scriptures, this kind of comprehensive servanthood emphasis is, in fact, a primary indication of the authenticity of our faith: "Religion that God our Father accepts as pure and faultless is this: to look after orphans and widows in their distress and to keep oneself from being polluted by the world" (James 1:27).

We are called to do "righteousness and justice" (Genesis 18:19 NASB). We are to be ministers of God's peace, instruments of His love, and ambassadors of His kingdom. We are to care for the helpless, feed the hungry, clothe the naked, shelter the homeless, visit the prisoner, and protect the innocent. We are to live lives of merciful service.

GOOD DEEDS

In writing to Titus, the young pastor of Crete's pioneer church, the apostle Paul pressed home this fundamental truth with a clear sense of persistence and urgency. The task before Titus was not an easy one. Cretan culture was terribly worldly. It was marked by deceit, ungodliness, sloth, and gluttony (Titus 1:12). Thus, Paul's instructions were precise. Titus was to preach the glories of grace, but he was also to make good deeds evident. Priestly mercy and selfless servanthood were to be central priorities in his new work:

> For the grace of God has appeared, bringing salvation to all men, instructing us to deny ungodliness and worldly desires and to live sensibly, righteously and godly in the present age, looking for the blessed hope and the appearing of the glory of our great God and Savior, Christ Jesus; who gave Himself for us, that He might redeem us from every lawless deed and purify for Himself a people for His own possession, zealous for good deeds. (Titus 2:11–14 NASB)

Paul tells Titus he should build his entire fledgling ministry around works of mercy: He was to be an example of good deeds (Titus 2:7). He was to teach the people to watch for chances to do good (3:1). They were all to "learn to devote themselves to doing what is good, in order that they might provide for daily necessities and not live unproductive lives" (3:14). Some within the church professed to know God, "but by their actions they deny him. They are detestable, disobedient and unfit for doing anything good" (1:16). Titus was to "rebuke them sharply, so that they will be sound in the faith" (1:13).

As a pastor, Titus had innumerable tasks that he was responsible to fulfill. He had administrative duties, doctrinal duties, discipling duties, preaching duties, counseling duties, and arbitrating duties. But intertwined with them all, fundamental to them all, were his servanthood duties.

TO THE UTTERMOST

Paul called himself a servant (Galatians 1:10). Similarly, James, Peter, Epaphroditus, Timothy, Abraham, Moses, David, and Daniel were all called servants.[7] In fact, even before they were called "Christians," all of the first century believers were called "servants" (1 Corinthians 7:22).

Whenever and wherever the Gospel has gone out, the faithful have emphasized the priority of good works, especially works of compassion toward the needy. Every great revival in the history of the church, from Paul's missionary journeys to the Reformation, from the Alexandrian outreach of Athanasius to the Great Awakening in America, has been accompanied by an explosion of priestly service. Hospitals were established. Orphanages were founded. Rescue missions were started. Almshouses were built. Soup kitchens were begun. Charitable societies were incorporated. The hungry were fed, the naked clothed, and the unwanted rescued. Word was wed to deeds.[8]

This fact has always proven to be the bane of the church's enemies. Unbelievers can argue theology. They can dispute philosophy. They can subvert history. And they can undermine character. But they are helpless in the face of extraordinary feats of selfless compassion.[9]

---

[7] James 1:1; 2 Peter 1:1; Colossians 4:12; 2 Timothy 2:24; Psalm 105:42; Nehemiah 9:14; Psalm 89:3; Romans 6:20.

[8] George Grant, *Bringing in the Sheaves: Transforming Poverty into Productivity* (Brentwood, TN: Wolgemuth & Hyatt, 1985).

[9] George Grant, *Third Time Around* (Brentwood, TN: Wolgemuth & Hyatt, 1990).

Thus, Martin Luther said: "Where there are no good works, there is no faith. If works and love do not blossom forth, it is not genuine faith, the Gospel has not yet gained a foothold, and Christ is not yet rightly known."[10]

Likewise, the Westminster Confession asserted:

> Good works, done in obedience to God's commandments, are the fruits and evidences of a true and lively faith: and by them believers manifest their thankfulness, strengthen their assurance, edify their brethren, adorn the profession of the Gospel, stop the mouths of the adversaries, and glorify God whose workmanship they are.[11]

All too often in our own day though, we have tended to decline those priestly responsibilities—yielding the work of service to government bureaucrats or professional philanthropists. Grave societal dilemmas that have always busied the church before—like defending the sanctity of life, caring for the aged, and protecting the helpless—have been mentally and practically separated from our other "spiritual" responsibilities. They have been relegated to the status of "issues," even declared "political" and put on the other side of the fence from us in "the separation of church and state."

From a biblical perspective, though, these things are not "issues"; they cannot be separated from our tasks as believer-priests. They are our tasks as believer-priests. They are central to our purpose and calling in the world.

Many Christians have observed—only partly in jest—that if God doesn't judge America soon, He's probably going to have to apologize to Sodom and Gomorrah. That may well be true—but not for the reason that we think. God did not judge Sodom and Gomorrah because of their rampant greed, perversity, and corruption. He judged them because, those who were charged with serving didn't (Ezekiel 16:49–50). If God's wrath ever does utterly consume America, it will be for precisely the same reason. When biblical service is replaced by its worldly counterfeits, the effects go far beyond rising taxes, bloated bureaucracies, welfare graft, urban blight, and sundered families. When we fail to do the priestly work of mercy and compassion, judgment becomes inevitable. Sava of Trnova, writing at the end of the seventh century, said:

> The chief spiritual works in the world are sevenfold: to admonish sinners, to instruct the ignorant, to counsel the doubtful, to comfort the sorrowful, to suffer wrongs patiently, to forgive injuries, and to pray for all men at all times. Thus, we are to feed the hungry, give drink to the thirsty, to clothe the naked, to ransom the captives, to shelter the homeless, to visit the sick, and to rescue the perishing, for only in these corporal acts of service may this world of carnality be guarded from the full consequences of judgment.[12]

The Bible tells us that if we will obey the command to be generous to the poor, we ourselves will taste joy. If we will serve the needy, God will preserve us. If we will offer priestly mercy to the afflicted, we ourselves will be spared. We will prosper, our desires will be satisfied, and we will even be raised up from beds of sorrow and suffering.[13] God will ordain peace for us, authenticate our faith, and bless our witness to the world.[14] But only if we will serve.

Charles Haddon Spurgeon, the great Victorian pastor, not only was a masterful pulpiteer, administrator, writer, and evangelist, he was a determined champion of the deprived and the rejected. He gave more than half of his incredibly busy schedule to one or another of the sixty organizations or institutions he founded for their care and comfort. Explaining his furious activity on behalf of the poor and needy, Spurgeon said:

> God's intent in endowing any person with more substance than he needs is that he may have the pleasurable office, or rather the delightful privilege, of relieving want and woe. Alas, how many there are who consider that store which God has put into their hands on purpose for the poor and needy, to be only so much provision for their excessive luxury, a luxury which pampers them but yields them neither benefit nor pleasure.[15]

[10] John Dillenberger, ed., *Martin Luther* (New York: Doubleday, 1961), 18.

[11] *Confession*, XVIII:2.

[12] *Terra Ecalivat*, VI: 82.

[13] Proverbs 14:21; Psalm 41:1-2; Proverbs 28:27; Proverbs 11:24; Proverbs 11:25; Psalm 41:3.

[14] Isaiah 26:12; James 2:14-26; Isaiah 58:6–12.

[15] George H. Neville, *Good Works* (Edinburgh: McGavock, 1956), 202.

Wherever committed Christians have gone, throughout Europe, into the darkest depths of Africa, to the outer reaches of China, along the edges of the American frontier, and beyond to the Australian outback, selfless care for the needy has been in evidence. In fact, most of the church's greatest heroes are those who willingly gave the best of their lives to the less fortunate. Service was their hallmark. Mercy was their emblem.

A LIFE OF SERVICE

According to the majority of eighteenth- and nineteenth-century historians, the most remarkable event during America's founding era did not take place on a battlefield. It did not occur during the course of the constitutional debates. It was not recorded during the great diplomatic negotiations with France, Spain, or Holland. It did not take place at sea, or in the assemblies of the states, or in the counsels of war.

In a humble demonstration of servanthood, the field commander of the continental armies surrendered his commission to the congressional authorities at Annapolis.

At the time, he was the idol of the country and his soldiers. The army was unpaid, and the veteran troops, well-armed and fresh from their victory at Yorktown, were eager to have him take control of the disordered country. Some wanted to crown him king. Others thought to make him a dictator—rather like Cromwell had been a century earlier in England.

With the loyal support of the army and the enthusiasm of the populace, it would have been easy enough for him to have made himself the ruler of the new nation. But instead, General George Washington resigned his officer's commission. He appeared before President Thomas Mifflin and his cabinet and submitted himself to their governance.

Though he had often wrangled in disagreement with his superiors over matters of military strategy, pay schedules, supply shipments, troop deployment, and the overlap of civil and martial responsibilities, there was never any question of his ultimate loyalty or allegiance. In the end, he always submitted himself to the authority God had placed over him.

And that was no mean feat.

Washington had faithfully served under eleven different American presidents at a time of severest crisis. The first two held office prior to the signing of the Declaration of Independence—Peyton Randolph of Virginia and Henry Middleton of South Carolina. The next six held office between the time of the Declaration and the ratification of the first constitution—John Hancock of Massachusetts, Henry Laurens of South Carolina, John Jay of New York, Samuel Huntington of Connecticut, Samuel Johnson of North Carolina, and Thomas McKean of Delaware. The last three held office under the Articles of Confederation—John Hanson of Maryland, Elias Budinot of New Jersey, and finally, Thomas Mifflin of Pennsylvania. Another four presidents would hold office during Washington's short interlude away from public life prior to the ratification of the current constitution—Richard Henry Lee of Virginia, Nathaniel Gorham of Massachusetts, Arthur St. Clair of Pennsylvania, and Cyrus Griffin of Virginia. During all those trying days, under each of those varied men, General Washington gave himself wholeheartedly to the loyal task of selfless service.

He obeyed orders. He rendered due respect. He yielded to the authority of lawful office and jurisdiction. He met the needs of the hour. He set aside personal ambition, preference, security, and at times, personal opinion in order to serve.

"His true greatness was evidenced," said the pundit Henry Adams, "in the fact that he never sought greatness, but rather service."[16] The dean of American historians, Francis Parkman, concurred that it was this "remarkable spirit of the servant" that ultimately "elevated him even higher in his countrymen's estimations than he already was."[17]

George Washington lived a life of service. He practiced what we today call servant-leadership. He would settle for nothing less. He would strive for nothing more. And he left the disposition of the matter of his life and fortune in the hands of God.

Though we generally think of mercy more in terms of charity or philanthropy, Washington's balanced and selfless perspective actually comes closer to the biblical ideal. Kindness, helpfulness, compassion, and

[16] B. L. Cartwright, *Washington* (Boston: Little, Brown, & Co., 1924), 166.
[17] Ibid.

care are the natural outgrowths of a servant's heart. Where personal ambition and a lust for self-fulfillment are subdued, true mercy is sure to follow.

GOOD SERVICE

The prophet Micah condemned the people of his day for their heartless defrauding and victimizing of the needy (Micah 2:1–2). He asserted that the imminent judgment of their land was due to their tolerance of sin, their blatant selfishness, and their refusal to undertake their servanthood responsibilities (3:2–4).

Instead, they were concerned only with their own comforts and pleasures (2:8–11). They were intent on their own personal peace and affluence, often at the cost of oppression and exploitation (3:5–11). They had thus violated the covenant (5:10–15).

Where there is no mercy there is no hope.

Thus, the Micah Mandate was not only a call to the people to repent and to return to the path of righteousness, it was a proclamation of reconciliation and healing. It was a promise of better things to come. The prophet asserted that the remnant would be regathered (Micah 4:6). The shame of affliction would be lifted (4:7). And the lost fortunes of the land would be restored (4:8).

Where there is mercy there is hope.

Therefore let us too be "zealous for good deeds" (Titus 2:14 NASB).

ZEALOUS FOR GOOD DEEDS

"He has showed you, O man, what is good. And what does the Lord require of you? To act justly and to love mercy and to walk humbly with your God" (Micah 6:8).

Through the ages, the great heroes of the faith were notable as much for their charity and kindness as they were for their doctrinal fidelity. They were invariably men and women of mercy who lived lives of selfless service. Examples abound:

Not only did *John Wycliffe* (1329–84) revive interest in the Scriptures during a particularly dismal and degenerate era with his translation of the New Testament into English, he also unleashed a grassroots movement of lay preachers and relief workers that brought hope to the poor for the first time since the peasants' land had been taken more than two generations before. Those common Lollards—as they were most often called—carried Wycliffe's determined message of grace and mercy to the entire kingdom, laying the foundations for the Reformation in England more than a century and a half later.

John Calvin (1509–64) established Geneva as the epicenter of the Reformation with his profound theological insight and his rich devotional piety. His careful and systematic codification of the biblical foundations for Reform was like a magnet for the best and brightest throughout Christendom. The city quickly became an island of intellectual integrity and economic prosperity. In addition, though, it became renowned for its charitable compassion. It was a kind of safe haven for all of Europe's poor and persecuted, dispossessed and distressed. There they found that Calvin had not only instructed the people in such things as the providence of God, but he had also taught them the importance of mercy in balancing the Christian life.

Dwight L. Moody (1837–99) was America's foremost evangelist throughout the difficult days that immediately followed the cataclysm of the War Between the States and disruption of Reconstruction. Literally thousands came to know Christ because the former shoe salesman faithfully proclaimed the Gospel wherever and whenever he had opportunity—pioneering the methods of both modern crusade evangelism and Sunday-school outreach. But in addition to preaching to the masses, he cared for the masses. He was responsible for the establishment of some one hundred and fifty schools, street missions, soup kitchens, clinics, colportage societies, and other charitable organizations. He believed it was essential that Christians proclaim the Gospel in both word and deed. As a result, his impact on the nation is still felt through many of those institutions that continue their vital work—nearly a century after his death.

Dozens of others could be cited throughout the wide span of history: Polycarp (d. 155), Ambrose (d. 397), Angelica of Brescia (d. 1540), Edmund Arrowsmith (d. 1628) David Brainerd (d. 1747), George Mueller (d. 1898), and Florence Nightingale (d. 1910). Each made the priestly message of their lips manifest by the servanthood message of their hands. Thus, each became an emblem of mercy in this often merciless world.

Do a Good Turn Daily

"He has showed you, O man, what is good. And what does the Lord require of you? To act justly and to love mercy and to walk humbly with your God" (Micah 6:8).

An entire catalog of Scripture exhorts us to act mercifully to those around us.[18] Do a brief concordance study—looking up the verses that deal with mercy, kindness, and compassion—to get a good overview of the subject. Try to make a list—from memory, if possible—of all the saints and heroes of the past whose stories of mercy, service, and compassion you have heard in sermons, Sunday school, missions conferences, Bible studies, or devotions. What does your list tell you about the importance and impact of mercy ministry on the overall history of the church? There are needs all around us. It doesn't matter what section of the country we live in. It doesn't matter what kind of neighborhood we call home. Single mothers silently struggle to make ends meet. Elderly couples try to get by on fixed incomes. Young families are stymied by debt, underemployment, illiteracy, physical handicaps, or prejudice. There are undernourished and poorly clothed children, third- and fourth-generation welfare dependents. There are hurting, lonely, desperate people. They may be right next door, down the street, around the block, across the tracks, or on the other side of town. But they are there. Stop. Look. Listen. See if you can't develop new eyes to see those needs where they are. Now, get busy. You may not have abundant resources or even much time to spare, but none of us is too strapped to care about—and then do something about—the needs of others.

Exodus 22:25	Proverbs 29:7	Romans 12:8–20
Leviticus 19:10	Proverbs 31:8–9	2 Corinthians 1:3–4
Leviticus 23:22	Isaiah 1:10–17	2 Corinthians 8:1–24
Leviticus 25:35–37	Isaiah 10:1–2	2 Corinthians 9:7
Numbers 18:24	Isaiah 32:6–8	Galatians 5:6
Deuteronomy 14:29	Isaiah 58:1–12	Galatians 6:2
Deuteronomy 15:1–2	Amos 5:1–27	Galatians 6:9–10
Deuteronomy 24:19–21	Matthew 5:16	Ephesians 2:8–10
Ruth 2:1–23	Matthew 7:12	Ephesians 5:2
Ruth 4:1-12	Matthew 10:8	2 Thessalonians 3:6–10
Psalm 41:1-3	Matthew 25:31–46	1 Timothy 5:8
Proverbs 11:25	Mark 12:44	1 Timothy 6:18–19
Proverbs 14:21	Luke 3:11	Titus 2:11–14
Proverbs 14:31	Luke 6:38	Titus 3:1
Proverbs 17:5	Luke 9:48	Titus 3:8
Proverbs 21:13	Luke 10:30–37	Titus 3:14
Proverbs 22:9	Luke 11:41	Hebrews 13:16
Proverbs 28:27	Luke 12:33–34	James 2:14–26
	Acts 20:35	1 John 3:17

---

*The essay originally appeared as a chapter in the book *The Micah Mandate*
   George Grant, *The Micah Mandate* (Chicago: Moody Press, 1995), 111–128.
**Reproduction rights granted by Moody Press.

---

[18] The following list is by no means comprehensive, but it may provide you with a good starting place for personal study.

LIVING AS IF PEOPLE MATTERED
ESSAY QUESTIONS

Answer the questions below on a separate sheet of paper and be prepared to review your answers in class. Reflection Questions will not be found in the text. These are merely designed to help you start thinking about issues from a worldview perspective.

1. What is the worldly function of service?

The corporate world treats service as a profit-producing utility. Good service is a tool used to ensure customer loyalty, management efficiency, and employee morale. Essentially, service is an intricate combination of courtesy and customer satisfaction. Service is simply realizing that the customer is always right and then going the extra mile. It is a principle-centered approach to human relationships and community responsibilities.

The political world also emphasizes service. Candidates often speak of offering themselves for public service rather than merely running for office. They invoke cheery images of community, military, and civic service as evidence of their suitability to govern the affairs of state. Once established in office, they initiate vast federal programs for national service, charging government bureaucracy with the task of domestic service. In the political arena, service is defined rather superficially as an expansive sense of public-spiritedness, good neighborliness, community-mindedness, or big-hearted cooperativeness. [SM p. 92]

2. What is the biblical function of service?

Biblical service isn't a tactic designed to boost profit margins, protect market shares, keep customers happy, or improve employee relations. It isn't a strategy designed to inculcate patriotism, strengthen community relations, or attract more investments. It is not a technique to pad resumes, garner votes, or patronize constituents. It isn't a style of leadership, a personality bent, or a habit of highly effective people.

Biblical service is a priestly function of mercy. The Hebrew word that is often used for service in the Old Testament literally means "to minister" or "to treat with affection." Similarly, the New Testament Greek word literally means "to care for" or to "offer relief." In both cases, the priestly connotations and merciful intentions of service are quite evident. In both cases, emphasis is on the interpersonal dimension rather than the institutional dimension, on mercy rather than management, on righteousness rather than rightness. Biblical service is far more concerned with taking care of souls than with taking care of business. [SM p. 92]

3. How are we to imitate God in his mercy and justness?

God cares for the needy and his people are to do likewise. God has comforted us, and we are to comfort others. God has forgiven us, and we are to forgive others. God has loved us, and we are to love others. He has taught us, and we are to teach others. He has borne witness to us, and we are to bear witness to others. He has laid down his life for us, and we are to lay down our lives for one

SM
99

Unit Three

another. These principles are demonstrated in Scripture (2 Corinthians 1:4; Ephesians 4:32; 1 John 4:11; Matthew 28:20; John 15:26–27; 1 John 3:16).

We are to demonstrate concern for the poor. We are to show pity toward the weak. We are to rescue the afflicted from violence. We are to put on "compassion, kindness, humility, gentleness and patience" (Colossians 3:12). We are to take up "the case of the stranger" (Job 29:16). We are to love our neighbors as ourselves (Mark 12:31), and "rescue those being led away to death" (Proverbs 24:11–12).

We are called to do "righteousness and justice" (Genesis 18:19 NASB). We are to be ministers of God's peace, instruments of his love, and ambassadors of his kingdom. We are to care for the helpless, feed the hungry, clothe the naked, shelter the homeless, visit the prisoner, and protect the innocent. Our lives should be characterized by merciful service. [SM p. 93–4]

4. What happened to the nation of Israel when they refused their responsibility to imitate God in mercy and justness? Does this principle hold true today?

Priestly privilege brings priestly responsibility. God promised that if Israel refused to take up that responsibility, he would revoke their privilege. If they refused to exercise reciprocal mercy, then God would rise up in his anger to visit the land with his wrath and displeasure, expelling them into the wilderness once again. On the other hand, if they fulfilled their calling to live lives of merciful service, then they would be blessed forever.

The principle still holds true. Those of us who have received the compassion of the Lord are to demonstrate tenderness to those all around us. This is precisely the lesson Jesus presented in the parable of the unmerciful slave (Matthew 18:23–35). The moral of the parable is clear. The needy around us are living symbols of our former helplessness and privation. We are therefore called to be living symbols of God's justice, mercy, and compassion. God has set the pattern by his gracious working in our lives. We are to follow that pattern by serving others in the power of the indwelling Spirit. [SM p. 93–4]

5. What responsibilities did Paul give to Titus in relation to the Cretan church?

Paul instructed this young pastor to preach the glories of grace and exhort the application of good deeds. However, this was no easy task. Cretan culture was terribly worldly, marked by deceit, ungodliness, sloth, and gluttony (Titus 1:12). Because of this, Paul tells Titus that he should build his ministry around works of mercy.

Titus was to be an example of good deeds (Titus 2:7). He was to teach the people to watch for chances to do good (Titus 3:1). They were all to "learn to devote themselves to doing what is good, in order that they might provide for daily necessities and not live unproductive lives" (Titus 3:14). As a pastor, Titus had innumerable tasks and responsibilities. He had administrative, doctrinal, discipling, preaching, counseling, and arbitrating duties. Yet intertwined with them all—fundamental to them all—were his servanthood duties. [SM p. 94]

6. How important have service and good works been to Christianity in the past?

Paul called himself a servant (Galatians 1:10). Similarly, James, Peter, Epaphroditus, Timothy, Abraham, Moses, David, and Daniel were all called servants. In fact, even before they were called "Christians," all of the first century believers were called "servants" (1 Corinthians 7:22).

Whenever and wherever the Gospel has gone out, the faithful have emphasized the priority of good works, especially works of compassion toward the needy. The mandate for Christians to serve others resulted in the formation of hospitals, orphanages, rescue missions, almshouses, soup kitchens, and charitable societies based upon the principle of good works. Christians fed the hungry, clothed the naked, and rescued the unwanted.

Good works were once seen as integral to being Christian. Thus, Martin Luther said, "Where there are no good works, there is no faith. If works and love do not blossom forth, it is not genuine faith, the Gospel has not yet gained a foothold, and Christ is not yet rightly known." [SM p. 94–6]

7. What has become of Christian good works in our own day?

We have tended to neglect our Christian responsibility of serving others, opting to relegate our duties to government bureaucrats and professional philanthropists. Generally speaking, societal dilemmas that once busied the church have today been handed over to secular organizations. In essence, such practical tasks such as defending the sanctity of life, caring for the aged, and protecting the helpless have been separated from our other "spiritual" responsibilities. They have been relegated to the status of "issues," even declared "political" and removed from our jurisdiction by "the separation of church and state." However, from a biblical perspective, we are taught that these things are more than "issues" and cannot be separated from our tasks as believer-priests. They are central to our purpose and calling in the world.

It is interesting to note the message Christian service sends to the unbelieving world at large. Unbelievers can disagree with our beliefs and dispute our history, but the church's living example of God's love and mercy (made evident by our deeds) is hard to ignore. The practical outworkings of selfless compassion speak with a voice that apologetics cannot imitate. However, this voice is often being silenced by our lack of obedience to the biblical command for Christian service. [SM p. 94–6]

8. Why were the actions of General Washington so momentous?

At the time of the British defeat, George Washington was an idol to the new nation and his soldiers. His men were not only willing to follow him as general, they were urging him to take control of the newly established and disordered country by declaring himself king.

General Washington could have taken control of the United States, but instead, he resigned his officer's commission. He appeared before President Thomas Mifflin and his cabinet and submitted himself to their governance. He did this despite the fact he had often disagreed with his superiors. He never questioned his ultimate allegiance. In the end, he consistently submitted to the authority God had placed over him, obeying orders, and setting aside personal ambition, preference, security, and even personal opinion in order to serve.

Though we generally think of mercy in terms of charity or philanthropy, Washington's balanced and selfless perspective actually comes closer to the biblical ideal. Kindness, helpfulness, compassion, and care are the natural outgrowth of a servant's heart. Where personal ambition and a lust for self-fulfillment are subdued, true mercy and humility are sure to follow. [SM p. 96–7]

9. **Why did the prophet Micah condemn the Israelites of his day and foretell their imminent judgment?**

The prophet Micah condemned the people of his day for their heartless defrauding and victimization of the needy (Micah 2:1–2). He asserted that their approaching judgment was due to tolerance of sin, blatant selfishness, and a refusal to undertake their servanthood responsibilities (Micah 3:2–4). Instead, they were concerned only with their own comforts and pleasures (Micah 2:8–11) and intent on personal peace and affluence, often as justification for oppression and exploitation (Micah 3:5–11). They had thus violated the covenant (Micah 5:10–15).

The Micah Mandate was not only a call to the people to repent and return to the path of righteousness—it was a proclamation of reconciliation and healing, a promise of better things to come. The prophet asserted that the remnant would be regathered to the land (Micah 4:6), the shame of affliction would be lifted (Micah 4:7), and the lost fortunes of the land would be restored (Micah 4:8). [SM p. 97]

10. **Reflection Question: How might this generation be able to serve those that are needy?**

[Answers will vary.]

COMMUNITY SERVICE ACTIVITY

Read Matthew 25:34–40 to the students and remind them of Christ's command that his followers become servants. Then ask them how they can let their light shine before men by serving others. Students are encouraged to be creative in their community service, finding ways to use the gifts God has given them to minister to others (many students, once exposed to the joy of serving others, will commit to long-term volunteer work).

This project, perhaps more than any other, forces the student to break out of his or her limited, selfish perspective and understand the reality of the body of Christ. Emphasize the importance of learning one's role in the body, and also stress cooperation. The student should learn that he or she can't change the world alone, but only with the help of God and the body of Christ.

"RESPONDING TO RELATIVISM"
WITH FRANK BECKWITH AND GREG KOUKL

I. What Is Moral Relativism?

"Moral relativism is the belief that ethics (morality) are simply reducible to either the culture or the individual—that is, there are no absolute or universal moral standards that apply to every person in every place and in every time." — Frank Beckwith

"Moral relativism is a kind of subjectivism… There are no moral rules that are outside the subject, that are objective features of the world, that we discover; rather, concepts of right and wrong are what individuals make up and invent for themselves. It's a personal choice when it comes to morality." — Greg Koukl

II. What Are Some Motivations for Moral Relativism?

A. Sometimes they want to get along with other people.

    1. *Problem #1:* They can't seem to _____get along_____ with the moral objectivists. They have to say that the objectivists are wrong.

    2. *Problem #2:* This assumes that it is a morally objective norm that we ought to get along with other people. But if relativism is true, there are no morally objective norms.

    3. *Problem #3:* This motive presupposes objective moral norms, such as tolerance. But there are no moral norms if relativism is true.

    4. *Problem #4:* Relativism robs meaning from such concepts as justice, fairness, and moral discourse. Even the word "tolerance" becomes meaningless.

B. Sometimes they want to engage in a certain immoral _____lifestyle_____.

III. Subjectivism and Objectivism

A. What does it mean for something to be "subjective?"

"It basically says that when it comes to moral questions—those questions of right and wrong, whether people are moral or immoral, ethical or unethical—the final standard is determined by what individual subjects decide. And so in moral relativism, it is not the case that moral rules are out there somewhere, that they are features of the universe, that they are objective realities in the world—kind of like math principles that we might discover—but rather they are personal preference items. They are the kinds of things that we choose because they resonate with our own self-interests or our own tastes. So, there is a sense in which when morals are viewed as relative, they are viewed more like tastes in ice cream than something like medicines. Medicines you choose to cure an objective illness. And if you choose the wrong medicine, you'll suffer from the illness and maybe die. But when it comes to ice cream, you don't choose ice cream to solve an external problem, you choose ice cream to satisfy a personal taste. And so in the area of moral relativism, morals then turn out to be relative to the subject, and subjects choose their own moral system, their own values system, based on what appeals to them." — Greg Koukl

SM
100

B. What does it mean for something to be "objective?"

"An objective claim is one that is true apart from my own mind. For example, that Ronald Reagan was president of the United States between 1981 and 1989 is true whether I believe it or not. It is objectively true. Now, objective doesn't mean publicly proved, it just means that it's something true apart from me. So let's say I know where a hidden treasure is. That may be something that nobody knows except me—and it has not been publicly proved, but it is something that is objectively true. Because if I were to die, that buried treasure would still be there, although nobody would actually know that it exists… So, subjective truths refer to our feelings, our perceptions, those things that we can only know in a first person context. Objective truths are truths that are true apart from whether I believe them or not, or whether I exist or not." — Frank Beckwith

IV. Preference Claims and Moral Claims

A. **Preference Claim**: what somebody _____likes_____ or _____dislikes_____

  1. A claim about what someone prefers

  2. Example—"I like vanilla ice cream."

B. **Moral Claim**: what somebody _____should_____ or _____should not_____ do

  1. A claim about what ought to be

  2. Example—"It is wrong to torture people."

  3. A person may *prefer* something that is *morally wrong*.

  "Part of the moral life is actually elevating your preferences so they can reach the standard of doing the right thing. To tell somebody, "Look, morality is simply what you prefer," is to advocate the morality of the sociopath. That is what the sociopath does; he does whatever he wants because he likes it. It's a dangerous thing to tell people." — Frank Beckwith

V. Three Main Types of Relativism

A. "_____Society Does_____" Relativism (Cultural Relativism)

  1. Different cultures have different moral values.

  2. Nobody has the right to say that one morality is better than the other.

  3. *Response*: Just because people disagree does not mean that no one is correct.

    i. Example—We used to think the earth was flat.

    ii. Example—We used to practice slavery.

B. "_____Society Says_____" Relativism (Conventionalism)

  1. We ought to do what society says we should do.

2. Each culture is its own source of morality.

3. *Response*:

    i. There could be nothing like an immoral society.

    ii. Morality is reduced to _____law_____ and _____power_____.

    iii. Moral reformers (e.g. Martin Luther King) are immoral because they defy the law.

C. "_____I Say_____" **Relativism** (Individual Ethical Relativism)

1. The individual is the deciding factor.

2. *Response*: If moral relativism were true, then…

    i. there would be no immoral individuals

    ii. there would be no heroes

    iii. there is no such thing as evil

    iv. there is no such thing as wrong-doing

    v. there is no such thing as justice or fairness

    vi. there is no moral obligation of tolerance

    vii. there is no sensibility to moral discourse

    viii. there is no way to morally improve

VI. Postmodernism

A. **Modernism**: morality is relative

B. **Postmodernism**: truth is relative

C. Epistemological Relativism

1. **Epistemology**: the study of how we know what we know—the study of knowledge

2. **Epistemological Relativism**: the idea that there is no objective knowledge of the world

    i. Example—Political correctness

    ii. *Response*:

        1) You allow them to rationalize their own prejudices and bigotries.

2) It's a _____self-refuting_____ claim.

    a) It is a claim that does not fulfill it own standards of truthfulness ("I have a brother who is an only child").

    b) To claim that epistemological relativism is universally true is to make a truth claim.

PART TWO

VII. Responses to Common Slogans

A. "Who are you to say?" or "Who are you to judge?"

"They have missed the point entirely. I don't expect people to believe my point of view just because I say it. I'm not speaking on my own authority. I'm trying to reason with them about moral rules." — Greg Koukl

"I think the claim or the proposition comes back on the person, because when they do that, *they're judging you*. So one way you can respond to it is, "Well, who are you to ask the question, 'Who are you to judge?' " And you're telling them, "Look, you are in the same position you are claiming I'm in. You're judging me!" — Frank Beckwith

"Look, I'm perfectly qualified to judge. I am a rational adult who is aware of certain moral principles. I think I'm perfectly qualified to judge. Who else do you want to judge things, dogs and cats? I mean, if human beings can't be the ones to make moral judgments, then who is left? I mean, in many ways, she's abdicating her responsibility. People who raise this question are abdicating their responsibility as human persons… 'I prefer to make no judgments whatsoever.' But of course, as we know, that turns out to be just another judgment." — Frank Beckwith

B. "You should be open-minded"

1. The assumption is that if you come to a _____conclusion_____, you are not open-minded.

2. If there is such a thing as the _____truth_____, then why be open-minded at all?

VIII. Moral Relativism in Our Society

A. _____**Values Clarification**_____: a theory of moral education that essentially tells kids to understand and appreciate their own *personal* values, and that there are really no objective moral values, that we each are sort of stuck with our own perspectives

"When you give my children the most difficult moral problems people can face in life, and then you tell them that there are no rules to guide them, that there is no morality to give insight to the circumstances, but instead, that it is up to them, that's not neutral. That is a moral point of view called moral relativism." — Greg Koukl

B. Multiculturalism

    1. _____**Weak**_____ **Multiculturalism**: reading and learning about diverse cultures around the world, and looking at the accomplishments of those cultures, and finding something that is good and true and beautiful in those cultures

    2. _____**Strong**_____ **Multiculturalism**: is the belief that all cultures are equal. No single culture has accomplished more than any other.

        i. What do we do with Nazi culture?

        ii. What do we do with cultures that engage in genocide and bizarre immoral practices?

C. Political Correctness

    1. _____**Speech codes**_____: rules of speech on college campuses that forbid students from making disparaging remarks about another student's religion, ethnicity, or gender

    2. *Response*:

        i. As Christians we can embrace a code that forbids harassing people.

        ii. Speech codes have been used on some universities to shut up legitimate discussion.

            1) Example—writing an editorial about homosexuality, even if respectful

            2) Harassing and/or coercing individuals to *accept* a morally liberal view

IX. Evolution, Science, and Morality

A. You don't need God for morals; morals are the kinds of things that have just simply evolved

B. *Response*: Morality can't be reduced to mere _____behavior_____.

"All evolution can do is describe why we behaved in certain ways in the past. What it can't do is tell us why we ought to be good in the future; it can't prescribe behavior, it can just describe behavior. And morality is not about description… it's about prescription. Morality is about what you and I ought to do in the future. And no evolutionary explanation can speak to that issue." —Greg Koukl

"The way we know about moral beliefs is that we discover them, and we discover them by reflecting on human nature, we discover them in Scripture. And sometimes they just are things that strike us as true. Think about when children play. Children many times are not taught when they are young about morality and ethics in any systematic way. And yet, when they play they'll say things like 'That's not fair!' They understand what fairness is. It's part of the way they're created." — Frank Beckwith

X. Same-Sex Marriage

A. Is it a question of liberty?

"It's really not a question about liberty, because when we talk about what freedom is, we have to ask the question 'What is the nature of freedom?' Is freedom simply license to do whatever I want, or does it mean the opportunity to do the right thing or to do the good? And I think there are two different views of freedom in our society." — Frank Beckwith

B. What is the nature of human sexuality?

"If human beings are the sorts of beings that are made with a purpose, and if gender has a purpose to it—that is, that men and women are the foundation of society. And that is to say when they are married they create the first government, so to speak… If, in fact, there is a unitive significance to marriage, then there really can be, in principle, no such thing as same sex marriage… because sex really means a union between a man and a woman." — Frank Beckwith

C. Understanding the battle of worldviews

"One worldview says, 'All sexual unions are equal as long as everybody consents'… The [Christian] view says that not all sexual unions are equal, that in fact, some are better than other, because in the case of heterosexual monogamy, it has unitive significance and serves as a foundation for society. Without that, we cannot expect to have a society in which children are nurtured and brought up in ways that would result in the benefit and good of society." — Frank Beckwith

D. Both views limit people

"The first view says that if you believe that men and women should be the exclusive members of a marriage, then you are narrow, intolerant, and bigoted, and you ought not to have your views figured in any way in the public square or reflected in any way in the law… The other view says the opposite about the same sex marriage proponent." — Frank Beckwith

E. Contrasting understanding of the nature of sexuality

"The same sex proponents are sexual Nihilists, or sexual egalitarians. They don't believe sex has an intrinsic purpose, it is simply there as an instrumental good for people to achieve pleasure… The other side says pleasure is an aspect of sexuality, but it is not the only aspect of it. It ultimately has intrinsic value because it has unitive significance as the foundation of society." —Frank Beckwith

F. *Response*: Use counter-intuitive examples

1. What about incest?

2. Could I marry my pet?

G. Shouldn't the state remain neutral?

    1. On abortion?

        "But now the state permits abortion. Isn't the state then saying that fetuses are not human persons; that they don't belong to the membership of the human community? Because, if they did belong as full-fledged members of the human community, then we ought to protect them. And the state ought to be in the process of doing so… [so] the state isn't neutral. The state is saying fetuses are *not* a part of our moral community, and for that reason we are not going to protect them from being harmed." — Frank Beckwith

    2. On same-sex marriage?

        "Once the state says all sexual unions are equal, it is not neutral. It is making a claim about the nature of human sexuality. And so by permitting same-sex marriage, or let's say polygamous same-sex marriage, or incestuous marriage, or some other bizarre union, they are in fact then treating all those unions as all equal in the eyes of the state. That *is* a position." —Frank Beckwith

PART THREE

XI. Tactics for Responding to Relativism

A. People can say they believe in relativism, but nobody can _____live_____ as a relativist.

B. *Tactic #1:* Self-refutation

    1. "You shouldn't push your morality on others"

    2. *Response*: _____Why not_____?

        "What this question does is push the burden of proof on the other person. The other person is going to have a very, very hard time answering the question why one person should not push their morality on another without at the same time imposing one of his own moral rules upon you." — Greg Koukl

C. *Tactic #2:* Pressing hot buttons

    "If people claim that there is no morality, then their own pet moral peeves can't really apply. They're going to have to surrender them; but people don't want to do that. And so one way to show that this person's point of view isn't really going to work is to press that button." — Greg Koukl

    1. True moral intuitions are shown by _____reactions_____ rather than by actions.

    2. Look for words like *should, ought, shouldn't,* and the like

        "If morals are relative, there are no *shoulds* and *oughts* of any kind; and every time a person utters a sentence that begins with *should* or *ought*, they are doing something incoherent according to their own professed view of morality." — Greg Koukl

D. *Tactic #3:* Forcing the tolerance issue

   1. "We should be tolerant"

   2. *Response*:

      i. If relativism is true, there is no moral rule that you ought to be tolerant.

      ii. Only moral objectivists can say that there is a moral rule like "you should be tolerant."

   3. Tolerance implies disagreement

      "Traditionally tolerance has implied condemnation. That is, if I tolerate you, *I am in fact saying you are wrong*, but I am willing to be civil with you and to get along with you." —Frank Beckwith

      "Today it has been translated to mean something like, 'Well, to judge somebody is to be intolerant,' which is odd, because I don't *tolerate* what I agree with. I agree with it! I only tolerate that which I disagree with." — Frank Beckwith

   4. Tolerance is not affirmation or approval.

      i. Christians may tolerate other religions, but we don't affirm them.

      ii. Much of what goes by the name of tolerance today is really coerced affirmation.

XII. God and Morality

   A. The argument from evil

      1. The most compelling argument against the existence of God?

      2. Actually, it is one of the best arguments in favor of the existence of God.

         i. What is the definition of "evil?"

         ii. Evil means that things aren't as they should be—they have departed from good.

         iii. That would mean that there is a standard for goodness.

            "I wouldn't have known what crooked was unless I knew what straight was." — C. S. Lewis

            "In order for somebody to complain about evil, there must be some transcendent standard of good that it departs from. That can only be the case if God exists." — Frank Beckwith

Unit Three

B. Can we have moral laws without God?

    1. Atheism teaches that only material things exist, but moral laws are not material.

    2. A law is something that is a <u>communication</u> between two persons.

        i. If laws are random mistakes, why obey them?

        "Or let's say I was playing a game of Scrabble and the letters randomly read, 'Go to Baltimore.' Would that mean that I should go? 'I better get on a plane and go to Baltimore?' I wouldn't take it seriously because I know that there is no mind behind the random collection of letters." — Frank Beckwith

        ii. Moral law, in order to have justification and force, has to have a mind behind it

XIII. Three Options Regarding Moral Laws

A. *Option #1:* Morals are <u>imaginary</u>.

B. *Option #2:* They happened by <u>chance</u>.

C. *Option #3:* They are designed and are purposed.

D. *Response*:

    1. *Option #1:* Believing morals are imaginary is moral relativism.

    2. *Option #2:* If morals happened by chance, "Why ought we to obey them?"

    3. *Option #3:* Moral rules do have a sense of 'oughtness' to them.

        i. Commands always have a commandee and a commander

        ii. Laws have a law-giver

        "This explains our feelings of guilt, our expectation of punishment; and further than that, it becomes pretty clear to people that if that's the case, when they violate a moral rule, which we do frequently, that we are not just breaking a rule, but we are offending the rule-maker. We have accountability." — Greg Koukl

"RESPONDING TO RELATIVISM"
VIDEO QUESTIONS

Answer the questions below on a separate sheet of paper and be prepared to review your answers in class.

1. What is moral relativism? What are some motivations for moral relativism? What are some problems with the motivations?

Moral relativism is the belief that ethics are reducible to either the culture or the individual. It is the belief that there are no absolute or universal moral standards that apply to every person in every place and in every time. Moral relativism is a kind of subjectivism. It purports that there are no moral rules that are outside the subject, that are objective features of the world, or that we discover. Rather, concepts of right and wrong are what individuals invent for themselves, making morality a personal choice.

Some individuals may hold to moral relativism in order to justify an immoral lifestyle, believing that if morality is personal or cultural, then they can behave almost any way they desire.

A second motivation for moral relativism is a desire to get along with others. If no moral system is universal, then one does not have to judge another's actions or beliefs as wrong. In fact, if moral relativism is true, then one cannot deem another's moral system as either good or bad. Herein lies the problem: both the desire to get along with others and the concept of tolerance are moral ideals. However, if moral relativism is true, then the moral principles of tolerance and cooperation are not universal. Those practicing moral relativism are then forced (if consistent) to be tolerant of another's intolerance and their own tolerance can be nothing but a preference. Likewise, a moral relativist cannot tell a moral objectivist that moral objectivism is wrong or bad (at least not universally).

2. What is objectivism? What is subjectivism? How do these ideas relate to moral relativism?

Something is objective if it exists apart from my own mind, i.e. something that exists even if I don't. Something is subjective if it is derived from my mind or emotions. For example, while a sore on my arm may be objective (in that it is not part of my imagination), only I experience the pain from the sore. While the sore is objective, the pain is subjective. No one else has access to my pain. Keeping this distinction in mind, moral relativism is the belief that moral rules are not features of the universe—that they are not objective realities in the world, like math. Rather, morality is a personal preference found within a subject or an individual.

3. What are moral claims? What are preference claims? How does this distinction relate to the subject of moral relativism?

A preference claim is a claim about what somebody likes or dislikes, based on preference. For example, the preference claims, "I like vanilla ice cream," or "I dislike chocolate ice cream," are statements about the speaker particularly and not about ice cream generally. Someone else may not even like ice cream. Such a position is neither right nor wrong, but is merely a fact about one's own preferences.

A moral claim is an assertion about what somebody should or should not do (based on what ought to be). For example, the moral claims, "It is wrong to torture people," or even "Slavery is immoral," are positions about reality in general and morality in particular. In fact, moral claims will be true or false regardless of who holds them. "Slavery is moral," for instance, is a claim that many would argue is false, because slavery is always wrong. Therefore, the foundational principle of moral claims is that they are true for everyone at all times.

With moral relativism there is often confusion between what a person may prefer and what is morally wrong. For example, some argue, "If you don't like abortion, then don't have one," or "If you don't like pornography, don't watch." However, objection to abortion or pornography, at least on the part of the moral objectivist, is not merely subjective about what one may or may not prefer, but rather objective or universal morality. In fact, a woman may prefer to have an abortion or a man may favor pornography and at the same time recognize that these acts are immoral.

4. **What are the three types of moral relativism? What are some of their problems?**

Cultural Relativism purports that since various societies differ on issues of morality, then a universal or objective system of morality must not exist. The main problem with this brand of moral relativism is that it assumes, because cultures disagree, that no one is actually right. Yet, disagreement does not mean that one party (or even both parties) can't be wrong. In fact, many cultures were once factually mistaken about the earth being flat. Cultures have also been objectively wrong about the practice of slavery.

According to **Conventional Relativism**, since there is no universal or objective system, you must treat the morality of the culture in which you find yourself as prescriptive. One of the major practical implications of this form of moral relativism is that society can never actually get better (or even worse). That is, whatever society dictates as right and wrong is right and wrong for that time and place. Therefore, social reformers are immoral individuals, and likewise, society cannot objectively get any better (or worse), it can only change.

Individual Moral Relativism purports that ethical systems are determined by the individual rather than dependent upon the culture. This type of moral relativism also maintains that there is no universal or objective moral standard for all persons at all times. In fact, there is no such thing as an objectively moral or immoral person. As long as we each follow our own rules, then we are being as moral as we can be.

5. **What is Epistemological Relativism? What are some problems with this position?**

Epistemological Relativism is the idea that there is no objective knowledge of the world—that we are all stuck with our own perspectives. This is more radical than moral relativism because epistemological relativism says that *everything* is relative, not just morality.

The biggest logical problem with this position is that it is self-refuting. To make a truth-claim that nothing is true is a contradiction of itself. This is a lot like saying that "Everything I say is false." But this begs the question, "What about that statement itself?" If it is a true statement, then it must, by its own definition, be false. This position also has a practical problem. If morality is subjective, then people, whether saints or sociopaths, are neither actually moral nor immoral. In fact, the sociopath is more consistent since he does whatever he feels like. The saint, on other hand, is following someone else's rules.

6. What are some common relativistic slogans? What are some problems with these slogans and possible responses?

One of the most common relativistic slogans is "Who are you to say?" or "Who are you to judge?" Generally this slogan is thrown at someone who expresses a moral claim about what is right and wrong. The first problem with the slogan is that it misses the point. To express a moral claim is not to say that it should be followed because of who said it, but because it is right on its own merits. Second, the implication is that no one should judge anyone else. Yet this implication is in itself a moral claim. Therefore, the slogan is itself a judgment made by individuals who believe that it is wrong to judge. Lastly, a good response to this slogan is to say that you are an intelligent human being and that it is up to us to discern what is moral and what is not. Someone has to judge right and wrong. Who else will do it if we do not?

Another common relativistic slogan is "You should be open-minded." G. K. Chesterton once wrote, "An open mind is like an open mouth: it is made to close on something solid." The assumption here is generally that if you have come to some conclusion, then you are closed-minded, a label no modern thinker wants to bear. This slogan is just another way of saying that no one can be right or at least that we cannot know if anyone is right. Therefore, one opinion about what is right/wrong or true/false is just as good as every other opinion. The problem is that no one really believes this. In fact, their minds are "closed" on the position of being "open-minded." They are also closed to the idea that you may know what is moral or true for everyone.

7. How has moral relativism advanced in our society? What are some problems and responses?

Society at large is interested in promoting multiculturalism, which seems to have two different definitions. Some see multiculturalism as the practice of learning about different cultures from around the world, studying their accomplishments, and perhaps even adopting some of their positive aspects into our own culture. However, others see multiculturalism as a mandate to treat all cultures as equal. The problem with this second type of multiculturalism is that it leaves us with no justification to condemn abhorrent cultural practices like genocide.

In secondary education, moral relativism is being championed through the doctrine of values clarification. This is the idea that there are no objective moral values; instead, we must each discover or create our own moral rules. This is often presented as a neutral position, yet is anything but neutral. By telling children that "it is up to them to decide," schools are actually promoting moral relativism, a moral position in itself.

In colleges, political correctness is often used as a means for promoting moral relativism. In fact, some campuses even have speech codes or rules about what students can and cannot say regarding certain people groups and practices. This, in effect, kills all debate about such topics as homosexuality. Students (Christian students most likely) are therefore not allowed to engage in dialogue about controversial subjects.

8. **Why can the state not take a neutral position on issues like same-sex marriage or abortion?**

> When it comes to same-sex marriage or abortion, there is no such thing as a neutral position. Once the state says that all sexual unions are equal or that a fetus is not a human person deserving protection, then the state has assumed a position. Likewise, if the state says that not all sexual unions are equal or that a fetus is a human person, then the state has assumed a position.

9. **What are some tactics for responding to moral relativism?**

> **Tactic #1**—Self-Refutation—Point out the logical inconsistency of moral relativism. If someone asserts that we shouldn't judge, ask them, "Why not?" Any response will be a moral imperative and thus a contradiction to the assumption that morality is relative to the individual.
>
> **Tactic #2**—Pressing Their Hot Button—If people claim that there is no morality, then their own moral pet peeves cannot apply. This means they can't use terms like "should," "ought," "shouldn't," and the like to support their position. Ask about environmentalism, abortion, homosexuality, euthanasia, and other controversial issues. If a moral relativist is consistent, then their positions on these topics can only be their personal opinions, like their preference for ice cream. Therefore, to say that homosexuality should be accepted would be like saying that only chocolate ice cream should be eaten.
>
> **Tactic #3**—Forcing the Tolerance Issue—Most moral relativists believe the way they do because they desire tolerance. However, if there are no moral rules, then even tolerance as a moral rule is out the window. Tolerance only makes sense if universal morals exist.
>
> Beyond this, the concept of tolerance itself has been misconstrued. To be tolerant does not mean that you must accept every moral position. Rather, it means that you should be civil toward those with whom you do not agree.

10. **How can evil be a proof of God's existence?**

> C. S. Lewis said, "I wouldn't have known what crooked was unless I knew what straight was." Someone cannot point to evil in the world as proof that God does not exist, because if we assume that there is no God, then we must also assume that there is no such thing as evil. Without God, morality is just a human invention, a set of arbitrary human rules that change from person to person and culture to culture. To Hitler in Nazi Germany, evil is being Jewish; for the majority of the rest of the world genocide is evil. If no one is objectively right, evil, just like morality, is merely based on preference. On the other hand, if there is a God who has set requirements in place for all of humanity, then there is a universal standard for morality, right/wrong, and good/evil.

"BIOTECHNOLOGY"
WITH JOHN STONESTREET

I. Understanding Our Times

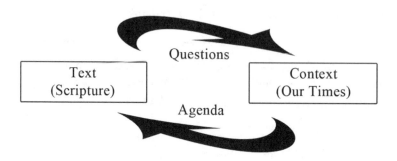

"There is nothing in Scripture about these things [Islam, stem cell research, xenotransplantation], but Scripture is full of stuff about these things. And we have to take the questions that emerge from our times, and that should drive us back to the text so that we can understand how we ought to live for 'such a time as this.'"

"If Christianity should happen to be true—that is to say, if God is the real God of the universe—then defending it may mean talking about anything and everything. Things can be irrelevant to the proposition that Christianity is false, but nothing can be irrelevant to the proposition that Christianity is true." — G. K. Chesterton

"Cloning and the biotech agenda are even worse news for human dignity than abortion. Not only are we taking upon ourselves the godlike prerogative of ending human life as we choose, but we also are attempting to appropriate the prerogative of making human life as we choose." — Charles Colson

II. What the Biotech Age Promises: (taken from Mitchell, *Bioethics in the New Millennium*)

A. Creation of life in a lab

B. Predetermination of the sex and genetic makeup of children

C. Pharmacogenomics

D. Programming of human genes

E. Identifying disease genes and genetically derived cures for cancer, AIDS, etc.

F. Repair of damaged spinal cords and brain cells

G. Cloning of mammals, including humans

H. Control of aging and obesity

I. Animals growing replacement organs for humans

J. Transgenic vegetables that will inoculate the world's poor against disease

K. Trees that can grow in a few years instead of decades

L. Plants that can produce substitutes for raw materials in plastic

M. Stronger materials, fibers, and adhesives

N. Wearable computers

O. Bionics

P. Bioelectric noses, ears, tongues, etc.

Q. Biosynthetic skin, blood, bones, muscles, etc.

III. What is Biotechnology?

A. **_____Bio_____**: Natural and living

B. **_____Technology_____**: Application of technique in an attempt to control, enhance, or manipulate

C. **Biotechnology**: Industrial use of living organisms or the application of technique to living organisms

IV. Different Areas of Biotechnology

A. Stem Cell Research

   1. **Stem Cells**: Cells in your body that have not been diversified and have not stopped reproducing

   2. Embryonic stem cells

      i. Kills the embryo when extracted

      ii. No scientific achievement

   3. Non-embryonic (or adult) stem cells

      i. Does not kill a human being

      ii. Has produced much scientific advancement

B. Genetics

   1. Human genome project

   2. Reproductive technology

C. **_____Xenotransplantation_____**: Use of animal tissues, organs, or cells transplanted to or used for contact with human subjects

D. **_____Transgenics_____**: Insertion of DNA of one species into the genetic code of another

E. Robotics

F. _____**Nanotechnology**_____: Engineering and manufacturing at the molecular level

   1. Medicine

   2. National defense

G. _____**Artificial Intelligence**_____: An artificial mechanism that can mimic human thinking

H. _____**Cybernetics**_____: Integration of man and machine

I. _____**Medical Technology**_____: Antibiotics, medicines, organ transplants, alternative medicines, etc.

J. _____**Life Issues**_____: Birth control, abortion, euthanasia, assisted suicide, etc.

PART TWO

V. Bioethics : Right conduct in the area of biotechnology

"Bioethics is at least thirty years behind biotechnology."

VI. The Challenges of Biotechnology

A. Biotechnology is carried out in the context of a false worldview.

"The most dangerous ideas in a society are not the ones that we argue, but the ones that we assume." — C. S. Lewis

"A worldview is not just a view of the world; a worldview gives you a view of yourself. And if you have a wrong view of yourself, then there are negative consequences from that."

B. We don't know what human is.

"The idols of the nations are silver and gold, made by the hands of men. They have mouths but cannot speak, eyes but they cannot see; they have ears but cannot hear, nor is there breath in their mouths. Those who make them will be like them, and so will all who trust in them." — Psalm 135:15–18

   1. We become what we worship.

      i. We worship stuff (e.g. music, celebrities, power, money, self, sex).

      ii. People have become stuff.

   2. People are seen only as machines.

      "The huge modern heresy is to alter the human soul to fit modern social conditions, instead of altering modern social conditions to fit the human soul." — G. K. Chesterton

   3. Only humans were created to bear God's image.

C. The Re-evaluation of humanity

    1. We judge the value of stuff by what it can do and what it looks like.

    2. We judge human beings by what they can do and what they look like.

    3. What makes humans valuable?

        i. Biblical Christianity: Human = _____*imago Dei*_____

            1) Humans are specially created in the image of God.

            2) God has endowed all humans with significant value.

            3) All humans have purpose and value.

                a) Value not based on what we can do

                b) Value not based on what we look like

                c) Value based on the fact that God has given us his image

        ii. Naturalism: Human = _____body_____

            1) Humans have no intrinsic value.

            2) Some humans have qualities that others do not.

            3) We decide which humans have value.

> "If we compared the characteristics of different individuals, irrespective of species… we would have to go much further down the evolutionary scale before we reached a point at which non-human animals had capacities as limited as the most severely retarded humans… Pigs, cows, and chickens have a greater capacity to relate to others, better ability to communicate, and far more curiosity, than most severely retarded humans." — Peter Singer, Princeton University bio-ethicist

D. The commodification of humanity

> "Intelligent, Athletic Egg Donor Needed for Loving Family. You must be at least 5'10" / Have a 1400+ SAT score / Possess no major family medical issues." Fee Offered: $50,000 — Ad from the *Harvard Crimson*

E. Are we really in control?

    1. 276 embryos failed [deformed fetuses] to produce Dolly

    2. Dolly ultimately euthanized

    3. Unused embryos are destroyed in human in-vitro fertilization

    4. Embryo ownership

5. Mix-ups during in-vitro fertilization

"Unless human choices control technology, technology will control human choices." — Andrew Kimbrell, *The Human Body Shop*

F. Not all knowledge is _____good_____ (Genesis 11)

"According to God, nothing is impossible for collective humanity."

VII. How to Live in a Biotech Age

A. Commit to the value of all *imago Dei*.

"It is a serious thing… to remember that the dullest and most uninteresting person you talk to may one day be a creature which, if you saw it now, you would be tempted to worship, or else a horror and a corruption such as you now meet, if at all, only in a nightmare. All day long we are, in some degree, helping each other to one or other of these destinations… There are no ordinary people. You have never talked to a mere mortal. Nations, cultures, arts, civilizations—these are mortal, and their life is to ours as the life of gnat. But it is immortals whom we joke with, work with, marry, snub, and exploit—immortal horrors or everlasting splendors." — C. S. Lewis

B. Send Christians to the "mission field" of biotechnology.

"What we want is not more little books about Christianity, but more little books by Christians on other subjects—with their Christianity latent. You can see this most easily if you look at it the other way around… it is not the books written in direct defense of Materialism that make modern man a Materialist; it is the materialistic assumptions in all the other books. In the same way, it is not books on Christianity that will really trouble him. But he would be troubled if, whenever he wanted a cheap popular introduction to some science, the best work on the market was always by a Christian." — C. S. Lewis

C. Be part of the educated public.

1. Learn terminology and follow new developments.

2. Offer hope (1 Peter 3:15).

See also ETHICS FACT SHEET

"BIOTECHNOLOGY"
VIDEO QUESTIONS

Answer the questions below on a separate sheet of paper and be prepared to review your answers in class.

1. **What is biotechnology? What does Scripture say about biotechnology?**

> The term biotechnology is derived from two words: bio + technology. The prefix "bio" refers to something living and "technology" refers to practical application of knowledge. Biotechnology is the industrial use of living organisms or the application of technique to living organisms. Strictly speaking, cars and elevators are biotechnology, just as are artificial hearts and artificial forms of intelligence.
>
> An important Christian principle is this: the Bible may not directly speak to a certain issue, but it most likely has something to say about every relevant issue. The Bible is a work that was compiled a long time ago, by cultures different than our own, written in a different language, a long way from here, to address issues relevant at a particular time. However, the Bible contains timeless truths and principles put forth by God to mankind. Although the Bible may not directly speak to abortion or stem cell research, it still has something to say about these subjects.

2. **What are stem cells? Why is research being done on stem cells?**

> Stem cells are cells that can 1) self-replicate indefinitely, and 2) can develop into other types of cells (e.g. red blood cells, white blood cells, platelets, etc).
>
> Medical researchers believe stem cells have the potential to cure diseases by repairing tissues or growing organs. Stem cell research is expected to make advancements in conditions such as Alzheimer's, Parkinson's, diabetes, spinal cord injury, heart disease, stroke, arthritis, and cancer.

3. **What are the differences between embryonic and non-embryonic stem cells? Which type of stem cells has produced scientific achievement?**

> Stem cells are often divided into two types: embryonic and non-embryonic (or adult) stem cells.
>
> Embryonic stem cells are the most controversial since the harvesting of these cells necessitates the killing of the embryo. In fact, some researchers have already manufactured embryos for the explicit purpose of extracting stem cells. If life truly does begin at conception, then innocent unborn human beings are being sacrificed in the hope of extending the lives of others. Beyond this, to date, embryonic stem cell research has not produced any scientific achievements.
>
> Non-embryonic (or adult) stem cells are far less controversial since these cells are harvested from such things as bone marrow or placentas and do not result in the extermination of human beings. Adult stem cell research has produced much scientific advancement.

Unit Three

SM
115

UNDERSTANDING THE TIMES

179

4. **What are some different areas of biotechnology? What are some promises that these areas hold? What are some concerns?**

- **Xenotransplantation**—Use of animal tissues, organs, or cells transplanted to or used for contact with human subjects
- **Transgenics**—Insertion of DNA of one species into the genetic code of another species
- **Nanotechnology**—Engineering and manufacturing at the molecular level
- **Artificial Intelligence**—An artificial mechanism that can mimic human thinking
- **Cybernetics**—Integration of man and machine
- **Medical Technology**—Antibiotics, medicines, organ transplants, alternative medicines, etc.
- **Life Issues**—Birth control, abortion, euthanasia, assisted suicide, etc.

[With respect to the last two questions, discuss xenotransplation, transgenics, artificial intelligence, and various life issues.]

5. **What is bioethics? What are some of the ethical challenges of biotechnology? What makes human beings valuable?**

Bioethics is right conduct in the area of biotechnology. Many believe that this area is around thirty years behind biotechnology in general, because we have only recently begun considering the moral implications of this field. The major challenge is that of worldview. More specifically, we need to examine which worldview provides our culture with its ethics and view of humanity?

Currently, we live in a society that views human beings as mere machines devoid of souls or real autonomy. This view of man stems from naturalism, a philosophical position which purports that all of reality is matter.

Our culture is also a context of idolatry in which *stuff* is idolized and coveted. In fact, we even view human beings as stuff with varying degrees of *extrinsic* value based on abilities and image. The biblical view, on the other hand, teaches that human beings are *intrinsically* valuable based on the fact that God has made them in his image. All of humanity is to be cared for, regardless of age, condition, looks, or abilities.

When people are valued by what they can do, euthanasia becomes a viable option for the infirm, mentally retarded, or elderly. When people are valued by what they can do, abortion seems to make sense because an unborn baby lacks *extrinsic* value.

IMAGO DEI ACTIVITY

Have your students pair off (but only with other students that are not programmed into their mobile phones, i.e. not good friends). Have them sit facing each other, knees touching. Tell them to stare at each other without looking away (this type of action is very uncomfortable in our culture, so most of the students will be forced to laugh in order to deal with the discomfort). After the laughing has died down, tell the students that the person in front of them is a valuable human being created in God's image. Ask the students to say that phrase to their partner.

DEAR DOUG
WRITING ASSIGNMENT

Hey there!

Well, I can't believe that we are almost halfway through the semester. Midterms are starting to loom and everybody's getting a little panicked. I'm barely holding my grades, so I've had to give up on some of the partying—but not football, never football.

I think we should start a club, the way our group keeps meeting spontaneously at the coffee shop! Paige even showed up today—guess her sorority didn't have any meetings today. As she and Sarah walked in the door, they were talking about the fact that there is no universal standard of right and wrong. Humans create their own ethics, Sarah said, and since these standards change from situation to situation—even from person to person—we need to be tolerant of everyone's beliefs and decisions. Paige said that it was wrong for people to force their beliefs on others. Do you believe there is a universal standard of right and wrong?

Nathan's argument was similar to what the girls stated, but he said that if we break our own ethical rules, we'd have to pay for it in our next life. He said that if our "good" deeds don't outweigh the "bad," we could come back as a toad or something. But does his idea of "karma" make sense?

Mark got all fired up about the differences between the wealthy and the poor. He defined wrong as anything the wealthy do to oppress the poor and right as anything that relieves the suffering of the underprivileged. But that would sanction everything from revolution to murder, as long as it was done for the "right" reasons. What are your thoughts?

Muhammad said there is a standard of right and wrong set by God and that if we break it we'll have consequences in this life and the next to deal with. He seemed to think that by doing enough good things we can outweigh the bad things we do and find Allah's favor. But is simply adding up good deeds a big enough standard to live by? I've always assumed that the Bible taught there was an external set of rules we had to live by, but I could be wrong. What does Christianity really teach about ethics?

Well, I gotta run. There's a big game tonight and not even cramming for tomorrow's quiz could make me miss it. Besides, I'm picking Amber up and we're going out for ice cream afterwards. You know how girls are… they want you to be on time, even if they aren't!

Keep in touch,
Doug

Unit Three

Doug has brought up five different subjects; below is a rough outline of possible responses.

1. Do you believe that there is a universal standard for right and wrong? (10 points)

> Secular and humanistic moral systems deny any superior divine moral lawgiver. Thus, man must ultimately construct his own moral system based on subjective preferences and reasoned insights. This leaves the moral relativist without an absolute or universal standard for judging actions. Without absolutes, humanity is left with only conflicting moral opinions.

2. Does the notion of karma make sense? (10 points)

> Ethical relativism, as one would expect, has led New Agers to blur the distinction between good and evil, right and wrong. Since Cosmic Humanism purports that no absolute standard of right or wrong exists, and since New Agers contend that they are God, they believe it is up to them to create their own moral systems. However, if everyone is part of the divine, then how can each of us have conflicting moral opinions? Moreover, if we are judged by our own moral standards, then why not create a moral system in which nothing is wrong? That would ensure that they would never return as a toad.

3. What do you think about basing moral standards on wealth? (10 points)

> While Christians believe that we should help the poor, we do not believe that the wealthy (especially non-Christians) should be forced to help the poor, especially by means that are themselves immoral. This utilitarian form of ethic merely trades one selfish act for an immoral one. This type of thinking leads to revolution, destruction, and death, but not change.

4. Is working to outweigh bad deeds with good an acceptable standard for moral behavior? (10 points)

> Both Christians and Muslims believe that God will one day judge the deeds of people. The difference is that Muslims see God's judgment in terms of scales, while Christians believe that even one bad deed will separate us from God. For this reason, God has provided a way for justification and a means for sanctification.

5. What is the Christian view of ethics? (10 points)

> God's moral nature is absolute and unchanging. God always hates evil and loves good. The Bible is of supreme importance because it tells us the difference between the two, providing a framework on which a completely unambiguous ethics must be built. According to Biblical Christianity, ethical relativism leads to destruction (Matthew 7:13). Christian ethics is inseparable from theology for the simple reason that Christian ethics is grounded in the character of God. Rather than believing in some ethical scheme bound to society's ever-changing whims, the Christian answers to a specific moral order revealed to man through both general revelation and the special revelation of the Bible and the person of Jesus Christ.

UNIT THREE TEST

'ETHICS' TEXTBOOK QUESTIONS

Matching: (1 point possible per answer [2 for 90-day])
some options may be used more than once or not at all; some questions may have multiple answers

1. __b/g__ Christianity

2. __b/h__ Islam

3. __a__ Secular Humanism

4. __c__ Marxism-Leninism

5. __a/f__ Cosmic Humanism

6. __d__ Postmodernism

a. Moral Relativism
b. Moral Absolutes
c. Proletariat Morality
d. Cultural Moral Relativism
e. Common Sense Realism
f. Karma
g. God's Nature
h. Allah's Will

Short answer: (8 points possible per answer [11 for 90-day])

7. Ethically speaking, what are Christians called to do?

> Christians are called to love God with all our hearts, souls, strengths, and minds and to love our neighbors as ourselves (Luke 10:27). This command, like all of the other commands in the Bible, implies that Christians have moral responsibilities.

8. In what two ways is the term jihad used?

> The term jihad is used in at least two ways by Muslims. First, it can be used to describe the battle against temptation and sin for the sake of self-control and the development of virtue. Second, it can define the battle against any and all who oppose Islam—the most self-sacrificing action a Muslim may undertake.

9. How did Karl Marx and Friedrich Engels view the issue of morality?

> Marx and Engels denied that morals were central in human life. Rather, they believed that biological and social evolution dictate and determine morality. What is moral or what is right or wrong is determined by evolution. If the bourgeois class hinders either biological or social evolution, then nature dictates the removal of that class.

10. What is the Marxist-Leninist morality of the future? How will it be determined?

> Marxism trusts that the future classless utopia will also deliver a new morality determined by the dialectic. In other words, morality is constantly evolving with the progression of time.

CD-ROM

11. What is the foundation for Cosmic Humanism's ethical system?

Cosmic Humanists approach ethics from their foundation of pantheism—they believe they are ultimately God. And since they are God; they get to write the moral rules. Thus, for the New Ager, there are no external moral precepts.

12. According to Postmodernists, how does a community create its own ethical standards?

Lyotard claimed to be content with "little narratives." By this he means that philosophical and moral truth (small "t") reside in the local community. This could be referred to as cultural or communal moral relativism.

LIVING AS IF PEOPLE MATTERED ESSAY
True or False: (2 points possible per answer)
if an answer is false, restate it to make it true

13. Christians are to imitate God in his mercy and justness by caring for the needy, forgiving others, bearing witness of Christ to others, and even laying down our lives for others.

True

14. According to both Martin Luther and the *Westminster Confession*, the demonstration of faith is not tied to good works.

False: According to both Martin Luther and the *Westminster Confession*, the demonstration of faith is tied to good works.

15. The church today has declined its priestly duties, yielding the work of service to government bureaucrats and professional philanthropists.

True

16. According to Ezekiel 16:49–50, God judged Sodom and Gomorrah for their lack of service.

True

17. The prophet Micah condemned the Israelites of his day for their tolerance of sin, blatant selfishness, and their refusal to serve.

True

"RESPONDING TO RELATIVISM" VIDEO
True or False: (2 points possible per answer)
*if an answer is false, restate it to make it true

18. Moral Relativism is the belief that morality is a personal preference found within an individual.

True

19. A subjective statement is true for everyone.

False: A subjective statement is true for <u>only the individual</u>.

20. The statement, "Homosexuality is morally good," is a moral claim.

True

21. A person can prefer something that is immoral.

True

22. Moral relativism is the belief that everything is relative.

False: <u>Epistemological</u> relativism is the belief that everything is relative.

23. "Society does" relativism and "society says" relativism purport that since different societies differ on various issues of morality, then a universal or objective system of morality must not exist.

True

24. "Who are you to judge?" is a judgment.

True

25. Strong multiculturalism is learning about diverse cultures around the world.

False: <u>Weak</u> multiculturalism is learning about diverse cultures around the world.

26. Evolution can only prescribe behavior.

False: Evolution can only <u>describe</u> behavior.

27. It is possible for the state to remain neutral on the issue of abortion.

False: It is <u>impossible</u> for the state to remain neutral on the issue of abortion.

"BIOTECHNOLOGY" VIDEO
Short answer: (8 points possible per answer [11 for 90-day])

28. What is bioethics?

Bioethics is right conduct in the area of biotechnology. Many believe that this area is around thirty years behind biotechnology in general because we have only recently begun considering the moral implications of this field.

29. What are the differences between embryonic and non-embryonic stem cells? Which type of stem cells has produced scientific achievement?

Embryonic stem cells are the most controversial since the harvesting of these cells necessitates the killing of the embryo. In fact, some researchers have already manufactured embryos for the explicit purpose of extracting stem cells. Thus, if life truly does begin at conception, then innocent unborn human beings are being sacrificed in the hope of extending the lives of others. Beyond this, to date embryonic stem cell research has not produced any scientific achievements.

Non-embryonic (or adult) stem cells are far less controversial since these cells are harvested from such things as bone marrow or placentas and do not result in the extermination of human beings. Adult stem cell research has produced much scientific advancement.

TEACHER
MANUAL

UNDERSTANDING THE TIMES

Unit Four

Topics:
Biology
Naturalism
Icons of Evolution
Intelligent Design

A Summit Ministries Curriculum

180-DAY SYLLABUS

DAY	IN CLASS	HOMEWORK	
1	WATCH "Biology" video		
2	READ <u>UTT</u> Textbook 'Biology 4.1'	READ <u>UTT</u> Textbook 'Biology 4.2'	
3	REVIEW <u>UTT</u> Textbook 'Biology 4.1–4.2' questions	READ <u>UTT</u> Textbook 'Biology 4.3'	
4	READ <u>UTT</u> Textbook 'Biology 4.4'		
5	REVIEW <u>UTT</u> Textbook 'Biology 4.3–4.4' questions	READ <u>UTT</u> Textbook 'Biology 4.5'	
6	READ <u>UTT</u> Textbook 'Biology 4.6'		
7	REVIEW <u>UTT</u> Textbook 'Biology 4.5–4.6' questions	ASSIGN Dear Doug Letter	
8	WATCH "Icons of Evolution" video P1		
9	WATCH "Icons of Evolution" video P2		
10	REVIEW "Icons of Evolution" video questions		
11	WATCH "Mysteries of Life's Origins" video P1		
12	WATCH "Mysteries of Life's Origins" video P1		
13	REVIEW "Mysteries of Life's Origins" video questions	READ *What is Darwinism?* essay	
14	REVIEW *What is Darwinism?* essay questions	Dear Doug Letter assignment DUE	
15	TAKE Unit Four Test		

90-DAY SYLLABUS

DAY	IN CLASS	HOMEWORK	
1	WATCH "Biology" video	READ <u>UTT</u> Textbook 'Biology 4.1–4.2'	
2	REVIEW <u>UTT</u> Textbook 'Biology 4.1–4.2' questions	READ <u>UTT</u> Textbook 'Biology 4.3–4.4'	
3	REVIEW <u>UTT</u> Textbook 'Biology 4.3–4.4' questions	READ <u>UTT</u> Textbook 'Biology 4.5–4.6'	
4	REVIEW <u>UTT</u> Textbook 'Biology 4.5–4.6' questions		
5	WATCH "Icons of Evolution" video P1		
6	WATCH "Icons of Evolution" video P2		
7	REVIEW "Icons of Evolution" video questions		
8	TAKE Unit Four Test		

UNDERSTANDING THE TIMES
BIOLOGY QUESTIONS

Answer the questions below on a separate sheet of paper and be prepared to review your answers in class.

BIOLOGY 4.1

1. **What are some problems with the theory of theistic evolution?**

The first problem with theistic evolution is that it is based on a bad interpretation of the Scripture. This method of bringing about life, especially mankind, seems cruel. Also, theistic evolution is particularly damaging to your view of Adam and Eve. If this account refers only to metaphoric or mythological characters, then it is hard to account for original sin and our need for Christ. Fourth, the theory of evolution in general is undergoing serious challenges from within the scientific community itself. [UTT 4.1.2–3]

[Ask them if they have had doubts regarding their beliefs in this area. Maybe they have thought that evolution, or at least a form of theistic evolution, sounded plausible. Assure them that it is okay to be honest about their doubts. Also, explain to the students that there are various beliefs about whether the creation took a literal 6 days or whether creation was gradual with Adam and Eve being the final act of creation. This is not theistic evolution. The purpose of this chapter is not to discuss these ideas, but rather if evolution (or a form of theistic evolution) has any scientific grounds.]

2. **What aspects of the Christian worldview were foundational to the development of science?**

Science is based on the assumption that the universe is orderly and can be expected to act according to specific and discoverable laws, a viewpoint that is tied directly to a Christian worldview. An ordered lawful universe would seem to be the effect of an intelligent cause, which was precisely the belief of most early scientists. [UTT 4.1.4]

3. **Define the following topics: teleology, DNA, spontaneous generation, Second Law of Thermodynamics, and gene pool. How do they relate to the debate over origins?**

[Answers will vary somewhat, but these main ideas need to be conveyed.]

- **Teleology**—the study of purpose and design. Science continually reveals the complexity of the various forms of life. Life in general operates like the most complex of machines, i.e. it seems to have been designed to perform particular complex purposes. [UTT 4.1.6]
- **DNA**—the storehouse containing all the genetic information necessary for life. DNA is a crucial part of all living matter, yet evolutionary theory is powerless to explain how it came into existence and why DNA evinces such phenomenal design. [UTT 4.1.7]
- **Spontaneous Generation**—the belief that non-life gave rise to living organisms. In order for life to have arisen due to random processes, non-living matter must have come alive at some point in time. It is the burden of the Darwinist to propose a rational theory for how this event could have occurred. [UTT 4.1.8]

- **Second Law of Thermodynamics**—scientific theory that states that although the total energy in the cosmos remains constant, the amount of energy available to do useful work is always decreasing. While the evolutionist calls for living organisms to grow more orderly as evolution progresses, the second law of thermodynamics assures us that order tends to disintegrate into disorder. [UTT 4.1.9]
- **Gene Pool**—the total genes of species. Evolutionists believe that no breeding limits exist within a gene pool because life forms must ultimately be able to break their "species barriers" to yield new species. Evolutionists have thus proposed that beneficial mutations are capable of breaking any barriers to change. However, evolutionists have not been able to demonstrate that mutations are capable of breaking these limits. [UTT 4.1.10]

4. **According to Walter Brown, what should we see in the fossil record if evolution is true?**

Brown makes the point that if the theory of evolution were true, then the fossil record should show continuous and gradual changes from the simplest (lower geological layers) to the most complex forms of life (higher geological layers). However, what scientists actually find are gaps and discontinuities that appear throughout the fossil record, with both simple and complex forms of life in the bottom and top layers—without any forms of life in between that could pass as "transitional." [UTT 4.1.11]

5. **What problems does the theory of punctuated equilibrium avoid? What problems must it face?**

Although the theory of punctuated equilibrium is able to avoid the problem of transitional forms, it still must be able to account for the problems of spontaneous generation, a lack of observed beneficial mutations, and the contradiction of the second law of thermodynamics. [UTT 4.1.12]

THEISTIC EVOLUTION ACTIVITY

Play the role of an evangelical who believes evolution was God's method of creating and developing life. Let the students struggle with this issue for a while. Then, have a student read aloud (or refer to their reading of) the introduction to the chapter on Biblical Christian biology while the other students follow along in their texts. Make sure they take note of the author's main objections to theistic evolution:

- Theistic evolution is based on a bad interpretation of Scripture. Particularly damaging is the implication that Adam and Eve are metaphoric or mythological characters.
- Evolutionary theory is undergoing serious challenges from within the scientific community.

BIOLOGY 4.2

6. **What is the Islamic view of creation?**

According to Islam, God has always existed. He is eternal and self-existent. He created everything and set the universe in order. [UTT 4.2.3]

7. According to Islam, how many days did creation take?

In some passages, creation is said to have taken six days; in others, the length of creation is given as eight days. [UTT 4.2.3]

8. According to Islam, did creation happen in literal days or longer periods of time?

Just as the Christian community is divided over whether to advocate an old or young earth, so Muslims are also divided on this subject. While many traditional Muslims take the reference to days literally, some contemporary Muslim spokesmen hold that the days of creation were long periods of time (though they do not normally advocate evolutionary theories). [UTT 4.2.4]

9. Do Muslims believe that the universe displays design?

The Qur'an describes the universe as finely ordered and illustrating God's magnificent mind in its design. Just like Christian apologists, Muslim apologists regularly appeal to the order of the universe as evidence for God's existence and creative activity. [UTT 4.2.6]

10. Does Islam incorporate a belief in evolution?

Though some modern Muslims believe that evolutionary theories accurately describe the history of the world and the origin of species, the majority of Muslims reject evolutionary theories on both religious and scientific grounds. [UTT 4.2.7]

BIOLOGY 4.3

11. What do the *Humanist Manifestos I* and *II* state about humanity's origins?

Humanist Manifesto I states, "Humanism believes that man is a part of nature and that he has emerged as the result of a continuous process." This belief is echoed in *Humanist Manifesto II*, which claims: "science affirms that the human species is an emergence from natural evolutionary forces." [UTT 4.3.1]

12. Why must "modern" science rule out creation? Does this reasoning pose a problem for evolution as well? Why or why not?

"Modern" science studies and theorizes only about things that can be observed and measured. This naturalistic restriction necessarily rules out the existence of the supernatural because the supernatural cannot lie beyond the natural world. It should be noted that by modern science's strict definition, it cannot consistently render judgment on the theory of evolution, because it can neither be measured nor observed. One-time-only historical events fall outside the parameters of the scientific method. [UTT 4.3.2]

13. **What is spontaneous generation? Why is this theory important to evolutionists?**

> Spontaneous generation is the evolutionary theory that life arose spontaneously from non-living matter by natural, random processes. Without this concept, Humanism would have to postulate a supernatural force to explain the existence of the first form of life. This, however, would contradict Secular Humanism's atheistic belief system. [UTT 4.3.4]

14. **Define the following topics: natural selection and struggle for existence (or survival). How do they relate to the debate over origins?**

> *[Answers will vary somewhat, but these main ideas need to be conveyed.]*
>
> - **Natural Selection**—The mechanism proposed by Darwin that naturally "selects" an organism's favorable characteristics and eliminates unfavorable ones through competition, predators, geography, time, etc. [UTT 4.3.5]
> - **Struggle for Existence**—Inherent in the idea of natural selection is the notion that those life forms best equipped to survive will win the struggle for existence. This allegedly explains why life forms have become better equipped to survive over time. [UTT 4.3.6]
> - **Mutation**—Evolutionists theorize that genetic mutations are responsible for introducing characteristics into a species, thus making it more fit to survive. Combining mutations with the theory of natural selection provides the means and mechanism for adaptation and evolution. [UTT 4.3.7]
>
> *[Discuss with your students what society would look like if we governed ourselves according to the "survival of the fittest" doctrine? Which people groups would probably be most at risk? Which would be the best off?]*

15. **Upon what six planks does Secular Humanist biology rest?**

> Secular Humanist biology rests on the theory of evolution, which is comprised of 1) spontaneous generation, 2) natural selection, 3) struggle for existence, 4) beneficial mutations, 5) adaptations, and 6) the fossil record. [UTT 4.3.10]

BIOLOGY 4.4

16. **Why was Charles Darwin's work so important to Karl Marx? What connection does Friedrich Engels make between Darwin and Marx?**

> Marx and Engels recognized the usefulness of Darwin's theory as a foundation for an entirely materialistic perspective on life. In a letter to Engels, Marx writes, "During… the past four weeks I have read all sorts of things. Among others Darwin's work on Natural Selection. And though it is written in the crude English style, this is the book which contains the basis in natural science for our view." Engels makes the same claim even more straightforwardly: "Just as Darwin discovered the law of evolution in organic nature, so Marx discovered the law of evolution in human history." [UTT 4.4.1–2]

17. **Where did Engels place his faith and was there any way to persuade Engels against spontaneous generation?**

> Louis Pasteur was able to disprove the theory of spontaneous generation, but apparently not to Engels's satisfaction. Although no proof could be found for spontaneous generation, and no rebuttal could be offered against Pasteur's finding, Engels still supported this theory wholeheartedly. In other words, Engels placed his faith in the possibility of spontaneous generation—disregarding whether it was scientific or not. [UTT 4.4.4]

18. **Why do Marxists ultimately deem Darwinism as inconsistent with their worldview?**

> When examined closely, Darwinian evolution of gradual change from species to species actually works contrary to the Marxist dialectic. According to dialectical materialism, whenever thesis and antithesis clash, the new synthesis created occurs rapidly, in the form of a jump, rather than in the form of a long, gradual process. Therefore, the theories of traditional and neo-Darwinism were eventually dropped by most Marxists and replaced by the theory of punctuated evolution. [UTT 4.4.6]

19. **What form of evolution does Marxism embrace?**

> Marxists expect evolution to work according to the dialectic—when thesis (a species) and antithesis (some aspect of the environment) clash, the synthesis (a new species) occurs rapidly. In 1972, the theory of punctuated equilibrium (or punctuated evolution) arose because it aligned with the dialectical process more closely than did Darwinian evolution. Punctuated evolution postulates that evolution worked itself out in periods of "punctuated" or speedy change, followed by periods of "equilibrium" or stasis. In the end, this theory contains room for jumps, rapid change, and chance and it is most consistent with the philosophy of dialectical materialism and the spirit of revolution within evolution. [UTT 4.4.6]

20. **What stunning indictment does Stephen J. Gould make against the fossil record? How does this relate to his theory of punctuated evolution?**

> Gould observed that the "stasis, or nonchange, of most fossil species during their lengthy geological lifespans was tacitly acknowledged by all paleontologists, but almost never studied explicitly because the prevailing theory treated stasis as uninteresting nonevidence for nonevolution… The overwhelming prevalence of stasis became an embarrassing feature of the fossil record, best left ignored as a manifestation of nothing (that is, nonevolution)." In other words Gould is admitting that the fossil record reveals a problem for the traditional and neo-Darwinian theories of evolution.
>
> Unable to fully relinquish the general theory of evolution, Gould suggested that slow and gradual change within a species is not supported by the fossil record simply because evolution is not slow and gradual. Rather, Gould (and Eldridge) theorize that the species remains relatively the same for long periods of time and then undergoes periods of relatively speedy change. Thus, scientists find numerous fossils, but few transitional forms. [UTT 4.4.6]

EVOLUTION EQUATION ACTIVITY

Write the following formula for evolution on board:

Time + Chance + Matter = All Life Forms

Tell students that for these three components to result in the production of all known life forms, the following three assumptions must be taken as fact (write these assumptions on the board):

1. Spontaneous generation occurred
2. All living species are interrelated
3. Lower forms of life gave rise to higher forms

Now explore the following questions with your students:

1. Which of these three assumptions can be verified by scientific investigation?
2. How have evolutionists since Darwin coped with the failure of the fossil record to bear out the third assumption?
3. Which of these three assumptions has been falsified by scientific investigation?

BIOLOGY 4.5

21. What is the main evolutionary concern for Cosmic Humanists? What is this approach called? Cosmic Humanists believe that mankind is moving upward toward an age of higher consciousness.

Because everything is ultimately energy, Cosmic Humanists believe that mankind will one day achieve unity with all of humanity and everything else, a kind of "collective consciousness." Not everyone in the world must embrace the New Age movement before it can become a reality—dedicated Cosmic Humanists can simply act as the catalyst for an evolutionary leap into utopia. This approach is called "Cosmic Evolution." [UTT 4.5.1]

22. How do Cosmic Humanists view science? In what ways do they believe it has been harmful? Do they believe science supports their ideas about reality?

Cosmic Humanists believe the traditional view of science—learning to control the laws of nature—has led to an assault on the balance of planetary harmony. Many Cosmic Humanists believe the scientific revolution that developed during the 1600s was responsible for the rape of the planet. They believe the new science of quantum mechanics (which is strictly theoretical and based on questionable theories) and other scientific discoveries support their pantheistic theology and nonnaturalistic philosophy. [UTT 4.5.2]

23. **How does the evolutionary view of Cosmic Humanism differ from the evolutionary theory purported by Marxist-Leninists and Secular Humanists?**

> Secular Humanists and Marxist-Leninists both believe that evolution is helping humanity progress toward a higher form of biological being. Cosmic Humanists, on the other hand, believe that evolution is helping humanity progress toward a higher consciousness or "New Age." The "science" of evolution provides the guarantee that all humanity will one day achieve this divine consciousness. [UTT 4.5.3]

24. **How is John White's version of the Second Coming different from the one described in the New Testament?**

> For White, Christ's final appearance will not be the moment when all people bow down to acknowledge the Lordship and sovereignty of Christ: "The final appearance of the Christ will be an evolutionary event. It will be the disappearance of egocentric, subhuman man and the ascension of God-centered Man. A new race, a new species, will inhabit the earth—people who collectively have the stature of consciousness that Jesus had." [UTT 4.5.3]

25. **What is the *Gaia Hypothesis*? How does this hypothesis undermine the Darwinian ideal of survival of the fittest?**

> The *Gaia Hypothesis* proposes that taken as a whole, earth behaves not as an inanimate sphere of rock and soil, but more as a biological organism that adjusts and regulates itself. Instead of competition and struggle for survival, the Gaia Hypothesis emphasizes the cooperative spirit of the entire biosphere. Lovelock suggested that the earth was not a "dead" habitat that happens to support life, but is itself a living, integrated system of soil, oceans, wind, and living things interacting together in harmony for the good of the whole. In addition, it runs counter to Darwinian evolution, which insists that life is a result of chance, not purpose. [UTT 4.5.4]

BIOLOGY 4.6

26. **What are three prominent theories of evolution? Why are many Postmodernists unwilling to endorse any particular theory of origins?**

> 1. **Classical Darwinism**—the gradual process of change by natural selection.
> 2. **Neo-Darwinism** (proposed in the 1930s)—Darwin's theory of natural selection combined with change generated by genetic mutation.
> 3. **Punctuated evolution/equilibrium** (proposed in the 1970s)—the theory that changes happen abruptly (geologically speaking) and are usually followed by longer periods of stasis. These abrupt changes are believed to occur in small isolated populations. [UTT 4.6.1]
>
> Each of these three theories of evolution is a metanarrative describing *how reality actually is* and *how life ultimately developed*. In general, Postmodernists are against promoting any overarching explanations of reality or, for that matter, origins.

This is precisely why Postmodernists at Boston University told the Nobel Prize winning evolutionist Steven Weinberg that evolution was merely his metanarrative, "evolution is merely a social construct, like every other schema—a creation of the human mind." [UTT 4.6.1]

27. What is Paul Feyerbend's opinion of how science works?

Feyerbend makes a number of points about the operation of scientific investigation and discovery:

- Many scientific "truths" that are accepted are eventually discarded.
- Data is never neutral, but will always be colored by the biases and agendas of scientists.
- Scientists usually work with unproven assumptions and filter data through their preconceived ideas.
- Theories are regularly tweaked and are constantly evolving.
- The scientific establishment is itself very politicized.

The title of Feyerbend's essay is "Anything Goes." Feyerbend doubts that anything decisive can be known definitively through science. He argues that science is not really knowledge at all. [UTT 4.6.2]

28. How does Thomas Kuhn describe the nature of scientific investigation?

Kuhn points out that science is not merely a progressive, incremental discipline that studies and records facts. Scientific "facts" can be understood and interpreted in a variety of ways depending on the worldview assumptions of the scientist.

Kuhn is also famous for pointing out how scientific theories lose favor. That is, theories don't usually die out because they are disproved; rather older theories usually die out with their proponents while new theories attract the attention of younger scientists, who promote these theories over the older ones. Current scientific theories are just that—*current* theories. Eventually the theories popular today will be replaced by more popular theories in the future. [UTT 4.6.2]

29. What do evolutionary Postmodernists believe about man's role in the process of evolution?

Unlike much of the earlier modernist Darwinists, Postmodernists who hold to evolution assert that the process did not "have man in mind." Humanity is not special nor can we claim that we are continually progressing in our evolution. In fact, Gould argues that homo sapiens are somewhat insignificant when compared with species such as bacteria, which "are—and always have been—the dominant form of life on earth." [UTT 4.6.3]

30. Although Christians acknowledge that scientists have biases and presuppositions, what reasons are given for believing that true knowledge about reality is possible?

To a degree, Christians can agree with Postmodernists: science is not the only source of knowledge, scientists do have biases and agendas, and scientific "truth" does seem to change with the shifting wind. However, unlike Postmodernists, Christians cannot deny that knowledge of the world is possible since we believe God has provided us with a source of knowledge in Scripture. Likewise, it seems logical that we can gain at least some basic knowledge of the world which he created:

- **Moreland**—"Science (at least as most scientists and philosophers understand it) assumes that the universe is intelligible and not capricious, that the mind and senses inform us about reality, that mathematics and language can be applied to the world, that knowledge is possible, that there is a uniformity in nature that justifies inductive inferences from the past to the future and from examined cases of, say, electrons, to unexamined cases, and so forth."

- **Kurtz** insists that rejecting objectivity is a mistake: "We think it profoundly mistaken because science does offer reasonably objective standards for judging its truth claims. Indeed, science has become a universal language, speaking to all men and women no matter what their cultural backgrounds."

- **Campbell**—"The methods used in the sciences have produced powerful explanations about how things work and innumerable useful applications, including technology even its harshest critics would never be without." [UTT 4.6.5]

CREATION/EVOLUTION ACTIVITY

It is essential that students understand that the creation/evolution debate is not relegated simply to some scientist's laboratory or some philosopher's study, but that it has real consequences in everyday life.

If you believe that you are the product of chance, you will most likely live that way (some have even attempted to build societies based on that idea). If you believe that a Designer created you and put you on earth for a distinct purpose, you will live in an entirely different way.

Distribute the "Implications of Creation and Evolution" handout found on your Teacher's CD-ROM in the "Handouts" folder. Contrast the ideas that follow from both opposing worldviews. Help your students understand these points.

"ICONS OF EVOLUTION"
VIDEO OUTLINE

I. Haeckel's Drawings

A. Artistic drawings of vertebrate embryos

1. Fraudulent drawings

2. Omits the earliest stages of development

3. Highlights stages and classes that look the most similar

4. Omits the classes that don't look similar

B. ____**Icons of evolution**____ : distortions of pro-evolution evidence found in textbooks

II. Galapagos Finches

A. Finch beaks change in size and shape

1. The changes are temporary.

2. They oscillate back and forth.

B. ____**Micro-evolution**____ : small changes within the species of a gene pool

C. ____**Macro-evolution**____ : the origin of fundamentally new organisms and plants

III. Four-Winged Fruit Flies

A. Anomaly: Fruit fly with two sets of wings

1. No muscles attached to wings

2. Hopeless cripple

3. Can only survive in the laboratory

4. Would be "selected out" by natural selection

5. Other fruit flies will not mate with them.

B. ____**Neo-Darwinism**____ : randomly occurring mutations provide the raw material needed for evolution

IV. Antibiotic Resistance

A. Bacteria strains resistant to antibiotics

  1. When the parent is re-introduced, the resistant bacteria disappear.

  2. The resistant bacteria is crippled.

B. _____**Fitness cost**_____: how well mutant bacteria survive when the antibiotic is removed

PART TWO

V. Homology

A. _____**Homology**_____: similarity in structure between different organisms

  1. The similarity shows that all living things have common ancestry.

  2. Complex life descended from simple life.

B. Darwin thought that similar animals shared similar genes.

C. Homologous structures can be produced by different genes.

  1. The body of the fruit fly

  2. The body of the wasp

D. Homologous structures can follow different patterns of development

  1. Shark gut—develops in upper cells of embryonic cavity

  2. Lamprey gut—develops in lower cells of embryonic cavity

  3. Frog gut—develops in upper and lower cells of embryonic cavity

VI. Cambrian Explosion

A. Biology textbooks

  1. Depict the progress of life from simple to complex

  2. Over hundreds of millions of years

B. _____**Cambrian explosion**_____: the sudden geological appearance of most major groups of animals

  1. Animals appeared with major differences.

  2. No fossil evidence that they came from a common ancestor

C. Chengjiang's fossils

    1. Complex life at the bottom

    2. Sudden appearance

    3. Pre-Cambrian fossils not ancestors

D. _____Hox_____ genes turned on after development

"ICONS OF EVOLUTION"
VIDEO QUESTIONS

Answer the questions below on a separate sheet of paper and be prepared to review your answers in class.

1. How do Haeckel's drawings seem to support Darwin's theory?

> One element required to prove the theory of evolution was to show a path of common descent. Darwin believed that he found this proof within the similarity of the earliest stages of life. Darwin, theorizing that organisms evolved over time from other organisms, believed that classes of animals within a particular phylum would be similar at the embryonic stage of development. He further theorized that it was only as these organisms developed that they began to look relatively dissimilar. The proposed similarity within a phylum of embryos was thought to demonstrate a common ancestry for organisms within a particular class.
>
> This supposed similarity within the embryos of a particular class is precisely what Haeckel's drawings seem to empirically indicate. Haeckel drew the stages of development for species which fell under the class of vertebrates such as fish, salamanders, turtles, chickens, and various mammals. All looked incredibly similar at the earliest stages of development, thus giving some reasonable proof to Darwin's conjecture about development from a common ancestor some.

2. What was the problem with Haeckel's drawings?

> Haeckel's drawings were published in the 1860s; however, soon after, his colleagues began to call the evidence into question. First, it turns out that Haeckel distorted the images of the embryos at the earliest stages of development to make them look more similar. Second, he only included embryos that would help Darwin's theory. For example, to represent amphibians he used a salamander rather than a frog, which would have looked quite different. Third, Haeckel was selective in Darwin's favor when he ignored two of the seven classes of vertebrates: jawless fish (such as the lamprey) and fish with cartilaginous skeletons (such as the shark). Finally, he omitted the embryos' earliest stages all together. Embryonic development actually starts out looking very dissimilar; midway through development looks vaguely similar, and then finally differs again in the adult stage.

3. Why is the change in a finch's average beak size a good example of natural selection?

> During times of drought, the population of finches on the Galapagos Islands declined drastically over a relatively short period of time. The reason for this phenomenon was that the only food available for the finches was large, thick seeds. The birds that died out were the birds with the smallest (and thus weakest) beaks. The few that survived were those with the largest (and thus strongest) beaks. These surviving birds then reproduced offspring with similar sized beaks. These finches in turn were equally able to crack though seeds and survived to produce similar offspring. This real life illustration demonstrates what most would call "natural selection" or the weeding out of the weakest animals in the competition for resources.

4. **What evidence do the Galapagos finches supply for macro-evolution?**

The theory of evolution (particularly macro-evolution) states that micro-changes can, over time, accumulate into macro-changes, i.e. natural selection, has the ability to build new species. Darwin's finches demonstrate the ability of natural selection to produce micro-changes within a species. However, these birds do not support the grander story of macro-evolution. The finches on the Galapagos never actually netted any change; their average beak size merely oscillated back and forth with the changing of the food supply. In this example, no new species ever emerged. There was (and is) merely fluctuation within a kind.

5. **What is neo-Darwinism?**

Darwin's original theory of evolution rested on the belief that natural selection could favor an organism with positive traits (or traits that help it survive) and could exclude an organism with negative traits (or traits that hinder its survival). According to traditional Darwinism, these traits arose from small inheritable variations within a species, e.g. the Galapagos finches. Therefore, according to traditional Darwinism, favorable traits arise from small variations in the heredity of a species and natural selection acts as the selecting agent to preserve these favorable traits. Neo-Darwinism, however, expanded Darwin's theory to include the occurrence of random genetic mutation. Thus, the ability to evolve need not rest on heredity alone; it could instead be sped up by accidental, yet favorable, molecular changes.

6. **What evidence does the four-winged fruit fly supply for neo-Darwinism?**

Neo-Darwinists hold up the four-winged fruit fly as an example of a favorable random genetic mutation. The problem with the four-winged fruit fly, however, is that its extra set of wings is not actually a favorable attribute. Its extra set of wings is a hindrance to the fruit fly's survival since these additional wings do not function. The anomaly of the four-winged fruit fly can only survive in the laboratory, and in nature it would be selected out. The four-winged fruit fly is actually a bad example of neo-Darwinism because the mutation is less than desirable.

7. **How can antibiotic resistance be demonstrated in the laboratory? What is the fitness cost?**

Antibiotics are chemicals that are produced by microorganisms, and that inhibit or kill the growth of other microorganisms such as bacteria. When an antibiotic is exposed to a Petri dish of bacteria colonies, the bacteria colonies usually die. However, this is not always the case. Sometimes bacteria strains survive. The phenomenon is called "antibiotic resistance."

These bacteria are resistant to antibiotics before the antibiotics are ever introduced to the colony of bacteria. Either the colony's cells are already encoded with antibiotic resistant enzymes or they arose earlier by accident from a DNA mutation. At first, these antibiotic resistant mutations seem beneficial, but since they alter essential molecules inside the cells, they can also be harmful. Without the antibiotics, these resistant bacteria colonies cannot compete with the non-resistant bacteria colonies. In a short period of time they will die. This trade off is known as "fitness cost."

8. **What evidence do antibiotic resistant bacteria provide for neo-Darwinism?**

> According to neo-Darwinism, DNA mutations provide raw material for evolution because they add variations to the process of descent with modification. However, in order for DNA mutations to be favored by natural selection, they must benefit the organism. In this case it does, at least in the short run. Yet this represents only a minor change within an existing species; and since the change is reversed when conditions return to normal, antibiotic resistance is at best an example of microevolution like the oscillating change in the average beak size of the finches of the Galapagos Islands. A new species of bacteria has never arisen from processes of mutation and natural selection.

9. **What is homology? Does the Darwinian theory of homology fit the available evidence?**

> Homology is the study of similarities in patterns of bones or structures of differing organisms. After Darwin, homology was redefined to mean similarity due to common ancestry. Darwin argued that the best explanation for homology was the biological descent with modification from a common archetype. Most scientists before Darwin (and those that today doubt Darwin) see such similarities as a plan in the mind of a Creator—not an ancient archetype, but a model.
>
> This could be compared to the manufacturing of automobiles. The 1953 and 1954 Corvette are different, yet very similar. Likewise, the 1955 model and the 1956 are also similar yet different. The reason for these similarities is that the manufacturers of all models had an archetype in mind. They used similar concepts.
>
> Neo-Darwinists have suggested that two mechanisms can account for homologous structures: similar development pathways and similar genes. However, there are instances of homologous structures that defy both proposed mechanisms. For example, homologous structures can be produced by different genes, as is the case with the body of the fruit fly and the wasp. Homologous structures can also follow different patterns of development, as is the case with the gut of the shark, lamprey, and frog.

10. **What is the Cambrian explosion? How does it challenge evolution's "bottom-up" progression of life?**

> The Cambrian explosion is the relatively sudden appearance of numerous simple and complex animals between 520 and 530 million years ago. The most striking feature of this event is that it turns Darwin's "bottom-up" progression of life on its head, for Darwin proposed an evolution of life from a few simple life forms to many more complex life forms. However, the Cambrian explosion does not fit this model. From this event we can see the sudden appearance of very complicated life forms. Some Darwinists have proposed that conditions before the Cambrian period may not have been favorable for preserving fossils or that the organisms were too soft to be preserved. However, a number of pre-Cambrian fossils have been found, including very simple organisms like bacteria. Instead of branching gradually from an original life form in a tree-like pattern, the fossil record actually looks upside down.

"MYSTERIES OF LIFE'S ORIGINS"
VIDEO OUTLINE

PART ONE

I. Fundamental Questions

    A. What brought life into existence?

        1. Chance and necessity?

        2. Purpose, plan, and design?

    B. Darwin saw life as the product of undirected natural forces.

        1. Time, chance, and natural selection

        2. Example: finch beaks

II. Doubts about Darwinism

    A. **Cells**: miniature molecular machines

    B. **Irreducible complexity**: if any part is removed, the system loses function

        1. Mouse trap (5 essential parts)

        2. Bacteria flagellum (40 essential parts)

    C. Intelligent Design

III. **Co-option**: natural selection's ability to borrow components from one machine to build another

    A. Borrowing from nothing

    B. Assembly sequence

    C. Irreducibly complex borrowed components

IV. How Did Life Begin?

    A. How do you get new living forms and structures from life that already exists?

    B. How did life originate in the first place?

V. Proteins: 30,000 distinct types made from a sequence of 20 different amino acids

    A. **Biochemical predestination**: life was inevitable due to attractions between amino acids

        1. Where did the genetic assembly instructions come from?

        2. How can proteins assemble without instructions from DNA?

VI. First Cell

    A. Chance alone

    B. Natural selection could not have existed before the first living cell.

VII. Cell Factory

    A. **DNA**: storehouse for instructions to build every protein in an organism

    B. **Transcription**: process where DNA is unwound to expose instructions for RNA

    C. **Messenger RNA**: carries the genetic information out of the cell

    D. **Translation**: process where information is translated and protein is built

    E. **Ribosome**: translates and builds specific amino acids from information

    F. Strain folded into protein

    G. Protein moved to where it is needed

VIII. The Design Inference

    A. Improbable object/event

    B. Recognizable pattern

    C. **Information**: small probability and specification

        1. **SETI**: searching for information

        2. **DNA**: world of information

Unit Four

"MYSTERIES OF LIFE'S ORIGINS"
VIDEO QUESTIONS

Answer the questions below on a separate sheet of paper and be prepared to review your answers in class.

1. What is irreducible complexity? What are some examples?

Irreducible complexity is the term for the functional necessity of all the components within a system. A system operating from multiple components is viewed as irreducibly complex—if it loses one part, then the entire system will no longer function. Irreducibly complex systems are systems that cannot function without all of their parts. These parts themselves serve no function apart from the whole system. Considering irreducible complexity, the notion that complex machines can gradually evolve from the collection of its parts is severely suspect, especially since these parts cannot function apart from the whole. Natural selection would have eliminated such things as a drive shaft or a propeller unless they served some purpose, but by themselves a drive shaft and a propeller serve no purpose.

This can be illustrated using the example of a mousetrap—a device that is composed of a catch, spring, hammer, holding bar, and platform. If any one of these parts is missing or defective, it will not work. All components of this entire complex system must be present simultaneously for it to perform its function: catching mice.

A thimble full of cultured liquid can contain more than four billion microscopic single-celled bacteria, each containing circuits, assembly instructions, and even miniature machines. Scientists have discovered a number of minute and complex machines such as molecular trucks that carry supplies from one end of the cell to the other, and machines that capture and transform energy from sunlight. In particular, the bacteria flagellum contains a molecular motor that drives bacteria through liquid. Each motor is a complex, water-cooled machine system of forty intricately arranged mechanical parts including: a u-joint, drive shaft, hook region, and propeller. This marvel of engineering moves at one thousand RPM, can stop on a dime, and reverse at one thousand RPM in the opposite direction. These are all examples of irreducibly complex systems.

Likewise, the body itself is full of microscopic machines. In fact, irreducibly complex cellular machines drive every function of the body. Functions such as hearing, seeing, smelling, tasting, feeling, blood clotting, respiratory action, and immune response require a host of miniature living machines.

2. What is co-option? What are some problems with the idea?

Co-option is the notion that natural selection is capable of borrowing components from one machine for the use of another machine. It is argued that irreducibly complex machines can evolve through co-option.

The problem is first a question of borrowing; from what other machines did these parts come? A second problem is the actual "assembly instructions" of the irreducibly complex machines themselves. The construction of such machines requires not only specific working parts, but also a precise sequence of assembly. This would be similar to the construction of a house where workers follow a detailed blueprint and plan for assembly. The foundation is poured before the walls are erected, plumbing

SM
127

206   **Unit Four**

and electrical fixtures are installed prior to enclosing the walls of the structure, windows must be hung before siding is applied, and shingles are attached only after plywood sheets are nailed to the rafters.

So it is with irreducibly complex systems such as the construction of a flagellum motor. A number of machines actually construct the flagellum motor according to a set of instructions. These machines themselves are also constructed by another set of complex machines. Everything must be present, exact, and done according to a particular sequence, or it will not function and the organism will most likely die.

3. How does Darwinism theorize that life first began? What are some problems with the idea?

If naturalism is true, then life must have originally come from non-life. Living organisms had to somehow come from non-living matter. The simplest form of life is a one-celled organism. To have a one-celled organism, Darwinists must be able to account for its different components—DNA, RNA, and the building blocks of cells—proteins. DNA and RNA store all the information, but it is protein that does all the "day-to-day" jobs like building, maintaining structural requirements, and producing enzymes. It is proteins that actually build the cellular structure.

Proteins are made from other substances called amino acids. There are twenty different amino acids that combine in various patterns to produce one of thirty thousand different known proteins. The theory of how life has evolved from non-life must first explain how amino acids appeared from nonlife, and then how amino acids were arranged into proteins.

The problem with any naturalistic explanation for the origin of the first protein is the origin of the information needed to design, arrange, and build the protein from amino acids. Or, put another way, how could the first proteins have been constructed without the information? Today, scientists know that amino acids are directed into proteins by the information found in DNA. Darwinists bear the burden of postulating how proteins could be formed absent from DNA.

It is possible that chance alone produced the first protein out of amino acids. However, the complexity and enormity of the information makes chance a virtual numeric improbability. Some have proposed that natural selection played a part in the formation of the first protein acting upon random variations of chemicals. However, by definition, natural selection only works on living organisms that reproduce (organisms that possess DNA), which saves favorable genetic code that is passed on to their offspring.

4. What is the process of protein production within the cell?

Within the center of the cell, we find tightly wound strains of what we call DNA—storehouses for the instructions used to build every protein in an organism. In a process known as transcription, a molecular machine first unwinds a section of the DNA helix to expose the genetic instructions needed to construct a specific protein molecule. Another machine then copies these instructions to form a molecule known as messenger RNA. When transcription is complete, the RNA strain carries the genetic information through the nuclear core complex—the gatekeeper for traffic in and out of the cell nucleus.

The messenger RNA strain is directed to a two-part molecular factory called a ribosome. After connecting itself securely, the process of translation begins. Inside the ribosome, a molecular assembly line builds a specifically sequenced chain of amino acids. These amino acids are transported from other parts of the cell, and then linked into chains which are often hundreds of units long. Their sequential arrangement determines which type of protein they manufacture. When the chain is finished, it is moved from the ribosome to a barrel shaped machine that folds it into the precise shape critical to its function. After the chain is folded into a protein, it is then released and shepherded by another molecular machine into the exact location where it is needed.

5. **What is design inference? What are some examples?**

Design inference is the logical process that human beings go through to decide if something was designed or not. If something is designed, then it must have intelligence behind it—someone or something doing the designing. For a pattern to be considered designed, it must be specific (or complex) and it must be highly improbable for it to have occurred randomly on its own. Human beings correctly detect the activity of intelligence whenever they observe a highly recognizable and improbable pattern in an object or event.

To use Mount Rushmore as a specific example, the images on the mountain face appear to have been planned, designed, and etched by intelligence—we come to this conclusion correctly because we see images of four former United States presidents on the mountain face. Human beings correctly assume design based on the fact that 1) there is a recognizable pattern of faces of presidents, and 2) it is highly improbable that these faces occurred by unguided chance.

Whenever these two things are present—small probability and specification (or recognizable pattern)—one can conclude the presence of information. This is exactly what the program SETI (Search for Extra-terrestrial Intelligence) is doing by listening for electromagnetic signals from space. The program is looking for information rich patterns—patterns that are improbable and recognizable. Usually, radio telescopes receive random noise or simple repetitive signals. However, if they ever received a signal containing information (like a large set of prime numbers—an improbable, recognizable pattern), they would logically conclude that it came from an intelligent source.

SETI has not found any information to date. However, scientists have found a wealth of information within the nucleus of the living cell. There is no entity in the known universe that stores and processes more information more efficiently than a DNA molecule. The Intelligent Design movement argues that it is highly logical to conclude that this information originated from an intelligent source.

WHAT IS DARWINISM?
BY PHILLIP E. JOHNSON

SUMMARY

The debate between creationism and Darwinism is often depicted as a dispute between naive biblical literalists, who ignore the overwhelming evidence for evolution, and scientifically enlightened intellectuals. But this is a caricature that serves the purpose of helping to perpetuate a worldview hostile to Christian faith: atheistic naturalism. The debate hinges on five key terms: creationism, evolution, science, religion, and truth. Instead of trying to Christianize evolution we ought instead to challenge the assumption that atheistic naturalism is true.

The popular television game show Jeopardy reverses the usual order of things. Instead of being asked a question to which they must supply the answer, contestants are given the answer and asked to provide the appropriate question. This format suggests an insight that is applicable to law, to science, and indeed to just about everything. More important than knowing all the answers is knowing what question is being asked.

That insight is the starting point for my inquiry into Darwinian evolution and its relationship to creation, because Darwinism is the answer to two very different kinds of questions. First, Darwinian theory tells us how a certain amount of diversity in life forms can develop once we have various types of complex living organisms already in existence. If a small population of birds happens to migrate to an isolated island, for example, a combination of inbreeding, mutation, and natural selection may cause this isolated population to develop different characteristics from those possessed by the ancestral population on the mainland. When the theory is understood in this limited sense, Darwinian evolution is uncontroversial and has no important philosophical or theological implications.

Evolutionary biologists are not content merely to explain how variation occurs within limits. They aspire to answer a much broader question—how complex organisms like birds, flowers, and human beings came to exist at all. The Darwinian answer to this second question is that the creative force that produced complex plants and animals is essentially the same as the mechanism producing variations in flowers, insects, and domestic animals before our very eyes. In the words of Ernst Mayr, the dean of living Darwinists, "Transspecific evolution [i.e., macroevolution] is nothing but an extrapolation and magnification of the events that take place within populations and species."

Neo-Darwinian evolution in this broad sense is a philosophical doctrine so lacking in empirical support that Mayr's successor at Harvard, Stephen Jay Gould, in a reckless moment once pronounced it "effectively dead. "Yet neo-Darwinism is far from dead. On the contrary, it is continually proclaimed in textbooks and the media as unchallengeable fact. How does it happen that so many scientists and intellectuals, who pride themselves on their empiricism and open-mindedness, continue to accept an unempirical theory as scientific fact?

DEFINING THE ISSUES

The answer to that question lies in the definition of five key terms—creationism, evolution, science, religion, and truth. Once we understand how these words are used in evolutionary discourse, the continued ascendancy of neo-Darwinism will be no mystery, and we need no longer be deceived by claims that the theory is supported by "overwhelming evidence." As we shall see, there are powerful vested interests in this area that thrive in the midst of ambiguity and confusion. Those who insist on defining terms precisely and using them consistently may find themselves regarded with suspicion and hostility, and even accused of being enemies of science.

Creationism

The first word is creationism, which means simply a belief in creation. In Darwinist usage, which dominates not only popular and professional scientific literature but also the media, a creationist is a person who takes the creation account in the Book of Genesis as true in the most literal sense. The earth was created in a single week of six 24-hour days no more than 10,000 years ago; the major features of the geological record were produced by Noah's flood; and there have been no major innovations in the forms of life since the beginning. It is a major theme of Darwinist propaganda that the only persons who have any doubts about Darwinism are young-earth creationists of this sort, who are always portrayed as rejecting the clear and convincing evidence of science to preserve a religious prejudice. The implication is that citizens of modern society are faced with a choice that is really no choice at all. Either they reject science altogether and retreat to a premodern worldview, or they believe everything the Darwinists tell them.

In a broader sense, however, a creationist is simply a person who believes in the existence of a creator who brought about the world and its living inhabitants for a purpose. Whether the process of creation took a single week or billions of years is relatively unimportant from a philosophical or theological standpoint. Creation by gradual processes over geological ages may create problems for biblical interpretation, but it creates none for the basic principle of theistic religion. Creation in this broad sense, according to a 1991 Gallup poll, is the creed of 87 percent of Americans. Is creation in this sense consistent with evolution?

Evolution

The answer is no, when evolution is understood in the Darwinian sense. To Darwinists evolution means naturalistic evolution, an insistence that science must assume that the cosmos is a closed system of material causes and effects, which can never be influenced by anything outside of material nature, such as God. In the beginning, an explosion of matter created the cosmos, and undirected, naturalistic evolution produced everything that followed. Thus, no intelligent purpose guided evolution. If intelligence exists today, that is only because it has itself evolved through purposeless material processes.

At bottom the theory must be based on chance, because that is what is left when we have ruled out everything involving intelligence or purpose. But theories invoking only chance are not credible. One thing everyone acknowledges is that living organisms are enormously complex—far more so than, say, a computer or an airplane. That such complex entities came into existence simply by chance is clearly less credible than that they were designed and constructed by a creator. To back up their claim that this appearance of intelligent design is an illusion, Darwinists therefore need to provide a building force that is mindless and purposeless. Natural selection is by far the most plausible candidate.

If we assume that random genetic mutations provided the new genetic information needed, say, to give a small mammal a start towards wings, and if we assume that each tiny step in the process of wing building gave the animal an increased chance of survival, then natural selection ensured that the favored creatures would thrive and reproduce. It logically follows that wings can and will appear as if by the plan of a designer. Of course, if wings or other improvements do not appear, the theory explains their absence just as well. The needed mutations didn't arrive, or "developmental constraints" closed off certain possibilities, or natural selection favored something else. There is no requirement that any of this speculation be confirmed by either experimental or fossil evidence. To Darwinists just being able to imagine the process is sufficient to confirm that something like that must have happened.

Biologist Richard Dawkins calls the process of creation by mutation and selection "the blind watchmaker," by which he means that a purposeless, materialistic designing force substitutes for the "watchmaker" deity of natural theology. The creative power of the blind watchmaker is supported only by very slight evidence, such as the famous example of a moth population in which the percentage of dark moths increased during a period when the birds were better able to see light moths against the smoke-darkened background trees. This may be taken to show that natural selection can change organisms, but not that it can create organisms that were not already in existence.

Even such slight evidence is more than sufficient, however, because evidence is not really necessary to prove something that is practically self-evident. The existence of a potent blind watchmaker follows deductively from the philosophical premise that nature had to do its own creating. There can be argument about the details, but if God was not in the picture something very much like Darwinism simply has to be true, regardless of the evidence.

Science

That brings me to my third term, science. We have already seen that Darwinists assume as a first principle that the history of the cosmos and its life forms is fully explicable on naturalistic principles. This reflects a philosophical doctrine called scientific naturalism, a necessary consequence of the inherent limitations of science. What scientific naturalism does, however, is transform the limitations of science into limitations on reality, in the interest of maximizing the explanatory power of science and its practitioners. It is, of course, entirely possible to study organisms scientifically on the premise that they were all created by God, just as scientists study airplanes and even works of art without denying that these objects are intelligently designed. The problem with allowing God a role in the history of life is not that science would cease, but rather that scientists would have to acknowledge the existence of something important that is outside the boundaries of natural science. For scientists who want to be able to explain everything, this is an intolerable possibility.

The second feature of scientific naturalism that is important for our purpose is its set of rules governing the criticism and replacement of a paradigm. A paradigm is a general theory, like the Darwinian theory of evolution, which has achieved general acceptance in the scientific community. The paradigm unifies the various specialties that make up the research community, and guides research in all of them. Thus, zoologists, botanists, geneticists, molecular biologists, and paleontologists all see their research as aimed at filling out the details of the Darwinian paradigm.

If molecular biologists see a pattern of apparently neutral mutations, which have no apparent effect on an organism's fitness, they must find a way to reconcile their findings with the paradigm's requirement that natural selection guides evolution. This they can do by postulating a sufficient quantity of invisible adaptive mutations, supposedly accumulated by natural selection. Similarly, if paleontologists see new fossil species appearing suddenly in the fossil record, and remaining basically unchanged thereafter, they must perform whatever contortions are necessary to force this recalcitrant evidence into a model of incremental change through the accumulation of micromutations.

Supporting the paradigm may even require what in other contexts would be called deception. As Niles Eldredge candidly admitted, "We paleontologists have said that the history of life supports [the story of gradual adaptive change], all the while knowing it does not."[1] Eldredge explained that this pattern of misrepresentation occurred because of "the certainty so characteristic of evolutionary ranks since the late 1940s, the utter assurance not only that natural selection operates in nature, but that we know precisely how it works." This certainty produced a degree of dogmatism that Eldredge says resulted in the relegation of paleontologists to the "lunatic fringe" who reported that "they saw something out of kilter between contemporary evolutionary theory, on the one hand, and patterns of change in the fossil record on the other."[2] Under the circumstances, prudent paleontologists understandably swallowed their doubts and supported the ruling ideology. To abandon the paradigm would be to abandon the scientific community; to ignore the paradigm and just gather the facts would be to earn the demeaning label of "stamp collector" (i.e., one who does not theorize).

As many philosophers of science have observed, the research community does not abandon a paradigm in the absence of a suitable replacement. This means that negative criticism of Darwinism, however devastating it may appear to be, is essentially irrelevant to the professional researchers. A critic may point out, for example, that the evidence that natural selection has any creative power is somewhere between weak and nonexistent. That is perfectly true, but to Darwinists the more important point is this: If natural selection did not do the creating, what did? "God" is obviously unacceptable, because such a being is unknown to science. "We don't know" is equally unacceptable, because to admit ignorance would be to leave science adrift without a guiding principle. To put the problem in the most practical terms: it is impossible to write or evaluate a grant proposal without a generally accepted theoretical framework.

The paradigm rule explains why Gould's acknowledgment that neo-Darwinism is "effectively dead" had no significant effect on the Darwinist faithful, or even on Gould himself. Gould made that statement in a paper predicting the emergence of a new general theory of evolution, one based on the macromutational speculations of the Berkeley geneticist Richard Goldschmidt.[3] When the new theory did not arrive as anticipated, the alternatives were either to stick with Ernst Mayr's version of neo-Darwinism or to concede that biologists do not know of a naturalistic mechanism that can produce biological complexity. That was no choice at all. Gould had to beat a hasty retreat back to classical Darwinism to avoid giving aid and

[1] Niles Eldredge, *Time Frames* (Portsmouth, NH: Heinemann, 1986), 144.

[2] Ibid., 93.

[3] Stephen Jay Gould, "Is a New and General Theory of Evolution Emerging?" *Paleobiology 6* (1980): 119–30, reprinted in Maynard Smith, ed., *Evolution Now: A Century after Darwin* (New York: W. H. Freeman, 1982).

comfort to the enemies of scientific naturalism, including those disgusting creationists. Having to defend a dead theory tooth and nail can hardly be a satisfying activity, and it is no wonder that Gould lashes out with fury at people such as myself who call attention to his predicament.[4] I do not mean to ridicule Gould, because I have a genuinely high regard for the man as one of the few Darwinists who has recognized the major problems with the theory and reported them honestly. His tragedy is that he cannot admit the clear implications of his own thought without effectively resigning from science.

The continuing survival of Darwinist orthodoxy illustrates Thomas Kuhn's famous point that the accumulation of anomalies never in itself falsifies a paradigm, since "to reject one paradigm without substituting another is to reject science itself."[5] This practice may be appropriate as a way of carrying on the professional enterprise called science, but it can be grossly misleading when it is imposed on persons who are asking questions other than the ones scientific naturalists want to ask. Suppose, for example, that I want to know whether God really had something to do with creating living organisms. A typical Darwinian response is that there is no reason to invoke supernatural action because Darwinian selection was capable of performing the job. To evaluate that response, I need to know whether natural selection really has the fantastic creative power attributed to it. It is not a sufficient answer to say that scientists have nothing better to offer. The fact that scientists don't like to say "we don't know" tells me nothing about what they really do know.

I am not suggesting that scientists have to change their rules about retaining and discarding paradigms. All I want them to do is to be candid about the disconfirming evidence and admit, if it is the case, that they are hanging on to Darwinism only because they prefer a shaky theory to having no theory at all. What they insist on doing, however, is to present Darwinian evolution to the public as a fact that every rational person is expected to accept. If there are reasonable grounds to doubt the theory, such dogmatism is ridiculous, whether or not the doubters have a better theory to propose.

To believers in creation, Darwinists seem thoroughly intolerant and dogmatic when they insist that their own philosophy must have a monopoly in the schools and the media. Darwinists do not see themselves that way, of course. On the contrary, they often feel aggrieved when creationists (in either the broad or narrow sense) ask to have their own arguments heard and considered. To insist that schoolchildren be taught that Darwinian evolution is a fact is, in their minds, merely to protect the integrity of science education; to present the other side of the case would be to allow fanatics to force their opinions on others. Even college professors have been forbidden to express their doubts about Darwinian evolution in the classroom, and it seems widely believed that the Constitution not only permits but actually requires such restrictions on academic freedom.[6]

Religion

To explain this bizarre situation, we must define our fourth term: religion. Suppose that a skeptic argues that evidence for biological creation by natural selection is obviously lacking, and that in the circumstances we ought to give serious consideration to the possibility that the development of life required some input from a preexisting, purposeful creator. To scientific naturalists, this suggestion is "creationist" and therefore unacceptable in principle, because it invokes an entity unknown to science. What is worse, it suggests the possibility that this creator may have communicated in some way with humans, perhaps with real prophets—persons with a genuine knowledge of God. Such persons could be dangerous rivals for the scientists as cultural authorities.

Naturalistic philosophy has worked out a strategy to prevent this problem from arising: it labels naturalism as science and theism as religion. The former is then classified as knowledge, and the latter as mere belief. The distinction is of critical importance, because only knowledge can be objectively valid for everyone; belief is valid only for the believer, and should never be passed off as knowledge. The student who thinks that 2 and 2 make 5, or that water is not made up of hydrogen and oxygen, or that the theory of evolution is not true, is not expressing a minority viewpoint. He or she is ignorant, and the job of education

---

[4] See Stephen Jay Gould, "Impeaching a Self-Appointed Judge," *Scientific American* (July 1992), 118–22. *Scientific American* refused to publish my response, but the response did appear in the March 1993 issue of *Perspectives on Science and Christian Faith: The Journal of the American Scientific Affiliation.*

[5] Thomas S. Kuhn, *The Structure of Scientific Revolutions* (Chicago: University of Chicago Press, 1970), 79.

[6] This issue is discussed in my article "What (If Anything) Hath God Wrought?" at www.arn.org.

is to cure that ignorance and to replace it with knowledge. Thus, students in the public schools must be taught at an early age that "evolution is a fact," and as time goes by they will gradually learn that evolution means naturalism.

The proposition that God was in any way involved in our creation is effectively outlawed, since naturalistic evolution is by definition in the category of scientific knowledge and what contradicts knowledge is implicitly false, or imaginary. That is why it is possible for scientific naturalists in good faith to claim on the one hand that their science says nothing about God, and on the other to claim that they have said everything that can be said about God. In naturalistic philosophy both propositions are at bottom the same. All that needs to be said about God is that there is nothing to be said of God, because on that subject we can have no knowledge.

Truth

Our fifth term is truth. Truth as such is not a particularly important concept in naturalistic philosophy. The reason for this is that "truth" suggests an unchanging absolute, whereas scientific knowledge is a dynamic concept. Like life, knowledge evolves and grows into superior forms. What was knowledge in the past is not knowledge today, and the knowledge of the future will surely be far superior to what we have now. Only naturalism itself, and the unique validity of science as the path to knowledge, are absolute. There can be no criterion for truth outside of scientific knowledge, no mind of God to which we have access.

This way of understanding things persists even when scientific naturalists employ religious-sounding language. For example, the physicist Stephen Hawking ended his famous book A Brief History of Time with the prediction that humanity might one day "know the mind of God." This phrasing gives some friends of mine the mistaken impression that he has some attraction to theism. In context, Hawking was not referring to a supernatural eternal agent, but to the possibility that scientific knowledge will eventually become complete and all-encompassing because it will have explained the movements of material particles in all circumstances.

The monopoly of science in the realm of knowledge explains why evolutionary biologists do not find it meaningful to address the question whether Darwinism is true. They will gladly concede that the theory is incomplete and that further research is needed. At any given point in time, however, the reigning theory of naturalistic evolution represents the state of scientific knowledge about how we came into existence. Scientific knowledge is by naturalistic definition the closest approximation of absolute truth available to us. To ask whether this knowledge is true is to miss the point, and to betray a misunderstanding of "how science works."

CHRISTIANS AND DARWINISM

So far I have described the metaphysical categories by which scientific naturalists have excluded the topic of God from rational discussion, and thus ensured that Darwinism's fully naturalistic creation story is effectively true by definition. There is no need to explain why atheists find this system of thought control congenial. What is more difficult to understand—at least at first—is the strong support Darwinism continues to receive in the Christian academic world. Attempts to investigate the credibility of Darwinist evolution are regarded with little enthusiasm by many leading Christian professors of science and philosophy, even at institutions that are generally regarded as theologically conservative. Given that Darwinism is inherently naturalistic and therefore antagonistic to the idea that God had anything to do with the history of life, and that it plays the central role in ensuring agnostic domination of the intellectual culture, one might have supposed that Christian intellectuals (along with religious Jews) would be eager to find its weak spots.

Instead, the prevailing view among Christian professors has been that Darwinism—or "evolution," as they tend to call it—is unbeatable, and that it can be interpreted to be consistent with Christian belief. In fact Darwinism is unbeatable as long as one accepts the thought categories of scientific naturalism that I have been describing. The problem is that those same thought categories make Christian theism, or any other theism, absolutely untenable. If science has exclusive authority to tell us how life was created, and if science is committed to naturalism, and if science never discards a paradigm until it is presented with an acceptable naturalistic alternative, then Darwinism's position is impregnable within science. Yet the same reasoning that makes Darwinism inevitable also bans God from taking any action within the history of the Cosmos, which makes theism illusory. Theistic naturalism is self-contradictory.

Some hope to avoid the contradiction by asserting that naturalism rules only within the realm of science, and that there is a separate realm called "religion" in which theism can flourish. The problem with this, as we have already seen, is that in a naturalistic culture scientific conclusions are considered to be knowledge, or even fact. What is outside of fact is fantasy, or at best subjective belief. Theists who accommodate scientific naturalism therefore may never affirm that their God is real in the same sense that evolution is real. This rule is essential to the entire naturalistic mindset that produced Darwinism in the first place.

If God exists he could certainly work through scientifically explainable processes if that is what he wanted to do, but he could also create by some means totally outside the ken of our science. Once we put him into the picture, there is no good reason to attribute the creation of biological complexity to random mutation and natural selection. Direct evidence that these mechanisms have substantial creative power is not to be found in nature, the laboratory, or the fossil record. An essential step in the reasoning that establishes that Darwinian selection created the wonders of biology, therefore, is that nothing else was available. Theism says that something else was available.

Perhaps the contradiction is hard to see when it is stated at an abstract level, so I will give a more concrete example. Persons who advocate the compromise position called "theistic evolution" are in my experience always vague about what they mean by "evolution." They have good reason to be vague. As we have seen, Darwinian evolution is by definition unguided and purposeless, and such evolution cannot in any meaningful sense be theistic. For evolution to be genuinely theistic it must be guided by God, whether this means God programmed the process in advance or stepped in from time to time to push it in the right direction. To Darwinists evolution guided by God is a soft form of creationism—that is to say, it is not evolution at all. To repeat, this understanding goes to the very heart of Darwinist thinking. Allow a preexisting supernatural intelligence to guide evolution, and this omnipotent being can do a whole lot more than that.

Of course, theists can think of evolution as God-guided whether naturalistic Darwinists like it or not. One problem with having a private definition for theists, however, is that the scientific naturalists have the power to decide what the term "evolution" means in public discourse, including the science classes in the public schools. If theistic evolutionists broadcast the message that evolution as they understand it is harmless to theistic religion, they are misleading their constituents unless they add a clear warning that the version of evolution advocated by the entire body of mainstream science is something else altogether. That warning is never clearly delivered, because the main point of theistic evolution is to preserve peace with the mainstream scientific community. Theistic evolutionists therefore unwittingly serve the purposes of the scientific naturalists by helping persuade the religious community to lower its guard against the incursion of naturalism.

We are now in a position to answer the question, What is Darwinism? Darwinism is a theory of empirical science only at the level of microevolution, where it provides a framework for explaining phenomena such as the diversity that arises when small populations become reproductively isolated from the main body of the species. As a general theory of biological creation Darwinism is not empirical at all. Rather, it is a necessary implication of a philosophical doctrine called scientific naturalism, which is based on the nonscientific assumption that God was always absent from the realm of nature. Evolution in the Darwinian sense is inherently antithetical to theism, although evolution in some entirely different and nonnaturalistic sense could conceivably (if not demonstrably) have been God's chosen method of creation.

To return to the game of Jeopardy with which we started, let us say that Darwinism is the answer. What, then, is the question? The question is: "How must creation have occurred if we assume that God had nothing to do with it?" Theistic evolutionists err in trying to Christianize the answer to a question that comes straight out of the agenda of scientific naturalism. What we need to do instead is challenge the assumption that the only questions worth asking are the ones that assume that naturalism is true.

---

*This essay originally appeared in the *Christian Research Journal*:

    Phillip Johnson, "What is Darwinism?," *Christian Research Journal* Vol. 19, No. 4, (1997), 20–26.

**Reproduction rights granted by the *Christian Research Journal*.

WHAT IS DARWINISM?
ESSAY QUESTIONS

Answer the questions below on a separate sheet of paper and be prepared to review your answers in class.

1. **What are the two tenets of Darwinian evolution?**

> First, Darwinism claims that the diversity in various complex living (yet already existent) organisms is a combination of inbreeding, mutation, and natural selection. For example, if a small group of birds happens to migrate to an isolated island, then variations may arise within this isolated population causing it to develop characteristics different from those of their ancestral population on the mainland. This component is known as microevolution (or natural selection) and is incontrovertible, having no important philosophical or theological implications. This aspect of evolution is observable and reproducible, both in controlled animal breeding and the classical example of natural finch variations on the Galapagos Islands.
>
> Second, Darwinism claims that this first process can be applied more broadly to explain how living organisms originally came into existence. This aspect, known as macroevolution (or "molecules-to-man evolution"), is an inconclusive and very controversial theory derived from naturalistic assumptions widely applied to empirical study. In other words, Darwinian scientists studying fossil evidence assume that nature is all that exists and then develop an alternative theory (to that of biblical creation) for the origin of the species based on that assumption—atheistic evolution. [SM p. 128]

2. **What defines a creationist?**

> In a broad sense, a creationist is simply a person who believes in the existence of a creator who brought about the world and its living inhabitants, whom he created in his image, for a purpose.
>
> A major theme of the Darwinian worldview is that the only people who have any doubts about Darwinism are young-earth creationists who reject the clear and convincing evidence of science to preserve a religious prejudice. Every creationist is caricatured as a young-earther who denies every aspect of evolution, even microevolution (natural selection). While there are both old-earth and young-earth creationists, both parties generally accept microevolution, but completely reject the theory of macroevolution ("molecules-to-man" evolution). [SM pp.128–9]

3. **What is Darwinian evolution?**

> Darwinists hold to a theory of naturalistic evolution—an assumption that the cosmos is a closed system of material causes and effects, which can never be influenced by anything outside of material nature, such as God.
>
> The foundation of this theory, therefore, must be random chance, which is all that remains when extra-material intelligence or purpose is disregarded. Darwinists insist that random genetic mutations in combination with the process of natural selection are able to explain the complexity, diversity, and appearance of design in life. [SM p. 129]

Unit Four

SM 134

4. **How does naturalism affect science?**

In the interest of being able to explain everything by naturalistic causes, Darwinists limit the nature of ultimate reality to naturalistic processes alone. Consequently, what should be viewed as valid supernatural theories are not even considered.

Science, by definition, is a means of objective inquiry. It is entirely possible to study life scientifically on the premise that God created the universe and all life in it. This is how scientists study airplanes and even works of art (i.e. with the assumption that these objects were intelligently designed and created). The problem with allowing God a role in the history of life is not that such a consideration would be unscientific, but rather that naturalistic science would be limited as to how much it could study and explain. [SM pp. 129–31]

5. **Why is the paradigm of naturalism revered so highly among Darwinists?**

Many scientists revere the paradigm (or worldview) of naturalism, because it is assumed to be an unbiased explanation of reality—naturalism is thought to explain only the obvious. Therefore, the naturalist assumes that every experiment, inquiry, or test simply helps us to discover and understand our naturalistic universe. This mindset is analogous to the way most Christians see the world. They assume that God created the world a priori, so that when they examine any part of the universe, they see it as discovering the person and work of God.

Just as the creationist reveres as indisputable the paradigm that "God is and God creates," the naturalist holds the paradigm that "the natural world is all that exists" as unquestionable doctrine. [SM p. 130]

6. **Why is Darwinism generally a dogmatic belief?**

Darwinists behave in an intolerant manner when they insist that naturalism must have a monopoly in the schools and the media. In fact, many Darwinists are often frustrated with creationists who ask that valid arguments against evolution be heard and considered in the public arena. They believe they are protecting the integrity of scientific education by insisting that school children be taught Darwinian evolution as fact when it is actually lacking sufficient proof. Darwinists insist that presenting any challenge to the Darwinian paradigm would allow religious fanatics a platform to preach their dogmatism. Ironically, this is exactly what the Darwinists want for themselves and their colleagues. [SM p. 131]

7. **What distinction do Darwinists make between religion and science?**

Scientific naturalists have created a dichotomy between science and religion. The former is classified as knowledge, and the latter as mere belief. The distinction is of critical importance, because only knowledge can be objectively valid for everyone—belief is valid only for the believer and should never be passed off as knowledge. The student who thinks that the theory of evolution is not true is not just expressing a minority viewpoint—he or she is ignorant, and the job of education is to cure that ignorance by replacing it with knowledge. Creationists who argue for serious consideration of the possibility that the development of life required some input from a preexisting, purposeful Creator are not even considered. Even atheists and agnostics who doubt evolution are equally dismissed. [SM pp. 131–2]

8. **What is the Darwinian view of truth?**

For the Darwinist, the closest thing to absolute truth is Darwinism. They will admit that their theory is incomplete and that further research is still needed to fill in some gaps, but they hold that only naturalism and science can lead us to absolute knowledge. Therefore, just as life has evolved, knowledge evolves and will someday grow into an all-explaining truth far superior to what we have now. [SM p. 132]

9. **Why are Christianity and Darwinism incompatible?**

Today, many Christians show strong support for Darwinism, believing that attempts to challenge the credibility of Darwinism are futile. Given Darwinism's inherent naturalistic basis, and therefore its utter antagonism to the idea that God had anything to do with the history of life, these two ideas should be seen as irreconcilable.

The prevailing view among Christian professors, however, is that Darwinism can be interpreted as consistent with Christian belief. The problem is that Darwinism, by definition, weakens the inherent theistic foundation of biblical creationism. If naturalist science has exclusive authority to tell us how life was created, and if science will never discard a paradigm until it is presented with an acceptable naturalistic alternative, then science will continue to exclude God. Theistic naturalism is therefore self-contradictory.

Some Christians try to avoid this contradiction by asserting that naturalism rules only within the realm of science, and that there is a separate realm called "religion" in which theism can flourish. The problem with this belief is that scientific conclusions are considered to be fact, while everything else outside of fact is, at best, subjective belief, and at worst utter fantasy. As a result, theists who accommodate scientific naturalism may never affirm that their God is real in the same sense that evolution is real. [SM pp. 132–3]

10. **What is Darwinism?**

Darwinism is a theory of empirical science which provides an explanation for the natural development of life—the origins of all living things on a macro level, and the diversity within species on a micro level. The theory of macroevolution ("molecules-to-man" evolution) is based on the measurable and observable phenomena of microevolution (natural selection). As a macro theory of biological creation, Darwinism is not empirical at all. Rather, it is a philosophical doctrine of naturalism based on the nonscientific assumption that the supernatural has always been absent from the realm of nature. Evolution, in the Darwinian sense, is inherently antithetical to theism. [SM p. 133]

DEAR DOUG

WRITING ASSIGNMENT

Hello again!

Last week before Thanksgiving break! I can hardly remember what life feels like without classes to worry about—nothing to do next week but sleep in and eat!

Speaking of classes, biology is driving me crazy. I have to read the textbook in order to pass the class, but it is so full of evolution that I hate to open it. The prof has been going on and on about how the facts of evolution have been scientifically proven and how college is supposed to be where our childish beliefs are replaced with the truth. Of course, everyone knew he was talking about me. I made the mistake last week of casually mentioning creation, and he hasn't missed a chance yet to bash it.

I have to tell you though… some of this stuff is starting to make sense. After all, evolution has a scientific basis, while creation is just a religious belief. I'm not sure how we can say that the Bible should take precedence over all the scientific evidence supporting evolution.

We were all talking about this the other day at lunch. Sarah said that scientists have pretty well proven that life evolved through a slow gradual process of natural selection, with random mutations making each generation better than the last one. Our biology professor did share some pretty good pieces of proof—finches, peppered moths, bacteria mutation, etc. But I'm just not sure if those examples explain evolution on a grand scale. Do you think Darwin's theory of evolution explains how life began?

Mark has been arguing with the professor, though. He thinks the original concept of evolution is too slow and that instead life evolved in big leaps separated by long static pauses. He says this explains why there is a lack of transitional life forms. But does this explain how we got here any better than regular Darwinism? Nathan agreed with Mark, but said he was being too "naturalistic"—that the physical side isn't as important as our steps toward becoming more enlightened and even divine. For a Christian, that kinda makes sense. At least Nathan believes we have a spiritual side. Do you think life is only a search for enlightenment?

Afterwards, Muhammad walked back to the dorm with me and told me that he didn't think we evolved. He asked me what I thought, but I wasn't sure how to answer him. I'd like to believe the Bible, but in this area, it just doesn't seem to be adequate, especially with all the verifiable evidence the biology prof uses. What does Christianity really have to say about how life began?

Thanks for being my resource on all these questions—I don't feel quite so awkward asking you. Anyway, gotta run. There's a paper I have to turn in before I leave, and maybe I can squeeze in lunch with Amber. I'd love to have you meet her sometime!

Talk to you later,
Doug

Doug has brought up four different subjects; below is a rough outline of possible responses.

1. Does Darwin's theory of evolution explain how life began? (12.5 points)

Darwin originally theorized that the process of natural selection could select out favorable variations within a species and discard unfavorable variations. Darwin further theorized that over vast amounts of time, species would gradually evolve into new species. However, Darwin had no theory regarding how variations arise in the first place, though he pointed to dog breeds as an example.

The primary problem with evolution is that it supposes that small changes can accumulate over vast periods of time to produce macro changes. In other words, it supposes that small changes within the species of dog could someday produce an entirely different species, like a horse. While microevolution (natural selection) does happen within species, macroevolution—one species evolving into another species—has no scientific basis.

2. Does punctuated equilibrium more adequately explain how life began? (12.5 points)

Another issue that plagues Darwin's theory is the lack of transitional fossils. Because of this obvious problem, many scientists have suggested an alternative theory to the slow and gradual accumulation of traits by natural selection—punctuated equilibrium. This theory suggests that the lack of transitional evidence is the result of a more rapid form of evolution. In other words, it is suggested that changes occur relatively quickly and thus leave few transitional fossils. This theory, however, comes with its own set of problems. First, punctuated equilibrium still relies upon the Darwinian mechanism of natural selection, but does not suggest a mechanism capable of producing accelerated changes.

Second, this theory is based on a *lack* of evidence rather than evidence. Darwinists are still presupposing naturalism and evolution; they are merely tweaking their assumptions to account for their worldview. However, this lack of evidence could indeed mean that any macro theory of evolution is untrue.

3. Is evolution toward divinity compatible with Christianity? (12.5 points)

This view of both evolution and humanity's potential divinity are not compatible with Christianity: God was supernaturally responsible for the creation of the world (Genesis 1) and requires that humanity worship him and not themselves (Exodus 20:2–6). Moreover, there is no objective scientific evidence that suggests that we have evolved by any Darwinian scheme.

4. What is the Christian view of biology? (12.5 points)

The Christian view of biology is known as "creationism"—the belief that God created the world. Since the creationist perspective postulates a designer, Christians believe this position most adequately accounts for the design and complexity seen in nature. Most Christians trust the account in Genesis as authoritative (see also Mark 10:6 and Colossians 1:16). Science and Christianity are demonstrated to be compatible and to declare in unison that God "created all things" (Ephesians 3:9). The Bible gives us information about God and his universe; science gives us information about God's universe.

UNIT FOUR TEST

'BIOLOGY' TEXTBOOK QUESTIONS

Matching: (1 point possible per answer [2 for 90-day])
*some options may be used more than once or not at all; some questions may have multiple answers.

1. __f__ Christianity

2. __f__ Islam

3. __b__ Secular Humanism

4. __c__ Marxism-Leninism

5. __g__ Cosmic Humanism

6. __c__ Postmodernism

a. Traditional Darwinism
b. Neo-Darwinian Evolution
c. Punctuated Evolution
d. Lamarckism
e. Paradigms of Destruction
f. Creationism
g. Cosmic Evolution

Fill in the Blank: (2 points possible per answer [4 for 90-day])

7. _____Teleology_____ is the study of design and purpose in nature.

8. _____DNA_____ is the storehouse containing all the genetic information necessary for life.

9. _____Spontaneous generation_____ is the theory that non-living matter gave rise to living organisms.

10. _____Second Law of Thermodynamics_____ states that although the total energy in the cosmos remains constant, the amount of energy available to do useful work is always decreasing.

11. _____Natural selection_____ is the natural process of choosing favorable characteristics and eliminating unfavorable ones through such things as competition, predators, geography, time, etc.

12. _____Mutation_____ is a change in genetic makeup.

Short answer: (5 points possible per answer [5 for 90-day])
13. What are some problems with the theory of theistic evolution?

The first problem with theistic evolution is that it is based on a bad interpretation of the Scripture. This method of bringing about life, and especially mankind, seems especially cruel. Also, theistic evolution is particularly damaging to one's view of Adam and Eve. If this account is no more than metaphoric or mythological characters, then it is hard to account for original sin and our need for Christ. Lastly, the theory of evolution in general is undergoing serious challenges from within the scientific community.

CD-ROM

14. Why must "modern" science rule out creation? Does this reasoning pose a problem for evolution as well? Why or why not?

"Modern" science studies and theorizes only about things that can be observed and measured. This naturalistic restriction necessarily rules out the existence of the supernatural because the supernatural cannot lie, for lack of a better term, beyond the natural world. Yet, it should be noted that by modern science's strict definition, it cannot consistently render judgment on the theory of evolution because it can neither be measured nor observed (i.e. one-time-only historical events fall outside the parameters of the scientific method).

15. What form of evolution does Marxism embrace?

Marxists expect evolution to work according to the dialectic—when thesis (a species) and antithesis (some aspect of the environment) clash, the synthesis (a new species) occurs rapidly. In 1972, an evolutionary theory that better fit the dialectical process was postulated: punctuated equilibrium or punctuated evolution, so called because it theorizes evolution as working itself out in periods of "punctuated" or speedy change, followed by periods of "equilibrium" or stasis. In the end, this theory contains room for jumps, rapid change, and chance. It is most consistent with the philosophy of dialectical materialism and the spirit of revolution within evolution.

16. How does the evolutionary view of Cosmic Humanists differ from the evolutionary theory purported by Marxist-Leninists and Secular Humanists?

Secular Humanists and Marxist-Leninists both believe that evolution is progressing humanity toward a higher form of biological being. Cosmic Humanists, on the other hand, believe that evolution is progressing humanity toward higher being or "New Age." The "science" of evolution provides the guarantee that all humanity will one day achieve divine consciousness.

17. Why are many Postmodernists unwilling to endorse any particular theory of origins?

Each of the three main theories of evolution is a "grand story" or metanarrative describing *how* reality actually is and *how* life ultimately developed. In general, Postmodernists are anti-metanarrative (they are against promoting any overarching explanations of reality or origins).

18. What do evolutionary Postmodernists believe about man's role in the process of evolution?

Unlike much of the earlier optimistic modernist Darwinists, Postmodernists who hold to evolution assert that the process did not "have man in mind." Humanity is not special, nor can we claim that we are continually progressing in our evolution. In fact, Gould argues that considering all the species that have ever lived, homo sapiens are somewhat insignificant when compared with such species as bacteria, which "are—and always have been—the dominant form of life on earth."

"ICONS OF EVOLUTION" VIDEO

Fill in the Blank: (2 points possible per answer [4 for 90-day])

19. _____ Icons of evolution _____ are the distortions of pro-evolution evidence found in textbooks.

20. _____ Microevolution _____ is the small changes within the species of a gene pool.

21. _____ Macroevolution _____ is the origin of fundamentally new organisms and plants from other forms of life.

22. _____ Neo-Darwinism _____ is the scientific theory which proposes that natural selection works in conjunction with genetic mutations to yield evolution within the species.

23. _____ Homology _____ is the study of the similarity in structures between different organisms.

24. _____ Cambrian Explosion _____ is the sudden geological appearance of most major groups of animals.

Short answer: (5 points possible per answer [5 for 90-day])

25. What evidence do the Galapagos finches supply for macroevolution?

The theory of evolution (particularly macroevolution) is that micro-changes can, over time, accumulate into macro-changes, i.e. natural selection has the ability to build new species. Darwin's finches do demonstrate the ability of natural selection to produce micro-changes within a species; however, these birds do not support the grander story of macroevolution. The Galapagos finches never actually netted any changes; their average beak size merely oscillated back and forth with the changing food supply. In this example, no new species ever emerged. There was (and is) merely fluctuation within a kind.

26. What evidence do antibiotic resistant bacteria provide for macroevolution?

According to neo-Darwinism, DNA mutations provide raw material for evolution because they add variations to the process of descent with modification. However, in order for DNA mutations to be favored by natural selection, they must benefit the organism. In the case of antibiotic resistant bacteria, it does, at least in the short run. However, this represents only a minor change within an existing species, and since the change is reversed when conditions return to normal, antibiotic resistance is at best an example of microevolution. A new species of bacteria has never arisen from processes of mutation and natural selection.

Unit Four

Unit Four (vertical tab)

Short answer: (5 points possible per answer)

27. What is irreducible complexity? Give an example.

Irreducible complexity is the term for the functional necessity of all the components within a system. Systems operating from multiple components are viewed as irreducibly complex—if it loses one part, then the entire system will no longer function. Irreducibly complex systems are systems that cannot function without all of their parts. These parts themselves serve no function apart from the whole system. Considering irreducible complexity, the notion that a complex machine can gradually evolve from the collection of its parts is severely suspect, especially since these parts cannot function apart from the whole. Natural selection would have eliminated such things as a drive shaft or a propeller unless they served some purpose, but by themselves a drive shaft and a propeller serve no purpose.

[*Previous examples include the mousetrap, the machines within the human body, and even the body itself.*]

28. What is design inference? What are some examples?

Design inference is the logical process that human beings go through to decide if something was designed or not. If something is designed, then it must have intelligence behind it—something or someone doing the designing. For a pattern to be considered designed it must be specific (or complex), and it must be highly improbable for it to have occurred randomly on its own. Human beings correctly detect the activity of intelligence whenever they observe a highly recognizable and improbable pattern in an object or event.

[*Previous examples include Mt. Rushmore, the SETI program, and the DNA molecule.*]

WHAT IS DARWINISM? ESSAY
True or False: (2 points possible per answer)
*if an answer is false, restate it to make it true

29. The creative theory of macroevolution logically follows from the empirical observations of microevolution.

False: The creative theory of macroevolution <u>assumes the existence</u> of phenomena that are categorically different from the phenomena of microevolution.

30. Creationism means a belief in creation.

True

31. According to Darwinian evolutionists, science assumes that the entire cosmos is fully explicable according to naturalistic principles.

True

32. Darwinian evolutionists believe that scientific knowledge is an unchanging absolute.

False: Darwinian evolutionists believe that scientific knowledge is a <u>dynamic concept</u>.

33. Naturalistic philosophers tend to classify science as knowledge and religion as mere belief.

True

34. For the creationist, there can be no criterion for truth outside of scientific knowledge.

False: For the <u>naturalist</u>, there is no criterion for truth outside of scientific knowledge.

35. The prevailing view among Christian professors is that Darwinism is unbeatable and must be interpreted to be consistent with Christian belief.

True

36. Some Christian professors try to avoid the contradiction between naturalism and religion by unifying the two under a single realm of objective knowledge.

False: Some Christian professors try to avoid the contradiction between naturalism and religion by <u>separating</u> Darwinism and Christianity into two separate realms: science and religion.

37. In the opinion of most Darwinists, theistic evolution redefines evolution to such an extent that it can no longer be legitimately identified with Darwinian evolution.

True

38. Darwinism is a naturalistic framework used to explain the development and diversity of life.

True

TEACHER
MANUAL

UNDERSTANDING
THE TIMES

Unit Five

A Summit Ministries Curriculum

(For this unit, the Worldview Paper replaces a unit test. If you wish to create your own test, questions for this unit are included in the Conclusion review on the Teacher's CD-ROM.) —

180-DAY SYLLABUS

DAY	IN CLASS	HOMEWORK	
1	WATCH "Psychology" video		
2	READ <u>UTT</u> Textbook 'Psychology 5.1'	READ <u>UTT</u> Textbook 'Psychology 5.2'	
3	REVIEW <u>UTT</u> Textbook 'Psychology 5.1–5.2' questions	READ <u>UTT</u> Textbook 'Psychology 5.3'	
4	READ <u>UTT</u> Textbook 'Psychology 5.4'		
5	REVIEW <u>UTT</u> Textbook 'Psychology 5.3–5.4' questions	READ <u>UTT</u> Textbook 'Psychology 5.5'	
6	READ <u>UTT</u> Textbook 'Psychology 5.6'		
7	REVIEW <u>UTT</u> Textbook 'Psychology 5.5–5.6' questions		
8	READ *Homosexuality, Fact or Fiction?* essay		
9	REVIEW *Homosexuality, Fact or Fiction?* essay questions		
10	READ *That Which is Unnatural* essay		
11	REVIEW *That Which is Unnatural* essay questions		
12	WRITE Worldview Paper		
13	WRITE Worldview Paper		
14	WRITE Worldview Paper		
15	Worldview Paper DUE		

90-DAY SYLLABUS

DAY	IN CLASS	HOMEWORK	
1	WATCH "Psychology" video	READ <u>UTT</u> Textbook 'Psychology 5.1–5.2'	
2	REVIEW <u>UTT</u> Textbook 'Psychology 5.1–5.2' questions	READ <u>UTT</u> Textbook 'Psychology 5.3–5.4'	
3	REVIEW <u>UTT</u> Textbook 'Psychology 5.3–5.4' questions	READ <u>UTT</u> Textbook 'Psychology 5.5–5.6'	
4	REVIEW <u>UTT</u> Textbook 'Psychology 5.5–5.6' questions	READ *Homosexuality, Fact or Fiction?* essay	
5	REVIEW *Homosexuality, Fact or Fiction?* essay questions		
6	WRITE Worldview Paper		
7	WRITE Worldview Paper		
8	Worldview Paper DUE		

UNDERSTANDING THE TIMES
PSYCHOLOGY QUESTIONS

Answer the questions below on a separate sheet of paper and be prepared to review your answers in class.

PSYCHOLOGY 5.1

1. Why does William Kirk Kilpatrick refer to Christianity and psychology as competing faiths?

Kilpatrick is referring specifically to secular psychology. Modern schools of psychology are based primarily on the works of atheists such as Freud, Skinner, Pavlov, Rogers, Maslow, and Fromm. Based on their assumption that there is no God, they conclude that man is only matter in motion and human beings do not possess souls. [UTT 5.1.1]

2. Why should Christians bring God's truth to the discipline of psychology?

Psychology is the study of the mind—no worldview other than Christianity has true insight into this spiritual realm. [UTT 5.1.1]

[Discuss the following points regarding popular secular psychology with your students:

Popular psychology is a deceived discipline because it adheres to the following misconceptions:
* *Denial of the Fall—it asserts that human beings are basically good, etc.*
* *Metaphysical monism—it denies that human beings possess a soul or conscience.*
* *Denial of the creaturehood of man—it does not place human beings under the Creator.*
* *Excuses guilt—it assumes that guilt comes from norms imposed by religions and society.]*

3. What is the Christian view of ontology (the study of being)? What is "unity of identity?"

The Bible view of ontology is dualistic: the view that human nature consists of two fundamental kinds of reality—physical (material or natural) and spiritual (supernatural).

Eccles asserts that dualism is the only explanation for the phenomena of consciousness. Since the physical substance of the brain is constantly changing, no unity of identity could exist if consciousness were a condition wholly dependent upon the physical brain. Something more than the physical brain, something supernatural, must exist. [UTT 5.1.2]

4. According to Christianity, what is the key to healing non-organic mental illnesses?

Christian psychologists insist that the best method for mental healing involves: (1) the confession and forgiveness of sin through Christ—1 John 1:9; (2) reconciliation with God—2 Corinthians 5:17–21; and (3) sanctification through the disciplining work of God's Spirit—1 Thessalonians 5:23 and Hebrews 12:1–11. [UTT 5.1.6]

SM
139

Unit Five

5. How do Secular Humanists and Christians differ in their views of suffering?

> Secular Humanists contend that suffering is to be avoided at all costs—we should all try to prevent being a victim to the pressures of society. Christians believe that suffering can be both purposeful and instructive (Romans 8:28; Psalm 119:71; Psalm 18:30; and Romans 11:33–36). [UTT 5.1.7]

PSYCHOLOGY 5.2

6. What do Muslims believe about being created in the "image of God?" What is their view of human nature?

> Muslims believe that although God breathed his Spirit into mankind, the only divine qualities entrusted to humans as a result of God's breath were those of knowledge, will, and action.
>
> Muslims believe that each person is born in a natural state of purity, with a true faith of Islam, but (in the case of all other religions) is falsely converted by his or her parents. [UTT 5.2.3]

7. What is the Islamic view of the Fall?

> According to Islam, the Fall was only a slip on Adam and Eve's part that was completely forgiven after their repentance. It had no further effect on the nature of man or the world. [UTT 5.2.5]

8. What is the Islamic view of Christ's work on the cross? How does one attain salvation in Islam?

> Islam rejects the atoning work of Jesus, even going so far as to deny that Jesus died on the cross. According to Islam, "each person must bear his own burden and responsibilities."
>
> Muslims believe that human beings have a naturally good nature and that we must work out our salvation through the guidance of God. [UTT 5.2.6–7]

9. What is the Islamic view of the Final Judgment and forgiveness?

> The Final Judgment will be a day of balancing good deeds against bad. If your good deeds outweigh your wrongdoings, there is a good chance you will enter paradise. However, it is not completely up to the person's deeds. Ultimately, it depends upon the mercy of Allah. [UTT 5.2.8–9]

10. What are the ramifications of denying Jesus' death on the cross?

> To deny Jesus' death is to deny his atoning work. If Jesus never died, there would be no resurrection from the dead. If Jesus was not resurrected from the dead, then there is no gospel, no hope of salvation, and the Christian faith is nothing but an empty fraud. [UTT 5.2.10]

11. **What is behaviorism? Why is Secular Humanism's rejection of behaviorist psychology inconsistent with its worldview?**

Behaviorism focuses on strictly material things—the brain, environmental stimuli, and tangible human responses to stimuli.

Secular Humanists, to be consistent, should embrace behaviorism—because of their assumption that the natural is all that exists, they should welcome a psychology that denies the supernatural. [UTT 5.3.1]

12. **Why do so few Secular Humanists accept behaviorism?**

Behaviorism is a stultifying theory that reduces men to mere automatons. Thus, it is neither an attractive theory nor one that matches up with day-to-day experience. Behaviorism also destroys the concept of free will, a necessary concept for freedom. [UTT 5.3.1]

13. **What do Secular Humanists believe about the innate nature of mankind?**

Secular Humanist psychology emphatically proclaims the innate goodness of man. Virtually every humanistic psychologist shares the view that society is responsible for the evil in mankind. [UTT 5.3.2]

[Contrast this view with the Christian view of man. Which worldview seems to account for the evil we see in the world today?]

14. **Why do Secular Humanist psychologists justify self-centeredness as a worthwhile goal? How does this contrast with the Christian view?**

Humanist psychologists believe the secret to better mental health lies in getting in touch with our unspoiled inner self. The humanist emphasis, then, is on self-reliance, even self-centeredness.

Humanist psychologists believe that this self-centered attitude is crucial for the mental health of the individual and for the eventual restructuring of society. [UTT 5.3.4]

[In contrast, Christians are to be Christ–centered. Our attentions should be focused on him, developing a heart of servanthood toward our fellow man, not to ourselves.]

15. **What is the Secular Humanist psychologist's source of ethics? How does this line of thinking tend toward elitism?**

> According to Secular Humanism, humanity must turn inward to discover goodness. The self-actualized person is the highest authority. Since there are relatively few of these enlightened people, those who are not yet self-actualized must look to them for guidance.
>
> Only the self-actualized few are fit to lead. Once in power, others should yield to them. "I propose that we explore the consequences of observing whatever our best specimens choose, and then assume that these are the highest values for mankind." — Abraham Maslow [UTT 5.3.6]

PSYCHOLOGY 5.4

16. **What aspects of behaviorism do Marxists accept? What aspects of behaviorism do they reject?**

> Marxists fear that a behaviorist psychology might not encourage the development of a communist society since it denies the possibility of man making a "conscious struggle" to achieve such a society. Free will is crucial for Marxist psychology. [UTT 5.4.4]

17. **How do Marxists avoid accepting the determinism dictated by behaviorism?**

> Marxist psychologists view the concept of speech—a "second signal system"—as the key to synthesizing behaviorism with free will. This concept of speech, as another stimulus, allows the Marxist to perceive humanity as shaped by environmental stimuli, such as their society. Speech is instrumental in defining and maintaining society and is a tool that allows us to shape the stimuli acting upon us, and thus our own environment. [UTT 5.4.4–5]

18. **According to Marxists, what is the major problem with society? Why?**

> According to Marxists, the major problem with society is capitalism since it inevitably leads to oppression. Capitalism promotes the existence of a ruling class (the bourgeois), which in turn breeds deviant behavior. Marxists believe that this behavior will always be manifested under capitalism and can only be eradicated by restructuring society into a communist ideal. [UTT 5.4.7]

19. **How does the Marxist view of the dialectic affect their psychology?**

> According to Marxist psychology, humanity's freedom to create whatever society we choose clashes with societal forces and other environmental factors that determine behavior. The individual's freedom (thesis) attracts to itself and struggles with man's behavioristic tendencies (antithesis). [UTT 5.4.8]

20. How do Marxists define freedom?

Freedom is simply an opportunity for the individual to choose whatever type of society will determine his or her behavior—it does not mean choosing his or her own behavior. [UTT 5.4.9]

PSYCHOLOGY 5.5

21. What role does psychology play in Cosmic Humanism?

Achieving higher consciousness is the central goal for any member of the New Age movement and only psychology provides the means for unlocking the secrets of this higher mindset. [UTT 5.5.1]

22. According to Cosmic Humanism, how do individuals achieve a healthy well-being?

Our consciousness affects both body and soul and only a constant state of higher consciousness can ensure our mental and physical well-being. Thus, psychology plays a crucial role in Cosmic Humanism's worldview not only because it can hasten our evolution to a collective God-consciousness, but also because it works to ensure perfect health for every individual. [UTT 5.5.1]

23. According to Cosmic Humanism, why do people suffer health problems?

Cosmic Humanists believe that an individual's mindset is responsible for his or her mental health. People suffering through painful sickness or disease are doing so because they have not yet achieved higher consciousness. However, if we are able to change our mindset, then we will be able to overcome health problems. [UTT 5.5.2]

24. According to Cosmic Humanism, where do criminal tendencies originate?

Cosmic Humanists believe that criminal tendencies come from a personal failing to recognize our divine status. They believe that criminals can be put in touch with their higher consciousness and thus become capable of leading healthy lives—spiritually, physically, and ethically. [UTT 5.5.2]

25. What methods do "fourth force" psychology employ to induce states of higher consciousness in willing individuals?

Fourth force psychology employs meditation, channeling, astrology, fire walking, Ouija boards, and aura readings. [UTT 5.5.3]

Unit Five

TEAPOT ACTIVITY

Bring a teapot to class and speak with a student before class to set up the following situation: Have the student present the question, "Which reality is real?" Ask the student to defend the view that the world is just an illusion. Then ask the rest of your students how they would go about helping the person to understand that his or her view of reality does not match with what we know about the real world. Remind your students that one way to find the answer to such a question is to test the alternatives to see which one fits the real world.

If your students are getting nowhere in this conversation, inform them that you have to resort to a drastic measure. Pull out the teapot and hold it over the student's head. Ask the class what they think the person will do if you pour it on them and why. The person who believes that this world is just an illusion cannot live consistently by that belief—he or she will move instead of getting burned by a hot liquid.

PSYCHOLOGY 5.6

26. How has the concept of soul become obsolete in the Postmodern era?

The traditional idea of an immaterial soul as the seat of our personal identity has been replaced with the Postmodern notion of socially constructed "selves." That is, if there is no God's-eye-view of what constitutes the individual, we must resort to the changing whims of our social condition to tell us who and what we are. Instead of viewing human beings as a "unified self," Postmodern psychologists look at the individual as a multiplicity of "selves." [UTT 5.6.1]

27. How do Gilles Deleuze and Felix Guattari view the soul?

Deleuze and Guattari reject the traditional idea that the soul is naturally whole, unified, or coherent. Instead, they postulate that it is a harmful illusion. They see the self as a flux of desires and intensities caught up in an ongoing process of change. [UTT 5.6.2]

28. What is the definition of "self" according to Jacques Lacan and Michel Foucault?

Jacques Lacan states: "Selfhood is really nothing but a fleeting, unstable, incomplete and openminded mess of desires which cannot be fulfilled." Lacan and Foucault propose that the stable, unified self has always been an illusion. In their view, our identity is the result of social factors—language, geography, family, education, government, etc. [UTT 5.6.3]

29. What is the theory of "multiple selves" according to Mitchell Stephens and Kenneth Gergen?

Stephens contends that human beings have no central personality to which our varied behaviors can be seen as just "sides." In other words, we are not anything in an absolute sense. Since we are not absolutely anything, we are free to construct whoever we want to be according to the situation.

Gergen likewise points out that in our technologically saturated society, with its multiple opportunities for personal interaction, it is impossible to know which is our "real self." We, as individuals, "play" many different roles at different times and with different people. A theory of multiple selves provides a way for those living in a postmodern world to adjust to the reality of their condition. [UTT 5.6.3]

30. What are some inherent problems with the notion of a socially constructed self?

In the area of law, crime, and punishment, Louis Sass points out that there are clear dangers in giving up that notion of a single self. First, we become absolved of the responsibility for our choices and actions, because different situations, and their accompanying behaviors, cannot be compared with each other or any absolute standard of right and wrong. Second, there is no such thing as normal or abnormal, since a constant view of self does not exist. Labeling certain behaviors as normal and others as abnormal establishes boundaries, which Postmodernists are notorious for avoiding. [UTT 5.6.4]

WORLDVIEW ROLE-PLAY ACTIVITY

The goal of this project is to have the students understand the different worldview positions well enough to present them to someone else and identify them when heard from a fellow student.

Have the students draw slips of paper that assign a different worldview to each one: Christianity, Islam, Secular Humanism, Marxism-Leninism, Cosmic Humanism, or Postmodernism. They should assume this role until the next time your class meets (or perhaps even longer). They are not to tell anyone who they are. However, they should react to situations and conversations in ways that are consistent with their assigned worldview. Classmates should try to identify these comments and the underlying worldview.

However, the students shouldn't just play their parts with others from the *Understanding the Times* class. Encourage them to "stay in character" with other friends and with their families. They should pay particular attention to how other people react. Do they agree or disagree with the things that are said? Do they even notice? Discuss the reactions at the next class.

HOMOSEXUALITY, FACT OR FICTION?
BY JOSEPH P. GUDEL

"People should live and let live!" "To each his own, let them live as they wish." "Let the gays have their freedom." "Whatever makes you happy, live with it."[1]

Comments like these are commonly heard when the topic of homosexuality comes up for discussion. The debate over homosexuality and homosexual rights has steadily grown over the past two decades and will only continue to do so.

In the course of this debate, however, numerous inaccuracies, half-truths, fallacies, and overt propaganda have been disseminated to the public as uncontested truth. It is the purpose of this article to examine these claims and separate fact from fiction. Before anyone can give intelligent and compassionate answers, the questions must be clarified and brought into focus. I believe that when this is done the impartial reader will be able to agree with the analogy made by Dr. James D. Mallory, a psychiatrist and the director of the Atlanta Counseling Center: "A physician would be guilty of malpractice if he didn't warn a diabetic of his condition because he didn't want to hurt his feelings. Simply letting the person continue eating excessive carbohydrates without proper treatment condemns him to a worsening physical condition. The most loving act one can do is point out that an abnormality exists, and offer help. This needs to be done—but not in a spirit of condemnation—with homosexuality."[2]

HOMOPHOBIA?

Homophobia is defined in *The Kinsey Institute New Report on Sex* as the "fear, dislike, or hatred of homosexuals."[3] The Greek word *phobia* denotes an "irrational fear." The word *homo* literally means "same," but the word is frequently used as a shortened form of *homosexual*—one who is sexually attracted to his or her own sex. Thus, strictly speaking, homophobia denotes an irrational fear or hatred of homosexuals. However, the gay rights movement (and, by-and-large, the media) places this label on anyone who opposes any of the movement's goals and objectives; specifically, anyone opposing the full acceptance of the homosexual lifestyle as healthy and "normal."

While indeed there are many people who hate or irrationally fear homosexuals, to say that anyone who opposes the homosexual lifestyle or disagrees with the gay rights political agenda is a homophobe is simply not true. This tactic is clearly intended to divert attention from the argument and onto the person. As we will see below, there are many who oppose homosexuality on psychological, sociological, medical, and moral grounds.

TEN PERCENT OF THE POPULATION?

Perhaps the most fascinating statistic cited (constantly and confidently) in research of homosexuality is that ten percent of the United States population is homosexual. The implication is that this is probably just as true in most other societies as well. I say this is fascinating because virtually nobody knows (or at least cites) where this statistic comes from.

The Family Research Institute asks, "How many homosexuals are there? *USA Today* said '25 million gay men and lesbians' [i.e., about 10% of the US population]. The *Washington Times* said '10 percent of American men are homosexual and 5 percent of women are lesbian.' The American Psychological Association assures us that homosexuality is 'an orientation found consistently in about ten percent of the male population and approximately five percent of the female population.'"[4]

Just this week, as I was preparing to put this article together, I watched "Teen Connection," a public broadcast program.[5] Its topic was "Sexual Orientation," with a panel consisting of a homosexual teenage

---

[1] Quotes from members of the studio audience on *The Geraldo Show*, "Can Gays and Lesbians Go Straight?" (June 11, 1991).
[2] James D. Mallory, "Homosexuality: Part III—A Psychiatrist's View," *Christian Life* (October 1977).
[3] June M. Reinisch, dir., *The Kinsey Institute New Report on Sex* (New York: St. Martin's Press, 1990), 147.
[4] *Family Research Report* (Family Research Institute, Washington DC), 1.
[5] *Teen Connection*, "Sexual Orientation," Wisconsin Public Television (May 19, 1992).

boy, the boy's mother, a young lady who is a lesbian, and an adult homosexual counselor. Within the course of an hour the ten percent figure was cited three times, being adduced as evidence of just how many people out there need our encouragement and understanding. They had a panel of phones for those who had questions or needed counseling themselves. I called in and asked them where the ten percent figure came from. The lady I spoke with did not know, and neither did another phone counselor she asked.

The truth is that this ten percent statistic comes from a report published more than 40 years ago—the famous 1948 study led by Alfred Kinsey.[6] The only problem with this report is that its findings were terribly flawed by the methodology used to collect the supposedly representative sample of the U.S. population.[7]

Why were his findings flawed? For several reasons, first and foremost being that approximately 25 percent of the 5,300 individuals Kinsey studied were prison inmates, "who by the nature of their confinement, couldn't have heterosexual intercourse." In addition, 44 percent of these inmates had had homosexual experiences while in prison.[8] This was hardly a representative sample of the American population.

But there were other major flaws in the group selected for the research. Kinsey admitted that "several hundred male prostitutes" were used in his sample. This alone would make a major difference in his findings.[9]

In addition there was clearly a "volunteer bias." In attempting to select a representative group to work with, one does not merely run an ad and accept anyone who responds. Research has shown that those responding to a study as intimate as the one Kinsey was doing would *not* be representative of the general population. In fact, the widely renowned psychologist Abraham Maslow pointed this out to Kinsey before his findings were published, but he refused to listen.[10]

To make matters worse, the people who refer back to this old and flawed study do not quote it accurately. Kinsey did not say that 10 percent of the entire U.S. population was homosexual. Rather, he affirmed that ten percent of white American males were "more or less" exclusively homosexual for at least three years of their lives between the ages of 16 and 65. The statistic for females was five percent. The actual percentage of those thought to be *exclusively* homosexual for their entire lives was only four percent of men and two or three percent of women, all based on his allegedly representative sample of the population.[11]

What are the real figures as far as we can tell today? One recent study of men conducted between 1984 and 1987 by David Forman, the senior staff scientist at the Radcliffe Infirmary (Oxford, England), found that only 1.7 percent of the sample study had ever had homosexual intercourse.[12] An even more recent study, conducted at the University of Chicago in 1989 and reported at the 1990 meeting of the American Association for the Advancement of Science, resulted in a figure "less than 1% exclusively homosexual."[13]

Are these results significant? Well, they are significant in at least setting the record straight as to the actual scope or parameters of the debate. There is quite a difference between one or two percent of the population being homosexual as opposed to ten percent of the population. Obviously, the higher the percentage cited as being homosexual, the more influence those in the gay rights movement can wield.

IS HOMOSEXUALITY AN ILLNESS? IS IT "NORMAL"?

An even more important question, though, is if homosexuality constitutes pathological behavior. Is it an illness? Gay rights groups continually assert that homosexuals are as "normal" as heterosexuals, that homosexuality is not an illness or psychological disorder. For example, Peri Jude Radecic, a member of the National Gay and Lesbian Task Force (NGLTF), asserted on the ABC news show *Nightline*, "Homosexuality is not an illness, it is not something that needs to be cured. We are normal, healthy people."[14]

[6] Alfred C. Kinsey, et al., *Sexual Behavior in the Human Male* (Philadelphia: Saunders, 1948).
[7] See Abraham Maslow and James M. Sakoda, "Volunteer Error in the Kinsey Study," *Journal of Abnormal and Social Psychology 47* (April 1952), 259–62.
[8] "The Ten Percent Solution, Part II," *Peninsula* 3:2 (October/November 1991), 7. Also see Judith A. Reisman and Edward W. Eichol, *Kinsey, Sex and Fraud* (Lafayette, LA: Huntington House, 1990), 23.
[9] Kinsey, 216.
[10] Maslow and Sakoda, 259–62.
[11] Reinisch, 140.
[12] Reisman and Eichol, 194.
[13] Ibid., 195.
[14] *Nightline*, ABC News (August 30, 1991).

Moreover, these groups universally contend that all competent psychiatrists and psychologists are in agreement on this. As proof of this, the American Psychiatric Association's (APA) 1973 declassification homosexuality as a mental disorder is always cited.

Before examining the contention that all competent psychiatrists and psychologists agree that homosexuality is normal and healthy, we need to look at the APA's 1973 decision for a moment. For 23 years homosexuality had been listed as a mental disorder by the APA. Why was it decided, at that particular point in time, that it was not pathological?

I do not have the space to go into a detailed analysis of the history leading up to the APA's decision.[15] Nonetheless, it is a misconception to think that this came about only after dispassionate and scholarly discussion, and only after listening equally to all sides of the issue. Also, it is important to note that the APA's vote was anything but unanimous.

In the three years leading up to the 1973 APA meeting, the previous national meetings had been repeatedly disrupted by gay activists. At the 1970 meeting in San Francisco certain sessions were broken up with shouts and jeers, prohibiting any rational discussion or debate.

At the APA's 1971 meeting in Washington, threats and intimidation accomplished what discussion could not. Ronald Bayer, in a work sympathetic toward homosexuality and the gay rights movement, recounts: "Using forged credentials, gay activists gained access to the exhibit area and, coming across a display marketing aversive conditioning [i.e., punishing an organism whenever it makes a particular response] techniques for the treatment of homosexuals, demanded its removal. Threats were made against the exhibitor, who was told that unless his booth was dismantled, it would be torn down. After frantic behind-the scenes consultations, and in an effort to avoid violence, the convention leadership agreed to have the booth removed."[16]

These tactics continued in the same manner at the APA's 1972 national meeting. It was against this backdrop that the association's trustees finally made its controversial 1973 decision. When a referendum on this was sent out to all 25,000 APA members, only a quarter of them returned their ballots. The final tally was 58 percent favoring the removal of homosexuality from their list of disorders.

Four years later, Dr. Charles Socarides—who was at the meetings and was an expert in the area of homosexuality, having treated homosexuals for more than twenty years—described the political atmosphere leading up to the 1973 vote. He writes that during this time, "militant homosexual groups continued to attack any psychiatrist or psychoanalyst who dared to present his findings as to the psychopathology [i.e., the study mental disorders from all aspects] of homosexuality before national or local meetings of psychiatrists or in public realms."[17] Elsewhere Socarides stated that the decision of the APA trustees was "the medical hoax of the century."[18]

Was this the end of the debate? Did the vast majority of "competent" psychiatrists agree with the APA's decision? In 1977 ten thousand members of the APA were polled at random, asking them their opinion on this. In an article entitled "Sick Again?" *Time* magazine summarized the results of the poll: "Of those answering, 69% said they believed 'homosexuality is usually a pathological adaptation, as opposed to a normal variation,' 18% disagreed, and 13% were uncertain. Similarly, sizable majorities said that homosexuals are generally less happy than heterosexuals (73%) and less capable of mature, loving relationships (60%). A total of 70% said that homosexuals' problems have more to do with their own inner conflicts than with stigmatization by society at large."[19]

But what about today? Has this issue been resolved in current medical opinion and research? Concerning this, Dr. Stanton L. Jones, professor of psychology at Wheaton College, states that there is a "mixed scorecard" among professionals on this. He writes: "I would not regard homosexuality to be a

---

[15] For those interested in the history leading up to the APA's 1973 removal of homosexuality from their *Diagnostic and Statistical Manual of Psychiatric Disorders*, see Ronald Bayer, *Homosexuality and American Psychiatry: The Politics of Diagnosis* (New York: Basic, 1981), 101–54; and William Dannemeyer, *Shadow in the Land* (San Francisco: Ignatius, 1989), 24–39.

[16] Bayer, 105–6.

[17] Charles W. Socarides, *Beyond Sexual Freedom* (New York: Quadrangle Books, 1977), 87. Prior to the 1973 vote, Dr. Socarides led the APA's task force studying homosexuality, which issued a report unanimously declaring homosexuality to be a disorder of psychosexual development. This report, considered to be too politically inflammatory, was shelved, only later being published as a "study group" report in 1974.

[18] Charles W. Socarides in Robert Kronemeyer, *Overcoming Homosexuality* (New York: Macmillan, 1980), 5.

[19] "Sick Again? Psychiatrists Vote on Gays," *Time* (February 20, 1978), 102.

psychopathology in the same sense as schizophrenia or phobic disorders. But neither can it be viewed as a normal 'lifestyle variation' on a par with being introverted versus extroverted."[20]

One may debate whether or not homosexuality is a pathological disorder, but it is clear that the APA's 1973 decision cannot be cited as medical consensus that homosexuality is a "normal" condition. Later in this article I will examine in some detail the assertion that homosexuality is a healthy lifestyle.

BORN GAY?

Perhaps the most dangerous myth disseminated today by the pro-homosexuality movement is that modern science has proven that homosexuality is innate and immutable. That is, homosexuals are *born* gay, much like being born left handed or with blue eyes. The inference, of course, is that if they are born that way, then homosexuality cannot be considered immoral or unnatural; the homosexual is just following his or her genes. However as Congressman William Dennemeyer put it, "if homosexuality is a perversion of what is natural, then homosexuals must look at their own conduct in an entirely different light and explain it in less satisfying terms."[21]

It is well beyond the scope of this article to summarize all the findings concerning the genesis of homosexuality. However, the scientific evidences for its origins are usually classified in terms of either biological causes (i.e., genetic/hormonal) or environmental factors (e.g., psychological causes, volitional, and so forth).

1. Biological Causes

The most recent research suggesting that homosexuality may be caused by biological factors came out in 1991 with the publication of some preliminary findings of Dr. Simon LeVay, a neuroscientist at the Salk Institute for Biological Studies in San Diego. His research consisted of studying the brains of 41 cadavers, including 19 homosexual males. He found that "a tiny area believed to control sexual activity [the hypothalamus] was less than half the size in the gay men than in the heterosexuals."[22]

This study was seized upon by many as "irrefutable evidence" that homosexuals are born gay, something the homosexual community has been proclaiming for many years. However, "instead of resolving the debate," a *Newsweek* article suggests, "the studies may well have intensified it. Some scientists profess not to be surprised at all by LeVay's finding of brain differences. 'Of course it [sexual orientation] is in the brain,' says Johns Hopkins University psychologist John Money, sometimes called the dean of American sexologists. 'The real question is, when did it get there? Was it prenatal, neonatal, during childhood, puberty? That we do not know.'"[23]

Other problems with his findings include: (1) all 19 of the homosexual men had died of AIDS, something that many researchers believe could very well account for or contribute to the differences; (2) there was no way to know the sexual history of the "heterosexual" men; (3) there is no way to determine if the smaller hypothalamuses were the *cause* or the *result* of homosexuality; and (4) Dr. LeVay, a homosexual himself, admitted that his study was not entirely a dispassionate scientific endeavor.[24]

2. Environmental Factors

There are probably just as many, if not more, psychiatrists and psychologists who believe that homosexuality arises from various environmental factors. The majority of these say that homosexuality's root causes are psychological, not biological. But these are not cited nearly as often by the media as the others—perhaps a pro-homosexual bias by the media? And they are virtually never even acknowledged by the homosexual community, because most homosexuals want to believe that they were born that way and had no choice (conscious or subliminal) in the matter.

In any case, some of the most noteworthy and respected researchers and therapists in the world deny that homosexuality is determined by biological factors. For example, therapists helping homosexuals who are

[20] Stanton L. Jones, "Homosexuality According to Science," in J. Isamu Yamamoto, ed., *The Crisis of Homosexuality* (Wheaton, IL: Victor, 1990), 107.
[21] Dannemeyer, 40–41.
[22] Charlene Crabb, "Are Some Men Born to Be Homosexual?," *U. S. News & World Report* (September 9, 1991).
[23] David Gelman, et al., "Born or Bred?" *Newsweek* (February 24, 1992).
[24] Simon LeVay on *The Phil Donahue Show*, "Genetically Gay: Born Gay or Become Gay?"(January 3, 1992).

unhappy with their condition can cite one case history after another showing that negative early childhood experiences are the one common factor found in almost all their patients. The vital factor here is that these people were raised in a very unloving home environment, never knowing love or acceptance from their father. According to these studies, the child's reaction to this rejection and lack of nurturing is formulated at a very early age, usually before five years old. The follow reference illustrates these findings.

William H. Masters (co-director of the Masters and Johnson Institute), Virginia E. Brown, and Robert C. Kolodny stated categorically in their 1982 work *Human Sexuality*: "The genetic theory of homosexuality has been generally discarded today."[25]

Robert Kronemeyer, in his work *Overcoming Homosexuality*, writes, "With rare exceptions, homosexuality is neither inherited nor the result of some glandular disturbance or the scrambling of genes or chromosomes. Homosexuals are made, not born 'that way.' I firmly believe that homosexuality is a learned response to early painful experiences and that it can be unlearned. For those homosexuals who are unhappy with their life and find effective therapy, it is 'curable.'"[26]

John DeCecco, professor of psychology at San Francisco State University and the editor of the 25-volume *Journal of Homosexuality*, expressed the same view in a 1989 *USA Today* article. "'The idea that people are born into one type of sexual behavior is entirely foolish,' says John DeCecco. Homosexuality, he says, is 'a behavior, not a condition,' and something that some people can and do change, just like they sometimes change other tastes and personality traits."[27]

One thing is clear: it is hardly an established scientific fact accepted by the entire medical field that homosexuality is solely or even primarily caused by biological factors. This brings us to the question just raised above: Can those who are homosexual change?

IS CHANGE IMPOSSIBLE?

The question of whether or not one should want to change his or her sexual preference will be addressed shortly. But before looking at the desirability of changing, we need to ascertain whether change is even possible. I say that this is important to investigate because a host of individuals concerned with homosexual issues deny that this is a possibility.

Those in the gay rights movement, as well as numerous researchers, psychotherapists, and so forth, decry any attempt to change the homosexual's sexual orientation or preference. Rick Notch, a homosexual man who at one time claimed to have become an ex-gay, stated on *The Geraldo Show*: "The only choice we have is to learn to accept ourselves and to find a way to live a responsible, moral life."[28] Dr. Richard Isay, a psychiatrist who heads the APA's committee on gay issues, likewise asserted: "The core orientation in a gay man cannot be changed."[29]

But even a perfunctory examination of the available testimonies and case studies shows that this simply is not true. First of all, do all of the other psychiatrists and psychologists agree with the assertion that change is not possible? By no means! In fact, most believe that change is possible. William H. Masters and Virginia E. Johnson, hardly homophobes, write in their work *Homosexuality in Perspective*: "Providing therapeutic support for the homosexually oriented man or woman who wishes to convert or revert to heterosexuality has been an integral part of the practice of psychotherapy for decades."[30]

Likewise, in the *Kinsey Institute New Report on Sex* (1990) we find the statement that "sexual orientation, whether heterosexual or homosexual, *is not readily changed* by any type of intervention" (emphasis added).[31]

---

[25] William H. Masters, Virginia E. Brown, and Robert Kolodny, *Human Sexuality* (Boston: Little, Brown, 1982), 319.

[26] Kronemeyer, 7.

[27] Kim Painter, "A Biological Theory for Sexual Preference," *USA Today* (January 1, 1989). Also see Alan P. Bell, et al., *Sexual Preference* (Bloomington, IN: Indiana University Press, 1981), 221. While not believing that biology determines sexual preference, neither do they believe that the parents somehow caused it. Instead, they believe there is a causal relationship in children having early "gender identity" problems and their becoming homosexual.

[28] Rick Notch, *The Geraldo Show* (June 11, 1991).

[29] Richard Isay, quoted on *20/20*, ABC News (April 24, 1992).

[30] William H. Masters and Virginia E. Johnson, *Homosexuality in Perspective* (Boston: Little, Brown, 1979), 333. Also, after a ten-year study of homosexuality they found that those desiring "conversion" to heterosexuality had only a 21 percent failure rate (p. 396). However, after making certain adjustments the conversion failure rate could be as high as 45 percent.

[31] Reinisch, 143.

Thus, while it is not easy, changing one's sexual orientation is nonetheless possible—which could not be the case if homosexuality was innate and immutable.

This was confirmed on a recent segment of ABC's *20/20*, which had a story dealing with Dr. Joseph Nicolosi. Nicolosi is a psychologist and psychotherapist who has been helping homosexual men convert to heterosexuality for a number of years now.[32]

I already referred above to the work of Dr. Robert Kronemeyer. If the interested reader pursues this work, he or she will find eight case histories cited—true accounts of people who sought relief from their lives of homosexual bondage (their own description of their lifestyles) and were converted to heterosexuality.[33]

Another area where we see the fruit of changed lives is in the numerous Christian ministries reaching out to homosexuals desiring help. Space limitations will not allow me to go into great detail. Those interested can find the references in the endnotes.

Are there really changed lives? There is Darlene Bogle, a woman who "struggled with lesbianism" for 17 years.[34] She was raised in an environment where she was sexually abused by different men and boys, the first at the age of three. Her parents divorced when she was only five. Her new stepfather frequently abused her, both verbally and physically. In her own words she was raised in "a home that lacked nurturing, that was void of positive role models and void of love."[35] Today, through the grace and mercy of God, she has been completely free for 15 years from her former lifestyle and is currently a counselor at Paraklete Ministries in Hayward, California.

There is Frank Worthen, a practicing homosexual for 25 years. In 1973 he turned back to Jesus Christ, who delivered him from that lifestyle. Since then he has remained free, without once falling back into his old secular behavior. Today he and his wife Anita are missionaries in the Philippines with Exodus International.[36]

There is Andrew Comiskey, a former homosexual who is now the director of Desert Stream Ministries.[37]

There is Joanne Highley, a lesbian from the ages of 13 to 23, who has now been freed from that lifestyle for the past 35 years. She has been married to the same man during those 35 years, is a mother and grandmother, and with her husband is co-director of L.I.F.E. Ministries in New York City.[38]

Are there really changed lives, people who were exclusively homosexual and became heterosexual? *Yes.* Have there not been those who have fallen back into their old lifestyles? Again, the answer is yes, which is to be expected. Just like in Alcoholics Anonymous, the road is rarely easy and involves a tremendous commitment by the individual seeking recovery and healing. Sometimes individuals stumble and never get back up again. Sometimes they stumble, get back up, and continue on in the process of recovery. And occasionally, individuals are healed instantly and never turn back again. But the fact remains that there are many former homosexuals, ex-gays, who have been transformed by the power of Jesus Christ.

A HEALTHY LIFESTYLE?

As noted above, those in the gay rights movement constantly assert that they are both normal and healthy individuals. We have already discussed the "normality" of homosexuality. The question of whether or not it is a healthy lifestyle can be addressed in two areas: promiscuity and actual sexual practices.

1. Promiscuity

If one agrees with the assertion that being promiscuous is not healthy, from either an emotional or physical standpoint, then homosexuality as typically practiced must be termed extremely unhealthy. *Homosexualties*, an official publication of The Institute for Sex Research founded by Alfred Kinsey, Alan Bell, and Martin Weinberg, reported that only ten percent of male homosexuals could be termed as "relatively monogamous"

[32] *20/20*, ABC News (April 24, 1992).
[33] Kronemeyer, 141–67.
[34] Darlene Bogle, "Healing from Lesbianism," in Yamamoto, 15.
[35] Ibid., 17.
[36] Bob Davies, "The Exodus Story: The Growth of Ex-gay Ministry," in Yamamoto, 47–59. Also see Kent Philpott, *The Gay Theology* (Plainfield, NJ: Logos International, 1977), 20–37.
[37] Andrew Comiskey, *Pursuing Sexual Wholeness: How Jesus Heals the Homosexual* (Lake Mary, FL: Creation House, 1989).
[38] Joanne Highley, L.I.F.E. Ministries, P.O. Box 353, New York, NY 10185.

or "relatively less promiscuous." Additional findings showed that 60 percent of male homosexuals had more than 250 lifetime sexual partners, and 28 percent of male homosexuals had more than 1,000 lifetime sexual partners. Another startling fact is that 79 percent admitted that more than half of their sexual partners were strangers.[39]

Just a few years after the publication of this report, Dr. William Foege, the director of the Centers for Disease Control, stated: "The average AIDS victim has had 60 different sexual partners in the past twelve months."[40] In contrast with this, "the average heterosexual male has—throughout his life—from five to nine sex partners."[41]

What about lesbian relationships? Are homosexual women less promiscuous than homosexual men? While less research has been done on lesbians, the data shows that they are much more monogamous than homosexual men. However, their relationships are still not very secure. Yvonne Zipter, a lesbian writing in Chicago's gay journal *Windy City Times*, in an article entitled "The Disposable Lesbian Relationship," notes that the "lasting lesbian relationship" is a "mythic entity."[42]

2. Sexual Practices

A second item that cannot be avoided in a discussion of the health aspects of homosexuality is the actual sexual practices of homosexuals. Are these healthy? Once again, the vast preponderance of medical evidence is resoundingly negative.

Many different medical sources document the physical aberrancy of homosexual sexual practices. The following information comes from an article entitled "Medical Perspective of the Homosexual Issue." It was written by Dr. Bernard J. Klamecki, a proctologist (rectal specialist) for more than 30 years.

Dr. Klamecki states in this article that when he began his medical practice in 1960, only one percent of his patients were homosexuals. By 1988 this number had grown to 25 percent of his patients, the majority being referred by a local gay free clinic. The following material comes from one who is known and respected by the homosexual community, a medical professional who has care and compassion for all his patients and who donates a good deal of his time to their service.

> I know well the medical and surgical pathology directly related to the sexual practices typical of active homosexuals, particularly anal intercourse (sodomy) and oral intercourse (fellatio)…
>
> Sexual practices typical of homosexuals can affect the oral cavities, lungs, penis, prostate, bladder, anus, perianal areas outside of the rectum, rectum, colon, vagina, uterus, pelvic area, brain, skin, blood, immune system, and other body systems… While none of the following practices is unique to homosexuals, they are nonetheless typical…
>
> Most common is anal intercourse (sodomy)… Foreign objects are often used in order to produce a different erotic sensation or to instigate a more violent sexual activity (sadomasochism). Objects that I have removed from the rectum and lower bowel include corncobs, light bulbs, vibrators, soda bottles, and varied wooden sticks.
>
> "Fisting" is when a fisted hand is inserted into the rectum, sometimes as far as the elbow, which produces varied sexually exciting sensations, strongly linking eroticism with pain…
>
> Oral intercourse (fellatio) is when the tongue is used to lick or tickle the outlet of the rectum for sexual excitement, arousing, or foreplay—Needless to say, bacteria may contaminate and infect the mouth. One other sexual practice is "Water Sports," in which urinating into the mouth or rectum is used as a sexual stimulant.
>
> Physical damage to the rectum may occur because of some of these practices… There is an anti-natural activity being performed when the rectum is the recipient of a penis or foreign object. Because of this activity, cracking of the tissue (fissuring), open sores (ulcers), boils (abscesses), and other infections can occur in the skin of the surrounding tissues…
>
> Persistent anal-rectal sexual activity can lead to various precancerous lesions such as Bowen's disease and Kaposi's sarcoma. Whenever tissues are traumatized, cracked, or abraded, they are vulnerable to bacterial infection.[43]

We believe this information is very vital for the case against the homosexual lifestyle. However, due to its graphic nature, the brown section has been blocked out in the student manual. If you decide to have your students read the essay in its entirety, it can be found on the Teacher's CD-ROM under "Handouts."

[39] Alan P. Bell and Martin S. Weinberg, *Homosexualities* (New York: Simon & Schuster, 1978), 308.

[40] Walter Isaacson, "Hunting for the Hidden Killers," *Time* (July 4, 1983), 51.

[41] Kronemeyer, 32.

[42] Yvonne Zipter, "The Disposable Lesbian Relationship," Chicago, *Windy City Times* (December 25, 1986).

[43] Bernard J. Klamecki, "Medical Perspective of the Homosexual Issue," in Yamamoto, 116–17.

Dr. Klamecki then continues, discussing the various bacterial diseases and viral diseases he regularly encounters with his homosexual patients—the most prominent being AIDS (the current figure is that 70 percent of Americans with AIDS are male homosexuals or bisexuals). In addition, he asserts that up to 86 percent of homosexual males use various drugs to enhance and increase their sexual stimulation.[44]

Is the homosexual lifestyle a healthy one? The information presented above just scratches the surface showing the pathological nature of these sexual practices. Much more could be shared (e.g., the homosexual is three times more suicidal than the heterosexual; a recent study shows the life expectancy of homosexual men and women *without AIDS* being about 33 years shorter than that of the heterosexual; and so forth),[45] but space will not permit it. I believe that any unbiased reader would have to admit that homosexuality is neither a healthy lifestyle nor a natural one.

THE CHRISTIAN'S TASK

Before closing I need to clarify that while I believe that homosexuality is anatomically aberrant, psychologically deviant, and morally bankrupt, it is also just as true that we are all sinners. The Bible states that we have *all* turned our backs on God and gone our own way. As Martin Luther once put it, we each "sin often and daily."

Except for the grace and mercy of God, each one of us would be left in our own little world of sin, alone and helpless. The good news, though, is that God has reached out to us, coming down to become one with us in our humanity, dying and rising again—that we may be free from the bondage of sin.

For anyone struggling with the bondage of homosexuality, or the bondage of any other sin, there is freedom available at the cross of Calvary. Our task as Christians is to lovingly reach out to all people with the gospel of Jesus Christ.

*This essay originally appeared in the Christian Research Journal:

    Joseph Gudel, "Homosexuality: Fact or Fiction," *Christian Research Journal* 15:1 (1992), 21–33.

**Reproduction rights granted by the Christian Research Journal.

[44] Ibid., 123, 119.

[45] Paul Cameron, William L. Playfair, and Stephen Wellum, "The Homosexual Lifespan," *Family Research Institute* (February 14, 1992).

HOMOSEXUALITY, FACT OR FICTION?
ESSAY QUESTIONS

Answer the questions below on a separate sheet of paper and be prepared to review your answers in class.

1. **How is homophobia defined in *The Kinsey Institute New Report on Sex*? According to this definition, are Christians homophobes? Why or why not?**

> *The Kinsey Institute New Report on Sex* defines "homophobia" as an irrational fear or hatred of homosexuals. Therefore, Christians are not (or least should not be) homophobes because although we recognize that homosexuality is sin, we are not called to hate anyone. [SM p. 141]
>
> *[Refer to Christ's words in Matthew 5:43–44 (cf. Luke 6:27–28). Although some homosexuals and/ or homosexual advocates may actually hate Christians, our response is supposed to be one of love and prayer.]*

2. **It is often cited that 10 percent of the population in the United States is homosexual; from where does this statistic come?**

> It seems that many who use this statistic do not know where it comes from. The truth of the matter is that it comes from a flawed 50-year-old study done by Alfred Kinsey—*Sexual Behavior in the Human Male* (1948). [SM pp. 141–2]

3. **Is the 10 percent figure accurate? Why or why not?**

> In this area, the study has at least three obvious problems: 1) Approximately 25 percent of the 5,300 individuals Kinsey studied were prison inmates who, because of their incarceration, could not have heterosexual intercourse. Almost half those prison inmates reported having homosexual experiences while in prison. 2) His representative study also included several hundred male prostitutes. 3) The study had volunteer bias. In other words, Kinsey ran ads asking for people to participate in his study on human sexual behavior. Common sense would seem to tell us that running an ad for such an intimate subject matter would lead to a disproportionate number of promiscuous respondents.
>
> It must also be noted that Kinsey did not say that 10 percent of the entire U.S. population was homosexual. Rather, he affirmed that ten percent of white American males were "more or less" exclusively homosexual for at least three years of their lives between the ages of 16 and 65. The statistic for females was five percent. The actual percentage of those thought to be *exclusively* homosexual for their entire lives was only four percent of men and two or three percent of women, all based on his allegedly representative sample of the population. [SM p. 142]

4. **What other studies have been done regarding the percentage of homosexuals in our society? What were their findings?**

> One study of men conducted between 1984 and 1987 by David Forman found that only 1.7 percent

Unit Five

of his sample had ever had homosexual intercourse. Another study conducted at the University of Chicago in 1989 resulted in a figure less than 1% exclusively homosexual. [SM p. 142]

5. **Does the APA's 1973 decision to remove homosexuality from its list of disorders substantiate the claim that homosexuality is normal? Why or why not?**

The fact that homosexuality was removed from the APA's list of disorders does not seem to substantiate the claim that homosexuality is normal. First, the removal was in part the result of pressure from homosexuals and not the result of scholarly debate. Second, the decision to declassify homosexuality was not unanimous. Only a quarter of the 25,000 APA members actually voted on this issue and of those that did, only 58 percent favored the removal of homosexuality from the list of disorders. Third, a later poll seems to reveal that the majority of the APA does not consider homosexuality to be normal. In 1977 ten thousand members of the APA were polled at random as to their opinion on this issue. In an article entitled "Sick Again?" *Time* magazine summarized the results of the poll: "Of those answering, 69% said they believed 'homosexuality is usually a pathological adaptation, as opposed to a normal variation,' 18% disagreed, and 13% were uncertain." [SM pp. 142–3]

6. **What is the best evidence for homosexuality being biological? What are the main problems with this evidence?**

A 1991 study by Dr. Simon LeVay of 41 cadavers, 19 of which were homosexual males, found that "a tiny area believed to control sexual activity [the hypothalamus] was less than half the size in the gay men than in the heterosexuals." The main problem with this study is best summed up by John Money, "The real question is, when did it get there? Was it prenatal, neonatal, during childhood, puberty? That we do not know." In other words, this study, if accurate, merely reinforces that there is a difference between heterosexual males and homosexual males. It does not, however, show that a homosexual is born homosexual.

Other problems are cited by the author. First, all nineteen of the homosexual men had died of AIDS, something that many researchers believe could very well account for or contribute to the differences. Second, there was no way to know the sexual history of the "heterosexual" men. Third, there was no way to determine if the smaller hypothalamus glands were the cause or the result of homosexuality. Fourth, Dr. LeVay, a homosexual himself, admitted that his study was not entirely a dispassionate scientific endeavor. [SM p. 143]

7. **Is there any evidence that would indicate an environmental cause for homosexuality?**

A number of researchers and therapists cite individual case studies and personal experiences to support the notion that homosexuality is, as Robert Kronemeyer states, "a learned response to early painful experiences and that it can be unlearned. For those homosexuals who are unhappy with their life and find effective therapy, it is curable." [SM pp. 143–4]

8. **Is it possible for homosexuals to revert or convert to heterosexuality? Cite at least one example.**

> It is certainly true that a number of homosexuals have changed from being exclusively homosexual to being heterosexual. Of course it must also be noted that a number of former homosexuals have fallen back into their old lifestyles. However, this is to be expected. Just like in Alcoholics Anonymous, the road is rarely easy and involves a tremendous commitment by the individual seeking recovery and healing. Sometimes individuals stumble and never get back up again. Sometimes they stumble, get back up, and continue on in the process of recovery. And occasionally, individuals are healed instantly and never turn back again. But the fact remains that there are many former homosexuals who have been transformed by the power of Jesus Christ. [SM pp. 145-6]

9. **For what two reasons is homosexuality not a healthy lifestyle?**

> First, promiscuity is neither emotionally nor physically healthy. There is a direct correlation between sexually transmitted diseases, such as AIDS, and the number of sexual partners one has/had. Second, typical homosexual sexual practices can adversely affect the following: oral cavities, lungs, penis, prostate, bladder, anus, perianal areas outside of the rectum, rectum, colon, vagina, uterus, pelvic area, brain, skin, blood, and immune system. Beyond this, it should be noted that 70 percent of Americans with AIDS are male homosexuals or bisexuals. Also, homosexuals are three times more suicidal than heterosexuals. Lastly, one study shows that the life expectancy of homosexual men and women *without AIDS* being about 33 years shorter than that of the heterosexual. [SM pp. 14–8]

10. **What is the Christian task in relation to homosexuals?**

> Our task as Christians is to lovingly reach out to all people with the Gospel of Christ. We must remember that all have sinned and even Christians continue to struggle with certain sins. In this area, we are all alike, but the Christian is not alone in his or her struggles. We have the power of the Almighty God to combat sin and he has given us a community of believers for strength, support, and guidance. Though this particular sin may make many of us uncomfortable, it is just as forgivable as every other deviation committed by mankind against the will of God. [SM p. 148]
>
> *[Discuss any personal experiences your students may have had with this issue.]*

LEPROSY ACTIVITY
Have the students read Mark 1:40–2, a story of how Jesus healed a man with leprosy. Based on this passage, discuss how Jesus would act today if confronted with a man who had AIDS. Referencing Leviticus 13, particularly verses 45 and 46, will help the students understand just how radical Jesus' reaction to the leper was. You may want to consider having them rewrite or retell the story for today with the disease being AIDS and not leprosy.

THAT WHICH IS UNNATURAL

BY JOSEPH P. GUDEL

THE GAY RIGHTS MOVEMENT'S POLITICAL AGENDA

In Part One of this series I went into some detail showing that even from a secular perspective the unbiased reader is forced to admit that homosexuality is neither a healthy nor a natural lifestyle. However, over the past 20 years or so there has been a growing gay rights movement within America. This movement has been militantly demanding not just the homosexuals' right to do whatever they wish to do behind closed doors, but, more importantly, that society fully accept their lifestyle as both healthy and normal, even demanding special rights and legislation as an "oppressed minority."

Concerning the demands of the gay rights movement, gay spokesperson Jeff Levi in a 1987 speech to the National Press Club in Washington stated: "We are no longer seeking just a right to privacy and a protection from wrong. We also have a right—as heterosexual Americans already have—to see government and society affirm our lives."[1]

As far back as 1975, in an article entitled "Gays on the March," *Time* magazine quotes gay activist Barbara Gittings, "What the homosexual wants, and here he is neither willing to compromise nor morally required to compromise—is acceptance of homosexuality as a way of life fully on a par with heterosexuality."[2] In response to this, *Time* wisely reflected: "It is one thing to remove legal discrimination against homosexuals. It is another to mandate approval… It is this goal of full acceptance, *which no known society past or present has granted to homosexuals*, that makes many Americans apprehensive" (emphasis added).[3]

In view of their stated goals, it is extremely significant that today there is legislation pending in the United States Congress which proposes to do just what the gay rights movement has demanded: fully legitimize homosexuality as an acceptable and sanctioned alternative lifestyle. The Senate version, sponsored by Senator Edward Kennedy, is bill S. B. 574. The House version, sponsored by Representative Barney Frank (an openly avowed homosexual), is measure H. R. 1430. [*Editor's Note: Neither of these bills passed.*]

For most Americans it is shocking simply to have a bill like this being considered in the halls of Congress.[4] What is even more amazing is that already it has approximately 140 congressional sponsors, as well as the full support of President Bill Clinton.[5]

If passed, this bill would make it illegal for any organization, including Christian businesses and churches, to refuse employment to practicing homosexuals. It would legalize same-sex "marriages," something not now recognized in any U.S. jurisdiction. [*Editor's Note: As of 2009, Massachusetts, Connecticut, Iowa, Vermont, and New Hampshire have legalized same-sex marriage, while the issue is actively being debated in California and Maine. In addition, New York, California, and Washington D.C. recognize same-sex marriages, although they are not currently performed in those states.*] Homosexual "couples" would have the right to adopt children. And every school system would have to include homosexuality as a positive alternative lifestyle in any sex education course offered.

Concerning the radical gay rights agenda now being advanced, Dr. John F. Harvey—a nationally known professor of moral theology at De Sales School of Theology and someone actively involved in counseling homosexual persons for over thirty years—writes: Homosexual activists… are not requesting merely the right to live their lifestyle in private, to be left alone; to use their own words, they want to convince all elements of society—even children—that "gay is as acceptable as straight"… I think that gay-rights legislation would harm children at an impressionable, malleable, and gullible age. There is plenty of evidence for the position that homosexual propaganda can sway young people into homosexual activity and, perhaps, permanent orientation in that direction.[6]

[1] Jeff Levi, in William Dannemeyer, *Shadow in the Land* (San Francisco: Ignatius, 1989), 86.
[2] "Gays on the March," *Time* (September 8, 1975), 43.
[3] Ibid.
[4] In a 1991 Gallup Poll, 61% of Americans believed that "tolerance of the gay lifestyle has been bad for society." *Nightline* (September 8, 1992).
[5] Gregory Bray, "Where Are Dems on Family Values?" Augusta, GA, *The Augusta Chronicle*, reprinted in the *Oshkosh Northwestern* (August 22, 1992).
[6] John F. Harvey, *The Homosexual Person* (San Francisco: Ignatius, 1987), 114–15.

As evidence that influencing children at a very early age is part of the gay rights agenda one need look no further than New York City's public school curriculum. Included in the curriculum materials are four pro-homosexual books aimed at very young children. One, *Heather Has Two Mommies*, is a children's book about a lesbian couple having a child through artificial insemination. Another book, *Daddy's Roommate*, describes a boy with divorced parents who visits his father and his father's new male roommate (obviously his lover). In a third book, *Gloria Goes to Gay Pride*, part of the text reads: "Some women love women, some men love men, some women and men love each other. That's why we march in the parade, so everyone can have a choice."[7]

The rationale for these books is found on page 145 of the city's "Children of the Rainbow" first-grade curriculum which states that teachers must "be aware of varied family structures, including . . . gay or lesbian parents," and "children must be taught to acknowledge the positive aspects of each type of household."[8]

In an article describing this, John Leo writes in *U.S. News and World Report,* "A line is being crossed here; in fact, a brand new ethic is descending upon the city's public school system. The traditional civic virtue of tolerance (if gays want to live together, it's their own business) has been replaced with a new ethic requiring approval and endorsement (if gays want to live together, we must 'acknowledge the positive aspects' of their way of life)."[9]

It is clear that the gay community wants much more than simply the right to privacy. But what about their civil rights? Are new laws really essential to protect those in the gay community? In answer to this Roger J. Magnuson, a nationally renowned trial lawyer, states: "Homosexuals have all of the same rights heterosexuals do. They are protected by the Bill of Rights, by federal and state statutes, and by common-law decisions. They have the same status before the law as do other citizens… The issue is not whether rights have been infringed. The issue is whether new rights, not previously recognized, should be created."[10]

There is no question about the homosexual's right to practice whatever deviations he or she wants to in the privacy of his or her own home. There are many questions, however, about their attempt to codify their behavior as acceptable and good, to force their lifestyle on the rest of society, and to influence those too young to understand the moral implications of this issue.

It is simply an emotional ploy to attempt to portray this issue as involving civil rights for an oppressed minority. No one would ever say it is a sin to be black or Hispanic, just as no one would say it is a sin to be female or to be physically handicapped. But God's Word does say it is a sin to engage in homosexual behavior, as we shall see below.

HOMOSEXUALITY AND THE CHURCH

Very few churches today come right out and affirm homosexuality as official church teaching. There are a few, though, which do. Foremost among these is the Metropolitan Community Church, founded by Troy Perry in 1968, largely for practicing homosexuals.

The only mainline denomination that has actually called for affirming and fully accepting homosexuals is the United Church of Christ (UCC). As far back as 1975 they voted to end any "discrimination" based on sexual preference and left it to individual UCC congregations to decide for themselves what they believed on this matter. In 1983 the UCC General Synod passed a resolution stating that "a person's sexual orientation is not a moral issue."[11] Finally, in 1991 the UCC General Synod approved the call for its congregations to "boldly affirm, celebrate, and embrace the gifts for ministry of lesbians, gays, and bisexual persons."[12]

Many other denominations are close to this view. Some, such as the Episcopal Church, have openly practicing homosexual clergy, with the full knowledge of their church's governing bodies. Others, such as the United Methodist Church (UMC), have officially rejected homosexual practice as incompatible with the Christian faith. However, at least 44 UMC congregations "have formally opened their doors to homosexuals" and called on their bishops to bless "same-sex union ceremonies."[13] Similarly, the Evangelical

---

[7] *Nightline.*
[8] John Leo, "Heather Has a Message," *U.S. News & World Report* (August 17 1992).
[9] Ibid.
[10] Roger J. Magnuson, *Are Gay Rights Right?* updated edition (Portland: Multnomah, 1990), 78.
[11] "UCC Admits Gay Church," *The Christian Century* (May 30, 1990).
[12] "Bar Homosexual Clergy, Conservative Disciples Say," *Religious News Service,* in *The Christian News* (Sept. 30, 1991).
[13] "UMC and Gay Unions," *The Christian Century* (June 27 1990).

Lutheran Church in America's 1991 study guide on sexuality affirms that "no absolutistic judgments can be drawn" concerning homosexuality.[14] However, the guide then goes on to promote "committed" homosexual relationships.[15] A new gay magazine which describes itself as a "journal for gay and lesbian Christians" has a 10-page listing of "Christian" churches and organizations that "welcome gays and lesbians into full membership and participation."[16]

Very few Christian denominations today have remained faithful to the Bible's clear affirmation that homosexuality is a sin. Among these would be the Roman Catholic Church, the Southern Baptist Convention, the Lutheran Church-Missouri Synod, the Wisconsin Evangelical Lutheran Synod, and the Greek Orthodox Church.

THE BIBLE AND HOMOSEXUALITY

The Authority of the Scripture

It is extremely revealing to note that almost every pro-gay group within the church shares one thing in common: *they reject the Bible as being fully the Word of God*. Of the above mentioned denominations which have accepted homosexuality or are sympathetic to it, none of them believe that we have God's inerrant Word in the Old and New Testaments. Likewise, the many pro-homosexual books that have come out almost all reject—or even ridicule—the church's historic stance on the inspiration and authority of Scripture.

Three different lines of attack on Scripture are found in the various pro-homosexual literature. The first is simply to ignore the biblical writers on the grounds that they were men who oftentimes made mistakes, and thus to reject what Scripture says as being morally authoritative. Thus John Barton states that "the Bible is not a code at all; it is a big baggy compendium of a book, full of variety and inconsistency, sometimes mistaken on matters of fact and theology alike."[17] And elsewhere, in John Boswell's widely cited work, we find, "In considering the supposed influence of certain biblical passages… one must first relinquish the concept of a single book containing a uniform corpus of writings accepted as morally authoritative."[18]

A second attack relates to the first—that is, the biblical writers were ignorant about homosexuality. They did not know all that we do today, it is argued, and so we must judge and interpret the Bible with our modern understanding of biology, psychology, sociology, and so forth. "With the quantum leaps that have been achieved in biology, psychology, and sociology, minds in the twentieth and twenty-first centuries must subject traditional religious arguments about nature to more thorough and critical analyses."[19]

It is not within the purview of this article to give a detailed defense of the inspiration and reliability of the Bible.[20] However, the simple response to these attacks is that both Judaism and Christianity have always held to the full authority of Scripture, as did Jesus Himself. In speaking of the Old Testament, for example, our Lord succinctly declared, "Scripture cannot be broken" (John 10:35). Parts of Scripture cannot be accepted while other parts are rejected. And in speaking of the guidance His apostles would receive, including guidance on their future writings (i.e., the New Testament), Jesus told them: "But the Helper, the Holy Spirit, whom the Father will send in My name, He will teach you all things, and bring to your remembrance all things that I said to you" (John 14:26; cf. 2 Tim. 3:16).

It is ludicrous to believe that the Creator of the universe, in guiding the biblical authors, was ignorant concerning the things we now know about homosexuality through modern biology, psychology, sociology, and so forth. To deny scriptural statements about homosexuality on these grounds is to completely deny God's superintendence in the authorship of Scripture.

---

[14] Evangelical Lutheran Church in America, *Human Sexuality and the Christian Faith* (Minneapolis: ELCA, 1991), 44.
[15] Ibid., 41–46.
[16] *Christus Omnibus*, premier issue, front cover and 18.
[17] John Barton, "The Place of the Bible in Moral Debate," *Theology* 88 (May 1985), 206.
[18] John Boswell, *Christianity, Social Tolerance, and Homosexuality* (Chicago: University of Chicago Press, 1980), 92.
[19] Jeannine Gramick, "What Is Natural?" in Robert Nugent and Jeannine Gramick, eds., *Building Bridges* (Mystic, CT: Twenty-Third Publications, 1992), 46. Also see Letha Scanzoni and Virginia Ramey Mollenkott, *Is the Homosexual My Neighbor?* (New York: Harper & Row, 1978), 71.
[20] See Norman L. Geisler and William E. Nix, *A General Introduction to the Bible* (Chicago: Moody, 1968).

A third type of attack is to state that it really does not matter what heterosexuals think the Bible says about homosexuality, because homosexuals must interpret Scripture in view of their own experiences. Hence, in the book *Building Bridges* we find the statement that "the Scriptures contain some insights that can be made known to the Christian community only through the testimony of lesbian and gay people." Thus homosexuals must "interpret the Scriptures in the light of their own experiences."[21]

The problem with this is that a person could justify *any* type of behavior by saying that Scriptures pertaining to a particular behavior can only be understood by those who engage in such behavior (e.g., incest, adultery, fornication, and even bestiality). Those who believe this should remember the words of our Lord, "Therefore take heed that the light which is in you is not darkness" (Luke 11:35).

Human Sexuality

Genesis 1–2

For those who believe that statements of the Bible are normative for our daily lives, the most important question to consider regarding homosexuality is: What was God's *purpose* in creating human sexuality? The answer to this question is more important than any other area of discussion.

From the very beginning of His revelation to humankind, God has revealed His order of creation, especially as it relates to sexuality. In Genesis 1 we are told that one purpose in creating the two sexes was *procreative*—through the sexual union of male and female we could reproduce the race: "Male and female He created them. Then God blessed them, and God said to them, Be fruitful and multiply; fill the earth and subdue it" (Gen. 1:27b–28).

More detail is provided in Genesis 2, however, where we are told that in addition to *procreation*, there is a *unitive* function of sexuality that has to do with fulfilling our need for companionship: "And the Lord God said, 'It is not good that man should be alone; I will make him a helper comparable to him'" (Gen. 2:18). Then, after God created Eve and presented her to Adam, Adam rejoiced in his God-given companion. The chapter concludes: "Therefore a man shall leave his father and mother and be joined to his wife, and they shall become one flesh" (Gen. 2:24–25).

In this second chapter several items emerge. First, man has need for companionship: "It is not good that man should be alone" (Gen. 2:18); second, God makes provision to meet this need: the creation of woman (2:19–23). Concerning this, Samuel Dresner, Visiting Professor at Jewish Theological Seminary, states: "Woman is formed and becomes his partner. In her, man finds completion."[22] And third, God ordains the institution of marriage. We are told that the man would (1) "leave his father and mother," (2) "cleave to his wife," and (3) "they shall become one flesh." Thus we find that heterosexuality is proclaimed to be God's natural order of creation.

In the New Testament, whenever the subject of sexuality comes up, the heterosexual norm of marriage is always upheld. For example, Jesus, in answer to a question, quoted Genesis 1 and 2: "Have you not read, that He who made them at the beginning 'made them male and female,' and said, 'For this reason a man shall leave his father and mother and be joined to his wife, and the two shall become one flesh'? So then, they are no longer two but one flesh. Therefore what God has joined together, let not man separate" (Matt. 19:4–6).

In addition, the apostle Paul reaffirms the norm of heterosexuality in several of his letters, also quoting the Genesis passages (e.g., Eph. 5:25–33; cf. 1 Cor. 7:2–3, 10–16; 1 Tim. 3:2, 12). And while some protest that we cannot take Genesis 1 and 2 as modern scientific treatises,[23] these chapters nonetheless teach us spiritual truths concerning God's intended order for His creation.

It is *only* in the heterosexual union of marriage that we find the fulfillment of God's intended order, both procreative *and* unitive. However, pro-homosexual writers argue that while homosexual activity in and of itself cannot be procreative it can still fulfill the unitive role of Genesis 2. In response to this Harvey writes:

---

21 Jeanine Gramick, "Lesbian/Gay Theology and Spirituality," *Building Bridges*, 190–91.

22 Samuel H. Dresner, "Homosexuality and the Order of Creation," *Judaism* 40: 3 (Summer 1991), 309; also see Richard F. Lovelace, *Homosexuality and the Church* (Old Tappan, NJ: Fleming H. Revell, 1978), 102 ff.

23 Ralph Blair, *Homosexualities* (New York: Ralph Blair, 1991), 13.

> Consider the three common forms of sexual activity between homosexual persons. Mutual masturbation in no way constitutes a physical union... Among female homosexuals some form of genital massage is used to bring the partner to orgasm, but this is not a physical union. In anal or oral intercourse between males the intromission of the penis in an opening of the body not meant to be used for the genital expression of sexuality cannot be called a true physical union... By way of contrast, the heterosexual union aptly symbolizes the psychological and spiritual union that ought to exist between a man and a woman.[24]

One does not need a Ph.D. to realize that homosexuality is anatomically aberrant; that is, there is a created biological order intended in our sexuality. As an editorialist at Harvard's Peninsula journal writes, "How can (homosexual) people be happy when they're persistently deceiving themselves, believing that it is just as natural for sperm to swim into feces as it is to swim into eggs?"[25] "The true religious goal of human sexuality can be seen, not as *satisfaction*, but as *completeness*."[26]

This fulfillment is unattainable in homosexuality. Now that we have considered God's positive purpose in creating human sexuality, we are ready to look at biblical texts which explicitly address homosexuality. Space precludes a detailed response to pro-homosexual interpretations of these passages. The interested reader can check the resources listed in the endnotes for further reading.

Leviticus 18 and 20

"You shall not lie with a male as with a woman. It is an abomination" (Lev. 18:22).

"If a man lies with a male as he lies with a woman, both of them have committed an abomination. They shall surely be put to death" (Lev. 20:13).

Although these prohibitions explicitly condemn homosexuality as an abomination before God, we are told that they are not relevant today. Why? First, the pro-homosexual interpretation is that since these condemnations are contained in the "Holiness Code" of Israel, they were only applicable to ancient Israelites, to keep them separate from the pagan practices of their neighboring tribes.[27]

Second, parts of this code are not kept today. Letha Scanzoni and Virginia Ramey Mollenkott assert that "consistency and fairness would seem to dictate that if the Israelite Holiness Code is to be invoked against twentieth-century homosexuals, it should likewise be invoked against such common practices as eating rare steak, wearing mixed fabrics, and having marital intercourse during the menstrual period."[28]

Much effort need not be expended answering these objections. First, God did not condemn certain behavior for the Israelites only because Israel was to be kept separate from Canaanite practice. Otherwise, if the Canaanites did not practice child sacrifice and bestiality, would these then have been all right for the Israelites? Of course not! Having sexual relations with an animal and killing one's child are inherently wrong and evil, even when they are not related to pagan worship; they are abominations before God. And yet, these specific prohibitions also are listed in this passage, both immediately before and after the condemnation of homosexuality (Lev. 18:21–23).

Other prohibitions listed in Leviticus include incest and adultery (Lev. 18:6ff; 20:10). Were these too only condemned because of the Canaanites? To argue in this fashion is dishonest and denies that there are eternal moral absolutes.

What of the fact that other parts of the Holiness Code in Leviticus are not kept today? Again, the answer is simple. The Holiness Code contained different types of commands. Some were related to dietary regulations or to ceremonial cleanliness, and these have been done away with in the New Testament (Col. 2:16–17; Rom. 14:1–3). Others, though, were moral codes, and as such are timeless. Thus incest, child sacrifice, homosexuality, bestiality, adultery, and the like, are still abominations before God.

We believe this information is very vital for the case against the homosexual lifestyle. However, due to its graphic nature, the brown section has been blocked out in the student manual. If you decide to have your students read the essay in its entirety, it can be found on the Teacher's CD-ROM under "Handouts."

Unit Five

---

[24] Harvey, 101.
[25] R. Wasinger, "If You're Gonna Call Me Names," *Peninsula* 3:2 (October/November 1991), 25.
[26] R. T. Barnhouse, *Homosexuality: A Symbolic Confusion* (New York: Seabury Press, 1977), in Natalie Shainess, "Homosexuality — Today," *Judaism* 32: 4 (Fall 1983), 414.
[27] Boswell, 100–106.
[28] Scanzoni and Mollenkott, 60–61.

<u>Romans 1:18–27</u>

"For this reason God gave them over to degrading passions; for their women exchanged the natural function for that which is unnatural, and in the same way also the men abandoned the natural function of the woman and burned in their desire toward one another, men with men committing indecent acts and receiving in their own persons the due penalty of their error" (Rom. 1:26–27).

If there were no other passage than this which condemns homosexuality, those engaged in this lifestyle would still be, in Paul's own words, "without excuse" (Rom. 1:20). Paul's intent in Romans 1–3 is to show that all have sinned, Jew and Gentile alike, and turned from God. It is not an accident that the apostle begins his argument with a reference to the Creator and His creation (1:16–20). His Jewish/Christian audience would immediately have connected this with Genesis 1–2, which, as we have seen, tells us not only about God's created order, but also about the complementary design of male and female within that order.

In his catalogue of sins (Rom. 1:18–32) Paul lists homosexuality and lesbianism first after idolatry not because they are the most serious sins, but because they are warning signs that a violation of reason and nature has occurred. Men have inverted God's order by worshipping the creature rather than the Creator, and as a signal of this error, like the blinking red light on the dashboard of a car which is functioning improperly, God has given them up to "dishonorable desires" in the inversion of their sexual roles.[29]

Two main arguments are raised against the historic understanding of this passage. The first is that Paul was not referring to true homosexuality here because he stated that they exchanged "the natural function for that which is unnatural." It is argued that for those with a true homosexual orientation, that is their "natural" sexual expression. Hence he could only mean heterosexuals who were leaving their heterosexual relations for what was against their natures.[30]

This argument involves an amazing anachronism. That is, those saying this are attempting to place a very recent twentieth century understanding of homosexuality back into the first century mindset of Paul. People in the first century did not think in terms of "sexual orientation." It is inconceivable for Paul to have even attempted to make a psychological differentiation such as this. Concerning this, Richard Hays writes: "The idea that some individuals have an inherent disposition towards same-sex erotic attraction and are therefore constitutionally 'gay' is a modern idea of which there is no trace either in the NT or in any other Jewish or Christian writings in the ancient world."[31]

The second attempt to refute Paul's clear condemnation of homosexuality argues that his words "unnatural" or "against nature" do not refer to a certain created order, but rather use "nature" in the sense of "current convention" or "current custom."[32] While "nature" is sometimes used in this fashion (e.g., 1 Cor. 11:14), the context of Paul's argument in Romans 1 clearly is that of creation and the natural order established by the Creator Himself (Rom. 1:20, 25). Thus Paul is asserting that homosexuality is a gross violation of God's natural design for His creation. In addition, it should be noted that the phrase "against nature" was used in connection with homosexual intercourse by both Philo and Josephus, contemporaries of Paul.[33]

<u>1 Corinthians:9 and 1 Timothy 1:10</u>

"Do you not know that the wicked will not inherit the kingdom of God? Do not be deceived: Neither the sexually immoral nor idolaters nor adulterers nor male prostitutes nor homosexual offenders… " (1 Cor. 6:9, NIV).

In both 1 Corinthians 6:9 and 1 Timothy 1:10 the apostle Paul states that those guilty of sexual immorality will not inherit the kingdom of God. At the time Paul wrote his letters there was no word in classical, biblical, or patristic Greek which corresponded with our English term "homosexual." Instead, homosexual behavior *was described* (e.g., Rom. 1:26–27). The words Paul uses here—*malakoi* ("male

---

[29] Lovelace, 92.

[30] Boswell, 109ff.

[31] Richard B. Hays, "Relations Natural and Unnatural: A Response to John Boswell's Exegesis of Romans 1," *The Journal of Religious Ethics* 14:1 (Spring 1986), 200; also see David F. Wright, "Homosexuality: The Relevance of the Bible," *Evangelical Quarterly* 61:4 (1989), 291–300.

[32] Boswell, 110ff.

[33] Philo, *Spec. Leg.* 3.39; Josephus, *Against Apion*, 2.273.

prostitute") and *arsenokoitai* ("homosexual offenders")—have been translated in different ways. Because of this those condoning homosexuality have tried to lessen the impact of these verses, saying that all Paul was condemning was either homosexual prostitution or pederasty (i.e., men having sexual relations with boys).[34]

Virtually every Greek lexicon, however, including all of the standard English ones, has understood these words (especially *arsenokoitai*) to be referring to homosexuality.[35] Arndt and Gingrich's lexicon says *malakoi* refers to persons who are "soft, effeminate, especially of catamites, men and boys who allow themselves to be misused homosexually."[36] Likewise, *arsenokoites* means "a male homosexual, pederast, sodomite."[37]

We also find these terms in classical Greek literature (e.g., Lucian and Aristotle) "sometimes applied to obviously gay persons."[38] As well, if Paul were only condemning certain types of homosexuality he would certainly have specified this. Instead, he used a term directly based on the Greek Septuagint translation of the prohibitions against homosexuality in Leviticus:

> *meta arsenos ou koimethese koiten*
> *gynaikos* (Lev. 18:22)
> *koimethe meta arsenos koiten*
> *gynaikos* (Lev. 20:13)[39]

Paul, a rabbi thoroughly trained in the Torah, was certainly mindful of these Levitical condemnations and the Septuagint translation of them when he chose his wording in 1 Corinthians and 1 Timothy.

Law and Gospel

Is homosexuality natural and healthy, as the gay rights movement wants us to believe? The answer from Scripture is no, and as Christians we must not be involved in homosexuality nor be among those who, as Paul warns, "approve of those" who are engaged in it (Rom. 1:32). The Roman Catholic church is correct in stating that homosexuality is "an intrinsic moral evil."[40]

At the same time, though, we must reach out to all people with the love of Jesus Christ and His gospel, which alone has the power to change lives. And we must speak out against hatred and violence directed toward any group, remembering that we are all sinners, worthy only of God's judgment. We all have sin in our lives, and we are all tempted in different ways (whether it be toward homosexuality, adultery, incest, greed, violence, pridefulness, or whatever else).

Paul used the Law to show us, his readers, our sin and the fearful judgment awaiting us. But then, to those who truly desired to follow after God, he announced the good news of the Gospel: "For the wages of sin is death, but the gift of God is eternal life, through Jesus Christ our Lord" (Rom. 6:23).

For all who accept this gift, including homosexuals, there is reconciliation to God, regeneration as His children, and "grace to help in time of need" (Heb. 4:16).

---

*This essay originally appeared in the *Christian Research Journal*:
    Joseph Gudel, "That Which is Unnatural: Homosexuality in Society, the Church, and Scripture," *Christian Research Journal* 15:3 (1993), pp. 9–15.
**Reproduction rights granted by the *Christian Research Journal*.

[34] Boswell, 106–7.
[35] Ibid., 341–42.
[36] Walter Bauer, *A Greek-English Lexicon of the New Testament and Other Early Christian Literature*, ed. William F. Arndt, trans. F. Wilbur Gingrich (Chicago: University of Chicago Press, 1957), 489.
[37] Ibid., 109.
[38] P. Michael Ukleja, "Homosexuality in the New Testament," *Bibliotheca Sacra* 140: 560 (October-December 1983), 351.
[39] Wright, 297ff.
[40] Joseph Ratzinger, *On the Pastoral Care of Homosexual Persons* (Boston: Daughters of St. Paul, 1986), 2.

THAT WHICH IS UNNATURAL
ESSAY QUESTIONS

Answer the questions below on a separate sheet of paper and be prepared to review your answers in class.

1. Of what are homosexual activists trying to convince society?

> Many homosexual activists are not merely contending for the right to live their lifestyle in private, but attempting to prove that a homosexual lifestyle is as acceptable as a straight lifestyle. They are not merely seeking tolerance, but acceptance—making homosexuality as a way of life fully equal with heterosexuality. [SM p. 150]

2. What types of legislation are homosexual activists trying to pass?

> Homosexual activists are seeking to pass gay-rights legislation, making it illegal to discriminate against homosexuals in any way. This would make it illegal for any organization (Christian or otherwise) to refuse employment to practicing homosexuals. Such activists are also seeking to legalize same-sex marriages and the adoption of children by homosexual couples. [SM p. 150]

3. How is the homosexual agenda being promoted in public schools?

> A number of schools are now using pro-homosexual curriculum materials in their schools. Some of these materials are aimed at very young children.
>
> For example, *Heather Has Two Mommies* is a children's book about a lesbian couple having a child through artificial insemination. Another book, *Daddy's Roommate*, describes a boy with divorced parents who visits his father and his father's new male roommate (obviously his lover). In a third book, *Gloria Goes to Gay Pride*, part of the text reads: "Some women love women, some men love men, some women and men love each other. That's why we march in the parade, so everyone can have a choice."
>
> The rationale for these books is found on page 145 of the first-grade curriculum "Children of the Rainbow," which states that teachers must "be aware of varied family structures, including… gay or lesbian parents," and "children must be taught to acknowledge the positive aspects of each type of household."
>
> The use of such materials demonstrates that some in the gay community desire more than just the right to privacy. They are seeking to promote (even indoctrinate) children into accepting such a lifestyle. [SM pp. 150–1]

SM
157

4. **Are new laws needed to protect homosexuals?**

No, homosexuals have all of the same rights that heterosexuals do. The United States Constitution, federal and state statutes, and common-law decisions protect homosexuals. Homosexuals have the same status before the law as every other citizen.

It is incorrect to compare the current status of homosexuals to that of African Americans or women's suffrage. Unlike African Americans and women in the past, a homosexual can vote and own property. Societal laws protect all citizens from bodily harm, not just heterosexuals. A homosexual can even marry, as long as he or she marries a member of the opposite sex; anything else, by definition, would not be 'marriage.' To argue that such 'restrictions' on marriage are discriminatory is something quite strange. In asking to redefine marriage, homosexual activists are actually asking for special treatment, not equal treatment. The issue is not whether rights have been infringed, but whether rights not previously recognized should be created. [SM p. 151]

5. **Point out three lines of attack being used by a number of Christian denominations to circumvent God's Word regarding homosexuality. What are some of the problems with these lines of attack?**

The first attack is to simply ignore the passages dealing with the immorality of homosexuality. This is usually based on the assumption that the Bible's human authors were simply mistaken about the issue, thus rejecting everything Scripture has to say about homosexuality.

A similar attack asserts that the biblical writers were ignorant about the subject of homosexuality. It is argued that these writers did not have all of the information on the subject that is available today in the areas of biology, psychology, sociology, and so forth. For example, had the writers of the Bible but known that homosexuality was genetic; they would not have prohibited it as sin.

A third type of attack is to state that it really does not matter what heterosexuals think the Bible says about homosexuality because homosexuals must interpret Scripture in view of their own experiences. In response to the first two attacks, it seems inconsistent to assert that our God is all-powerful, yet in guiding the biblical authors he somehow made mistakes regarding homosexuality. To deny scriptural affirmations regarding homosexuality is to deny God's superintendence in the authorship of Scripture. And if God does not wholly inspire the Bible, why give any part of it authority over your life?

In response to the third attack, if the Bible is to be personalized by our own likings, then every person could justify *any* type of behavior by appealing to his or her feelings on the issues (e.g., incest, adultery, fornication, and even bestiality). [SM pp. 151–3]

6. **What was God's purpose in creating human sexuality?**

It seems that there were at least two purposes for the creation of two sexes—procreation and union—and it is *only* in the heterosexual union of marriage that we find the fulfillment of God's intended order. In Genesis 1, there is a *procreative* element—through the sexual union of male and female we could reproduce the race: "Male and female he created them. Then God blessed them, and God said to them, 'Be fruitful and multiply; fill the earth and subdue it' " (Gen. 1:27b–28).

In Genesis 2, we are told that in addition to *procreation*, there is also a *unitive* function of sexuality that corresponds with our need for companionship: "And the Lord God said, 'It is not good that man should be alone; I will make him a helper comparable to him'" (Gen. 2:18). Then, after God created Eve and presented her to Adam, Adam rejoiced in his God-given companion. The chapter concludes: "Therefore a man shall leave his father and mother and be joined to his wife, and they shall become one flesh" (Gen. 2:24–25). [SM p. 153]

7. **Are the prohibitions against homosexuality in Leviticus still relevant today?**

While this prohibition is found within the section of Scripture known as the "Holiness Code," this does mean that this particular prohibition had been done away with in the New Covenant. In other words, although a number of restrictions found in the Holiness Code have been lifted in the New Testament age, this does not mean that *every* prohibition found within this section is obsolete for today. In fact, a number of prohibitions found in this section are indeed timeless. If this were not the case, then there would be no moral restrictions today against bestiality and child sacrifice.

Thus, the real question is if the restriction against practicing homosexuality was part of a timeless moral standard or just a temporary ordinance intended to set Israel apart from their pagan neighbors? Since homosexuality was later prohibited in the New Testament, it seems that the prohibition against homosexuality is an eternal ordinance. [SM pp. 154–5]

8. **What two arguments are raised against the historic understanding of Romans 1:18–27? How might the historic reading be defended?**

The first argument is built upon the assumption that a person is born with a sexual orientation— either homosexual or heterosexual—whichever preference we are born with is our "natural" orientation, making the opposite orientation "unnatural." It is argued that Paul was condemning homosexuals who were practicing heterosexuality and heterosexuals that were practicing homosexuality.

The main problem with this argument is that people in the first century did not think in terms of "sexual orientation." It hard to imagine Paul almost 2000 years ago making a case for homosexuality from a modern notion of sexuality.

The second argument claims that Paul's use of the words "against nature" does not refer to a certain created order, but rather to a violation of cultural custom. However, while this phrase is sometimes used in this fashion (e.g., 1 Cor. 11:14), the context of Paul's argument in Romans 1 clearly is that of creation and the natural order established by the Creator himself (Rom. 1:20, 25). Thus it is most likely Paul is asserting that homosexuality is a violation of God's natural design for his creation. [SM p. 155]

9. How should we translate the Greek words *malakoi* and *arsenokoitai*? Why?

> Virtually every Greek and English lexicon describes *malakoi* and *arsenokoitai* as terms referring to homosexuality. Arndt and Gingrich's lexicon says *malakoi* refers to persons who are "soft, effeminate, especially of catamites, men and boys who allow themselves to be misused homosexually." Likewise, *arsenokoites* means "a male homosexual, pederast, sodomite." These terms are also used in classical Greek literature (e.g., Lucian and Aristotle) referring to individuals who are obviously gay.
>
> Likewise, if Paul were only condemning certain types of homosexuality, as has been argued by some, he would certainly have specified this. Instead, he used a term directly based on the Greek Septuagint translation of the Levitical prohibitions against homosexuality. In other words, the Greek translation of the Old Testament uses the same term found in the Greek New Testament—basically *arsenos koiten gynaikos*. [SM pp. 155–6]

10. How should the Church respond to homosexuality and homosexuals?

> As Christians, we must not be involved in homosexuality nor ally ourselves with those who condone it. We must follow the strict command Paul gave the Romans—do not "approve of those" who are engaged in the sin of homosexuality (Rom. 1:32).
>
> However, at the same time, we must reach out to all people with the love of Jesus Christ and his gospel, which alone has the power to change lives. We must also speak out against hatred and violence directed toward any group, remembering that we are all sinners, worthy of judgment. We all have sin in our lives and are tempted in different ways (whether it be toward homosexuality, adultery, incest, greed, violence, pride, lying, coveting, or whatever else). But God has offered all human beings the gift of eternal life. [SM p. 156]

WORLDVIEW PAPER
WRITING ASSIGNMENT

REQUIREMENTS

Write a paper comparing the most fundamental elements of the six worldviews presented in this course. These elements include theology, philosophy, ethics, and biology. You should also explain how each of these elements logically interacts with the others (e.g. since Secular Humanists are atheists, they explain the origin of life by methods that exclude God—some form of evolution).

This paper should be 4–6 pages in length, double-spaced, Times New Roman 12 point font with 1 inch margins. You must use at least 3 sources (one source can be your textbook), and all citations must be documented with footnotes. The suggested outline for your paper is below:

    1. <u>INTRODUCTION</u> (25 points possible)
        • Define the term "worldview"
            1. In your own words
            2. Cite an expert
            3. Use an analogy (e.g. triangle, pyramid, bundle of sticks, tree, etc.)
            4. Do not merely list the disciplines
        • Practically explain how a person's worldview influences the way he or she lives (e.g. Christians pray because their worldview includes a belief in a personal God)

    2. <u>CHRISTIAN WORLDVIEW</u> (25 points possible)
        • Overview
        • Theology, philosophy, ethics, and biology

    3. <u>ISLAMIC WORLDVIEW</u> (25 points possible)
        • Overview
        • Theology, philosophy, ethics, and biology

    4. <u>SECULAR HUMANIST WORLDVIEW</u> (25 points possible)
        • Overview
        • Theology, philosophy, ethics, and biology

    5. <u>MARXIST-LENINIST WORLDVIEW</u> (25 points possible)
        • Overview
        • Theology, philosophy, ethics, and biology

    6. <u>COSMIC HUMANIST WORLDVIEW</u> (25 points possible)
        • Overview
        • Theology, philosophy, ethics, and biology

    7. <u>POSTMODERN WORLDVIEW</u> (25 points possible)
        • Overview
        • Theology, philosophy, ethics, and biology

    8. <u>CONCLUSION</u> (25 points possible)
        • Compare, contrast, and critique the above worldviews

TEACHER
MANUAL

UNDERSTANDING THE TIMES

Unit Six

Topics:
Community
Marriage and Family
Radical Feminism
Sociology

A Summit Ministries Curriculum

180-Day Syllabus

DAY	IN CLASS	HOMEWORK	
1	WATCH "Sociology" video		
2	READ <u>UTT</u> Textbook 'Sociology 6.1'	READ <u>UTT</u> Textbook 'Sociology 6.2'	
3	REVIEW <u>UTT</u> Textbook 'Sociology 6.1–6.2' questions	READ <u>UTT</u> Textbook 'Sociology 6.3'	
4	READ <u>UTT</u> Textbook 'Sociology 6.4'		
5	REVIEW <u>UTT</u> Textbook 'Sociology 6.3–6.4' questions	READ <u>UTT</u> Textbook 'Sociology 6.5'	
6	READ <u>UTT</u> Textbook 'Sociology 6.6'	ASSIGN Dear Doug Letter	
7	REVIEW <u>UTT</u> Textbook 'Sociology 6.5–6.6' questions	READ *Doing Life Together* essay	
8	REVIEW *Doing Life Together* essay questions		
9	WATCH "Love, Sex, and Marriage" video P1		
10	WATCH "Love, Sex, and Marriage" video P2		
11	REVIEW "Love, Sex, and Marriage" video questions		
12	READ *Domestic Tranquility* essay P1		
13	READ *Domestic Tranquility* essay P2		
14	REVIEW *Domestic Tranquility* essay questions	Dear Doug Letter assignment DUE	
15	TAKE Unit Six Test		

90-Day Syllabus

DAY	IN CLASS	HOMEWORK	
1	WATCH "Sociology" video	READ <u>UTT</u> Textbook 'Sociology 6.1–6.2'	
2	REVIEW <u>UTT</u> Textbook 'Sociology 6.1–6.2' questions	READ <u>UTT</u> Textbook 'Sociology 6.3–6.4'	
3	REVIEW <u>UTT</u> Textbook 'Sociology 6.3–6.4' questions	READ <u>UTT</u> Textbook 'Sociology 6.5–6.6'	
4	REVIEW <u>UTT</u> Textbook 'Sociology 6.5–6.6' questions		
5	WATCH "Love, Sex, and Marriage" video P1		
6	WATCH "Love, Sex, and Marriage" video P2		
7	REVIEW "Love, Sex, and Marriage" video questions		
8	TAKE Unit Six Test		

UNDERSTANDING THE TIMES
SOCIOLOGY QUESTIONS

Answer the questions below on a separate sheet of paper and be prepared to review your answers in class. Reflection Questions will not be found in the text. These are merely designed to help you start thinking about issues from a worldview perspective.

SOCIOLOGY 6.1

1. **According to the Bible, what are the three basic institutions of society? Why do sociologists differ when describing the origin of these institutions and their relationship to the individual?**

> According to the Bible, the three basic institutions of society are family, church, and state (government). Sociologists differ based on the assumptions inherent to their worldview. [UTT 6.1.1]

2. **According to Christianity, what is the source of humanity's problems?**

> Christianity describes human beings as creatures with the freedom to choose between right and wrong and to shape society. Problems arise when we choose to live in a way other than God intended. This often happens because of our alienation from God, others, and ourselves. [UTT 6.1.2]

3. **What scriptural references support the institutions of family, church, and state?**

> The Family
> - Genesis 2:20 (Adam and Eve)
> - Ephesians 5–6 (man, wife, children)
> - Ecclesiastes 9:9
> - Proverbs 18:22
>
> The Church
> - Romans 12
> - 1 Corinthians 12
> - Acts 20
> - Acts 2:47
> - Colossians 1:18
>
> Civil Government
> - Romans 13:1–4
> - Proverbs 8:15
> - Proverbs 24:21
>
> Friendships
> - 1 Corinthians 13
> - 1 Timothy 5
> - Romans 12
> - 1 Samuel 13ff (David and Jonathan)
>
> [UTT 6.1.6–8]

4. **Reflection Question: What impact did the Fall have on human relationships? How does this relate to the area of sociology?**

> We were created as social beings. At creation there were four main relationships that were in perfect harmony: Adam and Eve enjoyed a wonderful relationship with the Creator of the Universe (Relationship 1), Adam and Even understood clearly that they were created in the image of God (Relationship 2), Adam and Eve had an intimate, loving relationship with one another (Relationship 3), and they both understood their role in the creation as vice-regents and stewards (Relationship 4).

Unit Six

SM
161

The Fall destroyed these relationships. There was separation between God and man; the image of God was marred in man and the harmonious relationship between Adam and Eve had been altered forever. The first case of the "blame game" occurred: Adam blaming Eve and God for his sin. The relationship between man and the created world had been negatively affected as well. Though work was not part of the curse (Adam and Eve were to take care of creation before the Fall), work was made harder as a result.

All of these relationships were seriously affected by the Fall. The only way these relationships could be restored was through a work of redemption. That work of redemption was accomplished through Jesus dying on the cross for our sins. Because of this act we are no longer doomed to live lives of alienation, instead looking forward with hope to a day when we will live in glorified bodies and enjoy the blessings of a new heaven and new earth.

Bearing this "Grand Story" in mind, Christian sociology attempts to understand society in light of our free will and the consequences that followed our decision to turn from God. [UTT 6.1.2]

[Help your students understand that our lives are being played out within the context of the "Grand Story." Show them that the accounts of Creation (Act 1) and the Fall (Act 2) take place within the first two pages of the Bible. The rest of the story is about God redeeming his creation (Act 3). Ultimately, when history as we know it ends, believers will be in our glorified bodies enjoying a new heaven and a new earth with our eternal Creator (Act 4).]

5.   Reflection Question: **What does it mean to be created in the image of God and how was this image marred?**

God created mankind as his image-bearers with a non-physical dimension, including a mind (to know him), emotions (to love him), a will (to obey him), a moral awareness (to be able to make right choices), and a spirit (to communicate and have fellowship with him). These non-physical dimensions reflect the image of God.

We have lost the understanding, or openly mock, the idea of being made in the image of God. Lack of respect for this fact has led to such atrocities as slavery, abortion, euthanasia and infanticide. Lack of respect for human beings is not so much an affront to our worth, because we are sinful and deserving of judgment, as it is an offense to the Creator of the universe whose image we bear.

Consider this: I show you a photograph of my wife (insert appropriate person for your example). If you curse it, make fun of it, spit on it and tear it up, you will have to answer to me! "Why?" you ask. "After all, it's only a photograph." Yes, but it is a photograph of my wife! That is what makes all the difference. The picture itself—the paper and ink, etc.—is not of much value. It is worth only a few cents. What is of concern to me is not the picture itself but the one whom it represents.

Intrinsically, man is of little worth; he is certainly not of "infinite worth." No created finite being, whether fallen or unfallen, unredeemed or redeemed, could be. The warnings of Genesis 9 and James 3 do not stem from the fact of man's infinite worth; rather, they stem from the fact of God's infinite worth! To dishonor man and to abuse him is to dishonor and abuse God because he is made in God's image. That is what brings the warning and the penalty. It is *the One whose image and likeness man bears* that is of significance—not the man who bears that image and likeness. He is, in a sense, the photograph, but God loves man very much.

6. How do some Islamic writings characterize women?

Some Islamic texts teach that men and women are spiritually equal. However, other Islamic writings are not so charitable. For example, 1) some writings dictate that two women are needed for credible testimony versus only one man; 2) in the Sunnah, women are described as having less intelligence; and 3) according to Muhammad, most of the inhabitants in hell are women. [UTT 6.2.3]

7. What is the Islamic view of polygamy? Is polygamy the norm?

Most Muslims only have one wife but the Qur'an permits a man to have up to four wives (depending upon certain conditions). However, Muhammad had at least 9 wives, a discrepancy which has been difficult for Islamic apologists to resolve. [UTT 6.2.5]

8. How was Muhammad's disregard for the restriction on polygamy resolved?

Muhammad said he received revelations from God that permitted him this excess. [UTT 6.2.6]

9. What does the Bible have to say about polygamy?

Polygamy in biblical history is a reality that needs to be admitted and understood. While the creational intent of marriage seems opposed to the idea of polygamy (Adam and Eve were monogamous), polygamy was allowed for a time in Israel's history, though with certain restrictions. However, in the New Testament we find that leaders of the church, who are examples for us all, are commanded to be husbands "of one wife" (1 Timothy 3:2,12). Indeed, Jesus is the perfect example in that he has one bride (not "brides") which is the church, a relationship illustrating and illustrated by marriage (Ephesians 5:31–32). [UTT 6.2.8]

10. How do Muslims view the institution of the state? What two forms of government do Muslims promote?

Muslims do not see Islam as a social institution to be distinguished from the state. Instead Islam is a comprehensive reality encompassing the state just as much as does the mosque. However, the Muslim world is divided between those who favor nation-states (distinct nations, with distinct laws and constitutions from other nations) and those who favor pan-Islam (the vision that the Muslim community should be united, with diminished or non-existent national boundaries). [UTT 6.2.10]

11. How is sociology different from psychology? What problem do both secular psychologists and sociologists face?

While psychology's focus is on the individual, sociology's focus is on the society. Both disciplines face the unscientific nature of their approach. Just as Secular Humanist psychologists struggle to redefine science in a way that includes their approach while excluding a religious approach, Secular Humanist sociology struggles to fit the "scientific" label. [UTT 6.3.1]

12. What are some adjectives used by Secular Humanists to describe traditional marriage?

Secular Humanists often define traditional marriage as restrictive, old culture, inhibiting, social slavery, relic of the past, enslaving, victim, flawed, neurotic, insecurity. [UTT 6.3.4]

13. What must Secular Humanists use to reshape people's thinking socially and economically?

Because the classroom is the ideal place for Secular Humanists to further the "new" faith of Humanism, it becomes a prime avenue for activism. [UTT 6.3.6]

"I think that the most important factor moving us toward a secular society has been the educational factor. Our schools may not teach Johnny to read properly, but the fact that Johnny is in school until he is sixteen tends to lend toward the elimination of religious superstition. The average American child now acquires a high school education, and this militates against Adam and Eve and all other myths of alleged history." (Paul Blanshard quoted in Noebel, *Understanding the Times*, 441)

14. How does the new social order propose to handle childrearing?

A number of Humanist sociologists go so far as to suggest that the family in the new world order will no longer have to concern itself with childrearing, instead turning the next generation over to the government. They believe that this situation is a better alternative for all involved and that future generations will be more likely to stay in touch with their inherent goodness when raised in state-sponsored institutions. [UTT 6.3.5]

15. Reflection Question: How might state-sponsored childrearing change society?

[Answers will vary. Relate this to the problems we are having today concerning a lack of fathers in homes and broken families in general, but be sensitive to your students' various family situations.]

16. How does Marxism's reliance on evolution as a basis for its social theory influence its perception of the mechanisms of society?

Marxists believe that just as we are evolving biologically, we are also evolving sociologically. As humanity improves through the evolutionary chain of being, so does society. The scientific fact of biological evolution guarantees both the truth of Marxist social theory and the outcome of the process: a communist world. [UTT 6.4.1]

17. According to Karl Marx, what determines a person's consciousness?

"It is not the consciousness of men that determines their existence," writes Marx, "but their social existence that determines their consciousness." That is, our very consciousness is determined by a society predetermined by its economic system. [UTT 6.4.3]

18. How do Marxists view religion in relation to the evolution of society?

Marxists see religion as a stumbling block, hindering the development of the ultimate society. Therefore, Marxists seek ways to diminish the role and influence of religion. [UTT 6.4.6]

19. Once the proletariat has ushered in a socialistic system, what role does the Marxist sociologist envision education taking?

Marxist sociologists see the public system of education as a means to indoctrinate pupils in scientism. The educational system thus, in part, becomes a platform upon which the irreconcilability of science and religion is strongly stressed. [UTT 6.4.7]

[Take a few minutes to help students understand how education has been and continues to be used in other countries. We have discussed how Secular Humanism has influenced the public school system in the West. Discuss how children in Russia and China were/are educated under communist rule, and how children are educated in Islamic nations. Stress to the students that these children think differently than we do. They view the world through completely different lenses. Children raised in communist countries view the world through the lens of naturalism—no supernatural realm.]

20. How will children be cared for according to Marxist sociology?

The care of the children should become "a public affair." In communist thought, children are the entire community's responsibility. Thus, children are disengaged from the family and the school takes the place of home. The alienation of children from their parents helps ensure that children formulate their worldviews according to education provided by the Marxist state. [UTT 6.4.8]

Unit Six

21. What is the ultimate goal of Cosmic Humanist psychology and sociology?

Once every individual makes the evolutionary leap to collective godhood, Cosmic Humanists believe the disciplines of psychology and sociology will merge, i.e. both will study a society unified into one mind (the mind of God). [UTT 6.5.1]

22. What is the Cosmic Humanist view of traditional marriage and family?

Cosmic Humanists view traditional marriage and family as examples of outdated unenlightened institutions. They are regarded as too limiting and too hopelessly blind to universal sacredness to be useful in achieving full enlightenment. [UTT 6.5.2]

23. What does Shakti Gawain say about divorce in the New Age society?

Shakti Gawain believes we need to re-work our attitude about divorce to create a society more conducive to humanity's evolution to godhood: "People who divorce almost inevitably feel that they have failed, because they assume all marriages should last forever. In most such cases, however, the marriage has actually been a total success—it's helped each person to grow to the point where they no longer need its old form." [UTT 6.5.2]

24. What does Kevin Ryerson say about sexuality in the New Age society?

Cosmic Humanists note that humanity's evolution toward godhood has already begun and should not be halted by traditional views of society. Kevin Ryerson notes that moving forward requires a great deal of sexual freedom: "Sexuality, whether homosexual or heterosexual, is the exploring of the personalities of yourselves as incarnate beings, or as a spirit inhabiting the flesh. An individual's sexual preference should be viewed as neither good nor evil—such preferences are but the functioning of the body's dialogue to and with another." [UTT 6.5.2]

25. How do Cosmic Humanists view education?

They hope to encourage a "limitless" society by working within an already existing institution: our educational system. By teaching children the proper attitudes toward themselves and their consciousness, New Age educators believe that they can create a generation capable of ushering in the New Age. [UTT 6.5.3]

[Ask your students if they have heard reports where visualization, imaging, meditation, etc. have been used. Explain to them that New Age techniques are becoming more prevalent in the public school system. Explain that educational ideas do not arise out of a vacuum. There are always reasons behind techniques used.]

26. According to Michel Foucault, why is the social order important?

> Foucault maintains that living within the social order is the essence of life because one's culture determines one's self. The essence of life is another way of stating there is no unified self, but life is merely a summary of the cultural aspects of the social community. [UTT 6.6.1]

27. What do Postmodernists believe about the family, sexuality, traditional values, and the church? How is the Postmodernist view of sociology best defined?

> - **Richard Rorty** declares that Christian parents who teach their children about God are "frightening, vicious, and dangerous."
> - **Adam Phillips** says, "The only sane foregone conclusion about any relationship is that it is an experiment… "
> - **Michel Foucault**: "We must… ask why we burden ourselves today with so much guilt for having once made sex a sin."
>
> Since Postmodernists do not hold to objective universal standards, they consequently view the family and attitudes about sexuality as social constructions with no inherent moral obligation. Thus, they contend that there are no differences between homosexual practices and heterosexuality. What used to be considered perverted, abnormal, or deviant sexual behavior is actually only personal preference. And the church, which promotes traditional values, is seen as an enemy attempting to conform society to its own intolerant ideals.
>
> The Postmodernist view of sociology is best defined by the phrase "sexual egalitarianism." This expresses the idea that every individual defines sexuality and sexual relationships for himself or herself and that all sexual preferences are equally valid. [UTT 6.6.2]

28. According to Walter Truett Anderson, what role does education play within society? How do Postmodernists plan to equalize the playing field?

> Anderson contends that society's educational system should be used to promote human sensitivity in regards to other individuals regardless of race, sexual preference, or class identity. To make sure that white, heterosexual males don't continue in their privileged position in the educational system, "education should emphasize works not in the canon, it should focus on the achievements of nonwhites, females and the poor; it should highlight the historical crimes of whites, males, and the rich; and it should teach children that science's method has no better claim to yielding truth than any other method and, accordingly, that students should be equally receptive to alternative ways of knowing." [UTT 6.6.3]

Unit Six

29. How are Postmodernists seeking to restructure society?

> The Postmodern approach for restructuring society is to experience "new ways of living." Instead of overthrowing the government with some grand Utopian scheme—which could draw attention to one's socially constructed self—the new plan calls for challenging "power on a day-to-day level," or as Lyotard says, "gnaw away at the great institutionalized narrative apparatuses . . . by increasing the number of skirmishes that take place on the sidelines. That's what women who have had abortions, prisoners, conscripts, prostitutes, students, and peasants have been doing." [UTT 6.6.4]

30. Why is Dada art a good representation of the Postmodern mood? What words best describe Postmodern art and music?

> Dada's themes are about meaninglessness, which reflects the Postmodern nihilistic mood rather well. Similar themes prevalent in Postmodern art and music include waste and hopelessness. [UTT 6.6.5]

PRO-FAMILY ACTIVITY

Bring to class a variety of "women's magazines," TV guides, and newspapers. Divide the class into three separate groups and give each group a set of periodicals. Have them look for the following things about families.

For the TV guide people: How many shows feature an intact, non-blended family (mother, father, and children)? Which shows feature blended families? Which shows feature non-traditional families? How many shows feature families in a positive light? How many seem to mock traditional family roles (such as showing the father as a bumbling idiot or having the kids playing the parental role or disrespecting authority)? How many shows feature families in a negative light?

All others: Look for the following portrayals and keep tallies of how many times they occur (don't forget to look at advertisements also):

- women as mothers or caring for children
- men as fathers or caring for children
- men as providers for their families
- single parents
- monogamy as desirable

When the students have finished, go over their findings. Was a predominant view of the family reflected? If so, what was it? Was it hard to find families represented?

Doing Life Together

by Charles Moore

Fellowship is life, and lack of fellowship is death;
fellowship is heaven, and lack of fellowship is hell;
and the deeds that ye do upon the earth
it is for fellowship's sake that ye do them.
William Morris

If I've read the New Testament right, as followers of Christ, we are members of Christ's body (1 Cor. 12:14–21), and hence, by definition, we belong to each other. We cannot intentionally follow Christ solo. Interdependence, not independence, is God's pattern. In other words, there is no such thing as a lone ranger Christian. When we fail to connect with each other we are failing to connect with Jesus.

But what does it mean to *connect* with one another? Sadly, superficiality is a disease of our time. Shallow friendships and fragile relationships mark not only our society but also the church. Even our language betrays such superficiality. Consider how we use the word "fellowship" in Christian gatherings. In Acts 2:42 we read that the early Christians "devoted themselves to the fellowship." They did not occasionally have fellowship (verb). They *were* the fellowship (noun); marked by a shared life together. They were devoted *to each other*, and so they were being woven together in mutual care. It involved a common, daily, material life of unity and sharing. The early church experienced daily life *together* in Christ, and this was how they were constituted as a fellowship.

Biblically speaking, therefore, fellowship is far more than spilling coffee on one another on Sunday morning. It extends far beyond "getting together" and experiencing a rush of relational warm fuzzies during hyped-up religious happenings. Sadly, very few of us experience our life together as did the early Christians. They did not consider what they had as their own. Theirs was a common, daily, material life of unity and sharing. We, however, assemble and associate and meet at regular intervals, but our lives and pocket books are still very much our own. Our *lives* really don't intersect. We share commonly very little.

Re-Membering the Body

From what I have read and heard, right after the collapse of the Twin Towers, one might inadvertently come across a human body part, like a finger or a toe. The thought of dismemberment both shocks and repulses us. It not only is incongruous, but a severed body part is not quite human; removed from the body it is horrendously out of place.

Now if we would but step back and actually see how fractured and dismembered our country has become, how severed and alienated, and how conflicted and fearful we are of each other, if we could but see how frightfully alone we have become, we might become more repulsed and begin to see what it is that ails us both individually and socially. We might also discover anew the plan and purpose of God revealed in Christ's prayer for unity: "That they may be one, Father, as you and I are one… " (John 17:21ff).

Herein lies the gift and witness of Christ's body: the church on earth. God's people can, by their manner of life together, be the very thing the world cannot achieve on its own steam. But it is important to grasp that following Jesus is nothing if it is not a way, a life, a living, and a living together. It's all about *togetherness*. Consider, for example, the reciprocal pronoun "one another" (*allelon*) in the New Testament. This one word alone highlights the significance of doing life together:

- Outdo one another in showing honor (Rom. 12:10)
- Live in harmony with one another (Rom. 12:16)
- Admonish one another (Rom. 15:14)
- Greet one another with a holy kiss (Rom. 16:16)
- Wait for one another (1 Cor. 11:33)
- Have the same care for one another (1 Cor. 12:25)
- Be servants of one another (Gal. 5:13)
- Bear one another's burdens (Gal. 6:2)
- Comfort one another (1 Thess. 5:11)
- Build one another up (1 Thess. 5:11)
- Be at peace with one another (1 Thess. 5:13)
- Do good to one another (1 Thess. 5:15)
- Put up with one another in love (Eph. 4:2)
- Be kind and compassionate to one another (Eph. 4:32)
- Submit to one another (Eph. 5:21)

- Forgive one another (Col. 3:13)
- Confess your sins to one another (James 5:16)
- Pray for one another (James 5:16)
- Love one another from the heart (1 Pet. 1:22)
- Be hospitable to one another (1 Pet. 4:9)
- Meet one another with humility (1 Pet. 5:5)

Now when we reflect on the above list, one thing is clear: Virtually none of the above exhortations make sense without a serious level of *commitment* to one another. How are we to bear another person's burden unless the burden is known and unless we are willing to actually carry it? How are we to "put up with each other" unless we relate closely enough to get on each other's nerves? How are we to forgive one another unless we are in each other's lives enough to hurt and let down one another? How can we learn to submit to one another unless we struggle with differences? In other words, if we are to connect (or reconnect) our lives with one another, it will demand much more of us than we normally give. To be the church, and not just go to church, demands a great deal more than many of us are willing to give.

Few of us are ready to build up a common, committed life with others on a daily level, especially if it costs us a pay raise or causes us to forgo our personal preferences. If we are honest, we take our primary social cues from the broader culture. We consider our lives as "ours," independent of or above the church in some way. But experiencing genuine Christian community will never happen if you are hanging on to your own life or if your schedule only allows for a couple of "religious" meetings a week. New lifestyle habits will have to form. Sacrifices of convenience and of giving up private spaces and personal preferences will have to be made. It will involve making concerted choices so that others can more naturally and easily be in, and not just around, your life. Doing life together demands commitment. But it involves more than this. Without engaging in some very concrete practices, life together, instead of being a joy, may be hell.

LIFE TOGETHER

Commitment is the basis, but community in Christ is the aim. What might this look like in more concrete terms? What are the marks that signify authentic Christian fellowship beyond going to church on Sundays? What does a shared life really look like in which the Spirit bears its fruit?

Time

Perhaps the first fruit of commitment is *time*. Those who love one another spend time with each other. When I was in college and seminary I purposely took fewer credits than I could handle, just so I could make more time for others. As the years have gone by, finding time for others has become more difficult. A stark example of this occurred when I was living in an intentional Christian community in downtown Denver. A group of us, mostly in our thirties, lived in four duplexes right next to each other. We wanted to go on a back-packing trip together, but wouldn't you know, there was not one available weekend in the summer where we could all be together. Though we managed to share "space" together, our time was another matter.

Time is important because without being available to each other, fulfilling the biblical "one anothers" is virtually impossible. Take the construction metaphor of "building one another up." Building is a process that requires effort and persistence. Leaving a project undone will do damage to the materials. And if it is not done *together* who knows what will result? Or take the command to "do good to one another." It takes time to discern what is good for another person. I remember very well when I accidentally put a young college student into an emotional tailspin. I gave her a very strong challenge that completely backfired. I didn't realize she had been severely abused as a child and constantly struggled with suicidal feelings. If I had taken the time to know her better, I would have handled things very differently.

Time is crucial if we are really to "serve one another." Interestingly, the New Testament concept of service means performing lowly, thankless deeds—as a slave would do. This is what Jesus modeled when he washed his disciples' feet. The slave serves the master as *he* has need. Our gifts are less important than our readiness to serve. This hit home to me while I was in seminary. Jake, a fellow seminarian, and his wife Sharon were struggling to keep their home sane. They had two small boys, and Sharon had several medical needs. Their house, especially their kitchen, was a disaster. I was busy myself, but not at 10:30 PM. That was downtime before bed. I felt a nudge inside me that I should offer to do their dishes at that time. Did I want to? No. But a slave of Christ doesn't have the luxury of choosing which service to perform and when. They accepted my offer, and for two years this is what I did. Jake has been a life-long friend ever since.

Space

As important as time is, so is sharing space. This may or may not mean living with one another under the same roof. But it will mean finding practical ways of becoming more proximate with each other. The notion of a commuter marriage is an oxymoron. So is a commuter church. Unless we are physically present in each other's lives, unless our personal spaces are made available to one another, sharing life will only be skin deep.

Throughout history believers have found various ways of sanctifying space together. The earliest Christians formed neighborhoods within cities. The Celtic church created entire villages, sharing everything in common. Then there were various monastic orders, and during the Reformation radical reformers, like the Anabaptists, formed outright communities, some consisting of as many as 2,000 people. Today there are churches that revolve around cluster groups and there are groups like Jesus People USA in Chicago, or Community of Sojourners in San Francisco, or the Community of Jesus on Cape Cod, who have forged their own unique ways of drawing together in close proximity. Whatever its size, shape, or form, a living fellowship will seek very physical ways to share life together.

Of course, community demands more than sharing time and space. A fellowship of Christians is not the same things as a *Christian* fellowship. Doing life together must be done *in Christ*—in other words, in a way where Christ's authority holds sway. For this to happen, we must learn to listen to the Word—both in the Bible and as the Spirit speaks through others—and obey it *together*. Personal study of the Scriptures is vital, but God's Word has always been primarily addressed to his people—as a people! Interestingly, almost all the New Testament Epistles are written to churches! And when we think about the various "one another" commands, they can be fulfilled only if they are accomplished with others. Being under the Word is not just a matter of listening to a sermon together, but seeking with each other, by way of dialogue and prayer, what it means to obey Christ together. In my own church community, for instance, we regularly read the Scriptures together and then ask: "What must *we* do?" Recently, we felt convicted by how much unnecessary "stuff" we all had. So on a Saturday we all went through our houses, and with feedback from each other, got rid of piles of things that we really didn't need. We brought everything to one place to be either hauled away or sold. We did this all together in order to show God that we were serious about doing his Word. And by doing it together, we dealt a deathblow to the spirit of Mammon that wreaks so much havoc in our world. This was obviously not easy to do, but discipleship certainly isn't easy, and it definitely involves discipline (1 Cor. 9:24–27).

Resources

Another mark of life together is being open-handed with the excess that we have. "*Koinonia*" is not solely translated as "fellowship." In fact, its predominate use denotes the sharing of resources. The Macedonian and Achaian churches, for example, set up a common fund (*koinonian*) for the impoverished church in Jerusalem. Since the Gentiles shared (*ekoinonesan*) in the Jew's spiritual blessing, they in turn served their material need (Rom. 15:26,27; also 12:13). Out of their extreme poverty, they urgently pleaded with the apostles for the privilege of taking part (*koinonian*) in this service to the saints (2 Cor. 8:4). Such generosity marked a liberality of fellowship (*aploteti tes koinonias*—2 Cor. 9:13). It demonstrated the effectual working of God's grace (2 Cor. 8:1). On this basis and for this reason, Paul commands those of material means to generously extend their fellowship (*einai koinonikous*) by sharing with those in need (1 Tim. 6:17–19).[1]

For Paul, the right hand of fellowship (*koinonias*) authenticated his apostolic mission: he was committed to taking the gospel to the Gentiles and to obtaining funds for the needy in Jerusalem (Gal. 2:9,10). This sacrifice of sharing (*koinonias*), according to Paul, is what pleases God (Heb. 13:16).[2] Similarly, those receiving instruction in the gospel were to share (*koinoneito*) the good things of this life with their instructor (Gal. 6:6). For this reason Paul praises the Philippian church as ones who partook (*sugkoinonous*) in God's grace, who shared (koinonia) in the work of the gospel, and who were partners (*sugkononesantes*) in his

---

[1] It was only because of who the early church was *as a fellowship* that Paul could literally *command* the wealthier members to give generously. To hold back was a denial of their common life.

[2] The contribution for the needy Jewish Christians in Jerusalem, taken up by the Gentile Christians in the Hellenistic world was "a theological expression of the validity of his [Paul's] work among Gentiles, a sure sign that they had been completely accepted into God's work among the Jews." J. R. McRay, "Fellowship," *Evangelical Dictionary of Theology,* Walter E. Elwell, ed. (Grand Rapids, MI: Baker, 1984), 414.

troubles, for only they shared (*ekoinonesen eis logon*—lit. "opened an account") in giving to him and his companions the aid they needed (Phil. 1:5,7;4:14–16). This was indeed a "fragrant offering, an acceptable sacrifice, pleasing to God" (4:18).

The fellowship of the early church, therefore, was marked by how it shared material life together. It was this very practical expression of love that so impressed pagan society. Their love for one another was not in words, but in deeds—demanding real, physical sacrifices. It was assumed that those who belonged to Christ would have their material needs met (Acts 4:34; 2 Cor. 8:13–15). What a contrast to how we practice church today, where money matters are almost entirely private and personal.

This "none of your business" attitude can work both ways: for those who give and those who receive. Many years ago Cheryl, a good friend of mine who was a part of our local fellowship, lost her job. When she came to tell my wife and me about it, she was literally shaking, in tears, gripped with fear. After sharing with us, it dawned on me: Cheryl feels alone because, in terms of money, she was. It would be up to her to fend for herself. *She* lost her job, and *she* would have to find another. We as a fellowship hadn't lost a source of income; she had, and it was her welfare, not ours, that was on the line. She was no more willing to ask the church for help, than the church was willing to supply it. We were far from being a New Testament community.

I am currently a member of a community movement that consists of several intentional communities throughout the world. One thing we've vowed together is that amongst ourselves we will never charge each other money. Our services to each other are free. Why? Because we don't want money issues to divide or distract us. Nor do we want to be caught up in the snares of the world, which can so easily choke the inner life. Jesus said that we cannot serve both God and Mammon, and that if we seek first the kingdom of God and his justice, all our needs will be provided for (Matt. 6:33). We know which god the world worships; the church, by contrast, must do everything it can to show that it worships a very different God. What better way is there than to be free of the love of money?[3]

What so many Christians seem to miss is how it is possible to shape everyday life itself—including one's work—on the basis of faith. *In Christ*, all things can be made new, including those areas that tend to have a momentum all their own, as they especially do when it comes to career or business. If God's people would join together and redeem the workplace itself, both in terms of what is done and how, then a corporate work—a "Kingdom work"—of transformation can be achieved. A different social-spiritual material reality would emerge, one woven together by the diverse strands of everyday life where Jesus is proclaimed Lord, not just in word, but in deed.

Money and business matters are one thing, our homes are another. We mustn't forget how significant the injunction to "show hospitality to one another" is. It's a resource we often fail to use. It demands a different kind of personal investment—one that is often more telling. Showing hospitality is more than entertaining one another at our convenience. It means providing for each other's needs by offering what is most intimately "yours." Writing a check is easy compared to providing a night's lodging for someone who needs it. Eating at a restaurant with friends may be "fun," but what about taking the time and effort to prepare an equally nice meal? Giving hospitality communicates that you are giving your life, not just your possessions.

Accountability

Now all of this—be it our time, our space, our resources—demands a great deal of trust. Invariably, life together means not only building each other up, but letting each other down. For the struggle against sin, both within ourselves and how we are with each other, is an ongoing one. Life together requires that we be our brother's and sister's keeper.

At the very minimum, holding each other accountable demands that we speak the truth in love. Jesus instructed us clearly on this matter: if a brother is in sin, go to him. If he doesn't listen, get help. If he still

---

[3] One very practical way to show this is to find common ways to work together. Rondout House, in New York, consists of a group of Christians who run a cleaning and maintenance business together. Norwood Community, outside of Cincinnati, operates a café. Danthonia Community, in Australia, makes and sells custom signs together. Rose Creek Community in Tennessee runs a restaurant and a business in solar tinting, construction, and home improvement. Shepherdfield's Community, in Missouri, earns part of its living through organic homemade goods. And in my own community, Catskill Bruderhof, we manufacture specialized handicap equipment.

doesn't listen, then bring the matter to the whole church (Matt. 18:15–20). His point? Don't let sin destroy your brother or sister, nor let it mar my Body.

We have a "rule" in our community. It is paramount for experiencing real joy together. It goes as follows:

> There is no law but that of love (1 John 4:7–8). Love means having joy in others. Then what does being annoyed with them mean? It is thus out of the question to speak about another person in a spirit of irritation or vexation (Eph. 4:29–32). There must never be talk, either in open remarks or by insinuation, against another, against their individual characteristics—under no circumstances behind the person's back. Talking in one's own family is no exception.
>
> Without this rule of silence there can be no loyalty, no community. Direct address is the only way possible; it is the spontaneous service of love we owe anyone whose weaknesses cause a negative reaction in us (Eph. 4:2–3). An open word spoken directly to the other person deepens friendship and is not resented.

A truthful word spoken in love can be extremely powerful. A few years ago I met two fellow members of my community in a rather heated argument—right in the middle of work. Keith, one of our shop foremen, had made a bad machining mistake and had gotten overly defensive (and excited) about it. A few minutes later a couple of co-workers came over to try and sort things out. Then, all of a sudden, they all walked out of the factory. Later I learned that the whole scene was a result of something deeper, unrelated to work. Keith and his wife had been struggling in their marriage and it was starting to take its toll on Keith's general attitude on the floor. Fortunately, with the help of different ones in the community, they were able to find each other's hearts again.

To cite another example, some members of our community once spent a fair amount of money on hotel accommodations while on a mission trip. My wife and I got upset. Why hadn't that money, which we helped to earn, been put to better use? But in the course of our confrontation, and after several others had spoken honestly to us, we realized that our so-called concern was a cover up for cold-heartedness and self-righteousness. We weren't really interested in understanding their situation or their needs. We were more concerned with principles than with warm-blooded, everyday people. I'm glad we were called up short.

Having open, free and honest relationships demands work. And speaking the truth in love doesn't always work out. When Jim fell in love with Karen, who was married to Sean in our community in Denver, it was a burden to bear. But when they began to spend time together alone, and when Karen began to have feelings toward Jim, then something needed to be done. Neither, however, wanted Sean or others to know what was happening. And neither was willing to humble themselves to get help or to ask forgiveness. Sadly, two years later Karen and Sean divorced.

Karen and Jim were not solely to blame. If our community had been more committed to them, and had brought them up short and battled for their relationship openly, then the alluring power of sin might have been nipped in the bud. Recently, when some friends of mine inadvertently discovered a six-pack of beer in Greg's room, they right away talked to him about it. When it happened again, our whole fellowship confronted Greg. In so doing, we came to realize that it wasn't just drinking Greg struggled with, but a whole host of other things: vanity, sexual impurity, and loneliness. Fortunately, Greg wanted things to be different, and so he unburdened his conscience and heart with one of our pastors. He's been a new person ever since!

Forging life together in Christ with others is never easy. We fail each other—and God—all the time. This is why speaking truth in love must always be accompanied by forgiving one another. The Christian fellowship, the community, the church, or whatever one may call life together in Christ is ultimately the place of forgiveness. It is here that the cross comes alive. As Jean Vanier of the L'Arche Community, writes: "In spite of all the trust we may have in each other, there are always words that wound, self-promoting attitudes, situations where susceptibilities clash. That is why living together implies a certain cross, a constant effort, and an acceptance which is daily and mutual forgiveness."[4]

There's a reason why Jesus told his disciples to forgive seventy times seven times. Forgiveness is perhaps the most essential quality necessary for an ongoing and vibrant life with others. Without it our worship is not only false (Matt. 5:23–26), but we violate the very Body of Christ (1 Cor. 11:17ff). We

---

[4] Jean Vanier, *Community and Growth* (New York: Paulist Press, 1979), 10.

actually make a mockery of the cross. For in the cross, Jesus came to mend what is broken, and reconcile estranged relationships (Eph. 2:11ff). Harboring judgment, grudges, mistrust, and fear of each other denies the mystery of why Jesus came.

There are many other attributes one could list that mark being Christians together. But to reiterate, because disciples of Jesus follow a different road map than that of the world, the way in which we live and relate to each other will be markedly different. The path we are on is meant to be traveled together, for our destination is towards a kingdom the first fruits of which can already be felt and seen. Coming together in Christ, if it is real, can show the world that Jesus is Lord both in heaven and on earth.

BECOMING AN APOLOGETIC

It is a misnomer to think that a highly committed fellowship is an "exclusive" or a "reclusive" one. In fact, there is no greater witness to the reality of God's coming kingdom than a biblically formed life together. A fully functioning fellowship of love demonstrates the truth of the gospel far better than apologetic arguments over abstract ideas. As Stanley Hauerwas argues, "What is crucial is not that Christians know the truth, but that they be the truth." The strongest argument for Christianity's truthfulness consists of the lives it produces. Jesus was quite clear about this when he said, "All people will know that you are my disciples if you love one another" (John 13:35). What the world needs most is not words, but living testaments who embody the power of his love. Only our unity will convince the world of Christ's reality (John 17:22–23). For Jesus, the medium and the message are one.

As scientific theories are judged by the fruitfulness of the activities they generate, so is the Christian story. Christian truth is ultimately to be judged by the richness of moral character and the authenticity of relationship it generates. How else can the power of the gospel be *known* (1 Cor. 4:20)?

Therefore, it is how we are together, not just how smart or intellectually astute we are, that vindicates Christ. This is what characterized the witness of the early Christians and permeated the writing of all the early apologists. Athenagoras, for example, wrote:

> Among us you will find uneducated persons, and artisans, and old women, who, though in words are unable to prove the benefit of our doctrine, by their deeds exhibit the benefit arising from their persuasion of its truth. They do not rehearse speeches, but exhibit good works. When struck, they do not strike again; when robbed, they do not go to law. They give to those that ask of them, and love their neighbors as themselves.[5]

Athenagoras' words are not exaggerated. For example, the type of care the early Christians had for one another, revolutionary in comparison with pagan society, extended to all its members: to widows, orphans, the elderly and sick, those incapable of working and the unemployed, prisoners and exiles, Christians on a journey and all other members of the church who had fallen into special need. Care was also taken that the poor received a decent burial. Those no longer able to work received the support of the community.

Such care extended beyond the community's own ranks to include those abandoned and rejected by the unbelieving. For this reason, Christian compassion often received high praise, even from enemies of the faith. The Roman Emperor Julian writes:

> Why don't we notice that it is their [the Christians'] benevolence to strangers, their care for the graves of the dead and the pretended holiness of their lives that have done the most to increase atheism [i.e. Christianity]?… When these impious Galileans support not only their own poor but ours as well, everyone sees that our people lack aid from us.[6]

This failure, combined with the church's deeds, is what convinced the ancient world of Christianity's truth. The church's life together was its logic. Hence, Origen did not hesitate to say, "The evidences of Jesus' divinity are the Churches of people who have been helped."[7] It was not the rationality of its beliefs per se, but the lives the early church produced that persuaded the world. It was the church's ethical transformation that silenced her critics and their desperate accusations. This is how it always is. Christ's truth is both

---

[5] A. Roberts and J. Donaldson, eds., *The Ante-Nicene Fathers*, vol. II (Grand Rapids: Eerdmans), 134.
[6] W. C. Wright, *The Works of the Emperor Julian*, vol. 3 (LCL, 1923), 69,71.
[7] Henry Chadwick, *Origen: Contra Celsum* (Cambridge: Cambridge University Press, 1953), 150.

validated and vindicated when it is being lived out. A moral revolution, set in motion, not argument set in propositions, is what convinces.

Consider again the early church and the extraordinary role healing miracles played. For example, the apologist Origen takes for granted the healing power of Christ as he regularly saw with his own eyes those who were miraculously cured. And Cyprian, in his letter to Demetrianus, describes how the Spirit whips demons and drives them away from the believing. He thus challenges Demetrianus: "Come yourself and see how true it is what we say. You will see how we are entreated by those (i.e. the demons) whom you entreat and feared by those whom you fear and worship." In this vein, the church fathers repeatedly pointed out that the most profound miracles did not consist in people being healed of their infirmities but in their ability—against all human striving and expectation—to break with their pagan past and to embark on a new life.

In other words, the early Christians did not just believe in the power of Christ's resurrection, they lived in and by this power. C. S. Lewis writes, concerning the New Testament's resurrection narratives, that they "are not a picture of survival after death; they record how a totally new mode of being has arisen in the Universe. Something new had appeared in the Universe: as new as the first coming of organic life." A new mode of being has arisen, the first fruits of which were given to the Church to partake. For this reason, Clarence Jordan declares: "The crowning evidence that Jesus was alive was not a vacant grave, but a spirit-filled fellowship. Not a rolled-away stone, but a carried-away church." Such people were the direct evidence of the kingdom—the God movement.

While there is a place for demonstrating Christianity's truthfulness and historicity on certain documentary and experiential "facts," believers ultimately need to become the evidence—a living epistle—necessary to support its claims. Are the Scriptures reliable? How can this ever be answered unless there exists a people who consistently live by them and bear good fruit? Are miracles possible? Jesus' reply to John the Baptist was: "Look and see!" Do we live in such a way that the only satisfactory explanation for its existence is the power of God in its midst? Was Christ raised from the dead? Did he actually die for the world's sin? Well, are there or are there not communities of faith marked by the new life of the Spirit who reconciles all things?

CONCLUSION

In his book *Life Together*, Dietrich Bonhoeffer writes: "It is grace, nothing but grace, that we are allowed to live in community with Christian brothers and sisters." This but echoes the words of the Psalmist who wrote: "How good and pleasant it is when brothers live together in unity!" (Psalm 133:1). This gift of life together opens up the way to God and to our brother and sister.

This gift of community is not simply Christians who are really nice to their friends and the people they go to church with. In the end, Christian community is not even living together and sharing cars, money, and bagels. Genuine community is more like a movement where groups of people have been set free by Christ to pursue radically different agendas with their life and lifestyles.

The Apostle Paul reminds us that love is the greatest gift. This is precisely why Jesus gave up his body on the Cross and gave it back again in the Church. Doing life together in a way where we really need each other brings Christ and his kingdom very close to this earth. For Jesus once dwelt among us as a humble servant; and he continues to dwell among us in this same way. As Paul writes in Philippians, Jesus takes up residence in brothers and sisters, his corporate body, who, "being like-minded, having the same love, being one in spirit and purpose," consider others better than themselves and look to the interests of others above their own. It is they who "shine like stars in the universe" and hold out the word of life.

*This essay was commissioned by Summit Ministries for this curriculum.
** Reproduction rights granted by Charles Moore.

DOING LIFE TOGETHER
ESSAY QUESTIONS

Answer the questions below on a separate sheet of paper and be prepared to review your answers in class. Reflection Questions will not be found in the text. These are merely designed to help you start thinking about issues from a worldview perspective.

1. What is interdependence and why is it important? What makes us so independent?

> One of the defining characteristics of today's Western culture is the spirit of personal independence—an attitude that puts personal interests above everything else. The main goal in life becomes our own success, and the means of achieving this success is through personal accomplishments. For the Christian, however, the main goal in life is the glorification of God through obedience, character growth, and the dissemination of the Gospel. To achieve these goals Christians must work together in a spirit of interdependence, accepting that we do not belong to ourselves, but to God—that we function as an appendage of the body of Christ, rather than a separate entity. In fact, apart from such interdependence, the body of Christ is almost incapable of reaching its intended purpose. [SM p. 163]

2. What is fellowship? How does biblical fellowship differ from common Christian experience today?

> Sadly, the church has bought into the notion of personal independence. We have lost sight of the purpose of the church, denying the body to which we belong. The attitude of independence is not easy to break, but we can find comfort and direction through the example of the early church—a fellowship. In Acts 2:42 we read that the early Christians "devoted themselves to the fellowship." They did not occasionally have fellowship (verb). They *were* a fellowship (noun), marked by a shared life together. They were devoted *to each other*, and so were being woven together in mutual care. It involved a common, daily, material lifestyle of unity and sharing. The early church experienced daily life *together* in Christ and it was this that constituted them a fellowship. [SM p. 163]

3. How can we apply the "one another" statements in the Bible to a fellowship?

> *[This question should create a wide variety of answers. It is important to point out that virtually none of these exhortations make sense without a serious level of commitment to fellowship.]*
>
> Outdo one another in showing honor (Rom. 12:10)
> Live in harmony with one another (Rom. 12:16)
> Admonish one another (Rom. 15:14)
> Greet one another with a holy kiss (Rom. 16:16)
> Wait for one another (1 Cor. 11:33)
> Have the same care for one another (1 Cor. 12:25)
> Be servants of one another (Gal. 5:13)
> Bear one another's burdens (Gal. 6:2)
> Comfort one another (1 Thess. 5:11)

SM
170

Build one another up (1 Thess. 5:11)
Be at peace with one another (1 Thess. 5:13)
Do good to one another (1 Thess. 5:15)
Put up with one another in love (Eph. 4:2)
Be kind and compassionate to one another (Eph. 4:32)
Submit to one another (Eph. 5:21)
Forgive one another (Col. 3:13)
Confess your sins to one another (James 5:16)
Pray for one another (James 5:16)
Love one another from the heart (1 Pet. 1:22)
Be hospitable to one another (1 Pet. 4:9)
Meet one another with humility (1 Pet. 5:5) [SM pp. 163–4]

4. **How is *time* important to a life together as the fellowship? What are some examples from your own experience? What are some improvements you can make?**

Without being available to each other, it is virtually impossible to fulfill the biblical "one another" commands. Take, for example, the commands "be servants of one another" and "build one another up." It is almost impossible to serve members of the body while withholding your time from them. Likewise, it is difficult to edify members of the body without also investing the time required to build them up. [SM pp. 164–5]

[Examples will vary.]

5. **How is *space* important to a life together as the fellowship? What are some examples from your own experience? What are some improvements you can make? Why do we find it difficult to share our space with others?**

The majority of the various "one another" commands can be fulfilled only if they are accomplished with others. Thus, sharing space is as important as sharing time. This may or may not mean living with one another under the same roof, but it does mean finding practical ways to become closer to each other. Take, for example, the commands "comfort one another" and "be hospitable to each another." It is almost impossible to comfort your brother or your sister if you are not willing to share your space. Likewise, it would difficult to be hospitable to members of the body while you are absent from them. [SM pp. 165]

[Examples will vary.]

6. **How are *resources* important to a life together as the fellowship? What are some examples from your own experience? What are some improvements you can make?**

Another important element of life together (and perhaps the most difficult for those of us in the West) is the sharing of resources. Though this does not have to mean sharing everything in common (like the disciples in the book of Acts), it certainly means being more generous with what God has given us—and not just money, but our gifts and talents as well.

Take, for example, the commands "bear one another's burdens" and "do good to one another." It would be hard to bear another's burden without sharing some of your resources. Likewise, it would be difficult to do good to others in the body without giving of yourself. [SM pp. 165–6]

[Examples will vary.]

7. **How is accountability important to a life together as the fellowship? What are some examples from your own experience? What are some improvements you can make?**

All of these factors—time, space, and resources—demand a great deal of trust; invariably life together means not only building each other up, but letting each other down as well. The struggle against sin, both within our hearts and our relationships, is an ongoing one. Life together requires that we be our brothers' and sisters' keepers. Take, for example, the commands "admonish one another" and "love one another from the heart." It is difficult to correct each other unless we are let in on each other's struggles. Likewise, we do not truly love each other if our brothers and sisters are allowed to continue in sin. Equally important to accountability is forgiveness—"forgive one another" and "confess your sins to one another." This is one of the ways the body remains a pure witness to the world. [SM pp. 166–8]

[Examples will vary.]

8. **What role does church discipline play in accountability? How have you seen this work in your own fellowship? How should we look at failure?**

Jesus instructed us clearly on the matter of discipline within the church: if a brother is in sin, go to him. If he doesn't listen, get help. If he still doesn't listen, then bring the matter to the whole church (Matt. 18:15–20). If he is still unwilling to repent, then he must go. The hope is that the body will remain in a state of continued growth through admonishment and support—and when the body functions properly, this is exactly what we see. Sometimes this growth comes through correction and repentance and other times it must happen through excommunication. Ultimately, removing church society from a sinning believer is not a failure, but rests on the hope that he or she will repent and return to the body.

Forging a life together in Christ is never easy. We fail each other—and God—all the time. This is why speaking the truth in love must always be accompanied by forgiveness and restoration. The Christian fellowship is ultimately the place of forgiveness. This is why Jesus mentions the role of forgiveness right after discussing discipline. He told his disciples to forgive each other seventy times seven, emphasizing the vitality of this practice for the fellowship. [SM pp. 166–8]

[Examples will vary.]

9. **What does it mean to be an apologist? How did the early church practice this?**

Christianity is more than an intellectual faith—it also depends on action to be effective in the world. The members of the early church took the "one another" commands seriously and lived them in addition to preaching them. Similarly, the early Christian apologists discovered that the lifestyle they practiced did as much or more to win converts than the arguments they constructed. It is one thing to say you love Christ, but it is quite another thing to demonstrate this to an unbelieving world. When the body operates according to the principles of fellowship, it stands out as unique and different. We become a noticeable light within a selfish culture groping in darkness.

The care the early Christians showed for one another extended to all members—widows, orphans, the elderly and sick, the unemployed, prisoners and exiles, Christians on a journey, and other members of the church who had fallen into special need. Care was also taken that the poor received a decent burial. These "one another" principles were not saved for the church alone, but also included unbelievers and those abandoned or rejected by the world. As an "apologetic," a defense for the faith, these types of selfless acts performed by a body composed of former sinners merely added to the evidence of God's existence and ability to transform hearts. [SM pp. 168–9]

10. **Reflection Question: How can your fellowship be a more authentic apologetic in our culture today?**

[Answers will vary, but it is important to keep in mind that today's society is not substantially different than the culture of two thousand years ago.]

"LOVE, SEX, AND MARRIAGE"
WITH JEFF MYERS

PART ONE

I. The Story of the Family (Genesis 1:26–31)

II. God's Plan for Creation (Genesis 2:15–25)

    A. Bear God's image

    B. Name the animals—take responsibility

    C. Be fruitful and multiply

    D. Fill the earth and subdue (*kabash*) it—turn entire earth into a garden

III. Man's Rebellion (Genesis 3:1-15)

    A. Irresponsibility

    B. Paranoia

    C. Blame

IV. Satan's Plan

    A. The _____curse_____ ensured Satan's doom.

    B. Offspring (*zera*)

        1. One person who epitomizes the group

        2. Whole line of descendents as a group

    C. "The God of peace will soon crush Satan under your feet" (Romans 16:20).

V. Satan's Attack

"It can be demonstrated from history that no society has ever survived after its family life deteriorated." — Paul Popenoe

    A. Kill _____babies_____

    B. Make people fear or despise _____marriage_____

    C. Destroy existing marriages

    D. Promote _____promiscuity_____

E. "Alternatives" to marriage

F. Homosexuality

G. Pornography

H. Trivialize _____sex_____

I. Practice for _____divorce_____

J. Create a wedge between parents and kids

K. Get people to deceive themselves

<hr>

PART TWO

VI. Responding to Satan's Attacks

A. Understand this is a _____worldview_____ battle

   1. Secular Humanist View

      "All societies have long recognized that the family commitment is not merely biological, but rests on a complex foundation of contract, custom, and emotional commitment. Families have taken many forms—some, we have outgrown. The core of the modern family is two or more individuals who see themselves as a family, and who accept long-term responsibility for one another's health, security, independence, and happiness." — Council for Secular Humanism

   2. Marxist-Leninist View

      "With the transfer of the means of production into common ownership, the single family ceases to be the economic unit of society. Private housekeeping is transformed into a social industry. The care and education of the children becomes a public affair; society looks after all children alike, whether they are legitimate or not." — Frederick Engels

   3. Cosmic Humanist View

      "Relationships and families as we've known them seem to be falling apart at a rapid rate. Many people are panicky about this; some try to re-establish the old traditions and value systems in order to cling to a feeling of order and stability in their lives. It's useless to try to go backward, however, because our consciousness has already evolved beyond the level where we were willing to make the sacrifices necessary to live that way." — Shakti Gawain

4. Christian View

"The act of uniting a man and woman for life… marriage was instituted by God himself for the purpose of preventing the promiscuous intercourse of the sexes, for domestic felicity, and for securing the maintenance and education of children." — Webster's 1828 dictionary

    i. ____Covenant____ with community and God

    ii. As the means through which to fulfill the creation mandate (Genesis 1–2)

    iii. As a picture of ____Christ____ and the church (Ephesians 5:31–33)

B. Live out our God-given design

C. Commit to ____purity____ of body and mind

"Self-governing people require a robust culture founded on marriage and family, which nurtures the qualities that permit self-rule: deferred gratification, self-sacrifice, respect for kinship and law, and property rights. These qualities are founded upon sexual restraint, which permits people to pursue long-term interests, such as procreating and raising the next generation, and securing benefits for one's children." — Robert Knight

D. Model the love of Christ

E. Love kids

F. Be ____reconciled____ to one another

"People's hearts are seldom changed if they are not changed when young. Seldom indeed are men converted when they are old. Habits have long roots. Sin once allowed to nestle in your bosom will not be turned out at your bidding. Custom becomes second nature, and its chains are threefold cords not easily broken." — J. C. Ryle

"LOVE, SEX, AND MARRIAGE"
WITH JEFF MYERS

Answer the questions below on a separate sheet of paper and be prepared to review your answers in class.

1. What can we learn about the family in Genesis 1–3?

In the beginning, God created the cosmos and every living thing, including Adam. Out of God's entire creation, only Adam uniquely bore God's image and only Adam was given responsibilities over the rest of creation. God commanded Adam to name all the animals, take responsibility for them, and watch over his creation. Although God's creation was deemed good, Adam was told to make it better, i.e. turn the earth into a garden. To help Adam, God created Woman (who Adam renamed Eve).

Adam and Eve later disobeyed God by ignoring his only command—not to eat from the tree of knowledge. When God confronted them, each passed the blame onto another. Adam blamed his sin on Eve and God, while Eve blamed Satan. God ultimately cursed all three, as well the whole of his creation. Adam and Eve were still responsible for transforming creation, but their job would now be much harder. Moreover, God informed Satan that he would eventually be crushed by the offspring of Adam and Eve (ultimately Christ). This curse ensured Satan's doom!

2. What is Satan's plan to ensure his survival? How has this plan been implemented?

Since Satan will be crushed by the offspring of Adam and Eve, then Satan's best line of defense is to destroy the family. Perhaps this can be seen today by the state of the family throughout the world. 1) Currently over one million abortions are performed each year in the U.S. alone. 2) Popular culture and entertainment degrades marriage and promotes contempt among the sexes. 3) More than half of all marriages in the U.S. today end in divorce, which hurts not only the husband and wife, but also their children. 4) Promiscuity is encouraged and idolized in our culture. 5) Alternatives to marriage, like live-in lovers and homosexual relationships, are permissible. 6) Pornography is legal and growing exponentially every year. 7) Sex has been trivialized to an act of mere enjoyment. 8) Most individuals date around, in a sense "practicing divorce." 9) A wedge has been created by popular culture between parents and their children. 10) Finally, most people deceive themselves into believing that none of this will affect them.

3. What are the Secular Humanist, Marxist-Leninist, and Cosmic Humanist views of marriage and the family?

Secular Humanist view of marriage is that family changes over time. Secular Humanists recognize that while marriage was traditionally limited to a union between one man and one woman, this definition has evolved over time and will continue to adapt. The Marxist-Leninist view of marriage and the family is socialistic—marriage and the family are not particularly important. In fact, Marxists want children to be raised by the state. The Cosmic Humanist view of marriage and the family is that humanity has evolved beyond the traditional construction of these institutions and that it would be meaningless to attempt to move backwards.

4. What is the Christian view of marriage and the family?

> The Christian view of marriage and family is covenantal rather than individualistic. Marriage is a commitment to God—a promise that a husband and wife will maintain their marriage and family for the good of society. Marriage and the family are also the means through which we fulfill the creation mandate.
>
> *[Review Ephesians 5:31–33 with your students. Discuss how the picture of Christ relates to love and marriage.]*

5. How can we as Christians thwart Satan's attacks on marriage and the family?

> First, live out your God-given design. God created men and women with unique but complementary characteristics. Second, commit to purity of both mind and body. This ultimately means learning to be unselfish, but may also require abstaining from some forms of popular entertainment and changing the way you act or even dress. Third, learn to model the love of Christ. This will be a lifelong activity. Fourth, learn to love children as image-bearers and future culture shapers. Fifth, learn to be reconciled to one another. This means practicing forgiving others as well as seeking forgiveness for our sins.
>
> *[Discuss each of these points with your students in more detail. Ask your students how they might live out these points or if there any points they might add to this list.]*

SEASONS OF LIFE ACTIVITY

Ask the boys in the class to jot down the top five character qualities they will look for in a wife and the girls to write down the top five character qualities they would like to exhibit as a wife. As the students respond, write the character qualities on the board. If a quality is mentioned more than once, use tally marks to indicate duplicate responses.

Ask the girls in the class to jot down the top five character qualities they will look for in a husband and the boys to write down the top five character qualities they would like to exhibit as a husband. As the students respond, write the character qualities on the board. If a quality is mentioned more than once, use tally marks to indicate duplicate responses.

Print out and distribute the accompanying "Seasons of Life" handout found in the Teacher's CD ROM in the "Handouts" folder. Ask the students to make a timeline, placing the "seasons" of life listed above the age range where they would like to see that happen in their lives. These time frames, obviously, are ideal. Stages, or seasons, of life may overlap.

Now, have the students compare the lists of character qualities they have made with their time lines. Suppose they want to be married in five years. They just wrote down the character qualities they wanted to exhibit in marriage. Ask them *how* they will get those qualities. Will they suddenly appear when they say "I do?" Students should realize that the person they want to be in the future will *not* suddenly appear. The characteristics which are important for the future need to be built into their lives today. Although your students are probably not going to be married immediately, character needs to be developed now. The character that insures success in marriage also works to ensure success in all areas of life.

DOMESTIC TRANQUILITY
BY E. CAROLYN GRAGLIA

PART ONE

Since the late 1960s, feminists have very successfully waged war against the traditional family, in which husbands are the principal breadwinners and wives are primarily homemakers. This war's immediate purpose has been to undermine the homemaker's position within both her family and society in order to drive her into the work force. Its long-term goal is to create a society in which women behave as much like men as possible, devoting as much time and energy to the pursuit of a career as men do, so that women will eventually hold equal political and economic power with men. This book examines feminism's successful onslaught against the traditional family, considers the possible ramifications of that success, and defends a woman's choice to be a homemaker. Feminists have used a variety of methods to achieve their goal. They have promoted a sexual revolution that encouraged women to mimic male sexual promiscuity. They have supported the enactment of no-fault divorce laws that have undermined housewives' social and economic security. And they obtained the application of affirmative action requirements to women as a class, gaining educational and job preferences for women and undermining the ability of men who are victimized by this discrimination to function as family breadwinners.

A crucial weapon in feminism's arsenal has been the status degradation of the housewife's role. From the journalistic attacks of Betty Friedan and Gloria Steinem to Jessie Bernard's sociological writings, all branches of feminism are united in the conviction that a woman can find identity and fulfillment only in a career. The housewife, feminists agree, was properly characterized by Simone de Beauvoir and Betty Friedan as a "parasite," a being something less than human, living her life without using her adult capabilities or intelligence, and lacking any real purpose in devoting herself to children, husband, and home.

Operating on the twin assumptions that equality means sameness (that is, men and women cannot be equals unless they do the same things) and that most differences between the sexes are culturally imposed, contemporary feminism has undertaken its own cultural impositions. Revealing their totalitarian belief that they know best how others should live and their totalitarian willingness to force others to conform to their dogma, feminists have sought to modify our social institutions in order to create an androgynous society in which male and female roles are as identical as possible. The results of the feminist juggernaut now engulf us. By almost all indicia of well-being, the institution of the American family has become significantly less healthy than it was thirty years ago.

Certainly, feminism is not alone responsible for our families' sufferings. As Charles Murray details in *Losing Ground*,[1] President Lyndon Johnson's Great Society programs, for example, have often hurt families, particularly black families, and these programs were supported by a large constituency beyond the women's movement. What distinguishes the women's movement, however, is the fact that, despite the pro-family motives it sometimes ascribes to itself, it has actively sought the traditional family's destruction. In its avowed aims and the programs it promotes, the movement has adopted Kate Millett's goal, set forth in her Sexual Politics, in which she endorses Friedrich Engels's conclusion that "the family, as that term is presently understood, must go;" "a kind fate," she remarks, in "view of the institution's history.[2] This goal has never changed: feminists view traditional nuclear families as inconsistent with feminism's commitment to women's independence and sexual freedom.[3]

Emerging as a revitalized movement in the 1960s, feminism reflected women's social discontent, which had arisen in response to the decline of the male breadwinner ethic and to the perception—heralded in Philip Wylie's 1940s castigation of the evil "mom"[4]—that Western society does not value highly the roles of wife and mother. Women's dissatisfactions, nevertheless, have often been aggravated rather than alleviated by

---

[1] Charles Murray, *Losing Ground* (New York: Basic, 1984).
[2] Kate Millett, *Sexual Politics* (Garden City, NY: Doubleday, 1969), 127.
[3] This is a theme, for example, of Ellen Willis's *No More Nice Girls: Countercultural Essays* (Wesleyan University/University Press of New England, 1993).
[4] Philip Wylie, *Generation of Vipers* (New York: Holt, Rinehart, & Winston, 1942), 52–53.

UNDERSTANDING THE TIMES

the feminist reaction. To mitigate their discontent, feminists argued, women should pattern their lives after men's, engaging in casual sexual intercourse on the same terms as sexually predatory males and making the same career commitments as men. In pursuit of these objectives, feminists have fought unceasingly for the ready availability of legal abortion and consistently derogated both motherhood and the worth of full-time homemakers. Feminism's sexual teachings have been less consistent, ranging from its early and enthusiastic embrace of the sexual revolution to a significant backlash against female sexual promiscuity, which has led some feminists to urge women to abandon heterosexual sexual intercourse altogether.

Contemporary feminism has been remarkably successful in bringing about the institutionalization in our society of the two beliefs underlying its offensive: denial of the social worth of traditional homemakers and rejection of traditional sexual morality. The consequences have been pernicious and enduring. General societal assent to these beliefs has profoundly distorted men's perceptions of their relationships with and obligations to women, women's perceptions of their own needs, and the way in which women make decisions about their lives.

TRADITIONAL HOMEMAKING DEVALUED

The first prong of contemporary feminism's offensive has been to convince society that a woman's full-time commitment to cultivating her marriage and rearing her children is an unworthy endeavor. Women, assert feminists, should treat marriage and children as relatively independent appendages to their life of full-time involvement in the workplace. To live what feminists assure her is the only life worthy of respect, a woman must devote the vast bulk of her time and energy to market production, at the expense of marriage and children. Children, she is told, are better cared for by surrogates, and marriage, as these feminists perceive it, neither deserves nor requires much attention; indeed, the very idea of a woman's "cultivating" her marriage seems ludicrous. Thus spurred on by the women's movement, many women have sought to become male clones.

But some feminists have appeared to modify the feminist message; voices—supposedly of moderation—have argued that women really are different from men. In this they are surely right: there are fundamental differences between the average man and woman, and it is appropriate to take account of these differences when making decisions both in our individual lives and with respect to social issues. Yet the new feminist voices have not conceded that acknowledged differences between the sexes are grounds for reexamining women's flight from home into workplace. Instead, these new voices have argued only that these differences require modification of the terms under which women undertake to reconstruct their lives in accordance with the blueprint designed by so-called early radicals. The edifice erected by radical feminism is to remain intact, subject only to some redecorating. The foundation of this edifice is still the destruction of the traditional family. Feminism has acquiesced in women's desire to bear children (an activity some of the early radicals discouraged). But it continues steadfast in its assumption that, after some period of maternity leave, daily care of those children is properly the domain of institutions and paid employees. The yearnings manifested in women's palpable desire for children should largely be sated, the new voices tell us, by the act of serving as a birth canal and then spending so-called quality time with the child before and after a full day's work.

Any mother, in this view, may happily consign to surrogates most of the remaining aspects of her role, assured that doing so will impose no hardship or loss on either mother or child. To those women whose natures make them less suited to striving in the workplace than concentrating on husband, children, and home, this feminist diktat denies the happiness and contentment they could have found within the domestic arena. In the world formed by contemporary feminism, these women will have status and respect only if they force themselves to take up roles in the workplace they suspect are not most deserving of their attention. Relegated to the periphery of their lives are the home and personal relationships with husband and children that they sense merit their central concern.

Inherent in the feminist argument is an extraordinary contradiction. Feminists deny, on the one hand, that the dimension of female sexuality which engenders women's yearning for children can also make it appropriate and satisfying for a woman to devote herself to domestic endeavors and provide her children's full-time care. On the other hand, they plead the fact of sexual difference to justify campaigns to modify workplaces in order to correct the effects of male influence and alleged biases. Only after such modifications, claim feminists, can women's nurturing attributes and other female qualities be adequately expressed in and

Unit Six

truly influence the workplace. Manifestations of these female qualities, feminists argue, should and can occur in the workplace once it has been modified to blunt the substantial impact of male aggression and competitiveness and take account of women's special requirements.

Having launched its movement claiming the right of women—right allegedly denied them previously—to enter the workplace on an *equal* basis with men, feminism then escalated its demands by arguing that female differences require numerous changes in the workplace. Women, in this view, are insufficiently feminine to find satisfaction in rearing their own children but too feminine to compete on an equal basis with men. Thus, having taken women out of their homes and settled them in the workplace, feminists have sought to reconstruct workplaces to create "feminist playpens" that are conducive to female qualities of sensitivity, caring, and empathy. Through this exercise in self-contradiction, contemporary feminism has endeavored to remove the woman from her home and role of providing daily care to her children—the quintessential place and activity for most effectively expressing her feminine, nurturing attributes.

The qualities that are the most likely to make women good mothers are thus redeployed away from their children and into workplaces that must be restructured to accommodate them. The irony is twofold. Children—the ones who could benefit most from the attentions of those mothers who do possess these womanly qualities—are deprived of those attentions and left only with the hope of finding adequate replacement for their loss. Moreover, the occupations in which these qualities are now to find expression either do not require them for optimal job performance (often they are not conducive to professional success) or were long ago recognized as women's occupations—as in the field of nursing, for example—in which nurturing abilities do enhance job performance.

TRADITIONAL SEXUAL MORALITY TRADUCED

The second prong of contemporary feminism's offensive has been to encourage women to ape male sexual patterns and engage in promiscuous sexual intercourse as freely as men. Initially, feminists were among the most dedicated supporters of the sexual revolution, viewing female participation in casual sexual activity as an unmistakable declaration of female equality with males. The women in our society who acted upon the teachings of feminist sexual revolutionaries have suffered greatly. They are victims of the highest abortion rate in the Western world. More than one in five Americans is now infected with a viral sexually transmitted disease which at best can be controlled but not cured and is often chronic. Sexually transmitted diseases, both viral and bacterial, disproportionately affect women because, showing fewer symptoms, they often go untreated for a longer time. These diseases also lead to pelvic infections that cause infertility in 100,000 to 150,000 women each year.[5]

The sexual revolution feminists have promoted rests on an assumption that an act of sexual intercourse involves nothing but a pleasurable physical sensation, possessing no symbolic meaning and no moral dimension. This is an understanding of sexuality that bears more than a slight resemblance to sex as depicted in pornography: physical sexual acts without emotional involvement. In addition to the physical harm caused by increased sexual promiscuity, the denial that sexual intercourse has symbolic importance within a framework of moral accountability corrupts the nature of the sex act. Such denial necessarily makes sexual intercourse a trivial event, compromising the act's ability to fulfill its most important function after procreation. This function is to bridge the gap between males and females who often seem separated by so many differences, both biological and emotional, that they feel scarcely capable of understanding or communicating with each other.

Because of the urgency of sexual desire, especially in the male, it is through sexual contact that men and women can most easily come together. Defining the nature of sexual intercourse in terms informed by its procreative potentialities makes the act a spiritually meaningful event of overwhelming importance. A sexual encounter so defined is imbued with the significance conferred by its connection with a promise of immortality through procreation, whether that connection is a present possibility, a remembrance of children already borne, or simply an acknowledgment of the reality and truth of the promise. Such a sex act can serve as the physical meeting ground on which, by accepting and affirming each other through their bodies' physical unity, men and women can begin to construct an enduring emotional unity. The sexual

[5] *New York Times* (April 1, 1993). This study by the Alan Guttmacher Institute estimates that if "current trends continue, one-half of all women who were 15 in 1970 will have had [pelvic inflammatory disease] by the year 2000."

encounter cannot perform its function when it is viewed as a trivial event of moral indifference with no purpose or meaning other than producing a physical sensation through the friction of bodily parts.

The feminist sexual perspective deprives the sex act of the spiritual meaningfulness that can make it the binding force upon which man and woman can construct a lasting marital relationship. The morally indifferent sexuality championed by the sexual revolution substitutes the sex without emotions that characterizes pornography for the sex of a committed, loving relationship that satisfies women's longing for romance and connection. But this is not the only damage to relationships between men and women that follows from feminism's determination to promote an androgynous society by convincing men and women that they are virtually fungible. Sexual equivalency, feminists believe, requires that women not only engage in casual sexual intercourse as freely as men, but also that women mimic male behavior by becoming equally assertive in initiating sexual encounters and in their activity throughout the encounter. With this sexual prescription, feminists mock the essence of conjugal sexuality that is at the foundation of traditional marriage.

MARRIAGE AS A WOMAN'S CAREER DISCREDITED

Even academic feminists who are considered "moderates" endorse doctrines most inimical to the homemaker. Thus, Professor Elizabeth Fox-Genovese, regarded as a moderate in Women's Studies, tells us that marriage can no longer be a viable career for women. But if marriage cannot be a woman's career, then, despite feminist avowals of favoring choice in this matter, homemaking cannot be a woman's goal, and surrogate child-rearing must be her child's destiny. Contrary to feminist claims, society's barriers are not strung tightly to inhibit women's career choices. Because of feminism's very successful efforts, society encourages women to pursue careers, while stigmatizing and preventing their devotion to childrearing and domesticity.

It was precisely upon the conclusion that marriage cannot be a viable career for women that *Time* magazine rested its Fall 1990 special issue on "Women: The Road Ahead," a survey of contemporary women's lives. While noting that the "cozy, limited roles of the past are still clearly remembered, sometimes fondly," during the past thirty years "all that was orthodox has become negotiable." One thing negotiated away has been the economic security of the homemaker, and *Time* advised young women that "the job of full-time homemaker may be the riskiest profession to choose" because the advent of no-fault and equitable-distribution divorce laws" reflect, in the words of one judge, the fact that " society no longer believes that a husband should support his wife."[6]

No-fault divorce laws did not, however, result from an edict of the gods or some force of nature, but from sustained political efforts, particularly by the feminist movement. As a cornerstone of their drive to make women exchange home for workplace, and thereby secure their independence from men, the availability of no-fault divorce (like the availability of abortion) was sacrosanct to the movement. *Time* shed crocodile tears for displaced homemakers, for it made clear that women must canter down the road ahead with the spur of no-fault divorce urging them into the workplace. Of all *Time*'s recommendations for ameliorating women's lot, divorce reform—the most crying need in our country today—was not among them. Whatever hardships may be endured by women who would resist a divorce, *Time*'s allegiance, like that of most feminists, is clearly to the divorce-seekers who, it was pleased to note, will not be hindered in their pursuit of self-realization by the barriers to divorce that their own mothers had faced.[7]

These barriers to divorce which had impeded their own parents, however, had usually benefited these young women by helping to preserve their parents' marriage. A five-year study of children in divorcing families disclosed that "the overwhelming majority preferred the unhappy marriage to the divorce," and many of them "despite the unhappiness of their parents, were in fact relatively happy and considered their situation neither better nor worse than that of other families around them."[8] A follow-up study after ten years demonstrated that children experienced the trauma of their parents' divorce as more serious and long-lasting than any researchers had anticipated.[9] *Time* so readily acquiesced in the disadvantaging of homemakers and

---

[6] *Time* (Fall 1990).

[7] Ibid., 12.

[8] Judith S. Wallerstein and Joan Berlin Kelly, *Surviving the Breakup: How Children and Parents Cope with Divorce* (New York: Basic, 1980), 4–5, 10–11.

[9] Judith S. Wallerstein and Sandra Blakeslee, *Second Chances: Men, Women & Children a Decade After Divorce* (New York:

the disruption of children's lives because the feminist ideological parameters within which it operates have excluded marriage as a *proper* career choice. Removing the obstacles to making it a *viable* choice would, therefore, be an undesirable subversion of feminist goals.

That *Time* would have women trot forward on life's journey constrained by the blinders of feminist ideology is evident from its failure to question any feminist notion, no matter how silly, or to explore solutions incompatible with the ideology's script. One of the silliest notions *Time* left unexamined was that young women want "good careers, good marriages and two or three kids, and they don't want the children to be raised by strangers." The supposed realism of this expectation lay in the new woman's attitude that I don't want to work 70 hours a week, but I want to be vice president, and you have to change." But even if thirty hours were cut from that seventy-hour workweek, the new 'woman would still be working the normal full-time week, her children would still be raised by surrogates, and the norm would continue to be the feminist version of child-rearing that *Time* itself described unflatteringly as "less a preoccupation than an improvisation."[10]

The illusion that a woman can achieve career success without sacrificing the daily personal care of her children—and except among the very wealthy, most of her leisure as well—went unquestioned by *Time*. It did note, however, the dissatisfaction expressed by Eastern European and Russian women who had experienced as a matter of government policy the same liberation from home and children that our feminists have undertaken to bestow upon Western women. In what *Time* described as "a curious reversal of Western feminism's emphasis on careers for women," the new female leaders of Eastern Europe would like "to reverse the communist diktat that all women have to work." Women have "dreamed," said the Polish Minister of Culture and Arts, "of reaching the point where we have the choice to stay home" that communism had taken away."[11] But blinded by its feminist bias, *Time* could only find it "curious" that women would choose to stay at home; apparently beyond the pale of respectability was any argument that it would serve Western women's interest to retain the choice that contemporary feminism—filling in the West the role of communism in the East—has sought to deny them.

Nor was its feminist bias shaken by the attitudes of Japanese women, most of whom, *Time* noted, reject "equality" with men, choosing to cease work after the birth of a first child and later resuming a part-time career or pursuing hobbies or community work. The picture painted was that of the 1950s American suburban housewife reviled by Betty Friedan, except that the American has enjoyed a higher standard of living (particularly a much larger home) than has the Japanese. In Japan, *Time* observed, being "a housewife is nothing to be ashamed of." Dishonoring the housewife's role was a goal, it might have added, that Japanese feminists can, in time, accomplish if they emulate their American counterparts.

Japanese wives have broad responsibilities, commented Time, because most husbands leave their salaries and children entirely in wives' hands; freed from drudgery by modern appliances, housewives can "Pursue their interests in a carefree manner, while men have to worry about supporting their wives and children.[12] Typically, a Japanese wife controls household finances, giving her husband a cash allowance, the size of which, apparently, dissatisfies one-half of the men. Acknowledging that Japanese wives take the leadership in most homes, one husband observed that "things go best when the husband is swimming in the palm of his wife's hand." A home is well-managed, said one wife, "if you make your men feel that they're in control when they are in front of others, while in reality you're in control."[13] It seems like a good arrangement to me.

Ticknor & Fields, 1989). In *The Divorce Culture* (New York: Knopf, 1996), Barbara Dafoe Whitehead presents a heartrending picture of the blighting of children's lives and the permanent damage they suffer because of their parents' divorce. Rather than calling for a reform of no-fault that would reinstitute strict legal controls over divorce, she would rely on exhorting parents to behave more responsibly towards their children and each other.

[10] *Time* (Fall 1990).

[11] Ibid., 32. Christina Hoff Sommers has described the incredulity of American feminists when Russian women writers, alleging that socialism "had denied women their femininity," encouraged women "to pay more attention to their traditional role as 'keepers of the hearth,'" and proclaimed that they "have nothing to do with feminism." *Who Stole Feminism? How Women Have Betrayed Women* (New York: Simon & Schuster, 1994), 39–40.

[12] *Time* (Fall 1990).

[13] Nicholas D. Kristof, "Japan Is a Woman's World Once the Front Door Is Shut," *New York Times* (June 19, 1996). The contrast between Japanese women's public powerlessness and private authority is analyzed by Takie Sugiyama Lebra in *Japanese Women: Constraint and Fulfillment* (Honolulu: University of Hawaii Press, 1984).

Instead of inquiring whether a similar carefree existence might appeal to some American women, *Time* looked forward to the day when marriage would no longer be a career for Japanese women, as their men took over household and child-rearing chores, enabling wives to join husbands in the workplace. It was noted, however, that a major impediment to this goal, which would have to be corrected, was the fact that Japanese daycare centers usually run for only eight hours a day. Thus, *Time* made clear that its overriding concern was simply promoting the presence of women in the work force. This presence is seen as a good *per se*, without any *pro forma* talk about the economic necessity of a second income and without any question raised as to whether it is in children's interest to spend any amount of time—much less in excess of eight hours a day—in communal care.

IRONIES WITHIN FEMINISM

Feminist success in reshaping social attitudes has been facilitated by our media's eagerness to adopt and propagate the feminist perspective and by feminism's ability to piggyback on the black civil rights movement by portraying women as victims. In acquiring "minority" status, women (who are the sexual majority) secured preferential entitlement to educational and employment opportunities afforded to blacks and other minorities. Feminists have also promoted their goals through a large body of law developed under the rubric of "women's rights," much of it laid down by the United States Supreme Court in decisions invalidating distinctions on the basis of sex.

Contemporary feminism's remarkable ability to enlist social institutions in its war on the traditional family has entailed two ironies, the first relating to the women spearheading the attack and the second to feminist reliance on the black civil rights movement to obtain preferential treatment for women. As detailed in *The Sisterhood*,[14] the most influential leaders of the women's movement that was revived in the 1960s were Betty Friedan, Kate Millett, Germaine Greer, and Gloria Steinem. Including the international movement, Simone de Beauvoir was a fifth. Of these five women, only Betty Friedan had both married and borne children. But she was unhappy with her marriage and life in the suburban home, which she compared to a "comfortable concentration camp" in which the housewife performs "endless, monotonous, unrewarding" work that "does not require adult capabilities" and causes "a slow death of mind and spirit." She felt "like a freak, absolutely alone" and afraid to face her "real feelings about the husband and children you were presumably living for."[15]

Denying that contemporary women could "live through their bodies" and derive satisfaction from child-bearing as the "pinnacle of human achievement" that it was on Margaret Mead's South Sea Islands, Friedan recommended the path of women who remained in the workplace by "juggling their pregnancies" and relying on nurses and housekeepers. Characterizing her marriage as one based not "on love but on dependent hate," Friedan concluded that she could no longer continue "leading other women out of the wilderness while holding on to a marriage that destroyed my self-respect."[16] And so the self-proclaimed Moses from the New York suburbs obtained her divorce.

While Betty Friedan had tasted a life devoted to marriage and motherhood and pronounced it foul, the remaining four women were unacquainted with the experience. Kate Millett and Simone de Beauvoir, both bisexuals, agreed that women were prevented from becoming free human beings by the myths revering maternity and the expectations that women should personally care for their children. Gloria Steinem declared that she deliberately chose childlessness because "I either gave birth to someone else" or "I gave birth to myself."[17] Germaine Greer, who was the best known of the feminist sexual revolutionaries and wrote the very popular *The Female Eunuch*, was childless and argued that marriage was outmoded. Greer indicated a certain distaste for the female body, opining with respect to menstruation that women "would rather do without it."[18] Later, as a revisionist and to the regret of other feminists, she attacked sexual permissiveness and lauded motherhood and fertility. Her preference for abstinence, anal intercourse, and *coitus interruptus* over other contraceptive methods, however, suggested a lingering distaste for the womb as well as for

[14] Marcia Cohen, *The Sisterhood* (New York: Simon & Schuster, 1987).

[15] Betty Friedan, *The Feminine Mystique* (New York: Dell, 1984), 307–08, 381.

[16] Ibid., 140–41, 376, 381, 394.

[17] *Time* (May 2, 1988), 88. Steinem's name was on a list published of prominent women who had had an illegal abortion. Katherine Dalton, "Hard Cases," *The American Enterprise* (May/June 1995), 71.

[18] Germaine Greer, *The Female Eunuch* (New York: McGraw Hill, 1970), 43.

phallic potency.[19]

Although she never married or shared living quarters with him, Simone de Beauvoir maintained a lifelong liaison with Jean-Paul Sartre. Their relationship was based on sexual freedom for both, and as one commentator has described it, "her role was not unlike that of a eunuch in charge of a harem," inspecting the women who wished to have affairs with Sartre and "disposing of past sexual partners of his who became troublesome in their continued affection for him.[20] Simone de Beauvoir's life was a blueprint for the woman "liberated" through radical feminism: a bisexual[21] who was neither wife nor birth mother, but an aborted woman, a fact she disclosed in an advertisement by women who had obtained illegal abortions.[22]

Reflecting the female's hypergamous impulse, de Beauvoir allied herself with a man she considered her intellectual superior. Upon meeting Sartre as a university student, she recognized that he "had a deeper and wider knowledge of everything," "a true superiority over me." She recalled "the calm and yet almost frenzied passion with which he was preparing for the books he was going to write." In comparison, her "frantic determination seemed weak and timid" and her "feverish obsessions," "lukewarm." Their early discussions, she said, were "the first time in my life that I had felt intellectually inferior to anyone else;" "Day after day, and all day long I set myself up against Sartre, and in our discussions I was simply not in his class;" "he soon demolished" my theories and in "the end I had to admit I was beaten."[23] De Beauvoir's evident excitement at being bested by this superior man is familiar to women (it was not entirely with regret that I realized my future husband might beat me in an argument). This excitement can serve women well. But while losing to a superior man may enhance a woman's sexual as well as intellectual satisfaction, whatever intellectual pleasure a heterosexual man may derive from being bested by a superior woman, he is unlikely to find the experience sexually affirmative.

Eschewing marriage and childbirth, de Beauvoir undertook to live a life of the intellect on the basis of presumed equality with a man she believed to be superior and who achieved greater fame. When compared to "great men," she said, the woman of achievement seems mediocre,"[24] a view echoing Beatrice Webb's assertion that women lacked "that fullness of intellectual life which distinguishes the really able man."[25] According to Paul Johnson, Sartre's superiority was more apparent than real: de Beauvoir was "in a strictly academic sense, abler." She almost beat Sartre for first in the philosophy degree, the examiners thinking her "the better philosopher." Johnson thinks her "in many respects a finer" writer, her novel, *Les Mandarins*, being "far better than any of Sartre's."[26]

It has been the norm for women to ally themselves with men who achieve greater market success than they. David M. Buss has established the biological basis for our attraction to the powerful, superior men best able to protect and care for us while we bear children.[27] Her affinity for a superior man well serves a woman who enjoys the many rewards afforded by marriage and child-bearing. But it must surely bring discontent to the woman who confines her life to seeking achievement in the workplace as the equal of that superior man. Not only was de Beauvoir unmarried and childless, but "there are few worse cases," says Johnson, "of a man exploiting a woman." She "became Sartre's slave from almost their first meeting and remained such for all her adult life until he died;" yet, although she was his "mistress, surrogate wife, cook and manager, female bodyguard and nurse," she never held "legal or financial status in his life." Their sexual relationship, moreover, ended in the mid-1940s as she became a "sexually-retired, pseudowife," while he pursued innumerable affairs with ever younger mistresses, one of whom, in his ultimate humiliation of de Beauvoir, he legally adopted so that she was his sole heir and literary executor.[28]

[19] Germaine Greer, *Sex and Destiny: The Politics of Human Fertility* (New York: Harper & Row, 1984), 124–43, 149–53, 353–55, 363–64.

[20] *Insight* (June 8, 1987), 62–3.

[21] De Beauvoir's adopted daughter, Sylvie Le Bon, published de Beauvoir's letters to Sartre which discussed her sexual trysts with young female students. Simone de Beauvoir, *Letters to Sartre*, edited and translated by Quintin Hoare (New York: Little, Brown, 1992). After charges were brought by the parents of one of her female students, de Beauvoir was barred from the university and lost her license to teach anywhere in France. Paul Johnson, *Intellectuals* (New York: Harper, 1988), 238–39.

[22] *Time* (April 28, 1986), 77.

[23] Simone de Beauvoir, *Memoirs of a Dutiful Daughter* (New York: Harper, 1974), 340–44.

[24] Simone de Beauvoir, *The Second Sex* (New York: Knopf, 1978), 711.

[25] Norman and Jeanne MacKenzie, eds., *The Diary of Beatrice Webb: Two* (Cambridge, MA: Belknap, 1983), 52.

[26] Johnson, *Intellectuals*, 235.

[27] David M. Buss, *The Evolution of Desire: Strategies of Human Mating* (New York: Basic, 1994), 19–48.

28 Johnson, *Intellectuals*, 235, 239, 251. Ronald Hayman, a biographer of Sartre, has noted that in a fifty-year friendship, the

In *The Coming of Age*, de Beauvoir attested to the bitterness of life's fruits, describing old age as "life's parody" and "a degradation or even a denial of what has been." "What," she repined, "is the point of having worked so hard if one finds that all is labour lost" and "if one no longer sets the least value upon what has been accomplished?" Those old people who do not "give up the struggle" but stubbornly persevere, continued her lament, "often become caricatures of themselves."[29] Only with great difficulty, one must think, can it be otherwise for those who forgo the bearing of children that can fill our lives with the richest meaning, enabling us to greet old age with equanimity and the expectation that we too will "come proud, open-eyed and laughing to the tomb."[30] To trade the rewards of child-bearing for an aborted fetus and production of intellectual constructs—however great their merit—seems, to some of us, an unsatisfactory exchange.

Upon this exchange—in theory, if not fact—were grounded the lives of all, save one, who spearheaded the contemporary feminist movement. Their qualifications to speak for women as a class are rarely questioned, however, nor are they viewed simply as representing the interests of lesbians and other women who forgo marriage and reproduction. The one exception, Betty Friedan, had concluded that a life devoted largely to marital and maternal responsibilities could never be satisfying. It was these jaundiced abdicants from traditional femininity who led the assault on the traditional wife and mother, the kind of woman only one had ever been, and none would choose to be. Their aim was to make this woman's domestic role untenable; their method was to revile, disdain, and calumniate her. Which leads us to the second irony of their offensive.

Feminism's ability to piggyback upon the black civil rights movement has greatly facilitated women's acquisition of educational, job, and other market preferences. Yet, the principal weapon feminists have employed to devalue the housewife's status has been an attack based on stereotypical analysis, arrant bigotry, and undisguised contempt, all the antithesis of respect for the worth and integrity of each individual that was the wellspring of our civil rights movement. To see this clearly, one need only substitute the word "African-American," "Jew," or "Hispanic" for the word "housewife" in the statements of Betty Friedan and her sisters in the movement. These feminists (who surely thought themselves good people and committed to liberal values) would recoil from characterizing any other group in society in the degrading terms they have routinely applied to the housewife.

PART TWO

FEMINISM'S FALSIFICATION OF REALITY

Contemporary feminism is the creation of women who rejected the traditional family and traditional femininity, who were career-oriented, and who either rejected motherhood altogether, or believed it should play a very subordinate role in a woman's life. The ideology they developed is based on misrepresentation of the facts—feminism's falsification of reality. Feminist success has depended on convincing both men and women that a woman's devotion to home and children is a sacrifice, a virtually worthless pursuit which affords no opportunity to use the energies and intelligence of even an average woman.

A crucial step towards inculcating this attitude has been to foster the belief that mothers previously stayed at home to rear their children only because they had no alternative. The allegation that women have been discriminatorily denied jobs has been, of course, the predicate for giving women job preferences within the legal framework of affirmative action remedies. But this allegation also has been essential to the task of convincing younger generations of women that, if older generations had been permitted to do so, they themselves would have pursued careers rather than staying at home to rear their children.

The major complaint of working mothers is usually not workplace discrimination in the ordinary sense, but their exhaustion, lack of leisure time, and the discrepancy between their own image of what being a good mother entails and the reality of their lives. One feminist response has been to demand alteration of workplace requirements to accommodate child-rearing responsibilities. In addition to these palliative

sexual relationship lasted only about sixteen. Ronald Hayman, "Having Wonderful Sex, Wish You Were Here," *The New York Times Book Review* (July 19, 1992).

[29] Simone de Beauvoir, *The Coming of Age* (New York: Putnam, 1972), 539, 540.

[30] William Butler Yeats, *Vacillation* (1932).

measures, feminists have also undertaken to alter the traditional image of a good mother. They began by creating the myth that the decision of women of an earlier generation to decline participation in the workplace did not arise from their own vision of motherhood; rather, they stayed at home with their children only because they had been denied any opportunity to enter or succeed in the workplace. To feminists, who were certain they themselves would never willingly stay at home to rear children, this myth was believable and accorded with the view of sociologist Jessie Bernard that a woman who said she enjoyed being a homemaker had to be somewhat mentally disturbed.

Feminist myth-making meant that women of my generation who had willingly exchanged market production for child-rearing found ourselves represented as victims in analyses designed to document the denial of career opportunities to women. Workplace discrimination in fact played no part in the decisions many of us made to cease working outside the home. We were impelled to stay with our children by the strong emotional pull they exercised on us and because we thought our presence in the home was the single best guarantee of their well-being. A life caring for them at home, we often discovered, was good for us as well. We were confident, moreover, that society respected us and believed us to be engaged in a valuable activity—not acting as sacrificial victims—when we functioned as full-time homemakers.

It is this confidence that contemporary feminism has destroyed by successfully propagating the idea that homemakers' activities are largely valueless, convincing younger generations of men and women that society disdains a woman's domestic role. Yet feminism has been less successful in expunging women's own image of a good mother and relieving working mothers of their ambivalence and feelings of guilt about leaving their children. While workplace modifications can help accommodate working mothers, they offer, at best, mild palliatives for those mothers who do yearn to be with their children and for those children who never find an adequate replacement for lost maternal care.

Workplace modifications can usually only compensate slightly for what is often a mother's nearly insupportable burden of dual responsibility. Instituting these changes serves a very important function, nevertheless, by helping assuage mothers' guilt. The message conveyed through these changes is that society is willing to impose the cost upon taxpayers and consumers because it believes a mother should work outside the home and that her presence at home would be of little value to either mother or child. Reinforcing this message is the fact that costs of workplace modifications benefiting working mothers will be disproportionately borne by one-income families which must pay for, while not sharing in, these benefits.

Like all special interest groups, feminists seek subsidies for themselves. Their economic interests and professional advancement have been greatly enhanced by claims of past societal discrimination against women, including the claim of being forced to assume a sacrificial role as homemaker.

My own experience differs sharply from the tales feminists tell. I was a practicing lawyer in the 1950s. From the time in junior high school when I decided to become a lawyer until I ceased working in order to raise a family, I always received unstinting encouragement and support. It was scarcely possible that someone from the working class, living on the edge of poverty with a divorced mother, could have succeeded otherwise. My entire college and law school educations were funded by scholarships and my employment. Teachers and counselors in high school and college energetically assisted in my efforts to secure these scholarships and other aid, without ever questioning the suitability of my aspirations for a woman. Not once in all the sessions where we discussed my educational options and planned how I would pay for them was this issue ever raised.

Contrary to the received opinion that society consistently discouraged women's market activity, I found social acquaintances were extremely supportive, while employers and many colleagues generously encouraged my pursuit of a career. At the same time, those of my female friends in the 1950s who were traditional housewives little resembled the stereotype, so effectively popularized by Betty Friedan, of intellectually shallow, bored, underachieving child-wives. Nor do I believe the stereotype accurately applied to me when I, too, became a homemaker.

Attending law school and practicing law during a period when feminists would have us believe women were systematically discriminated against, I was treated as well as, and I sometimes thought even better than, the men with whom I was competing. But feminists tell a very different story. Justice Ruth Bader Ginsburg, for example, upon her nomination to the United States Supreme Court, reiterated the feminist mythology. Paying homage to her mother, Justice Ginsburg expressed the hope that she herself would be

UNDERSTANDING THE TIMES

all her mother "would have been had she lived in an age when women could aspire and achieve." Reflected in these words are the feminist assumptions that women can "achieve" only through market production and that failure to achieve within the workplace cannot have been a willing choice. Cannot Justice Ginsburg conceive that her mother may not have wanted to sacrifice the time at home with her child that would have been required to gain what that child has achieved?

The nominee also attested to the discrimination she faced when, having graduated from Columbia University Law School (on the Law Review and tied for first in her class), "not a law firm in the entire city of New York bid for my employment as a lawyer." It was reported—surely inaccurately—that she had to take a job as a legal secretary.[31] The phrasing of her remarkable statement raises the question whether, resume in hand, she had actually sought a job with every law firm in New York City or simply waited to receive "bids."

When I graduated from the same law school several years before justice Ginsburg (also on the Law Review, but not first in my class) and began my job search, I received an offer from a major Wall Street law firm. As I recall, most of the fourteen women in my class sought and obtained legal positions,[32] although only two of us were on the Law Review and none was first in the class. It is true that the other woman on the Law Review (who was Jewish) did not share my good fortune of receiving an offer from any of the major Wall Street law firms, which did discriminate at that time against Jews and other ethnics. My future husband, for example, who graduated with me—also on the Law Review and with a virtually identical record but without the advantage of being a "Pennington"—was among the many men who could claim they were so discriminated against. Many Jewish graduates during that period, including women, took jobs with what were known as the midtown Jewish law firms, and it seems hardly possible that this avenue was foreclosed to a woman who had graduated first in her class. If her complaint is that she received no offers from major Wall Street firms, my own experience and that of my classmates would indicate the controlling variable was not her sex. It is, of course, more beneficial to plead sex, rather than ethnic, discrimination. Reparation for the latter still leaves her in competition with all the men who share her ethnicity.

Similarly, Barbara Aronstein Black, at the time Dean of Columbia Law School, discussed what it was like for her and other women to go to law school when they did not think they could get jobs or have a career: "We all knew that once we attempted to move into practice (but of course I never did), we would meet active discrimination. That was perfectly clear, and we were pretty angry about it."[33] But we did *not* all know this; it was *not* perfectly clear. The then-Barbara Aronstein graduated from Columbia Law School the year after I did. I never was part of such discussions and never doubted that I could obtain a good legal job and pursue a career for as long as I wanted. Like most of my classmates, male and female, I set out with my resume and obtained a job. Those women, who, like Barbara Aronstein Black, were Jewish or members of other ethnic groups, did know—just as similarly situated men knew—that for them the job search would be harder and that they were unlikely to receive offers from major Wall Street law firms. The distinction then usually made—but certainly not always—was between white, Anglo-Saxon Protestants and ethnics, not between men and women.[34] Now that it has become fashionable to plead one's victimization at every opportunity, what I find most interesting is that my classmates who were disadvantaged because of their ethnicity rarely did seem angry, but only determined to overcome whatever obstacles they faced.

Feminist Susan Brownmiller entered Cornell University as a freshman the year after I had finished my undergraduate work there and gone on to law school. In a letter to the *Cornell Alumni News* of April 1973,

---

[31] *New York Times* (June 15, 1993). Although this lead article on her nomination stated that her first job was as a "legal secretary," a letter from the Columbia Law Women's Association detailing her alleged victimization by sex bias states that when "she could not find a job in a law firm commensurate with her credentials," she served "as law clerk to Judge Edmund L. Palmieri of the United States District Court, Southern District of New York." This is confirmed in *Columbia, The Magazine of Columbia University* (Summer 1980) and it was so reported in *The Wall Street Journal* (June 15, 1993).

[32] The same is true for women graduates of Harvard Law School. Because she transferred to Columbia in her final year at Harvard Law School, Justice Ginsburg is a member of the Harvard Law class of 1959. On the occasion of that class's 25th reunion, an examination of the careers of its female members disclosed that "most of the women in the class ended up following career paths similar to the men—law firm partners, judges, academics, public-interest lawyers and in-house corporate lawyers. In the late 1970s and 1980s, many found themselves established as the senior women in their field—and enjoying the benefits." Jill Abramson, "Class of Distinction," *The Wall Street Journal* (July 20, 1993).

[33] "Barbara Aronstein Black: A Conversation," *The Observer* (Columbia Law School Alumni Association, August 1986), 4.

[34] Ethnicity would sometimes be overlooked in the presence of other factors—for example, the ability to bring business to the firm.

Brownmiller wrote that when she entered Cornell in 1952, "I had secret hopes of going to Law School. Two years later I abandoned that goal as a rather unseemly ambition for a woman." She does not say who made her believe this ambition was unseemly—perhaps it was her family. I doubt it was any of the faculty or administrators with whom I dealt at Cornell. After my first year, I was given a job that enabled me to earn my room and board without working so many hours that I would be unable to maintain the grades required for my full-tuition scholarship; this job was given only to students whose ambition was thought serious and seemly. The Registrar at Cornell Law School took my aspirations very seriously. My only doubt about those aspirations was that it might be foolish for one as poor as I to continue her education. The Registrar always encouraged me to pursue my ambitions, and he helped me to choose the law schools where I should apply and then to decide between Harvard, Yale, Columbia, and Cornell. That these law schools accepted me and offered me scholarships and other aid belies the claim that being a lawyer was considered unseemly for a woman.

My own career pursuits elicited a vastly more tolerant reaction four decades ago than is now evoked by a decision to devote oneself to being a full-time mother and housewife, a choice that, in recent years, has usually been depicted as a waste of time and talent. What were once considered valuable and respected activities—raising children, attending to a husband's needs, and managing a household—the present society created by contemporary feminism views as benighted and beyond rational justification. No woman with a brain in her head, feminists have largely convinced society, could possibly be happy devoting herself to what they portray as worthless, even degrading, activities. No woman, as Justice Ginsburg implied, would *willingly* live a life of such limited achievement.

Feminists have inaccurately depicted women's past lives both in home and workplace and falsely claimed that the intensive devotion of a woman at home cannot significantly benefit her marriage and children. But feminists are accurate when they deny that women should be expected to become mothers. The denial seems superfluous, however, since it has rarely been asserted that motherhood must be every woman's destiny. Monasteries and nunneries, for example, have been among the social institutions recognizing that reproduction is not expected of everyone. Clearly, some women are not suited to motherhood and some mothers prefer delegating child-rearing to others in order to pursue a career or other interests. The insidiousness of the women's movement is that, while claiming—and being perceived by society—to speak for all women, it has represented only these two groups.

THE AWAKENED BRUNNHILDE

The woman who wishes to rear her children within a traditional marriage, to whom contemporary feminism has been an implacable enemy, I call the "awakened Brunnhilde." Best-known from Richard Wagner's *The Ring often Nibelung*, Brunnhilde is a warrior maiden who was transformed by her love for the hero Siegfried. The Brunnhilde I seek to defend is a woman who finds that the satisfactions of full-time commitment to being a wife and mother outweigh the rewards of pursuing a career. This realization is part of what I call her awakened femininity.

But Brunnhilde's choice, according to societal consensus, is a sacrifice. It is viewed as a sacrifice because society has acquiesced in feminism's depiction of the homemaker's role as worthless, boring, unrewarding, unfulfilling, and incapable of using a woman's talents. Even those who support this choice as being in children's best interest will speak of it as a sacrifice. For women like me, however, the sacrifice lies in precisely the opposite choice. It would have been a virtually unendurable sacrifice for me to have left my children with anyone (including my husband who, while possessing many virtues, was ill suited to a mother's role) in order to remain in the workplace.

I have been happy in every period of my adult life: attending college and law school, practicing law, staying at home to raise a family, and creating a new life once my family responsibilities had largely ended. Yet those many years I spent as a mother at home from the birth of my first child until the last left for college were the best, the ones I would be least willing to have forgone. Feminists recount endless tales of women's oppression throughout the ages, but one of the greatest injustices to women is feminists' own success in convincing society to treat as a sacrifice what for some women can be the most rewarding occupation of their lives.

By undermining the status and security of awakened Brunnhilde, contemporary feminism has inflicted undeserved injury upon many good women. And society itself has been weakened by its curtailing of women's domestic role, which contributes substantially possibly more than any other single activity—to societal health and stability. All indicia of familial well-being demonstrate that our society was a significantly better place for families in the decade before the feminist revival—when the primary concerns of most mothers were their husbands, their children, and their home. Those of us who concluded that our marriages and families would thrive better if we devoted ourselves to home and children rather than to market production find our belief validated by studies showing that "when women can support themselves, there is a lesser degree of bonding between husband and wife and more relaxed sexual mores" and that "the higher the relative degree of power attributed by respondents to the male partner, the lower the rate of marital dissolution."[35] These findings are consistent with the long-known fact that the women "with high incomes and/or graduate degrees have the highest divorce rate—a rate far higher than successful men."[36]

Our belief is also confirmed by several findings of a recently concluded long-term study of married couples: (1) husbands "who do more household tasks are less satisfied with the way the tasks are distributed," and this division of tasks "is associated with declines in their love for their wives;" (2) the "more fathers in dual-earner marriages are involved with child care, the more negativity in the marriage," and those fathers "who report more negative interaction tend to be less satisfied with the division of child care tasks and also tend to be less in love with their wives;" and (3) the extent to which husbands who are the sole bread-winners are involved in child care is unrelated to the amount of negativity toward their wives, and "the more single-earner fathers are in love with their wives, the more (rather than less) involved they are in child care and leisure activities alone with their children.[37]

That mothers provide daily care for their children is in the interest of those men who would resist the feminist effort to refashion them into mother-substitutes, a role for which men are usually not well-suited. It is in the interest of those children who would have both a father and a mother, each filling different roles, and who would be spared the daycare and surrogate mothering that can be a source of misery and are likely to be inferior to care at home from a competent and contented mother. And it is in the interest of those women who could find a motherhood that is unencumbered by marketplace commitments to be an incomparable joy.

Admittedly, life at home with their children cannot be a joy—either incomparable or ordinary—for women who regard that life as a sacrifice. It is not my purpose to convince these women otherwise. Such persuasion, my own experience has taught me, is more likely to spring from their own physical and emotional experience than from discussion. It is the experiences in her marital relationship, together with the experiences of pregnancy and childbirth—forces more subtle than intellectual reasoning—that will usually awaken a woman's response to her children and then mold the dimensions of that response.

I use the term "awakened femininity" to describe Brunnhilde's response to her sexual experiences and to her children. The purpose of the feminist endeavor was to discourage a response like Brunnhilde's and encourage what I call women's "spiritual virginity." This is the term I use to describe a response that permits a woman to resist the emotional pull exerted by her child so that she can continue her life as a market producer after childbirth. At the same time as feminists promoted the sexual revolution that mocked women's premarital sexual virginity and marital chastity, they vilified and disadvantaged those women who refused to adopt a feminist "spiritual virginity," but chose, instead, to become homemakers and child-rearers.

Clearly, some women do experience full-time child-rearing as a joy, not a sacrifice, even when their initial decision to stay at home is prompted by the altruistic motive that this will be best for their children. That these women should find life at home to be enjoyable and rewarding is, I contend, at least reasonable. It is, therefore, scarcely debatable that society should support, not undermine, their lives at home. In the interests of such women, their families, and society, we should begin to restore the level playing field that the women's movement has destroyed.

[35] Kingsley R. Browne, "Sex and Temperament in Modern Society: A Darwinian View of the Glass Ceiling and the Gender Gap," *Arizona Law Review* 37 (1995), 995, n.112, 1089, n.810.

[36] George Gilder, *Sexual Suicide* (New York: Quadrangle, 1973), 67.

[37] Ted L. Huston, "Path to Parenthood," *Discovery: Research and Scholarship at The University of Texas At Austin* 14 (1996), 59, 63.

We must recognize that proposals with an initial appeal can often have detrimental effects on traditional families and must therefore be resisted by those who want to support such families. The proposed equal rights amendment, for example, would have forbidden denial of "equality of rights under the law... on account of sex." It was intended to make sex distinctions identical to distinctions on the basis of race so that men and women—like blacks and whites—would have to be treated alike for all purposes. The amendment was intended, like many of the judicial decisions reached under the Fourteenth Amendment's equal protection clause, to promote the feminist goal of an androgynous society. It would forbid, among other things, the existence of publicly run schools, classes, or athletic activities for one sex only and require drafting of women for military service, including combat. Feminists sought the amendment to signify that our nation endorsed the aim of the National Organization for Women to disfavor the traditional family with a breadwinner husband and homemaker wife. Like no-fault divorce laws, the amendment was designed to force women to abandon their traditional roles and refashion themselves after the feminist role models who promoted it.

Similarly, government-funded child care programs must inevitably harm traditional families. The greatest financial need in our society exists in households with children. It is not this financial need, however, which leads the women's movement to endorse government-funded child care, but its firm belief that a woman's proper place is in the work force, rather than in the home caring for her children. Financial hardships of families with children could be alleviated by increasing the federal income tax exemption for dependents or providing family allowances (through tax credits or some other method) that would benefit *all* families with children, including those in which the mother stays at home. Such reforms would lighten the financial burden of one-wage-earner families and permit some women to leave the work force.

But any outcome that enables women to exchange market activities for life at home is disfavored by the women's movement. It consistently argues, instead, for government-funded institutional child care that would require expenditures rivaling social security and Medicare. The lure of subsidized child care, together with the resulting tax burden imposed on all families, would serve feminist goals by encouraging women to continue working and enticing women into the work force who prefer caring for their children at home. Through the legislation they seek, feminists demonstrate their preference for a government policy that disfavors families where the mother remains at home with her children by taxing these families in order to pay for child care, as well as other benefits, for families in which the mother works outside the home. Acting upon their belief that women should do market work rather than care for their children, feminists advocate discriminatory methods designed to deprive women of a real choice and push them into living in accordance with the feminist ideology.

In *1984*, George Orwell describes an old man in a pub who, having survived revolution and purges, is one of the "last links that now exist with the vanished world of capitalism." When told by the barman that there are no pints of beer, the old man responds that "a pint's the 'alf of a quart, and there's four quarts to the gallon," to which the barman replies that he'd never heard of them: "liter and half liter—that's all we serve."[38] All that is now served by the reigning cultural elite are views like feminist Karen DeCrow's: "No man should allow himself to support his wife—no matter how much she favors the idea, no matter how many centuries this domestic pattern has existed, no matter how logical the economics of the arrangement may appear, no matter how good it makes him feel... It will diminish and destroy affection and respect... Love can flourish between adults only when everyone pays his or her own way."[39]

Contained within DeCrow's brief statement is the entire feminist ideology. Andrea Dworkin had earlier stated it even more briefly, asserting that "to have what men have one must be what men are."[40] This ideology dictates that marriage should not be an institution in which a man and a woman assume different, complementary roles, but a relationship like that of roommates, each fully and independently committed to market production—something resembling a homosexual relationship, yet between heterosexuals. DeCrow assumes that only a paycheck can fulfill a woman's half of the marital bargain. To Brunnhilde, however, the arrangement DeCrow proposes, in which the woman (who for all purposes could just as well be another man) must pay her own way, has two fatal flaws: first, the arrangement requires child-rearing by surrogates;

[38] George Orwell, *1984* (New York: Harcourt, Brace, 1949), 86–87.
[39] Letters to the Editor, *The New York Times Magazine* (May 31, 1992).
[40] Andrea Dworkin, *Intercourse* (New York: Free Press, 1987), p. 100.

second, it discards the different, complementary roles that she believes are most likely to produce a stable marriage, enlivened by satisfying sexuality. DeCrow's market-oriented roommates, who are little more than clones of each other, are the least likely to satisfy what Roger Scruton identified—Brunnhilde believes accurately—as the foundation of heterosexual sexual excitement: "the energy released when man and woman come together is proportional to the distance which divides them when they are apart."[41]

That this feminist ideology is now substantially institutionalized in our society is evidenced by the wide acceptance of Justice Ginsburg's assumption that what can properly be considered achievement occurs only within the marketplace. A woman who seeks an alternative achievement within the domestic arena is dismissively described by Ginsburg—in words reflecting the same ideological assumptions as those of DeCrow and Dworkin—as being "reduced to dependency on a man."[42] It is beyond the ken of these feminists to perceive the homemaker—in the way I have always viewed myself—not as being "reduced," but as happily being spared the market work which would have required an unbearably constricted maternal role.

Feminism's ideological victory has been a significant factor in producing the conditions cited by public school administrators when recommending full-day public school education for very young children because government institutions must take responsibility for children at ever younger ages. One administrator, for example, stated at a public hearing that children are no longer being reared by their families since the family "as we once knew it, has been destroyed." The family, he said, "is gone" and so "we are going to have to do something else." "You can forget the family part."[43] But not all those mothers whose employment has contributed to creating this situation celebrate it as the social advance it is to feminists. Some of these mothers, instead, acknowledge a strong yearning to be at home with their children and guilt because of the choices they have made.[44]

If this maternal yearning is ever to influence behavior, it must be powerful enough to overcome the feminist triumph that has entrenched within our society views of elite opinion-makers like those expressed by justice Ginsburg and Karen DeCrow. The traditional family that the women's movement targeted as its enemy is, like the pints and quarts of *1984*, on its way to extinction. While not yet dead and gone, as the school administrator claimed, it will be unless those who believe in the value of this family structure attempt to reverse feminism's victory. Such an attempt will not succeed until society begins again to respect and support—rather than disfavor, patronize, and demean—the woman who undertakes a traditional role and the man who makes it possible for her to do so.

---

*The essay originally appeared as a chapter in the book *Domestic Tranquility: A Brief Against Feminism*:
   E. Carolyn Graglia, *Domestic Tranquility: A Brief Against Feminism* (Dallas: Spence Publishing, 1998), 1–30.
**Reproduction Rights granted by E. Carolyn Graglia and Spence Publishing.

[41] Roger Scruton, *Sexual Desire: A Moral Philosophy of the Erotic* (New York: Free Press, 1986), 273.

[42] *New York Times* (June 27, 1993).

[43] Transcript of Proceedings, United States Commission on Civil Rights, Forum on Early Childhood Education, Dallas, TX (May 20, 1989), 90, 103.

[44] These are the typical reactions of the working mothers and women considering motherhood who were surveyed by anthropologist Katherine S. Newman in her study of a New York suburban community. *Declining Fortunes: The Withering of the American Dream* (New York: Basic, 1993). In *Feminism Is Not the Story of My Life* (New York: Doubleday, 1996), 194, Elizabeth Fox-Genovese describes how "the pull between family and work can drive working mothers to distraction" and "the feelings of guilt may become almost too much to bear."

DOMESTIC TRANQUILITY
ESSAY QUESTIONS

Answer the questions below on a separate sheet of paper and be prepared to review your answers in class.

1. **What are the similarities and differences between radical feminists and moderate feminists?**

First, while the early radical feminists asserted that there are no fundamental differences between men and women, some of today's more moderate feminists are willing to admit this. However, both eras of feminism still insist that a woman can only find fulfillment in the workplace.

Second, while the early radical feminists discouraged childbearing, some of today's more moderate feminists are not against bearing children. However, this new branch of feminism is steadfast in its assumption that mothers should not care for their children. Childcare is the proper domain of institutions and paid employees. [SM pp. 176–7]

2. **What are two consequences of the mass migration of women into the workforce?**

Feminists have sought to reconstruct the workplace to create a more conducive environment for female qualities such as sensitivity, caring, and empathy. Thus, contemporary feminism has endeavored to uproot the woman from her home-based role of providing daily care to her children and has instead planted her and her nurturing attributes in the workplace. The qualities that are most likely to make women good mothers are thus redeployed away from their children and into workplaces that must be restructured to accommodate them. The irony is twofold. First, children—the ones who could benefit most from their mothers' nurturing—are deprived of those attentions and left only with the hope of finding an adequate replacement for their loss. Second, the occupations in which these qualities are now forced to find expression either do not require them for optimal job performance or were long ago recognized as women's occupations—the field of nursing, for example—in which nurturing abilities enhance job performance. By this exchange, both the home and the workplace are ultimately damaged. [SM p. 177]

3. **What are the consequences of the feminist-supported sexual revolution?**

First, the women in our society who acted upon the teachings of feminist sexual revolutionaries have suffered physically. They are victims of the highest abortion rate in the Western world. Moreover, one in five Americans is now infected with a viral sexually transmitted disease which can at best be controlled, but not cured.

Second, this sexual revolution rested on the assumption that sexual intercourse involves nothing more than a pleasurable physical sensation, that it possesses no symbolic meaning and no moral dimension, thus leading to the corruption of the very nature of sex. This makes sexual intercourse a trivial event and compromises the act's ability to fulfill its most important function after procreation—bridging the gap between males and females, who often seem separated by many differences, both biological and emotional. [SM pp. 177–8]

Unit Six

4. **What have been the consequences of no-fault divorce laws?**

First, no-fault divorce has made the job of homemaker risky. A woman who chooses to invest her resources in her family, home, and children risks being left destitute if her husband should file for divorce. This is precisely why many in the feminist movement have fought for no-fault divorce, which has, in part, forced women to exchange the home for the workplace as a means of protecting their future financial security.

Second, no-fault divorce has removed one of the barriers to divorce. In the past, the complications of separation impeded divorce, making it a distasteful process to begin. This, in turn, usually benefited the children by helping to preserve their parents' marriage. (A number of studies seem to indicate that children are better off living with two unhappy parents than a broken family). However, no-fault divorce made it much easier to file, resulting in many more broken homes and marriages. [SM pp. 178–9]

5. **What is the irony of feminism's alignment with the black civil rights movement?**

Feminism's ability to piggyback upon the black civil rights movement has greatly facilitated women's acquisition of educational, career, and other market preferences. Yet, the principal weapon feminists have employed to devalue the housewife's status has been an attack based on stereotypical analysis, arrant bigotry, and undisguised contempt—the antithesis of a respect for the worth and integrity of each individual that was the wellspring of our civil rights movement. To see this clearly, one need only substitute the word "African-American," "Jew," or "Hispanic" for the word "housewife" in the statements of Betty Friedan and her sisters in the movement. These feminists (who surely thought themselves good people committed to liberal values) would recoil from characterizing any other group in society in the degrading terms they routinely applied to the housewife. [SM pp. 180–1]

6. **What myth has helped lead to feminism's success?**

Feminism's success has depended on convincing both men and women that a woman's devotion to home and children is a worthless sacrifice. Feminism promoted the myth that women of an earlier generation stayed at home with their children only because they had been denied an opportunity to enter or succeed in the workplace. Feminist myth-making painted earlier generations of women as victims.

In reality, most women before feminism were confident that society respected their work and believed it to be valuable. They did not see themselves in any way as sacrificial victims, but functioned confidently as full-time homemakers. It is this confidence, however, that contemporary feminism has worked so hard to destroy by propagating the idea that homemakers' activities are largely valueless. This has convinced an entire generation of men and women to disdain a woman's domestic role. [SM pp. 182–3]

7. Why does the feminist movement support government-funded child care?

The feminist movement supports government-funded child care because one of their core beliefs is that a woman's proper place is in the work force, rather than in the home caring for her children. Government-funded childcare would help alleviate the financial burden for families with two working parents. [SM p. 187]

8. Why do feminists refuse to support incentives that would benefit a single-income family?

The feminist movement does not support incentives for single income families for the same reason they do support government-funded childcare—feminists want women out of the home and in the workplace. Incentives such as increasing the federal income tax exemption for dependents or providing family allowances (through tax credits or some other method) would benefit all families with children, including those in which the mother stays at home. Such reforms would lighten the financial burden of one-wage-earner families and permit some women to leave the work force. But any outcome that enables women to exchange market activities for life at home is disfavored by the women's movement. It consistently argues, instead, for government-funded institutional childcare that would require expenditures rivaling social security and Medicare. The lure of subsidized childcare, together with the resulting tax burden imposed on all families, would serve feminist goals by enticing women into the work force who prefer caring for their children at home. [SM pp. 187–8]

9. What type of marital relationship is most likely produced by feminism's dictum that "a woman must pay her own way?"

This ideology dictates that marriage should not be an institution in which a man and a woman assume different, complementary roles. Rather it encourages a relationship much like that of roommates or homosexuals, each fully and independently committed to market production. [SM p. 188]

10. What problems can arise from this type of marital relationship?

There are at least two potentially fatal flaws with this arrangement. First, it requires child rearing by surrogates, and second, it discards or ignores the different, complementary roles that exist between a husband and wife, conditions that are most likely to produce a stable marriage. [SM p. 188]

[To the second point, discuss some of the differences (and similarities) between men and women.]

DEAR DOUG
WRITING ASSIGNMENT

Hello again!

A new semester has begun! I'm determined not to slack off this year—let's just say my grades pointed out exactly how many parties I went to. My new class sheet says I'm signed up for economics, law and politics, history, and sociology this spring.

That last class is going to be interesting, just from looking at the textbook. We've already had a coffee discussion about it and everyone brought up lots of issues. I walked in late and they were talking about the church's effect on society. Mark was saying that religion is a hindrance to progress—it dumbs people down so they can't influence change in society. Sarah agreed because she thinks women aren't allowed enough power in the church. I've never thought of Christians as being outdated.

Mark was also saying that the government should take a much larger role in raising kids so that they aren't brainwashed by their parents into believing in religion. Sarah thought that was a great idea because it would free women from the constraints of the home. Without children tying them down, they would be able to exercise the same power and sexual freedoms as men. I'm not sure I agree with them, though. What do you think about the government taking on the full responsibility of educating children?

Nathan and Paige pretty much agreed, adding that the church is sexist and homophobic—it doesn't care about anything but rules and regulations and being perfect. Paige said religion in general limits what women can do and Nathan told a story about a gay friend of his who got kicked out of church because of his lifestyle. I guess I've never seen church from that angle… at least I didn't see it that way in our youth group. How would you respond to that accusation?

In addition to all this, I had a fight with Amber. I took her out last night and during dinner we started talking about what we wanted to do after college. Her plan had a lot to do with career and nothing at all about marriage. When I asked her about it, she said that would be like throwing away everything women have gained over the past several decades.

I must've had a strange look on my face, because she stopped eating and jumped into this tirade about how there really isn't any difference between the sexes—men have just been forcing their will on women and women have let them get away with it. Then she headed into abortion and how women everywhere deserve the right to decide what happens to their own bodies, not religious fanatics or the government. By the time she ran out of steam, I didn't have a clue what to say. How's a Christian supposed to handle this issue, anyway? Seems to me any side I take I'm going to be wrong, just because I'm a guy.

Sorry to dump all this on you just after we both got back in the school routine, but I really need some advice. Does the Bible have anything to say about social issues like feminism and the role of the church in society?

Later,
Doug

Doug has brought up four different subjects; below is a rough outline of possible responses.

1. **Should the state take a greater role in raising the nation's children? (12.5 points)**

> Although state involvement in child rearing is a relatively recent phenomenon, the Bible declares that it is primarily the parents' role and responsibility to raise their children. Yet socialism teaches that this responsibility should primarily belong to the state in order to better indoctrinate its people, especially the next generation, with its primary beliefs and goals.

2. **How would you respond to the accusation that the Church is sexist and homophobic? (12.5 points)**

> It is best to be honest and admit that some individuals who have claimed to be (and perhaps even were) Christians are guilty of hating homosexuals. However, the Bible seems to clearly discourage discrimination—all are sinners and are in need of God's forgiveness and guidance. This does not mean that Christians are called to accept or be silent about homosexuality or any other sin. On the contrary, we are called to speak truth, but with an attitude of love and concern for their soul and well-being.
>
> A number of individuals influenced by radical feminism believe that raising children is a sacrifice and waste of talent. Thus, when they look at Christian families and see women "stuck in the home raising kids," they can't help but view Christianity as outdated and sexist. However, this view assumes that children are an inconvenience and that child rearing is an unfulfilling endeavor, a position that seems far more intolerant and discriminatory than Christianity.

3. **How should a Christian approach the issue of feminism? (12.5 points)**

> It is important to note that Christ and the early Christian church sought to change the way women were viewed in society—some of Jesus' most loyal followers were women and Paul taught that *all* were equal in Christ regardless of sex, nationality, or social status (Galatians 3:28–29, an assertion which was anything but PC at the time). Christianity is thus a religion that recognizes that both men and women have equal value in the eyes of God, while at the same time appreciating that we are different.

4. **What is the Christian view of sociology? (12.5 points)**

> Christian sociology is based on the proposition that both the individual and the social order are important to God, mankind, and society. Christ died and rose again for each person as an individual. God also ordained social institutions, the three most important of which are family, church, and state, to teach love, respect, discipline, work, and community. Christian sociology focuses both on society as a means for human cooperation in accordance with God's will and on the individual as a vital part of various social institutions in society.

UNIT SIX TEST

'SOCIOLOGY' TEXTBOOK QUESTIONS

Matching: (2 points possible per answer [5 for 90-day])
some options may be used more than once or not at all; some questions may have multiple answers

1. __a__ Christianity

2. __b__ Islam

3. __c__ Secular Humanism

4. __e__ Marxism-Leninism

5. __c__ Cosmic Humanism

6. __d__ Postmodernism

a. Traditional Family, Church, State
b. Polygamy, Mosque, Islamic State
c. Non-traditional Family, Church, State
d. Sexual Egalitarianism
e. Classless Society

Short answer: (4 points possible per answer [10 for 90-day])

7. **According to Christianity, what is the source of humanity's problems?**

> Christianity describes human beings as creatures with the freedom to choose between right and wrong and to shape society. The Christian view grants individuals much more control over their society, but it also burdens us with much more responsibility.

8. **How do Muslims view the institution of the state? What two forms of government do Muslims promote?**

> Muslims do not see Islam as a social institution to be distinguished from the state. Instead, Islam is a comprehensive reality encompassing the state just as much as does the mosque. However, the Muslim world is divided between those who favor nation-states (distinct nations, with distinct laws and constitutions from other nations) and those who favor pan-Islam (the vision that the Muslim community should be united, with diminished or non-existent national boundaries).

9. **How does Marxism's reliance on evolution as a basis for its social theory influence its perception of the mechanisms of society?**

> Just as Marxists believe that we are evolving biologically, we are also evolving sociologically. As humanity improves through the evolutionary chain of being, so also does society. The scientific fact of biological evolution guarantees both the truth of Marxist social theory and the outcome of the process: a communist world.

CD-
ROM

10. How do Marxists view religion in relation to the evolution of society?

The Marxists see religion as a stumbling block, hindering the development of the ultimate society. Therefore, Marxists seek ways to diminish the role and influence of religion.

11. How will children be cared for according to Marxist sociology?

The care of the children should become "a public affair." In communist thought, children are the entire community's responsibility. Thus, children are disengaged from the family and the school takes the place of home. The alienation of children from their parents helps ensure that children formulate their worldviews according to education provided by the Marxist state.

DOING LIFE TOGETHER ESSAY
True or False: (3 points possible per answer)
*if an answer is false, restate it to make it true

12. Independence is God's desire for the members of his body.

False: <u>Interdependence</u> is God's desire for the members of his body.

13. In the Scriptures, fellowship is primarily a verb used to denote a time when Christians meet together.

False: In the Bible, fellowship is primarily a <u>noun</u> used to denote the shared life of believers.

14. The "one another" exhortations make sense only with a serious level of commitment to the community.

True

15. The "one another" statements require Christians to devote time, space, and resources to the fellowship.

True

Unit Six

16. **The New Testament concept of service means performing lowly, thankless deeds—as a slave would do.**

True

17. **Overcoming our independence requires not only offering our resources to others in need, but also being willing to ask others for help.**

True

18. **The "one another" statements require Christians to hold each other accountable.**

True

19. **If a brother or sister is in sin, we must take the issue to the church.**

False: If a brother or sister is in sin, we must confront him or her. It is only after we take the issue to others that we are to take it to the whole church.

20. **Speaking truth in love must always be accompanied by forgiving one another.**

True

21. **To be an apologist means to argue with others often.**

False: To be an apologist means to demonstrate the truth of Christ through a transformed life.

"LOVE, SEX, AND MARRIAGE" VIDEO
Short answer: (4 points possible per answer [10 for 90-day])

22. **What can we learn about the family in Genesis 1–3?**

In the beginning, God created the cosmos and every living thing, including Adam. Out of God's entire creation, only Adam bore God's image and only Adam was given responsibility over the rest of creation. God commanded Adam to name all the animals, take responsibility for them, and watch over his creation. Although God's creation was deemed good, Adam was told to make it better, i.e. turn the earth into a garden. To help, God created Woman (who Adam named Eve).

Adam and Eve later disobeyed God by ignoring his only command—not to eat from the tree of knowledge. When God confronted them, each passed the blame onto another. Adam blamed his sin on Eve and God, while Eve blamed Satan. God ultimately cursed all three, as well the whole of his creation. Adam and Eve were still responsible for transforming creation, but their job would now be made harder. Moreover, God informed Satan that he would eventually be crushed by the offspring of Adam and Eve (ultimately Christ). This curse ensured Satan's doom!

23. What is the Christian view of marriage and the family?

The Christian view of marriage and family is covenantal rather than individualistic. Marriage is a commitment to God—a promise that a husband and wife will maintain their marriage and family for the good of society. Marriage and the family are also the means through which we fulfill the creation mandate.

DOMESTIC TRANQUILITY ESSAY
True or False: (3 points possible per answer)
*if an answer is false, restate it to make it true

24. Radical feminism purports that a woman can only find identity and fulfillment in a career.

True

25. Radical feminism purports that a woman should place the responsibilities of family over all else.

False: Radical feminism purports that <u>there is no worth in traditional homemaking.</u>

26. One of the consequences of the feminist-supported sexual revolution is a higher rate of sexually transmitted diseases and abortions.

True

27. One of the consequences of the feminist-supported sexual revolution is a moral and symbolic corruption of sex.

True

Unit Six

28. One of the consequences of no-fault divorce is that it has made the career of homemaker more attractive to women.

False: One of the consequences of no-fault divorce is that it has made the career of homemaker <u>financially risky</u>.

29. Feminism's plight is similar to the black civil rights movement.

False: Feminism's plight is <u>not</u> similar to the black civil rights movement.

30. The myth that a woman's devotion to her career was a sacrifice has helped lead to feminism's success.

False: The myth that a woman's devotion to her <u>children</u> was a sacrifice has helped lead to feminism's success.

31. The feminist movement is in support of government-funded childcare.

True

32. Feminists do not support incentives that would benefit a single-income family because feminists do not want women in the workforce.

False: Feminists do not support incentives that would benefit a single-income family because feminists <u>do</u> want women in the workforce.

33. One consequence of the view that a woman must pay her own way in the marital relationship is that childrearing is delegated to surrogates.

True

TEACHER
MANUAL

UNDERSTANDING
THE TIMES

Unit Seven

Topics:
Arts
Entertainment
Law

A Summit Ministries Curriculum

180-Day Syllabus

Day	IN CLASS	HOMEWORK	
1	Watch "Law" video		
2	Read <u>UTT</u> Textbook 'Law 7.1'	Read <u>UTT</u> Textbook 'Law 7.2'	
3	Review <u>UTT</u> Textbook 'Law 7.1–7.2' questions	Read <u>UTT</u> Textbook 'Law 7.3'	
4	Read <u>UTT</u> Textbook 'Law 7.4'		
5	Review <u>UTT</u> Textbook 'Law 7.3–7.4' questions	Read <u>UTT</u> Textbook 'Law 7.5'	
6	Read <u>UTT</u> Textbook 'Law 7.6'		
7	Review <u>UTT</u> Textbook 'Law 7.5–7.6' questions	Assign Dear Doug Letter	
8	Watch "Entertainment" video P1		
9	Watch "Entertainment" video P2		
10	Review "Entertainment" video questions		
11	Read *The Creative Arts* essay P1		
12	Review *The Creative Arts* essay questions P1		
13	Read *The Creative Arts* essay P2		
14	Review *The Creative Arts* essay questions P2	Dear Doug Letter assignment Due	
15	Take Unit Seven Test		

90-Day Syllabus

Day	IN CLASS	HOMEWORK	
1	Watch "Law" video	Read <u>UTT</u> Textbook 'Law 7.1–7.2'	
2	Review <u>UTT</u> Textbook 'Law 7.1–7.2' questions	Read <u>UTT</u> Textbook 'Law 7.3–7.4'	
3	Review <u>UTT</u> Textbook 'Law 7.3–7.4' questions	Read <u>UTT</u> Textbook 'Law 7.5–7.6'	
4	Review <u>UTT</u> Textbook 'Law 7.5–7.6' questions		
5	Watch "Entertainment" video P1		
6	Watch "Entertainment" video P2		
7	Review "Entertainment" video questions		
8	Take Unit Seven Test		

UNDERSTANDING THE TIMES
LAW QUESTIONS

Answer the questions below on a separate sheet of paper and be prepared to review your answers in class.

LAW 7.1

1. Why do law systems that reject God as Lawgiver ultimately fail?

Atheistic systems of law ultimately fail because they do not recognize humanity's dignity as created in God's image and its fallen nature. [UTT 7.1.1]

2. Why does public trust in law disappear if the fundamental principles of law are undermined? How could this affect other areas of life?

When law is not considered sacred (i.e. first established by the ultimate Lawgiver), it is also not considered binding. If fallen human beings are in charge of creating law, we will constantly recreate it to better suit our selfish needs.

Our disregard for man-made law can cause us to adopt an arbitrary attitude toward other areas in our lives, most notably ethics. [UTT 7.1.2]

When law is seen as arbitrary, changing, and pragmatic, authority is reduced to mere power ("might makes right").

3. Why do Christians believe that law exists? Why do Christians believe it is possible to develop a just system of law?

The Biblical Christian approach to law grounds it firmly in God as the ultimate Lawgiver. Christians also believe that since humanity is in rebellion against God, absolute laws are required to curb that rebellion (though Christians recognize that the implementation of these laws will always be imperfect because of our fallen nature). [UTT 7.1.3]

4. In what two ways has God revealed his law to mankind?

God has revealed his law through nature (or natural law) and special revelation (or divine law). Natural law provides humanity with a general concept of right and wrong, while divine law as given in the Bible fleshes out this skeletal framework so that we can know what God considers lawful. General and special revelation, while not providing specific answers to all situations, provide humanity with the guidance necessary to create a reasonably just system of law. [UTT 7.1.4]

Unit Seven

SM
193

5. **What are the five basic precepts of Christian law?**

> The Christian view of law is based on five key principles:
>
> 1. The source of all divine law is the character of God.
> 2. The moral order proceeds out of the character of God. This order is as real as the physical order and reflects God's nature—his holiness, justice, truth, love, and mercy.
> 3. We are created in the image of God and therefore have significance (life is not an afterthought). God established human government to protect human life, rights, and dignity (Genesis 9:6).
> 4. When Jesus Christ took human form (John 1:14), human life took on even greater significance. God the Creator became God the Redeemer.
> 5. Someday Jesus Christ will judge the whole human race according to a universal standard of good and evil (Acts 17:31, Romans 1:16, 2 Corinthians 5:10). [UTT 7.1.5]

BASIS FOR LAW ACTIVITY

Use the verses given below to develop principles for a legal system:

Malachi 2:9	Impartial adjudication of the law
1 Timothy 5:21	No favoritism
Exodus 22:9	Restitution by the guilty party
Ezra 7:26	Punishment for disobeying the law
Acts 10:34–35	God's impartiality
Galatians 3:28	Equality before the law racially and sexually
James 2:1–7	Equality before the law economically
Isaiah 1:16–17	Justice for the oppressed
1 Timothy 5:8	Family responsibility enforced
Matthew 5:21–22	Dignity of human life
Acts 5:1–4	God judges dishonesty
Ephesians 4:28	Thief to go to work, provide for others
Exodus 20:13–16	Murder, adultery, theft, etc.
Romans 13:1–4	Government to punish sin (assume law to define sin)
Acts 17:31	All men are accountable to God
Deuteronomy 1:17	Rich and poor to be heard
Leviticus 19:15	Impartial justice

True/False questions for further discussion:

1. "The Christian should try to make all sinful acts illegal."
   False—Overloads the legislative system and is too specific

2. "Law, order, and a safe society will always result from passing tougher laws."
   False—Tougher punishment (if fairly and swiftly applied) will discourage crime, but the law cannot make us righteous.

3. "Earthly justice should point us to the final judgment and encourage us to live rightly."
   True—Punishment, justice, and restoration after repentance should be included. Restoration includes not only compensation to the offended person, but restoration of God's order.

4. "The goal of law is to remove sin."
   False—Law cannot redeem humanity. Law should promote justice, maintain liberty, stabilize a fallen society, and point out our need for a Savior.

5. "Law should be tied to religion."
   True—Law is tied to morality and ethics, which are always rooted to a religious worldview.

LAW 7.2

6. **What is Shari'ah law? What are its main tributaries? What is *fiqh*?**

Shari'ah law is the body of laws Muslims believe apply to the human race. *Fiqh* is their endeavor to understand and follow those laws. Shari'ah law is based on principles found in the Qur'an, Sunnah, Ijma', and the Qiyas. [UTT 7.2.2]

7. **Which legal schools do the Sunnis promote? Which legal schools do the Shi'ites promote? Why do the legal traditions of the Shi'ites give them an edge over their Sunni counterparts in contemporary culture?**

The Sunnis subscribe to Shafi'i, Hanifi, Asbahi, and Hanbal legal schools, while the Shi'ites subscribe to the Ja'fari legal school. In contrast to Sunni legal practices, the Shi'ite religious leaders are recipients of the religious taxes of the people. The Shi'ites therefore have financial independence from the government, an advantage that the Sunnis rarely have. This grants Shi'ite mosques greater independence and Shi'ite religious leaders greater political power. [UTT 7.2.7]

8. **What are the five categories of behavior within Shari'ah law?**

1. *Commanded* **acts are required or obligatory**—disobedience is worthy of punishment, in this life and the next, and obedience is rewarded in eternity. This applies to the five pillars of Islam and perhaps participation in jihad.

2. *Recommended* **acts are deemed commendable, though not required.** Failure to do these does not incur punishment, though obedience to recommended laws is worthy of reward (usually in paradise, though social commendation can be significant in this life). This includes charitable acts above and beyond those commanded, extra prayers or fasting, and other good deeds.

3. *Forbidden* **acts are strictly prohibited.** To participate in forbidden acts is to become worthy of punishment (most often in this life). To avoid such acts is to be worthy of reward (most often in paradise). Forbidden acts include thievery, sexual immorality, and drinking wine.

4. *Disapproved* **acts are discouraged to one degree or another.** Participating in disapproved acts does not result in punishment, but avoiding them may be worthy of reward (usually in the afterlife). Many Muslims put divorce in this category.

5. *Indifferent* **acts are those that earn neither punishment nor reward.** [UTT 7.2.8]

9. **How does the Islamic view of humanity and law differ from the view held by Christianity? What form of government does the Islamic view usually produce? How does India's system of government differ from most Islamic governments?**

Christians believe that humanity should not be trusted with too much power. Thus in Western nations power is usually distributed among various facets of government. In contrast, Islam (which teaches that mankind is not corrupt) generally believes that individuals who can be counted on to resist temptation should take charge of the government. Thus, Islamic political institutions are only as just and ethical as the people who run them. This view of mankind's goodness, when applied to government, usually produces dictatorships or monarchies and results in a lack of personal freedoms.

The government of India is a counter example to this, since the foundation for freedom and democracy was laid down by the British during the 19th century (a time when Great Britain was still inclined toward a biblical view of mankind as sinful beings created in the image of God). [UTT 7.2.9]

10. **Can the Muslim community find a basis for individual freedom within its religion? What examples are given as restrictions of these freedoms?**

The idea of freedom of expression is not part of Muslim legal tradition. Historically, Muslim countries operating under Shari'ah law and Muslim legal scholarship have given a certain amount of freedom to Muslim men, but have limited the freedoms of Muslim woman and non-Muslims in general. Restrictions for non-Muslims have included prohibitions against building Christian churches, restrictions against Christian prayer, and prohibitions barring the dissemination of Christian materials. [UTT 7.2.9]

LAW 7.3

11. **What is the basic assumption upon which Secular Humanist law is founded?**

Secular Humanist law is founded on the basic assumption that God does not exist and that humanity is perfectible. Therefore, our focus, according to this view, must be on creating an environment that encourages further evolutionary progress. [UTT 7.3.1]

12. **What are some key foundational principles of Secular Humanist law?**

Secular Humanist law is founded on key principles such as rejection of the supernatural, an eternal destiny, eternal consequences for behavior, and traditional morality. In the end, Secular Humanists see human beings as highly evolved animals capable of setting up and following their own moral systems. [UTT 7.3.2]

13. What is natural law?

> The theory of natural law, traditionally defined, states that there is one true morality (one proper way for us to behave) that is both independent of us and discoverable by us. [UTT 7.3.4]

14. How do the theistic and Secular Humanistic views of natural law differ?

> Theism believes that natural law exists and that it was written by God and implanted in our conscience (though revealed in greater detail through special revelation). While some Secular Humanists dismiss the idea of natural law altogether. Others believe that something similar to natural law actually exists (though it is the product of our evolutionary progress) and is ever changing. [UTT 7.3.4]

15. What view of law must consistent Humanists accept? What danger is inherent in such a view?

> Secular Humanists must embrace positive law, which appoints the state as the ultimate source of legal truth. This is dangerous, however, because of the potential for the government to take advantage of its position and power. [UTT 7.3.6]
>
> When we form laws based upon our own whims, rather than on universal principals found within Scripture, tragic consequences follow. For example:
> * Dred Scott Case—stated that slaves are property, not people (1857)
> * Roe v. Wade—denied the right of life to the unborn (1973)
>
> *[Make sure your students understand that there is a place for a form of positive law within society. Red lights and stop signs are forms of positive law—they are not directly derived from divine law but are intended to protect the citizenry.]*

ORIGINS OF LAW ACTIVITY

This activity will compare Humanist notions of rights and law with the ideas expressed in the opening lines of the Declaration of Independence. Distribute the "Declaration of Independence" handout found on your Teacher's CD-ROM in the "Handouts" folder.

As you read, there will be numbers signifying assumptions the founders held. Ask the students what these assumptions are and then have them compare these assumptions with those expressed by Secular Humanists. You will probably want to create a chart on the board resembling the one below.

Humanist	#	Declaration of Independence
Rejects natural law	1	Refers to natural law
Rejects God as author of freedom	2	Upholds God as granting freedom to nations

Rejects general revelation	3	Upholds natural law, truth evident to all men, and general revelation
Evolution as the origin of man	4	Creation as the origin of man
Humanity and the state as the source of basic truth and rights	5	God the Creator as the source of basic truth and rights
Government determines rights and molds society for man's good	6	Government responsible to secure and preserve God-given rights
Government as the controller of the people	7	The people delegate power to the state
Government as the ultimate legal authority	8	If government fails to secure God-given rights, the people must alter or abolish it

Note that God is the source of natural law and human rights. If these came from the state, the state would have the right to take them away or alter them.

LAW 7.4

16. According to Marxism, where do rights and laws originate?

Marxists perceive rights and laws as arising from mankind and society, rather than from the moral order of a supernatural Being. According to Marxists, as soon as mankind formed a society and the rudimentary economic structure involving class distinctions, two things came into existence simultaneously: law and the state. This implies that law arose at a specific point in history, sometime after the emergence of man on the evolutionary scene. [UTT 7.4.2]

17. What is bourgeoisie law? What two problems do Marxists have with bourgeoisie law? How do Marxists propose that society overcome the corrupt rule of bourgeoisie law?

According to Marxists, bourgeoisie law is formulated by the ruling class of a capitalistic society. Marxists contend that bourgeoisie law 1) invariably discriminates against the propertyless working class and 2) breeds protest in the form of lawlessness. Accordingly, capitalistic society is more responsible for lawlessness than the individual. Indeed, criminals need feel no remorse for their actions, since the unjust bourgeois society leaves them no alternative but to lash out against it.

The only clear-cut solution is for the working class to overthrow the bourgeoisie, thereby allowing the proletariat to make the laws. In fact, Marxists believe that the working class is justified in ignoring modern capitalistic laws in the pursuit of equality. [UTT 7.4.3]

Unit Seven

18. **How is Marxist legal theory similar to Secular Humanist law? How does Marxist legal theory differ from that of the Secular Humanist?**

Although a number of Marxists deny that their legal theory is positivistic, the foundation of Marxist law is in mankind and the state. In this sense, both Marxists and Humanists deny any absolute legal foundation in the person of God. However, Marxists add economics to their legal theory. Marxists see the modern capitalistic society as financially oppressive. By basing laws on the will of the proletariat, Marxists believe they can create a society that is less financially exploitative. Moreover, Marxist law takes on a class and party distinctive as well. While Secular Humanists simply believe that the state is responsible for establishing rights and promoting justice, Marxists believe that the proletarian state is the only government capable of promoting justice, thus legally requiring a state led by the proletariat. [UTT 7.4.4–6]

19. **What is the ultimate source for determining justice in a Marxist society?**

Marxists declare the proletariat to be the only true source of justice and require the proletariat to gain power to correct old, unjust bourgeois law. Thus, the state is seen as the ultimate source of justice only when the dictatorship of the proletariat (working class) has been established, making the ultimate source for justice neither the proletariat class nor the state but Marxism itself. [UTT 7.4.6]

20. **What is the ultimate fate of law in the future communist utopia?**

Marxists expect the state to wither away as a socialist society moves toward communism. However, if the state withers away, then the source of all justice will disappear as well. A positive view of law that calls for the disappearance of the state must also call for the disappearance of law. [UTT 7.4.7]

LAW 7.5

21. **According to Cosmic Humanists, where does all authority reside and why?**

According to Cosmic Humanists, all authority resides within each individual (i.e. god). Since every person is God and God is every person, humanity can only decide the legality of an action by getting in touch with its inner God. [UTT 7.5.1]

22. **According to Cosmic Humanism, what is sacrificed when we choose to honor a set of rules other than our own inner truth?**

Our own godhood is sacrificed. [UTT 7.5.1]

23. What must societies abandon to become more conducive to a Cosmic Humanist view of law?

Personal power can only be perfectly exercised in societies that have abandoned all law. [UTT 7.5.1]

24. Under the Cosmic Humanist legal perspective, what makes an action right or wrong?

Any action we might choose is perceived as lawful as long as it is an action true to the god within. Once humanity has achieved collective consciousness, we will all be co-creators of reality, working in harmony according to our own authority. [UTT 7.5.2]

25. What problems do Cosmic Humanists have with a Christian view of law?

In regards to law, Cosmic Humanists purport that everything and everyone is god and that as gods we should create and follow our own legal rules. To do otherwise is to deny our higher consciousness. Cosmic Humanists deny the Christian view of law, which maintains both an external authority (God) and a specific moral order based on his nature. [UTT 7.5.2]

LAW 7.6

26. Why are Postmodernists opposed to Western law? What do they desire to see in its place?

Postmodernists insist that Western law, which grew out of Christianity and the Enlightenment, reflects "white male bias." They attack the concepts of reason and objective truth, preferring instead the more subjective "ways of knowing" supposedly favored by women and minorities (e.g. storytelling). It is the Postmodern position that all legal rules are actually indeterminate. Therefore, Postmodernists are intent on eliminating the religious and transcendent qualities from Western law. They desire more fragmentation, more subjectivity, and less morality (e.g., Judeo-Christian and deontological morality). They intend to create and use their brand of "social justice" for left-wing political purposes. [UTT 7.6.2]

27. What is the Critical Legal Studies movement?

Critical Legal Studies (CLS) is a movement that publishes critiques of more traditional systems of law. CLS is focused on promoting progressive (even radical) political change. The CLS slogan is "critique is all there is." Using Derrida's deconstruction principle, Postmodernists deconstruct every law to discover its subjective meaning (no matter what the law objectively states) and its inherent bias. [UTT 7.6.3]

28. In what ways have the ideas of Michel Foucault and Jacques Derrida influenced CLS?

> CLS extends the Postmodern insight of social construction to law. The Postmodern thesis is that reality is socially constructed by the powerful in order to perpetuate their own hegemony. As one radical feminist puts it, "Feminist analysis begins with the principle that objective reality is a myth. Of course, if objective reality is a myth, so is an objective standard for law."
>
> From Foucault, Postmodern legal radicals draw the assertion that what counts for objective knowledge is a power relation, i.e. one category of people benefiting at the expense of another category of people. In other words, Foucault sees all relationships between people as power relationships. Universal or common standards of legal judgment do not exist. Any claim to universal truth is merely a mask for exercising political power over women and minorities. [UTT 7.6.3]

29. How is Susan Estrich's view of law different from the traditional view?

> Estrich takes her cue from Marx, Nietzsche, and Foucault by implying that law is simply a tool of political power. Marx said, "Political power, properly so called, is merely the organized power of one class for oppressing another." Estrich implies that she will use the law in any way necessary to get what she wants. Thus, the law is no longer a God-ordained, objective standard by which to judge our actions and maintain an ordered society, but a weapon to beat political opponents into submission to your way of thinking. [UTT 7.6.3]

30. What techniques do Postmodernists prefer over objective reasoning and why?

> Postmodernists prefer rhetoric and story telling over objective reasoning. Logic and dispassionate reasoning are seen as tools of white male bias used to subjugate "the outsider"—women, blacks, gays, etc. Rhetoric and story are used to effect political change regardless of any scientific arguments to the contrary.
>
> Rational argument in the courtroom is now replaced by the emotional power of stories. Putting it simply, Postmodernists view objectivity and reason as the domain of white males and the white male establishment as the cause of all social ills and oppression in Western civilization. The Postmodernist purpose is to correct this situation by using law to disenfranchise those who are in positions of power. [UTT 7.6.4]

"ENTERTAINMENT"
WITH JOHN STONESTREET

I. Christianity and Culture

    A. <u>   Offended   </u> by culture

       1. Tend to withdraw

       2. We are neither in the world nor of the world

       3. Scopes Monkey Trial

         "We really took the approach, by and large as the church, that we couldn't handle the tough questions and that we were going to get made fun of, so we withdrew from the culture… Today Christians are much better known for what they are against than what they are for."

    B. <u>   Distracted   </u> by culture

      "For the first time in recorded history there is no significant difference between the way Christians and non-Christians live their lives and make decisions." — George Barna

       1. We become just like our culture

         i. We forget about morality

         or

         ii. We take everything the world is doing and put "Christian" on it

       2. We are in the world and of the world

    C. <u>   Distressed   </u> by culture

      While Paul was waiting for them in Athens, he was greatly distressed to see that the city was full of idols. So he reasoned in the synagogues… as well as in the marketplace day by day… 'Men of Athens, I see that in every way you are very religious. For as I walked around and looked carefully at your objects of worship… ' — Acts 17

       1. We need to know both the word of God and the world of God

       2. We are to be *in* the world but not *of* the world

II. Exegeting Entertainment

A. It is an overwhelming and culture-shaping force in our world

"It is not any 'ism' but entertainment that is arguably the most pervasive, powerful, and ineluctable force of our time—a force so overwhelming that it has finally metastasized into life." — Neal Gabler

"I feel like I have a duty. I, as an architect, have a need to impose my worldview on the culture." — Courtney Love

"We don't shoot for fourteen year-olds, we own them." — President of MTV

"If a man were permitted to write the ballads of a nation, he need not care who writes its laws." — Andrew Fletcher

"First art will imitate life, then life will imitate art, then life will find its very meaning from the arts." — Unknown

B. How entertainment shapes culture:

1. It _____embodies_____ worldview ideas

   "The most dangerous ideas in a society are not the ones being argued, but the ones that are assumed." — C. S. Lewis

2. It _____changes_____ how we know and think:

   i. The rapid pace discourages reflection and evaluation

   ii. Images and ideas given and juxtaposed out of context fragment and trivialize life

   iii. Celebrity-ism, escapism, and addiction

   "We risk being the first people in history to have been able to make their illusions so vivid, so persuasive, so 'realistic' that they can live in them." — Daniel Boorstin

---

PART TWO

III. Approaching Entertainment

A. Wrong "Christian" approaches

1. Avoid it and it will go away

2. Just listen/watch "_____Christian_____" music and movies

   i. What is a Christian song or movie?

   ii. Entertainment changes how we know and think

   "Entertainment makes us silly." — Neil Postman

"If entertainment makes us silly, then Christian entertainment makes us silly Christians… Instead of having a meaningful time with the Lord, we listen to a CD."

"A good song, a good movie, and a good book take you deeper into life. A bad song, a bad movie, and a bad book distract you from life."

3. The Rating System (G, PG13, R, etc.)

4. Cusswords + Sex = Acceptability

5. **Wrong Question:** "Where do I draw the _____line_____?"

"Life is not a line; life is a direction… We are either running toward life or running toward death."

B. **The right approach:** "How should I live as a Christian in an entertainment-based culture?"

1. *With the right goal*: cultural impact

2. *With the right mind*: engaged, not "_____amused_____"

   i. Recognize and utilize where possible the culture's search for meaning

   ii. Live above the triviality

   iii. Do not condone sin, but warn of it

3. *With the right framework*: Scripture (Philippians 4)

i. Form	→	Quality (Is it well done?)	→	Excellent
ii. Content	→	Message (What is it saying?)	→	True
iii. Function	→	Effect (What is its purpose?)	→	Noble

4. *With the right tool*: discernment

5. Use available resources for selectivity

"ENTERTAINMENT"
VIDEO QUESTIONS

Answer the questions below on a separate sheet of paper and be prepared to review your answers in class.

1. **What are two bad approaches Christians have taken with regards to culture? What is wrong with these approaches?**

The first bad approach is to be *offended* by culture and to withdraw. This was the approach taken by many Christians in the early to mid 1900s. As Christianity fell out of favor, Christians withdrew and avoided the world. Yet, Christ's example is to be *in* the world, but not *of* the world. By withdrawing from culture, we aren't *in* the world.

Another bad approach is to be *distracted* by culture and immersed within it. This is the approach taken by many Christians today. Rather than being offended by culture, Christians embrace it. We either forget about being godly or borrow from the ideas of the world and label them "Christian." Yet, Christ's example is to be *in* the world, but not *of* the world. By embracing the culture we are *of* the world.

2. **How should Christians approach culture? How did Christ and Paul approach culture?**

A better approach to handling our culture is to be distressed and bothered by it. There are numerous false philosophies promoted by our current culture about sin, truth, and religion and many individuals are embracing and living out these bad ideas. This fact should bother us just as it bothered Christ. He did not avoid sinners—he loved them, talked to them, ate with them, and shared a message of hope. This is the approach Christians should take toward culture—to be in the world, but not of the world.

Another example of this principle in action is found in Acts 17 when Paul journeyed to Athens. At the time, Athens was the cultural center of the day—host to numerous philosophies, religions, idolatry, and perverted forms of sexuality. It was a culture that was as bad, if not worse, than our modern culture. Yet Paul visited Athens to tell its citizens about Christ. He neither avoided the culture nor adopted its pagan practices. Instead, he was concerned about what was going on there and presented evidence and reasons for adopting a different worldview—Christianity. He studied their idols, knew the works of their poets and philosophers, and used this cultural information as a bridge toward the gospel. In other words, Paul not only knew the Bible, he also knew the culture. Christians need to know both the word of God and the world of God.

3. **In what two ways does entertainment shape culture?**

First, entertainment presents and often embodies messages—it communicates ideas to those being entertained.

[Discuss some popular movies, books, and music with your students.]

SM
198

UNDERSTANDING THE TIMES

Second, entertainment changes how we as a culture think. Today there are more forms of entertainment than ever before—movie theaters, video rentals, pay-per-view, online movies, cable, satellite, libraries, bookstores, radio stations, audio-books, sporting events, video games, computer games, etc. This overabundance of entertainment barely gives us time to think about the ideas the arts embody and communicate. Sometimes we are convinced by philosophies portrayed in entertainment and we don't even know it.

Similarly, today images and ideas are portrayed out of context and in a manner that trivializes life. In other words, entertainment can skew reality by what it portrays. For example, news is no longer news. News networks run feature stories about entertainment and celebrities. Today, catastrophic tragedies are as newsworthy as the lives of celebrities, movies portray the enjoyment (but not the consequences) of pre-marital sex, and video games make killing fun.

Entertainment promotes the idolization of celebrities, making popularity and physical attractiveness life goals. It also promotes escapism—a substitute to reality—and can become addictive. Today we are so used to entertainment that silence can be disturbing.

4. **What are some faulty ways Christians can approach entertainment? What is wrong with these approaches?**

First, some Christians avoid entertainment entirely and hope that it will just go away. The problem is that entertainment (like culture) will not just go away. No matter how hard we try to ignore it, we will continue to bump up against it from time to time. This is perhaps why so many Christians turn away from their faith when they get to college. They have been so sheltered from the world that when they get out on their own, the enticement of the world all at once is just too much to combat.

A second faulty approach is listening to and watching only "Christian" entertainment, as if there is a line between sacred and secular. C. S. Lewis did not write just for Christians, but that is precisely what most "Christian" entertainers do. God wants Christian artists to use their talents for the benefit of everyone, not just other Christians. Moreover, this approach skirts the fundamental problem with entertainment (both "Christian" and non-Christian)—we use it to distract us from living.

Entertainment becomes a tool for escaping reality. Instead, art should be used to enrich one's life. A good song, movie, or book can take you deeper into life. A bad song, movie, or book distracts you from life.

A third faulty approach is relying solely on the movie industry rating system to determine acceptability. There are some R-rated films that have redeeming value and some G-rated films that do not.

A fourth faulty approach is counting cusswords and sexual content and applying a good/bad value based on this equation. There are a number of movies and songs that have no references to sex and use no dirty words but promote a non-Christian worldview.

The fundamental problem with all of these approaches is that they look for a definitive line to avoid crossing. Life and purity are not lines; we are either running toward life and purity or running toward death and impurity. We are either seeking art that is life-giving or we are using art to entertain sin and escape life.

5. What is a good approach Christians can take with entertainment?

We need to approach entertainment with the right goal, mindset, and framework.

The Right Goal—are we using entertainment to entertain thoughts of sin or to enrich our lives?

The Right Mind—are we using entertainment to turn our brains off or to learn about the culture? Entertainment is our culture's form of art. Within cultural expression we find artists searching for answers in life. Sometimes they find good answers and sometimes they do not. Sometimes sin is present and sometimes it is not. But we should not condemn non-Christians because they do not act like Christians. We need to understand where they are in life (and entertainment can help with this) and then have compassion for them as they search and struggle.

The Right Framework—are we judging entertainment from a biblical perspective? Entertainment and art should be judged by the following criteria: quality, message, and effect. Is the form well done? Is the content true? Is the function noble?

ENTERTAINMENT ACTIVITY

Bring in a list of the top 20 or so TV programs or musical hits, and photocopy it or put it on an overhead. Of the top ten, which do the students watch regularly? Why? Rate each program on a scale of 1–10, with "10" being friendly to the Christian worldview and "1" being antagonistic toward Christianity.

Explain that programs and songs don't even have to mention "religion" to take a stance on Christianity. Pro-Christian programs would portray ideas and characters consistent with biblical principles, while anti-Christian programs would portray ideas and characters inconsistent with biblical principles. Where do the majority fall? Where along the scale should Christians draw the line on what they will "set before their eyes?"

THE CREATIVE ARTS
BY LELAND RYKEN

PART ONE

This is the final essay in a series that defines a Christian worldview and applies that framework to leading areas of intellectual life. We must not allow the final position of this essay to mislead us into thinking that the creative arts are the extraneous "dessert" in a person's worldview, an intellectual delicacy that cannot hope to compare in importance to such staples as philosophy and the physical and social sciences.

Creativity and imagination permeate all human activity. It is important to note at the outset, therefore, that the qualities that I attribute to the creative arts are present in other intellectual pursuits as well. My focus will be on the arts; I leave it to each reader to decide how widely my statements apply to the humanities in general and the social and natural sciences.

THE PLACE OF THE ARTS IN A WORLDVIEW

The creative arts play a crucial role in shaping the worldview of every person and culture. They are an implied declaration that a worldview consists of more than abstract ideas or theoretical concepts. A world picture is a map of reality made up of images, symbols, myths and stories as well as theoretical concepts. Contemporary psychology has given us such terms as *preconceptual sensing* and *nonverbal cognition* and *the right side of the brain* to identify what I will call images.

The arts are rooted in the image-making and image-perceiving nature of people. People do not live by ideas alone. They also express their affirmations and denials through the paint on a canvas, the tension and release of sound, and poems and stories. A noted theologian has said that "we are far more image-making and image-using creatures than we usually think ourselves to be and… are guided and formed by images in our minds… Man… is a being who grasps and shapes reality… with the aid of great images, metaphors, and analogies."[1]

Who can doubt it? People organize their lives and make their decisions partly in terms of such images as heroes and villains, cross and altar, national emblem and patriotic legend, love song and hymn, landscape painting and portrait. These images have an ideational aspect to them but also communicate meanings that do not become focused into the form of theoretical propositions.[2]

By their very nature, therefore, the arts serve the salutary function of reminding people, including Christians, that to regard their worldview as being solely the domain of theoretical thought is to invite unawareness about themselves. People may not accede to the accumulation of possessions, but if their minds are filled with images of big houses and fancy clothes, their actual behavior will run in the direction of materialism. People may theoretically believe in the ideals of chastity and faithful wedded love, but if their minds are filled with images of exposed bodies and songs of seduction, their sexual behavior will have a large admixture of lust and sexual license in it.

Unless we recognize the powerful role of images in a worldview, our worldview and the behavior it produces will continue to be the muddled things they often are. We also need to recognize that the quality of our life and character is heavily affected by the quality of the images that we habitually take into our minds and imaginations.

The contribution that the arts make to a person's worldview is rooted in the fact that they all employ a "language" of images. The visual artist, for example, uses physical materials such as paint and stone to produce images that we can see and touch. Music employs physical instruments to produce sounds that we hear with our ears and feel in our muscles. Poets use words to evoke imagined sensations, objects and emotions. And storytellers describe such tangible realities as people performing actions in physical settings.

---

[1] H. Richard Niebuhr, *The Responsible Self* (New York: Harper & Row, 1963), 151–52, 161.

[2] Michael Polanyi's way of saying this is that "we can know more than we can tell" (*The Tacit Dimension* [Garden City, NY: Doubleday, 1966], 4).

The Imagination

The human faculty or capacity that enables the arts to image forth reality in this way is the imagination. Imagination is what the arts share. By "imagination" I mean simply the image-making and image-perceiving capacity that we all have; I do not have in mind any particular theory of artistic creativity or mental association. Modern aesthetic theory is based on the imagination as the key to everything, and it has stressed two aspects of the imagination.

Imagination implies, first of all, the notion of "image," that is, sensory concreteness or experiential immediacy. The arts are a *presentational* form. Instead of talking about human experience, they present the experience. The arts show rather than tell. They incarnate their meanings in concrete images of human experience or the external world. Instead of primarily asking our intellects to grasp an idea, the arts ask us to undergo an experience, which may or may not eventuate in a proposition or concept. The fiction writer Flannery O'Connor has said regarding her particular art form that "the whole story is the meaning, because it is an experience, not an abstraction."[3] We can view the arts as analogous to a picture accompanying the instructions for assembling an appliance or piece of furniture: if we have a good picture, we may not even need the written instructions.

The second thing that imagination implies is a fictional or imaginary element. Fictional literature is the most obvious illustration of the "made up" quality of art, but in fact all art is an imaginary reconstruction of actual reality. Looking at a painted landscape is never the same as standing in an actual landscape. Music gives us combinations of sounds that we never encounter in real life. Only in poems do people speak in rhyme and regular meter.

The arts are never a mere copy of life. They are always a distillation of some aspect of reality. All artists use techniques of highlighting, omission, selectivity, exaggeration, arrangement and juxtaposition to heighten our perception of some aspect of life. Music, for example, artificially produces arrangements of sounds that awaken feelings of serenity or exultation or reverence. A painting can give us a heightened sense of something as common as flowers and household utensils, as in the still-life paintings of the Dutch realists. Literary tragedy distills the essence of human suffering and silhouettes it with clarity.

The arts, in short, are based on a grand paradox. They are imaginary constructions that "distort" reality in order to increase our awareness of it. In the words of Pablo Picasso, "Art is a lie that makes us realize truth."[4] Or as Samuel Johnson put it, works of fiction "are not mistaken for realities, but… bring realities to mind."[5] The truth that the arts are particularly adept at capturing is enduring, elemental human experience. Whereas the newspaper and history book tell us what *happened*, the arts tell us what *happens*—the reality that never goes out of date because it is universal in human experience.

Imagination and the Bible

If we now ask how the artistic imagination fares in a Christian worldview, it is at once apparent that Christianity affirms the artistic enterprise. The Bible itself endorses both the image-making and imaginary impulses of the arts. There are four main lines of evidence to support this claim.

The first is that God is portrayed in the Bible as a creator of images. A dominant theme throughout the Old Testament is God's creation of the natural world of created objects. These visible images, in turn, are said to communicate truth about God himself (Psalm 19:1–4; Romans 1:19–20). The New Testament counterpart is the Incarnation of Jesus, who is declared to be God in tangible human form.

We should note secondly the literary nature of the Bible. The one thing that the Bible is not is what we so often picture it as being—a theological outline with proof texts attached. The bulk of the Bible consists of stories, poems, visions and letters, all of them literary forms. When asked to define neighbor, Jesus told a fictional story (Luke 10:25–37). When he wished to teach a lesson in servanthood, he washed his disciples' feet (John 13:1–20). Jesus taught religious truth by making up stories about sheep and pearls and seed and fish. Oliver Cromwell rightly said that Jesus "Spoke things." Jesus trusted the ability of literary images to convey religious truth when he told his disciples to "remember Lot's wife" (Luke 17:32). The Bible repeatedly affirms the image-making tendency of the arts.

[3] Flannery O'Connor, *Mystery and Manners*, eds. Sally and Robert Fitzgerald (New York: Farrar, Straus & Giroux, 1961), 73.
[4] Pablo Picasso, *The Arts*, May 1923.
[5] Quoted in Charles Kaplan, ed., *Criticism: The Major Statements* (New York: St. Martin's Press, 1975), 264.

Third, the Christian sacraments of communion and baptism have also been important in attempts to arrive at a Christian aesthetic (philosophy of the arts). The Christian sacraments affirm the sign-making impulse of the arts. The sacraments, after all, use the physical elements of water, bread, and wine to express and impart spiritual realities. While the Christian sacraments do not lend sanction to every manifestation of the creative imagination in a fallen world, they do nonetheless confirm the principle that images and symbols can express truth to the glory of God and the edification of people.

A fourth biblical validation of the arts is the descriptions of worship that we find especially in the Old Testament. Worship in the Bible is surrounded by a wealth of music and visual and verbal art.[6] As the Old Testament worshipers approached the Temple in Jerusalem, they saw two gigantic freestanding bronze pillars over twenty-five feet high (1 Kings 7:15–22). These monoliths had no architectural function other than to be beautiful and suggest by their aesthetic properties something of the grandeur, stability and power of God. The pillars were specimens of one prominent type of art in the Temple, namely, abstract or nonrepresentational art.

Representational and symbolic art were also present in Old Testament worship. The ten stands of bronze at the Temple were engraved with lions, oxen and palm trees (1 Kings 7:27–37). Sculptures of winged cherubim were prominent in both the tabernacle (Exodus 25:18–20; 26:31) and the Temple (1 Kings 7:29). Symbolic art also abounded, with such tangible objects as a golden table for the sacred bread, a golden altar, lampstands of pure gold and basins serving as visual symbols of such spiritual realities as communion with God, sacrifice, revelation, and cleansing.

There can be no doubt that the tabernacle and Temple were the Old Testament believer's most intense encounter with artistic beauty. If we doubt this, we need only read the chapters of the Bible that describe the visual properties of these places (Exodus 25–31; 35–39; 1 Kings 5–7; 2 Chronicles 2–4). The descriptions testify to an overwhelming value accorded to beauty. Some of the artistic embellishment in these places of worship awakened the worshipers' awareness of the other great source of beauty in their life—nature, as seen, for example, in the carved flowers about which we read repeatedly (1 Kings 7).

The beauty associated with the tabernacle and Temple included the purely imaginary as well as the realistic. The pomegranates on Aaron's robe were colored blue, purple and scarlet. In nature there are no blue pomegranates. One of the most attractive artifacts at the Temple was a molten sea forty-five feet in circumference, filled with water and resting on twelve statuesque oxen (1 Kings 7:23–26). Where in the real world can one find a sea held up on the backs of oxen? Francis Schaeffer rightly comments that "Christian artists do not need to be threatened by fantasy and imagination… The Christian is the one whose imagination should fly beyond the stars."[7]

Music was as prominent at the Temple as were the visual arts. David appointed four thousand musicians to conduct the music of the Temple (1 Chronicles 23:5). The Psalms, moreover, are a Temple hymnbook. If we catalog the musical instruments mentioned in the Psalms, they show the same wide use of available art forms that the visual arts in the Temple do.

It is no wonder that Christianity has been the most artistic religion in the world. Much of its doctrine has been enshrined in music, visual symbol, poem and story. The authoritative book of this revealed religion is itself a largely literary work in which story, character, and image are the customary ways of embodying truth. For more than fifteen centuries of Western history, Christianity provided the main influence and content for the creative arts. That it lost its dominance is one of the tragedies of both Western civilization and Christendom. That the arts will someday regain their lost place among Christians is a thing to be hoped.

PERSPECTIVE IN THE ARTS

The main thesis of the entire book—that a person's worldview affects all human pursuits—emphatically applies to the creation and study of the arts. The arts by their very nature are value-laden. They embody and express human values. Even the aspects of human experience that painters and composers and writers choose for artistic portrayal are an implied comment about what is important and worthy of attention.

[6] The best discussions are by Gene Edward Veith, Jr., *The Gift of Art* (Downers Grove, IL: InterVarsity, 1983) and Francis A. Schaeffer, *Art and the Bible* (Downers Grove, IL: InterVarsity, 1974).
[7] Schaeffer, *Art and the Bible*, 61.

Unit Seven

And once they have selected their subject, artists express an attitude toward the subject. The arts are *affective*: they are constructed so as to encourage an audience to share the artist's way of experiencing or perceiving reality. Works of art by their nature awaken attitudes or feelings of sympathy, aversion, approval, and disapproval toward the whole range of human experience.

While the importance of perspective in works of art is probably a truism, it is too often overlooked that the *study* of art, music and literature is just as influenced by perspective. Critics and teachers of the arts have a bias, too. They even reveal a bias in the works they choose to discuss or include in a course syllabus. And once they have chosen their works, they reveal a perspective in the aspect of a work that they single out for comment and in the attitudes they express toward the topics they have chosen for scrutiny. What critics and teachers of the arts *omit* from discussion can tell us as much about their bias as what they include. It would be a drastic mistake, therefore, to think that what a literature or art teacher says about works of art is any more "objective" than what a teacher of philosophy or biology says.

If art is inherently value-laden, so is the assimilation of art. As readers, viewers and listeners, we assimilate works of art within the framework of our personal experiences and worldview. Experiencing and interpreting works of art are subjective activities. The final meaning of a painting or symphony or story is a fusion of what the work itself puts before a person and the content that a person is able to bring to the words on a page or the sound from an instrument or the colors and objects on a canvas.

If experiencing art is this subjective, we are free as consumers of art to be ourselves when we read and listen and look. We do not need to repress our values or apologize for having a worldview when we read a novel or visit an art gallery or attend a concert. We do, however, need to be self-aware about our responses. We should acknowledge the presuppositions that lead us to see certain elements in a work of art, and we need to extend the same charitable privilege to people who do not share those presuppositions and therefore respond differently.

Current aesthetic theory stresses the idea of "interpretive communities"—groups of people who view the creative arts from a common core of interests and assumptions and values. Christians are one such interpretive community. They are not inherently better artists or critics than other people are. But they have their own "agenda" of interests springing from their coherent worldview. They also share beliefs and attitudes that they bring to their artistic and critical pursuits. The purpose of this essay is to delineate the Christian principles that have a special relevance to the arts.

As an organizing framework, we should note that artists perform three interrelated activities: (1) they create aesthetic objects and artistic form (2) they present human experience for our contemplation; and (3) they offer an interpretation of the experiences they present. Perspective affects all three activities, which I will discuss individually.

ARTISTIC CREATIVITY IN CHRISTIAN PERSPECTIVE

Human creativity is active in all human pursuits, but it has always, and rightly, been especially regarded as an attribute of the arts. For one thing, the arts are the province of the imagination, and the imagination is never limited solely to observable reality. Oscar Wilde once commented that art "has flowers that no forests know of, birds that no woodland possesses… She can work miracles at her will, and when she calls monsters from the deep they come. She can bid the almond-tree blossom in winter, and send the snow upon the ripe cornfield."[8] Artists are the orators of the imagination. A work of art is a new creation that cannot be fully explained by any previously existing model.

In addition to the creative element of the arts, the related qualities of form, beauty, technique and craftsmanship are an essential ingredient of art. The elements of artistic form that all of the arts share are theme or centrality, pattern or design, organic unity (also called unity in variety or theme and variation), repetition or recurrence, rhythm, balance, contrast or tension, symmetry, harmony or "fittingness," unified progression and coherence. No single work of art needs to possess all of these, and some are more appropriately applied to one of the arts than the others. Nor should we limit these elements of artistic form to classical or Platonic aesthetic standards. Modern art also possesses its version of these formal qualities, even when artists claim that they are not using them.

[8] Oscar, Wilde, "The Decay of Lying," as reprinted in *The Modern Tradition: Backgrounds of Modern Literature*, eds. Richard Ellmann and Charles Feidelson, Jr. (New York: Oxford University Press, 1965), 20.

The elements of artistic form are what the arts share. They differ in the medium by which they incarnate them. Music presents these elements of form through the medium of sound, literature through words, and painting through color, line and texture.

Artistic beauty or proficiency consists of the skillful composition and manipulation of the elements of aesthetic form. Such proficiency in the control of artistic technique is an important part of the value that we attach to the arts; sometimes the creation of beauty is virtually the whole point of a work of art. This is especially true of much abstract or nonrepresentational art. Abstract art such as the symmetrical designs of a Persian carpet, an ornamental wrought-iron railing, or music without words have as their main purpose to present an artistic pattern for the pleasure of the beholder or listener.

And even in representational art, where part of the attention is focused on some aspect of human experience or external reality, the technical excellence remains an important part of the total effect. "Our primal aesthetical experience," writes one aesthetic theorist, is "a response of enchantment to 'beauty' (in a very wide sense of the term)."[9]

To gauge the importance of creativity and form in the artistic enterprise, we need only note the statements and practices of artists. They attribute creativity to a process of inspiration, however conceived. The revisions and refinements that they continue to lavish on their unfinished works are almost always directed toward a better crafted artistic form and rarely toward the ideational content of the work.

The poet Dylan Thomas wrote over 200 manuscript versions of his poem "Fern Hill." Beethoven sketched and resketched his compositions. Leonardo da Vinci drew a thousand hands. The Christian poet Gerard Manley Hopkins theorized that the purely artistic dimension of poetry exists "for its own sake and interest even over and above its interest of meaning."[10] And even when artistic excellence is not the main purpose of art, as when art is used in religious worship, for example, the formal beauty of a work enhances its effectiveness.

When we ask how the high value that the arts place on creativity and artistic form fits into a Christian worldview, it is apparent at once that the two are in total accord. In contrast to much of the prevailing cultural climate of our time, biblical Christianity asserts that human creativity and artistry are not only desirable but indispensable.

The Doctrine of Creation

The starting point for thinking Christianly about creativity and beauty is the doctrine of creation, especially as described in the first chapter of the Bible. We learn in these verses that God himself is a creator who pronounced his handiwork "very good" (Genesis 1:31). Equally important is the precise kind of nature of world that God created. It is a world that is beautiful as well as functional.

From a purely utilitarian point of view, God need not have created a world filled with symmetrical shapes and beautiful colors and pleasing sounds and varied textures. What we find in the visible creation is evidence not only of a functional mind but also an artistic imagination.

What kind of environment did God intend people to inhabit? Genesis 2:9 tells us: When God created Paradise, he "made to grow every tree that is pleasant to the sight and good for food." The conditions for human welfare are double—aesthetic and functional. Along with nature, the human arts have been the largest source of beauty in people's lives.

Not only did God create a universe filled with beautiful forms, he also created people in his own image (Genesis 1:26–27). Exactly what does this mean? Theology has rightly stressed human rationality, morality and holiness as the things that people share with God. But in its narrative context in Genesis 1, where we first hear about God's image in people, something else is even more obvious, namely, the idea of creativity.

[9] Auriel Kolna, "Contrasting the Ethical with the Aesthetical," *British Journal of Aesthetics* 12 (1972):340. Although the word *beauty* has fallen out of vogue in scholarly circles, partly because it is inappropriate to modern art whose subject is ugliness, I am unwilling to relinquish the term for the simple reason that I have found again and again that it is the term with which ordinary people resonate. Whatever synonym we might choose, we obviously need some term by which to term *beauty* can continue to serve this function has been argued by Guy Sircello, *A New Theory of Beauty* (Princeton, NJ: Princeton University Press, 1975).
[10] Gerard Manley Hopkins, "Poetry and Verse," as quoted in *Gerard Manley Hopkins: The Major Poems*, ed. Walford Davies (London: J. M. Dent and Sons, 1979), 38.

The classic study of what the image of God in people means to aesthetic theory is Dorothy L. Sayers' book *The Mind of the Maker*, where we read this regarding the Genesis statement about God's image in people:

Had the author of Genesis anything particular in his mind when he wrote? It is observable that in the passage leading up to the statement about man, he has given no detailed information about God. Looking at man, he sees in him something essentially divine, but when we turn back to see what he says about the original upon which the "image" of God was modeled, we find only the single assertion, "God created." The characteristic common to God and man is apparently that: the desire and the ability to make things."[11]

The image of the creative God in people is the theological reason why people create. The doctrines of creation and the image of God in people affirm human creativity as something good in principle. Abraham Kuyper once wrote,

As image-bearer of God, man possesses the possibility both to create something beautiful, and to delight in it… The world of poetic ideas, can have no source other than God; and it is our privilege as bearers of His image, to have a perception of this beautiful world, artistically to reproduce, and humanly to enjoy it.[12]

Can a Christian in good conscience do something as non-utilitarian as spending an afternoon at an art gallery or an evening at a concert? Can a student justify the time spent taking a course in fiction writing or painting or music composition? In a Christian scheme of things, the answer is clear: to be artistically creative, and to enter into the creativity of others, is to exercise the image of God within oneself.

The Doctrine of Stewardship

The Christian doctrine of stewardship leads to the same conclusion. A steward is a person put in charge of the resources of his or her master. Christian stewardship means serving God with the talents with which he has endowed us (see especially the parable of the talents in Matthew 25:14–30). A duty of cultivation attaches to every ability and capacity that we possess.

What, then, are the talents with which God has endowed the creative artist? The classic answer is given in Exodus 31:3–5 in the description of the building of the tabernacle. We read that the Lord filled Bezalel "with the Spirit of God, with ability and intelligence, with knowledge and all craftsmanship, to devise artistic designs, to work in gold, silver, and bronze, in cutting stones for setting, and in carving wood, for work in every craft." These are the gifts of the artist. To cultivate them is to exercise stewardship. It is worthy of note, too, that "God called Bezalel" to exercise his creative ability (Exodus 31:2). The creation and study and dissemination of art is a calling. The "creation mandate" that God gave to Adam and Eve when he told them to exercise dominion over the creation (Genesis 1:26–30) is by extension also a cultural mandate to rule human culture in the name of God.

It is evident from what I have said that thinking Christianly about the arts involves rejection of the utilitarian mindset that scorns aesthetic form and beauty. The non-utilitarian aspect of the arts is not a mark against them. God did not create a purely utilitarian world. He filled his creation with much that is simply beautiful and delightful. When he created the perfect human environment, it included every tree that is pleasant to the sight (Genesis 2:9). The garments of Aaron were embellished "for glory and for beauty" (Exodus 28:2). We should note that well: beauty is worthy in itself, just as truth and goodness are.

The embellishments of the Temple served no architectural weight bearing function. They simply beautified the place. As H. R. Rookmaaker writes in his monograph *Art Needs No Justification*, "God gave humanity the skill to make things beautiful, to make music, to write poems, to make sculpture, to decorate things… Art has its own meaning. A work of art can stand in the art gallery and be cherished for its own sake. We listen to a piece of music simply to enjoy it."[13] Art nearly always has a gratuitous, more-than-functional quality to it. By its very nature it involves a willingness to go beyond the purely utilitarian.

---

[11] Dorothy L. Sayers, *The Mind of the Maker* (Cleveland, OH: World Publishing, 1956), 34.

[12] Abraham Kuyper, *Calvinism* (Grand Rapids, MI: Eerdmans, 1967), 10.

[13] H. R. Rookmaaker, *Art Needs No Justification* (Downers Grove, IL: InterVarsity, 1978), 38–39.

While it is an overstatement to attribute automatic moral effects to the arts, one of the virtues that the arts tend to foster is an inherent rejection of the materialism and acquisitiveness that are always threatening to overwhelm the human race. Because the enjoyment of artistic beauty is essentially non-utilitarian, it draws a boundary around human acquisitiveness and clears a ground in which people can recover and celebrate distinctively human values. Any worldview that finds a place for artistic delight has a built-in curb against the purely acquisitive mindset that sees value only in practical activities that serve a utilitarian function.

Creativity and the Fall

We must, of course, not overstate the case for artistic creativity. Human creativity did not escape the effects of the Fall. Artistic creativity, too, is subject to moral and intellectual criticism. A painting or song or novel has no claim to our reverence or admiration simply because it is the product of human creativity. We must differentiate between noble and ignoble manifestations of the creative impulse.

One criterion is the purpose or *telos* that governs an artist's effort. Art composed to feed an artist's greed for fame or wealth has a less noble purpose than art designed to serve one's fellow humans or to glorify God. Art that caters to the coarse taste for pornography is less worthy than creativity that aims to dignify and refine human taste.

Another criterion for judging the worthiness of human creativity is the effect of art on its audience. We rightly admire art, music and literature whose effect is to make people more sensitive, moral or humanly refined. And we should judge negatively art whose effect is to encourage people to behave selfishly, immorally or coarsely.

Yet another standard by which we can judge artistic creativity is aesthetic excellence. Poorly executed paintings or musical compositions or stories might be the products of someone's creativity, but they do not for that reason merit our admiration. Technical excellence, on the other hand, is one of the very aims of artistic creativity. In fact, the lack of artistic excellence detracts from the impact of the Christian content.

Artistic creativity is a great gift, but it is not inherently sacred or good. For at least a century now, non-Christian enthusiasts for the arts have tended to find in art a substitute for the Christian religion. Nietzsche virtually deified free creativity. The romantic poets regarded the imagination as the religious faculty by which we have contact with the supernatural. Such people elevate the imagination to a religious role that the Bible reserves for a person's "heart" or "soul."

Artistic creativity can never hold such an esteemed place in a Christian worldview. There is wisdom and beauty but not salvation in a sonnet. Art can satisfy some of the same longings that religion does. It speaks to the human capacity for illumination, mystery, order, and beauty. But a Christian finds the ultimate satisfaction of these longings in God, not in art. It is this conviction that lies behind this statement of C. S. Lewis:

> The Christian will take literature a little less seriously than the cultured Pagan… The unbeliever is always apt to make a kind of religion of his aesthetic experiences… But the Christian knows from the outset that the salvation of a single soul is more important than the production and preservation of all the epics and tragedies in the world.[14]

The Christian religion encourages a balanced view toward artistic creativity. To a technological world that values only what is utilitarian, Christianity declares that whatever is beautiful, whether it is a tree or a sonata, has worth in itself because a creative God has conferred the capacity for artistry on his human creatures. To enthusiasts for the arts who make an idol of the imagination and its products, Christianity asserts that God the Creator is always separate from his creation, whether nature or culture.

---

[14] C. S. Lewis, *Christian Reflections* (Grand Rapids, MI: Eerdmans, 1967), 10.

THE PORTRAYAL OF HUMAN EXPERIENCE IN THE ARTS

The arts take human experience as their subject. They are above all the expression of human response to reality. When a painter paints a landscape, he or she is suggesting something of the human response to nature. Music is particularly adept at expressing the inner weather of the human emotions or condition. Literature is even more comprehensive in its ability to present the contours of human experience in the world. The novelist Joseph Conrad wrote, "My task... is, by the power of the written word to make you hear, to make you feel—it is, before all, to make you see."[15] So rooted are the arts in reality that the oldest and most influential of all aesthetic theories has regarded the arts as an imitation of reality.

Creative artists are sensitive observers of reality. "The writer should never be ashamed of staring," writes novelist Flannery O'Connor.[16] The American painter Andrew Wyeth once told an interviewer, "I love to study the many things that grow below the corn stalks and bring them back into the studio to study the color. If one could only catch that true color of nature—the very thought of it drives me mad."[17] The creative artist's vocation is to stare at the created and human worlds and to lure the rest of us into a similar act of contemplation.

The arts stay close to the way things are in the world. The knowledge that they convey is an experiential knowledge of the physical and human worlds. Whether or not this is a knowledge worth having depends on one's values and worldview. Plato viewed such knowledge as rather frivolous, a knowledge hardly worth having.

A Christian viewpoint disagrees with this denigration of physical and human reality. It does so partly on the basis of the doctrine of creation. Things are real because God made them. And because he made them, they are worthy of study and celebration and love. Not only did God make things. He created people in such a way that they perceive them as much through their physical senses as their minds. The color and smell of a rose are not irrelevant or illusory.

The Christian doctrine of Incarnation points in the same direction. When Jesus took on human form in order to redeem people, he demonstrated that earthly, human experience is of immense worth. Christianity is not escapist. It does not substitute a heavenly world for the earthly one. It brings a spiritual reality into the earthly order.

Simply at the level of subject matter, then, the Christian doctrines of creation and Incarnation have far-reaching implications for the arts. Visual artists are assured that their preoccupation with the scenes and people and colors that they paint or mold are worthy of such attention. Musicians need not doubt the significance of the human feelings and attitudes embodied in their sounds. Poets and storytellers and dramatists can be convinced that their portrayal of the whole range of human experience in the natural and social worlds is a worthwhile endeavor. Christian artists can take all of life as their subject, just as the writers of the Bible did.

VALUES AND REALITY: THE ARTIST'S PERSPECTIVE

We might think that the mere subject matter of an artistic work is philosophically neutral and that perspective enters only when artists add their interpretive slant to the subject of portrayal. But the worldview of creative artists emerges even from the subjects they select for portrayal. The details that an artist includes in the limited confines of a single work carry a burden of meaning larger than themselves and are understood to be representative of a bigger sense of life. Artistic subject matter implies a statement about both values and reality.

In the realm of *values*, artists imply what they regard as worthy of human attention whenever they put brush to canvas or pen to paper. Why did the French painter Courbet shock the artistic norms of his day by painting common stonebreakers and a peasant burial? Because his very choice of such subject matter implied that true worth resides in people of humble social standing instead of people with aristocratic status.

---

[15] From the preface of Joseph Conrad, *The Nigger of the Narcissus* (New York: Collier Books, 1962), 19.
[16] O'Connor, *Mystery and Manners*, 84.
[17] Quoted by Virginia Stem Owens in *The Christian Imagination*, ed. Leland Ryken (Grand Rapids, MI: Baker, 1981), 380.

Bach wrote church music on sacred themes because he valued supremely the worship of God. Wordsworth's nature poems, simply at the level of subject matter, express his attitude toward what is important in human experience.

What an artist chooses to portray is a comment about *reality* as well as values. Artists create out of the habitual furniture of their minds. What they exclude is as important as what they include. Writers whose poems or stories never portray God, spiritual reality or Christian values exhibit, simply at the level of subject matter, a secular worldview. We can tell by looking at the table of contents of the works of Mendelssohn and Handel that their view of reality was Christian. Flannery O'Connor theorized that "it is form the kind of world the writer creates, from the kind of character and detail he invests it with, that a reader can find the intellectual meaning of a book."[18]

We might think that abstract or nonrepresentational art and music are free from perspective, but they, too, are an implied comment about reality. A symphony in which organization dominates the composition conveys a different sense of life from a symphony in which disorganization dominates. A vastly different worldview emerges from the intricate harmony of a Persian tapestry and most modern abstract art. When a graduate student who works in abstract sculpture recently had his work critiqued by his department, he was asked why his nonrepresentational sculptures possessed an order and gracefulness and clean lines so atypical of prevailing contemporary trends. His answer was that his sculpture expressed his Christian view of the world as ultimately orderly.

Artistic content is inherently laden with perspective. Christians have a picture of reality and a value system stemming form their Christian worldview. As they assimilate works of art, therefore, they should self-consciously assess the adequacy of artistic pictures of the world in terms of a Christian framework.

The central tenets in that worldview are the existence of God and an unseen spiritual world, the worth of physical reality, the value of the individual person and social institutions, the fact of human evil and fallenness, the availability of God's redemptive grace, and a view of human history as being under God's purposeful providence and headed toward a goal.

As Christians look at the subject matter of artistic works through the lens of their convictions, some of the objects they see come into focus. Other objects remain out of focus. In either case, art has served its useful purpose; it has furnished the recipient with an occasion to exercise intellectual discrimination on questions of values and reality. Some value systems and views of reality are wrong, but Christians have an obligation to understand the world in which they minister.

THE INTERPRETATION OF REALITY IN WORKS OF ART

Artists do more than present human experience; they also *interpret* it from a specific perspective. Works of art make implied assertions about reality. This is simply one of the conventions with which people approach the artistic enterprise, whether as creators or recipients. The primary convention of the arts is what aesthetic theorist Jonathan Culler calls "the rule of significance," meaning that we should look on works of art "as expressing a significant attitude to some problem concerning man and/or his relation to the universe."[19] Artists intend meanings, and audiences can scarcely avoid looking for them.

Art's Implied Assertions

Works of art make implied assertions, just as history and science and philosophy do. For convenience, we can say that the arts make implied claims about the three great issues of life:

1. Reality: what really exists, and what is its nature?
2. Morality: what constitutes right and wrong behavior?
3. Values: what really matters, and what matters most and least?

For purposes of illustration, I turn first to a pair of nineteenth-century English painters, Constable and Turner. They both chose nature as their paintings convince us not simply that physical nature is an important

[18] O'Connor, *Mystery and Manners*, 75.
[19] Jonathan Culler, *Structuralist Poetics: Structuralism, Linguistics, and the Study of Literature* (Ithaca, NY: Cornell University Press, 1975), 115.

part of reality but also that it is something of great worth in human experience.

But along with these similarities we notice obvious differences in how Constable and Turner interpreted nature. What do we see as we look at Constable's famous paintings of Salisbury Cathedral? We see the beauty and harmony of nature. We see nature in a religious light and as the friend of people. The human and natural worlds are unified. Constable himself said that he painted nature as benevolent because he sensed God's presence in nature.

Turner offers quite a different interpretation of nature. His colors are more intense, his brush strokes much broader and more passionate. There is an element of terror in many of his nature scenes. One of his paintings shows a gigantic avalanche ready to overwhelm a matchbox cabin under it furious weight. In such a painting nature is not nurturing, as in paintings by Constable and the Dutch realists, but hostile. The one is not necessarily more Christian than the other, though we should not minimize how artists select details that suggest their overall view of human possibilities in the universe.

For a literary illustration, consider the following sonnet, entitled "God's Grandeur," by Gerard Manley Hopkins:

> The world is charged with the grandeur of God.
> It will flame out, like shining from shook foil.
> It gathers to a greatness, like the ooze of oil
> Crushed. Why do men then now not reck his rod?
> Generations have trod, have trod, have trod;
> And all is seared with trade; bleared, smeared with toil;
> And wears man's smudge and shares man's smell: the soil
> Is bare now, nor can foot feel, being shod.
>
> And for all this, nature is never spent;
> There lives the dearest freshness deep down things;
> And though the last lights of the black West went
> Oh, morning, at the brown brink eastward, springs—
> Because the Holy Ghost over the bent
> World brooks with warm breast and with ah! bring wings.

The subject of the poem is the permanent freshness of nature. The perspective from which we view that reality is the grandeur of God. What really exists? According to this poem, the physical world of sun and trees and the spiritual world that includes the Triune God are equally real. What constitutes moral and immoral behavior? To live morally is to live in reverence before God's creation. To desecrate nature in pursuit of selfish acquisitiveness is immoral. What values are most worthy of human pursuit? God's nature.

The Audience's Responsibility

If works of art are this laden with meaning, what are the implications for those who constitute the audience of the arts? Today it is commonplace to appropriate works of art in terms of our own values, morality and view of reality. A Christian worldview asserts specific ideas in all three areas. To assimilate the arts in a Christian way means to interact with their implied assertions within a framework of Christian doctrine, as derived from the Bible.

Because the three big subject areas of the arts are God, people and nature, it is especially crucial for Christians to have a grasp of Christian truth about these topics whenever they encounter works of art. In a Christian view, God is the ultimate reality and object of devotion. God is the one who has created everything that exists in the universe. Several important corollaries follow. One is that God is transcendent over reality and never to be equated with the creation. Another is that since God is the ultimate source and end of reality, everything else derives its identity from God. Thus people are the creatures of God, moral goodness consists of doing God's will, history is the outworking of God's purposes, human institutions such as state and family are ordained by God, and so forth.

Christianity postulates a threefold view of people: good and worthy in principle because God made them in his image, evil or fallen by virtue of their sinful actions, and capable of restoration by God's grace.

Judged by such a standard, any view of people is inadequate if it sees them as *only* evil or *only* good. In a Christian scheme, people are evil by their inclinations but good as they participate in God's grace. In either case, human choice is both possible and necessary. A lot of art is *truthful* without telling the whole *truth*. It accurately portrays part of the truth about human nature, but still falls short of a Christian perspective because it fails to do justice to the comprehensive balance in a Christian view of people.

The Christian view of nature runs parallel to the view of people. Nature was created by God and it is under his providential control. This means on the one hand that nature itself is not divine and on the other that it is worthy of love and reverence. A lot of artistic portrayals of nature err in either overvaluing or undervaluing it. Medieval painting and music were so preoccupied with heaven and angels and Madonnas and grace that they suffer from an unbiblical denigration of nature. The reverse has been true of the arts during the last two centuries.

At the heart of the Christian worldview is a balance or tension between good and evil, hope and despair, optimism and pessimism. Is a work of art unchristian in its viewpoint if it portrays only a sense of despair or discord? Isn't the Fall a keystone of Christian doctrine? If so, why should Christians not endorse the protest music and literature and painting that are so dominant in the twentieth century?

The best framework that I have seen for grappling with this issue is Francis Schaeffer's commonsensical suggestion that Christianity consists of two themes.[20] One is the pessimistic fact of sin, despair and lostness in human experience. The other theme is the hope, meaningfulness and redemptive potential in life. A Christian worldview embraces both halves of this tension. The sense of life that emerges from artistic works is less than Christian if it omits either side of the tension. The garbage can behind the house and the rose bush in front of the house are equally real.

To summarize, artists inevitably offer a perspective on such basic human issues as what really exists, how people should act and what values are worthy of human devotion. The obligation of Christian artists is to convey a Christian viewpoint in their stories and paintings and musical compositions. The task of all Christians is to discern and evaluate the perspectives that artists offer for their approval whenever they read of look or listen.

TRUTH IN ART

We are now in a position to consider the question that inevitably arises when art is considered in terms of a worldview. Do the arts tell the truth? There is no single answer to the question because there are various types or levels of truth in art. There is a range of ways in which a work of art can be true or false. I will discuss them under the headings of human values, representational truth, and ideational or perspectival truth.

Human Values

To begin, the arts as a whole tell us the truth about what is foundational in human experience. Simply at the level of content, the arts keep calling us back to bedrock humanity. The arts are probably the most accurate index to human preoccupations, values, fears and longings that we possess. If we wish to know what people want and do not want, we can go to their stories and poems and songs and paintings.

This is why we often feel that we have learned more from art than from life. In real life the essential patterns and values are usually obscured by the sheer complexity and pressures of living. The arts, however, awaken our awareness of the central realities of human experience—realities such as nature and God and family and love and pain. A work of art is a distillation of experience in which the irrelevancies are stripped away. The knowledge that the arts give us is rarely new information but rather a bringing to consciousness of what we already know but to which we become oblivious in daily living.

The arts are therefore a great organizing force in human life. When people say that the arts help them to understand or make sense of life, they usually mean the ability of the arts to cut through the clutter and put them in touch with what is enduring in human experience. This, then, is one level of truth in the arts: truthfulness to the fears, longings, and values of the human race. The arts possess such truth regardless of the philosophical perspective of an artist. Such knowledge about human experience is a type of truth that Christians need; it is one of their bonds with the human race.

---

[20] See Schaeffer, *Art and the Bible*, 56–59.

Representational Truth

A second level of truth in the arts is representational truth, by which I mean truthfulness to the way things are in the world. Artists are sensitive observers of reality. They present human experience in their chosen artistic medium. Whenever a writer or composer or visual artist accurately captures the contours of human experience or external reality, we can say that the resulting work of art is true to reality.

A work of art can be true at this level even though the perspective from which the subject is viewed might be wrong. As with the previous level of truth (art as a truthful repository of what is most essential in human experience), we can make very large claims for the truth of art in its faithfulness to reality. We have all looked at paintings or read stories and poems that struck us as false to reality, to the way things are, but the overwhelming majority of art is true to reality.

Of course the arts are not "photographically" real. They use artistic techniques of highlighting, selectivity, omission, juxtaposition, and distortion in their portrayal of reality. There is a certain indirection to art. Thus the "truthfulness" of a painted portrait of a person is not measured in terms of photographic realism but in terms of whether it captures the reality of grief or serenity or the beauty of the human face. Coleridge's *Rime of the Ancient Mariner* contains such fantastic elements as ghosts and surrealistic landscapes and an albatross with supernatural powers. But these elements of fantasy accurately suggest such realities as sin, guilt, alienation, and renewal. The imaginative details in a work of art are a lens or window through which we look at life.

Perspectival Truth

The third level at which the truthfulness of a work of art needs to be tested is the level of perspective or implied assertion. I noted earlier that artists inevitably offer an interpretation of the human experiences that they portray. Not all art forms are equally laden with perspective. Literature, because it consists of words, is the most consistently perspectival. Music, being the most nonrepresentational, is least likely to bear ideational perspective. The visual arts fall somewhere between the two.

The perspectives or themes embodied in artistic works range from a general sense of life at one end of the spectrum to very specific assertions at the other. At the general end, artistic perspective consists of such attitudes as order or lack of it, hope or despair, the presence or absence of a supernatural reality, meaning or futility. As works of art become more explicitly laden with perspective, they embody specific ideas about God, people, society and nature, or about what constitutes good and bad behavior, or about what values are worthy and unworthy of human devotion.

As people assimilate a work of art, they do so in terms of their own worldview. They measure the perspective in works of art by their own convictions. The more committed they are to a standard of truth that they regard as authoritative, the more consciously they will assess art in terms of their own worldview.

Two-Stage Criticism

Christians surely fall into the category of people committed to a standard of truth. The methodology for integrating one's encounter with works of art and one's Christian faith has been succinctly summarized in T. S. Eliot's theory that the criticism of artistic works

> should be completed by criticism from a definite ethical and theological standpoint… It is… necessary for [Christians] to scrutinize… works of imagination with explicit ethical and theological standards… What I believe to be incumbent upon all Christians is the duty of maintaining consciously certain standards and criteria of criticism over and above those applied by the rest of the world; and that by these criteria and standards everything… must be tested.[21]

Notice that Eliot envisions a two-stage process of criticism. First we must receive the work on its own terms and allow it to say what it really says. Then we must exercise our prerogative of agreeing or disagreeing with the artist's interpretation of reality and experience.

What are the "explicit ethical and theological standards" by which Eliot thinks Christians should

[21] T. S. Eliot, "Religion and Literature," reprinted in *The Christian Imagination*, ed. Ryken, 142, 153.

assess the truth content of art? They are based ultimately on the Bible, the only final authority for belief in what is, after all, a *revealed* religion. The insights of Christian creeds based on the Bible and Christian thinkers who are gifted to codify and state the implications of biblical doctrine become important elements in a person's understanding of a Christian worldview. In the application of Christian doctrine to specific artistic assertions about life, biblical revelation obviously needs to be supplemented by human reason in any Christian critique of art.

Judging the truthfulness of the implied assertions of art is a form of intellectually testing the spirits to see if they are from God. The criteria by which the ideational or perspectival truth of art is judged are the same intellectual standards as applied to the other disciplines. The arts, for all their beauty and delightfulness and imaginative power, do not allow us to take a holiday from the mind. The task of completing artistic criticism with a Christian assessment of an artist's perspective or worldview needs to be informed by insights from philosophy, theology, ethics and psychology. It can never rest solely on aesthetic considerations.

Common Grace

The truthfulness of a work of art does not depend on an artist's Christian orthodoxy. The doctrine of common grace asserts that God endows all people, believers and unbelievers alike, with a capacity for goodness, truth, creativity and so forth. All truth is God's truth. It is not suspect if it happens to be expressed by non-Christian artists.

The Bible itself affirms that unbelieving artists can express truth. In the New Testament, Paul several times quotes with approval from pagan Greek poets.[22] When Solomon needed visual artists who could express the beauty of holiness, he hired the best available artists, who happened to be pagans.[23] As John Calvin wrote regarding the application of the doctrine of common grace to the arts, "All truth is from God; and consequently, if wicked men have said anything that is true and just, we ought not to reject it; for it has come from God."[24]

Does art tell the truth? There is no single answer to the perennial question. A lot of misleading eulogistic overstatements and denigrating understatements have been made about the truthfulness of art by people who ignore the range of ways in which art can be true and false.

Virtually all art tells us the truth about the foundational preoccupations, values, fears and longings of the human race. Most art is true as a representation of some aspect of human experience or external reality. At the level of intellectual perspective or interpretation of reality, most of the world's art, music and literature has not measured up to a Christian standard of truth.

Of course it is possible to state the theme of a work of art so broadly that virtually no one, including Christians, would disagree with the statement. But when pressed more specifically at the level of implied philosophical assertion, most art through the centuries has deviated from Christian doctrine, despite the predominantly Christian tenor of European culture during the Middle Ages and Renaissance.

Not all art is Christian in viewpoint, but it is always of interest to Christians because it clarifies the human situation to which the Christian faith speaks. Encountering the moral and philosophic viewpoints of artistic works is an avenue to understanding the people with whom we live and the culture that is our daily environment. Measuring those viewpoints by a Christian norm serves as an invaluable catalyst to a Christian's thinking about human issues.

WHY CHRISTIANS NEED THE ARTS

The arts serve many functions in human culture. They are functions that Christians should welcome and that they avoid to their own harm.

One of the functions of art can be summed up under such related words as refreshment, recreation, entertainment, and the enjoyment of artistic form or beauty. The arts are a celebration of life. The goal of our excursions into the realm of imaginative art is to send us back to real life with a renewed zest for it. The

---

[22] The passages include Acts 17:28; 1 Corinthians 15:33; and Titus 1:12. For commentary on the importance of this data for aesthetic theory, see my book *Triumphs of the Imagination: Literature in Christian Perspective* (Downers Grove, IL: InterVarsity, 1979), 161–63.

[23] See Veith, *The Gift of Art*, pp. 57–58, for the details.

[24] John Calvin, *Commentaries on the Epistles to Timothy, Titus, and Philemon*, trans. William Pringle (Grand Rapids, MI: Eerdmans, 1948), 300–301.

arts awaken us to the hidden beauty of the world and are themselves an extension of that beauty. The arts affirm the humanness of humans. Even when the subject of art is human evil, suffering, and ugliness, the artistic skill with which the subject is rendered is a tribute to human achievement.

The arts are useful as well as delightful. They are a great ordering force in human culture. As the arts present human experience for our contemplation, they intensify our involvement with life, heighten our awareness, expand our range of experiences, and enlarge our human sympathies and compassion. The arts sharpen and reward the senses and do justice to the emotional and imagining side of human nature. They give shape to our own experiences, thereby satisfying the human urge for adequate expression of insights and feelings.

Because the arts are interpretive in nature, they speak to our intellect. They offer a diagnosis, definition and explanation for the human condition. With their implied assertions about life, the arts force us to think, ponder alternative views of life, to commit ourselves to our own convictions of truth. They provide the materials for us to exercise and expand our own angle of vision.

These are the gifts of art. They are even more important to Christians than to non-Christians because to the human reasons for art a Christian can add an even more ultimate rationale—the glory of God. This, indeed, is the appointed consummation of the arts. The person who can revere the ultimate source and end of human creativity has an added reason to cherish the ability of the arts to intensify human awareness and compassion, to enhance human enjoyment and understanding.

---

*This essay originally appeared in the book *The Making of a Christian Mind*:
   Leland Ryken, "The Creative Arts," *The Making of a Christian Mind*, ed. Arthur Holmes (Downers Grove, IL: InterVarsity, 1985), pp. 105–131.
**Reproduction rights granted by Leland Ryken.

The Creative Arts
Essay Questions

Answer the questions below on a separate sheet of paper and be prepared to review your answers in class.

PART ONE

1. What role do the arts play in affecting worldviews?

The arts play a crucial role in shaping the worldview of people and culture. To understand this, we must first recognize that a worldview consists of more than just abstract ideas or theoretical concepts. A worldview is also shaped by images, symbols, myths, and stories. People do not live by ideas alone—they also express their affirmations and denials through the paint on a canvas, the tension and release of sound, and poems and stories.

The arts are rooted in mankind's image-making and image-perceiving nature. People organize their lives and make their decisions partly in terms of such images as heroes and villains, crosses and altars, national emblems and patriotic legend, love songs and hymns, landscape paintings and portraits. While these images have an ideational aspect to them, they also communicate meanings that do not become focused into theoretical propositions.

Unless we recognize the powerful impact of images on a worldview, our worldview and the behavior it produces will continue to be muddled. We also need to recognize that the quality of our life and character is heavily affected by the quality of the images that we habitually take into our minds and imaginations.

For example, people may not accede to the accumulation of possessions, but if their minds are filled with images of big houses and fancy clothes, their actual behavior will run in the direction of materialism. People may theoretically believe in the ideals of chastity and faithful wedded love, but if their minds are filled with images of exposed bodies and songs of seduction, their sexual behavior will have a large admixture of lust and sexual license in it. [SM p. 199]

2. How does imagination relate to art?

The human faculty that enables art to become reality in our minds is the imagination. Imagination is simply the image-making and image-perceiving capacity that we all have. The arts are thus imaginary constructions that "distort" reality in order to increase our awareness of it.

Imagination implies, first of all, the notion of "image," that is, sensory concreteness or experiential immediacy. The arts are a *presentational* form. Instead of talking about human experience, they present the experience. The arts show rather than tell. Instead of primarily asking our intellects to grasp an idea, the arts ask us to undergo an experience, which may or may not lead to a proposition or concept.

The second thing that imagination implies is a fictional or imaginary element. The arts are never a mere copy of life. They are a distillation of some aspect of reality. All artists use techniques of highlighting, omission, selectivity, exaggeration, arrangement, and juxtaposition to heighten our perception of some aspect of life. Music, for example, artificially produces arrangements of sounds that awaken feelings of serenity, exultation, or reverence. A painting can give us a heightened sense of something as common as flowers and household utensils, as in the still-life paintings of the Dutch realists. Literary tragedy distills the essence of human suffering and silhouettes it with clarity. [SM p. 200]

3. **In what ways does the Bible endorse both the image-making and imaginary impulses of the arts?**

First, God is portrayed in the Bible as a creator of images. A dominant theme throughout the Old Testament is God's creation of the natural world. These visible images, in turn, are said to communicate truth about God himself (Psalm 19:1–4; Romans 1:19–20). The New Testament presents the Incarnation of Jesus, who is declared to be God in tangible human form.

We should note secondly the literary nature of the Bible. The Bible is *not* what we so often picture it as being—a mere theological outline with proof texts attached. The bulk of the Bible consists of stories, poems, visions, and letters, all of them literary forms. When asked to define *neighbor*, Jesus told a fictional story (Luke 10:25–37). When he wished to teach a lesson in servanthood, he washed his disciples' feet (John 13:1–20). Jesus taught religious truth by making up stories about sheep and pearls, seed, and fish. Oliver Cromwell rightly said that Jesus "Spoke things." Jesus trusted the ability of literary images to convey religious truth when he told his disciples to "remember Lot's wife" (Luke 17:32). The Bible repeatedly affirms the image-making tendency of the arts.

Third, the Christian sacraments of communion and baptism have been important in defining a Christian aesthetic (philosophy of the arts). The Christian sacraments affirm the sign-making impulse of the arts. The sacraments, after all, use the physical elements of water, bread, and wine to express spiritual realities. While the Christian sacraments do not sanction every manifestation of imagination in a fallen world, they nonetheless confirm the principle that images and symbols can express truth to the glory of God and the edification of people.

A fourth biblical validation of the arts is the descriptions of worship that are contained in the Bible, especially in the Old Testament. Worship in the Bible is surrounded by a wealth of music and visual and verbal art. As the Old Testament worshipers approached the Temple in Jerusalem, they saw two gigantic freestanding bronze pillars over twenty-five feet high (1 Kings 7:15–22). These monoliths had no architectural function other than to be beautiful and suggest by their aesthetic properties something of the grandeur, stability, and power of God. The pillars were specimens of one prominent type of art in the Temple, namely, abstract or nonrepresentational art. [SM pp. 200–1]

4. **What role does one's worldview play in interpreting and experiencing art?**

One does not interact with art in a vacuum. As readers, viewers, and listeners, we assimilate works of art within the framework of our personal experiences and worldview. We interpret and experience art from our own unique vantage point, making the experience and interpretation of works of art a subjective action. The final meaning of a painting or symphony or story is a fusion of what the work itself puts before a person and what the person brings to the work. Thus, we should acknowledge the presuppositions that lead us to see certain elements in a work of art and extend the same charitable privilege to others, who may not share those presuppositions and therefore respond differently. Individuals with differing values, experiences, and worldviews interpret works of art differently. For example, we as Christians bring a set of presuppositions when we interpret art. We are not inherently better artists or critics than other people are, but we have our own agenda springing from our coherent worldview. [SM pp. 201–2]

5. **Besides creativity, what essential elements do the arts share in common?**

In addition to the creative element, the arts share the "elements of artistic form"—theme or centrality, pattern or design, organic unity (also called unity in variety or theme and variation), repetition or recurrence, rhythm, balance, contrast or tension, symmetry or harmony, unified progression, and coherence. No single work of art needs to possess all of these. Some are more appropriately applied to one facet of the arts than the others, and they may differ in the medium by which they are brought to life. For example, music presents these elements of form through the medium of sound, literature through words, and painting through color, line, and texture. [SM pp. 202–3]

6. **Besides rationality, morality, and holiness, what other aspect do human beings share in common with God?**

We share creativity in common with our Creator. As God's image-bearers, we possess the ability to create and delight in what has been created (either by God or human hands). Thus, Christians can in good conscience participate in non-utilitarian activities such as the arts. In fact, to do so is to exercise the image of God placed within each of us. [SM pp. 203–4]

7. **What do the arts have to do with the doctrine of stewardship?**

We often only hear the responsibility of stewardship applied to the wealthy, as God has given them the ability to generate wealth and allows them to possess it for a time. The principle of stewardship then, as applied to finances, is concerned with what the affluent do with their wealth. Are they merely hoarding it or are they using it wisely for kingdom purposes?

This same principle applies to us all, including those who are artistically gifted. If a steward is a person put in charge of his master's resources and if Christians are called to be stewards of everything God has allowed them to possess, then it would follow that the Christian artist has a responsibility to use the talents the Creator has given to him in a holy manner to glorify God. [SM pp. 204–5]

8. **How can the arts foster a rejection of materialism and acquisitiveness?**

Since the enjoyment of artistic beauty is essentially non-utilitarian, it draws a boundary around human acquisitiveness and clears a ground in which people can recover and celebrate distinctively human values. Any worldview that finds a place for artistic delight has a built-in curb against the purely acquisitive mindset that sees value only in practical activities that serve a utilitarian function. [SM pp. 204–5]

9. **How do we judge between noble and ignoble human creativity?**

First, we can examine the purpose or *telos* that governs an artist's effort. Art composed to feed an artist's greed for fame or wealth has a less noble purpose than art designed to serve mankind or to glorify God. Art that caters to a coarse taste for pornography is less worthy than creativity that aims to dignify and refine human taste.

Second, we can judge the effect of the art on its audience. We rightly admire art, music, and literature that have the effect of making people more sensitive, moral, or refined. Likewise, we should judge negatively art that encourages people to behave selfishly, immorally, or coarsely.

Third, we can evaluate the artist's aesthetic excellence. Poorly executed paintings, musical compositions, or stories might be the products of someone's creativity, but they cannot merit our admiration for that reason alone. Technical excellence, on the other hand, is one of the very aims of artistic creativity, and a lack of artistic excellence actually detracts from the impact of Christian content. [SM p. 205]

10. **Is artistic creativity inherently sacred or good?**

Artistic creativity is a great gift, but it is not inherently sacred. For centuries, non-Christian enthusiasts for the arts have tended to make art a substitute for religion. Nietzsche virtually deified free creativity. The romantic poets regarded imagination as the religious faculty by which we have contact with the supernatural. Such people elevate imagination to religious roles that the Bible reserves for a person's heart or soul. Artistic creativity can never hold such an overly esteemed place in a Christian worldview. While there is wisdom and beauty in a sonnet, it cannot save the reader. Art can satisfy some of the same longings that religion does, as it speaks to the human capacity for illumination, mystery, order, and beauty, but a Christian finds the ultimate satisfaction of these longings in God. [SM p. 205]

PART TWO

11. **What role do *values* and *reality* play in the arts?**

In the realm of *values*, artists emphasize what they regard as worthy of attention whenever they put brush to canvas or pen to paper. Likewise, what an artist chooses to portray is a comment about *reality* as well. Artists create out of the habitual furniture of their minds—what they exclude is as important as what they include. Writers whose poems or stories never portray God, spiritual reality, or Christian values exhibit a secular worldview simply based on their subject matter.

Artistic content is inherently laden with perspective. Christians have a picture of reality and a value system stemming from their Christian worldview. As they assimilate works of art, therefore, they should consciously assess the adequacy of artistic perspectives of the world in terms of a Christian framework. The central tenets of a biblical worldview are the existence of God, the value of the individual person and social institutions such as marriage, the fact of human depravity, the availability of God's redemptive grace, and a view of human history as being under God's purposeful providence and headed toward a goal. [SM p. 206]

12. What are the three big subject areas of the arts and what is the Christian view of these subjects?

The three big subject areas of the arts are God, people, and nature. It is important for Christians to have a biblical understanding of these subjects when evaluating works of art in their portrayals of these areas.

Biblical Christianity states that God is the ultimate reality and the object of our devotion. God created everything that exists in the universe. He is transcendent over reality and can never be equated with the creation. Since God is the ultimate and complete source of reality, everything else derives its identity from God. Thus, people are God's creations, moral goodness consists of doing God's will, history is the outworking of God's purposes, human institutions—such as state and family—are ordained by God, and so forth.

Christianity also postulates a threefold view of people: worthy in principle because God made them in his image, evil by virtue of their sinful actions, and capable of restoration by God's grace. Judged by such a standard, any view of mankind is inadequate if it sees them as *only* evil or *only* good. In a Christian scheme, people are evil by their inclinations, but good as they participate in God's grace. The Christian view of nature runs parallel to the view of people. Nature was created by God and therefore under his providential control. This means that nature is not divine of itself, but is worthy of love and reverence. A lot of artistic portrayals of nature err in either overvaluing or undervaluing it. [SM pp. 207–8]

13. What three types of truth are discussed in relation to the arts? How is each unique?

Human Values—To begin, the arts as a whole tell us the truth about foundational human experience. The arts are probably the most accurate index to human preoccupations, values, fears, and longings that we possess.

The arts are therefore a great organizing force in human life. When people say that the arts help them to understand or make sense of life, they usually mean the ability of the arts to cut through the clutter and put them in touch with the fundamentals of human experience. This, then, is one level of truth in the arts: truthfulness to the fears, longings, and values of the human race. The arts possess such truth regardless of the philosophical perspective of an artist. Such knowledge about human experience is a type of truth that Christians need—one of their bonds with the human race.

Representational Truth—A second level of truth in the arts is representational truth—truthfulness to the way things are in the world. Artists are sensitive observers of reality. They present human experience in their chosen artistic medium. Whenever a writer or composer or visual artist accurately captures the contours of human experience or external reality, we can say that the resulting work of art is true to reality.

Of course the arts are not "photographically" real. They use artistic techniques of highlighting, selectivity, omission, juxtaposition, and distortion in their portrayal of reality. Thus the "truthfulness" of a painted portrait of a person is not measured in terms of photographic realism but in terms of how well it captures the reality of grief, serenity, or the beauty of the human face.

Perspectival Truth—The third level at which the truthfulness of a work of art needs to be tested is the level of perspective or implied assertion. Artists inevitably offer an interpretation of the human experiences that they portray. However, not all art forms are equally laden with perspective.

The perspectives or themes embodied in artistic works range from a general sense of life at one end of the spectrum to very specific worldview assertions at the other. On the general end, artistic perspective consists of such attitudes as order or lack of it, hope or despair, the presence or absence of a supernatural reality, meaning, or futility. As works of art become more explicitly laden with perspective, they embody specific ideas about God, people, society, and nature, what constitutes good and bad behavior, or what values are worthy and unworthy of human devotion.

People assimilate a work of art in terms of their own worldview—they measure the perspective in works of art by their own convictions. The more committed they are to a standard of objective truth, the more consciously they will assess art in terms of their own worldview. [SM pp. 209–10]

14. How should a Christian judge the truthfulness of art?

First, we must receive the work on its own terms and allow it to say what it really says. Then we must exercise our prerogative of agreeing or disagreeing with the artist's interpretation of reality and experience.

Judging the truthfulness of the implied assertions of art is a form of intellectually testing the spirits to see if they are from God. The criteria by which the ideational or perspectival truth of art is judged are the same intellectual standards that should be applied to other disciplines. The arts, for all their beauty and imaginative power, do not allow us to take a holiday from the mind. The task of biblically assessing an artist's perspective or worldview needs to be based on insights from philosophy, theology, ethics, and psychology. It can never rest solely on aesthetic considerations. [SM p. 210]

15. Why do Christians need the arts?

The arts are a celebration of life. The goal of our excursions into the realm of imaginative art is to send us back to real life with renewed zest. The arts awaken us to the hidden beauty of the world and are themselves an extension of that beauty. The arts affirm the humanness of humans. Even when the subject of art is human evil, suffering, and ugliness, the artistic skill with which the subject is rendered is a tribute to human achievement.

The arts are useful as well as delightful. They are a great ordering force in human culture. As the arts present human experience for our contemplation, they intensify our involvement with life, heighten our awareness, expand our range of experiences, and enlarge our human sympathies and compassion. The arts sharpen and reward the senses and do justice to the emotional and imagining side of human nature. They give shape to our own experiences, thereby satisfying the human urge for adequate expression of insights and feelings.

These gifts of art are even more important to Christians than to non-Christians because to the human reasons for art a Christian can add an ultimate rationale—the glory of God. This is the appointed consummation of the arts. The person who can revere the ultimate source and end of human creativity—God's glory—has an added reason to cherish the ability of the arts to intensify human awareness and compassion and to enhance human enjoyment and understanding. [SM pp. 211–12]

TALK SHOW ACTIVITY

Set this up in traditional talk show style, and assign roles to your class: one student as host, two to three as guests on the opposing sides, and perhaps one as the "expert" who is "supposed" to remain neutral. Divide the class into two groups, each supporting an opposing side and let them think up arguments in favor of their perspective, as well as the "life story" of the students who will appear as guests on the show.

At the beginning of the show, let the guests tell their stories and answer questions from the host, then field questions from the audience (students should remember which side of the issue they are on). Allow the host to be in charge of directing the discussion (pick your host carefully or play the role of host yourself).

Some possible topics include:

- **Music lyrics**—is banning some songs censorship or simply upholding the standards of society?
- **What is art?**—anything that I want to express, or something I create that reflects the truth or goodness of God?
- **Pornography**—is outlawing it a denial of free speech or protection of women and children?
- **TV programming**—should we just turn off programs we don't like or get the producers to stop making them? Are there other options?

DEAR DOUG
WRITING ASSIGNMENT

Hey there!

Just when you think spring might be around the corner, February changes your mind! Last week I was ready to break out the sunscreen, but now I'm back to wearing a sock cap and long underwear. Next time, remind me to pick a college someplace warm… like Hawaii.

At least brisk weather makes a steaming cup of coffee more inviting—and where there's coffee, there's discussion! This week we were talking about some issues our law professor brought up in class. He had stated that mankind is the author of all laws, and Sarah agreed with him. She said that she didn't believe that laws came from a higher power, but were created by society. I've always assumed that most laws had their foundation in God and the Bible. Who do you think makes the laws?

Nathan thought her basic idea was correct, but he changed it a bit. He said that we don't write laws because of society, but for ourselves—that the laws you should keep are the ones you believe in. This didn't really make sense to me, though. I mean, that would let someone who didn't think stop signs applied to him put everyone else on the road in danger. Are there laws that apply to everyone in every situation?

Nathan's comment got Paige started. She said that the people in power write laws, pretend they are objective, and then use them to enforce their will on society. It's like the religious right passing laws against gay marriage, she said. I had never thought about it that way before. Are laws only based on the beliefs of the people in power?

After listening to everyone else, Muhammad spoke up. He was adamant that law comes from Allah and that only laws based on principles found in the Qur'an and Islamic tradition can be trusted. How are laws from biblical principles different than laws taken from the Qur'an?

I guess everyone agreed that laws have to have a credible source in order to be trustworthy. We just differed on the source itself—Muhammad said the Qur'an, Sarah and Nathan said humanity or society, and Paige said whoever's in power. But none of these sources seem big enough. What is the Christian position on law?

All right, enough serious thinking for now… my brain is starting to hurt. I wonder—can a brain cramp become permanent, like those faces my mother said would stick if I kept making them?!

Talk to you later!
Doug

Unit Seven

Doug has brought up five different subjects; below is a rough outline of possible responses.

1. **Are governments the ultimate authority for creating laws? (10 points)**

> If laws are left to the whims of the state, then law would need to be redefined as non-universal in scope. It is the government's role to create laws, which must reflect divine law and be consistent with natural law.

2. **Are legal standards limited to the determination and interpretation of each individual? (10 points)**

> If legal standards are left to the whims of the individual, then there would cease to be one set of universal laws that apply to everyone. We would be left with some six billion sets of laws. Moreover, such a system would be impossible to enforce—to what would two disagreeing individuals appeal? It is the individual's responsibility to understand and abide by the laws of their land. If these laws are contrary to God's revealed law or character, the Christian, indeed any citizen, should refuse to abide by such laws.

3. **Are laws based solely on the beliefs of those in power? (10 points)**

> Those in power are in a position to create laws, and those laws often flow directly out of their worldview. The key, however, is for officials to remember that they are not the ultimate authority in matters of law. Man-made laws should always be thoroughly grounded in God's moral laws.

4. **Are Islamic teachings and traditions a reliable source for universal law? (10 points)**

> Ethics and law are intimately connected. In Islam, ethics are not derived from the character of Allah; rather, things are good or bad because Allah says they are. Islamic teachings and traditions concerning the law are based upon the same principle. There is no unchanging standard by which to judge good or bad laws because they are derived from the prerogative of Allah.

5. **What is the Christian view of law? (10 points)**

> Christian or divine law consists of both natural and biblical law originating in the very character of our righteous and loving God. Divine law is eternal because God is eternal and someday God will use it to judge the world (Acts 17:31) according to both natural and revealed law (Romans 2:12f). God established human government and the rule of law primarily to keep humanity's sinful nature and passions in check (Romans 13:1–4). Because of the Fall, human history reflects a continuing human effort to substitute man-made law for God's law. Christians believe that when God's laws are obeyed, humanity and its societies thrive. The Christian concept of human rights involves the biblical doctrine of man's creation in the image of God. These rights, which necessitate specific responsibilities, are unalienable. God's Word and nature's law are sufficient for mankind to establish a legal system that exemplifies man's creative image without negating his depravity.

Unit Seven Test

'Law' Textbook Questions

Matching: (1 points possible per answer [5 for 90-day])
some options may be used more than once or not at all; some questions may have multiple answers

1. __f__ **Christianity**

2. __e__ **Islam**

3. __d__ **Secular Humanism**

4. __a__ **Marxism-Leninism**

5. __b__ **Cosmic Humanism**

6. __c__ **Postmodernism**

a. Proletariat Law
b. Self-Law
c. Critical Legal Studies
d. Positive Law
e. Shari'ah Law
f. Divine/Natural Law

Short answer: (7 points possible per answer [7 for 90-day])

7. In what two ways has God revealed his law to mankind?

God has revealed his law through nature (or natural law) and special revelation (or divine law). Natural law provides humanity with a general concept of right and wrong, while divine law as given in the Bible fleshes out this skeletal framework so that we can know what God considers lawful. General and special revelation, while not providing specific answers to all situations, provide humanity with the guidance necessary to create a reasonably just system of law.

8. What are the five basic precepts of Christian law?

The Christian view of law is based on five key principles:

1. The source of all divine law is the character or nature of God.
2. Out of the character of God proceeds the moral order. This order is as real as the physical order and reflects God's character—his holiness, justice, truth, love, and mercy.
3. Mankind is created in the image of God and therefore has significance, i.e. life is not an afterthought. God established human government to protect human life, rights, and dignity (Genesis 9:6).
4. When Jesus Christ took human form (John 1:14), human life took on even greater significance. God the Creator became God the Redeemer.
5. Christian law is also based on the fact that some day God, through Jesus Christ, will judge the whole human race according to a right standard of good and evil (Acts 17:31, Romans 1:16, 2 Corinthians 5:10).

Unit Seven

CD-ROM

9. **How does the Islamic view of humanity and law differ from the view held by Christianity? What form of government does the Islamic view usually produce?**

> Christians believe that people should not be trusted with too much power. Thus in Western nations power is usually distributed among various facets of government. In contrast, Islam (which teaches that mankind is not corrupt) generally promotes a model of government based on the belief that government can be run by impeccable individuals who can be counted on to resist temptation. Thus, Islamic political institutions are only as ethical as those who run them.
>
> This view of mankind's goodness, when applied to government, usually produces dictatorships or monarchies. A subsequent result is usually a lack of personal freedoms.

10. **What is the basic assumption upon which Secular Humanist law is founded?**

> Secular Humanist law is founded on the basic assumption that God does not exist and that humanity, as an evolving animal, is perfectible. Therefore, our focus, according to this view, must be on creating an environment that encourages further evolutionary progress.

11. **What is bourgeoisie law? What two problems do Marxists have with bourgeoisie law? How do Marxists propose that society overcome the corrupt rule of bourgeoisie law?**

> According to Marxists, law is formulated by the ruling class of a capitalistic society. Marxists contend that bourgeoisie law 1) invariably discriminates against the propertyless working class and 2) breeds protest in the form of lawlessness. Accordingly, capitalistic society is more responsible for lawlessness than the individual. Indeed, criminals need feel no remorse for their actions, since the unjust bourgeois society leaves them no alternative but to lash out against it.
>
> The only clear-cut solution is for the working class to overthrow the bourgeoisie, thereby allowing the proletariat to make the laws. In fact, Marxists believe that the working class is justified in ignoring modern capitalistic laws in the pursuit of equality.

12. **How is Marxist legal theory similar to Secular Humanist law? How does Marxist legal theory differ from that of the Secular Humanist?**

> Although a number of Marxists deny that their legal theory is positivistic, the foundation of Marxist law is in mankind and the state. In this sense, both Marxists and Humanists deny any absolute legal foundation in the person of God. However, Marxists add economics to their legal theory. Marxists see the modern capitalistic society as financially oppressive. By basing laws on the will of the proletariat, Marxists believe they can create a society that is less financially exploitative. Moreover, Marxist law takes on a class and party distinctive as well. While Secular Humanists simply believe that the state is responsible for establishing rights and promoting justice, Marxists believe that the proletarian state is the only government capable of promoting justice, thus legally requiring a state led by the proletariat.

Unit Seven

13. According to Cosmic Humanists, where does all authority reside and why?

According to Cosmic Humanists, all authority resides within each individual (i.e. god). Since every person is God and God is every person, humanity can only decide the legality of an action by getting in touch with its inner God.

14. What is the Critical Legal Studies movement?

Critical Legal Studies (CLS) is a movement that critiques more traditional systems of law. CLS is focused on promoting progressive (even radical) political change. The CLS slogan is "critique is all there is." Using Derrida's deconstruction principle, Postmodernists deconstruct every law to discover its subjective meaning (no matter what it objectively states) and its inherent bias.

"ENTERTAINMENT" VIDEO

Short answer: (7 points possible per answer [7 for 90-day])

15. What are some faulty ways Christians can approach entertainment? What is wrong with these approaches?

First, some Christians avoid entertainment entirely and hope that it will go away. The problem is that entertainment (like culture) will not just go away. No matter how hard we try to ignore it, we will continue to bump up against it from time to time. This is perhaps why so many Christians turn away from their faith when they get to college. They have been so sheltered from the world that when they are on their own, the enticement of the world all at once is too much to fight.

A second faulty approach is listening to and watching only "Christian" entertainment, as if there is a line between sacred and secular. C. S. Lewis did not write just for Christians, but that is precisely what most "Christian" entertainers do. God wants Christian artists to use their talents for the benefit of everyone, not just other Christians. Moreover, this approach skirts the fundamental problem with entertainment (both "Christian" and non-Christian)—we use it to distract us from living. Entertainment becomes a tool for escaping reality. Instead, art should be used to enrich one's life. A good song, movie, or book can take you deeper into life. A bad song, movie, or book distracts you from life.

A third faulty approach is relying solely on the movie industry rating system to determine acceptability. There are some R-rated films that have redeeming value and some G-rated films that do not. A fourth faulty approach is counting cusswords and sexual content and applying a good/bad value based on this equation. There are a number of movies and songs that have no references to sex and use no dirty words but promote a non-Christian worldview.

The fundamental problem with all of these approaches is that they look for a line between acceptable and not acceptable. Life and purity are not lines; we are either running toward life and purity or running toward death and impurity. We are either seeking art that is life-giving or we are using art to entertain sin and escape life.

16. What is a good approach Christians can take with entertainment?

We need to approach entertainment with the right goal, mindset, and framework.

The Right Goal—are we using entertainment to entertain thoughts of sin or to enrich our lives?

The Right Mind—are we using entertainment to turn our brains off or to learn about the culture? Entertainment is our culture's form of art. Within cultural expression we find artists searching for answers in life. Sometimes they find good answers and sometimes they do not. Sometimes sin is present and sometimes it is not. But we should not condone non-Christians because they do not act like Christians. We need to understand where they are in life (and entertainment can help with this) and then have compassion for them as they search and struggle.

The Right Framework—are we judging entertainment from a biblical perspective? Entertainment and art should be judged by the following criteria: quality, truth, and message. Is the form well done? Is the message true? Is the purpose noble?

THE CREATIVE ARTS ESSAY
True or False: (2 points possible per answer)
*if an answer is false, restate it to make it true

17. Imagination is the making and perceiving capacity that we all have.

True

18. Utility is what the arts share in common.

False: <u>Imagination</u> is what the arts share in common.

19. God is portrayed in the Bible as a destroyer of images.

False: God is portrayed in the Bible as a <u>creator</u> of images.

20. The bulk of the Bible consists of stories, poems, visions, and letters, all of them literary forms.

True

21. Differing individuals with differing values, experiences, and worldviews interpret works of art differently.

True

22. God created a world that is functional and wholly divine.

False: God created a world that is functional and <u>beautiful</u>.

23. According to the doctrine of stewardship, an artist bears a responsibility to be utilitarian.

False: According to the doctrine of stewardship an artist bears a responsibility to <u>use his or her talents for kingdom purposes</u>.

24. We can judge between noble and ignoble human creativity by the effect the work of art has on its audience.

True

25. We can judge between noble and ignoble human creativity by the purpose that governs an artist's effort.

True

26. The arts make implied assertions about epistemology, morality, and values.

False: The arts make implied assertions about <u>reality</u>, morality, and values.

27. We must agree or disagree with an artist's interpretation of reality and experience.

True

28. We must receive the work on its own terms and allow it to say what it really says.

True

UNDERSTANDING THE TIMES

Unit Eight

Topics:
Abortion
Euthanasia
Politics

A Summit Ministries Curriculum

180-Day Syllabus

DAY	IN CLASS	HOMEWORK	
1	WATCH "Politics" video		
2	READ UTT Textbook 'Politics 8.1'	READ UTT Textbook 'Politics 8.2'	
3	REVIEW UTT Textbook 'Politics 8.1–8.2' questions	READ UTT Textbook 'Politics 8.3'	
4	READ UTT Textbook 'Politics 8.4'		
5	REVIEW UTT Textbook 'Politics 8.3–8.4' questions	READ UTT Textbook 'Politics 8.5'	
6	READ UTT Textbook 'Politics 8.6'		
7	REVIEW UTT Textbook 'Politics 8.5–8.6' questions	ASSIGN Dear Doug Letter	
8	WATCH "The Case Against Abortion" video P1		
9	WATCH "The Case Against Abortion" video P2		
10	WATCH "The Case Against Abortion" video P3		
11	REVIEW "The Case Against Abortion" video questions		
12	READ *The Shifting Focus in the Abortion Debate* essay		
13	REVIEW *The Shifting Focus...* essay questions	READ *The Battle for Life* essay	
14	REVIEW *The Battle for Life* essay questions	Dear Doug Letter assignment DUE	
15	TAKE Unit Eight Test		

90-Day Syllabus

DAY	IN CLASS	HOMEWORK	
1	WATCH "Politics" video	READ UTT Textbook 'Politics 8.1–8.2'	
2	REVIEW UTT Textbook 'Politics 8.1–8.2' questions	READ UTT Textbook 'Politics 8.3–8.4'	
3	REVIEW UTT Textbook 'Politics 8.3–8.4' questions	READ UTT Textbook 'Politics 8.5–8.6'	
4	REVIEW UTT Textbook 'Politics 8.5–8.6' questions		
5	READ *The Shifting Focus in the Abortion Debate* essay		
6	REVIEW *The Shifting Focus...* essay questions	READ *The Battle for Life* essay	
7	REVIEW *The Battle for Life* essay questions		
8	TAKE Unit Eight Test		

UNDERSTANDING THE TIMES
POLITICS QUESTIONS

Answer the questions below on a separate sheet of paper and be prepared to review your answers in class. Reflection Questions will not be found in the text. These are merely designed to help you start thinking about issues from a worldview perspective.

POLITICS 8.1

1. **What two aspects of human nature did America's founding fathers understand?**

America's founding fathers took into account both humanity's fallen nature and humanity's bearing of God's image when forming their new government. [UTT 8.1.3]

[Some points in this lesson are similar to principles discussed in the chapter on law. Students need to see the contrasting views of the origin and purpose of the state and the importance of recognizing the Fall when thinking politically. Scripture provides principles to be applied within all political systems.]

2. **Why does mankind need a civil government?**

Since every person is inherently sinful, our evil inclinations must be kept in check by laws and a government capable of enforcing such laws. [UTT 8.1.3]

3. **How can mankind be protected from government abuses?**

First, it is prudent to design a government around a system of checks and balances. Second, government leaders must see themselves as accountable not only to their citizens but also to the sovereign God. [UTT 8.1.3]

4. **Reflection Question: What are some current government activities that go beyond the limited sphere suggested by the text?**

[Answers will vary. Some examples include education, welfare, and economic controls.]

5. **Reflection Question: What explanations can be made for why Christians are hesitant to be involved in politics? What logically follows if Christians retreat from political involvement?**

Political involvement is seen by many as a worldly, corrupt, and unspiritual priority. However, if Christians retreat, those with non-biblical worldviews will control the arena of politics.

Unit Eight

POLITICS ACTIVITY

Uses the verses given below to develop principles for a Christian view of politics:

Romans 13:1–4	Christians are to submit to the governing authority which is established by God (to rebel against authority is to rebel against God). Rebellion brings judgment from God and sometimes from the state. If one does good, he should not have to fear the state. Government is accountable to God to punish wrongdoers and protect the righteous. Taxation to support government is appropriate.
1 Timothy 2:1–3	Christians are to pray and submit.
Exodus 18:13–26	Decentralized authority is effective; representative government is efficient.
1 Peter 2:13–14	Christians are to submit to those in authority and those in authority are to punish the evil and protect the good.
Psalm 103:19	God is the Sovereign King over all.
Daniel 6	Obey God over the state when the state's law conflicts with God's.
Proverbs 16:10–13	A king should rule with integrity.
Proverbs 20:26	A king should punish the wicked.
Proverbs 22:11; 25:4–5	A king is to befriend the honest and remove the wicked from his courts.
Proverbs 29:2	Righteous rule produces a joyful populace while corruption brings public groaning.
Proverbs 29:4	Justice promotes political stability and corruption and bribery bring the government down.
Proverbs 29:14	A king must rule both poor and rich without bias.
Proverbs 24:23–25	A king must rule impartially.
Proverbs 21:1	A king's heart can be turned by the Lord.
Proverbs 31:8–9	The needs of the poor, needy, and those who cannot speak for themselves must be honored.
Proverbs 31:3–5	A ruler must avoid alcohol abuse or the state will suffer.

6. **What are two ways in which the term *jihad* can be used?**

1. *Jihad* can be used to describe striving and struggling in the name of Allah. Muslims who try to live according to the guidance given by Islam thus strive to promote the message of Islam through their words and actions and are obeying the principal of jihad.

2. Some Muslims believe that to strive and struggle for Allah, it may be necessary at times to give one's life or even kill in order to preserve the truth of Islam. Therefore, to some, *jihad* implies a readiness to kill and/or die for the sake of Allah. [UTT 8.2.1]

7. **How did the attitudes of Jesus and Muhammad differ toward those who opposed them?**

While Jesus told his disciples not to take up swords against those who oppose him, Muhammad told his disciples to fight those who opposed them. [UTT 8.2.3]

8. **What reason do some Muslims offer in defense of bloodshed in the name of Allah? Does this argument seem plausible in light of history?**

Muslims in defense of past jihadist bloodshed often assert that the early conquests of Muhammad and his companions were purely defensive in nature. However, the history of Islam clearly reveals that *jihad* has never been primarily defensive, but primarily offensive. [UTT 8.2.5]

9. **What are four points that support the belief that violent forms of *jihad* are intended to be in force until Islam is a global reality?**

1. **Creation and Original Islam**—Ever since Adam and Eve's "mistake" in the Garden, Allah has been trying to bring the world back to the original state of Islam—submission to Allah.
2. **Prophets of Islam**—Ever since the beginning of time, Allah has provided prophets to draw humans back into submission to Islam.
3. **Born Muslims**—Every human being is born Muslim but is led astray—therefore, Muslims need to speak to all the nations of the world to correct these errors of belief and practice.
4. **Global Islam**—In conjunction with the first three beliefs is the hope and expectation that all nations will eventually submit to Allah and become Muslim nations.

Given these four points, some Muslims believe that violence is necessary to restore Allah's original intention for his creation. [UTT 8.2.6]

10. **For what reason were the Crusades fought? How should Christians handle this issue?**

Christians should neither completely downplay nor ignore the horrific nature of the Crusades. In the name of God, numerous Muslims and Crusaders lost their lives and little was accomplished.

Unit Eight

While there is little doubt that the Crusades are a scar on institutional Christianity and that actions were taken during the Crusades that did not honor God, it is imperative that we understand the reasons for the Crusades: They began as a *response* to Muslim aggression. Muslim armies had moved north, taking Jerusalem and threatening the Christian Byzantine Empire. Eastern Christians called on the Western Christians for aid in the face of Muslim aggression. The later Spanish crusades, intending to rout Muslim armies from Spain, were called *reconquistas* (re-conquests). They intended to *take back* land and free those captive to Muslim intruders.

Second, institutional Christianity has recognized, apologized, and renounced the atrocities of the Crusades committed on their behalf. Christians no longer promote Crusades, but a number of Muslims still call for *jihad*. The difference can be found in the teaching of Muhammad and Jesus. Jesus, unlike Muhammad, did not call for war (in fact he called for peace and submission). [UTT 8.2.8]

POLITICS 8.3

11. How does the Secular Humanist conception of democracy differ from the more common attitude?

For Secular Humanists, democracy extends beyond the realm of government. In fact, they believe the principle of democracy should color every aspect of life. The autocratic principle creates superiors and inferiors, i.e. one is dominant and the other submissive. Secular Humanists would like to do away with this division entirely through equalization. For example, many Humanists promote "equalization" within families (parent-child) and schools (teacher–pupil). Equalization implies the removal of levels of authority and variations of quality (relativism). [UTT 8.3.1–2]

12. Why do Secular Humanists favor globalism?

Because humanity is seen as the highest of all evolved animals and simply one among many parts of the world's single ecosystem, we are viewed as violating our place in nature when we attempt to divide the ecosystem into states and nations. Thus, according to Humanism, mankind should live in one community, without national borders and differing state policies. Indeed, a peaceful world government appears to be inevitable, given that we are constantly evolving to a higher state and are now capable of controlling our own evolution. [UTT 8.3.2–3]

13. Why do most Secular Humanists call for universal disarmament and expanded power for the United Nations?

Secular Humanists contend that the most effective way to move toward globalism is by disarmament and expanding the control of the U.N. Humanists believe that once disarmed, nations will be more willing to cooperate and less ready to enforce nationalistic boundaries. Also, since the U.N. is currently the only truly global organization, it is the best candidate for a secular world government. (This is because Humanism is based on the false assumption that human beings are basically good and that it is our environment that makes us evil.) [UTT 8.3.4]

14. Why does Humanistic globalism call for the international compromise of ideologies?

Secular Humanists believe that in order for globalism to work, ideologies will have to be compromised. This requirement of "compromise" is rooted in their definition of democracy (i.e. overall equalization). For Humanists, the mere fact that some ideologies perceive themselves as "more right" than others is contrary to the notion of democracy. Individuals must stop worrying about which ideology or worldview might be ethically correct and simply agree to be tolerant of everyone. This stems from the Secular Humanist stance that no ethical belief is any better than any other (except perhaps the belief in moral relativism). [UTT 8.3.6]

15. How can Secular Humanism justify defending its ideology while viewing other ideologies as opposed to democracy?

Secular Humanism claims that tolerance of ethical systems and ideologies must exist before globalism can succeed. By claiming that Humanism is open-minded, whereas all other ideologies are dogmatic and far too dependent upon absolutes, Humanism in essence sees no inconsistency in promoting its own ideology over those championed by other groups. [UTT 8.3.6]

POLITICS 8.4

16. How do Marxists view the notion of democracy?

"Democracy is a *state*," explains Lenin, "which recognizes the subordination of the minority to the majority, i.e., an organization for the systematic use of *force* by one class against another, by one section of the population against another." Marxists view the struggle to control the forces of production as the dynamic force behind mankind's development. According to Marxism, a socialist economy lays the foundation for the best form of democracy (although Marxists view democracy as little more than a necessary evil). A socialist government will tend to discourage class antagonism, since it will be founded on an economic system that is a step closer to abolishing classes. The socialist democracy is more appealing than a capitalist democracy, but is not the ideal (which will only come with the utopia of communism). [UTT 8.4.1]

17. For the Marxist, what is the ideal state?

The ideal state for the Marxist is no state at all. Marxists perceive the state, whether a democracy or a dictatorship, as a vehicle for maintaining class antagonism. "Political power," writes Marx, "is merely the organized power of one class for oppressing another." From this perspective, the state exists because class antagonism exists; however, once this antagonism is eradicated, the state will no longer be necessary. [UTT 8.4.2]

18. According to Marxism, what is the first step in the transition from capitalism to communism?

Before the utopia of communism becomes a reality, the means of production must pass from the bourgeois to the state. Marx writes, "Between capitalist and communist society lies the period of the revolutionary transformation of the one into the other. Corresponding to this also is a political transition period in which the state can be nothing but the *revolutionary dictatorship of the proletariat*." Thus the first step away from oppressive capitalism and toward utopian communism is a revolution followed by a proletariat-led dictatorship. [UTT 8.4.3]

19. Why is a proletariat dictatorship crucial for obtaining communism? What is the role of the communist party in this dictatorship?

Proletariat dictatorship is essential for at least two reasons: 1) it is needed to consolidate the means of production in the hands of the state, which in turn takes society on the first step toward the abolition of classes. And 2) it is necessary because the proletariat will have seized power through a revolution and will need a dictatorship to thwart bourgeois efforts to reclaim power. [UTT 8.4.3]

According to the Marxist, the dictatorship of the Marxist-Leninist is synonymous with the dictatorship of the proletariat. As the authors of *Socialism as a Social System* admit, Marxist-Leninist theory and the experience of history show conclusively that the working class can carry out its historic mission only if led by a strong, well-organized party. [UTT 8.4.5]

20. According to Marxism, how did the state come into being? What is the ultimate fate of the state under communism? What is the ultimate political aim of Marxism?

Marxists view the state as a transitory phenomenon. At some point in mankind's social development the state arose with the system of capitalism. Thus, the state is a necessary tool for the capitalist who promotes class antagonism. However, as capitalism and class distinctions disappear, so too will the state. As Lenin stresses, "Only in the communist society, when the resistance of the capitalists has been completely crushed, when the capitalists have disappeared, when there are no classes… only then the state… can cease to exist and *it becomes possible to speak of freedom*." [UTT 8.4.6]

Marxists believe that the establishment of a new world order—world communism—and the withering away of the state are inevitable steps in our biological and social evolution. The new world order is an evolutionary advance over nations, states, tribes, and other such distinctions. [UTT 8.4.7]

POLITICS 8.5

21. What is the political goal of Cosmic Humanism?

Cosmic Humanists believe humanity is evolving toward a collective consciousness, one that will transcend all material and individual boundaries—including national and political boundaries. World government is a natural evolutionary step in this dissolution of boundaries. "Unlike many historical expressions of the one-world idea," says David Spangler, "which focus… upon the establishment of a world government, the vision of the New Age qua planetary civilization arises less out of politics than out of what is called the holistic vision. This is the awareness that all life is interrelated and interdependent, that the formative elements of creation are not bits of matter but relationships, and that evolution is the emergence of ever more complex patterns and... relationships." [UTT 8.5.1]

22. Why do Cosmic Humanists believe that a New World Order is guaranteed?

The New World Order is guaranteed by evolution, which is not just a physical process—it is a total spiritual development. Human beings cannot help but evolve into higher species; neither can we help but evolve into a higher state of consciousness. [UTT 8.5.2]

23. What type of government system will humanity have in the New World Order?

Neither democracy nor totalitarianism is offered as a potential system of world government by New Agers. This is due to the fact that New Agers believe that each person is evolving the capacity for self-government. When we achieve a collective consciousness, world government will be synonymous with self-government. [UTT 8.5.3]

24. What is the fate of centralized government, according to Cosmic Humanism?

Because of the higher consciousness presently evolving in all mankind, centralized government will eventually wither away. In the projected New Age, we will all decide what is right for us, without reference to institutional limits. [UTT 8.5.3]

25. Reflection Question: Does the New World Order sound like anarchy? Will this system of government ever work?

Although the Cosmic Humanists do not agree that their vision for the New World Order is a recipe for anarchy, it clearly is. Their utopian dream is not based on a realistic understanding of the concept of the Fall and the reality of our sinfulness.

POLITICS 8.6

26. What is the Postmodernist position toward politics?

Michel Foucault and Richard Rorty both uses the term "progressive politics," while Richard Rorty uses the term "leftism" to describe their politics. For Postmodernists, politics is not centered around political parties, utopian visions, or some ultimate telos; rather progressive politics is a tool of experimentation, a way to break traditional social norms, and a means for achieving social justice and leftism is overall credulity toward Christian values. [UTT 8.6.2]

27. What is identity politics?

Identity politics seeks to advance the interests of particular groups in society that have been perceived to be the victims of social injustice. In this way, the *identity* of the oppressed group gives rise to a political basis around which they then unite. [UTT 8.6.3]

28. What is an example of identity politics in action? Does identity politics strive to establish truthful theories?

Examples of identity politics in action include the feminist and gay rights movements. In the sixties radical feminists identified women as victims of male oppression. As Kelley Oliver admits, the goal of feminist theory "should be to develop strategic theories—not true theories, not false theories, but strategic theories." Since there is no "correct" theory, then all that is left is to promote a theory that strategically gets done what you want to accomplish. [UTT 8.6.3]

29. How do Postmodernists manipulate language to achieve their political goals?

Another strategy often used in the pursuit of Postmodern political goals is the manipulation of language. Someone once noted that we will either master words or be mastered by those who do. Postmodernists have mastered the manipulation of words to such an extent that what used to be considered shameful, immoral, or bad behavior is now heralded as progressive. [UTT 8.6.5]

30. According to Postmodernists, what is social justice? How is social justice to be achieved?

The goal of progressive politics is to produce social justice, i.e. giving oppressed groups their "due" within society. The Postmodern understanding of social justice revolves around the notion of "oppressed groups" or what Derrida and Rorty call "others"—the poor, unemployed, migrants, Hispanics, blacks, women, gays, and lesbians. Social justice is to be achieved through laws, education, and the redistribution of wealth. [UTT 8.6.5]

"THE CASE AGAINST ABORTION"
WITH SCOTT KLUSENDORF

I. Task #1: Restore Meaning to the Word "Abortion"

A. Our current culture

   1. <u>**Visual**</u> culture: We live in a culture that thinks and learns visually.

     i. We predominantly learn through images.

     ii. We no longer learn through books and linear thought.

   2. <u>**Postmodern**</u> culture: Postmodernism, simply stated, says that there is no objective truth.

     i. Debate is no longer over what happens to the fetus, if the fetus feels pain, or if abortion is moral.

     ii. Debate is now about the circumstances of individual women and the right to privacy.

     iii. Truth has been reduced to personal experience.

     iv. Christians have not been a movement of thinkers.

   3. <u>**Avoidance**</u> culture: We live in a culture that wants difficult life problems to "just go away."

"Our generation is the first generation of people [that] having demanded the right to kill its children through abortion is now demanding the right to kill its parents through doctor-assisted suicide." — Greg Cunningham

B. The challenge we face

"How do we communicate truth on abortion to a culture that thinks and learns visually, that wants difficult life problems to 'just go away,' and thinks that truth on abortion is elusive and is nothing more than a personal story or subjective experience?... The answer is we have to show the culture abortion; it is not enough to talk about it... We don't use images in place of good arguments; rather we use them to support our arguments."

   1. Tell people what they are about to see; don't trick them.

   2. Tell them there is no narration, only instrumental music.

   3. Stress the fact that our Lord is eager to forgive the sin of abortion.

Unit Eight

II. Task #2: Simplify the Abortion Debate

A. What is the unborn?

1. The debate is not over choice and who gets to decide.

2. When someone kills a toddler, everyone agrees that a human was killed.

3. Are fetuses human beings like toddlers?

4. You cannot answer the question "Can I kill this?" until we ask the question, "What is it?"

B. Tactic: _____Trot out the toddler_____

"Every time someone gives you an objection to the pro-life view or offers you a justification as to why abortion ought to be allowed, ask yourself if this works as a good argument for killing a toddler."

Note: This tactic is not designed to show that the fetus is a human. It is designed to show that this is the question and that everything else is irrelevant, for example:

1. Unwanted children

2. Psychological pain/rape

3. Back-alley abortions

   "If the unborn aren't human, then no justification for elective abortion is necessary. If they are human, then no justification for elective abortion is adequate." — Gregory Koukl

C. Showing that the unborn are human

1. Scientific evidence

   i. _____**The Law of biogenesis**_____: Living things reproduce after their own kind.

      "How is it possible for human parents to produce an offspring that is not human but later becomes human?"

   ii. Some individuals claim that the unborn are biologically human, but not persons.

      "What is the difference between being a human and being a person?"

2. Philosophic evidence

   i. _____**Size**_____: Large people are not more human than small people.

   ii. _____**Level of development**_____: A four-year-old is not less human than a fourteen-year-old.

Unit Eight

iii. _____**Environment**_____: A newborn in an incubator is not less human than a child outside the womb.

iv. _____**Degree of dependency**_____: People on insulin are less viable but no less human.

"[For] any physical change to your body that does not kill you, you remain yourself through that change, because you have a human nature that was present from the moment you were conceived that allows us to say that we are the same person now that was conceived 19 or 20 years ago. The only difference is function—your abilities have changed but your essential nature is the same."

III. Task #3: Responding to Five Common Objections

A. Pro-abortion rhetoric assumes the unborn are not human.

1. _____**Begging the question**_____: When people assume what they are trying to prove

"The statement 'a woman has a right to an abortion' assumes there is no child in her womb that also has a right to live."

"The statement 'a woman has a right to control her own body' assumes there is only one body involved in the act of abortion."

2. They are asserting rather than arguing

i. _____**Assertion**_____: A claim without evidence

ii. _____**Argument**_____: A claim supported with evidence and/or reasons

3. Tactic: _____Raising the roof_____

"In order for an argument to be valid it must have walls supporting it. You want to force them to provide walls [justification] for their house [assertion]."

4. Tactic: _____Ghostbusters_____

"Sometimes there is an invisible wall in an argument. For example, some assert that 'the Bible is silent on abortion; therefore it is fine.' Now the Bible doesn't expressly condemn cutting up your neighbor and feeding him to sharks, or drive-by shootings, or lynching homosexuals, but does that mean we are morally correct if we do those things?"

Ask, "Are you saying that whatever the Bible doesn't expressly condemn, it permits?"

B. Pro-abortion rhetoric often attacks the character of pro-lifers rather than refuting the argument.

1. _____**Ad Hominem fallacy**_____: Attacking the person rather than the argument

i. You're a man.

"Arguments don't have genders, people do."

ii. How many unwanted babies have you adopted?

2. Tactic: _____Columbo_____

"How does my alleged unwillingness to adopt a child justify an abortionist killing one? The issue is, 'What is the unborn?'"

PART THREE

C. Pro-abortion rhetoric confuses moral claims with preference claims.

1. _____**Moral**_____ claim: Does not address what we like, but what we believe is true or right.

2. _____**Preference**_____ claim: Has nothing to do with what is true or right, but with what we personally like.

"Here is the problem: we are saying to the culture that abortion is wrong and they are hearing we like chocolate ice cream rather than vanilla. They are taking our truth claim and changing it into a preference claim."

"When we are talking about what is right and wrong, we are not talking about what we like. In fact, there are a lot of things I would like to do, but I do not do because it would be morally wrong. And morality is about not doing some things we would *like* to do. That is why the bumper sticker 'don't like abortion; don't have one' is so off the mark. Imagine me saying 'don't like owning slaves, that's fine don't own one.'"

3. Why relativism fails

i. It cannot live up to its own standard.

"When someone says 'You shouldn't force your view on me,' they are forcing their view on you… "When someone says 'You shouldn't force your view on me,' your reply is, 'Why not?' Any answer they give you will be an example of them forcing their view on you."

ii. You can't say anything is right or wrong, including intolerance.

D. Pro-abortion rhetoric confuses functioning as a person with being one.

1. Rights are not based on current capacity but inherent capacity.

"If our rights are based on functional ability, we are all on a gigantic bell curve. We start off with very little rights of personhood; as we age and mature and reach our physical and intellectual peaks we have maximum rights of personhood and then as we grow old and decline we lose personhood… It also results in savage inequality… Keep in mind there is a difference between functioning as a person and being a person."

2. The issue of personal identity

"Ask, 'Were you ever an unborn child?' If the answer is yes, they have conceded a fundamental point of the pro-life view, that is, that human identity is a continuum from conception to death. If they answer that they were never an unborn child, ask them, 'What were you?'"

E. Pro-abortion rhetoric disguises its true position.

    1. The case of rape

        "Would you be willing to fight with me to end the practice of abortion for every instance except rape?"

        "Rape is a tragic thing but should the child be executed for the crime of its father? Or is it fair to demand that the child be killed so that its mother can feel better?... Would it be okay to kill a two-year old so its mother can feel better?"

    2. The real issue is not rape, incest, or anything else. It is, "What is the unborn?"

IV. Questions and Answers

A. How can we respond to those who say that they are personally against abortion but would not make it illegal?

"You personally oppose abortion because it takes the life of an innocent human baby, but you think it should be legal to kill babies?"

B. How can we respond to the claim that "Even if we outlaw abortion, people will still get them?"

"Laws against rape don't stop all rape, but we still have laws against it. Laws against car theft don't stop all cases of car theft but it does stop most of them. The law is a moral teacher."

C. How should we respond to pregnancies that endanger the life of the mother?

"It is better to save one person than lose both."

D. How can we respond to partial-birth abortion?

"First, these abortions are done for convenience. Second, if the mother's life is in danger why would the doctor use a three-day technique... If this is a life or death situation for the mother, you could do a c-section in a matter of minutes."

"THE CASE AGAINST ABORTION"
VIDEO QUESTIONS

Answer the questions below on a separate sheet of paper and be prepared to review your answers in class.

1. **What three negative characteristics of our current culture complicate the abortion debate?**

> Today we learn predominantly through images rather than through books and linear thought. We also live in a Postmodern culture, one that is skeptical of truth. The abortion debate is no longer over what happens to the fetus, if she feels pain, or if abortion is moral. The debate is now over the question of truth and personal privacy. Lastly, we also live in an avoidance culture, a culture that desires to have difficult problems just go away. It is easier to abort a baby than care for her or to end the lives of the elderly than to be burdened by them.

2. **How do we restore meaning to the word "abortion" in our culture?**

> The abortion debate should be centered on one question, "What is the unborn?" Or another way to put it, "What are we killing?" If the unborn are not human, then there should be no restrictions on abortion whatsoever. However, if the fetus is an innocent human being, then she deserves the same right to life as her mother. Most pro-choice objections skirt this central question.
>
> To bring the debate back around to the nature of the fetus, use the "Trot out the Toddler" tactic. Every time someone gives an objection to the pro-life view or offers a justification as to why abortion ought to be allowed, ask if this objection would work as a good argument for killing a toddler.

3. **How do we simplify the abortion debate?**

> The abortion debate should be centered on one question, "What is the unborn?" Or another way to put it, "What are we killing?" If the unborn are not human, then there should be no restrictions on abortion whatsoever. However, if the fetus is an innocent human being, then she deserves the same right to life as her mother. Most pro-choice objections skirt this central question.
>
> To bring the debate back around to the nature of the fetus, use the "Trot out the Toddler" tactic. Every time someone gives an objection to the pro-life view or offers a justification as to why abortion ought to be allowed, ask if this objection would work as a good argument for killing a toddler.

4. **How do we convey both scientifically and philosophically that the unborn are human beings?**

> Some will try to argue that the unborn are not human. However, the opposite can be proven using science and philosophy. First, if the fetus is not a human, then what species is it? According to the Law of Biogenesis creatures reproduce only after their own kind—humans beget humans, frogs beget frogs, etc. Some may assert that the unborn are human beings, but not persons. Force them to support such a claim. Ask them, "What is the difference between being a human and being a person?"

Second, there are only four differences between the unborn and adults and none of those differences nullify a fetus's humanity:

- **Size**—a fetus is smaller than an adult, but so is a toddler
- **Level of Development**—a fetus is less developed than an adult, but a toddler is less developed than a teenager
- **Environment**—a fetus is in a womb, but how does one's location change his or her nature?
- **Degree of Dependency**—a fetus is not viable on its own, however neither is a toddler or a person on insulin

5. **What are five common pro-abortion objections to the pro-life position and how might one best respond?**

First, some pro-choice advocates beg the question (i.e. assume what they are trying to prove) or make assertions (i.e. claims without evidence) rather than offering support for their position. Point out assumptions and bring the issue back to the nature of the unborn, i.e. force a pro-choice advocate to erect a supporting wall (or reasons) for their position.

Second, some pro-choice advocates commit ad-hominem fallacies rather than respond to pro-choice arguments. For example, some may claim that a man has no right to speak on abortion because he is male. However, this fact has nothing to do with the nature of the fetus. This can be demonstrated by asking questions such as, "What does my gender have to do with whether or not abortion is murder?' Third, some pro-choice advocates confuse moral claims with preference claims. Whenever this happens, make sure they are aware that your pro-life position is not necessarily your preference, but that you think your position is true—that the unborn are human beings and that it is just as wrong to kill unborn human beings as it is to own slaves.

Fourth, some pro-choice advocates confuse functioning as a person with being a person. They may argue that since a fetus does not function as an adult that she is not human. Use the S.L.E.D. acronym to point out the flaws with this thinking. Moreover, point out that if our rights are based on functional ability, we are all on a gigantic bell curve of personhood. We start off with very little rights of personhood; as we age and mature and reach our physical and intellectual peaks we have maximum rights of personhood; then as we grow old and decline we lose personhood. This view of personhood seems absurd to most individuals.

Fifth, some pro-choice advocates are actually disguising their true position. This is often demonstrated when a pro-choicer argues that abortion should remain legal because some women become pregnant through rape. However, when asked if they would be willing to fight to end the practice of abortion for every instance except rape, they usually assert that abortion should be legal for all, thus revealing that rape is not actually the issue.

PRO-LIFE ACTIVITY
Ask the students to name as many pro-abortion slogans and arguments they can recall. Write all of these slogans and arguments on the board for the students to examine. Ask the class to identify all the pro-abortion defenses that actually deal with question—"Is the baby a human being?"

Objects on this page are no smaller than they appear.

If you can read this, you are too close to your workbook.

THE SHIFTING FOCUS
OF THE ABORTION DEBATE
BY FRANCIS J. BECKWITH[1]

Pro-lifers in the United States have always assumed that if they could demonstrate beyond a reasonable doubt that the fetus is a human person, then it would be only a matter of time before the courts and legislatures would declare nontherapeutic abortion—the willful destruction of a living fetus—unjustified homicide. Thus the pro-life view would be vindicated and nontherapeutic abortion would once again be illegal.

Even pro-abortion Supreme Court Justice Harry Blackmun, who wrote the majority opinion in *Roe v. Wade* (1973), agrees with this assumption: "If the suggestion of personhood [of the unborn] is established, the appellant's case, of course, collapses, for the fetus's right to life is then guaranteed specifically by the [Fourteenth Amendment]."[2] The scholarly and popular literature produced by evangelicals on the issue of abortion seems to make this assumption as well.[3]

In 1985, however, evangelical philosopher Robert Wennberg[4] defended a moderate pro-choice position employing an argument first presented in 1971 by MIT philosopher Judith Jarvis Thomson. Thomson argued that even if the fetus is a human person, abortion—at least in the early months of pregnancy—is *still* morally justified.[5] Unfortunately, nearly all the books published by evangelical opponents of abortion since the release of Wennberg's *Life in the Balance* (with the exception of recent works by John and Paul Feinberg,[6] Keith J. Pavlischek,[7] and myself[8]) have failed to address this important argument.[9]

This is so despite the fact that this argument—though nearly a quarter of a century old—is now being suggested by a number of legal scholars as a way to circumvent the problems of fetal personhood which they believe were mishandled in *Roe v. Wade*.

THOMSON'S ARGUMENT: THE FETUS'S PERSONHOOD DOES NOT MATTER

In her 1971 article, which by 1986 had become "the most widely reprinted essay in all of contemporary philosophy,"[10] Professor Thomson argued that even if the fetus is fully a human person with a right to life, this does not mean a woman must be forced to use her bodily organs to sustain its life. It is much the same, we are told, as the case in which one does not have a right to use another's kidney if one's kidney has failed. Consequently, a pregnant woman's removal of a fetus from her body, even though it will probably result in its death, is no more immoral than an ordinary person's refusal to donate his or her kidney to another in need of one, even though this refusal will probably result in the death of the prospective recipient. Thomson illustrates her position with the following story:

[1] This article under a different title was presented at the conference "The Christian Stake in Bioethics" (May 19–21, 1994), at Trinity Evangelical Divinity School, Deerfield, Illinois. Another version of this article (titled "From Personhood to Bodily Autonomy: The Shifting Legal Focus in the Abortion Debate") was published in *Bioethics and the Future of Medicine*, Nigel Cameron, David Schiedermayer, and John Kilner, eds. (Cumbria, UK: Pasternoster Press, 1995).

[2] Justice Harry Blackmun, "The 1973 Supreme Court Decisions on State Abortion Laws: Excerpts from Opinion in Roe v. Wade," in *The Problem of Abortion*, Joel Feinberg, ed. (Belmont, CA: Wadsworth, 1984), 195.

[3] See, for example, Harold O. J. Brown, *Death Before Birth* (Nashville: Thomas Nelson, 1977); Francis A. Schaeffer and C. Everett Koop, *Whatever Happened to the Human Race?* (Old Tappan, NJ: Revell, 1979); and John Warwick Montgomery, *Slaughter of the Innocents* (Westchester, IL: Crossway, 1981).

[4] Robert Wennberg, *Life in the Balance: Exploring the Abortion Controversy* (Grand Rapids: Eerdmans, 1985).

[5] Judith Jarvis Thomson, "A Defense of Abortion," in *The Problem of Abortion*, 173–87. All references to Thomson's article in this essay are from this book. This article was originally published in *Philosophy and Public Affairs* 1 (1971): 47–66.

[6] John S. Feinberg and Paul D. Feinberg, *Ethics in a Brave New World* (Wheaton, IL: Crossway, 1993), 66–69.

[7] Keith J. Pavlischek, "Abortion Logic and Paternal Responsibilities: One More Look at Judith Thomson's 'A Defense of Abortion,'" *Public Affairs Quarterly* 7 (October 1993): 341–61.

[8] Beckwith, *Politically Correct Death: Answering the Arguments for Abortion Rights* (Grand Rapids: Baker, 1993), chapter 7.

[9] See, for example, R. C. Sproul, *Abortion: A Rational Look at an Emotional Issue* (Colorado Springs, CO: NavPress, 1990); Randy Alcorn, *Pro Life Answers to Pro Choice Questions* (Portland: Multnomah, 1992); and F. LaGard Smith, *When Choice Becomes God* (Eugene, OR: Harvest, 1990).

[10] According to her editor, William Parent, in Judith Jarvis Thomson, *Rights, Restitution, and Risk* (Cambridge: Harvard University Press, 1986), vii.

SM
225

You wake up in the morning and find yourself back to back in bed with an unconscious violinist. A famous unconscious violinist. He has been found to have a fatal kidney ailment, and the Society of Music Lovers has canvassed all the available medical records and found that you alone have the right blood type to help. They have therefore kidnapped you, and last night the violinist's circulatory system was plugged into yours, so that your kidneys can be used to extract poisons from his blood as well as your own. The director of the hospital now tells you, "Look we're sorry the Society of Music Lovers did this to you—we would never have permitted it if we had known. But still, they did it, and the violinist now is plugged into you. To unplug you would be to kill him. But never mind, it's only for nine months. By then he will have recovered from his ailment, and can safely be unplugged from you." Is it morally incumbent on you to accede to this situation? No doubt it would be very nice of you if you did, a great kindness. But do you *have* to accede to it? What if it were not nine months, but nine years? Or still longer? What if the director of the hospital says, "Tough luck, I agree, but you've now got to stay in bed, with the violinist plugged into you, for the rest of your life. Because remember this. All persons have a right to life, and violinists are persons. Granted you have a right to decide what happens in and to your body, but a person's right to life outweighs your right to decide what happens in and to your body. So you cannot ever be unplugged from him." I imagine that you would regard this as outrageous.[11]

Thomson's argument makes some very important observations that have gone virtually unnoticed. She is asking, "What happens if, for the sake of argument, we allow the premise [that the unborn are fully human or persons]? How, precisely, are we supposed to get from there to the conclusion that abortion is morally impermissible?"[12] That is to say, from the fact that a certain living organism is fully a human person, how does it logically follow that it is *never* permissible to kill that person?

Although a near unanimous number of ethicists maintain that it is *prima facie* wrong to kill an innocent human person, a vast majority agree that there may be some circumstances in which taking a human life or letting a human being die is justified, such as in the event of a just war, capital punishment, self-defense, or withdrawing medical treatment. Thomson's argument, however, includes abortion as one of these justified circumstances. She maintains that, since pregnancy constitutes an infringement by the fetus on the pregnant woman's personal bodily autonomy, the ordinary abortion—though it results in the death of an innocent human person—is not *prima facie* wrong.

One can immediately appreciate the appeal of this argument, especially in light of what is arguably the most quoted passage from *Roe*: "We need not resolve the difficult question of when life begins. When those trained in the respective disciplines of medicine, philosophy, and theology are unable to arrive at any consensus, the judiciary, at this point in the development of man's knowledge, is not in a position to speculate."[13] The Court, however, did not choose to employ Thomson's argument, though there is little doubt that it was brought to its attention. Consequently, the *Roe* Court assumed the major premise of the pro-life position: If the fetus is a person, then abortion in almost every case is unjustified homicide. This, according to a growing number of scholars, was a fatal mistake—a mistake that energized the right-to-life movement.

It appears that the first leading legal scholar to have recommended Thomson's argument to the judiciary was Michigan Law School professor, Donald Regan, in a law review article that appeared in 1979.[14] More recently, Professor Laurence Tribe of Harvard Law School, whose influence on the Court's liberal wing is well-known, suggested in a 1990 book on abortion that the Court should have seriously considered Thomson's argument. Tribe writes: "Perhaps the Supreme Court's opinion in Roe, by gratuitously insisting that the fetus *cannot* be deemed a 'person,' needlessly insulted and alienated those for whom the view that the fetus is a person represents a fundamental article of faith or a bedrock personal commitment… The Court could instead have said: Even if the fetus *is* a person, our Constitution forbids compelling a woman to carry it for nine months and become a mother."[15]

In his highly acclaimed book *The Culture of Disbelief* (1993), Stephen Carter of Yale Law School also recommended Thomson's argument:

[11] Thomson, "A Defense of Abortion," 174–75.
[12] Ibid., 174.
[13] Blackmun, 195.
[14] Donald Regan, "Rewriting Roe v. Wade," *Michigan Law Review* 77 (1979).
[15] Laurence Tribe, *Abortion: The Clash of Absolutes* (New York: W. W. Norton, 1990), 135.

As many theorists have recognized, the right to choose abortion, if indeed it survives, must be based on an approach that allows abortion *even if the fetus is human*—instead of an approach that denies that humanity under cover of the pretense that the definition is none of the state's business. The conclusion of fetal humanity by no means ends the argument; it simply forces the striking of a balance… My point is that the only fair way around a successful legislative effort to define the fetus as human—the only option that does not deride religiously based moral judgments as inferior to secular ones—is to argue for a right to abortion despite it. And an argument of that kind does not require an attack on the religious motivations of any abortion opponents.[16]

In addition to what has already been mentioned, a subtle philosophical shift seems to have occurred on the Supreme Court as well as society at large, which would indicate an openness to Thomson's argument. First, in a 1985 article Justice Ruth Bader Ginsburg, who was a Clinton appointee to the Supreme Court, chided the Court for appealing to the right to privacy rather than the equal protection clause in its grounding of abortion rights. She argued that since women are unique in their ability to be burdened by pregnancy—giving men a distinct advantage in social and political advancement—women should have the right to abortion based on the constitutional principle that all people, regardless of gender, deserve equal protection under the law. Thus, Ginsburg argued, by permitting women to undergo abortions on the basis of the equal protection clause, the Court would have made a clear stand for gender equity on firm constitutional grounds rather than basing its decision on the controversial and constitutionally vague right to privacy.[17]

Second, consider the recent physician-assisted suicide cases in Washington state and Michigan, in which a judge in the first case and a jury in the latter acquitted physicians who had killed consenting patients by appealing to an almost absolute principle of personal autonomy. The judge in Washington claimed she could find this principle in the 14th Amendment, the same place Justice Blackmun found the right to privacy in order to constitutionally ground *Roe*.

Third, in the 1992 case that upheld *Roe* as precedent, *Casey v. Planned Parenthood*, the Court asserted the following about the meaning of the 14th Amendment:

> Our law affords constitutional protection to personal decisions relating to marriage, procreation, family relationships, child rearing, and education… These matters, involving the most intimate and personal choices a person may make in a lifetime, choices central to personal dignity and autonomy, are central to the liberty protected by the Fourteenth Amendment. At the heart of liberty is the right to define one's own concept of existence, of meaning, of the universe, and of the mystery of human life. Beliefs about these matters could not define the attributes of personhood were they formed under compulsion by the State.[18]

Evidently the Supreme Court has chosen to abandon a rigorous defense of philosophical argument in the free marketplace of ideas only to replace it with a New Age mantra ("define your own reality") in the convenience store of slogans.

In any event, there is little doubt that a shift is occurring in the abortion debate. This shift should be addressed by those who oppose abortion as well as those who, regardless of their stand on abortion, see Thomson's argument as a threat to the moral force of parental obligations. Let us, therefore, take a critical look at Professor Thomson's argument.

WHY FETAL PERSONHOOD MATTERS

Although there are a number of problems with Thomson's argument, the following five are sufficient for the judiciary to reject it from consideration.

[16] Stephen L. Carter, *The Culture of Disbelief: How American Law and Politics Trivialize Religious Devotion* (New York: HarperCollins, 1993), 257–58.

[17] Ruth Bader Ginsburg, "Some Thoughts on Autonomy and Equality in Relation to *Roe v. Wade*," *University of North Carolina Law Review* (1985).

[18] Justice O'Connor, Justice Kennedy, and Justice Souter, "Planned Parenthood v. Casey (1992)," *The Abortion Controversy: A Reader*, Louis P. Pojman and Francis J. Beckwith, eds. (Boston: Jones & Bartlett, 1994), 54.

1. Thomson assumes that all moral obligations are voluntary.

By using the violinist story as a paradigm for all relationships, Thomson implies that moral obligations must be voluntarily accepted in order to have moral force. Thus she mistakenly infers that all true moral obligations to one's offspring are voluntary.

Consider the following story. Suppose a couple has a sexual encounter that is fully protected by several forms of birth control short of abortion (condom, the Pill, IUD, and so forth), but nevertheless results in conception. Instead of getting an abortion, the mother of the conceptus decides to bring it to term, although the father is unaware of this decision. After the birth of the child the mother pleads with the father for child support. Because he refuses, she seeks legal action and takes him to court. Although he took every precaution to avoid fatherhood—thus showing that he did not wish to accept such a status—according to nearly all child support laws in the United States he would still be obligated to pay support *precisely because* of his relationship to this child.[19]

As Michael Levin points out, "All child-support laws make the parental body an indirect resource for the child. If the father is a construction worker, the state will intervene unless some of his calories he extends lifting equipment go to providing food for his children."[20]

For this reason, Keith Pavlischek argues that "given the logic of" Thomson's argument, "the most reasonable course to follow would be to surrender the defense of paternal support laws for those children whose fathers would rather have had their children aborted." This "will lend some credence not only to the pro-life insistence on the corollary—that an intimate connection exists between the way we collectively relate to the unborn and the way we relate to our children after birth—but also to the claim made by pro-life feminists that the abortion mentality simply reaffirms the worst historical failings, neglect, and chauvinism of males."[21]

2. A case can be made that the unborn *does* have a prima facie *right to her mother's body.*

Assuming there is such a thing as a special obligation to one's children that does not have to be voluntarily accepted to have moral force, it is obvious that the unborn entity in ordinary circumstances (that is, with the exception of significant life-endangerment to the mother) *does* have a natural *prima facie* claim to her mother's body. There are several reasons to suppose that the unborn entity had such a natural claim.

First, unlike Thomson's violinist, who is artificially attached to another person in order to save his life and is therefore not naturally dependent on any particular human being, the unborn entity is a human being who is by her very nature dependent on her mother. This is how human beings *are* at this stage of their development.

Second, this period of a human being's natural development occurs in the womb. This is the journey we all must take and is a necessary condition for any human being's post-uterine existence. And this fact alone brings out the most glaring disanalogy between the violinist and the unborn: the womb is the unborn's *natural* environment, whereas being artificially hooked-up to a stranger is *not* the natural environment for the violinist. It would seem, then, that the unborn has a *prima facie* natural claim upon its mother's body.

Third, this same entity, when it becomes a newborn, has a natural claim upon her parents to care for her, regardless of whether her parents "wanted" her (see the above story of the irresponsible father). This is why we prosecute child abusers, people who throw their babies in trash cans, and parents who abandon their children.

Although it should not be ignored that pregnancy and childbirth entail certain emotional, physical, and financial sacrifices on the part of the pregnant woman, these sacrifices are also endemic *of parenthood in general* (which ordinarily lasts much longer than nine months). And these sacrifices do not justify the execution of troublesome infants and younger children whose existence entails a natural claim to certain financial and bodily goods that are under the ownership of their parents. If the unborn entity is fully human, as Thomson is willing to grant, why should the unborn's natural *prima facie* claim to her parents' goods differ *before* birth from what it will be *after* departing her mother's womb?

---

[19] See Carolyn Royce Kastner and Lawrence R. Young, eds., *In the Best Interest of the Child: A Guide to State Child Support and Paternity Laws,* (Child Support Enforcement Beneficial Laws Project, National Conference of State Legislatures, 1981).
[20] Michael Levin, review of *Life in the Balance* by Robert Wennberg, *Constitutional Commentary* 3 (Summer 1986): 511.
[21] Pavlischek, 343.

Of course, a court will not force a parent to donate a kidney to her dying offspring. But, as in the case of the unconscious violinist, this sort of dependence on another's body is highly unusual and is not part of the ordinary parental obligations associated with the *natural* process of human development.

Professor Stephen Schwarz points out that "the very thing that makes it plausible to say that the person in bed with the violinist has no duty to sustain him; namely, that he is a stranger unnaturally hooked up to him, is precisely what is absent in the case of the mother and her child." That is to say, the mother "does have an obligation to take care of her child, to sustain her, to protect her, and especially, to let her live in the only place where she can now be protected, nourished, and allowed to grow, namely the womb."[22]

It is evident that Thomson's violinist illustration undermines the *deep natural bond* between mother and child by making it seem no different than two strangers artificially hooked-up to each other so that one can "steal" the service of the other's kidneys. Rarely if ever has something so human, so natural, so beautiful, and so wonderfully demanding of our human creativity and love been reduced to such a brutal caricature.

This is not to say that the unborn has an *absolute* natural claim to her mother's body, but simply that she has a *prima facie* natural claim. One can easily imagine a situation in which this natural claim is outweighed by other important *prima facie* values, such as when pregnancy significantly endangers the mother's life.

3. Thomson ignores the fact that abortion is indeed killing, not merely withholding treatment.

Thomson makes an excellent point in her use of the violinist story; namely, there are times when withholding and/or withdrawing medical treatment is morally justified. For instance, one is not morally obligated to donate his kidney to Fred (one's next-door neighbor) simply because Fred needs a kidney in order to live. In other words, one is not obligated to risk his life so that Fred may live a few years longer. Fred should not expect that. If, however, one donates a kidney to Fred, one will have acted above and beyond the call of duty, since he will have performed a supererogatory moral act. But this case is not analogous to pregnancy and abortion.

Levin argues that there is an essential disanalogy between abortion and the unplugging of the violinist. In the case of the violinist (as well as one's relationship to Fred's welfare), "the person who withdraws [or withholds] his assistance is not completely responsible for the dependency on him of the person who is about to die, while the mother is completely responsible for the dependency of her fetus on her. When one is completely responsible for dependence, refusal to continue to aid is indeed killing."

For example, "if a woman brings a newborn home from the hospital, puts it in its crib and refuses to feed it until it has starved to death, it would be absurd to say that she simply refused to assist it and had done nothing for which she should be criminally liable."[23] Just as the withholding of food kills the child after birth, in the case of abortion it is the *abortion* that kills the child. In neither case is there any ailment from which the child suffers and for which highly invasive medical treatment (with the cooperation of another's bodily organs) is necessary in order to cure this ailment and save the child's life.

Or consider the case of a person who returns home after work to find a baby at his doorstep (as was the case in the film *Three Men and a Baby*, starring Tom Selleck, Ted Danson, and Steve Guttenberg). Suppose that no one else is able to care for the child, but this person only has to care for the child for nine months. (After that time a couple will adopt the child.) If we assume with Thomson that the fetus is as much a person as you or me, would "withholding treatment" (i.e., nourishment and protection) from this child and its subsequent death be justified on the basis that the homeowner was only "withholding treatment" from a child who could not benefit him, and for whom he did not ask? Is any person, born or unborn, obligated to sacrifice his life because his death would benefit another person?

Is it accurate to think of abortion as the withholding of support or treatment? Professors Schwarz and R. K. Tacelli make the important point that although "a woman who has an abortion is indeed 'withholding support' from her unborn child... abortion is far more than that. It is the active killing of a human person—by burning him, by crushing him, by dismembering him."[24] Euphemistically calling abortion the "withholding of support or treatment" makes about as much sense as calling suffocating someone with a pillow the withdrawing of oxygen.

---

[22] Stephen D. Schwarz, *The Moral Question of Abortion* (Chicago: Loyola University Press, 1990), 118.

[23] Michael Levin, *Feminism and Freedom* (New Brunswick: Transaction Books, 1987), 288–89.

[24] Stephen D. Schwarz and R. K. Tacelli, "Abortion and Some Philosophers," *Public Affairs Quarterly* 3 (April 1989), 85.

4. Thomson's argument ignores family law.

Thomson's argument is inconsistent with the body of well-established family law, which presupposes parental responsibility of a child's welfare. And, of course, assuming as Thomson does that the unborn are fully human, this body of law would also apply to parents' responsibility for their unborn children.

According to legal scholars Dennis J. Horan and Burke J. Balche, "All 50 states, the District of Columbia, American Samoa, Guam, and the U.S. Virgin Islands have child abuse and neglect statutes which provide for the protection of a child who does not receive needed medical care." They further state that "a review of cases makes it clear that these statutes are properly applied to secure emergency medical treatment and sustenance (food or water, whether given orally or through intravenous or nasogastic tube) for children when parents, with or without the acquiescence of physicians, refuse to provide it."[25] Evidently, "pulling the plug" on a perfectly healthy fetus, assuming that it is a human person, would clearly violate these statutes.

In a case in New York, for example, the court ruled that the parents' actions constituted neglect when they failed to provide medical care to a child with leukemia: "The parent... may not deprive a child of lifesaving treatment, however well-intentioned. Even when the parents' decision to decline necessary treatment is based on constitutional grounds, such as religious beliefs, it must yield to the State's interests, as *parens patriae*, in protecting the health and welfare of the child."[26] The fact is that the "courts have uniformly held that a parent has the legal responsibility of furnishing his dependent child with adequate food and medical care."[27]

It is evident, then, that child-protection laws reflect our deepest moral intuitions about parental and community responsibility and the utter helplessness of infants and small children. These moral scruples are undoubtedly undermined by "brave new notions" of a socially contracted "voluntaristic" family (Thomson's view). Without such scruples the protection of children and the natural bonds and filial obligations that undergird family life (and, through it, society itself) will become a thing of the past. This seems too high a price to pay for "bodily autonomy."

5. Thomson's argument implies a "macho" view of bodily control that is inconsistent with true feminism.

Some pro-life feminists have pointed out that Thomson's argument and/or the reasoning behind it, which is supposed to be consistent with feminism, is actually quite anti-feminist.[28] In response to a similar argument from a woman's right to control her own body, one feminist publication asked the question, "What kind of control are we talking about? A control that allows for violence against another human being is a macho, oppressive kind of control. Women rightly object when others try to have that kind of control over them, and the movement for women's rights asserts the moral right of women to be free from the control of others." After all, "abortion involves violence against a small, weak and dependent child. It is macho control, the very kind the feminist movement most eloquently opposes in other contexts."[29]

Professor Celia Wolf-Devine makes the observation that "abortion has something... in common with the behavior ecofeminists and pacifist feminists take to be characteristically masculine; it shows a willingness to use violence in order to take control. The fetus is destroyed by being pulled apart by suction, cut in pieces, or poisoned."

Wolf-Devine goes on to point out that "in terms of social thought... it is the masculine models which are most frequently employed in thinking about abortion. If masculine thought is naturally ... oriented toward power and control, then the interests of the fetus (who has no power) would naturally be suppressed in favor of the interests of the mother. But to the extent that feminist social thought is egalitarian, the question must be raised of why the mother's interests should prevail over the child's... Feminist thought about abortion

---

[25] Dennis J. Horan and Burke J. Balch, *Infant Doe and Baby Jane Doe: Medical Treatment of the Handicapped Newborn*, Studies in Law and Medicine Series (Chicago: Americans United for Life, 1985), 2.

[26] Quoted in ibid., 2–3, regarding Storar, 53 N.Y. 2d 363, 380–81, 420 N.E. 2d 64, 73, 438 N.Y.S. 2d 266, 275 (1981).

[27] Horan and Balch, 3–4.

[28] Although not dealing exclusively with Thomson's argument, Celia Wolf-Devine's article is quite helpful. "Abortion and the 'Feminine Voice,'" *Public Affairs Quarterly* 3 (July 1989). See also Sidney Callahan, "Abortion and the Sexual Agenda," *Commonweal* 113 (25 April 1986); and Janet Smith "Abortion as a Feminist Concern," Jeff Lane Hensley, ed., *The Zero People* (Ann Arbor: Servant, 1983).

[29] *Sound Advice for All Pro-life Activists and Candidates Who Wish to Include a Concern for Women's Rights in Their Prolife Advocacy: Feminists for Life Debate Handbook* (Kansas City, MO: Feminists for Life, no date), 15–16.

has… been deeply pervaded by the individualism which they so ardently criticize.[30]

Despite the recent suggestion in legal scholarship that fetal personhood ought not be the question that determines the morality of abortion, we have seen that if such a move is carried out by the courts the result would be morally and legally disastrous. For this reason, opponents of abortion ought to master the contents of this article and be prepared to engage this old philosophical, though new legal, challenge to human dignity.

---

*This essay originally appeared in the *Christian Research Journal*:
Francis Beckwith, "The Shifting Focus in the Abortion Debate: Does the Humanity of the Unborn Matter Anymore?," *Christian Research Journal* Vol. 17, No. 3 (1995), pp. 17–19, 32–34.
** Reproduction rights granted by the *Christian Research Journal*.

---

[30] Wolf-Devine, 86–87.

THE SHIFTING FOCUS
OF THE ABORTION DEBATE
ESSAY QUESTIONS

Answer the questions below on a separate sheet of paper and be prepared to review your answers in class.

1. **In relation to the personhood of the fetus, how has the abortion debate shifted?**

> The 1973 *Roe v. Wade* decision granted women in the United States a legal right to abort their babies. This decision was based upon the supposed ambiguity surrounding the personhood of the fetus. It was reasoned that since neither science nor philosophy could determine whether the fetus was human, a women's rights should trump those of a possible non-human-being. Therefore, most pro-lifers have spent the majority of their efforts trying to establish the personhood of the unborn. Today, however, it appears that this is no longer the central issue. In fact, a good number of pro-choice defendants now grant that the fetus is indeed human. Thus, the core of the debate has shifted away from the humanity of the unborn. [SM p. 225]

2. **Granting the personhood of the fetus, how does Thomson support the pro-choice position?**

> Thomson's position is that abortion does take the life of a human person, but that taking this life is not immoral. She compares this with the taking of lives in cases of war, capital punishment, self-defense, or withholding medical treatment upon the patient's insistence. Thus, Thomson argues that a woman should have the option to refuse the responsibility of caring for a fetus—a person that will die without care, but at the same time a person that no mother is obligated to care for in the first place. After all, Thomson reasons, it is the fetus that has attached itself to the mother and no one has ever been under any type of moral obligation to care for someone else. [SM pp. 225–6]

3. **On what basis does Justice Ruth Bader Ginsburg base her belief in a right to abortion? What about *Casey v. Planned Parenthood*?**

> Both Justice Ginsburg and the Supreme Court in the *Casey* case granted that a fetus might indeed be a human being. However, Ginsburg did not see this a viable reason to protect the fetus. Ginsburg saw this an issue of equality. That is, if women are forced to carry their children to term, then they will not be as apt to compete with men in the marketplace. The *Casey* case had basically the same effect, although it deemed the question of personhood open, i.e. to be "[defined by] one's own concept of existence." Therefore, the question of a fetus's personhood was a subjective issue to be answered by a mother's own personal convictions. [SM p. 227]

4. **What are the first two objections made against Thomson's argument?**

> First, Thomson assumes that moral obligation must be voluntary in order to carry moral force. She asserts that a mother should not be obligated to use her body to care for (and be attached to) another

SM
232

Unit Eight

human being. However, countries make laws obligating individuals to do just such a thing. For example fathers are *required* to provide child support, even if they do not desire to be attached to their child or took precautions not to have children. If we were to accept Thomson's argument, fathers paying child support would have good grounds to argue that they should not be obligated to take care of their offspring.

Second, it would seem that the unborn child does indeed have a natural right to her mother's body. It is here that Thomson's analogy falls short—the violinist is *artificially* attached to another person, while every child is *naturally* attached to its mother at the fetus stage of human development. Building on this point, an infant or a toddler also has a natural right to his or her parent's goods after birth. Parents cannot refuse their children food, shelter, or clothing. They have an obligation to provide for their children, and their children have an expectation to receive at least basic provisions. [SM pp. 228–9]

5. What other objections are made against Thomson's argument?

Third, Thomson's analogy ignores the fact that abortion is the active killing of another human being and not merely the *passive* withholding of treatment. Her analogy stresses the refusal to lend one's body to another human being, yet this does not correspond with abortion—the killing of a fetus.

Fourth, Thomson's argument seems to be against the very spirit of feminism—a movement born out of the supposed (and to some degree actual) oppression of women by men. Feminism was a reaction against the oppression of the weak by the powerful. In Thomson's world, women are to do unto their unborn children that which was done unto them—they are to exercise control over the downtrodden by means of violence and oppression. [SM pp. 229–31]

CRISIS PREGNANCY ACTIVITY

You are a telephone operator for a pro-life crisis pregnancy center. The center offers free pregnancy tests and counseling, hoping to keep women from having abortions. How might you respond to the following calls?

- **Tina:** A 32-year-old woman, pretty sure she is pregnant. She already has 3 kids. Her husband, Tom, is physically abusive, and she was just about to leave him to get her other kids away. She has a minimum wage job and doesn't have any idea how she will support another child. She really wants an abortion because she doesn't want to bring another child into this mess.

- **Janelle:** A 17-year-old high school student. Her parents want her to get an abortion because her dad is an elder in the church and it would be best if nobody knew about the pregnancy. She's not really sure what she thinks. Her boyfriend wants her to keep the baby, but he hasn't said he'll marry her.

- **Shannon:** An 19-year-old with a full-ride scholarship to college this fall. She has had an abortion before and just wants to schedule another one. She is firmly pro-choice in all her views and cannot be persuaded otherwise.

- **Ann:** A 24-year-old who has only been married a year and is just beginning to get a foothold in her job as an engineer. A baby doesn't fit her plans right now, so she and her husband decided they would have an abortion now and then work on getting pregnant again in about five years.

THE BATTLE FOR LIFE
BY RAYMOND G. BOHLIN AND KERBY ANDERSON

THE HISTORY OF EUTHANASIA

The debate over euthanasia is not a modern phenomenon. The Greeks carried on a robust debate on the subject. The Pythagoreans opposed euthanasia, while the Stoics favored it in the case of incurable disease. Plato approved of it in cases of terminal illness.[1] But these influences lost out to Christian principles as well as the spread of acceptance of the Hippocratic Oath: "I will neither give a deadly drug to anybody if asked for it, nor will I make a suggestion to that effect."

In 1935 the Euthanasia Society of England was formed to promote the notion of a painless death for patients with incurable diseases. A few years later the Euthanasia Society of America was formed with essentially the same goals. In the last few years, debate about euthanasia has been advanced by two individuals: Derek Humphry and Dr. Jack Kevorkian.

Derek Humphry has used his prominence as head of the Hemlock Society to promote euthanasia in the United States. His book *Final Exit: The Practicalities of Self-Deliverance and Assisted Suicide for the Dying* became a bestseller and further influenced public opinion.

Another influential figure is Jack Kevorkian, who has been instrumental in helping people commit suicide. His book *Prescription Medicide: The Goodness of Planned Death* promotes his views of euthanasia and describes his patented suicide machine which he calls "the Mercitron." He first gained national attention by enabling Janet Adkins of Portland, Oregon, to kill herself in 1990. They met for dinner and then drove to a Volkswagen van where the machine waited. He placed an intravenous tube into her arm and dripped a saline solution until she pushed a button which delivered first a drug causing unconsciousness, and then a lethal drug that killed her. Since then he has helped dozens of other people do the same.

Over the years, public opinion has also been influenced by the tragic cases of a number of women described as being in a "persistent vegetative state." In the U.S. the first was Karen Ann Quinlan. Her parents, wanting to turn the respirator off, won approval in court. However, when it was turned off in 1976, Karen continued breathing and lived for another ten years. Another case was Nancy Cruzan, who was hurt in an automobile accident in 1983. Her parents went to court in 1987 to receive approval to remove her feeding tube. Various court cases ensued in Missouri, including her parents' appeal that was heard by the Supreme Court in 1990. Eventually they won the right to pull the feeding tube, and Nancy Cruzan died shortly thereafter. Most recently in 2005, Terri Schiavo's fate was sealed by the U.S. 11th circuit court of appeals, which granted Terri's husband the right to remove her feeding tube. The decision was unsuccessfully challenged by Terri's parents.

Seven years after the Cruzan case, the U.S. Supreme Court had occasion to rule again on the issue of euthanasia. On June 26, 1997 the Supreme Court rejected euthanasia by stating that state laws banning physician-assisted suicide were constitutional. Some feared that these cases (*Glucksburg v. Washington* and *Vacco v. Quill*) would become for euthanasia what *Roe v. Wade* became for abortion. Instead, the justices rejected the concept of finding a constitutional "right to die" and chose not to interrupt the political debate (as *Roe v. Wade* did), and instead urged that the debate on euthanasia continue, "as it should in a democratic society."

VOLUNTARY ACTIVE EUTHANASIA

It is helpful to distinguish between "mercy killing" (or active euthanasia) and what could be called "mercy dying" (or passive euthanasia). Taking a human life is not the same as allowing a terminal patient to die, that is, allowing nature to take its course. The former is immoral (and perhaps even criminal), while the latter is not.

However, drawing a sharp line between these two categories is not as easy as it used to be. Modern medical technology has significantly blurred the line between hastening death and allowing death. Certain analgesics, for example, ease pain, but they can also shorten a patient's life by affecting respiration. An

---

[1] Plato, *Republic* 3. 405.

artificial heart will continue to beat even after the patient has died and therefore must be turned off by the doctor. So the distinction between actively promoting death and passively allowing nature to take its course is sometimes difficult to determine in practice. But this fundamental distinction between "mercy killing" and "mercy dying" is still an important philosophical distinction.

Another concern with active euthanasia is that it eliminates the possibility for recovery. While this should be obvious, somehow this problem is frequently ignored in the euthanasia debate. Terminating a human life eliminates all possibility of recovery, while passively ceasing extraordinary means may not. Miraculous recovery from a bleak prognosis sometimes occurs. A doctor who prescribes active euthanasia for a patient may unwittingly prevent a possible recovery he did not anticipate.

A further concern with this so-called voluntary active euthanasia is that these decisions might not always be freely made. The possibility for coercion is always present. Richard D. Lamm, former governor of Colorado, said that elderly, terminally ill patients have "a duty to die and get out of the way." Though those words were reported somewhat out of context, they nonetheless illustrate the pressure many elderly feel from hospital personnel.

The Dutch experience is also instructive. A survey of Dutch physicians was done in 1990 by the Remmelink Committee. They found that 1,030 patients were killed without their consent. Of these, 140 were fully mentally competent and 110 were only slightly mentally impaired. The report also found that another 14,175 patients (1,701 of whom were mentally competent) were denied medical treatment without their consent and died.[2]

A more recent survey of the Dutch experience is even less encouraging. Doctors in the United States and the Netherlands have found that though euthanasia was originally intended for exceptional cases, it has become an accepted way of dealing with serious or terminal illness. The original guidelines (that patients with a terminal illness make a voluntary, persistent request that their lives be ended) have been expanded to include chronic ailments and psychological distress. They also found that 60 percent of Dutch physicians do not report their cases of assisted suicide (even though reporting is required by law) and about 25 percent of the physicians admit to ending patients' lives without their consent.[3]

INVOLUNTARY ACTIVE EUTHANASIA

Involuntary active euthanasia requires a second party who makes decisions about whether active measures should be taken to end a life. Foundational to this discussion is an erosion of the doctrine of the sanctity of life. Ever since the Supreme Court ruled in *Roe v. Wade* that the life of unborn babies could be terminated for reasons of convenience, the slide down society's slippery slope has continued even though the Supreme Court has been reluctant to legalize euthanasia.

The progression was inevitable. Once society begins to devalue the life of an unborn child, it is but a small step to begin to do the same with a child who has been born. Abortion slides naturally into infanticide and eventually into euthanasia. In the past few years doctors have allowed a number of so-called "Baby Does" to die—either by failing to perform lifesaving operations or else by not feeding the infants.

The progression toward euthanasia is inevitable. Once society becomes conformed to a "quality of life" standard for infants, it will more willingly accept the same standard for the elderly. As former Surgeon General C. Everett Koop has said, "Nothing surprises me anymore. My great concern is that there will be 10,000 Grandma Does for every Baby Doe."[4]

Again the Dutch experience is instructive. In the Netherlands, physicians have performed involuntary euthanasia because they thought the family had suffered too much or were tired of taking care of patients. American surgeon Robin Bernhoft relates an incident in which a Dutch doctor euthanized a twenty-six-year-old ballerina with arthritis in her toes. Since she could no longer pursue her career as a dancer, she was depressed and requested to be put to death. The doctor complied with her request and merely noted that "one doesn't enjoy such things, but it was her choice."[5]

---

[2] R. Finigsen, "The Report of the Dutch Committee on Euthanasia," *Issues in Law and Medicine* (July 1991), 339–44.

[3] Herbert Hendlin, Chris Rutenfrans, and Zbigniew Zylicz, "Physician-Assisted Suicide and Euthanasia in the Netherlands: Lessons from the Dutch," *Journal of the American Medical Association* 277 (June 4, 1997): 1720–2.

[4] Interview with C. Everett Koop, "Focus on the Family" radio broadcast.

[5] Robin Bernhoft, quoted in *Euthanasia: False Light*, produced by IAETF, P.O. Box 760, Steubenville, OH 43952.

WHY PEOPLE SEEK EUTHANASIA

Why is such a large segment of our society enamored with the possibility of physician-assisted suicide? While there can be many roads that will lead to this conclusion, the primary one is fear. People today fear being at the mercy of technology, of being kept alive with no hope of recovery by machines. Few seem to realize that it is already legal for a terminally ill patient to refuse life-prolonging measures. We must realize that there is a difference between simply allowing nature to take its course when someone is clearly dying and taking direct measures to hasten someone's death. Former Surgeon General C. Everett Koop acknowledges,

> If someone is dying and there is no doubt about that, and you believe as I do that there is a difference between giving a person all the life to which he is entitled as opposed to prolonging the act of dying, then you might come to a time when you say this person can take certain amounts of fluid by mouth and we're not going to continue this intravenous solution because he is on the way out.[6]

Extraordinary measures are not required to keep a dying person alive at all costs. But some people fear exactly that. Removing this fear will take a lot of the wind out of the euthanasia sails.

Secondly, people fear the pain of the dying process. Intractable pain is a real fear, but few people today realize that most of the pain of terminally ill patients can be dealt with. Many doctors, particularly in the U.S., are not aware of all the measures at their disposal. There are new ways of administering morphine, for example, that can achieve effective pain management with lower doses and therefore a lower risk of respiratory complications.

Dr. Paul Cundiff, practicing oncologist and hospice care physician with 18 years of experience treating dying patients says,

> It is a disgrace that the majority of our health care providers lack the knowledge and the skills to treat pain and other symptoms of terminal disease properly. The absence of palliative care training for medical professionals results in sub-optimal care for almost all terminally ill patients and elicits the wish to hasten their own deaths in a few.[7]

But many would even be willing to live with the pain if they knew that they would not be left alone. The growth in the hospice movement will help alleviate this fear as well. The staff at a hospice is trained to deal not only with physical pain, but with psychological, social, and spiritual pain as well. If you have seen pictures of the many people Jack Kevorkian has assisted to commit suicide, you cannot help but notice that these are lonely, miserable people. Pain has had little to do with their desire to commit suicide.

As a nation we have in large part abandoned our elderly population. When God commanded Israel to honor their fathers and their mothers, this was understood to mean primarily in their older years. Extended families no longer live together even when the medical needs of parents are not severe or terribly limiting. No one wants to be a burden or to be burdened.

WHY LIFE IS WORTH LIVING

As we discuss the issue of euthanasia and physician-assisted suicide, it is critical that we not only understand what is going on in the world around us but that we also understand what the Bible clearly teaches about, life, death, pain, suffering, and the value of each human life.

First, the Bible teaches that we are made in the image of God and therefore, every human life is sacred (Genesis 1:26). In Psalm 139:13–16 we learn that each of us is fearfully and wonderfully made. God himself has knit us together in our mother's womb. We must be very important to him if he has taken such care to bring us into existence.

Second, the Bible is very clear that God is sovereign over life, death, and judgment. In Deuteronomy 32:39 The Lord says, "See now that I myself am He! There is no god besides me, I put to death and I bring to life, I have wounded and I will heal, and no one can deliver out of my hand." Psalm 139:16 says that it

[6] C. Everett Koop, "The Surgeon General on Euthanasia." *Presbyterian Journal* (Sept. 25, 1985):8.
[7] David Cundiff, quoted in review of *Euthanasia is NOT the Answer: A Hospice Physician's View* by Debbie Decker, *CURRENTS in Science, Technology, and Society*, 1(2):20.

is God who has ordained all of our days before there is even one of them. Paul says essentially the same thing in Ephesians 1:11.

Third, to assist someone in committing suicide is to commit murder and this breaks God's unequivocal commandment in Exodus 20:13.

Fourth, God's purposes are beyond our understanding. We often appeal to God as to why some tragedy has happened to us or someone we know. Yet listen to Job's reply to the Lord in Job 42:1–3:

> I know that you can do all things; no plan of yours can be thwarted. [You asked,] 'Who is this that obscures My counsel without knowledge?' Surely I spoke of things I did not understand, things too wonderful for me to know.

We forget that our minds are finite and his is infinite. We cannot always expect to understand all of what God is about. To think that we can step in and declare that someone's life is no longer worth living is simply not our decision to make. Only God knows when it is time. In Isaiah 55:8–9 the Lord declares, "For my thoughts are not your thoughts, neither are your ways my ways. As the heavens are higher than the earth, so are my ways higher than your ways and my thoughts higher than your thoughts."

Fifth, our bodies belong to God anyway. Paul reminds us in 1 Corinthians 6:15,19 that we are members of Christ's body and that we have been bought with a price. Therefore we should glorify God with our bodies. The only one to receive glory when someone requests doctor-assisted suicide is not God, not the doctor, not even the family but the patient for being willing to "nobly" face the realities of life and "unselfishly" end everyone else's misery. There is no glory for God in this decision.

Lastly, suffering draws us closer to God. In light of the euthanasia controversy, listen to Paul's words from 2 Corinthians 1:8:

> We were under great pressure, far beyond our ability to endure, so that we despaired even of life. Indeed, in our hearts we felt the sentence of death. But this happened that we might not rely on ourselves but on God, who raises the dead.

Not only does He raise the dead but there is nothing that can separate us from His love (Romans 8:38). For an inspiring and thoroughly biblical discussion of the euthanasia issue, read Joni Earickson Tada's book *When is it Right to Die?* (Zondervan, 1992). Her testimony and clear thinking is in stark contrast to the conventional wisdom of the world today. We must do the same.

WHAT WILL YOU DO? WHAT CAN YOU DO?

The Christian Medical and Dental Society has produced an excellent resource on physician-assisted suicide titled *The Battle for Life*.[8] As a part of the package they provide several cases to test your grasp of the principles involved and to help Christians be aware of the tough decisions that have to be made. I would like to share two of those with you and then discuss what you can do now to combat the "right to die" forces in this country.

Test Case 1:

Your 80 year-old grandmother has been fighting cancer for some time now and feels the emotional strain. She feels like she'll become a burden to the family. Her doctor notes that she seems to have lost her desire to live. Should she be able to have her doctor give her a prescription expressly designed to kill her? This is precisely what the courts have legalized and precisely what God's word says is wrong. It is wrong because it would be taking her life into our hands and violating God's sovereignty. Because physician-assisted suicide goes beyond letting someone die naturally to actually causing the death, it violates God's commandment, "You shall not murder." There is a clear distinction between allowing death to take its natural course in

---

[8] *The Battle for Life* is an educational resource kit produced by the Christian Medical and Dental Society. The kit includes an award winning video, *Euthanasia: False Light*, a leader's presentation guide with discussion questions, handouts for Christian and secular audiences, overhead transparencies, biblical principles summary, research synopsis, cassette tape of public service announcements, and bulletin inserts. The $30 kit is available from the Christian Medical and Dental Society, P.O. Box 5, Bristol, TN, 37621, Phone (615) 844-1000, FAX: (615) 844-1005. The kit can also be purchased through Probe Ministries.

someone who is clearly dying with no hope of a cure, and taking specific measures to end someone's life. There comes a time when the body is imminently dying. Bodily functions begin to shut down. At this point, people should be made as comfortable as possible, be supported and encouraged by their family and doctors, and allowed to die. This is death with dignity. Taking a lethal injection or breathing poisonous carbon monoxide takes life out of God's hands and into our own.

Test Case 2:

Your spouse has an incurable fatal disease, has lost control of bodily functions, and is unable to communicate. Special treatment and equipment can extend your spouse's life for a few weeks or even months but will involve much pain and exhaustion. Would it be morally right for you to not arrange for the treatment? Many would accept a decision not to arrange for treatment because that would not be killing but simply allowing death to take its natural course. Such decisions are not always clear-cut, however, and a physician and family members must take into account the pros and cons of intervention versus a faster natural death. Sometimes we rationalize that we need to keep the patient alive as long as possible because God may still work a miracle. But just how much time does God need to work a miracle? If God is going to intervene He will do so on His time and not ours.

Now that we have a better understanding of the issues, you may be wondering just what we can do about this threat among us. Three things:

Pray — Pray that God will turn the hearts of people back to Himself and back to protecting life. Pray for righteousness and justice in our legal system, that we enact laws that preserve life, punish the guilty and protect the innocent.

Speak Out — Present this information to other groups. Talk with your friends and family and discuss the reasons for protecting life. Contact your state and federal legislators and tell them to stand against physician-assisted suicide.

Reach Out — Visit the elderly, care for those who can't care for themselves, comfort the sick. Consider joining or starting a church ministry to the elderly, handicapped, or other individuals with special needs. As Christians we must lead the way with our hearts and actions and not just our words. If we devote our energies to providing quality and loving care and effective pain control, the euthanasia issue will die from a lack of interest.

---

*This essay originally appeared as two separate essays on the *LeaderU* website:
    Raymond G. Bohlin, "Euthanasia: The Battle for Life"
    Kerby Anderson, "Euthanasia"
**Reproduction rights granted by Raymond G. Bohlin and Kerby Anderson.

Unit Eight

THE BATTLE FOR LIFE
ESSAY QUESTIONS

Answer the questions below on a separate sheet of paper and be prepared to review your answers in class.

1. **What is active euthanasia? What is passive euthanasia?**

> Active euthanasia (also known as mercy *killing*) occurs when a medical professional deliberately acts to cause the death of a patient. This is usually done through the administration of drugs or other such means. Passive euthanasia (also known as mercy *dying*) occurs when a medical professional withdraws extraordinary medical treatment consequently allowing a patient's demise. The former act is killing and usually illegal while the latter is not. Terminating a human life eliminates all possibility of recovery, while passively ceasing extraordinary means may not. Miraculous recovery from a bleak prognosis sometimes occurs. [SM pp. 233–4]

2. **What is voluntary euthanasia? What is involuntary euthanasia? What are some concerns connected with each?**

> Voluntary euthanasia occurs when an uncoerced patient chooses to end his or her life. Involuntary euthanasia occurs when a second party makes the decision about whether active or passive measures should be taken to end a patient's life.
>
> One concern with voluntary euthanasia is that it may not always be the patient's initial choice, that is some patients may be pressured (either directly or indirectly) to "get out of the way." Similarly, a doctor or relative may choose involuntary euthanasia for reasons of convenience or financial strains. Caring for the sick and the elderly require an investment of both time and money. [SM pp. 233–4]

3. **What are some similarities between the society's general acceptance of euthanasia and the practice of abortion?**

> At least two similarities exist between the debates over abortion and euthanasia. First, many today limit human worth to viability and productivity. The unborn, elderly, and infirm are neither capable of taking care of themselves nor are they deemed to have a quality existence because they cannot function as "normal" healthy adults. Thus, the lives of the unborn, elderly, and infirm are no longer valued as highly as they once were.
>
> A second issue is that of convenience. We live in a society that desires for difficult, costly, and time intensive problems to just go away. Thus, the easiest solution to the "inconvenience" of the unborn, elderly, and infirm is death. [SM p. 234]

SM
238

4. Why do individuals seek euthanasia?

First, a person seeking euthanasia may fear being kept alive by machines even when he or she has no hope of recovery. For the most part this fear is unfounded. Few seem to realize that it is already legal for a terminally ill patient to refuse life-prolonging measures. In other words, no one can force a person who is dying to be kept alive by extraordinary measures, rather if they desire, they have the right to let nature take its course.

Second, a person may fear pain. While the fear of pain is normal, this worry is no longer as valid as it once was. Few people today realize that most of the pain of terminally ill patients can be dealt with.

Third, a person may seek euthanasia because they fear being alone. To a large extent the society in general, and perhaps the church in particular, has abandoned the elderly. We no longer take seriously the command to honor our fathers and mothers. Extended families no longer live together even when the medical needs of parents are not severe or terribly limiting. No one wants to be a burden or to be burdened in our selfish society, including Christians. One recent change to this pattern has been the growth of the hospice movement. The staff at a hospice is trained to deal not only with physical pain, but also with psychological, social, and spiritual pain that accompanies being lonely. [SM p. 23–35]

5. How does the Bible teach that all life is valuable?

First, the Bible teaches us that all human beings are made in God's image. This means that all human life is sacred (Genesis 1:26–31).

Second, the Bible is clear that God is sovereign over life, death, and judgment. It is his place to determine who lives and who dies, not ours (Deuteronomy 32:39).

Third, to assist someone in suicide is to commit murder (Exodus 20:13). [SM pp. 235–6]

[Review with your students the above passages as well as Job 42:1–6 and 1 Corinthians 6:12–20. Discuss how these passages relate to Christians and the question of euthanasia.]

DEAR DOUG
WRITING ASSIGNMENT

It's me again!

I'm finally getting back into the swing of college life. It's been a little tough balancing everything so there's time left over for fun, but I think I've got it licked. Oh, yeah, the big news is I got a job—I'm working four evenings a week at a restaurant about a block from the dorm. Nice place, with good customers.

Nathan and I had everyone over last night to watch a movie. Can you picture the six of us crammed into a college dorm room? We were draped everywhere, but it was great! Paige brought the popcorn and Mark brought the movie, some new futuristic action-adventure.

When it was over, we started talking about what the world would look like in a couple of decades. Sarah thinks we'll have a unified global government... after all, the first steps have already been taken, when you consider the UN and Europe's adoption of the Euro. Everyone's always talking about "world peace" and this would be one way to get it, but I'm worried about how to keep it from becoming tyrannical. What do you think about a worldwide government?

Muhammad believes that a global government would only be possible under the control of Islamic leaders—a government unified by religious fervor. That didn't sit too well with me, since Christianity and Islam don't seem to mix. What are your thoughts on a global Islamic government?

Nathan supported having a single global power, but wanted to know what would happen to everyone's individual rights. Mark said we would only have those rights granted to us by the state, at which point Paige jumped on him. She wanted to know how they were going to protect women's rights. Nothing is certain in life, she said, and she wanted to make sure that she would keep total control over her own body.

That got the girls started on the topic of abortion and why the religious fanatics can't just leave women alone. Sarah said that it's her body and nobody should tell her what to do with it. A fetus is not really human until it's born, after all, and a mistake like getting pregnant shouldn't mess up her life and career. Paige added that legalized abortion is saving all those women who would die having back-alley abortions if the laws were overturned. By the time the conversation was over, both of them were pretty disgusted with the pro-life movement. How is a Christian supposed to deal with the issue of abortion anyway?

The whole issue of government and politics is pretty new to me. I mean, I've only been old enough to vote for a couple of years. Does Christianity have a position on politics?

Well, I've gotta get changed and head out to work.

Talk to you later!
Doug

Doug has brought up four different subjects; below is a rough outline of possible responses.

1. What do you think the ramifications of a global secular government would be? (12.5 points)

> The problem with a global secular government is that it is based on a false view of the world, namely a failure to recognize God's providence, sovereignty, and truth. Such a system will inevitably have problems because it elevates humanity's role in the making of laws, fails to pay homage to God, and downplays our depravity.

2. What do you think the consequences of a worldwide Islamic government would be? (12.5 points)

> A global Islamic government could very easily lead to the global oppression of women and a loss of religious freedom and free speech—nothing could be said against Allah or Muhammad.

3. How should a Christian approach the issue of abortion? (12.5 points)

> The central issue of the abortion debate hinges upon this: all human life, no matter how small, is valuable because humans uniquely bear the image of God. If abortion were only the removal of tissue from a woman's body, then there would be no issue. However, if abortion is the ending of human life (and what else could it be?), then the practice is murder. That being said, Christians must also seek to speak this truth in love. Part of our message must be that God is capable of forgiving all of our sins and that none of us are any better than another.

4. What is the Christian view of politics? (12.5 points)

> Biblical Christianity recognizes the state as a God-ordained institution (Genesis 9:6, Romans 13:1–7, 1 Peter 2:13–17). Christians believe in the depravity of humanity (Jeremiah 17:9) and our moral responsibility, and therefore realize that government is a necessary institution—even to the imposition of the death penalty (Genesis 9:6, Romans 13:1–4). However, government has limited obligations, not totalitarian powers. The Bible calls for limited government, falling somewhere between no government (anarchy) and total government (totalitarianism). Caesar has his role, but God has also appointed separate roles for the family and the church.

Unit Eight

UNIT EIGHT TEST

'POLITICS' TEXTBOOK QUESTIONS

Matching: (1 point possible per answer [3 for 90-day])
some options may be used more than once or not at all; some questions may have multiple answers

1. __g__ **Christianity**

2. __b/i__ **Islam**

3. __e/j__ **Secular Humanism**

4. __c/l__ **Marxism-Leninism**

5. __d__ **Cosmic Humanism**

6. __a/f__ **Postmodernism**

a. Progressive Politics
b. Global Islam
c. Communist World Government
d. New World Order
e. Secular World Government
f. Leftism
g. Justice, Freedom, Order
h. Libertarianism
i. Theocracy
j. Liberalism
k. Green Party
l. Statism

Short answer: (6 points possible per answer [6 for 90-day])
7. **Why do Secular Humanists favor globalism?**

> Because humanity is seen as the highest of all evolved animals and simply one among many parts of the world's single ecosystem, we are viewed as violating our place in nature when we attempt to divide the ecosystem into states and nations. Thus, according to Humanism, mankind should live in one community, without national borders and differing state policies. Indeed, a peaceful world government appears to be inevitable, given that we are constantly evolving to a higher state and are now capable of controlling our own evolution.

8. **How do Marxists view the notion of democracy?**

> "Democracy is a state," explains Lenin, "which recognizes the subordination of the minority to the majority, i.e., an organization for the systematic use of force by one class against another, by one section of the population against another." Marxists view the struggle to control the forces of production as the dynamic force behind mankind's development. According to Marxism, a socialist economy lays the foundation for the best form of democracy (although Marxists view democracy as little more than a necessary evil). A socialist government will tend to discourage class antagonism, since it will be founded on an economic system that is a step closer to abolishing classes. The socialist democracy is more appealing than a capitalist democracy, but is not the ideal (which will only come with the utopia of communism).

9. **According to Marxism, how did the state come into being? What is the ultimate fate of the state under communism? What is the ultimate political aim of Marxism?**

Marxists view the state as a transitory phenomenon. At some point in mankind's social development the state arose linked with capitalism. Thus, the state is a necessary tool for the capitalist who promotes class antagonism. However, as capitalism and class distinctions disappear, so too will the state. As Lenin stresses, "Only in the communist society… when the capitalists have disappeared, when there are no classes… only then the state… can cease to exist and *it becomes possible to speak of freedom*."

Marxists believe that the establishment of a new world order—world communism—and the withering away of the state are inevitable steps in our biological and social evolution. The new world order is an evolutionary advance over nations, states, tribes, and other such distinctions.

10. **Why do Cosmic Humanists believe that a New World Order is guaranteed?**

The New World Order is guaranteed by evolution, which is not just a physical process—it is a total spiritual development. Human beings cannot help but evolve into higher species; neither can we help but evolve into a higher state of consciousness.

11. **What type of government system will humanity have in the New World Order?**

Neither democracy nor totalitarianism is offered as a potential system of world government by New Agers. This is due to the fact that New Agers believe that each person is evolving the capacity for self-government. When we achieve a collective consciousness, world government will be synonymous with self-government.

12. **What is the Postmodernist position toward politics?**

Michel Foucault and Richard Rorty both uses the term "progressive politics," while Richard Rorty uses the term "leftism" to describe their politics. For Postmodernists, politics is not centered around political parties, utopian visions, or some ultimate telos; rather progressive politics is a tool of experimentation, a way to break traditional social norms, and a means for achieving social justice and leftism is overall credulity toward Christian values.

13. **According to Postmodernists, what is social justice? How is social justice to be achieved?**

The goal of progressive politics is to produce social justice, i.e. giving oppressed groups their "due" within society. The Postmodern understanding of social justice revolves around the notion of "oppressed groups"—the poor, unemployed, Hispanics, blacks, women, gays, and lesbians. Social justice is to be achieved through laws, education, and the redistribution of wealth.

"THE CASE AGAINST ABORTION" VIDEO

Short answer: (6 points possible per answer)

14. How do we simplify the abortion debate?

> The abortion debate should be centered on one question, "What is the unborn?" Or another way to put it, "What are we killing?" If the unborn are not human, then there should be no restrictions on abortion whatsoever. However, if the fetus is an innocent human being, then she deserves the same right to life as her mother. Most pro-choice objections skirt this central question.
>
> To bring the debate back around to the nature of the fetus, use the "Trot out the Toddler" tactic. Every time someone gives you an objection to the pro-life view or offers you a justification as to why abortion ought to be allowed, ask if this objection would work as a good argument for killing a toddler.

15. How do we convey both scientifically and philosophically that the unborn are human beings?

> Some will try to argue that the unborn are not human. However, the opposite can be proven using science and philosophy.
>
> First, if the fetus is not a human, then what species is it? According to the Law of Biogenesis, creatures reproduce only after their own kind—humans beget humans, frogs beget frogs, etc. Some may assert that the unborn are human beings, but not persons. Force them to support such a claim. Ask them, "What is the difference between being a human and being a person?"
>
> Second, there are only four differences between the unborn and adults and none of those differences nullify a fetus's humanity:
> - **Size**—a fetus is smaller than an adult, but so is a toddler.
> - **Level of Development**—a fetus is less developed than adult, but a toddler is less developed than a teenager.
> - **Environment**—a fetus is in a womb, but how does one's location change his or her nature?
> - **Degree of Dependency**—a fetus is not viable on its own, however neither is a toddler or a person on insulin.

THE SHIFTING FOCUS IN THE ABORTION DEBATE ESSAY

True or False: (4 points possible per answer [4 for 90-day])
*if an answer is false, restate it to make it true

16. In relation to the abortion debate regarding the personhood of the fetus, the central question is no longer the humanity of the fetus.

> True

17. **Thomson supports the pro-choice position by arguing that the fetus is not a person and that it is also an intruder on the women's body.**

> False: Thomson supports the pro-choice position by arguing that the fetus is a person <u>but</u> that it is also an intruder on the women's body.

18. **The advancement of racial equality and the right to personal autonomy are now popular defenses for abortion rights.**

> False: The advancement of <u>gender</u> equality and the right to personal autonomy are now popular defenses for abortion rights.

19. **Thomson's argument for abortion rights assumes that moral obligations must be enforced in order to carry moral weight.**

> False: Thomson's argument for abortion rights assumes that moral obligations must be <u>voluntary</u> in order to carry moral force.

20. **Thomson's argument for abortion rights ignores the fact that abortion is the active (rather than passive) killing of a human being.**

> True

THE BATTLE FOR LIFE ESSAY

True or False: (4 points possible per answer [4 for 90-day])
*if an answer is false, restate it to make it true

21. **Active euthanasia is the killing of another human being.**

> True

22. **Passive euthanasia eliminates the patient's possibility of recovery, while actively ceasing extraordinary means may not.**

> False: <u>Active</u> euthanasia eliminates the possibility of recovery, while passively ceasing extraordinary means may not.

23. Voluntary active euthanasia requires a second party who makes the decision about whether active measures should be taken to end the life of another.

False: <u>Involuntary</u> active euthanasia requires a second party who makes the decision about whether active measures should be taken to end the life of another.

24. People seek euthanasia because they fear being kept alive, they fear medicine, and they fear being alone.

False: People seek euthanasia because they fear being kept alive, they fear <u>pain</u>, and they fear being alone.

25. Christians have a duty to take care of the elderly.

True

TEACHER
MANUAL

UNDERSTANDING THE TIMES

Unit Nine

Topics:
Economics
Radical Environmentalism
Stewardship
Welfare

A Summit Ministries Curriculum

180-Day Syllabus

DAY	IN CLASS	HOMEWORK	
1	WATCH "Economics" video		
2	READ <u>UTT</u> Textbook 'Economics 9.1'	READ <u>UTT</u> Textbook 'Economics 9.2'	
3	REVIEW <u>UTT</u> Textbook 'Economics 9.1–9.2' questions	READ <u>UTT</u> Textbook 'Economics 9.3'	
4	READ <u>UTT</u> Textbook 'Economics 9.4'		
5	REVIEW <u>UTT</u> Textbook 'Economics 9.3–9.4' questions	READ <u>UTT</u> Textbook 'Economics 9.5'	
6	READ <u>UTT</u> Textbook 'Economics 9.6'		
7	REVIEW <u>UTT</u> Textbook 'Economics 9.5–9.6' questions	READ *Heart, Soul, and Money* essay	
8	REVIEW *Heart, Soul, and Money* essay questions	ASSIGN Dear Doug Letter	
9	WATCH "Radical Environmentalism" video		
10	REVIEW "Radical Environmentalism" video questions		
11	READ *Principles of a Christian...* essay		
12	REVIEW *Principles of a Christian...* essay questions		
13	WATCH "The Dangerous Samaritan" video		
14	REVIEW "The Dangerous Samaritan" video questions	Dear Doug Letter assignment DUE	
15	TAKE Unit Nine Test		

90-Day Syllabus

DAY	IN CLASS	HOMEWORK	
1	WATCH "Economics" video	READ <u>UTT</u> Textbook 'Economics 9.1–9.2'	
2	REVIEW <u>UTT</u> Textbook 'Economics 9.1–9.2' questions	READ <u>UTT</u> Textbook 'Economics 9.3–9.4'	
3	REVIEW <u>UTT</u> Textbook 'Economics 9.3–9.4' questions	READ <u>UTT</u> Textbook 'Economics 9.5–9.6'	
4	REVIEW <u>UTT</u> Textbook 'Economics 9.5–9.6' questions	READ *Principles of a Christian...* essay	
5	REVIEW *Principles of a Christian...* essay questions		
6	WATCH "The Dangerous Samaritan" video		
7	REVIEW "The Dangerous Samaritan" video questions		
8	TAKE Unit Nine Test		

UNDERSTANDING THE TIMES
ECONOMICS QUESTIONS

Answer the questions below on a separate sheet of paper and be prepared to review your answers in class.

ECONOMICS 9.1

1. What is the distinction between socialism and the free market system?

> The major difference between socialism and capitalism is economic freedom, as Ron Nash outlines, "the right of people to exchange things voluntarily, free from force, fraud, and theft... Socialism, on the other hand, seeks to replace the freedom of the market with a group of central planners who exercise control over essential market functions." [UTT 9.1.2]
>
> *[Some Christians use Acts 2—where it says that the early Christians "had all things in common"—to support the claim that Christians should favor socialism. However, it should be noted that socialism always achieves its goals by force and coercion, while Acts 2:45 clearly states that people "were sharing." Second, this collection was set aside for kingdom purposes and was freely given as an act of a love. Third, the property was shared among the disciples, not surrendered to the state. Fourth, this practice was not mandated for all Christians. As we see elsewhere, the Apostles requested donations from other Christians and never required converts to turn over their material possessions.]*

2. What biblical support is offered for private property? What happens when private ownership is denied?

> Many verses in the Bible support or assume the notion of private ownership and stewardship of property—Deuteronomy 8; Ruth 2; Isaiah 65:21–22; Jeremiah 32:42–44; Micah 4:1–4; Luke 12:13–15; Acts 5:1–4; Ephesians 4:28; and Exodus 22:1. To highlight a few:
>
> 1. The commandment "Thou shalt not steal" assumes that individuals are allowed to own things which others should not take.
> 2. The fact that Scripture requires restitution for theft assumes that people not only have the right to own property, but also when that right is violated that proper material amends should be made (even if it requires selling yourself into slavery—Exodus 22:1ff).
> 3. The right to property stems from our duty to work (Genesis 3:17–19). In fact Proverbs 10:4 states, "Lazy hands make a man poor, but diligent hands bring wealth."
>
> Since God grants us private ownership of certain aspects of his creation, we each become accountable to God for the way in which we use our property. Every person's responsibility as a steward is to maximize the Owner's return on his investment by using it to serve others (Matthew 25:14–30). But publicly owned property destroys our sense of responsibility to use our possessions wisely, because there is no incentive for selfish humanity to treat property wisely. [UTT 9.1.3]
>
> *[For a practical example ask your students which is cleaner—their home bathroom or the public restroom in the park? When everything is held in common, there is no sense of personal gain or loss. What is everyone's responsibility becomes no one's responsibility.]*

Unit Nine

3. **What is the principle of comparative advantage? How does competition stifle mankind's sinful tendencies?**

Principle of comparative advantage—every member of a free market society can produce valuable goods or services by specializing in areas where he or she enjoys the greatest advantage. Productive activities are directed toward meeting the needs of as many people as possible.

Benefits of a free market economy include:
1. Creates cooperation—individuals can more successfully operate in a free market because they can focus their energies on production that is the most beneficial to society as a whole. This in turns creates more goods and services at lower prices.
2. Promotes self-worth—the free market preserves an individual's dignity by giving men and women the opportunity to contribute to the welfare of society. Comparative advantage allows everyone to be the best producer of some service or good.

Competition requires meeting the needs of others better than anyone else. It promotes cooperation through the division of labor, which benefits society as a whole. [UTT 9.1.4]

4. **What are two mistaken assumptions often made about the wealthy?**

Some people assume that the rich gained their wealth by taking from the poor. Although this is sometimes the case, poverty does not always result from exploitation. As Scripture points out, sometimes poverty is the result of misfortune (e.g. accidents, injuries, illness, etc.) or is the result of indigence and sloth (Proverbs 6:6–11; 13; 24:30–34; 28:19). Second, the free market encourages the wealthy to invest their wealth in productive enterprises, thus making jobs, goods, and services available for others. [UTT 9.1.7]

5. **What is the relationship between freedom and the economic system a country employs?**

Socialist systems require more bureaucracies and more powerful centralized governments to initiate its plans. In contrast, the capitalist system requires far less political power because the government is not needed to control incomes, prices, production, etc. Under capitalism it is the citizens who are free to determine how they will spend their money and how they will use their resources. [UTT 9.1.7]

ECONOMICS 9.2

6. **What similarities exist between the Islamic and Christian approaches to economics?**

Both Christians and Muslims believe that human beings are created by God, were delegated authority over creation, and will one day will give an accounting of how they have used the good resources God has provided (see Genesis 1:28).

The belief in final judgment (one of the five pillars of Islam) places all actions under divine scrutiny: no action is hidden from Allah (Qur'an 9:105), and he is the most just of all (95:8). Allah expects

Muslims to feed the poor, give alms, help orphans, provide loans without interest to fellow Muslims, not hoard food, and not gamble. But Islamic economics is not just a meager series of prohibitions; while Muslims are to work hard and share their wealth with fellow Muslims in need, they can gain income, amass wealth, and enjoy all good things. [UTT 9.2.2]

7. **What are the four foundational principles of Islamic economics as described by Syed Hawab Haider Naqvi?**

1. **Unity**—Economic resources must never be used contrary to the vision of the universal unity of the Ummah, the Muslim community.
2. **Equilibrium**—Justice and kindness are to be reflected in all social institutions, including economic life. Justice and kindness relate not only to economic transactions but also to caring for the less fortunate members of society.
3. **Free will**—Humans are responsible for their beliefs and actions. Such responsibility presupposes that humans have wills so they can choose to do what is right or what is wrong.
4. **Responsibility**—Responsibility corresponds to free will. Not only are Muslims responsible to God, they are also responsible to fellow Muslims. Muslims believe that by giving they become better people and fulfill our moral responsibilities to God, themselves, and their fellow human beings. Some even believe that generosity can atone for sins. [UTT 9.2.4–7]

8. **What economic system do Muslims favor?**

Muslim economists contend that their economic system is neither socialism nor capitalism—they reject socialism's negation of private property, but also reject capitalism's absolute view of private property. In Naqvi's words, "As to the ownership of private property, especially of land ownership, it has been restricted in various ways. For instance, individuals cannot own uncultivated lands, forests, grazing grounds, mines, etc. All these must be owned by the public authority for public welfare."

Not surprising, for all the above to be worked out and to make sure that one's labor is correct, the state will have to play a very prominent and important role in the Islamic economy. This is not merely in terms of instituting justice in economic dealings, but even meddling in the ways and means of production, distribution, and risk. Therefore, Muslim economists seem to favor some form of government intervention. [UTT 9.2.1]

9. **What do the terms *zakat* and *jizrah* mean?**

Zakat is alms Muslims give to provide for poor Muslims. *Jizrah* is taxes levied against unbelievers living within the Islamic community. [UTT 9.2.9–10]

10. **How does Islam treat inheritance? What is the Islamic view of charging interest?**

While Islam respects the right to own property, that right terminates on the owner's death and is distributed over the next two generations, with certain considerations made for the widower (who receives one-half of estate) or the widow (who receives one-quarter of the estate). [UTT 9.2.12]

Traditionally, it has been believed that to charge interest on loans to fellow Muslims is forbidden. However, this may be changing as more and more Muslims are interpreting the passages to mean unfair interest, or usury. [UTT 9.2.13]

FINANCIAL STEWARDSHIP ACTIVITY

Ask the students to write out a monthly budget, keeping biblical principles in mind. Distribute the "Getting a Grip on Money" handout found in the *Teacher's CD-ROM* in the "Handouts" folder. There are two columns on the form, the first for their current income and expenses, and the second for what they would like to bring in or spend.

Students may have a hard time getting a handle on what they are spending, though they'll probably know how much money they are receiving. Help them contemplate how much money they spend on fast food, soft drinks, and vending machine items. It may not seem like much to spend just $1 a day on candy and soft drinks (many students spend much more). But if you were to save that much ($365) each year from age 17 to age 30, you would have over $10,000. The purpose of this exercise is not to make the students stingy or greedy, but to make them aware that their decisions have consequences. You may also want to challenge your students to use some of what they are spending on junk food to help feed a child overseas or you can pool resources to help feed the hungry in your area.

ECONOMICS 9.3

11. Why do a number of current leading Secular Humanists favor capitalism?

A number of current leading Secular Humanists have come out in favor of capitalism over socialism after witnessing the tragic outcome of the economic system in practice. Marvin Zimmerman writes, "I contend that the evidence supports the view that democratic capitalism is more productive of human good than democratic socialism." And Robert Sheaffer agrees, "No intellectually honest person today can deny that the history of socialism is a sorry tale of economic failure and crimes against humanity." [UTT 9.3.1]

12. Why did most of Secular Humanism's earliest proponents favor socialism?

Most of the early Humanists were proponents of socialism for at least two reasons: Corliss Lamont, John Dewey, and others all believed that the economic system of socialism was more moral than capitalism. In his earlier years, Sidney Hook wrote, "In my case, as in so many others, allegiance to socialism at first appeared to be primarily the articulation of a feeling of moral protest against remediable evils that surrounded us." [UTT 9.3.3]

Similarly, most of the earliest Humanists believed that capitalism was a failure highlighting that it breeds materialism, strips mankind of its humanity, and creates artificial scarcity. [UTT 9.3.4]

Unit Nine

13. On what form of economics does almost every Humanist agree?

Most of Secular Humanism's earliest supporters—Lamont, Dewey, Hook, Fromm, and Sellars—were all socialists of one form or another. More recently, however, a number of Secular Humanists—Kurtz, Zimmerman, Sheaffer, and Hook—have spoken out in favor of capitalism. But all Secular Humanists, whether leaning toward capitalism or socialism, seem to favor some form of government interventionism and the redistribution of wealth. [UTT 9.3.2]

14. Why do many Secular Humanists believe in interventionism?

Still, Hook, and other Humanists cannot bring themselves to completely abandon some form of socialism. The reason is their commitment to the goodness of man. Their view expects man to be able to overcome evil—and evil is, theoretically, the one thing preventing a socialist economy from working. However, human history clearly demonstrates that socialism has never worked very well. Therefore, the blame for its failure must be placed in another area. [UTT 9.3.2]

15. How do Secular Humanists propose that we achieve a more "equal" society?

Lamont, Dewey, Fromm, and Sellars all call for a redistribution of wealth in the form of a "guaranteed income" for every person. [UTT 9.3.5]

ECONOMICS 9.4

16. According to Karl Marx, what two flaws within capitalism cause it to be exploitative?

Marx describes the first flaw of capitalism as the "surplus of labor." The bourgeoisie make their profits not by selling their product at a price above the cost of materials plus labor, but rather by paying the workers less than a fair amount for their labor. The second flaw of capitalism according to Marx is its chaotic nature. Under socialism the state can control every aspect of the economy (from production to distribution), but under capitalism the economy is controlled by the free market. Marx claims that only a planned economy could truly discover the best methods of production and distribution. [UTT 9.4.2]

17. According to Marxism, what will be the fate of capitalism?

The capitalist system, according to Marxists, will simply exploit more and more people until virtually everyone becomes a member of the proletariat. Eventually the working class will get fed up and overthrow the wealthy minority. Marxists further believe that this destruction of capitalism and the victory of the proletariat is ultimately guaranteed by the dialectic: the thesis (bourgeoisie) and the antithesis (proletariat) must clash and create a synthesis—socialism. [UTT 9.4.3]

18. What is the difference between socialism and communism?

Socialism is only the first step toward communism. Like capitalism before it, socialism is a necessary evil. It is a period of time in which the government owns all property, controls wages, regulates production, and ultimately controls a nation's entire economy. This transitional phase will come to an end when classes and economic distinctions have disappeared. At that time, every citizen will peacefully own all things in common, eliminating the need for a government and laws.

The basic difference is best summed up by Moscow's *Political Dictionary* (1940): "Socialism is the first phase of communism. The principle of socialism is: from each according to his abilities, to each according to his work… Under communism the basic principle of society will be: from each according to his abilities, to each according to his need." [UTT 9.4.4]

19. Why must a transitional phase necessarily exist between capitalism and communism?

Engels addressed this question by asking, "Will it be possible to abolish private property at one stroke?" and then answered: "No… the proletarian revolution, which in all probability is impending, will transform existing society only gradually, and be able to abolish private property only when the necessary quantity of the means of production has been created." Because both the abolition of private property and the refining of the means of production must happen gradually, the move to communism requires a transitional phase. [UTT 9.4.5]

20. What do Marxists believe the benefits of communism will be?

Marxists claim that communism provides more freedom than any other system. We will finally achieve perfection and will therefore no longer need government or laws to keep us in check. Another benefit will be the redistribution of wealth. The current divisions of labor merely allow the rich to get richer and the poor to get poorer. This environment thus creates hostility and crime which will be eradicated under communism. Another advantage claimed by Marxists is communism's ability to motivate workers. A capitalistic system must deal with the problem of unemployment; under communism, however, every citizen will be given a constitutional right to work and allowed to work where he or she sees fit without the worry of finances or finding and keeping a job. [UTT 9.4.7]

ECONOMICS 9.5

21. Why are Cosmic Humanists vague when defining their ideal economic system?

Just like with politics and law, the degree of autonomy the individual will experience in the New Age cannot be bound by the limitations of any present-day economic system. [UTT 9.5.1]

22. How do Cosmic Humanists encourage individuals to decide on a vocation?

> Cosmic Humanists encourage people to ask, "What is my inner voice calling me to do?" Since the inner voice is the voice of God, that call will lead to the proper vocation. [UTT 9.5.1]

23. According to Cosmic Humanism, what is the best way to achieve a higher income?

> According to New Age gurus, the more enlightened a person becomes, the more money and success he or she will accrue. As Shakti Gawain proclaims, "The more you are willing to trust yourself, and take the risks to follow your inner guidance, the more money you will have. The universe will pay you to be yourself and do what you really love!" [UTT 9.5.2]

24. According to Cosmic Humanists, what does God desire for us?

> Marianne Williamson says, "God does not demand sacrifice." Rather, God wants us to prosper materially. By getting in touch with our higher consciousness, we can ensure a higher income. [UTT 9.5.2]

25. According to New Agers, why can the enlightened trust the world to bring them material possession?

> According to Marianne Williamson, we can trust the world to grant us material blessings because "our purpose on this earth is to be happy, and because we, as part of God, ultimately control reality." [UTT 9.5.2]

ECONOMICS 9.6

26. What is the "decentered self" and why is it important to Postmodern economics?

> According to Postmodern psychology, human beings are fictions with no unified self or permanent understanding of who we are; rather, what we call human beings are merely social constructions. The goals of Postmodern economics are 1) to eliminate the oppressive distinction between men and women and 2) to elevate the economic realities of differently gendered subjects, such as women, homosexuals, bisexuals, etc. This would include creating more equitable work environments for all subjects (i.e., women, homosexuals, etc.) in the military, the clergy, and in any area that is presently monopolized by heterosexual men. [UTT 9.6.2]

Unit Nine

27. Why do Postmodernists denounce capitalism? How do Postmodernists propose that we fix the problems inherent in capitalism?

> Postmodernists view capitalism as a "male-dominated" economic system which inevitably produces "one-sided" individuals who lack the ability to perceive the whole. In other words, capitalism speaks primarily to heterosexual maleness and "oppresses" all others. Since men will not willingly give up their economic power over women, the poor, etc., the government must intervene to see that economic justice is available to all. A state-planned economy is such an intervention. [UTT 9.6.3]

28. What is interventionism?

> Some Postmodernists favor socialism while a number of others favor capitalism. Some Postmodernists even critique both capitalism and socialism yet fail to offer any type of alternative. However, all Postmodernists seem to favor some form of government interventionism. Interventionism is not a totally state-planned economy nor a completely free market economy, but a combination of the two, where the state plays a role in redistributing wealth created in a partially or mostly free market environment. [UTT 9.6.4]

29. Since all economic theories have problems, what do Postmodernists claim should be done?

> According to Postmodernists, the best route for economics is constant experimentation. With ever-changing situations and communities, the best approach is to never be married to any one way; there is always the possibility of inventing something new that will better serve the people. [UTT 9.6.5]

30. Why are Postmodernists hesitant to offer a positive economic theory?

> Postmodernists are hesitant to argue that their worldview shows the way forward and are content with conversations and encounters. Since there is no "truth" about the "real" world or the "nature" of mankind, it is hard to arrive at a "correct" view of economics. [UTT 9.6.5]

HEART, SOUL, AND MONEY
BY CRAIG BLOMBERG[1]

INTRODUCTION

More than a billion people out of earth's six billion inhabitants live in desperate poverty. Natural disasters, war, corrupt governments, lack of education, disease, unfair trade laws, and false religions all play their part in creating this situation. Conservatively, at least 200 million (one-fifth) of these poor are Bible-believing, born-again Christians.

In North America, trends over the last thirty years demonstrate an increasing disparity between rich and poor, irrespective of which political party has been in power at any given time. More and more, the growing gap between rich and poor follows racial lines: whites and Asians growing richer; blacks and Hispanics growing poorer.

Meanwhile middle- and upper-class Americans, including Christians, have markedly changed their spending patterns. We now eat out on average for nearly 30% of all our meals, compared to only 10% a mere twenty years ago. The amount of money spent on such nonessentials as sports and recreation, lawn care, video and computer games, home entertainment centers, pets and dieting has skyrocketed. At the same time Christians' per capita giving to charitable causes of all kinds has steadily declined in the last forty years from just under 4% of their total annual income to barely above 2%.

We are in the midst of the largest transfer of wealth in human history from the World War II generation to their children, the baby boomers. The possibilities of funding Christian ministry to address people's spiritual and physical needs at home and abroad are at an all-time high. But all the trends suggest that overall those inheriting this wealth are spending the vast majority of it on themselves, either to get out of all-time, global record levels of debt or to continue to fuel their self-centered interests.

Christian trend-watchers have made two staggering calculations. On the one hand, if every American Christian simply tithed, the additional amount of money that would be raised above and beyond current giving levels would be enough to eradicate world poverty in our lifetime. Of course, the sinful behavior of fallen humanity would prevent this from ever fully happening, but we could certainly make substantially greater progress than we currently are making. Second, the average age of major donors in both church and para-church organizations is now, for the first time ever, well over sixty-five. Current Christian work is being funded largely by retired people, who lived a more frugal lifestyle a generation ago. Thus, unless patterns of Christian giving change dramatically, a majority of currently existing ministries will close their doors for lack of finances within one generation.

Astonishingly, while all this is happening, some Christian leaders are promoting a "health-wealth" gospel that pretends that it is God's desire for the already affluent Western Christian to become even richer. In striking contrast, every once in a while someone else seems to argue that well-to-do Christians should trade places with the poor. Both of these extremes prove unbiblical and probably discourage some of the rest of us from taking any action at all.

I have written on this subject, therefore, because I have discovered that many Christians today are not willfully choosing to be disobedient to the Scriptures in the area of financial stewardship. They merely are unaware of the Bible's teaching on the topic and often unaware of the plight of the world and the kinds of trends I have just described. Many gladly increase their giving after a careful study of the Bible and current realities.

HISTORICAL BACKGROUND TO NEW TESTAMENT PASSAGES

In order to accurately understand the biblical instruction on any subject, but especially this one, we need to understand the context in which the message was communicated. First and foremost, unlike our relatively large middle class of America today, in Jesus' time about 80% of the Jews were poor, hoping each year's

[1] This essay was adapted from a study guide of the same name by Craig Blomberg published by College Press (www. collegepress.com) in 2000. For an expanded study of this topic or to find the sources for Dr. Blomberg's facts stated in this essay, please consult his book *Neither Poverty nor Riches: A Biblical Theology of Possessions* (InterVarsity, 1999).

crops would get them through that year. For these believers the Lord's prayer "give us this day our daily bread," was a present reality and an understandable request.

By the first century, a tiny handful of Jewish and Roman landlords owned vast tracts of land in Palestine. Small landowners found it harder and harder to get by. Eventually many of them sold their property and went to work as hired hands of the rich, tilling the same land they once owned. When they were unable to pay their taxes, they took out loans and amassed debts on which they often had to default. In the most acute cases, some were thrown into debtors' prisons. Some even died there.

While the Jewish synagogues and temple regularly took up collections to benefit their poor, the Greco-Roman world, pertinent to the background of the traveling apostles, had no equivalent institutions. The Roman empire in general lacked any kind of welfare system. Greco-Roman ways of thinking often viewed poverty as the fault and just punishment of the poor. So it was very common for people to become disabled or diseased, homeless and helpless, with few if any people in the empire who cared.

Both the Jewish and Greco-Roman cultures reflected widespread frustration with the economic disparities between rich and poor that increased in severity throughout the first century. Little wonder, then, that many Jews looked for a military Messiah who would help them overthrow Rome and reestablish an independent state of Israel in which they could revert to the more just laws and practices of their Scriptures. Many of them became disenchanted with Jesus, who claimed to be the Messiah but had little interest in political revolution. Little wonder, too, that many Greeks and Romans warmed to the apostles' message of equality in Christ across the wide, humanly created socioeconomic divides of their world.

However, we should recognize that at least some of Jesus' twelve disciples were more middle-class than poor. Matthew's tax collecting business probably vaulted him into this class, though through ill-gotten gain if he resembled others of his day. James and John, the sons of Zebedee, may have come from one of the handful of more prosperous fishing businesses, because Mark 1:20 speaks of their family having "hired men." Even households with meager resources often had one servant, rescuing him or her from total poverty, but more than one "employee" in a household suggested some measure of prosperity.

Just as we ought not think of all twelve of the disciples and Jesus as uniformly poor, neither may we imagine them as having permanently divested themselves of all their property. True, Peter can declare, "We have left everything to follow you!" (Mark 10:28). But he will later lead a group of the disciples back to their fishing boats after the resurrection (John 21:3), demonstrating that they had not sold their property but merely left it for a time. Likewise when Jesus says, "The Son of Man has nowhere to lay his head" (Matt. 8:20), this does not mean that he is homeless. Mary still lived in Nazareth (Joseph may have died by this time), and Jesus himself seems to have had a house in Capernaum (Mark 2:1). Instead, Jesus is stressing his voluntarily chosen path of itinerant ministry.

Further insight into how Jesus and the twelve supported themselves comes from Luke 8:1–3, in which we read of several wealthy women who supported the little traveling troupe out of their personal means. A pair of apparently secret followers of Jesus who were also extremely rich were Joseph of Arimathea and Nicodemus (Matt. 27:57; John 19:38–40—the amount of spices used to anoint Jesus' body came close to that used in the burial of kings). Thus when we read in 2 Corinthians 8:9 that "you know of the grace of our Lord Jesus Christ, that though he was rich, yet for our sakes he became poor, so that you through his poverty might become rich," we are not to understand literal poverty and riches to be in view. Christ in his incarnation gave up the incomprehensible privilege of sitting at the Father's right hand to be humiliated as a human and ultimately executed. That is how he became "poor." Similarly, we become rich in spiritual blessings, not necessarily earthly ones, as we become disciples of Christ.

Major Themes

Any attempt to summarize the dominant emphases in any large swathe of biblical material inevitably oversimplifies. So, too, our comments here do not adequately encompass the wealth of detail discussed in the books from which this essay derives. Nonetheless, these broad strokes should help provide a framework through which to think about stewardship in general and your personal stewardship in particular. In the body of this paper, we will consider the five most important conclusions to emerge from a survey of the Bible's teaching on material possessions.

1. Material possessions are a good gift from God meant for his people to enjoy.

The Scriptures begin and end with one of the most important principles about possessions in the Bible. Like all of the rest of the material world, God created them as something good to be enjoyed by all humanity (Genesis 1:4, 10, 12, 18, 21, 25, 31). Unique among his creation, humans were fashioned in God's image and called to be stewards of everything else God had created (vv. 26–28). Even after the Fall, that calling does not give us permission to be cruel to animals or to destroy the environment, but it does grant us authority over "animal, vegetable, and mineral" to mold and reshape creation in ways that make our lives more productive and rewarding.

Throughout the Old Testament, Job, Abraham, David, Solomon and a variety of other figures demonstrate that riches and godliness can coexist, at least for a time. The very fact that God promised Israel the land of Canaan, with its abundant natural resources, demonstrates his commitment to providing the blessings of the material world as a pre-eminent, good gift for his people (Numbers 14:8). The proverbial literature offers riches as a reward for wholesome work. The New Testament likewise recognizes an increasing number of well-to-do Christians throughout the early history of Christianity who host churches in their homes, make business trips and fund itinerant ministries. The community of disciples shares its material resources with one another, not so that all will be equally impoverished, but so that there will be 'no needy persons among them' (Acts 4:34). This is part of the principle behind those with extra giving to those who lack. That those of us who have more than others should work to help those who have less to have at least a little more to enjoy. Even in the harshest of scenarios, the very luxuries that can lead to the demonic (Revelation 17–18) will be available for all of God's redeemed people in a very material age to come (Revelation 21–22).

Thus Paul concludes 1 Timothy by commanding "those who are rich in this present world not to be arrogant nor to put their hope in wealth, which is so uncertain, but to put their hope in God" (6:17). But he balances this with the reminder that God "richly provides us with everything for our enjoyment." Paul is no ascetic, the material world still includes good gifts for God's people, and Christ does not call a majority of his followers to permanently divest themselves of all of their property. Verse 18 explains how we can enjoy a measure of prosperity with a good conscience—when we simultaneously are "rich in good deeds," "generous and willing to share."

2. Material possessions are simultaneously one of the primary means of turning human hearts away from God.

It is not impossible to be both rich and Christian, but consistently throughout biblical and church history, lower percentages of believers are found among the richer than among the poorer segments of society.

Adam and Eve coveted the attractive but forbidden fruit of the garden, and everything was corrupted or cursed quickly thereafter. Possession of, or desire for, too many material goods leads to rejection of God, interpersonal hostility and exploitation or neglect of the poor. Thus most of the property laws of the Torah set limits on the amounts to be accumulated. The celebration of the Jubilee year (Leviticus 25:8–55) alone would have allowed for a family to start afresh once a lifetime (once every 50 years), no matter how irresponsibly they had handled their finances or how far into debt they had fallen. However, it is uncertain whether this special sabbatical year was ever observed. Therefore the loss of ancestral properties to wealthy aristocrats who bought up vast tracts of land forever altered the economic landscape and widened the gap between rich and poor.

The enormous wealth of the monarchy, even though enjoyed by some like David who remained faithful to God, fuelled social injustice and prophetic critique. Ezekiel 22:29, Micah 2:2, and Amos 5:11–12 are three of numerous passages that stress how the rich in Israel were trying to get richer at the expense of the poor. Instead of honoring the Torah's commitment that inheritance remain within families so that all can own at least modest amounts of property, numerous illegal and unethical maneuvers were being concocted to concentrate wealth in the hands of fewer and fewer.

Not all poor people follow God and not all rich people deny him, but increasingly the Israelites experience what many other cultures have recognized throughout history: levels of religious commitment are consistently higher among the less well-to-do, who recognize they must depend on God for their wellbeing, than among the affluent, who think their buying power can meet all of their human needs.

For Jesus, mammon was God's rival. In addition to his statement in Matthew 6:24, Jesus taught this to his followers in a number of parables. In the parable of the Sower, one of the kinds of soils that proves unfruitful is that which is crowded by thorns and thistles. Jesus explains that the seed sown here corresponds to those who "hear the word; but the worries of this life, the deceitfulness of wealth, and the desires for other things come in and choke the word" (Mark 4:18–19). In the parable of the Rich Fool (Luke 12:13–21), an inheritance dispute leads Jesus to warn about covetousness (vv. 13–15). Then he illustrates by telling the story of a farmer who had an unexpected bumper crop and had to build extra barns to store it all (vv. 16–20). Six times in the text, the man speaks about himself with the first-person pronoun "I." Never does he suggest that any of this surplus ought to help the needy who, as we have seen in the introduction, would have constituted about 80% of the peasants and villagers surrounding him. Suddenly, his life comes to an end and he can't take his riches with him. Jesus concluded, "This is how it will be with those who store up things for themselves but are not rich toward God" (v. 21).

This same idea leads Paul to proclaim, "The love of money is the root of all kinds of evil" (1 Timothy 6:10). Paul does not say that "money is the root of all evil" but speaks of "the love of money." The love of money is one important root, but not the only one, of all kinds of evil. Still, we must not lose the force of Paul's warning. Even translated correctly, as in the NIV, the verse still reminds us of all the ways wealth or its pursuit distracts us from godly priorities in our lives. In 1 Timothy 3:3 and 8, under the criteria for church leaders, Paul includes the prohibitions against being lovers of money and pursuing dishonest gain. The terms used are both synonyms for being greedy. Thus we should not be surprised when in Titus 1:11 false teachers are described as seeking dishonest gain, while in 2 Timothy 3:2,4 the terrible people that will arise in the last days are said to be lovers of money and lovers of pleasure.

James (4:13–17) rebukes well-to-do believers for planning an entire year or more of their lives without taking God's will into account. These businesspeople may well be part of the small middle class of the ancient Roman empire rather than truly wealthy, but either way the point is that the early Christians were not uniformly poor. But the "practical atheism" of the behavior of these traders closely parallels the long-term planning of middle-class people, including Christians, in our world today. The book of James contains an implicit criticism of the behavior of wealthy (at least not poor) Christians that reminds us that affluent Christians have particular obstacles they must overcome. They are tempted to think that their material possessions can replace God, that they deserve better treatment than poorer people do, and that life can be secured against all crises.

Both 2 Peter and Jude describe false teachers whose influence Christians should avoid. Among their evil character traits appears "greed" (2 Peter 2:3,14). Second Peter 2:14–15 describes them literally as "well trained in covetousness!" Jude 11 speaks of those who "rushed for profit into Balaam's error," a reference to Numbers 25 and 31:16 in which the pagan prophet who had earlier refused to curse Israel (Numbers 22–24) later seduced her into idolatry. In each of these contexts, it is interesting to see how sins of out-of-control spending are combined with references to sexual immorality. Both involve one's inability to delay gratification of one's wants and desires. Fulfilling one's immediate urges is all that counts for such people. It has been said that in our culture, too, one of the best barometers of Christian obedience is how a person uses his or her "wallet and zipper."

3. A necessary sign of a life in the process of being redeemed is transformation in the area of stewardship.

This will look different for every Christian, and it is dangerous to compare or contrast ourselves with anyone else, but over time some noticeable change in this arena will occur if a person is truly being indwelt by the Holy Spirit. Ultimately, one's entire life should be dedicated to God, but a particularly telling area for determining one's religious commitment involves one's finances. The wealthy but godly patriarchs and kings of the Old Testament are, without exception, said to have shared generously with the poor and needy. Even though none of the patriarchs—Abraham, Isaac, Jacob, and Joseph—ever experiences the complete fulfillment of this promise, each lives in the land for part of his life and amasses enormous wealth. Early on in the Bible, then, we learn that it is possible to be both rich and obedient to God (Genesis 20:14–16; 24:35; 26:13; 30:43; 47:27). At the same time, Genesis points out that the patriarchs are also generous in sharing their wealth with needier people around them (Genesis 13:1–18; 14:20,23; 32:13–16; 41:57).

Similar accounts are found in the historical books of the Old Testament. Those blessed by God with wealth during Israel's tenure within the Promised Land regularly and generously share that wealth with the poor. Boaz in the little book of Ruth and Nehemiah after the return from exile (especially Nehemiah 5) are two often neglected examples. One of the most frequent refrains of the Torah, Psalms, and Prophets is God's concern for the 'widow, fatherless, alien and poor', a concern which should lead his people ruthlessly to avoid every form of exploitation and to seek ways to meet the genuine needs of the marginalized and to address the causes of their misery. By way of contrast, one of the sins that makes someone like Ahab so wicked is his endless covetousness, so that he has Naboth, a small landowner near his palace, murdered just so he can add that property to his already vast holdings (1 Kings 21).

The book of Job reminds us that sometimes the wicked prosper and the righteous are impoverished (Job 21:7–21; 24:1–12). So Job keeps his possessions in proper perspective: "Naked I came from my mother's womb, and naked I shall depart. The Lord gave and the Lord has taken away; may the name of the Lord be praised" (1:21). Less well known is the fact that Job was always generous in sharing his possessions with the poor and often opposed injustice (29:12–17; 31:16–23). Thus he can declare, "If I have put my trust in gold or said to pure gold, 'You are my security,' if I have rejoiced over my great wealth, the fortune my hands had gained… so that my heart was secretly enticed… then these also would be sins to be judged, for I would have been unfaithful to God on high" (31:24–28).

In the New Testament, Jesus simply presupposes the practice of giving from one's surplus to help those who do not have daily essentials and some to enjoy. This comes through most clearly in the Sermon on the Mount: "So when you give to the needy… " (Matthew 6:2–3). Riches (or any amount of money) should not be our greatest goal. Instead, as Jesus teaches in the parables of the Hidden Treasure and the Pearl of Great Price, one must be prepared to give up whatever it takes, including material possessions, to enter the kingdom (Matthew 13:44–46). In the Good Samaritan, compassion for the helpless victim across ethnic and racial lines is illustrated by open-ended financial help (Luke 10:34–35).

Luke and Paul enjoin generous almsgiving. As part of Paul's farewell address to the Ephesian elders at Miletus, "I have not coveted anyone's silver or gold or clothing. You yourselves know that these hands of mine have supplied my own needs and the needs of my companions. In everything I did, I showed you that by this kind of hard work we must help the weak, remembering the words the Lord Jesus himself said: 'It is more blessed to give than to receive'" (Ephesians 20:33–35). Instead of endlessly amassing wealth for oneself, the ideal in most of the first-century empire (and in the modern West!), Paul quotes an otherwise unknown saying of Jesus that it is better to give some of one's wealth away.

First Corinthians 16:1–4 introduces a topic that will consume much of Paul's attention in his second letter to Corinth—a collection for the still impoverished Christians in and around Jerusalem. Here is the first reference in the New Testament, chronologically, to Christians gathering on the first day of the week (Sunday) rather than on the Jewish Sabbath (Saturday). And part of their weekly worship was to involve an offering. "Passing a collection plate" has formed a part of Christian worship services ever since.

Second Corinthians 8–9 forms the longest, sustained teaching passage in the New Testament on Christian stewardship. Here Paul returns to his instructions regarding the collection for Jerusalem, applying principles that give guidance for the church's giving in every era of her history. The Corinthians were initially eager to participate but have now lagged behind in fulfilling their pledges. The poorer Macedonian Christians have actually given more in a shorter period of time. So Paul encourages the Corinthians to complete what they started (8:1–11). En route he makes clear that this giving is the voluntary outgrowth of the larger Christian process of sanctification (vv. 4–5). It is a demonstration of the grace of God and of believers' spiritual giftedness (vv. 1,7). And it is the least we can do when we think of how much Jesus gave up in leaving his heavenly home and becoming incarnate and dying for our sakes (v. 9).

The epistle of James is best known for its hard-hitting teaching about faith and works. More ink has been spilled since the Protestant Reformation about James 2:18–26 than over all the rest of the letter put together. Martin Luther established the pattern by questioning whether James belonged in the canon of Scripture since it appeared to contradict Paul's teaching on salvation by grace through faith alone. Modern scholars of many theological persuasions have agreed that Paul does not contradict James: both recognize that true saving faith will produce tangible fruit (cf. Galatians 5:6).

But what is often lost sight of in this discussion is the context in which James's teaching about faith without works being dead emerges. In 2:14–17, James uses the illustration of help for the materially needy

Unit Nine

fellow Christian as the prime example of whether one performs the kinds of works that demonstrate the genuineness of one's faith. Interestingly, whereas the word "brother" in ancient Greek (and elsewhere in James) regularly functioned generically to include both men and women, here James explicitly adds the Greek word for "sister" (*adelphe*) in verse 15. As with the widows in 1:27, women in general were more likely to be impoverished and outcast in the biblical cultures, but James makes it clear that God does not approve.

The Greek also clarifies what remains ambiguous in English translations of verse 14. In the question, "Can such faith [professed belief in one God without any change of behavior, including helping the poor] save them?" the Greek uses an adverb (*me*) that implies a negative answer: "No, such 'faith' is not true saving faith." Put bluntly, if a person claims to be a Christian, is aware of the acute physical needs of desperately poor believers at home or abroad, is in any position to help, but never does a single thing except wish them well, that person's inaction disproves his or her profession of faith.

Two common misinterpretations of Scripture need to be dealt with before moving to the next point. First, there exists the mistaken idea of equating 'spiritual growth' with growth in material possessions. Not surprisingly, Christians who think that it is God's ideal for all believers to be rich regularly cite the arrangements God made with Israel during Old Testament times. What they fail to observe is that God made these arrangements with no other nation. Whereas the prophets can rebuke foreign nations for their injustice or mistreatment of the poor, demonstrating that the principles of the Mosaic Law apply at some level to all peoples, no other piece of geography is ever called a Promised Land. No other people are ever formed into a "theocracy," a country in which, even when there are human kings, God reigns and can overrule a king's command. Interestingly, the New Testament repeats all of the broad principles that we find in the Old Testament with respect to poverty and wealth with one notable exception. No Christian is ever promised material prosperity as the result of adequate obedience to Christ!

Another mistake is to read more into Acts 2:44 than the context permits. Acts 2:44 says, "All the believers were together and had everything in common." Verses 45–46 qualify the apparently absolute statement of the previous verse by explaining how people periodically sold property to meet various needs. Apparently not everyone sold everything as an entrance requirement for joining the church. It is interesting that the clause in verse 45, which could be translated "to each according to his need" combines with one in Acts 11:29—"from each according to his ability" to form the two halves of Karl Marx's famous Communist manifesto. Marx after all had thoroughly studied Christianity before rejecting it. It has been argued that Marx's ideal is indeed Christian and that what doomed it to failure were his means of implementing it: by coercion and legislation rather than voluntary cooperation and by divorcing it from its religious underpinnings. At any rate, if we cannot deduce a timeless, unalterable system for addressing issues of rich and poor from Acts 2, neither should we go to the opposite extreme and call the early Christian "communalism" an ill-advised, failed experiment. Luke as narrator makes it clear that he believes God has approved of and blessed these arrangements (Acts 2:47; 4:33; 5:13–14).

4. There are certain extremes of wealth and poverty that are in and of themselves intolerable.

These vary from person to person and culture to culture but involve, on the one hand, unused and unusable surplus and, on the other hand, the inability to meet even one's basic human needs of adequate food, clothing, shelter, and access to health care. It is one thing to generate income which is then channeled into kingdom purposes (Luke 16:9; 19:11–27); it is quite another to accumulate and hoard resources which are likely to be destroyed or disappear before being put to good use (Luke 16:19–31; James 5:1–6). In the latter case, such a surplus prevents others from having a better opportunity for a reasonably decent standard of living. Such hoarding or accumulation is sin, and if left unchecked proves damning (Luke 12:31–21; 16:19–31).

God created the material world completely good, but humanity in its sin regularly abuses that world so that all of creation is now in a corrupted state. Laws, therefore, must be enacted to keep human greed and violence in check. God does not believe in pure *laissez-faire economics*.[2] Sinful human beings, including

---

[2] *Laissez-faire economics* is defined as "an economic doctrine that opposes governmental regulation of or interference in commerce beyond the minimum necessary for a free-enterprise system to operate according to its own economic laws." Taken from *The American Heritage Dictionary of the English Language*, fourth ed. (New York: Houghton Mifflin, 2000).

Christians, will find ways to amass goods for themselves at the expense of the poor and needy of the world under any economic system. We must therefore recognize that all we have is on loan from God and that he calls us to be good stewards of all of it. Precisely because private property is a desirable good, we should work to see that everyone in the world has a fair shot at owning at least enough to live with some decency.

A closer look at James 5:1–6 may be helpful. James employs the literary figure of speech known as "apostrophe" to address rhetorically people who are probably not physically present to hear James's letter read as it circulated among his churches. Here he clearly is speaking about the rich non-Christian, and he is equally clearly warning them about the horrifying judgment that awaits them when Christ returns if they do not repent. What is frightening is to observe what is true in our world that was not the case in James's day—numerous, perhaps even a majority of American Christians living "on earth in luxury and self-indulgence" and fattening themselves "in a day of slaughter" (verse 5).

Lest we think this is referring only to the excessively wealthy, we must observe what made the rich landlords' behavior so heinous in this text: they were growing wealthier at the expense of the impoverished day-laborers (we might call them migrant workers in the U.S. or sweat-shop employees in the Two-Thirds World). In America alone, in the last thirty years, the number of poor and homeless has steadily grown, even as the number of upper middle-class and wealthy has skyrocketed. Abroad, even greater inequities abound. For example, in the mid-1990s Michael Jordan earned more money in promoting shoes for Nike™ than did Nike's entire 18,000 person Indonesian workforce that produced those shoes. But unless Western Christians become more informed and refuse to support companies that act like this, they remain unwitting coconspirators in the very crimes James condemned in his day!

In addition to rebuke, the New Testament contains appropriate instructions for wealthy Christians as they consider giving to kingdom work. Perhaps the most important section of 2 Corinthians 8–9 comes in 8:12–15. Here Paul seems to teach the principle that some have called "the graduated tithe." If ever there were a context in which one would expect a New Testament author to speak about tithing, if Christians were required to give exactly 10% of their income, this would be it. Instead Paul talks about giving "according to your means" (v. 11) and "according to what one has" (v. 12). To what do these expressions refer? Verses 13–15 hint at the answer. Paul is not calling on the more affluent to trade places with the less affluent but wants to create "equality" (vv. 13, 14).

The Greek word used here (*isotes*) could also be translated "that which is fair or equitable." Paul cites the illustration of the Israelites collecting manna in the wilderness. "Equality" for them did not mean that each person collected or consumed the same amount, but that no one had "too much" or "too little." Similarly, Paul does not imagine all Christians having the identical amount of material possessions. But he does recognize that many have unused surplus that qualifies as "too much," while others cannot even meet their basic needs and thus have "too little." To require the poorest of believers in our world today to give ten percent of their income would often just create added hardship for them. To permit affluent believers to give only ten percent would often let them off the hook well before their giving had become truly generous or sacrificial. Thus it seems reasonable to suggest that the implementation of Paul's principles here should call on Christians who earn more than others to give a higher percentage of their income to the Lord's work, including caring for the poor.

First Timothy 5 contains considerable teaching on stewardship that is often overlooked. While much attention is devoted in Christian churches to the "offices" of overseer and deacon dealt with in chapter 3, the similar "office" of widow in chapter 5 is almost never studied. Widows, as examples of the most dispossessed in Paul's world, who have no family members to care for them and who are too old to work, should be supported by the church (vv. 3–5). On the other hand, working-age relatives have the responsibility to provide for elderly or infirm family members. This is the context of verse 8, which thus says nothing about a man having to be the breadwinner for his nuclear family. (The word "anyone" in verse 8 is simply a generic pronoun referring to men and women alike.) That an adult who refuses to obey this command "has denied the faith and is worse than an unbeliever" does not mean they have lost their salvation, merely that they are acting less nobly than the pagan world around them which uniformly recognized this responsibility to care for needy relatives. Contemporary application can take many forms because of the changes in our society and the numerous methods available for providing for the elderly, but it does mean that children have a lifelong responsibility to their parents to see that they are properly taken care of.

A particularly clear example of the principle of moderation comes with God's provision of manna for the Israelites in the wilderness (Exodus 16:18), an episode cited by Paul as he encouraged the Corinthians to greater generosity in the giving (2 Corinthians 8:15). The principle of moderation lies behind the redistribution of property in sabbatical and Jubilee years and behind the prophetic critique of life under the monarchy and aristocracy of Israel. Its reduction of disparity between the 'haves' and 'have-nots' inspired early Christian communalism in Acts and ongoing collection for the poor throughout the New Testament. The principle of moderation explains Jesus' and Paul's concerns to live simply, particularly while engaged in ministry, so as to afford no unnecessary cause for bringing the gospel into disrepute. And it summarizes a large swathe of wisdom literature, particularly as epitomized in Proverbs 30:8: 'Give me neither poverty nor riches.'

Finally, in light of the biblical mandate to give to the poor and moderation, we must not neglect—nor overstate—the biblical example of occasional extravagance. The Song of Solomon primarily discusses the appropriate delights of sexual union within the context of a king's marriage to his beloved. But its picture of their lavish wedding (3:6–11) reminds us that once-in-a-lifetime ceremonies are often proper places for more extravagant expenditures. The question for many Americans, and especially Christians, today is whether the exception has become the norm.

5. Above all, the Bible's teaching about material possessions is inextricably intertwined with more "spiritual" matters.

No one is ever saved by stewardship; all the charitable giving in the world does not make one right with God if a person does not trust in Jesus as Savior and Lord. On the other hand, someone who never gives to the Lord's work or cares for the poor in any way demonstrates that nothing has ever happened in their lives that could qualify as "regeneration." Nor do we find any ungodly poor people exalted as models for emulation. The rich are not necessarily wicked, but frequently surplus goods have led people to imagine that their material resources can secure their futures so that they ignore God, from whom alone comes any true security. That was certainly a recurring trend in ancient Israel. Conversely, when the Jews found themselves in desperate circumstances, they more often than not turned back to God. It has not always been so in the history of humanity, but it frequently has been.

The good news of the kingdom that Jesus proclaimed is consistently "holistic." Jesus was concerned with both body and soul. All the charitable deeds in the world prove meaningless if a person is not a true follower of Christ; that individual will still be damned for all eternity. On the other hand, anyone who professes to be a disciple must demonstrate the reality of that profession by transformed living, including in the areas of personal spending and giving. Different people will experience that transformation in different ways and to different extents, but the person who never displays any concern for the Lord's work and for the poor and who never gives anything to help them by definition is not someone whom the power of the Spirit has touched. So it is wrong to claim, as some do, that Jesus does not envision any rich Christians. But it is correct to observe that the Gospels never depict a well-to-do person who is a genuine believer and yet who is not simultaneously generous in giving of his or her treasure.

In his summary of the sins of the "world"—the fallen nature of contemporary humanity—John lists "the cravings of sinful people, the lust of their eyes and the boasting of what they have and do" (1 John 2:16). The New Living Translation captures these thoughts even more powerfully: "the lust for physical pleasure, the lust for everything we see, and pride in our possessions"! To avoid these powerful forces within each of us, we must give from our surplus. First John 3:17–18 puts it quite bluntly: "If anyone of you has material possessions and sees a brother or sister in need but has no pity on them, how can the love of God be in you? Dear children, let us not love with words or tongue but with actions and in truth."

APPLICATIONS

The possibilities are enormous and the list of what Christians could do nearly endless. But it may help to list a few practical suggestions that most all readers of this essay could implement or implement further (now or in the future).

(1) Maintaining a budget helps people to see where their money is going. The more detailed records we keep, the more we can identify purchases that are not truly necessities so as to free up more money for

our giving. We must beware of our culture's daily attempts to seduce us through advertising into thinking that luxuries are necessities. Many Christians could easily spend less on housing, cars, recreation, home entertainment centers, phone and computer-related technologies, heating and cooling their environments, lawn care, and food (recall our comments in the Introduction on eating out) without sacrificing a generally comfortable lifestyle. Most would be surprised how many additional funds would be freed up for Christ and his kingdom.

(2) Avoiding debt wherever possible should be another priority. Most Americans could live most of their lives without ever owing debts on anything besides property and, at times, cars, or schooling. Credit cards should never be used if a person cannot pay the bills interest-free at the end of a month. Those who have already amassed crippling debts should take whatever action is necessary to implement a realistic plan to get out of debt as quickly as possible; Christian financial counselors can help.

(3) The graduated tithe offers an excellent opportunity for those whom God blesses with growing incomes (above the annual cost-of-living increases) to give higher percentages to the Lord's work. A young person or couple just beginning full-time employment can commit to giving 10%, and, without necessarily following any fixed tables, commit to increasing that percentage as their income grows. Others can start wherever they are and commit to similar increases. Churches should model similar practices. If a congregation is not yet giving 10% of its total income in a year to missions, it could begin with that commitment and then pledge to add 1% a year whenever their income increases.

(4) Christians must choose churches to belong to, in part, on the basis of how those churches spend their money. They should look for congregations that give generously to the poor and to outreach at both home and abroad. Because few churches are ever likely to give enough support to these areas to make enough difference in our world, believers should consider giving to individuals and organizations that more directly help the needy on top of their giving to their churches. Groups like World Vision, Food for the Hungry, Compassion International, and others are particularly successful and reputable organizations in this respect.

CONCLUSION

Countless other possibilities remain. But, in closing, it is worth stressing that attitudes are crucial in all this as well. Does reading an essay like this leave you resentful of the areas of your life into which it has "pried"? If so, it might be good to reflect on all the ways God has been enormously generous with you in your life, above all in providing salvation by grace which we could never have earned. Can we be any less generous in helping others, spiritually and materially? Do you feel a measure of guilt as a result of this study? Some may claim that they are being "manipulated by guilt." If that is the case, then it is important to realize that there is both true guilt and false guilt. If you are already being generous in giving from your surplus, you may need to focus on those portions of Scripture that stress how God gives us material possessions as good gifts for us to enjoy! Relax, put away your false guilt, and delight in God and his goodness. On the other hand, if you realize that there are numerous ways you could free up more money for the Lord and you just haven't been doing it, then guilt is a healthy and biblical motivation. Repent, change your ways, and then you can justifiably "feel good" about yourself!

---

*This essay originally appeared as a booklet produced by College Press Publishing Company.
  Craig L. Blomberg, *Heart, Soul, and Money: A Christian View of Possessions* (Joplin, MO: College Press, 2000).
**Reproduction rights granted by Craig L. Blomberg.

HEART, SOUL, AND MONEY
ESSAY QUESTIONS

Answer the questions below on a separate sheet of paper and be prepared to review your answers in class. Reflection Questions will not be found in the text. These are merely designed to help you start thinking about issues from a worldview perspective.

1. **What biblical evidence is there for the idea that Jesus and his disciples were not likely materially poor?**

> Scripture tells us that Matthew was a tax collector, a business which probably vaulted him into the middle class, though through ill-gotten gain if he resembled others of his day. Similarly, James and John, the sons of Zebedee, may have come from one of the handful of more prosperous fishing businesses, because Mark 1:20 speaks of their family having "hired men." Even households with meager resources often had one servant, rescuing him or her from total poverty, but more than one "employee" in a household suggested some measure of prosperity. And of course Joseph of Arimathea and Nicodemus seem to have been extremely rich (Matt. 27:57; John 19:38–40—the amount of spices used to anoint Jesus' body came close to that used in the burial of kings).
>
> Neither the disciples nor Jesus seemed to permanently divest themselves of all their property. Luke 8:1–3 describes how Jesus and his disciples were supported on the road. Several wealthy women supported them out of their personal means. Peter claims to have left everything, (Mark 10:28), but he will later lead a group of the disciples back to their fishing boats after the resurrection (John 21:3). Jesus says, "The Son of Man has nowhere to lay his head" (Matt. 8:20), but Mary still lived in Nazareth (Joseph may have died by this time) and Jesus himself seems to have had a house in Capernaum (Mark 2:1). [SM p. 246]
>
> *[Ask your students how this subject has affected their thinking regarding Jesus, the disciples, and personal possessions. What does this mean for God's concern for the poor?]*

2. **What are the first two biblical themes discussed by Dr. Blomberg? What are two biblical texts or ideas the author uses to support these themes?**

> **Theme 1**—Material possessions are a good gift from God meant for his people to enjoy
> * God created a world as something good to be enjoyed by all humanity (Genesis 1:4, 10, 12, 18, 21, 25, 31).
> * God promised Israel the land of Canaan with its abundant natural resources, demonstrating his commitment to providing the blessings of the material world as a pre-eminent, good gift for his people (Numbers 14:8).
> * The community of disciples shared their material resources with one another—not so that all will be equally impoverished—but so that there will be "no needy persons among them" (Acts 4:34). Those of us who have more than others should work to help the less fortunate have at least a little more to enjoy.
> * God "richly provides us with everything for our enjoyment" (1 Timothy 6). Paul is no ascetic and Christ does not call a majority of his followers to permanently divest themselves of all of their property. Verse 18 explains how we can enjoy a measure of prosperity with a good conscience—when we are "rich in good deeds," "generous and willing to share."

SM
254

Unit Nine

- Even in the harshest of scenarios, the very luxuries that can lead to the demonic (Revelation 17–18) will be available for all of God's redeemed people in a very material age to come (Revelation 21–22). [SM pp. 247–8]

Theme 2—Material possessions are one of the primary means of turning human hearts away from God
- Adam and Eve coveted the attractive but forbidden fruit of the garden, and everything was corrupted or cursed quickly thereafter. Possession of, or desire for, too many material goods leads to rejection of God, interpersonal hostility, and exploitation or neglect of the poor.
- Property laws of the Torah set limits on the amounts to be accumulated. The celebration of the Jubilee year (Leviticus 25:8–55) alone would have allowed for a family to start afresh once a lifetime (once every 50 years), no matter how irresponsibly they had handled their finances or how far into debt they had fallen.
- The enormous wealth of the monarchy, even though enjoyed by some like David who remained faithful to God, fuelled social injustice and prophetic critique. Ezekiel 22:29, Micah 2:2, and Amos 5:11–12 are three of numerous passages that stress how the rich in Israel were trying to get richer at the expense of the poor.
- Matthew 6:24, the parable of the Sower, and the parable of the Rich Fool (Luke 12:13–21).
- Paul's proclamation, "The love of money is the root of all kinds of evil" (1 Timothy 6:10). In 1 Timothy 3:3 and 8, Paul prohibits church leaders from being lovers of money and pursuing dishonest gain.
- James (4:13–17) rebukes well-to-do believers for planning an entire year or more of their lives without taking God's will into account. They are tempted to think that their material possessions can replace God; that they deserve better treatment than poorer people; and that life can be secured against all crises.
- 2 Peter 2:3,14 and Jude 11 [SM pp. 247–8]

3. **What are the third and fourth biblical themes discussed by Dr. Blomberg? What are two biblical texts or ideas the author uses to support these themes?**

Theme 3—A necessary sign of a life in the process of being redeemed is that of transformation in the area of stewardship

Transformation shows most clearly in one's giving to the work of the Lord (local churches and Christian ministries) and to the poor (directly or through organizations working with the poor). The patriarchs, Job, Boaz, Nehemiah, and Paul are all good examples of people giving some personal resources to others who needed it. The book of James teaches that "faith" without works for the brother and sister lacking basic needs, is not saving faith. [SM pp. 247–8]

Theme 4—There are certain extremes of wealth and poverty which are in and of themselves intolerable.

These vary from person to person and culture to culture but involve, on the one hand, unused and unusable surplus, and on the other hand, the inability to meet even one's basic human needs of adequate food, clothing, shelter, and access to health care. It is one thing to generate income which is then channeled into kingdom purposes (Luke 16:9, 19:11–27); it is quite another to accumulate and hoard resources which are likely to be destroyed or disappear before being put to good use (Luke 16:19–31, James 5:1–6). In the latter case, such a surplus prevents others from having a better opportunity for a reasonably decent standard of living. Such hoarding or accumulation is sin, and if left unchecked proves damning (Luke 12:13–21, 16:19–31). [SM p. 250–52]

4. **In relation to the topic of stewardship, what should one look for when choosing a church?**

Blomberg recommends we look for churches that give generously to the poor and to outreach at both home and abroad. However, he also notes we may never find a church giving 'enough' by our standards, so we can contribute personally to organizations like World Vision, Compassion International, Samaritan's Purse, etc. [SM p. 253]

[Regarding personal finances, see if any of your students feel guilty (refer back to the "Conclusion" section). Is it true, appropriate guilt, or is it false guilt?]

5. **Reflection Question: How do you keep the needs of poor brothers and sisters in mind when we live in a relatively affluent culture?**

What we spend time thinking about will be where we see needs. If we regularly look at things we can buy (e.g., in catalogs, at the mall, or on internet sites) that will be our focus and most likely where our money will go. In order to begin (or continue) thinking about helping the poor, we need to keep the needs of the poor in front of us. To do this, it may be helpful to partner with a local church that serves a poor section of town, or with a homeless shelter, or other local organizations working with the poor. Many opportunities are available internationally. Contact the organizations listed in the article to find out more about receiving regular updates about poor brothers and sisters around the world. Find a missionary working among materially poor Christians in this country or another. Receive their updates and pray for those believers, and as this article points out, if possible, help meet their physical needs.

"RADICAL ENVIRONMENTALISM"
WITH CAL BEISNER

I. Environmentalism

    A.   **Radical Environmentalism**   : Biocentric (nature as central concern)

    B.   **Conventional Environmentalism**   : Anthropocentric (man as central concern)

    "Radical Environmentalism sees life—all biology (human, animal, plant) as a matter of concern—at an equal level. Whereas old line environmentalism saw our responsibility toward nature as a matter of our responsibility toward ourselves. We wanted to conserve resources and preserve beautiful places for… the benefit of future generations. Christian environmentalism should be neither. It should be theocentric."

    C.   **Christian Environmentalism**   : Theocentric (God as central concern)

    "Christian environmentalism should be theocentric (God is at the center of our concern and our responsibility to the world around us stems from God)… then man, and then the rest of creation."

      1. World created for God's enjoyment (Job)

      2. World created for mankind (Psalm 115:16)

II. Types of Radical Environmentalism

    A. Green political parties

      1. Favor socialism as nature's only hope

      2. Work through the political process using legislation, treaties, etc.

      3. Tied to respectable organizations—*Environmental Defense Fund*, *Sierra Club*, etc.

    B. Deep ecologists

      1. Pantheists: All life is fundamentally one

      2. Spiritual and religious (druidism, goddess worship, eastern religions)

      3. Darwinian

      4. Tied to radical organizations—*Green Peace*, *Earth First*, *Sea Shepherds*, etc.

      5.   **Biological Egalitarianism**   : All life is fundamentally equal

      "Man is no more important than any other species and it may well take our species to set things straight." — Dave Foreman, *Earth First* founder

SM
255

C. Animal rights movement

    1. Avoid all killing of animals (for any reason, even food)

    2. Darwinian

    3. No qualitative distinction between species

    4. Assume that animals must have rights if they are to be treated humanely

III. Radical Environmentalism vs. Christianity

A. Population

    1. Radical environmentalists

        i. People are naturally destructive—they consume resources and emit pollutants

        ii. Human population should be reduced

    2. Christianity

        i. People are created in God's image and creative

        ii. Population growth is a blessing

B. Animals

    1. Radical environmentalism

        i. Animals must not be harmed

        ii. Animals and human beings have equal rights to life

    2. Christianity

        i. Animals are for food

        ii. Human beings are created higher than animals

C. Nature

    1. Radical environmentalism

        i. Man is part of nature

        ii. Nature is good and perfect, man is the only destructive element

        iii. Human population must be reduced

2. Christianity

    i. Nature has been given to man to watch over and care for

    ii. Nature was good, but has been cursed

    iii. Man must restore the earth from the curse (part of the great commission)

IV. Summary of Radical Environmentalism

A. All life, including man, is one

B. Man is a part of nature, not above it

C. Man is an intruder on the earth, using up resources and polluting

D. Favor reducing human population

"RADICAL ENVIRONMENTALISM"
WITH CAL BEISNER

Answer the questions below on a separate sheet of paper and be prepared to review your answers in class.

1. **What is radical environmentalism? How are radical environmentalism, conventional environmentalism, and Christian environmentalism different?**

> Radical environmentalism describes a number of fringe environmental movements that tend to regard humanity as a mere animal. Some radical environmentalists resort to non-traditional forms of activism.
>
> *Radical environmentalism* is biocentric—it considers creation to be the central point of concern regarding environmental issues. *Conventional environmentalism* is anthropocentric—it considers humanity to be the central point of concern regarding environmental issues. *Christian environmentalism* is theocentric—it considers God to be the central point of concern regarding environmental issues. Christians therefore recognize that God created the world for his enjoyment and humanity's use. Christians should also realize that God has placed humanity in charge of looking after his creation.

2. **What are three types of radical environmentalism?**

> The first radical environmental movement is the green party. The greenies tend to be less radical than other groups, but favor socialism as the best means of solving environmental concerns. This group attempts to accomplish its ends by working through the political system—legislation, treaties, etc. They are often loosely connected with more respectable environmental groups like *Environmental Defense Fund, Sierra Club*, etc.
>
> The second radical environmental movement is known as deep ecology. This group is religious in nature, instead of political. Most of its followers adhere to some form of pantheism and promote druidism, goddess worship, and the like. This group also tends to be very Darwinian, considering human beings to be evolved animals. Deep ecologists are often connected with more radical environmental groups like *Green Peace, Earth First, Sea Shepherds*, etc.
>
> The third radical environmental movement is the animal rights movement. Like the deep ecologists, this group has been heavily influenced by Darwinism and logically contends that human beings are merely animals. Unlike the deep ecologist, however, the animal rights movement asserts that no animals should ever be harmed, even for food. Animal rights advocates assume that animals will only be treated humanely if they are granted rights similar to those possessed by human beings.

3. **How do radical environmentalism and Christianity differ about population?**

> Radical environmentalism views humanity as a destructive plague only capable of consuming resources and emitting pollutants, so most radical environmentalists want to vastly reduce the human population. The Christian worldview values human beings as bearers of God's image. Christians take God's call to fill and subdue the earth seriously, and consider human population growth a blessing.

SM
258

418 **Unit Nine**

Unit Nine

4. How do radical environmentalism and Christianity differ about animals?

Radical environmentalism views animals and human beings as equal. Animal rights activists contend that no animal should be harmed for any reason (including for food) and that animals and human beings have the same rights to life and happiness. The Christian worldview sees animals as a source of food (since the fall). Christians believe that human beings were created lower than God, but higher than animals.

5. How do radical environmentalism and Christianity differ about nature?

Radical environmentalism views man as merely a part of nature. Nature, however, is often viewed as perfect, while man is viewed as destructive. Christianity views nature as a creation of God distinct from mankind. Christians acknowledge that God has placed human beings in a unique position as stewards of his creation. We likewise recognize that neither nature nor humanity is perfect this side of the Fall. Moreover, God has called humanity to care for the environment as well as use it.

STEWARDSHIP ACTIVITY

Have the students get out a piece of paper, and write down their most treasured possession. If they can't think of one, ask them "If your house were on fire, and you could save only one thing you own, what would it be?" Then tell them that a friend borrowed the thing they just wrote down, and when it was returned it looked like an asteroid had crashed into it. In ten words or less, have them write down their reaction. (It may be entertaining to share these with the class!)

Remind the students that they are stewards—someone who manages another's property or financial affairs. As Christians, we are taking care of the money and possessions that God has loaned to us. Ask the students if they can think of some biblical principles that would apply to how God wants us to deal with our money and possessions. Some examples are:

- Keep your priorities straight—God comes first
  Matthew 6:24–25—You can't serve both God and money
- Don't worry about possessions
  Matthew 6:25ff—God will take care of you
- Use what you are given for God's glory
  Matthew 25:14ff—Parable of the talents
- Give generously back to God
  1 Corinthians 9:6–7—God loves a cheerful giver
- Give generously to others
  Matthew 5:42—If someone asks you, give to him
- Be content with what you have
  Philippians 4:12–13—Paul learned to be content in any circumstance
  1 Timothy 6:6–10—Wanting to be rich and striving after money will ruin you

PRINCIPLES OF A CHRISTIAN ENVIRONMENTAL ETHIC

BY JOHN C. BERGSTROM

"Where do you live?" is a question most people have been asked many times. When answering this question, our automatic response is most likely to think about the place where our homes made out of brick, wood, or stone are located. How would God answer the question of where each one of us lives? What physical home or homes has God given to all people?

The Bible teaches that when we put our faith and trust in Jesus Christ, he will lead us to an eternal heavenly home prepared by God. But, until we are called to live forever with God in our heavenly homes, we must live within the physical homes God has provided for us. These physical homes include the entire planet earth, the various natural environments found on the planet, our towns and cities, and the houses or apartments where we lay our heads down at night to sleep.

Thus, upon further reflection, the question of "Where do you live?" can be answered from a number of different perspectives and is perhaps a much more thought-provoking question than one may initially imagine. The perspective we are most interested in for this paper is the concept of the entire planet earth and different natural environments as places God has deliberately and carefully designed as homes for the people, plants, and animals he has created.

Because we all live on the same planet and are ultimately dependent on the natural fruits of the earth for life-support, everyone has a stake in how elements of nature and natural systems are used and managed. When a specific natural resource or environmental issue or problem arises, individuals and groups often disagree on the appropriate course of action to resolve the issue or problem. At the core of these disagreements are different values and beliefs related to nature itself, and the use and management of nature by people. Scholars in the humanities, social sciences, and physical and biological sciences have emphasized that environmental issues and problems are fundamentally interrelated with ethical issues and problems.[1] Consequently, we are hearing more voices saying that in order to solve environmental issues and problems, people need to develop and follow an appropriate "moral basis" for dealing with nature. This recognizes a basic tenant of human behavior taught in the Bible: true change starts from within a person's heart, mind, and spirit and works outwardly as reflected by attitudes and actions. In all areas of our lives, the substance of our inner faith determines the living out or practice of our faith.

The system of values and beliefs that influences how a persons thinks and acts is known as that person's ethical system or ethics. The purpose of this paper is to discuss three general principles of a Christian environmental ethic and applications of this ethic to natural resource and environmental stewardship. The three general principles of a Christian environmental ethic are: 1) God created and therefore values all of his works of creation (Principle of Creation Value); 2) God created and sustains all elements and systems in his creation within particular orders to meet certain ongoing purposes (Principle of Sustained Order and Purpose); and 3) Everything in the created world and universe is subject to corruption by sin and ultimate redemption through Jesus Christ (Principle of Universal Corruption and Redemption).

CHRISTIAN ENVIRONMENTAL ETHIC PRINCIPLES

The three general principles of a Christian environmental ethic are consistent with a careful study of God's Word found in the Holy Bible as illuminated by a number of historical and recent authors.[2] The meaning and biblical basis for these principles are discussed in more detail in this section.

---

[1] See for example Herman E. Daly, "The Steady-State Economy," *Valuing the Earth: Economics, Ecology, Ethics* (Cambridge, MA: MIT Press, 1993); Paul H. Santmire, *The Travail of Nature* (Philadelphia, PA: Fortress Press, 1985); Francis Schaeffer, *Pollution and the Death of Man: The Christian View of Ecology* (Wheaton, IL: Crossway, 1992); Ruth Goring Stewart, *Environmental Stewardship* (Downers Grove, IL: InterVarsity, 1990); Fred VanDyke, David C. Mahan, Joseph K. Sheldon, and Raymond H. Brand, *Redeeming Creation: The Biblical Basis for Environmental Stewardship* (Downers Grove, IL: InterVarsity, 1996); and Lynn White, Jr., "The Historical Roots of Our Ecological Crisis," *Science*, Volume 155, March 1967, 1203–1207.

[2] See for example Schaeffer, *Pollution and the Death of Man* and VanDyke, et. al., *Redeeming Creation.*

SM
259

420   **Unit Nine**

Principle of Creation Value

The Principle of Creation Value first recognizes that God created the heavens and earth and all things found therein (Genesis 1; Psalm 146:6; Acts 14:15). For example, Revelation 4:11 states: "You are worthy, our Lord and God, to receive glory and honor and power, for you created all things, and by your will they were created and have their being."[3] The Bible also teaches that although God allows people to utilize elements of nature, God retains ownership of all his creation (Psalm 89:11; Leviticus 25:23; Colossians 1:15–16). For example, Psalm 24:1 states; "The earth is the Lord's, and everything in it, the world, and all who live in it."

The Bible teaches that God loves and enjoys all that he has created. Psalm 145:16–17 reads: "You open your hand and satisfy the desires of every living thing. The Lord is righteous in all his ways and loving toward all he has made." Thus, an important implication of the Principle of Creation Value from an ethical standpoint is that God places value on elements of nature independent of human use and human-centered values (Genesis 1:25; Psalm 104:31; Psalm 148:9–13). This God-centered inherent value of nature is termed *theistic intrinsic value.*[4]

Plato's philosophy influenced the Gnostic view of the physical world that arose within the first century Christian church. Followers of Gnosticism taught that the spiritual world contains all that is good, and that everything in the physical or material world is bad.[5] Thus, under Gnosticism, nature would have a negative value and is something that should be disregarded in a person's life.

Christians in the modern church who say that "nature really doesn't matter because it's part of the physical world" are carrying on the heritage of Plato and the Gnostics. This position, which has a very low view of nature's value, is not supported by the Scriptures. As pointed out by Schaeffer,[6] the greatest testimony to the lasting value and importance of the physical world is that Jesus Christ's physical body was resurrected from the dead and exists today in the unseen spiritual world. In the new heaven and earth that God will someday create, Scripture teaches that in addition to Christians being given new, resurrected bodies, nature will also be renewed. As discussed in more detail later in the paper, both people and nature will therefore have existence and value in eternity.

The other extreme position on the value and importance of the physical world and nature that Christians should not fall into is one that improperly elevates the status of nature to being equal to or even above people. The "equality between people and nature" viewpoint in considered first. In modern times, certain secular environmental ethics or philosophies such as "deep ecology" teach that people and nature have equal status and value in the world.[7] Such viewpoints on the parity between people and nature can enter into the church as erroneous teaching.[8] Scripture teaches that although God values nature, he places a special higher value on people who he "crowned with glory and honor" as the climax of his creation (Genesis 1:26–30; Psalm 8:5–8). The "nature above people" viewpoint is considered next.

Romans 1:20–23 states: "For since the creation of the world God's invisible qualities—his eternal power and divine nature—have been clearly seen, being understood from what has been made, so that men are without excuse. For although they knew God, they neither glorified him as God nor gave thanks to him, but their thinking became futile and foolish hearts were darkened. Although they claimed to be wise, they became fools and exchanged the glory of the immortal God for images made to look like mortal man and birds and animals and reptiles." This passage refers to people who knew or at least knew of God but elevated nature to be objects or idols of worship. The worship of anything in nature violates the Second Commandment in which God states: "You shall not make for yourself an idol in the form of anything in heaven above or on the earth beneath or in the waters below. You shall not bow down to them or worship them" (Exodus 20:4–5).

---

[3] All Scripture references are taken from the New International Version (Grand Rapids, MI: Zondervan, 1985).

[4] Christopher B. Barrett and John C. Bergstrom, "The Economics of God's Creation," *Bulletin of the Association of Christian Economists*, Issue 31, Spring 1998, 4–23.

[5] Colin Brown, *Philosophy and the Christian Faith* (Downers Grove, IL: InterVarsity, 1968).

[6] Schaeffer, *Pollution and the Death of Man.*

[7] Donald VanDeVeer and Christine Pierce, *The Environmental Ethics and Policy Book* (Belmont, CA: Wadsworth Pub., 1998).

[8] See for example Kevin L. Burrell, "The Ethics of Environmentalism," *Faith and Practice*, Volume 2, Fall 1996, 16–24; and Tony Campolo, *How to Rescue Earth without Worshiping Nature* (Nashville: Thomas Nelson, 1992).

Principle of Sustained Order and Purpose

The Principle of Sustained Order and Purpose implies that God originally created all elements of nature to fit and function together in an orderly fashion within interrelated systems to meet certain ongoing purposes. God's direct involvement in natural systems did not end after the original creation period described in Genesis 1. The triune God continues to hold together or sustain the functioning of nature, accomplishing his intended order and purpose of all nonliving and living elements of nature and natural systems.

What are the various purposes of nature according to the Bible? One of the reasons God created and continues to sustain nature, as discussed above under the Principle of Creation Value, is for God himself to love and enjoy. Another purpose is to help meet people's needs such as food and shelter (Genesis 2:15; Genesis 9:3). A third major purpose of nature is to glorify and reveal God to people everywhere (Psalm 19:1–4; Romans 1:18–20). For example, Psalm 19:14 states: "The heavens declare the glory of God; the skies proclaim the work of his hands. Day after day they pour forth speech; night after night they display knowledge. There is no speech or language where their voice is not heard. Their voice goes out into all the earth, their words to the ends of the world."

To meet their intended purposes, God created and sustains all of creation within particular orders. The first large-scale Creation ordering of interest is the biblical hierarchy between God, people, and nature. Understanding and applying a Christian environmental ethic requires a proper interpretation of Biblical verses establishing and describing this basic hierarchy. A key verse is Genesis 1:28, which states: "So God created man in his own image, in the image of God he created him, male and female he created them. God blessed them and said to them, 'Be fruitful and increase in number; fill the earth and subdue it. Rule over the fish of the sea and the birds of the air and over every living creature that moves on the ground.'"

Genesis 1:28 establishes that in God's basic ordering of Creation, people have dominion over nature. However, this verse also clearly states that people are creations of God. As creations of God, people are under the authority or dominion of God. Thus, from the perspective of God's authority and control, people and nature are in the same class or order—all of Creation, including people, must submit to God's plans and ways. The basic biblical relationships and ordering between God, people, and nature are illustrated in Figure 1. A similar illustration is provided and discussed by Schaeffer.[9]

Figure 1. Principle of Sustained Order and Purpose
General Biblical Hierarchy

God

People

Nature

The Created World

In Figure 1, it is first shown that there is a fundamental separation between God and his creation including people. God is above people and nature and both people and elements of nature such as plants and animals must interact and live together within the same created world governed by God's ways and plans. Thus, people share a common heritage and bond with plants, animals, and other elements of nature as fellow creations of God. People, like plants and animals, must also cope with living in a physical world and universe created and controlled by God.

The diagram also illustrates that within the physical world and universe, people are above nature. People are above nature by the grace and will of God only—not by our own power and ingenuity. God created people in his image to exercise Godly dominion over nature. Godly dominion over nature, as discussed in more detail later in the paper, means that people act as stewards or caretakers of nature who are ultimately responsible to God for their use and management of nature.

---

[9] Schaeffer, *Pollution and the Death of Man.*

In addition to the major large-scale relationships or orders between God, people, and nature illustrated in Figure 1, God created and sustains elements of nature within particular orders to meet deliberate purposes. The food chain system shown in Figure 2 illustrates how living and nonliving elements of nature in an ecosystem fit and function together to provide life-support for each other.

Figure 2. God's Order within Nature:
Simple Food Chain or System

As illustrated in Figure 2, living plants take nutrients from the soil. Herbivores such as rabbits or deer eat plants for food. Carnivores such as mountain lions eat other animals for food. When plants and animals die, microorganisms in the environment decompose the plant and animal body material into basic chemicals that go back into the soil. These chemicals are then taken up by plants for nutrients completing the cycling of life-supporting chemicals through the environment.

People are also dependent on the food chain and chemical cycling systems illustrated in Figure 2. The linkages and interrelationships between people and elements of nature and natural systems are illustrated at a broader scale in Figure 3. Figure 3 illustrates the planet earth home God has provided for all of us, and the global interrelationships between people and nature.

Figure 3. Global Interrelationships between
People and Nature on God's Earth

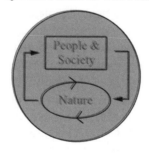

The scientific study of natural life-support systems falls under the realm of ecology. The word ecology is derived from the Greek root words *eco-* meaning "house" and *-logy* meaning "study." Ecology can therefore be literally interpreted to mean "house study" or the "study of the house." The "house" being referred to here is the planet earth and its natural systems. Before describing how the earth's natural systems provide life-support, consider the artificial life-support systems that people build into the various dwellings we call home at a small scale.

The actual physical dwellings in which we live were constructed by people with certain life-support systems in mind. These artificial life-support systems include: air circulation systems to regulate oxygen (O_2) and carbon dioxide (CO_2) levels so that indoor air is healthy to breathe; water systems to provide safe and secure drinking water supplies; heating and cooling systems to regulate indoor temperatures at healthy levels; and waste disposal systems that help to prevent illness by safely and regularly removing potential germ-producing human wastes and garbage.

The planet earth and different environments such as forests, deserts, oceans, lakes, and rivers were created by God with natural life-support systems in his mind and design. God built several major chemical cycles into our planet earth home. Each of these cycles helps to provide all that is needed to support life on earth. For example, the carbon and oxygen cycle helps to provide breathable air and regulate global temperatures at livable levels. The hydrologic cycle helps to provide water to drink and for a multitude of other purposes.

The different chemical cycles also contribute to the provision of mineral resources such as coal, oil, and natural gas that we use as fuel for transportation, electricity, and heating. These cycles also support renewable resources such as trees and fish and wildlife. We use trees for consumptive uses such as lumber and to support non-consumptive uses such as recreation and aesthetic enjoyment. We use fish and wildlife for consumptive uses such as harvesting ocean fish for food and hunting of wildlife on public and private lands. We also use fish and wildlife for non-consumptive recreational uses and aesthetic enjoyment such as wildlife observation and photography.[10]

When people use elements of nature for commercial production and consumption, and even recreational and aesthetic enjoyment, some level of waste by-products enter the environment. Smokestacks into the air and effluent discharge pipes into rivers are obvious evidence of these waste by-products. When people use a forest or park for recreation, waste by-products are emitted into the air from automobiles, RVs, ATVs and motorboats. Solid wastes in the form of litter are also often left behind. God has built waste assimilation and treatment capabilities into natural systems. For example, scientists have documented the natural ability of wetlands to filter chemicals out of water that are potentially harmful to human health. However, excessive use of a particular natural system such as a wetland area by people for waste by-product disposal may threaten the continued ability of that natural system to assimilate and treat wastes.

The God-given role of people as caretakers or managers of elements of nature and natural systems is illustrated through several linkages. People manage nature, for example, by cultivating the land to grow and harvest crops for food through agriculture and to grow and harvest trees for wood products through forestry. People manage lakes and rivers for producing electricity, providing drinking water and supporting many types of recreational activities such as boating and swimming. People may also be involved in managing entire ecosystems to provide fish and wildlife habitat and other broad environmental services such as protection of regional air and water quality or even regulation of global climate.

People also manage nature through waste and pollution management and policy. For example, people design and build waste treatment facilities to filter harmful materials out of human sewage waste water before the water is discharged into the environment. People also design and implement "best management practices" for reducing waste run-off from construction sites, farms, and forest and mining operations. Other people are trained and hired to develop and enforce policies and laws for regulating the discharge or emissions of waste by-products into the environment from a variety of sources including point sources (e.g., manufacturing plants) and non-point sources (e.g., automobiles).

This section discussing the Principle of Sustained Order and Purpose has emphasized that God created people and nature with order and purpose. In God's ordering, people are over nature, meaning that people may take from nature to meet their needs. However, God also expects people to give back to nature, as one of God's intended purposes for people is to act as responsible caretakers of nature.

Principle of Universal Corruption and Redemption

The Principle of Universal Corruption and Redemption has familiar implications with respect to the relationship between men and women created in God's image by God their Creator. The Scriptures are clear that all men and women have sinned and fall short of God's expectations for a righteous life. Thus, we are all in need of forgiveness and saving faith through a personal relationship with Jesus Christ (1 John 1:8–9). The Scriptures also teach that all of creation has been corrupted by sin (Romans 8:20–22). The effects of this universal corruption include not just separation of people from God, but also separation of people from themselves, each other, and nature.

The separation of people from nature as a result of sin entering the world at the time of the Fall of Mankind taught in the Bible (Genesis 3) is of particular interest to the topic of this paper. First, this separation

---

[10] Barrett and Bergstrom. "The Economics of God's Creation."

occurs at a physical level. Nature provides beneficial services to people, but since the Fall nature can also be the source of physical harm to people; the physical harm caused by tornadoes and hurricanes is a graphic example. The Fall also has resulted in a spiritual separation between people and nature. Prior to the Fall, God, people, and nature had close spiritual fellowship with each other. The introduction of sin into the world and its corrupting effects on all of God's created works broke apart this fellowship.

For people, forgiveness and saving faith through Jesus Christ assures personal redemption of the believer before God, and restoration of the believer's relationship and fellowship with God. Scripture teaches that God will also redeem nature and restore the relationship and fellowship between God, people, and nature in the eternal world. God's plan for redeeming nature is reflected in the creation covenant.[11] The creation covenant is God's promise to redeem, restore, and renew the physical world in the new heaven and earth that he will create when the earth we now call home no longer exists (2 Peter 3:13; Revelation 21:1).

In the New Testament, Romans 8:19–23 speaks to the creation covenant, saying: "For the creation waits in eager expectation for the sons of God to be revealed. For the creation was subjected to frustration, not by its own choice, but by the will of the one who subjected it, in hope that the creation itself will be liberated from its bondage to decay and brought into the glorious freedom of the children of God. We know that the whole creation has been groaning as in the pains of childbirth right up to the present time. Not only so, but we ourselves, who have the firstfruits of the Spirit, groan inwardly as we wait eagerly for our adoption as sons, the redemption of our bodies." This passage teaches that the physical universe including nature is not destined for eternal destruction when the world we now live in ends when Jesus Christ returns. Rather, when God gives Believers new bodies in the new heaven and earth, He will also provide a new beginning for nature and rest of the physical world.

In the new heaven and earth, nature will be restored to its pre-Fall magnificence and perfection. In this new Creation of God, both people and nature will be freed from the sufferings caused by the imperfections of the world we live in today, including death and decay. People and nature will also no longer battle against each other as so often is the case in our world today.

In the Old Testament, there is a precedent for divine covenants or promises that incorporate nature. Consider, for example, this passage from Genesis 9: "Then God said to Noah and to his sons with him: 'I now establish my covenant with you and with your descendants after you and with every living creature that was with you—the birds, the livestock and all the wild animals, all those that came out of the ark with you—every living creature on earth. I establish my covenant with you: Never again will all life be cut off by the waters of a flood; never again will there be a flood to destroy the earth'" (Genesis 9:8–11). The beautiful natural rainbow is God's sign and reminder of His covenant with Noah not to destroy life on earth again with a great flood. This covenant clearly includes plants and animals and every "living creature on earth."

The creation covenant referred to in Romans 8 can be thought of as an extension of God's covenant with Noah that includes a promise to protect and sustain both people and nature. God's concern for protecting and sustaining all living creatures was illustrated by Jesus Christ who, when speaking about sparrows, said that "not one of them will fall to the ground apart from the will of your Father" (Matthew 10:29). Providing for the continued and restored existence of nature in the new heaven and earth is consistent with what the Bible teaches about God's love and concern for all of his large and small works of Creation.

PRACTICING A CHRISTIAN ENVIRONMENTAL ETHIC THROUGH STEWARDSHIP

The three general principles of a Christian environmental ethic have practical implications for the role of people as caretakers or managers of nature. The Bible teaches that as caretakers or managers of nature, people are to practice good stewardship. The words "steward" and "stewardship" are used throughout the Old and New Testaments (Genesis 15:2, 44:1; 1 Chronicles 28:1; Matthew 20:8; 1 Corinthians 4:2; Luke 12:42, 16:1–2). The word used for steward in the Bible can also be interpreted as manager or servant.

When the word for steward (manager, servant) is used in the Bible, it refers to a person who is put in charge of taking care of something that does not belong to him or her. This meaning is consistent with the *Webster's Dictionary* definition of a steward as "one employed in a large household or estate to manage domestic concerns." As stewards of nature, people have been appointed by God to manage the "domestic environmental concerns" of our planet earth home.

[11] See again Schaeffer, *Pollution and the Death of Man* and VanDyke, et al, *Redeeming Creation*.

According to the Bible, general characteristics and responsibilities of a steward include being faithful, wise, and responsible. The steward should be concerned with meeting daily needs and is not to abuse or waste what he or she has been put in charge of managing. The steward is to maintain self-control (not overindulging), be a "problem-solver," and follow the household or estate owner's wishes and instructions with respect to management (Luke 12:42–46, 16:1–9).

How are stewards held accountable according to the Bible? Proper management actions are rewarded with "true riches" (spiritual riches). Improper actions are punished (something is taken away). Stewards in charge of more are held more accountable, especially if they do wrong when they know better.

Stewardship and the Principle of Creation Value

Under the Principle of Creation Value, all of God's creations are important and valuable to God. People hold a special particular value to God as living beings created in his image (Genesis 1:26–30). Part of God's provision for the well-being of people is the use of plants, animals, minerals and other elements of nature for meeting our material needs. These uses, for example, include farming the land to meet food and fiber needs and harvesting trees from forests to meet wood product needs.

When using elements of nature for human benefit, the Christian environmental steward keeps in mind that all of creation ultimately belongs to God and is valuable to God independent of human use. This knowledge, when put into practice, means that the Christian environmental steward respects and even loves elements of nature out of respect and love for their Creator, the Triune God—Father, Son and Holy Spirit.

Godly respect and love for elements of nature leads the Christian environmental steward to be a responsible caretaker of nature who does not abuse or misuse what has been entrusted into his or her care by God. The Christian steward or manager of a farm, forest, park or natural area, for example, would not deliberately kill plants and animals under his or care without good reason. Although the Christian environmental steward demonstrates Godly love and care for nature, he or she does not worship nature, only God who is its Creator.

Stewardship and the Principle of Sustained Order and Purpose

Genesis 1 establishes that although both people and nature are created works of God and under God's authority, God has given people dominion over nature. But, how are people to exercise this dominion? God created people in his own image—as his representatives on earth. Because we are under God's authority in all things, we are to do God's will when exercising our dominion over nature.

In Genesis 1:28, God tells people to subdue nature. The word "subdue" is translated from the Hebrew word *kabash*, which means to make to serve, by force if necessary. But "subdue" does not mean "abuse," just as the phrase "rule over" in the Bible does not mean "exercise tyranny over." Some specific instructions pertaining to managing nature are given in Genesis 2:15, which says, "The Lord God took the man and put him in the Garden of Eden to work it and take care of it." The phrase "to work it" means "to till it" or "to cultivate it," and the general meaning is to use productively. The phrase to "take care of it" means "to keep," "to guard," or "to exercise great care over." The intent of "keeping, guarding, caring over" is to sustain the function for which the element of nature or natural system being cared for was originally designed. Sustaining the original God-designed functions of nature is a very important objective from theological, ethical, and practical standpoints.

In summary, the "good steward" according to the Bible will manage nature in a wise, self-controlled, and non-wasteful manner, always taking care to sustain the original functions of elements of nature and natural systems. The "poor steward," in contrast, lacks self-control, is wasteful and irresponsible, and cannot be trusted to take proper care of what he or she has been put in charge of managing. The "poor steward" allows the original functions of elements of nature or natural systems to be degraded or ruined.

In the "natural economy" of God's creation, human use and management of natural environments can have positive or negative consequences. Negative consequences of poor use and management can be illustrated by thinking about the end results of not properly maintaining the life-support systems built into a house or apartment building. The most serious consequence of this poor management is that the health and well-being of the dwelling's occupants would likely suffer. In extreme cases, such as when improper use or management of heating equipment allows CO_2 in the indoor air to build up to unhealthy levels, death of the dwelling's occupants may result.

If we misuse and mismanage nature, the ability of nature to support provision of goods and commodities of consumptive or non-consumptive value to people may be significantly reduced. In extreme cases, essential life-support systems may be degraded to the point that plant, animal, and human health and life are seriously threatened.[12] However, if we use and manage nature properly as God expects us to, natural systems can continue to provide essential life-support services and various goods and commodities of consumptive or non-consumptive value to people.

Unfortunately, the poor management or stewardship model often describes how men and women of the world improperly exercise their dominion over nature. An example of poor stewardship from agriculture is farming a tract of land until the soil is totally "burned out" and incapable of further production. An example from forestry is over-harvesting a forest so that new trees can no longer be grown. Exceeding the capacity of air and water resources to absorb and disperse pollution so that air and water become unsafe to consume is an example of poor stewardship in the environmental pollution management area.

The Christian environmental steward understands that the elements of nature or natural systems that he or she may be involved in using or managing are ultimately controlled by God according to his ways and plans. Whether he or she is involved in the use and management of farmland, forestland, parks, natural areas, or air and water resources on a large scale, the Christian environmental steward realizes that human uses and management of nature that run counter to God's ways and plans are detrimental to nature and ultimately to people. There is also a realization that whenever we go our own way rather than following God, he is grieved by our actions.

To carry out his or her responsibilities, the Christian environmental steward attempts to learn as much as he or she can about the God-intended order and purpose of nature. This effort includes learning about individual elements of nature, and how these elements of nature function within natural systems created and sustained by God. The Christian environmental steward puts this knowledge into practice by doing his or her best to use and manage nature within the boundaries of God's ways and plans.

Stewardship and the Principle of Universal Corruption and Redemption

An important overarching implication of the Principle of Universal Corruption and Redemption for the practice of Christian environmental stewardship is that everyone who is involved in the study, use, and management of nature is corrupted by sin. Dealing with the effects of sin in our own lives and the lives of others represents a major challenge to Christians involved in the use and care of nature through education, administration or direct management in the field. To effectively meet this challenge, the Christian manager of nature applies Biblical values and guidance to manage both nature and people in a positive manner.

The Christian environmental steward also acknowledges that God will redeem both people and nature in the new heaven and earth. Knowing that God intends one day to redeem nature (rather than completely destroy it, as some in the church today may think) should motivate Christians to view and act differently towards nature. Christians should also be involved as much as possible in the process of redeeming nature here and now on earth as an expression of our own redemption and salvation and the "living out" of our faith (Philippians 2:12–13; James 2:14–25). In the case of a Christian forester or ecologist, for example, being involved in the restoration of a healthy forest ecosystem is consistent with and honors God's ultimate plan for redeeming nature. In contrast, being responsible for widespread and complete destruction of a particular forest ecosystem does not seem consistent with nor honors God's plan for redeeming nature.

PRINCIPLES AND PRACTICE OF A CHRISTIAN ENVIRONMENTAL ETHIC: CONCLUSIONS

We are faced in the world today with many natural resource and environmental issues and problems. There are issues and problems related to managing nature and the natural resources provided by nature to provide food for eating, paper for writing, lumber for construction, and areas for people to participate in outdoor recreation and experience aesthetic enjoyment of nature. There are issues and problems related to protecting nature from many sources of degradation or damage by people.[13] If nature is degraded or damaged by people (or even by itself), there are issues and problems related to how to go about repairing or mitigating the environmental damage.

---

[12] Calvin B. DeWitt, "Seven Degradations of Creation," *Perspectives* (February 1989), 4–8.
[13] Ibid.

Christians are in a unique position to offer thoughtful solutions to the natural resource and environmental problems and issues we face in the world today. As mentioned at the beginning of this paper, there is growing recognition on the part of people from a variety of professional and personal backgrounds that effective, long-term solutions to natural resource and environmental problems and issues requires an appropriate moral basis for action. God's word found in the Holy Bible provides this moral basis in the form of a Christian environmental ethic that results in responsible and caring stewardship of all of God's creation.

The foundation of a Christian environmental ethic are the Principle of Creation Value, the Principle of Sustained Order and Purpose, and the Principle of Universal Corruption and Redemption. To practice effective Christian environmental stewardship, we must work on increasing our knowledge of these principles from biblical, scientific and practical policy and management perspectives. But stale book knowledge of these principles is not enough to get the job done.

In Romans 12:2, the Apostle Paul says, "Do not conform any longer to the pattern of this world, but be transformed by the renewing of your mind. Then you will be able to test and approve what God's will is—his good, pleasing and perfect will." This passage implies that before we can effectively manage or take care of nature according to God's ways and plans, we must renew our minds. This renewal process first requires that we become new persons through a personal relationship with Jesus Christ as Savior and Lord. As it is said in the Scriptures, "if anyone is in Christ, he is a new creation; the old has gone, the new has come!" (2 Corinthians 5:17).

Once we have become a new creation or person in Christ, our minds and thinking can be and are renewed in many areas of our lives. In the area of environmental stewardship, a deep personal understanding of the way God loves and sustains all of His creation gives us a new and proper perspective of the temporal and eternal value and purposes of nature. This understanding, when taken to heart, transforms how we view and carry out our God-given role as caretakers of nature.

Christian caretakers of nature may be farmers, foresters, or fishermen who manage and harvest the land and waters of the earth in a productive and sustainable manner. They may be professional biologists, botanists, ecologists, or other environmental scientists who study nature and develop scientific solutions to problems and challenges related to managing specific parts of nature or entire natural systems. They may be toxicologists or other human health specialists who study the effects of environmental pollutants on people in order to develop waste management and pollution control strategies that protect and maintain our health and quality of life.

Christian caretakers of nature may be professional economists, sociologists, or political scientists who study economic and social systems in order to help solve problems and challenges related to people's use of natural resources and impacts on the environment. They may also be philosophers or theologians who help us to understand the proper biblical perspectives on the worth and purposes of people and nature. Professors at colleges and universities and teachers at secondary schools can also be Christian caretakers of nature through teaching, research, and public service activities that focus on providing needed information and equipping others to meet natural resource and environmental problems and challenges now and in the future in a Christian manner.

The above listing of possible professions of Christian caretakers of nature is meant to be illustrative, not exhaustive. The fact of the matter is that every Christian can and should be a Christian caretaker of nature no matter what his or her vocation or position in life happens to be. What characteristics distinguish the Christian caretaker of nature from others involved in the caring for and managing of nature? The proper model for the stewardship of nature from a biblical perspective is the Christian stewardship model (Genesis 2; Luke 12:16).

The Christian steward of nature first recognizes that nature, like everything else in heaven and earth, was created by God, belongs to God, and is valued by God for itself. The Christian steward helps to utilize nature as God intended in the service of both God and people. When making use of nature, the Christian steward recognizes that he or she has a responsibility to manage or take care of nature in a way that is not wasteful or destructive of the original functions of nature designed by God.

The Christian steward respects plants, animals, and other elements of nature in their created order out of respect for the Triune God—Father, Son and Holy Spirit—who created and continues to sustain the entire earth and universe. The Christian steward also respects and values nature because he or she knows that both people and nature will share in redemption and renewal in the new eternal heaven and earth. Respecting and valuing nature never makes nature the object of a Christian steward's worship. Rather, credit and honor and worship always go to the Creator of nature and not nature itself in the same way that credit and honor for a magnificent piece of art work do not go to the artwork itself, but to the artist who created it.

---

*This essay originally appeared on the *LeaderU* website:
    John C. Bergstrom, "Principles of an Christian Environmental Ethic."
**Reproduction rights granted by John C. Bergstrom.

PRINCIPLES OF A
CHRISTIAN ENVIRONMENTAL ETHIC
BY JOHN C. BERGSTROM

Answer the questions below on a separate sheet of paper and be prepared to review your answers in class.

1. What is the Principle of Creation Value?

> The Principle of Creation Value simply states that creation has a value to God. This can be subdivided into three points. First, we, as God's people, must recognize that God created all—both man and nature (Genesis 1; Psalm 146:6; Acts 14:15; Revelation 4:11). Second, although God allows people to utilize elements of nature, he alone retains ownership of his creation (Psalm 24:1; Psalm 89:11; Leviticus 25:23; Colossians 1:15–16). Third, God places value on elements of nature independent of human use and human-centered values, i.e. nature has intrinsic value apart from its utilitarian value (Genesis 1:25; Psalm 104:31, 148:9–13). [SM pp. 260–1]

2. What are three non-biblical views of nature?

> The first non-biblical viewpoint asserts that nature doesn't really matter. This view finds its roots in Gnosticism—an early church heresy that still plagues us today. One core belief of the Gnostics was that the spiritual world contains all that is good and the physical world (or nature) all that is evil. Those in the modern church who say nature doesn't matter because it is part of the physical world are carrying on the heritage of the Gnostics. Scripture does not support this position. In fact, the greatest testimony to the contrary is the lasting value and importance the physical world played in the person of Jesus Christ. He was born, lived, and died a human being in a physical body, which was resurrected from the dead and exists today in the unseen spiritual world. Furthermore, in the new heaven and earth that God will someday create, Scripture teaches that in addition to Christians being given resurrection bodies, nature will also be renewed.
>
> A second position is that of deep ecology, which maintains that people and nature have equal status and value in the world. Although Scripture teaches that God values nature, he places a much higher value on humanity (Genesis 1:26–30; Psalm 8:5–8).
>
> A third position places nature above humanity and indeed equal to God. Romans 1:20–23 refers to people who knew of God, but worship nature in place of its creator. The worship of anything in nature violates the Second Commandment, in which God states, "You shall not make for yourself an idol in the form of anything in heaven above or on the earth beneath or in the waters below. You shall not bow down to them or worship them" (Exodus 20:4–5, NIV). [SM pp. 260–1]

3. What is the Principle of Sustained Order and Purpose?

> The Principle of Sustained Order and Purpose states that God originally created all elements of nature to function together in an orderly fashion within interrelated systems to meet certain ongoing purposes. In other words, God has a continued interest in his creation. This can be subdivided into

three purposes. First, God enjoys and loves his creation. Second, it provides for the physical needs of humanity through such things as food, water, and shelter (Genesis 2:15, 9:3). Third, nature reveals some of the glories of God to people everywhere (Psalm 19:1–4; Romans 1:18–20).

God created people and nature with an intended order and purpose. God set people above nature, meaning that we may take from nature to meet our needs. However, God also expects people to give back to nature, as one of God's intended purposes is for us to act as responsible caretakers of nature. [SM pp. 261–4]

4. What is the hierarchy between God, people, and nature?

There is a fundamental separation between God and his creation. Genesis 1:28 establishes that in God's basic ordering of creation people have dominion over nature. However, Genesis 1:28 also clearly states that people are creations of God and thus are under the authority or dominion of God. Therefore, God has dominion over his entire creation, and he has granted people dominion over nature. People are only above nature by the grace and will of God, not by our own power and ingenuity. We are granted the right and responsibility to be caretakers of nature. [SM pp. 261–2]

5. How do people manage nature?

Our God-given role to be caretakers or managers of nature and natural systems is illustrated through several linkages. People manage nature, for example, by cultivating the land to provide crops for food through agriculture and trees for wood products through forestry. People manage lakes and rivers to produce electricity, provide drinking water, and support many types of recreational activities such as boating and swimming. People may also be involved in managing entire ecosystems to maintain fish and wildlife habitats and other broad environmental services, such as protection of regional air and water quality or regulation of global climate.

People also manage nature through waste and pollution management. For example, people design and build waste treatment facilities to filter harmful materials out of wastewater before it is discharged into the environment. People also design and implement "best management practices" for reducing waste runoff from construction sites, farms, and forestry and mining operations. Other people are trained to develop and enforce policies for regulating the discharge or emissions of waste by-products into the environment from a variety of sources, including point sources (e.g., manufacturing plants) and non-point sources (e.g., automobiles). [SM pp. 263–4]

6. What is the Principle of Universal Corruption and Redemption?

The Scriptures are clear that all human beings have sinned and fall short of God's expectations for a righteous life. Thus, we are all in need of forgiveness and saving faith through a personal relationship with Jesus Christ (1 John 1:8–9). The Scriptures also teach that all of creation has been corrupted by sin (Romans 8:20–22). The effects of this universal corruption include not just separation from God, but also the separation of people from themselves, each other, and nature.

Nature provides beneficial services to people, but since the Fall nature can also be the source of physical harm to people—tornadoes and hurricanes are graphic examples of this. The Fall has also resulted in a spiritual separation between people and nature. Prior to the Fall, God, people, and nature had close spiritual fellowship with each other. The introduction of sin into the world and its corrupting effects on all of God's created works broke apart this fellowship.

For people, forgiveness and saving faith through Jesus Christ assures personal redemption of the believer before God and restoration of the believer's relationship and fellowship with God. Scripture teaches that he will also redeem nature and restore the relationship and fellowship between himself, people, and nature in the eternal world (Romans 8:20–23). [SM pp. 264–5]

7. **What does it mean to be a steward?**

The Bible teaches that as caretakers or managers of nature, people are to practice good stewardship. The words "steward" and "stewardship" are used throughout the Old and New Testaments of the Bible (Genesis 15:2, 44:1; 1 Chronicles 28:1; Matthew 20:8; 1 Corinthians 4:2; Luke 12:42, 16:1–2). The word used for steward in the Bible can also be interpreted as manager or servant. When this term is used in the Bible, it refers to a person who is given the responsibility of taking care of something that does not belong to him or her. As stewards of nature, people have been appointed by God to manage the "domestic environmental concerns" of our planet.

According to the Bible, general characteristics and responsibilities of a steward include being faithful, wise, and responsible. The steward should be concerned with meeting daily needs and is not to abuse or waste what he or she has been put in charge of managing. The steward should maintain self-control (not overindulge), be a "problem-solver," and follow the household or estate owner's wishes and instructions (Luke 12:42–46, 16:1–9). [SM pp. 265–7]

8. **How can we practice stewardship in relation to the Principle of Creation Value?**

When using elements of nature for human benefit, the Christian environmental steward should keep in mind that all of creation ultimately belongs to God and is valuable to him independent of human use. This knowledge, when put into practice, means that the Christian environmental steward respects and even loves elements of nature out of respect and love for their Creator, the Triune God—Father, Son, and Holy Spirit. Godly respect and love for nature leads the Christian agricultural, forestry, or environmental manager to be a responsible caretaker who does not abuse or misuse what has been entrusted by God into his or her care. A Christian who manages a farm, forest, park, or natural area, for example, would not deliberately kill plants and animals under his care without good reason. Although the Christian environmental steward demonstrates godly love and care for nature, he or she does not worship nature, but gives all glory to God as its Creator. [SM p. 265]

9. **How can we practice stewardship in relation to the Principle of Sustained Order and Purpose?**

The biblical principle of stewardship states that people should manage nature in a wise, self-controlled, and non-wasteful manner, always taking care to sustain the original functions of the natural systems. In contrast, a poor steward lacks self-control, is wasteful and irresponsible, and cannot be trusted to take proper care of what he or she has been put in charge of managing.

Unfortunately, human beings often improperly exercise their dominion over nature. An example of poor stewardship from agriculture is farming a tract of land until the soil is totally "burned out" and incapable of further production. An example from forestry is over-harvesting and mismanaging a forest so that new trees can no longer be grown. Exceeding the capacity of natural resources to absorb and disperse pollution so that air and water become unsafe is an example of poor stewardship in the area of pollution management.

The Christian environmental steward understands that God ultimately controls natural systems they may use or manage according to God's ways and plans. Whether involved in the management of farmland, forestland, parks, natural areas, or air and water resources at a large-scale, the Christian environmental steward realizes that human uses for nature that run counter to God's ways and plans are detrimental to both the world and themselves. There is also a realization that whenever we go our own way, rather than following God, he is grieved by our actions. [SM pp. 265–6]

10. How can we practice stewardship in relation to the Principle of Universal Corruption and Redemption?

The Christian environmental steward acknowledges that everyone who is involved in the study, use, and management of nature is corrupted by sin. The effects of sin in our lives and the lives of others represent a major challenge to Christians involved in the use and care of nature. To effectively meet this challenge, the Christian manager of nature applies biblical values and guidance to direct both nature and people in a positive manner.

The Christian environmental steward also acknowledges that God will redeem both people and nature in the new heaven and earth. Knowing that God intends one day to redeem nature rather than completely destroy it, as some in the church today may think, should motivate Christians to act differently towards nature. Just as Christians should be actively involved in their own process of redemption by "living out their faith," they should also be involved as much as possible in the process of redeeming nature here on earth. In the case of a Christian forester or ecologist, being involved in the restoration of a healthy forest ecosystem is consistent with God's ultimate plan for redeeming nature. In contrast, being responsible for widespread destruction of a particular forest ecosystem does not honor God's plan. [SM pp. 266–7]

STEWARDSHIP ACTIVITY

As we have seen, Christians are called to be stewards. This call doesn't just affect how we deal with the earth, or use our money, but how we react to every resource we have been given. If we have an attitude of stewardship in every area of life, that will carry over into our treatment of the environment.

For this exercise, explain the idea above to the students, and then distribute the "How Do You Rate?" handout found on the *Teacher's CD-ROM* in the "Handouts" folder. Have the students list their resources in each of the categories indicated. In the next column, have them rate their stewardship of the resource on a scale from 1–10, with "10" meaning they are taking the best possible care of that resource, or using it in the best possible way, or striving for excellence every time they use it. "1" means they couldn't really care less about it. In the final column, the student should write down one thing they can do that would raise their "Stewardship Rating" in that category into the 7–10 range. If their rating is already there in that category, they should note one thing that would send them into the 10+ category!

"THE DANGEROUS SAMARITAN"
WITH MICHAEL BAUMAN

"If you are a Christian, you have an interest in aiding the poor wisely. That is a harder job than you might think it is, because when it comes to aiding the poor, good intentions are not enough."

"If you want to do the right thing, you must learn to think with your head and not just your heart. Good public policy comes from clear thinking."

I. Minimum Wage Laws

"We forget that a wage is not just a selling price for a worker; it is a purchase price for an employer. So we pass laws that prevent the least desirable workers from selling their services at a price that prospective employers (and ultimately you the consumer) can afford to pay."

    A. <u>Artificially</u> high prices forces consumers to look elsewhere (e.g. $30k Fords)

    "When you put an artificially high price on someone's service, you put them out of business. You make it impossible for them to get a job, because no one is going to want to pay that price for their service."

    B. Ultimately harms rather than helps

        1. Forces wage raises all the way up the corporate ladder

        2. Forces an increase in the price of the company's product

        3. The consumers may no longer want to buy the product

        4. The company may be forced out of business

        5. Minimum wage laws always lead to greater unemployment

    C. Good examples are Ray Croc and Dave Thomas

        1. Provide fast food for the poor

        2. Provide job opportunities for the poor

        3. Provide an opportunity for skills

        "You can't make a career flipping hamburgers, but you can start a career by flipping hamburgers. Because you get those important marketplace skills like punctuality, teamwork, appearance, deference, accuracy, dependability—you can get all those skills plus gain a reference and a little money to boot."

        "12 percent (almost 1/8th) of the entire American workforce has worked for McDonalds or Wendy's at one time or another."

II. Rent Control Laws

A. Create incentives for landowners to _____convert_____ property (e.g. condos)

   1. Supply and demand

      i. Reduces the supply of cheap apartments

      ii. Aids the wealthy, injures the poor

   2. Can lead to homelessness

B. Quality of apartments can deteriorate

   1. Landowners cannot afford maintenance

   2. The condition of an apartment will always reflect its _____price_____

C. Creates incentives for landowners to _____sell_____ (e.g. parking lot)

III. Welfare Programs

A. Transferring of money

   1. The intention is to alleviate suffering

   2. The intention is to help the poor escape poverty

> "Since we started the welfare society programs in America in the late 1960s under Lyndon Johnson until today, we have transferred somewhere above 9 trillion dollars… and all the while poverty got worse because poverty is not a money problem… don't ever think that poverty is a money problem."

> "If you took the money earmarked for welfare in the national budget this year and gave it directly to all those people the government designates as poor, you could raise every man, woman, and child in America above the poverty line and have 54 billion dollars left over."

   3. _____Moral hazard_____: When insurance against a disaster actually creates an incentive for the disaster to occur

      i. Fire insurance can cause fires (e.g. restaurant is worth more if set on fire)

      ii. Life insurance can cause death (e.g. beneficiaries better off if the insured is dead)

      iii. Medical insurance can causes illness (e.g. treatment for petty sicknesses)

> "Welfare is in some ways poverty insurance, and if your welfare insurance pays off too well, you are going to cause the very problem you are trying to alleviate."

B. Payment for illegitimacy

"One of the rules of government is this: whatever you tax you get less of; whatever you subsidize you get more of... We pay people to have illegitimate children... Inside the inner cities in urban American more than 80% of all black children were born without fathers to take care of them. Our welfare programs have actually made black men, in their families, unnecessary... Poverty circles around broken homes, especially homes led by single mothers... We are encouraging people to do the very things that make them poor and keep them poor."

  1. Worse in Sweden

  2. Incentive for mothers not to get married and to have children with different men

  3. Incentive for fathers to have sex outside marriage, government will pick up the tab

IV. False Charity

  A. Success is not an entitlement; it is an achievement.

  B. Bearing false witness against the wealthy.

  1. The rich haven't stolen from the poor.

  2. The rich didn't get wealthy by cheating.

  C. Capitalism

  1. Does not begin with greed

  2. It begins with your neighbor

      i. Must offer your neighbor a product he wants at a price he can afford

      ii. The marketplace requires people to act decently.

  D. Paul: "If you don't work, you don't eat."

  E. Donate money to organizations that are part of the solution, not part of the problem

V. Improving Welfare Programs

  A. Transfer welfare programs to contributors and away from government bureaucrats

  B. Redefine poverty

  1. 40% own their own homes, 70% own their own cars, 60% own two or more televisions

  2. Poor used to mean a lack of food, shelter, and/or clothing

  3. Poverty programs ought not offer dollars

C. Re-educate politicians and poor

    1. Politicians should promote morality and responsibility

    2. Politicians should remember that welfare payments can be psychologically addictive

      "It is not a shame to be poor; it is a shame to be lazy and unproductive."

D. Provide tax credits for companies that hire and train welfare beneficiaries.

E. Welfare reform proposals should be local, timely, and situation specific.

F. Churches should provide food, shelter, and clothing.

    1. Provide example

    2. Know the people you are helping

    3. Know how they got where they are

    4. Be good stewards

    5. Make them change their lives

    6. Don't injure those you are trying to help

"THE DANGEROUS SAMARITAN"
VIDEO QUESTIONS

Answer the questions below on a separate sheet of paper and be prepared to review your answers in class.

1. **What are three ways in which minimum wage laws can hurt the poor? How are Ray Croc and Dave Thomas counterexamples of this?**

Minimum wage jobs can hurt the poor in at least three ways:

First, the basis of economics is supply and demand. If supply goes up, prices go down. If demand goes up, prices go up. In effect, the market sets its own prices for goods and services. A business cannot sell a product that consumers do not want nor can they sell a product at a price consumers are unwilling to pay. For example, if the government were to set the price of all Ford cars at $30,000, you would likely buy a Chevy, GMC, or foreign automobile. This equilibrium of economics works the same for employee wages. If the government sets an artificial minimum wage for employees, then employers (such as Ford) may not be able to afford such employees. As a result, a company may cut employees, move jobs overseas, hire illegal immigrants, or even close down.

Second, forcing an increase in base employee pay can lead to increases in employee pay all the way up the corporate ladder. For example, if a company had 5 employee pay levels: $5/hour, $7/hour, $9/hour, $11/hour, and $13/hour respectively, and the minimum wage was artificially set as $7/hour, then overnight the first and second tiers are making the same income, yet tier two is actually worth more. Thus, tier two employees will likely seek higher wages, which leads to a chain reaction all the up to the top of the ladder. The result is a new company pay scale: $7/hour, $9/hour, $11/hour, $13/hour, and $15/hour respectively.

[Calculate the monthly and yearly effect this would have on a company with 1,500 employees (500 tier one, 400 tier two, 300 tier three, 200 tier four, and 100 tier five).]

Third, to offset the cost of minimum wage restrictions, a company may be forced to raise the price of its products. The problem, however, is that the company may be forced to raise their prices above what the consumer is willing to pay.

What we need are more people to create "starter" jobs for the poor. The businesses of Ray Croc and Dave Thomas are good counterexamples to minimum wages laws. Through McDonalds and Wendy's, the poor can *afford* to eat out, *earn* an income, and *gain* skills and experience. And these employees are paying into the tax system rather than taking money out.

---

2. **What are two ways in which rent control laws can hurt the poor?**

Rent control laws can hurt the poor in two ways: First, these laws create an incentive for landowners to convert their properties rather than rent them. For example, a landlord may decide to convert his properties into higher priced condos, making fewer affordable housing options available to the poor. In effect, this could lead to cheaper housing for the more affluent. Second, rent control laws can lead to a decrease in the quality of housing. If the landlord is not able to earn enough to keep up with regular maintenance, then the quality of the accommodations will diminish.

SM
274

Unit Nine

3. **How can welfare programs hurt the poor?**

Essentially, welfare programs redistribute wealth. The government collects money from taxpayers and redistributes it—some money goes directly to the poor through welfare checks and food stamps, some of it goes to assistance programs, public health care, and job training, and some of the money pays the salaries and operational expenses of the welfare programs.

Interestingly enough, if we took all the money earmarked for welfare in the national budget this year and gave it directly to those people the government designates as poor, we could raise every man, woman, and child in America above the poverty line and have 54 billion dollars left over! Since the late 1960s we have spent over 9 trillion dollars on poverty, only to watch it get worse. In the end, poverty is not a money problem.

One of the rules of government is whatever you tax you get less of and whatever you subsidize you get more of. The government pays mothers to have illegitimate children. Inside the inner cities in urban America more than 80% of all black children were born without fathers to take care of them. We are encouraging people to do the very things that make them poor and keep them poor. In essence, welfare has created what insurance companies call a moral hazard. That is, welfare has offered the poor the incentive and the means to remain in poverty. An insurance company will not insure a property for more than it is worth, because it does not want to give the insurer a reason to collect. The government, however, offers the poor a financial incentive to remain poor and act immorally. For example, a single mother receives financial benefits for each child born out of wedlock and those of different fathers.

4. **What are some false ideas people hold about capitalism and the wealthy?**

Success is not an entitlement; it is an achievement. No one deserves wealth; it is earned. The unskilled and lazy are not entitled to receive without effort what others have worked hard to earn. Moreover, many of us have a false perception of how the rich became wealthy. The vast majority of the wealthy did not steal or cheat their way to wealth. In fact, a capitalistic society promotes the exact opposite. Capitalism is not about greed—it is about offering your neighbors a desired product at a price they are willing to pay. Capitalism is the equal trade of one item for another. If a business owner charges too much, sells something no one wants, or treats his or her employees and customers rudely, the business is likely to fail. If, however, they offer the public something desirable at an affordable price and are polite, they will likely succeed.

5. **What are six ways to improve welfare programs?**

One of the first problems with welfare programs is that they have become bureaucratic businesses. At one time the church headed up charity efforts because it cared about the poor. Today, people earn their livelihood running huge government programs that are merely sinkholes for money. If we are going to actually help the poor, this situation will need to change.

Second, we need to redefine the term poverty. At one time being poor meant lacking one of the three basic elements needed for survival—food, clothing, or shelter. But today 40% of the "poor" own their own homes, 70% own their own cars, and 60% own two or more televisions.

Third, we need to re-educate politicians. Under most current welfare systems, politicians do not promote morality and responsibility. Instead, they promote out-of-wedlock children and children from multiple fathers. Government welfare programs encourage situations that perpetuate poverty.

Fourth, the government could provide tax credits for companies that hire and train welfare beneficiaries.

Fifth, welfare programs should be local, timely, and situation specific.

Sixth, the church should remember its role in caring for the poor and it should do it in a way that changes lives. The church is called to know the poor and seek to understand how they got into their situation. The church, unlike the state, is to care for the poor, the dying, and the elderly. We are to set an example of love and grace to our neighbors that all might see the power of God in us.

WELFARE ACTIVITY

Help your students to get a feel for the difficulties of those trapped on welfare by playing the role a single mom who is on welfare. Your class should try to convince you that it is better to be working than to be on welfare. What would they say to her?

As they bring up suggestions and ideas, reveal the reasons you are on welfare: you got pregnant early, didn't finish school, have three children, etc. Note that your welfare check and other assistance barely cover rent, food, and clothing for your kids. You have never had a job, and really have no job skills. You're willing to get a job, but you have no form of transportation and can't find anything that will pay more than you're getting through welfare. Moreover, if you get a job, you'll have to pay for child care. Give the students guidance to help them understand some of the following points:

- While she can't change the past, she needs to take responsibility for making current decisions
- The mother, not society, is responsible for herself
- Ask the students how they or their church could help this woman and why they should get involved
  1. Students: baby sitting, fixing up her living quarters, giving her a ride to work on their way to school, etc.
  2. Church: offering child care while she's getting back on her feet, providing food or low cost housing, giving financial assistance, providing counseling to keep wrong choices from being made in the future, education on financial management, job training, or job placement.

DEAR DOUG
WRITING ASSIGNMENT

Hello again!

Wow, I realized this morning that we only have a month and a half before the semester is over. It doesn't seem like the weeks could have sped by that fast, but they have. There's just a hint of spring in the air. Nothing big yet—like flowers blooming—but enough to get you thinking of summer! Speaking of which, spring break is coming up. I don't have any big plans—just a few days back at home.

Nathan's loved the milder temps we've had the past week. It seems to have brought out this tree-hugger streak in him that I can't quite relate to. He's been going on and on about protecting the environment and saving the whales and ending pollution. He says that since we are all one with nature, we're only harming ourselves by misusing the earth's resources. He's even gone vegan, though I can't see how not eating a hamburger is going to save the world. Does the Bible have anything to say about environmentalism?

Sarah's thing this week has been helping the poor. Both she and Mark think that government welfare programs are the only way to correct the imbalance between rich and poor. Mark, of course, blamed the gap on capitalism. He even said it is the state's moral responsibility to take care of the poor. I've always thought the church had a duty to help the less fortunate, but if it'll come out of my taxes anyway, maybe I don't need to contribute to the church relief fund. What do you think about welfare?

The longer Sarah and Mark talked the more they decided the government should take over in order to redistribute wealth evenly. Mark even suggested having the state own everything so the people could learn to share things equally. He said that owning land and property causes greed and greed leads to immorality. This sounds awfully close to communism. Do you think such a "socialistic" system can work?

I guess I haven't thought much about economics… been too busy worrying about my credit card bill. Does Christianity have anything to say about economics?

By the way, Amber and I are back together. She wouldn't talk to me for weeks after our fight, but I saw her at the library last week and invited her to a concert with a big group of us. She met me there and we went out for Chinese afterward. We talked and laughed like nothing had happened. I hope we can keep moving forward, because I really missed her.

Later,
Doug

Doug has brought up four different subjects; below is a rough outline of possible responses.

1. **What is a biblical view of environmentalism? (12.5 points)**

> At its core, a biblical view of environmentalism entails stewardship. We were put on the earth to subdue (master) and cultivate (take care of and even make better) it. Christians should be at the forefront of the environmental movement, always keeping in mind a correct understanding of creation's role in God's economy. There is a hierarchy of creation, and the environment has been put under the dominion of mankind. Using good science, we should be about the business of caring for and utilizing the resources abundant upon the earth for the benefit of mankind and the glory and honor of God.

2. **Is it the state's responsibility to provide for the poor? (12.5 points)**

> Biblically speaking, it has never been the government's role to care for the poor. This responsibility has always been within the purview of the church (James 1:27). However, as the church has neglected its responsibility to the needy, the government has filled the gap. Historically, however, the church did a better job. Current tax-sponsored social programs are in the business of giving handouts, while the church was concerned with helping the poor get back on their feet. The current system lacks accountability as well as opportunities for mentoring. It has become a trap for the poor, often offering incentives for immoral behavior and laziness.

3. **What would be the results of a socialistic society? (12.5 points)**

> While socialism theoretically seems like a good idea, in practice it has been tried numerous times and proven to yield horrific results. In implementing a socialistic system, the government takes over more control, leaving its citizens with less freedom. Likewise, socialistic systems diminish motivation and creativity, which in turn decrease production and increase poverty.

4. **What is the Christian view of economics? (12.5 points)**

> Based on the biblical principles of our sinful nature and the concept of justice, the most desirable economic system from a Christian perspective promotes justice by protecting the rights of individuals from infringement by others. If humanity were inherently good, we might not have to worry about individuals denying the rights of others; but we are not inherently good. Therefore, the Christian believes the best economic system would contain basic checks and balances that can guarantee the protection of human rights. Applying this criterion, the Christian believes the free enterprise system is more compatible with biblical truths than other economic systems. Economic systems that punish injustice and grant people responsibility—in terms of private property and economic decisions—can allow individuals the freedom to act with all the dignity of beings created in God's image. This, according to the Christian view, is the important end of economic theory: offering us not riches or luxury, but the freedom to seek fulfillment through an understanding of our role in God's universe.

Unit Nine Test

'Economics' Textbook Questions

Matching: (1 point possible per answer [2 for 90-day])
some options may be used more than once or not at all; some questions may have multiple answers

1. __d__ Christianity

2. __d__ Islam

3. __a__ Secular Humanism

4. __b/c__ Marxism-Leninism

5. __e__ Cosmic Humanism

6. __a__ Postmodernism

a. Interventionism
b. Socialism
c. Communism
d. Stewardship
e. Universal Enlightened Production
f. Laissez-faire

Short answer: (5 points possible per answer [7 for 90-day])

7. **What is the principle of comparative advantage? How does competition stifle our sinful tendencies?**

> Principle of comparative advantage—every member of a free market society can produce valuable goods or services by specializing in areas where he or she enjoys the greatest advantage. Productive activities are directed toward meeting the needs of as many people as possible.
>
> Competition requires meeting the needs of others better than anyone else. It promotes cooperation through the division of labor, which benefits society as a whole. Another benefit is the fact that it promotes the worth of each individual. The free market preserves each person's dignity by granting us the opportunity to contribute to the welfare of society.

8. **What is the relationship between freedom and the economic system a country employs?**

> Socialist systems require more bureaucracies and more powerful centralized governments to initiate its plans. In contrast, the capitalist system requires far less political power because the government is not needed to control incomes, prices, production, etc. Under capitalism it is the citizens who are free to determine how they will spend their money and how they will use their resources.

9. **What economic system do Muslims favor?**

> Muslim economists contend that their economic system is neither socialism nor capitalism—they reject socialism's negation of private property, but also reject capitalism's absolute view of private property.

Unit Nine

CD-ROM

UNDERSTANDING THE TIMES

443

Not surprising, for all the above to be worked out and to make sure that one's labor is correct, the state will have to play a very prominent and important role in the Islamic economy. This is not merely in terms of instituting justice in economic dealings, but even meddling in the ways and means of production, distribution, and risk. Therefore, Muslim economists seem to favor some form of government intervention.

10. According to Marxism, what will be the fate of capitalism?

The capitalist system, according to Marxists, will simply exploit more and more people until virtually everyone becomes a member of the proletariat. Eventually the working class will get fed up and overthrow the wealthy minority. Marxists further believe that this destruction of capitalism and the victory of the proletariat is ultimately guaranteed by the dialectic: the thesis (bourgeoisie) and the antithesis (proletariat) must clash and create a synthesis—socialism.

11. What is the difference between socialism and communism?

Socialism is only the first step toward communism. Like capitalism before it, socialism is a necessary evil. It is a period of time in which the government owns all property, controls wages, regulates production, and ultimately controls a nation's entire economy. This transitional phase will come to an end when classes and economic distinctions have disappeared. At that time, every citizen will peacefully own all things in common, eliminating the need for a government and laws.

12. According to Cosmic Humanism, what is the best way to achieve a higher income?

According to New Age gurus, the more enlightened a person becomes, the more money and success he or she will accrue.

13. Since all economic theories have problems, what do Postmodernists claim should be done?

According to Postmodernists, the best route for economics is constant experimentation. With ever-changing situations and communities, the best approach is to never be married to any one way; there is always the possibility of inventing something new that will better serve the people.

Heart, Soul, and Money Essay

True or False: (4 points possible per answer)
*if an answer is false, restate it to make it true

14. Christians give, on average, 25% of their income to Christian ministries.

> False: Christians give, on average, <u>just over 2%</u> of their income to Christian ministries.

15. Jesus and his disciples were supported by wealthy individuals.

> True

16. Material possessions are a good gift from God meant for his people to enjoy.

> True

17. "Money is the root of all evil."

> False: The <u>love of money</u> is <u>*a* root of all kinds</u> of evil.

18. The Bible teaches that the more affluent are to trade places with the less affluent.

> False: The Bible teaches that the more affluent are to <u>help</u> the less affluent.

19. There are certain extremes of wealth and poverty which are in and of themselves intolerable.

> True

"Radical Environmentalism" Video

Short answer: (5 points possible per answer)

20. What are three types of radical environmentalism?

> The first radical environmental movement is the green party. The greenies tend to be less radical than other groups, but favor socialism as the best means of solving environmental concerns.

This group attempts to accomplish its ends by working through the political system—legislation, treaties, etc. They are often loosely connected with more respectable environmental groups like *Environmental Defense Fund*, *Sierra Club*, etc.

The second radical environmental movement is known as deep ecology. This group is religious in nature, instead of political. Most of its followers adhere to some form of pantheism and promote druidism, goddess worship, and the like. This group also tends to be very Darwinian, considering human beings to merely be evolved animals. Deep ecologists are often connected with more radical environmental groups like *Green Peace*, *Earth First*, *Sea Shepherds*, etc.

The third radical environmental movement is the animal rights movement. Like the deep ecologists, this group has been heavily influenced by Darwinism and logically contends that human beings are merely animals. Unlike the deep ecologist, however, the animal rights movement asserts that no animals should ever be harmed, even for food. Animal rights advocates assume that animals will only be treated humanely if they are granted rights similar to those possessed by human beings.

PRINCIPLES OF A CHRISTIAN ENVIRONMENTAL ETHIC ESSAY
True or False: (4 points possible per answer [5 for 90-day])
*if an answer is false, restate it to make it true

21. Someday all of creation will be renewed.

True

22. One of the reasons God created and continues to sustain nature is for his own love and enjoyment.

True

23. God has dominion over his entire creation, and he has granted people dominion over nature.

True

24. God created people and nature with order and purpose.

True

25. A steward is a person who is put in charge of taking care of something that does not belong to him or her.

True

"THE DANGEROUS SAMARITAN" VIDEO
Short answer: (5 points possible per answer [7 for 90-day])

26. How can welfare programs hurt the poor?

One of the rules of government is whatever you tax you get less of and whatever you subsidize you get more of. The government pays mothers to have illegitimate children. Inside the inner cities in urban America more than 80% of all black children were born without fathers to take care of them.

We are encouraging people to do the very things that make them poor and keep them poor. In essence, welfare has created what insurance companies call a moral hazard. That is, welfare has offered the poor the incentive and the means to remain in poverty. An insurance company will not insure a property for more than it is worth, because it does not want to give the insurer a reason to collect. The government, however, offers the poor a financial incentive to remain poor and act immorally. For example, a single mother receives financial benefits for each child born out of wedlock and those of different fathers.

27. What are some false ideas people hold about capitalism and the wealthy?

Success is not an entitlement; it is an achievement. No one deserves wealth; it is earned. The unskilled and lazy are not entitled to receive without effort what others have worked hard to earn. Moreover, many of us have a false perception of how the rich became wealthy. The vast majority of the wealthy did not steal or cheat their way to wealth. In fact, a capitalistic society promotes the exact opposite. Capitalism is not about greed—it is about offering your neighbors a desired product at a price they are willing to pay. Capitalism is the equal trade of one item for another. If a business owner charges too much, sells something no one wants, or treats his or her employees and customers rudely, the business is likely to fail. If, however, they offer the public something desirable at an affordable price and are polite, they will likely succeed.

Unit Nine

UNDERSTANDING THE TIMES

Unit Ten

Topics:

History

Historical Jesus

Historical Revisionism

Scriptural Reliability

A Summit Ministries Curriculum

180-DAY SYLLABUS

DAY	IN CLASS	HOMEWORK	
1	WATCH "History" video		
2	READ <u>UTT</u> Textbook 'History 10.1'	READ <u>UTT</u> Textbook 'History 10.2'	
3	REVIEW <u>UTT</u> Textbook 'History 10.1–10.2' questions	READ <u>UTT</u> Textbook 'History 10.3'	
4	READ <u>UTT</u> Textbook 'History 10.4'		
5	REVIEW <u>UTT</u> Textbook 'History 10.3–10.4' questions	READ <u>UTT</u> Textbook 'History 10.5'	
6	READ <u>UTT</u> Textbook 'History 10.6'		
7	REVIEW <u>UTT</u> Textbook 'History 10.5–10.6' questions	READ *Censoring the Past* essay	
8	REVIEW *Censoring the Past* essay questions	ASSIGN Dear Doug Letter	
9	WATCH "The Reliability of Scripture" video P1		
10	WATCH "The Reliability of Scripture" video P2		
11	REVIEW "The Reliability of Scripture" video questions P1		
12	REVIEW "The Reliability of Scripture" video questions P2		
13	WATCH "The Historical Jesus" video		
14	REVIEW "The Historical Jesus" video questions	Dear Doug Letter assignment DUE	
15	TAKE Unit Ten Test		

90-DAY SYLLABUS

DAY	IN CLASS	HOMEWORK	
1	WATCH "History" video	READ <u>UTT</u> Textbook 'History 10.1–10.2'	
2	REVIEW <u>UTT</u> Textbook 'History 10.1–10.2' questions	READ <u>UTT</u> Textbook 'History 10.3–10.4'	
3	REVIEW <u>UTT</u> Textbook 'History 10.3–10.4' questions	READ <u>UTT</u> Textbook 'History 10.5–10.6'	
4	REVIEW <u>UTT</u> Textbook 'History 10.5–10.6' questions	READ *Censoring the Past* essay	
5	REVIEW *Censoring the Past* essay questions		
6	WATCH "The Historical Jesus" video		
7	REVIEW "The Historical Jesus" video questions		
8	TAKE Unit Ten Test		

UNDERSTANDING THE TIMES
HISTORY QUESTIONS

Answer the questions below on a separate sheet of paper and be prepared to review your answers in class.

HISTORY 10.1

1. How important is historical validation to Christianity?

> Christians believe that the Bible is God's revealed Word in the form of a trustworthy book grounded in history. Either Christ is a historical figure and the Bible is a historical document that describes God's communications with humanity and records events in the life of Christ, or the Christian faith is bankrupt (1 Corinthians 15:14). To shatter Christian doctrine and the Christian worldview, one need only shatter its historical underpinnings. [UTT 10.1.1]

EYE-WITNESS ACTIVITY

Help students understand the importance of this study by asking, "How would your life change if you found out today that the Bible were not true?" Get them thinking about how it would change their education, standards, and what they do on weekends. Some of those changes might seem pleasant, like the lifting of restrictions. But it would al- so mean that the students have no purpose here on earth, aren't worth anything as individuals, and have no hope for the future. Help them to see that our entire lives are based on the reliability of God's revelation to us in the Bible. Fortunately, we can know that the basis for our lives is sure.

2. What are two common objections made against the Bible's reliability? How do Christians respond?

> The first objection commonly raised is that of authorship. Was the Bible written by eyewitnesses of historical events, or were some books written years after the fact by individuals attempting to boost Christianity's reliability? Today's scholars have little doubt that the books of the Bible were written largely by eyewitnesses. William F. Albright, a leading twentieth-century archaeologist, writes, "In my opinion, every book of the New Testament was written by a baptized Jew between the forties and the eighties of the first century (very probably sometime between about A.D. 50 and 75)." Likewise H. G. Wells, a confirmed atheist, acknowledged that "the four gospels… were certainly in existence a few decades after [Christ's] death."
>
> However, a second objection arises. Perhaps, say some critics, the Bible was an accurate historical document as it was originally written—but it has been copied and re-copied for thousands of years, and so it has been warped by the inevitable mistakes of copyists. However, within the discovery of the Dead Sea Scrolls, archaeologists have been able to show that ancient documents may be reliably copied—these documents were at least 1000 years older then the oldest Old Testament copies in existence yet were virtually identical. [UTT 10.1.2]

Unit Ten

3. **What external evidence exists to support the historicity of Jesus Christ?**

> Christ was treated as a historical figure by early historians other than Christians. Around A.D. 93, the Jewish historian Josephus referred to Jesus at least twice in his *Antiquities of the Jews*. In one instance, he recorded that the high priest Annas "assembled the Sanhedrin of the judges, and brought before them the brother of Jesus, who was called Christ, whose name was James."
>
> Another early historian, Cornelius Tacitus, wrote around A.D. 112 about "the persons commonly called Christians," and also stated, "Christus, the founder of the name, was put to death by Pontius Pilate, procurator of Judea in the reign of Tiberius: but the pernicious superstition, repressed for a time broke out again, not only through Judea, where the mischief originated, but through the city of Rome also." [UTT 10.1.3]

4. **Who witnessed Christ's resurrection? What effect did his resurrection have upon the disciples?**

> The resurrected Christ was witnessed by more than 500 people, including Mary, Peter, and ten other apostles. It transformed a group of scared and skeptical men into courageous evangelists who proclaimed the Resurrection in the face of threats on their lives. [UTT 10.1.4]
>
> *[Discuss whether someone would devote their lives to a cause, even unto death, if they did not truly believe what they stood for. Also, discuss the difference between a Muslim dying for Allah and the apostles' willingness to die for Christ. Muslims believe in something they have been taught, second-hand knowledge that they devote their lives to in hopes of reaching paradise. The apostles saw the resurrected Christ; their conversion was not by second-hand information.]*

5. **According to Christianity, what is the purpose of history?**

> For the Christian, history is linear. Time began with creation, we rebelled against God and creation fell, and God provided a means of redemption for us—Jesus Christ. Presently history is moving toward a specific climax—the Day of Judgment (Acts 17:31; Romans 2:11–16). At this point, Christ's victory over sin will become apparent to all and Christians throughout history will be allowed to share in his triumph. [UTT 10.1.5]

HISTORY 10.2

6. **What is the history of Muhammad's life?**

> - Born in A.D. 570 into a culture characterized by polytheism and animism.
> - A spiritual man, he started encountering visions that he thought were Satanic; eventually, he was convinced by his wife, Khadija, that they were from God.
> - In A.D. 610 he was visited by the angel Gabriel and commissioned to be a prophet of God.
> - Muhammad's teachings clashed with the city's merchants (men would travel to Mecca to worship their tribal deities, trading goods and spending money). He fled to Medina in A.D. 622.

- After several skirmishes with the Meccans, Muhammad and a force of 10,000 were able to defeat Mecca without a battle, cleanse the Ka'ba of its idols, and establish Islam. [UTT 10.2.1–10.2.2]

7. **How did the two dominant Islamic factions come into existence?**

After Muhammad died (A.D. 632), his followers were faced with the problem of succession. The conflict resulted in the two major factions of Islam. Some insisted that the successor should be elected by popular vote. These became the Sunni Muslims, who currently comprise about eighty percent of Muslims worldwide. The Shi'ite Muslims believed that the successor should be someone related to Muhammad, a family member or descendant. [UTT 10.2.4]

8. **What is Sufism?**

Sufi Islam historically has expressed a more spiritual, less legalistic form of Islam. Because of this, Sufism has been, and continues to be, a major force in the spread of Islam throughout the world. [UTT 10.2.5]

[Briefly discuss with your students the other offshoots of Islam.]

9. **According to Muslims, what is the purpose of history and the vision for the future?**

Just as God created the world, he superintends it throughout time, guiding it toward an expression of his will. In concert with this belief is the Muslim hope that Islam will one day span the globe, with all peoples and nations being Muslim. [UTT 10.2.8–9]

10. **How will Muslims attain this vision for the future?**

To attain this vision, Muslims will employ jihad, for it is "a Divine institution or warfare to extend Islam into the Dar al-harb (the non-Islamic territories described as the 'abode of struggle' or disbelief) or to defend Islam from danger." [UTT 10.2.9]

HISTORY 10.3

11. **How does Secular Humanism's belief in evolution influence its optimism for the future?**

For the Secular Humanist, all of history is a development from non-life to life, from simple to more complex, from mindless to mind, from animal to human, from pond scum to Shakespeare, from amoral to moral. If, as Humanists believe, all reality is an evolutionary pattern that has moved upward step by step to create rational thought and morality in the highest species, then mankind's history must also be a progressive march toward a better world, i.e., as the evolutionary process continues, so must progress continue. Civilization constantly improves and ultimately carries the human race (or whatever race evolution dictates) into some type of better community. [UTT 10.3.2]

12. How does Secular Humanism's belief in naturalism influence its optimism for the future?

Oddly enough, this denial of the supernatural and a source of meaning in history pushes the Humanist toward historical optimism. While it seems that such a denial would generate pessimism, it instead spurs the Secular Humanists to pin all their hopes on history and the future, because the progress of humanity becomes the only meaningful goal. The Humanist's atheism, instead of leading them into the trap of nihilism, makes them dependent on the progress of human history to provide meaning for mankind. [UTT 10.3.2]

13. In order to shape history, what must mankind do, according Secular Humanism?

In order to grant us the power to control our own destiny and maintain an optimistic attitude toward history, Secular Humanists believe we must abandon their belief in environmental influences and stress our role in shaping history. [UTT 10.3.4]

14. According to Secular Humanists, which ideologies are worthy of shaping history? Why?

Since Secular Humanists assert that systems of thought evolve, then some ideologies are hopelessly outdated and unsuited to modern problems. For example, any worldview that accepts the existence of the supernatural is scoffed at. Thus, Humanists portray Christianity as a primitive ideology that might have been relevant in ancient history but is useless today. Secular Humanism alone is the ideology most relevant for advancing the evolution of mankind. Humanism is the dominant ideology and becomes the single causal agent for effecting change in mankind's destiny. [UTT 10.3.5]

15. According to Secular Humanism, what is mankind's role in shaping the future?

Secular Humanism assigns us the tasks of being "creator" and "redeemer." According to Humanism, only mankind is capable of creating (guiding evolution) and redeeming humanity (optimistic view of future). Ultimately, we may be replaced with a higher life form (e.g. new species or computers), but for now we must play the role once delegated to the gods. [UTT 10.3.6]

HISTORY 10.4

16. What term describes the Marxist view of history? What is this view?

Marxists see evolution as continuously encouraging development and progress in living things; therefore, they assume that we have been constantly improving ourselves and will continue to progress in the future. Marxism's "scientific" approach to biology leaves no room in its worldview for God, especially a God who might influence history. For this reason, the Marxist view of history is called historical materialism. Historical materialism states that only matter exists, that history is the account of matter in motion and that matter moving according to specific laws drives the progress of the world. [UTT 10.4.1]

17. According to Karl Marx, what is the real force behind history?

Karl Marx says simply, "It is not the consciousness of men that determines their existence, but, on the contrary, their social existence determines their consciousness." If you want to get at the real driving force behind history, you must look beyond the ideas of men to the true reality—the material world. Economics is the only dynamic force in history. Governments, courts, philosophies, and religions are based on a society's economic system and therefore affect history only to the extent that economics shapes their ability to guide our development. [UTT 10.4.2–10.4.3]

18. Why do Marxists believe that global communism is inevitable? How does the dialectic play a role?

Since Marxists believe that everything is determined by natural deterministic laws that direct the evolution of economic systems toward a paradisiacal end, the future state of global communism is inexorable. No amount of human will can stop the collapse of capitalism, the rise of socialism, and the steady transition from socialism to communism. Marxism perceives mankind's efforts toward any other end as useless and insignificant, declaring that it is determined for us to achieve utopia (a communist society) despite all efforts and desires to the contrary. Marxists believe that the dialectic has guided society through certain phases in a constant upward spiral through the dialectic of thesis, antithesis, and synthesis. This cycle guarantees inevitable progress toward a communist utopia— slavery, feudalism, capitalism, socialism, and some day communism. [UTT 10.4.4–10.4.5]

19. What effect does the belief in historical determinism have on free will?

Under historical determinism, free will becomes drastically truncated—we are free in the sense that we can influence history by striving to achieve communism, but we are determined in the sense that we can affect history in no other way and are headed toward communism whether we like it or not. Communism is inevitable, as dictated by the laws of history, which, in turn, are governed by the dialectic. [UTT 10.4.5]

20. According to Marxists, what does the future look like? What is the fate of the dialectic?

Marxists believe that under communism all class distinctions will be abolished. Further, the dialectic has (theoretically) improved our economic structures (and consequently, societies and ideas) throughout history, but as soon as the dialectic leads the whole world to communism, the ultimate mode of production and exchange will have been achieved and the need for the dialectic will have been erased. [UTT 10.4.6]

21. What do Cosmic Humanists place their faith in for a better future?

In a very real sense, members of the New Age movement place their faith in cosmic evolution as humanity's savior. This faith in evolution cause the Cosmic Humanists to view human history as an ascent from lower to higher levels of consciousness. Each step in our evolution is a jump upward. It is a jump upward because the God-force within the universe pulls it upward. [UTT 10.5.1]

22. How do Cosmic Humanists view the role of Christianity?

Cosmic Humanists believe that Christianity might have helped us in our quest for godhood in the past, but that it is now outdated and must be abandoned. [UTT 10.5.2]

23. According to Cosmic Humanism, what is the goal of evolution?

God is the goal of evolution. God wants us to become himself (or herself or itself); and it is God who is the source of the evolutionary force and God who is the destination. [UTT 10.5.3]

24. Are all Cosmic Humanists satisfied with an evolutionary explanation? Why or why not?

Dissatisfied with a purely evolutionary explanation, some Cosmic Humanists have postulated the appearance of a spiritual Savior who will guide humanity to higher consciousness and utopia. According to Yott, a Savior appears every two thousand years or so, but eventually a mighty Master Soul will come to earth to light the way up to the throne of perfect man. [UTT 10.5.3]

25. According to David Spangler, what role does each individual have in history?

Each individual is a co-creator with history and is involved in a process of conscious and participatory evolution. [UTT 10.5.4]

HISTORY 10.6

26. What is the Postmodern approach to history?

Postmodernists use the term *historicism* to describe the view that all questions must be settled within the cultural and social context in which they are raised. Both Lacan and Foucault argue that each historical period has its own knowledge system and individuals are unavoidably entangled within these systems. Answers to life's questions cannot be found by appealing to some external truth, but only the norms and forms within each culture that phrase the question. [UTT 10.6.1]

27. How did Michel Foucault approach history?

Foucault, like most Postmodernists, doubts that there is such a thing as "truth." Indeed, one of his major theses was that truth and knowledge were nothing other than claims to power by one particular group or another. Thus, for Foucault an accurate and objective telling of the past is impossible. From this Foucault seems to have reasoned, that if history is merely an un-objective fiction and a play for power, then what we call history should (and does) promote an ideology. In the end, for Foucault, history serves to promote the power of repressed groups—homosexuals, sadists, masochists, prisoners, and the clinically insane. [UTT 10.6.2–10.6.3]

28. What is historical revisionism?

The rewriting/editing of the past to serve an ideological purpose is called historical revisionism. Today this practice is seen with "feminist histories," i.e., attempts to expose a male-dominated, patriarchal past and point the way for empowering women. Likewise, we see "homosexual histories," i.e., responses to homophobic repressions in order to provide equality for homosexuals. Every repressed group has its own revision of history. [UTT 10.6.3]

29. How does the Postmodern approach to history mimic the Marxist approach?

While Marxists focus on the proletariat rising against the bourgeoisie, Postmodernists focus on one gender, race, or socially identifiable group's struggle against some other. [UTT 10.6.4]

30. How does the Postmodern approach to history differ from the Marxist approach?

One significant difference between Postmodernist and Marxist approaches to history regards whether history has an inherent meaning. Marxists advocate *historical materialism*, complete with the vision that human history eventually will arrive at a purely communistic (i.e., classless) society. But the Postmodernist view of history is distinctly a-teleological (i.e., without a purpose). [UTT 10.6.4]

CENSORING THE PAST

BY GARY DEMAR

There is a lot of talk today about censorship. Recent art exhibits, funded by tax dollars and promoted by the National Endowment for the Arts, have come under severe attack. Many Americans rightly criticize these exhibits as inappropriate, certainly for viewing, but most assuredly for government support and funding. Museums, government-funded artists, Hollywood activists, homosexual groups, and the government-funded NEA (National Endowment for the Arts)[1] are crying "censorship" over such protests.

Another battle is raging over the selling of pornography in popularly trafficked bookstores. Rev. Donald Wildmon and his American Family Association have targeted Waldenbooks, a subsidiary of K-Mart, for selling pornography. Harry Hoffman, president of Waldenbooks, says that Wildmon and others like him "want to censor and stop the sales of constitutionally protected publications they deem objectionable."[2]

Protests against pornography and government-funded art are not acts of censorship. Censorship is a mandate by the civil government which prohibits the publication, sale, or distribution of material it deems to be politically harmful. As civil libertarian Nat Hentoff describes it, "Legally, censorship in violation of the First Amendment can only take place when an agent or agency of the state—a public school principal, a congressman, a President—suppresses speech."[3]

It is not censorship for a government to refuse to pay for objectionable material. In the case of pornographic "art," the protestors are only asking that their tax money not be used to fund the offensive material. Rev. Wildmon is not asking the government to prohibit Waldenbooks from selling *Playboy* and *Penthouse*; he is only calling on concerned citizens to stop doing business with K-Mart and its subsidiaries.[4] He wants the same freedoms that the pornographers are claiming belong only to them. Wildmon writes: "We don't want K-Mart, *Playboy*, and *Penthouse* drawing the line for the rest of us. The First Amendment belongs to all Americans, not just to pornographers."[5]

THE CENSOR BAND WAGON

Literature of all types has been scrutinized by numerous groups from different ends of the political and religious spectrum. Those on the political left have denounced classic works like Charles Dickens's *Oliver Twist* as being "anti-semitic." William Shakespeare's *King Lear* has been condemned as "sexist." *Tom Sawyer*, Mark Twain's coming-of-age classic, has suffered a double blow with denouncements of "racism" and "sexism." Beatrix Potter's *The Tale of Peter Rabbit* and *The Tale of Benjamin Bunny* have been criticized "because they are about 'middle-class rabbits.'"[6]

In 1988, librarians in Cobb County, Georgia, removed the Nancy Drew and Hardy Boys mysteries from the library shelves. The librarians cited lack of shelf space as the reason for the exclusion of the popular mystery series. Mary Louis Rheay, director of the Cobb County Library System, tells a different story, saying that "series books are poorly written and do not meet library standards for book selection."[7] In 1994 the library board in Wellesley, Massachusetts, voted 5 to 1 to keep *Playboy* on the shelves. The board said the magazine, like all its material, is protected by free speech provisions. "There is something in the library to offend everyone," librarian Anne Reynolds said. "We cannot be in the position of censoring everything. Those days are gone." Trustee Carol Gleason, who voted to remove the magazine, said, "If minors cannot buy the magazine in a store, why should they be able to obtain it in the library?"[8]

---

[1] Miriam Horn with Andy Plattner, "Should Congress censor art?," *U.S. News and World Report* (September 25, 1989); Bo Emerson, "Civil War over Censorship: Morality is the Issue on Battlefield of Culture," *Atlanta Journal/Constitution* (July 25, 1990); and "Four artists to NEA: Who are you to judge?," *The Atlanta Constitution* (March 19, 1991).

[2] Harry Hoffman, "Protect the Right to Buy and Sell Books," *USA Today* (April 25, 1990).

[3] Nat Hentoff, *Free Speech for Me—But Not for Thee* (New York: HarperCollins, 1992), 2.

[4] Those who promote liberal causes are not opposed to boycotts of companies and products they deem objectionable. See Cathy Lynn Grossman, "Boycotting is popular resort for activists," *USA Today* (October 11, 1994).

[5] Donald C. Wildmon, "Protect the Right to Boycott Pornography," *USA Today* (April 25, 1990).

[6] Joseph W. Grigg, "'Peter Rabbit' banned from London schools," *Atlanta Journal/Constitution* (April 7, 1988).

[7] Peggie R. Elgin, "Hardy Boys banned from Cobb libraries," *Marietta Daily Journal* (January 13, 1988).

[8] "Residents want 'Playboy' out of library," *Marietta Daily Journal* (October 18, 1994).

WHO DRAWS THE LINE?

An ad hoc public school committee supported the removal of books by Dr. James Dobson, a Christian psychologist, from the library of the Early Childhood Family Education Program of the Mankato, Minnesota, school system. They were removed because the staff "disagreed with Dobson's views on child discipline, which includes an endorsement of spanking, and because of the religious nature of his philosophy."[9]

Donated books are often refused by libraries because of religious content. *The Closing of the American Heart*, written by Dr. Ronald H. Nash, was donated to the Haggard Library in Plano, Texas, by a group of concerned citizens. Nash is a former professor of religion and philosophy at Western Kentucky University who presently teaches at Reformed Theological Seminary in Orlando, Florida. He has also served as an advisor to the United States Civil Rights Commission. Why was his book refused? Certainly not because of his academic and professional credentials. Book donations had to pass the library's evaluation criteria.[10] *The Closing of the American Heart* did not pass because of its Christian perspective.

Each year People for the American Way (PAW), a liberal political advocacy group, publishes a report on censorship and "book banning." Most of the books which are brought into question deal with occultic themes, promiscuous sexual content, and advocacy of homosexuality. Most of the protestors are parents who send their children to government-controlled (public) schools. PAW considers such parental concern over what children read "attacks on the freedom to learn."[11] What PAW does not tell its unsuspecting audience is that incidents of so-called censorship are negligible compared to the number of schools and libraries in existence. For example, the most challenged book, *Scary Stories to Tell in the Dark*, "was challenged only 7 times out of 84,000 public schools and never removed." In fact, Kristi Harrick, press secretary for the Family Research Council, reports that "none of the most challenged books were censored."[12]

Eric Buehrer, a former public-school teacher and president of Gateways to Better Education in Lake Forest, California, states that "PAW has confused the issues of material selection and censorship. What used to be called discernment is now called censorship."[13] Why is it called "censorship" when parents apply standards for book selection but called "meeting library standards" when a librarian evaluates a book?

Judgments are constantly made as to what children should read and what books should appear on library shelves. As we've seen, librarians appeal to "library standards" when selecting books. There is nothing wrong with having "standards."

Unfortunately, these "library standards" are neither applied consistently in libraries and schools nor always reported in the same way by the press.[14] It seems that when concerned Christian parents voice objections to the content of books, they are said to be censors. But when books with Christian themes are refused by libraries or when teachers are denied the right to read a Bible silently during a reading period,[15] we learn that the rejection is based upon the religious nature of the literature. Rarely are such actions by libraries and schools said to be "censorship" by even the strongest opponents of book banning.

WILL THE REAL CENSORS PLEASE STAND UP?

It is instructive how one segment of our society screams "censorship" every time its views are questioned, but when Christians claim "censorship" of the facts of history, they are ignored by the guardians of the First Amendment.

Liberal media coverage of world events is just one example of the anti-Christian bias of mainstream contemporary society. Consider journalistic coverage of events in Eastern Europe. Rev. Laszlo Tokes, the Hungarian pastor who sparked the Rumanian Revolution, stated that "Eastern Europe is not just in a political revolution but a religious renaissance." How many people read in their local newspapers or

---

[9] Willmar Thorkelson, "Book Ban Considered," *Washington Post* (September 1, 1990).

[10] Reported in "Texas Report," a supplement to the *Christian American* (July/August 1992).

[11] Andrew Mollison, "Group says efforts to ban schoolbooks focus on alleged satanic, occult content," *Atlanta Constitution* (August 29, 1991).

[12] "PAW Cries Censor-Wolf: Attempt to Keep Parents Out of Schools, Says FRC," *Family Research Council Press Release* (August 31, 1994).

[13] Quoted in "The Great 'Censorship' Hoax," *Citizen* (September 19, 1994).

[14] David Shaw, "Abortion Bias Seeps Into News" and Al Knight, "School races turn nasty," Denver Post (October 10, 1993). Knight writes: "The term *religious right*, in the hands of PAW and other groups, has become one of the most elastic political labels in memory. It is routinely stretched to include nearly anyone who might be motivated by conservative, religious, or moral concerns."

[15] John W. Whitehead, *The Rights of Religious Persons in Public Education* (Wheaton, IL: Crossway, 1994), 112–13.

saw on the evening news that Rev. Tokes believed he had been saved from execution through "divine intervention"? Explicitly Christian themes are regularly excluded from news articles: "References to 'Jesus,' the 'Christian spirit,' and Czechoslovakia's role as the 'spiritual crossroads of Europe' were omitted from excerpts of President Vaclav Havel's New Year's Day address. *The New York Times*, *The Washington Post*, and *Newsweek* were among the sinful censors."[16]

None of these examples should surprise the informed Christian. The present educational establishment, to cite just one group, has been obscuring the past so that our children have no way of comparing the facts of history with the distorted version promoted by biased secular historians.

CENSORSHIP AT WORK IN THE CLASSROOM

Public school textbooks are fertile ground for the seeds of willful historical deception. Paul C. Vitz, professor of psychology at New York University, spent months of careful analysis of sixty textbooks used in elementary schools across the country. The study was sponsored by the National Institute on Education. The texts were examined in terms of their references to religion, either directly or indirectly. "In grades 1 through 4 these books introduce the child to U.S. society—to family life, community activities, ordinary economic transactions, and some history. None of the books covering grades 1 through 4 contain one word referring to any religious activity in contemporary American life."[17] Dr. Vitz offers an example of how this translates into the real world of classroom instruction:

> Some particular examples of the bias against religion are significant. One social studies book has thirty pages on the Pilgrims, including the first Thanksgiving. But there is not one word (or image) that referred to religion as even a part of the Pilgrims' life. One mother whose son is in a class using this book wrote me to say that he came home and told her that "Thanksgiving was when the Pilgrims gave thanks to the Indians." The mother called the principal of this suburban New York City school to point out that Thanksgiving was when the Pilgrims thanked God. The principal responded by saying "that was her opinion"—the schools could only teach what was in the books![18]

In 1986 school children in Seattle, Washington, were given a large dose of revisionist history in the booklet *Teaching about Thanksgiving*. The children were told that "the Pilgrims were narrow-minded bigots who survived initially only with the Indians' help, but turned on them when their help wasn't needed anymore." The Pilgrims "had something up their sleeves other than friendship when they invited the Indians to a Thanksgiving feast, and it was the Indians who ended up bringing most of the food, anyway."[19] The booklet has obvious biases and is filled with historical inaccuracies. For example, supposedly Increase Mather preached a sermon in 1623 where he reportedly "gave special thanks to God for the plague of smallpox which had wiped out the majority of Wampanoag Indians, praising God for destroying 'chiefly young men and children, the very seeds of increase, thus clearing the forests for a better growth.'"[20] This sermon could not have been preached by Increase Mather, at least not in 1623, because he was not born until 1639.

The rewriting of history has even reached the pages of the Sunday comics. A story recently appeared about "Squanto and the First Thanksgiving." As all children know, Squanto was a great help to the Pilgrims. But was Squanto so much of a help that the first Thanksgiving was given in his honor? According to the author of the Squanto column, we learn that "the Pilgrims so appreciated Squanto's generosity that they had a great feast to show their thanks."[21] William Bradford, governor of Plymouth and the colony's first historian, continually makes reference to "the Lord Who never fails," "God's blessing," and "the Providence of God," in times of both plenty and want.[22] How uncharacteristic it would have been for the Plymouth settlers to ignore thanking God during a time of harvest. Edward Winslow, in his important chronicle of the history of

[16] Barbara Reynolds, "Religion is Greatest Story Ever Missed," *USA Today* (March 16, 1990).
[17] Paul C. Vitz, *Censorship: Evidence of Bias in Our Children's Textbooks* (Ann Arbor, MI: Servant Books, 1986), 1.
[18] Ibid., 3.
[19] Carey Quan Gelernter, "The Real Thanksgiving," *Seattle Post-Intelligencer* (November 23, 1986).
[20] Ibid.
[21] "Squanto and the First Thanksgiving," Rabbit Ears, *Atlanta Journal/Constitution* (November 27, 1994).
[22] William Bradford, *Bradford's History of the Plymouth Settlement: 1608–1650*, rendered into modern English by Harold Paget (Portland, OR: American Heritage Ministries, 1988).

Plymouth, reports the following eyewitness account of the colony's thanksgiving celebration:

> Our harvest being gotten in, our governor sent four men out fowling, that so we might, after a special manner, rejoice together after we had gathered the fruit of our labors. They four in one day killed as much fowl as, with a little help beside, served the company almost a week. At which time, among other recreations, we exercised our arms, many of the Indians coming among us, and among the rest their greatest king, Massasoit, with some ninety men, whom for three days we entertained and feasted; and they went out and killed five deer, which they brought to the plantation, and bestowed on our governor, and upon the captain and others. And although it be not always so plentiful as it was at this time with us, yet by the goodness of God we are so far from want, that we often wish you partakers of our plenty.[23]

Squanto was an example of God's providential care of the Pilgrims. He taught them how to farm in the New World and led them on trading expeditions. There is no doubt that these early Christian settlers thanked the "Indians" in general and Squanto in particular for their generosity in supplying venison to supplement the Pilgrims' meager Thanksgiving rations. As the historical record shows, however, thanksgiving was ultimately made to God. "Governor Bradford, with one eye on divine Providence, proclaimed a day of thanksgiving to God, and with the other eye on the local political situation, extended an invitation to neighboring Indians to share in the harvest feast… This 'first Thanksgiving' was a feast called to suit the needs of the hour, which were to celebrate the harvest, thank the Lord for His goodness, and regale and impress the Indians."[24]

CENSORSHIP THROUGH CREATIVE EDITING

Dr. Vitz is not the only person to uncover the way public school texts minimize the role that Christianity played in the founding of our nation. Consider how a teacher's guide for the high school history text *Triumph of the American Nation*, published in 1986, omits material from the Mayflower Compact without informing the teacher that the document has been edited. In discussing the document students are left with an incomplete understanding of what motivated these early founders because they do not have all the facts. The Mayflower Compact is depicted solely as a political document with its more striking religious elements deleted. Here is the document as presented by the textbook company. The bold face portions are missing from the textbook version:

> In the name of God, Amen. We whose names are underwritten, **the loyal subjects of our dread sovereign lord, King James, by the grace of God, of Great Britain, France, and Ireland, King, Defender of the Faith, etc.,** having undertaken **for the glory of God and advancement of the Christian faith and honor of our king and country,** a voyage to plant the first colony in the northern parts of Virginia, do **by these presents** solemnly and in the presence of God, and one another, covenant and combine ourselves together into a civil body politic… [25]

These brave men and women had more on their minds than political freedom. Missionary zeal and the advancement of the Christian faith were their primary motivations as they risked life and property to carve out a new home in an uncertain wilderness.

The critics of America's early Christian origins have steadily removed such references from textbooks and have created a tense legal environment that frightens many teachers from even raising evidence contradicting the censored texts. Will a member of the ACLU threaten legal action against a teacher who decides to cite original source material to support a view that differs from the historical perspective of the textbook?

---

[23] Edward Winslow, "How the Pilgrim Fathers Lived," *CD Sourcebook of American History* (Mesa, AR: Candlelight Publishing, 1992), 2:116. Also see Mourt's *Relation: A Journal of the Pilgrims of Plymouth*, ed. Jordan D. Fiore (Plymouth, MA: Plymouth Rock Foundation, 1985), 67–69.

[24] Diana Karter Appelbaum, *Thanksgiving: An American Holiday, An American History* (New York: Facts on File Pub., 1984), 9.

[25] This editing was exposed in *Education Update*, Heritage Foundation, 10:3 (Summer 1987). Quoted in Robert P. Dugan, *Winning the New Civil War: Recapturing America's Values* (Portland, OR: Multnomah, 1991), 149–50.

HOLLYWOOD HISTORY

The entertainment industry has entered the field of creative editing in an animated version of the story of Pocahontas, the Native American woman who pleaded with her father to spare the life of John Smith. Pocahontas later became a Christian and married another colonist, John Rolfe. But this episode will all be deleted from an animated retelling of the story. Kendall Hamilton of *Newsweek* offers the following report on the newly designed and politically correct Pocahontas:

> The film's P.C. prospects are… helped by the exclusion of Pocahontas's potentially, er, problematic later years, in which she was kidnapped by settlers and, after converting to Christianity, married one of her captors. Male domination fantasy! Subversion of morally superior indigenous culture! Well, maybe, but [Producer James] Pentecost says such considerations weren't a factor: "We didn't really sidestep any of it for any reason other than this was the most direct way to tell the story and the clearest." Pass the peace pipe.[26]

While this might be the *official* explanation from Disney, my guess is that the studio was pressured by Native Americans to hide Pocahontas's "mistake" of rejecting her native religion.

WILLIAM HOLMES MCGUFFEY'S ECLECTIC READERS

A study of the historical record reveals that religion played a major role in the development of the public school curriculum. "Textbooks referred to God without embarrassment, and public schools considered one of their major tasks to be the development of character through the teaching of religion. For example, the *New England Primer* opened with religious admonitions followed by the Lord's Prayer, the Apostles' Creed, the Ten Commandments, and the names of the books of the Bible."[27]

The most widely used textbook series in public schools from 1836 to 1920 were William Holmes McGuffey's *Eclectic Readers*. More than 120 million *Readers* were sold during this period. The *Readers* stressed religion and its relationship to morality and the proper use of knowledge. In an introduction for a reissue of the *Fifth Reader*, historian Henry Steele Commager writes:

> What was the nature of the morality that permeated the *Readers*? It was deeply religious, and… religion then meant a Protestant Christianity… The world of the *McGuffeys* was a world where no one questioned the truths of the Bible or their relevance to everyday contact… The *Readers*, therefore, are filled with stories from the Bible, and tributes to its truth and beauty.[28]

Competing textbooks of the same era contained varying amounts of biblical material, but *McGuffeys* contained the greatest amount—"more than three times as much as any other text of the period."[29] Subsequent editions of the *Readers*—1857 and 1879—showed a reduction in the amount of material devoted to biblical themes. Even so, the 1879 edition contained the Sermon on the Mount, two selections from the Book of Psalms, the Lord's Prayer, the story of the death of Absalom (2 Samuel 18), and Paul's speech on the Areopagus (Acts 17). The Bible was still referred to as "'the Book of God,' 'a source of inspiration,' 'an important basis for life,' and was cited in support of particular moral issues."[30]

ANTISEPTIC TEXTS

Since the nineteenth century, secularists have been gradually chipping away at the historical record, denying the impact Christianity has had on the development of the moral character of the United States. In 1898 Bishop Charles Galloway delivered a series of messages in the Chapel at Emory College in Georgia. In his messages he noted that "books on the making of our nation have been written, and are the texts in our colleges, in which the Christian religion, as a social and civil factor, has only scant or apologetic mention.

---

[26] Kendall Hamilton, "No Red Faces, They Hope," *Newsweek* (November 21, 1994).
[27] Whitehead, *Rights of Religious Persons in Public Education*, 41–42.
[28] Quoted in Ibid., 42.
[29] John H. Westerhoff, "The Struggle for a Common Culture: Biblical Images in Nineteenth-Century Schoolbooks," *The Bible in American Education*, eds. David L. Barr and Nicholas Piediscalzi (Philadelphia, PA: Fortress Press, 1982), 32.
[30] Ibid., 28.

This is either a fatal oversight or a deliberate purpose, and both alike to be deplored and condemned. A nation ashamed of its ancestry will be despised by its posterity."[31]

The 1980s saw an even greater expurgation of the impact the Christian religion has had on our nation. So much so that even People for the American Way had to acknowledge that religion is often overlooked in history textbooks: "Religion is simply not treated as a significant element in American life—it is not portrayed as an integrated part of the American value system or as something that is important to individual Americans."[32] A 1994 study of history textbooks commissioned by the federal government and drafted by the National Center for History in the Schools at UCLA concluded that religion "was foolishly purged from many recent textbooks."[33] In 1990, Warren A. Nord of the University of North Carolina wrote:

> What cannot be doubted is that our ways of thinking about nature, morality, art, and society were once (and for many people still are) fundamentally religious, and still today in our highly secular world it is difficult even for the nonreligious to extricate themselves entirely from the webs of influence and meaning provided by our religious past… To understand history and (historical) literature one must understand a great deal about religion: on this all agree. Consequently, the relative absence of religion from history textbooks is deeply troubling.[34]

The removal of the topic of religion from textbooks is not always motivated by a desire to slam Christianity. Textbook publishers fear special interest groups that scrutinize the material for any infraction, whether it be religious, racial, sexual, or ethnic. For example, "the 1990 Houghton Mifflin elementary series first made special efforts to include material (and in state hearings received savage criticism from militant Jews, Muslims, and fundamentalist Christians)."[35] The easiest way to placate these diverse groups is to remove all discussion of the topic. This deletion of material is either outright censorship or else a reluctance to fight ideological wars, but whatever the case, failure to deal factually with the past distorts a student's historical perspective. This has happened to such an extent that even when religious themes are covered "their treatments are uniformly antiseptic and abstract."[36]

---

*This essay originally appeared as a chapter in the book *America's Christian History: The Untold Story*

Gary DeMar, *America's Christian History: The Untold Story* (Atlanta: American Vision, 1994), pp. 21–34.

**Reproduction rights granted by Gary DeMar and American Vision.

---

[31] Charles B. Galloway, *Christianity and the American Commonwealth* (Nashville: Methodist Episcopal Church, 1898), 15.
[32] Joan Delfattore, *What Johnny Shouldn't Read: Textbook Censorship in America* (New Haven, CT: Yale Univ. Press, 1992), 85.
[33] This is also the conclusion of the editorial writers of the *Marietta Daily Journal*: "History needing revision" (October 30, 1994). The National Standards for United States History has called for the restoration of the role religion played in the founding of America while pushing a "politically correct" agenda in nearly everything else. See Lynne V. Cheney, "The End of History," *Wall Street Journal* (October 20, 1994).
[34] Quoted in *History Textbooks: A Standard and Guide*, 1994–95 Edition (New York: American Textbook Council, 1994), 32.
[35] Ibid.
[36] Ibid., 33.

CENSORING THE PAST
ESSAY QUESTIONS

Answer the questions below on a separate sheet of paper and be prepared to review your answers in class.

1. How does censorship compare to protesting?

> Government censorship is defined as a governmental mandate that prohibits the publication, sale, or distribution of material it deems politically harmful. Legally, censorship in violation of the First Amendment can only take place when an agent of the state suppresses protected speech.
>
> Therefore, protesting against businesses that sell pornography is not censorship and neither is the government's refusal to fund the production of objectionable art. However, whenever a morally conservative group informs the public about businesses that sell pornographic materials, they are often accused of censorship. Likewise, protesting taxpayers are not calling for censorship whenever they object to governmental funding of questionable artists and art exhibits. [SM p. 281]

2. How does censorship compare to discernment?

> Librarians and parents alike use discernment when choosing books—they make material selections based on a particular criteria or worldview. Libraries do this when they chose what books to put on their shelves and parents do this when deciding which books their children should and should not read. Likewise, conservative groups use standards when they call into question books that promote such things as sexual promiscuity, the occult, or homosexuality. In fact, liberal groups have their own standards when choosing books, finding a number of Christian books and authors "questionable." [SM pp. 282–3]

3. What are some examples of historical revision in public schools?

> Paul C. Vitz spent months carefully analyzing sixty textbooks used in elementary schools across the country. The texts were examined in terms of their references to religion, either directly or indirectly. "In grades 1 through 4 these books introduce the child to U.S. society—to family life, community activities, ordinary economic transactions, and some history. None of the books covering grades 1 through 4 contain one word referring to any religious activity in contemporary American life."
>
> Other examples of revisionist history include the booklet *Teaching about Thanksgiving*. From this booklet children in Seattle were told that "the Pilgrims were narrow-minded bigots who survived initially only with the Indians' help, but turned on them when their help wasn't needed anymore." The Pilgrims "had something up their sleeves other than friendship when they invited the Indians to a Thanksgiving feast, and it was the Indians who ended up bringing most of the food, anyway." [SM pp. 283–4]

SM
287

4. **What is an example of censorship through omission in public schools?**

> The teacher's guide for the high school history text *Triumph of the American Nation*, published in 1986, omits material from the Mayflower Compact without informing the teacher that the document has been edited. Students, in discussing the document, are left with an incomplete understanding of what motivated these early founders because they do not have all the facts. The Mayflower Compact is depicted solely as a political document with its more striking religious elements deleted. However, these brave men and women had more on their minds than political freedom. Missionary zeal and the advancement of the Christian faith were their primary motivations as they risked life and property to carve out a new home in an uncertain wilderness. [SM pp. 283–4]

5. **What were curriculum materials like in public schools before the middle of the twentieth century?**

> In the past, religion played a major role in the development of the public school curriculum. Textbooks referred to God without embarrassment, and public schools considered one of their major tasks to be the development of character through the teaching of religion. For example, the *New England Primer* opened with religious admonitions followed by the Lord's Prayer, the Apostles' Creed, the Ten Commandments, and the names of the books of the Bible. Similarly, the most widely used textbook series in public schools from 1836 to 1920 was William Holmes McGuffey's *Eclectic Readers*, more than 120 million of which were sold during this period. The *Readers* stressed religion and its relationship to morality and the proper use of knowledge. [SM p. 285]

"THE RELIABILITY OF SCRIPTURE"

WITH TODD COTHRAN

PART ONE: THE OLD TESTAMENT

I. Three Categories of Evidence

  A. Transmission

  B. Archaeological record

  C. Fulfilled prophecy

II. Transmission

  A. Jewish scribes

    1. Reproduction process

    2. Error prevention

  B. God's will

  "Moses wrote all the words of the Lord." — Exodus 24:4

  Joshua also "wrote these words in the Book of the Law of God." — Joshua 24:26

  Samuel "told the people the ordinances of the kingdom, and wrote them in the book and placed it before the Lord." — 1 Samuel 10:25

  "Take for yourself a large tablet and write on it in ordinary letters." — Isaiah 8:1

  C. _____ Dead Sea Scrolls _____ (1947)

  "Even though the two copies of Isaiah discovered in Qumran Cave 1 near the Dead Sea in 1947 were a thousand years earlier than the oldest dated manuscript previously known (A.D. 980), they proved to be word for word identical with our standard Hebrew Bible in more than 95 percent of the text. The 5 percent of variation consisted chiefly of obvious slips of the pen and variations in spelling." — Archer Gleason, *A Survey of Old Testament Introduction*

III. Archaeology

  A. Ebla Tablets (1974)

    1. Greatly weakens the Documentary Hypothesis

    2. Written _____ 1,000 _____ years before Moses

B. Archaeology suggests or proves…

    1. That Israel derives its ancestry from   Mesopotamia   (Genesis 11:27–12:4)

    2. That language arose from a common origin

    3. That   Jericho   and several others cities thought to be legend actually existed

    4. That the Hittite civilization…

        i. Existed at time of Abraham

        ii. Lasted over 1,200 years (doctorate from University of Chicago)

C. Latest discoveries

    1. **Tell Dan** in northern Galilee—found remains of a black basalt stele (stone slab)

        i. "The King of Israel"

        ii. "House of   David   "

    2. **Tell es-Safi** (the biblical city of "Gath of the Philistines")—found small ceramic shard that mentions two names remarkably similar to the name "   Goliath   "

    "The science of modern archaeology and historical philology actually provides verification of the most ancient biblical texts. Whereas… throughout the nineteenth century and almost up to the Second World War, systematic criticism of the Old Testament texts tended to destroy their historicity, and to reduce the Pentateuch, in particular, to mere myth or tribal legend, the trend over the last half-century has been quite in the opposite direction." — Paul Johnson, *The Quest for God*

IV. Fulfilled Prophecy

A. Provides more than   2,000   prophecies that validate its historical claims

B. All biblical prophecies concerning events up to the present time have come to pass.

C. Messianic Prophecies

    1. His   birthplace

    "But as for you, Bethlehem Ephrathah, too little to be among the clans of Judah, from you One will go forth for Me to be ruler in Israel." — Micah 5:2

    "They said to him, 'In Bethlehem of Judea; for this is what has been written by the prophet: "And you Bethlehem, land of Judah are by no means least among the leaders of Judah; for out of you shall come forth a ruler who will shepherd my people Israel."'" — Matthew 2:5–6

Unit Ten

2. His _____attitude_____ toward accusers

"He was oppressed and He was afflicted, Yet he did not open His mouth; like a lamb that is led to the slaughter, and like a sheep that is silent before its shearers." — Isaiah 53:7

"Then Pilate said to Him, 'Do you not hear how many things they testify against You?' And He did not answer him with regard to even a single charge, so that the governor was quite amazed." — Matthew 27:13–14

3. His _____burial_____ in a rich man's tomb (Joseph of Arimathea: Matthew 27:57–60)

"His grave was assigned with wicked men, yet He was with a rich man in His death, because He had done no violence, nor was there any deceit in His mouth." — Isaiah 53:9

4. His _____resurrection_____

"For Thou wilt not abandon my soul to Sheol; neither wilt Thou allow Thy Holy One to undergo decay." — Psalm 16:10

"Brethren, I may confidently say to you regarding the patriarch David that he both died and was buried, and his tomb is with us to this day. And so, because he was a prophet, and knew that God had sworn to him with an oath to seat one of his descendants upon his throne, he looked ahead and spoke of the resurrection of the Christ, that He was neither abandoned to Hades, nor did His flesh suffer decay." — Acts 2:29–31

D. 60 major prophecies and 270 ramifications

   1. *Objection*: Many prophecies were manufactured after the fact

   2. *Objection*: Many prophecies are obscure

TOPIC	OT PROPHECY	NT FULFILLMENT
Born of seed of woman	Genesis 3:15	Galatians 4:4
Line of Abraham	Genesis 12:2	Matthew 1:1
Line of Jacob	Numbers 24:17	Luke 3:23, 34
Line of Judah	Genesis 49:10	Matthew 1:2
Line of Jesse	Isaiah 11:1	Luke 3:23, 32
Line of David	2 Samuel 7:12–16	Matthew 1:1
Virgin Birth	Isaiah 7:14	Matthew 1:23
Birthplace	Micah 5:2	Matthew 2:6
Sold for 30 Shekels	Zechariah 11:12	Matthew 26:15

Forsaken by disciples	Zechariah 13:7	Mark 14:50
Silent before accusers	Isaiah 53:7	Matthew 27:12–19
Crucified with thieves	Isaiah 53:12	Matthew 27:38
No bones broken	Psalm 22:17	John 19:33–36
Scourging and death	Isaiah 53:5	John 19:1, 18
Rich man's tomb	Isaiah 53:9	Matthew 27:57–60
Resurrection	Psalm 16:10; 22:22	Matthew 28:6
Ascension	Psalm 68:18	Luke 24:50–53

PART TWO: THE NEW TESTAMENT

I. Objection One: Oral tradition is unreliable

A. Oral tradition was held in the highest regard.

B. Jewish children were taught to remember oral material accurately.

C. Oral tradition was handed down collectively to the entire community.

D. Exodus 24:4; Joshua 24:26; 1 Samuel 10:25; Isaiah 8:1; 1 Corinthians 14:37; Revelation 1:19

II. Objection Two: Written by men

A. Writers were inspired by God

"Biblical inspiration may be defined as God's superintending of the human authors so that, using their own individual personalities—and even their writing styles—they composed and recorded without error His revelation to humankind in the words of the original autographs."
— Ron Rhodes, *Answering the Objections of Atheists, Agnostics and Skeptics*

B. To what extent were the writers controlled by the Holy Spirit?

"Prophecy [or Scripture] never had its origin in the will of man, but men spoke from God as they were carried along by the Holy Spirit." — 2 Peter 1:21

Paul said he spoke "not in words taught us by human wisdom but in words taught by the Spirit, expressing spiritual truths in spiritual words." — 1 Corinthians 2:13

III. Objection Three: Writers were biased

A. Some of the most reliable reports of the Nazi Holocaust were from Jews.

"We did not follow cleverly invented stories when we told you about the power and coming of our Lord Jesus Christ, but we were eyewitnesses of his majesty." — 2 Peter 1:16

"That which was from the beginning, which we have heard, which we have seen with our eyes, which we have looked at and our hands have touched—this we proclaim concerning the Word of life." — 1 John 1:1

B. Other considerations

    1. Apostles had little to _____gain_____ and almost everything to _____lose_____

    2. New Testament writers gave up their lives in defense of what they saw.

    3. They kept in _____embarrassing_____ details about themselves

        i. Jewish people's unfaithfulness to God

        ii. Peter denying Christ three times

        iii. Peter being addressed as Satan

        iv. Disciples scattering when Christ was arrested

        v. Thomas's doubt about the resurrection

IV. Objection Four: Too much time had passed

A. The time between these two events (the writing of the original and the copying of the oldest extant manuscript) is extremely short

    1. Important because the shorter the time, the more reliable a text is considered

        i. Ancient classics have an average gap of over _____1,000_____ years

        ii. A 700-year gap is considered good among works of antiquity

    2. **John Ryland's manuscript** (oldest copy of New Testament)

        i. Contains fragments from John (John 18:31–33, 37–38)

        ii. Dates to approximately A.D. 117–138

    3. **Bodmer Papyri**

        i. Contains most of the Gospels of Luke and John

        ii. Dates to approximately A.D. 200

    4. **Chester Beatty Papyri**

        i. Contains almost all of the New Testament (including large portions of the Gospels)

        ii. Dates to approximately A.D. 250

5. **Codex Sinaiticus** (The British Museum)

    i. Contains the entire NT and parts of the OT

    ii. Dates to approximately A.D. 340

6. **Codex Vaticanus** (Vatican Library)

    i. Contains most of the Bible

    ii. Dates to approximately A.D. 325–350

7. **Codex Alexandrinus** (The British Museum)

    i. Contains most of the Bible

    ii. Dates to approximately A.D. 450

8. **Codex Bezae** (Cambridge University Library)

    i. Contains parts of the NT and most of the Gospels (written in Greek and Latin)

    ii. Dates to approximately A.D. 450–550

B. The New Testament compared to other documents of antiquity

AUTHOR	DATE WRITTEN	EARLIEST COPY	NUMBER OF COPIES	ACCURACY OF COPIES
Caesar	1st century B.C.	A.D. 900	10	———
Tacitus	A.D. 100	A.D. 1100	20	———
Thucydides	5th century B.C.	A.D. 900	8	———
Herodotus	5th century B.C.	A.D. 900	8	———
Homer	9th century B.C.	———	643	95%
New Testament	1st century A.D.	2nd century A.D.	5,000+	99+%

C. Non-Christian accounts

    1. **Tacitus** (ca. A.D. 55–120): Roman historian, *Annals*

    2. **Suetonius** (ca. A.D. 120): Roman historian, *Life of Claudius*

    3. **Josephus** (A.D. 37–97): Jewish Historian, *Antiquities*

    4. **Pliny the Younger** (A.D. 112): Roman governor, *Epistles X*

    5. **Jewish Talmud** (commentary on Jewish law, completed A.D. 500)

    6. **Lucian** (second century A.D.): Greek satirist

D. General reports of Jesus and Christianity

    1. Provocative teacher, a wise and virtuous man from the region of Judea

    2. Reportedly performed miracles and made prophetic claims

    3. Jewish leaders condemned him for acts of sorcery and apostasy

    4. Crucified by the Roman procurator Pontius Pilate

    5. Christians reported that he had risen from the dead

    6. Roman Christians charged with crimes and met horrific persecution

    7. First-century Christians worshiped Jesus Christ as God

    8. Disciples were known for their courage and virtue

> "To be skeptical of the resultant text of the New Testament books is to allow all of classical antiquity to slip into obscurity, for no documents of the ancient period are as well attested biographically as the New Testament." — John Warwick Montgomery, *History and Christianity*

> "The excessive skepticism of many liberal theologians stems not from a careful evaluation of the available data, but from an enormous predisposition against the supernatural." — Millar Burrows, *What Mean These Stones?*

V. Truth: Myths and legends did not have sufficient time to develop and be recorded

A. Gospels (Matthew, Mark, Luke/Acts, and John)—probably written in early 50s and 60s

B. None mention noteworthy events between A.D. 60 and 70

    1. Persecution of Christians instigated by the Roman emperor _____Nero_____ (mid-60s)

    2. The martyrdom of James (brother of Jesus), Peter, and Paul (62–66)

    3. The fall of Jerusalem and destruction of the Temple under Roman general Titus (70)

C. Conclusion: Span of two full generations is insufficient

VI. Eyewitness Accounts of Historical Events

A. Luke 1:1–4; John 19:35; 1 Corinthians 15:3–8; Galatians 1:11–12; 2 Peter 1:16; 1 John 1:1–2

B. Actively attempted to squelch rumors before they could spread (John 21:22–25)

If the Gospel writers had departed from historical fact (either by exaggeration or outright invention), hostile witnesses familiar with the events of Jesus' life could have and would have exposed them.

VII. Other Known Mythical Writings

A. The Bible is neither bizarre nor frivolous, as in Greek mythology

B. Jesus' miracles were always done within the context of his ministry, specifically to give glory to God and to meet legitimate human need.

"THE RELIABILITY OF SCRIPTURE"
VIDEO QUESTIONS

Answer the questions below on a separate sheet of paper and be prepared to review your answers in class.

PART ONE

1. What was significant about the 1947 discovery of the Dead Sea Scrolls?

> Before the Dead Sea Scrolls were found, the oldest existing Old Testament text dated to around A.D. 900. This date, hundreds of years after Christ, left much more room for criticism of the reliability of the Old Testament text. The discovery of the scrolls, which contained fragments of almost every book in the Old Testament, put to rest most of those criticisms. Many of the newly-found manuscripts dated to around 150 B.C., nearly one thousand years older than the Masoretic manuscript. The fact that the two copies of Isaiah found at Qumran are 95% identical to the next oldest manuscripts from nearly a thousand years later proves the reliability of the Old Testament text (the variations consisted chiefly of obvious slips of the pen and differences in spelling).

2. How does archaeology support the reliability of the Old Testament?

> There are many archaeological discoveries that support the reliability of the Old Testament. The Ebla Tablets found in 1974 prove that written language existed nearly 1,000 years prior to Moses. This greatly weakens the Documentary Hypothesis, which posits that written language was developed after Moses, therefore discounting his authorship the Pentateuch.
>
> Archaeological discoveries have proven 1) that Israel derives its ancestry from Mesopotamia, which is what the Bible states in Genesis 11:27–12:4; 2) that language arose from common origin; 3) that Jericho and several other cities thought to be legendary actually existed; and 4) that the Hittite civilization, once thought to predate Abraham in contradiction of the biblical text, actually existed in Abraham's day and lasted over 1,200 years.

3. What are some of the latest discoveries that support the reliability of the Old Testament?

> In 1993, near Tell Dan in northern Galilee, the remains of a black basalt slab were found with "The King of the Israel" and "House of David" inscribed on them. Also recently at Tell es-Safi (near the biblical city of Gath of the Philistines), shards were found that mention two names remarkably similar to "Goliath." These two recent discoveries lend even more credence to the argument that the Old Testament is a reliable historical book.

4. How should we respond to the claim that many prophecies were manufactured after the fact?

> Scholars are practically unanimous that the books of the Old Testament were completed years before the birth of Christ.

5. **How should Christians respond to the claim that many prophecies are so obscure that a variety of events could be interpreted as fulfillment?**

> Literally hundreds of very precise messianic prophecies were fulfilled in an exact way in the person of Jesus Christ. The probability of just eight such prophecies being fulfilled by one person is 1 in 10 to the 17th power. An example of this would be to cover the entire state of Texas with silver dollars two feet deep, mark one, and ask a blindfolded volunteer to pick the marked silver dollar.

PART TWO

6. **How should Christians respond to the claim that the oral tradition from which the New Testament was written was unreliable?**

> We need to remember that the culture in which the Jews lived is not like today, where we have the internet, digital voice recorders, and an assortment of other recording devices. Oral tradition was vital in the dissemination of information and was held in the highest regard. Customs, practices, and teachings were handed down from generation to generation. Jewish children were taught to remember oral material accurately. Also, oral tradition was handed down collectively to the entire community of believers, which served to keep oral accounts accurate.

7. **What is meant by the phrase "the Scriptures were inspired by God?"**

> Biblical inspiration is defined as God's supervision of the human authors of Scripture so that—fully utilizing their own individual personalities and writing styles—they composed and recorded without error his revelation to humanity in the words of the original autographs. 2 Peter 1:21 says that the writers of Scripture were "carried along" by the Holy Spirit.

8. **What are some problems with the claim that the New Testament is unreliable because the gospel writers were biased?**

> First, the claim that giving an account of something you believe in passionately necessarily forces you to distort history is a fallacy. Some of the most reliable reports of the Nazi Holocaust were from Jews who wanted to insure it was reported correctly, so a similar event would never happen again.
>
> Second, Scripture itself refutes accusations of bias. Peter says, "We did not follow cleverly invented stories when we told you about the power and coming of our Lord Jesus Christ, but we were eyewitnesses of his majesty" (2 Peter 1:16). John likewise asserts: "That which was from the beginning, which we have heard, which we have seen with our eyes, which we have looked at and our hands have touched—this we proclaim concerning the Word of life" (1 John 1:1).
>
> Third, the apostles had little to gain and almost everything to lose in proclaiming Jesus as Lord and Savior. In fact, many of the New Testament writers gave up their lives in defense of the truth they witnessed. Lies would not have been motivation enough for them to lay down their lives rather than deny the truth of their writings.

Fourth, the New Testament includes embarrassing details about the writers themselves, such as Peter denying Christ three times, the disciples scattering like faithless cowards when Christ was arrested, and Thomas's doubt about the resurrection of Jesus.

9. **How should Christians respond to the objection that the New Testament is unreliable because too much time passed between the original authorship and the date of the earliest copy?**

The shorter the time between the date a document was originally written (the autograph) and the date of its first extant copy (or manuscript), the more reliable a text is considered. For most ancient classics, an average gap of over 1,000 years separates the original work and its earliest existing copy (but that could extend to as much as 1,400 years). A 700-year gap is considered good among works of antiquity.

The oldest copy of any portion of the New Testament in existence today is the John Ryland manuscript, which contains fragments from John 18 and dates to between A.D. 117–138. The Bodmer Papyri contain parts of the New Testament, including the majority of the Gospels of Luke and John, and date to approximately A.D. 200. The Chester Beatty Papyri contain almost all the New Testament and date to approximately A.D. 250. In all of these instances, the gap between original autograph and extant manuscript is less than three hundred years.

With over 5,000 Greek manuscripts, the New Testament is unparalleled by any other ancient text in manuscript support. No one denies the accuracy of the writings of Caesar, and yet the earliest copy is nearly 1,000 years later than the original writings.

10. **How can Christians be sure that the Gospels do not contain myth and legend?**

Because of the early emergence of the Gospels and the sources behind them, myths and legends did not have sufficient time to develop and be recorded in their accounts. Scholars agree that even two full generations is insufficient for myth and legend to distort historical fact. We can be fairly certain that the Gospels were written in the mid-60s, since the Gospels do not mention the persecution of Christians by Nero, the martyrdom of the early church's central leaders James, Peter, and Paul, or the fall of Jerusalem, including the destruction of the Jewish Temple under Titus in A.D. 70. These are significant events that would have been recorded if the Gospels had been written after they occurred.

"THE HISTORICAL JESUS"
WITH KEVIN BYWATER

I. Critical Timeline

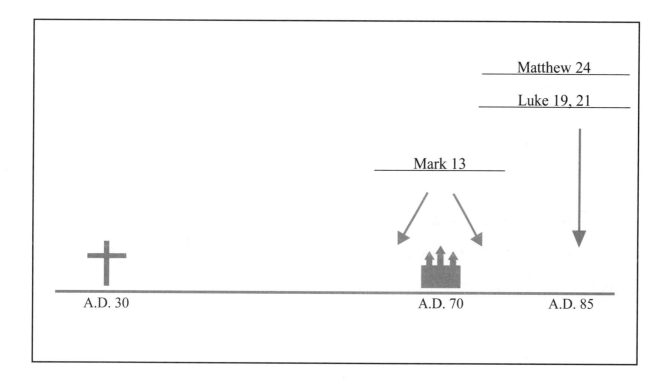

Matthew 24

Luke 19, 21

Mark 13

A.D. 30

A.D. 70

A.D. 85

II. Synoptic Gospels: Mark, Matthew, and Luke

   A. Dated after 70 A.D. by some scholars

   B. _____**Olivet Discourse**_____: A speech in which Jesus predicts the destruction of the temple within one generation

   C. Temple demolished in 70 A.D.

III. Methodological Naturalism: the process of interpreting history as purely natural events

   A. Assumption: God does not intervene in history.

   B. Miracles and prophecies do not occur.

   C. Jesus' prophecy must have therefore been added by someone else after the event.

IV. Jesus Seminar: a group of scholars and others who vote on the saying of Jesus

    A. **_Scientism_**: Truth can only be know through science

    B. Prophecy is actually historical fiction or retrojected legends.

V. **Reconstructing History**

    A. When was Acts written?

        1. Consider Luke's dual focus: Peter (1–12), then Paul (13–28)

        2. Consider Luke's tendencies: persecutions and deaths of leaders

           i. Jesus (2:23)

           ii. Stephen (7:60)

           iii. James (12:2)

        3. No mention of _____Paul's_____ death—A.D. 64

        4. Acts was likely written before A.D. 64

    B. When was Luke written?

        1. Luke/Acts was a two volume set

        2. Luke was therefore written before Acts (possibly A.D. 62)

    C. When was Mark written?

        1. Luke most likely used Mark as a source

        2. Mark was therefore written before Luke (possibly A.D. 60)

VI. **Additional Warrants for Earlier Dates**

    A. No mention of _____Nero's_____ persecution (A.D. 64–68)

    B. No mention of the fall of _____Jerusalem_____ (A.D. 70)

        1. No residue indicating it was past event

        2. No New Testament book mentions it as past

VII. Gospels' Tendencies Regarding Fulfilled Prophecy

    A. Old Testament prophecies as fulfilled

        1. Throughout Matthew

        2. Luke 24:25–27

    B. Consider the sufferings and resurrection of Jesus

        1. Prophesied: e.g., Matthew 16:21

        2. Noted as fulfilled:

            i. His sufferings:

                1) Peter disowning Jesus three times (Mark 14:74)

                2) On the road to Emmaus (Luke 24:6–8)

            ii. His resurrection:

                1) Matthew 28:6

                2) Mark 16:6

                3) Luke 24:6–8

                4) John 20:9

    C. Yet not even a hint indicating that the Olivet Discourse had been fulfilled

VIII. Why Do Critics Date Matthew and Luke So Late?

    A. Anti-Semitism—e.g. Matthew 23

        1. Christians kicked out of synagogues in A.D. 85

        2. After A.D. 85 Christians added anti-Semitic language to the words of Christ

        3. _____Jews_____ condemning Jews was normal and prophetic

            i. Isaiah 1:21

            ii. Jeremiah 3:6

            iii. Jeremiah 9:26

            iv. Isaiah 1:4

    B. What we find in the Gospels is thus not anti-Semitism

Unit Ten

IX. Presence of What Became Irrelevant

    A. Temple service

    B. Sabbath

X. Lack of What Later Was Relevant

    A. Circumcision of Gentiles

    B. Marriage to unbelievers

    C. Spiritual gifts

    D. Church structure

    E. Roles of women

    F. Food restrictions

XI. Additional Indicators of Historicity

    A. Diversity among the Gospel accounts

    B. Retention of embarrassing elements

        1. Was Jesus unable to heal? (Mark 6:5–6)

        2. Is Jesus good? (Mark 10:18)

        3. His family opposed him (Mark 3:21)

        4. He was baptized by John

    C. The quality and purpose of the miracles

    D. Distinction between Christian prophets and the words of Jesus

        1. John (Revelation 2–3)

        2. Agabus (Acts 11:28; 21:10–11)

        3. Paul (1 Corinthians 7:10,12)

XII. Final Observations

A. The Gospel accounts are _____summaries_____ and _____paraphrases_____

B. What language did Jesus speak? _____Aramaic_____

C. In what language were the gospels written? _____Greek_____

D. What does this imply?

    1. The gospels are translations

    2. Some of their differences may thus be explained

"THE HISTORICAL JESUS"
VIDEO QUESTIONS

Answer the questions below on a separate sheet of paper and be prepared to review your answers in class.

1. **Why do critical scholars date the Synoptic Gospels after A.D. 70?**

> *[Read through Christ's prediction in Matthew 24.]*
>
> A number of biblical scholars today interpret history through the lens of methodological naturalism, thus limiting history to natural events and refusing to allow for the possibility of miracles. Therefore, since the Synoptic Gospels mention the destruction of the temple (the Olivet Discourse is found in Mark 13, Matthew 24, and Luke 19 and 21), the works must have been written after that event took place (i.e. after A.D. 70) and the prophecy merely attributed to Jesus to make it seem as if he actually predicted the event.

2. **What is the Jesus Seminar? How do they interpret Scripture?**

> The Jesus Seminar is a group of scholars, Hollywood scriptwriters, and others who, skeptical of the supernatural claims within Scripture, instead favor naturalism, the theory of evolution, and, ultimately, scientism. Scientism is the belief that only scientific claims are true and everything else is suspect. Thus, the Jesus Seminar views history and the predictive prophetic sayings of Christ as just historical fiction or words attributed to Jesus by later Christians after his death.

3. **What case can be made for dating Acts and the Synoptic Gospels before A.D. 70?**

> First, the book of Acts tells the story of the formation and growth of the church through the lives of two central characters—Peter (1–12) and Paul (13–28). Along the way, the author tends to highlight certain events, namely persecutions and the death of leaders. For example, the death of Jesus (2:23), Stephen (7:60), and James (12:2) are all mentioned as relevant events. However, the death of Paul in A.D. 64 is never mentioned, leading many scholars to infer that the book was written while Paul was still alive.
>
> Second, the gospel of Luke and the book of Acts were written as an historical two-volume account of the church. The gospel of Luke surveys the life and death of Jesus, while the book of Acts records the formation of the early church and the lives of its leading men. Thus, Acts follows Luke. Therefore, if Acts was written before A.D. 64, then Luke must have been written prior to A.D. 64 as well.
>
> Third, a majority of scholars believe that Matthew and Luke used Mark as a source. This theory is derived by the similar (and sometimes exact wording) that is found between Mark and Luke, and Mark and Matthew. Therefore, if Luke used Mark, we can conclude that Mark was written before Luke, which was written before Acts, which was written before the death of Paul in A.D. 64.

4. **What are some additional considerations for dating Acts (and consequently the Synoptic Gospels) before A.D. 70?**

> Besides the death of Paul, one would reasonably expect Acts to mention the persecution of Nero (A.D. 64–68) or the fall of Jerusalem and the destruction of Herod's Temple itself (both A.D. 70). However, even though Acts frequently records persecutions, we find no mention of either of these momentous events having taken place by the completion of the work, the latter being a world-changing event for both Jews and Christians alike.

5. **What are the Synoptic Gospels' tendencies toward the recording of prophecies?**

> The Gospels tend to mention fulfilled prophecy—for example, Peter denying Jesus (Mark 14:72), Christ's suffering (Luke 24:6–8), and his resurrection (Matt 28:6). However, none of the Gospels mention the fulfillment of the Olivet Discourse.
>
> *[Ask your students for other examples of prophecies mentioned and then fulfilled in the Gospels.]*

6. **Why do critics date Matthew and Luke around A.D. 85?**

> *[Review Matthew 23 and the seven woes.]*
>
> Around A.D. 85 Christians were excommunicated from Judaism and synagogue worship. This act greatly angered the early Christians and created anti-Semitic feelings. It is therefore theorized by critical scholars that these later Christians added harsh words to the lips of Jesus because, according to their vision of Jesus, he would have never said such things. Thus, they conclude that Matthew and Luke were written around A.D. 85.
>
> Their reconstruction is based on the idea that Jesus was a "really nice guy" and would not offend anyone. This of course raises the question of why then anyone would want to crucify him.

7. **Are the Gospels anti-Semitic?**

> Since the atrocities of the Jewish holocaust, our modern culture has become very sensitive to language spoken and actions taken against Jews. While anti-Semitism exists and while it is true that Jesus spoke harshly against Israel, he was not anti-Semitic. Christ himself was a Jewish prophet, and harsh criticism and correction was regular practice for God's messengers. Consider the following Old Testament examples:
>
> - Isaiah 1:21
> - Jeremiah 3:6
> - Jeremiah 9:26
> - Isaiah 1:4
>
> In light of the Old Testament precedence, to call a Jew anti-Semitic because he is following regular Jewish customs seems unwarranted, especially when we also consider that Jesus wept for Israel.

Unit Ten

8. **If the Gospels were written later, what might we expect to find that we do not?**

> If the Gospels were written later, one might expect to find a number of relevant topics addressed. There were a number of topics that later Christians struggled with that are simply not addressed in the Gospels: circumcision of Gentiles, marriage to unbelievers, spiritual gifts, church structure, roles of women, and food restrictions. If later Christians had written the Gospel accounts as history, then why would they not have addressed these time-relevant issues?
>
> Also, one might reasonably expect the absence of topics that became irrelevant for later Christians, such as temple service and Sabbath observance.

9. **What are some additional indicators for the historicity of the Gospels?**

> If the Gospels were written late in the first century and if the Gospel writers were adding to the words of Jesus, then we could reasonably expect to find a number of issues represented quite differently.
>
> First, there is some disparity among the Gospel accounts, making them somewhat difficult to harmonize (for example, the accounts of the empty tomb). Why not correct these seeming discrepancies?
>
> Second, within the Gospels we find a number of embarrassing accounts. Why not remove these?
>
> - Was Jesus unable to heal? (Mark 6:5–6)
> - Is Jesus good? (Mark 10:18)
> - His family opposed him. (Mark 3:21)
> - The baptism of Jesus by John, did Jesus sin?
>
> Third, why not embellish the accounts of his miracles?
>
> Fourth, why not attribute more sayings and teachings to Jesus? We find in a number of places within the Bible qualifications or instances where particular authors are very careful to distinguish between what Jesus had said and what they had said.
>
> - John (Revelation 2–3)
> - Agabus (Acts 11:28; 21:10–11)
> - Paul (1 Corinthians 7:10, 12)
>
> These are issues that the church had to struggle through during its earliest years. They are embarrassing, yet they were retained. They are things that we would expect to be described differently if they had been made up. However, these elements exist and it is reasonable to conclude that they were retained because they were words and deeds that actually took place.

10. How might Christians explain some of the differences among the accounts of the Gospels?

First, it is important to keep in mind that the Gospel accounts are summaries and paraphrases. That is, we do not have everything that Jesus said. His speeches, which are found within the Gospels, are only highlights. It would have been impossible to record or memorize everything that he communicated. Not only is this acceptable, it is the nature of history.

Second, it is important to understand that the oldest manuscripts we possess are written in Greek, but Jesus most likely spoke Aramaic. Thus, the Gospel accounts were translated from Aramaic to Greek to English. This does not mean that what we have is inaccurate; it merely means that when different translators translate, they translate differently.

[Discuss Paul's speech at the Areopagus (Acts 17:22–34) and Matthew, Mark, and Luke's explanation of the Parable of the Sower (Matthew 13:18–23; Mark 4:13–20; Luke 8:11–15).]

DEAR DOUG
WRITING ASSIGNMENT

Hey there!

Spring—it's so close I can almost taste it! I'm about ready to crawl out of my skin from being cooped up all winter doing nothing but studying. I'll be so glad when finals are over—I won't have to read a textbook for months!

Speaking of which, I've got a history exam I'm supposed to be cramming for right now. The gang met at the library last night to discuss some questions the professor gave us to research and write about. I guess I've always thought history was dull, but that everything written down actually happened... well, was based on fact at least. But Paige said that history isn't objective at all, since it's always told from the perspective of the winner. Do you think that is true?

Sarah said that there's no point to history, since everything that happens in life is based on chance. I would've put that attitude down to the blues (she got dumped last week), but Mark agreed with her. He said that the only way history means anything is if mankind helps to guide it in a positive direction. Do you agree that history doesn't have a point?

While we're on the subject, Nathan asked me the other day if I thought the stories in the Bible were actually true or if they were just myths people wrote to communicate truth. When I said that I've always believed the events in the Bible actually took place, he asked me what proof I had. I couldn't give him anything satisfying. I've never questioned what my Sunday school teachers told me. How do you know that the Bible is accurate and reliable?

I suppose history is important, but I'm more interested in the present. I mean, history's already happened and can't be changed, but that doesn't necessarily mean it's not important. Does Christianity have anything to say about history?

By the way, you probably want to know the latest on Amber and me. We've been hanging out together a lot, but she seems different somehow. She's quicker to get mad at me when the slightest hint of religion crosses my lips. I'm not sure what to do exactly. Your letters have gotten me more interested in worldviews and the Bible, and I don't want to slip back into being a wimpy Christian. But I've gotten really close to Amber and don't want to lose her either. I'm just not sure what to do. Anyway, I've got to go... procrastination is getting me nowhere!

Keep in touch,
Doug

Doug has brought up four different subjects; below is a rough outline of possible responses.

1. Is history merely a medium for perpetuating the viewpoint of the group in power? (12.5 points)

> While history can be "spun" or even "edited" to promote groups in power, actual historical events have taken place and reveal to us truths about reality and humanity's state of affairs. For example, either there was an historical event called the Fall or there wasn't. Either a man who claimed to be God's only Son and the way to salvation was born over two thousand years ago or he wasn't.

2. Does history have a purpose? (12.5 points)

> Unlike atheistic worldviews that see history as meaningless (other than the meaning they give to it) and pantheistic worldviews that see history as circular (reincarnation, for instance), the Christian worldview sees history as linear and progressing toward something. Christians see history as "The Grand Story" of creation, fall, and redemption. While the first pages of the Bible deal with creation and the fall, the rest of the Bible looks at God's plan for redeeming his fallen people. The Old Testament points to the cross and the redeeming work of Christ, while the New Testament gives us the details of the fulfillment of that promised redemption and renewal.

3. How do you know that the Bible is accurate and reliable? (12.5 points)

> There is much intra- and extra-biblical evidence that supports the claim that the Bible is both accurate and reliable. The many fulfilled prophecies from the Old Testament, archaeological evidence, and manuscripts such as the Dead Sea Scrolls attest to the Old Testament's reliability. The New Testament has even more support in terms of ancient manuscripts. There are over 5,000 Greek manuscripts alone and nearly 30,000 other documents that attest to its accuracy, such as the writings of Josephus, Polycarp, Eusebius, Tertullian, Origen, and others. In addition to the textual support, there are good reasons to believe that the Bible, the New Testament specifically, is not the creation of deceitful disciples, myth, or overzealous scribes.

4. What is the Christian view of history? (12.5 points)

> Christianity is rooted in history, and without its historical roots there would be no Christian worldview (1 Corinthians 15:14). The history contained in the Bible is accurate and describes events that actually occurred. All in all, the historical Bible (the written Word) and Jesus Christ (the living Word) are the two cornerstones of the Christian worldview. If the Bible isn't history, or if Jesus Christ isn't "God with us" (Matthew 1:23), Biblical Christianity crumbles.

UNIT TEN TEST

'HISTORY' TEXTBOOK QUESTIONS

Matching: (1 point possible per answer [2 for 90-day])
some options may be used more than once or not at all; some questions may have multiple answers

1. __a__ **Christianity**

2. __b/d__ **Islam**

3. __e__ **Secular Humanism**

4. __f/i__ **Marxism-Leninism**

5. __g__ **Cosmic Humanism**

6. __c/h__ **Postmodernism**

a. Creation, Fall, Redemption
b. *Jihad*
c. Historicism
d. Historical Determinism
e. Historical Evolution
f. Historical Materialism
g. Evolutionary Godhood
h. Historical Revisionism
i. Economic Determinism

Short answer: (6 points possible per answer [7 for 90-day])
7. **According to Christianity, what is the purpose of history?**

> For the Christian, history is linear. Time began with creation, we rebelled against God and creation fell, and God provided a means of redemption for us—Jesus Christ. Presently, history is moving toward a specific climax—the Day of Judgment (Acts 17:31; Romans 2:11–16). At this point, Christ's victory over sin will become apparent to all and Christians throughout history will be allowed to share in his triumph.

8. **According to Muslims, what is the purpose of history and the vision for the future?**

> Just as God created the world, he superintends it throughout time, guiding it toward an expression of his will. In concert with this belief is the Muslim hope that Islam will one day span the globe, with all peoples and nations being Muslim.

9. **How does Secular Humanism's belief in evolution influence its optimism for the future?**

> For the Secular Humanist, all of history is a development from non-life to life, from simple to more complex, from mindless to mind, from animal to human, from pond scum to Shakespeare, from amoral to moral. If, as Humanists believe, all reality is an evolutionary pattern that has moved upward step by step to create rational thought and morality in the highest species, then mankind's history must also be a progressive march toward a better world, i.e., as the evolutionary process continues, so must progress continue. Civilization constantly improves and ultimately carries the human race (or whatever race evolution dictates) into some type of better community.

10. Why do Marxists believe that global communism is inevitable? How does the dialectic play a role?

Since Marxists believe that everything is determined by natural deterministic laws that direct the evolution of economic systems toward a paradisiacal end, the future state of global communism is inexorable. No amount of human will can stop the collapse of capitalism, the rise of socialism, and the steady transition from socialism to communism. Marxism perceives mankind's efforts toward any other end as useless and insignificant, declaring that it is determined for us to achieve utopia (a communist society) despite all efforts and desires to the contrary.

Marxists believe that the dialectic has guided society through certain phases in a constant upward spiral through the dialectic of thesis, antithesis, and synthesis. This cycle guarantees inevitable progress toward a communist utopia—slavery, feudalism, capitalism, socialism, and some day communism.

11. According to Marxists, what does the future look like? What is the fate of the dialectic?

Marxists believe that under communism, all class distinctions will be abolished. Further, the dialectic has (theoretically) improved our economic structures (and consequently, societies and ideas) throughout history, but as soon as the dialectic leads the whole world to communism, the ultimate mode of production and exchange will have been achieved and the need for the dialectic will have been erased.

12. What is the Postmodern approach to history?

Postmodernists use the term *historicism* to describe the view that all questions must be settled within the cultural and social context in which they are raised. Both Lacan and Foucault argue that each historical period has its own knowledge system and individuals are unavoidably entangled within these systems. Answers to life's questions cannot be found by appealing to some external truth, but only the norms and forms within each culture that phrase the question.

13. What is historical revisionism?

The rewriting/editing of the past to serve an ideological purpose is called historical revisionism. Today this practice is seen with "feminist histories," i.e., attempts to expose a male-dominated, patriarchal past and point the way for empowering women. Likewise, we see "homosexual histories," i.e., responses to homophobic repressions in order to provide equality for homosexuals. Every repressed group has its own revision of history.

CENSORING THE PAST ESSAY
True or False: (2 points possible per answer [5 for 90-day])
*if an answer is false, restate it to make it true

14. Protesting against businesses that sell pornography or the government's refusal to fund the production of objectionable art is considered censorship.

> False: Protesting against businesses that sell pornography or the government's refusal to fund the production of objectionable art is <u>not</u> censorship.

15. Librarians and parents use discernment when they choose particular books over others.

> True

16. Censorship through preservation is the misrepresentation of historical facts.

> False: Censorship through <u>revision</u> is the misrepresentation of historical facts.

17. Censorship through omission is the exclusion of particular historical facts.

> True

18. In the past, religion played a major role in the development of public school curricula.

> True

"THE RELIABILITY OF SCRIPTURE" VIDEO
True or False: (2 points possible per answer)
*if an answer is false, restate it to make it true

19. There are many archaeological discoveries that support the reliability of the Old Testament.

> True

20. Archaeologists are still searching for the city of Jericho.

> False: Archaeologists <u>have found</u> the ancient city of Jericho

21. The prophecies of the Old Testament are general in nature and not specific.

False: The prophecies of the Old Testament were <u>very specific</u> in nature.

22. The Dead Sea Scrolls do not support the claim that the Bible is reliable.

False: The Dead Sea Scrolls <u>strongly substantiate</u> the claim that the Bible is reliable.

23. The Dead Sea Scrolls match the Masoretic text verbatim.

False: The Dead Sea Scrolls <u>contain a 5% variation (some spelling errors and pen slips)</u> from the Masoretic text.

24. Jewish people did not depend on oral tradition, rather, they wrote everything down.

False: Jewish people <u>were taught to remember</u> oral material.

25. Many prophecies were manufactured after the fact.

False: Scholars agree that the Old Testament was complete by 400 B.C.

26. Just because someone feels passionately about what they are writing doesn't mean it isn't reliable.

True

27. The Apostles had everything to gain and nothing to lose by changing the facts about Jesus's life.

False: The Apostles had <u>little</u> to gain and <u>almost everything</u> to lose by proclaiming the story of Jesus and his resurrection.

28. The Gospels include embarrassing details about some of the Apostles.

True

29. When God claims that the biblical authors were inspired, what he means is that the writers were so moved by wondrous acts of Jesus that they felt compelled to write.

> False: Peter and Paul both tell us that the words they spoke were not the words of men but rather were from God by way of his Spirit.

30. There are many ancient texts that have the same bibliographic support as the New Testament.

> False: There are <u>no</u> ancient texts that have the same bibliographic support as the New Testament.

31. The disciples did not act any differently after Christ's resurrection than they did before.

> False: The disciples <u>were transformed from fearful cowards to bold and courageous proclaimers of the Gospel</u> after Christ's resurrection.

32. The time between the original writings of the New Testament and subsequent manuscripts is a relatively short period of time.

> True

33. A 700-year gap between the original writing and a copied manuscript is considered good among works of antiquity.

> True

"THE HISTORICAL JESUS" VIDEO
Short answer: (6 points possible per answer [7 for 90-day])

34. Why do critical scholars date the Synoptic Gospels after A.D. 70?

> A number of biblical scholars today interpret history through the lens of methodological naturalism, thus limiting history to natural events and refusing to allow for the possibility of miracles. Therefore, since the Synoptic Gospels mention the destruction of the temple (the Olivet Discourse is found in Mark 13, Matthew 24, and Luke 19 and 21), the works must have been written after that event took place (i.e. after A.D. 70) and the prophecy merely attributed to Jesus to make it seem as if he actually predicted the event.

35. What case can be made for dating Acts and the Synoptic Gospels before A.D. 70?

First, the book of Acts tells the story of the formation and growth of the church through the lives of two central characters—Peter (1–12) and Paul (13–28). Along the way, the author tends to highlight certain events, namely persecutions and the death of leaders. For example, the death of Jesus (2:23), Stephen (7:60), and James (12:2) are all mentioned as relevant events. However, the death of Paul in A.D. 64 is never mentioned, leading many scholars to infer that the book was written while Paul was still alive.

Second, the gospel of Luke and the book of Acts were written as an historical two-volume account of the church. The gospel of Luke surveys the life and death of Jesus, while the book of Acts records the formation of the early church and the lives of its leading men. Thus, Acts follows Luke. Therefore, if Acts was written before A.D. 64, then Luke must have been written prior to A.D. 64 as well.

Third, a majority of scholars believe that Matthew and Luke used Mark as sources. This theory is derived by the similar (and sometimes exact wording) that is found between Mark and Luke, and Mark and Matthew. Therefore, if Luke used Mark, we can conclude that Mark was written before Luke, which was written before Acts, which was written before the death of Paul in A.D. 64.

Unit Ten

WORLDVIEW TEACHER MANUAL TRAINING

UNDERSTANDING THE TIMES

Conclusion

Topics:
Evangelism
Leadership

A Summit Ministries Curriculum

180-DAY SYLLABUS

DAY	IN CLASS	HOMEWORK	
1	WATCH "Worldview Witnessing" video	READ UTT Textbook 'Conclusion 11.1-11.2'	
2	REVIEW "Worldview Witnessing" video questions	READ UTT Textbook 'Conclusion 11.3'	
3	READ UTT Textbook 'Conclusion 11.3'		
4	REVIEW UTT Textbook 'Conclusion 11.3' questions	READ UTT Textbook 'Conclusion 11.4'	
5	READ UTT Textbook 'Conclusion 11.5-11.6'	READ UTT Textbook 'History 10.5'	
6	REVIEW UTT Textbook 'Conclusion 11.4-11.5' questions		
7	WATCH "Secrets of the World Changers" video P1–2		
8	WATCH "Secrets of the World Changers" video P3–4		
9	WATCH "Secrets of the World Changers" video P5–6		
10	REVIEW "Secrets of the World Changers" video questions		
11	TAKE Final Test		
12			
13			
14			
15			

90-DAY SYLLABUS

DAY	IN CLASS	HOMEWORK	
1	WATCH "Worldview Witnessing" video	READ UTT Textbook 'Conclusion 11.3'	
2	REVIEW "Worldview Witnessing" video questions	READ UTT Textbook 'Conclusion 11.4-11.5'	
3	TAKE Final Test		
4			
5			

Conclusion

"WORLDVIEW WITNESSING"
WITH KEVIN BYWATER

I. _____Apologetics_____: The defense of the Christian faith; to present reasons for why you believe what you believe

    A. Engaging the war of worldviews

        1. Jude 3

        2. 1 Peter 3:15–16

        3. Acts 17:2–4

    B. You can either _____dodge_____ the bullets or _____disarm_____ your opponent

    C. Difficulties in apologetics

        1. Too many _____issues_____

        2. Too little time

        3. Too much _____fear_____

II. **What happens when worldviews clash?**

    A. _____Convert_____

    B. Cower

    C. _____Compromise_____

    D. Confirm

III. **Developing probing and persuasive apologetics:**

    A. Attitude: Refutation vs. _____Persuasion_____

    B. Strategy: _____Questions_____ vs. Statements

C. Probing the Worldview Iceberg:

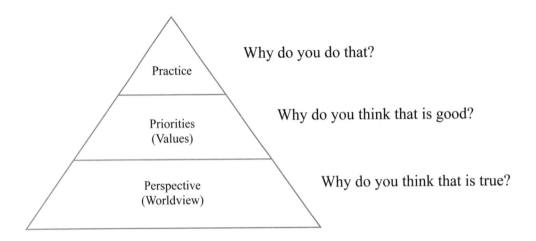

Practice — Why do you do that?

Priorities (Values) — Why do you think that is good?

Perspective (Worldview) — Why do you think that is true?

D. Some discerning and "disarming" questions:

1. What do you mean by _____that_____?

2. How did you come to that _____conclusion_____?

    i. Where did you get that information?

    ii. How do you know that to be true?

3. Have you ever considered _____[blank]_____?

    "Remember the 'golden rule' of asking questions: Ask of others only what you're willing for them to ask of you."

IV. Testing worldviews

A. Look for logical inconsistencies

B. Look for _____self-refuting_____ ideas

C. Is the worldview actually livable?

D. It must be able to explain _____reality_____

"WORLDVIEW WITNESSING"
VIDEO QUESTIONS

Answer the questions below on a separate sheet of paper and be prepared to review your answers in class.

1. **What is apologetics? What are three key verses used in the discussion of apologetics? How are these verses applied?**

Apologetics is the defense of the Christian faith.

[Read each of these passages and try to supply some context.]

In Jude 3, Jude notes that he wanted to write to his audience about their common faith in Christ, but he instead had to write and urge them to contend for the faith since there were false teachers and teachings in their midst. Jude thus defends Christian doctrine.

In 1 Peter 3:15–16, Peter informs his audience that they need to "always be prepared to give an answer" to everyone who asks about their faith. Beyond this, Peter instructs that such a reason should be given with "gentleness and respect" so that one can be above the attitude of those attacking Christianity. Even our actions are an apologetic for faith.

In Acts 17:2–4 Luke records the habits of the missionary Paul. It was Paul's custom to argue that Jesus was Lord and that Christ's ministry was prophesied beforehand. He thus attempts to persuade Jews, Godfearers [Greek converts to Judaism], and Greeks of the truth of Christianity.

2. **What four things can occur when worldviews clash?**

First, a person can convert to the other side. This is not necessarily a bad thing, since this means that people can convert to the truth. Of course, this also means that people can convert to falsehood. Second, a person can cower, become afraid, and withdraw from the struggle of ideas. Third, a person can compromise and adopt bits and pieces of other worldviews with their Christian worldview. Fourth, a person can be confirmed or further convinced of the truth of Christ.

3. **How does one persuade using apologetics?**

One of the first strategies of apologetics should be persuading rather than refuting. Persuasion is obviously more difficult, but if it can become our goal, then we have a better chance of winning hearts rather than mere arguments. Therefore, it is important to maintain a Christian attitude while dialoging with a non-believer or asking questions. By asking questions rather than making blunt statements, one can force the other person to actually consider a Christian point of view without seeming argumentative. Another advantage of asking questions is that it forces the other person to think through and ultimately defend their own point of view.

Conclusion

SM 309

4. **What are some questions that can help us understand another's worldview? What are some discerning and disarming questions that can help others think through their worldview?**

If we are seeking to understand one's worldview, then a series of questions can often lead us from their practices to their perspectives. What we are looking for is the foundational reasons for what they believe.

For example, if someone is participating in pre-martial sex, we could ask the simple question, "Why do you do that?" Their response may be that it is fun or enjoyable, to which we could respond with a deeper question, "Why do you think that is good?" Hopefully sooner or later you can get to their worldview through questions. They may assert that the purpose of life is to maximize pleasure and reduce pain. To this response, we could further probe, "Why do you think that is true?"

Some other good questions to use in dialogue are the following:
- "What do you mean by that?"—This question forces clarity of terms or ideas.
- "How did you come to that conclusion?"—This question forces out a methodology or reveals the process of one's thinking.
- "Where did you get that information?"—This question is helpful for statistical assertions, etc. that people purport.
- "How do you know that to be true?"—Like the previous question, this question seeks sources or reasons.
- "Have you ever considered [blank] ?"—This question allows an alternative perspective to be considered.

5. **What are some good tests for worldview viability?**

- Look for logical inconsistencies. If a belief is true, then it must be logical. For example, a belief must satisfy the Law of Non-contradiction, which states that a belief cannot be both true and false at the same time and in the same sense. One cannot logically hold a worldview where in some cases they believe in God and in others they do not.
- Look for self-refuting ideas or beliefs that defeat themselves. One cannot hold to the belief that nothing is true and at the same time assert that such a belief is true.
- Is the worldview actually livable? Does it work in the real world? Some people assert that human beings are basically good. However, few of us live out this belief (case in point, we lock our doors at night).
- It must be able to explain reality. That is, it must line up with what we experience. Some may argue that God does not exist and reality is the result of evolution. Yet, this belief does not seem to conform to the design we see in nature.

UNDERSTANDING THE TIMES
CONCLUSION QUESTIONS

Answer the questions below on a separate sheet of paper and be prepared to review your answers in class.

CONCLUSION 11.3

1. Why does it take faith to be an atheist?

Many atheists deny theism because they claim it takes too much faith to believe in an unseen God. However, atheists themselves cannot escape the need for faith. According to the naturalistic worldview, not only did unintelligent matter produce the mind, but it also *feigns* the appearance of design. From the complexity of DNA to the intricate communicative dance of the bumblebee, what *appears* to be design is merely the product of random chance. To hold such a worldview takes a great deal of faith in things unseen—an eternal existence of matter/energy, chance producing design, simple life evolving into complex life, unintelligent matter producing intelligence, etc. [UTT 11.3.2]

2. According to naturalism, which came first: mind or matter? Why?

The atheist believes that matter predated and eventually produced the mind. Many atheists deny the existence of God because they claim that science renders such a belief illogical. However, both science and reason give credence to theism. The naturalistic worldview posits that an eternal universe composed entirely of matter and energy somehow arranged itself in an increasing order of complexity (which is contrary to the Second Law of Thermodynamics). Non-life yielded life, simple life evolved into advanced forms, which finally produced the intelligence seen in mankind. [UTT 11.3.2–3]

3. What are evolution's two biggest hurdles? Why?

Evolution must be able to 1) demonstrate spontaneous generation and 2) account for the lack of transitional forms of life.

For evolution to be true, life must somehow have originated from non-life. Evolution must explain how amino acids appeared from non-life and how amino acids were arranged into proteins without the guidance of DNA. Moreover, every such experiment involves intelligent life forms (i.e. scientists) manipulating factors to yield the necessary *random* results. For example, even though scientists believe that oxygen has been plentiful since the beginning, all of these experiments are performed in environments depleted of oxygen because oxygen destroys organic compounds. Yet not one experiment to create life from non-life has been successful.

A second hurdle for the theory of evolution is the lack of transitional fossil evidence. At least Darwin was scientifically honest when he first formulated the theory, noting that if fossil evidence is not found to support his theory, then his theory must be abandoned. Today, evolutionists either dogmatically *assume* the theory is true or adopt the theory of punctuated evolution—a theory which postulates that the lack of transitional fossil forms supports the theory. [UTT 11.3.5–7]

4. **Is there ample evidence for humanity's sinful nature?**

> The Bible teaches that humanity, left to its own devices, naturally gravitates toward selfish and sinful ends. On the other hand, most secular worldviews place the problem of sin on the shoulders of society rather than the individual. These worldviews posit that mankind is inherently good and that if society could be correctly altered, this inherent goodness would be evident. However, in attempts to prove this belief, Marxists and Secular Humanists alike have merely proven the Christian position. Tens of millions have been sacrificed in the name of communism and countless millions more in the debate over personhood (i.e., the convenience of abortion). [UTT 11.3.8–9]

5. **What problems stem from the promotion of non-traditional families?**

> Christians believe that the family is the glue that holds society together. As the family goes, so goes society. Current examples of this are everywhere today: poverty is epidemic among families headed by single women; young men and women between 17 and 24 years old are far more likely to abuse drugs or commit crimes if they come from fatherless homes; legalized abortion has cheapened human life to the point that Americans are no longer shocked by euthanasia; and child abuse rates have risen right along with abortion rates. [UTT 11.3.9]

6. **What are some inconsistencies inherent in the Marxist utopian worldview in general and socialism in particular?**

> As with the rest of the Marxist worldview, there are a number of inconsistencies in its theories regarding civilization and its institutions. If we are but helpless pawns of the dialectic, why bother to encourage workers to revolt—won't societal change happen inevitably when the dialectic demands it? Further, does the dialectic just stop working once the perfect society (i.e., communism) is attained? Or will communism draw a new antithesis to itself and clash to form another synthesis? In other words, because the synthesis is transitory, even utopia will be transitory and must logically give way to another social order.
>
> A larger problem is created by the Marxist's insistence that socialism is an improvement over capitalism. Socialism robs mankind of any incentive to better himself because it is contrary to human nature's built-in sense of justice. Those who are lazy and do not produce—whether grades in school or cars on an assembly line—should not receive an equal result with those who do. In the end, socialism discriminates against the competent, the hardworking, the productive, and encourages envy and laziness among poor men and women who might, in a capitalist society, achieve productivity and cultivate feelings of self-worth rather than jealousy.
>
> Further, socialism does not hasten the abolition of class distinctions (as Marxists claim it will), but creates a new elite. For example, the former Soviet Union created a class known as the nomenklatura or the government elite who owned everything—the factories, markets, transportation systems, etc. Instead of destroying class distinctions, socialism created a completely authoritarian class.
>
> The greatest flaw in the Marxist and the Secular Humanist socialistic schemes is that it expects to replace the precise free market mechanism with that of central planners. They trust that enough economists can make the proper decisions about what to produce and how much of it to produce,

Conclusion

and assign various prices, as efficiently as the constant adjustments made by the laws of supply and demand. Not only does this claim appear unworkable in theory, it has been proven totally unworkable in practice in numerous socialist countries. There are not enough smart, moral people to know all the economic factors to make such decisions. [UTT 11.3.10–11]

7. **What does Christianity postulate as the root of humanity's problems? How does Christianity propose to transform society?**

The Christian worldview understands that the problems of this world lie not on faulty societal structures and governments, but in the inherent sinfulness of mankind. Thus, Christianity offers a cure—the opportunity to break the bonds of sin—not by trusting in men or government, but by acknowledging the human lust for control and turning to the lordship of Christ for help. [UTT 11.3.12]

8. **What legal problems arise from the Secular Humanist and Marxist worldviews? How do Christians view the discipline of law?**

Secular Humanists and Marxists place legal responsibility solely in the hands of the State—a move which leads to a pitfall similar to that of self-law—legal relativism. Because government is an ever-changing entity, law cannot remain absolute. For law to remain constant, for the word justice to mean anything in a rational, legal sense, law must have an unchanging basis. Only an absolute foundation can create absolute laws like, "It is always unlawful and morally wrong for a judge to take a bribe." "It is always and universally wrong for an adult to sexually molest and torture a child for fun." Other systems of law can only declare, "It is unlawful, in the present circumstances, to take a bribe," or "Thou shalt not commit bribery… ordinarily."

The danger of legal relativism should be obvious to all. It is no exaggeration to say that under positivist law, an individual might one day awaken to find that green eyes have been decreed illegal, and be executed that morning for breaking legal code. When the state is the only basis for law, any law may be conceived. Examples of this truth may be seen throughout society. Hitler, Stalin, and many others used positive law to murder millions—passing laws to eliminate Jews, gypsies, the sick, landowners, Christians, or anyone they had an urge to destroy—which fundamentally means anyone who stood in the way of their absolute domination of every person and action in society. Conversely, Christian law applied to society results in practical and just legal structures. Christian law is based on the character of God, a moral order, man created in the image of God, and the coming of Jesus Christ in flesh. [UTT 11.3.13]

9. **What is scientism? What problems arise from this belief when applied to ethics?**

Scientism is the belief that all knowledge and truth can be and should be discovered through the discipline of science. If science is unable to investigate an area, then it has nothing to do with truth.

The first problem associated with scientism is that science *cannot* reasonably be the sole source of truth and knowledge. For example, science cannot study God (or even the absence of a God). Neither can it study ethics or even truth and epistemology itself.

The second problem that arises from scientism is closely associated with the first—proponents of this view inevitably attempt to apply the scientific method to unscientific questions like those found in theology, ethics, and the origins debate. And desiring science to be omniscient, they go beyond the findings of science, and conclude that God does not exist, that morality is a human invention, and that all the cosmos and the life within it originated from naturalistic and random processes. And, as the past has shown us, when these conclusions are applied in the real world we get genocide, oppression, and nihilism.

In the end, science has nothing to say about terms such as justice, love, and courage. Science can no more reveal a meaningful foundation for these terms than it can explain a man and a woman falling in love. So, despite railing against absolute codes and traditional morality, the secular worldviews inevitably fall back on some form of Christian ethics when postulating specific moral suggestions. Science had nothing to do with forming the foundation for biblical morality. God's character is the foundation for Christian law and ethics—and as a result, Christian legal and ethical systems fit the facts of reality and provide genuine guidance for the man seeking to act rightly. [UTT 11.3.14–16]

10. What problems arise from scientism when applied to psychology?

When scientism is applied to study of mankind, humanity is reduced to mere matter, the mind and soul regarded as illusions, and free will regarded as a myth. In other words, no person wills to do anything because there is nothing physical within a human being which is able to escape the law of causation. Therefore, every "choice" we make is just an illusion. What appears to be a "choice" is actually the mechanical process of cause and effect. I cannot help but believe scientism is an incorrect view of the world, and naturalists cannot help but believe that it is. Neither of us can "freely" change our minds, though some natural process (e.g. firing synapses or whatever) may someday make it appear that I have.

Interestingly enough, most Secular Humanists and Marxists downplay or even ignore this inevitable conclusion simply because it seems illogical, and moreover, they fear its implications.

In a sense, this is what Secular Humanists and Marxists are forced to do when coping with the real world. Their worldviews describe the universe one way, but they cannot live in accordance with their views. Secular worldview proponents leave their atheism and materialism on the shelf and embrace the concept of absolutes and free will when interacting with the community. [UTT 11.3.18–19]

CONCLUSION 11.4

11. What two things should Christians keep in mind when defending the biblical worldview?

According to 2 Timothy 2:24–26, we must present the truth in order set free those who have been captured by deceptive philosophies, and secondly, we are to be kind and gentle as we do so. Both our message content and our character are important. [UTT 11.4.1]

12. Why is religious pluralism logically impossible?

The Law of Non-contradiction states specifically that two things cannot be the same and different at the same time and in the same way. In other words, something cannot be both true and false at the same time. When we apply the Law of Non-contradiction to the religions of the world, we find that Hindus, Buddhists, Jews, and Muslims deny what Christians affirm: that Jesus is God incarnate, the third person of the Trinity. Either Jesus is, in fact, a member of the Trinity, or he is not. If he is not, then Christians are wrong about their belief and those of other religions are right. On the other hand, if Christians are right, then the other religions are wrong. It cannot be both ways. While it is possible all the religions of the world are false, it is a *certainty* that they cannot all be true. [UTT 11.4.2]

13. What is wrong with the parable of the elephant?

The parable assumes 1) that each man can discern only part of the truth about the elephant and 2) that we know something the blind men don't—there is a real elephant everyone is touching.

While the first assumption relies on the belief that no one possesses complete knowledge, the second presupposes that objective knowledge about the nature of God does exist and that someone knows what the elephant (or God) is really like. But here we find a contradiction. On the one hand, the story claims that we—the blind men—only have limited knowledge. But if everyone is blind, no one can know the ultimate shape of the elephant. We need the perspective of someone who is not blind, a privileged position that the New Ager claims for himself. But how is it that the New Age adherent knows the truth and the rest of us don't? As it turns out, this story does not *prove* the point it is trying to make—it merely *illustrates* what Cosmic Humanists already believe to be true. [UTT 11.4.3]

14. Why can ethical relativists not live consistently?

Whether they recognize it or not, ethical relativists cannot live consistently with their own moral position. The first step in defending a Christian view of ethics requires showing how other views are not valid. When someone says all morals are relative, the simplest way to deflate that idea is to ask, "Relative to what?" As soon as anyone attempts to answer that question by giving a fixed reference point, he or she has just provided an "absolute" standard and thus ceases to be a relativist.

Another way to help people realize they actually do believe in moral absolutes is to take from them something they value, like a wallet or mp3 player. When they object to this, turn the tables and ask, "Why are you upset? You're not trying to force *your* morality on *me*, are you?" When it comes to things people hold dear, all become moral absolutists. [UTT 11.4.4]

15. What are a couple of areas of commonality Christians can use when speaking with someone who has been captured by the New Age worldview?

When approaching someone who has been captured by the New Age worldview, we can affirm his or her desire for greater spirituality in the midst of our materialistic culture. Their longing for inspiration and wonder in life is legitimate, as is their craving for a sense of personal worth. Yet we also need to explain that they are selling themselves short by seeking personal fulfillment in a non-personal

Conclusion

source—the New Age cosmic-energy-force-God. Only a personal God can meet their deepest need for love and unconditional acceptance.

In addition, we can agree with the New Age concern for karma as it reflects our innate sense of justice—the idea of reaping what you sow, as the Bible mentions in Galatians 6:7. Yet, the idea of karma does not measure up to the Bible's assertion that our past faults can be forgiven and that we can be united with the God who created us to have a relationship with him. [UTT 11.4.5]

CONCLUSION 11.5

16. Why is the Postmodern view of reality self-defeating?

The Postmodernist asserts that words construct rather than reflect reality. Thus, the popular slogans "that's just your interpretation" or "that may be true for you, but not for me." These slogans insinuate that differing individuals have differing views of reality and that no one's interpretation is any better than anyone else's. However, these slogans are promoted as truth and their underlying belief are held as "true." In the end real life is not open to infinite interpretations. [UTT 11.5.2]

17. What is wrong with the Postmodern view of language?

If each community determines what is true through its use of language, which community gets to decide between rival communities when it comes to conflicting ideas? Take for example such disputed ideas as suttee (the Hindu practice of burning widows on their deceased husband's pyre), exterminating the Jewish race, or abolishing private ownership of property? Since no community can claim to be "right" on any of these or other issues, the result is an increased competition for which group will dominate over the others. [UTT 11.5.3]

18. Why is the Postmodern rejection of truth and metanarratives incompatible with Christianity?

According to a Christian worldview, "truth" exists. Nearly everything about Christianity is *universal* in scope and application. God created the whole universe, including men and women. Sin is a *universal* condition affecting every human being. God loved the whole world, including every human being. Christ died for the sins of the *whole world*, not just one or two particular communities. Christians are to love God with all their heart and mind and their fellow human beings around the *whole world*.

And most importantly, God chose to communicate the truth about himself and his world through words contained in the Scriptures along with the language of the heavens (Psalm 19). God's words do not depend upon a reader's interpretation. Instead, the reader is to interpret the Bible according to God's intention. [UTT 11.5.4]

19. How are Postmodernists inconsistent when it comes to the subject of "social justice?"

On the one hand Postmodernists claim that no metanarrative can capture the essence of truth. Yet, at the same time they claim that a leftist vision of social justice is "right" for the world. But this begs the question, how can their view be correct?" Why try to rescue minority races from oppression? What's wrong with oppression? And what gives them the right to impose their views on others? The best they can say is, "We don't like it." [UTT 11.5.5]

[Discuss with your students the role Christianity has played in promoting "social justice" around the world. 11.5.6.]

20. How is the Postmodernist approach to history inconsistent?

Postmodernists claim that all historical accounts are merely fictions created for a political purpose and that all historians are biased, confined within their own social setting. Historians, of course, have a worldview, some vision of political improvement, and a host of emotional investments. This always has been the case. Thus the Postmodernist is correct to assert that biased historians have misidentified as well as mischaracterized historical events. However, this assertion assumes that such historians have "gotten it wrong."

While it is the case that some historians have misconstrued history to convince others of a certain perspective of past events, the fact that we can even *know* this has occurred illustrates that history is not entirely inaccessible. That narratives of the past can be *corrected* illustrates that history should not be equated with fictional accounts such as imaginative novels.

It is clear that individuals, communities, and governments have misconstrued history for the purpose of either gaining power or covering up their misdeeds. For example, the former Soviet Union controlled the writing of textbooks and taught children Joseph Stalin was the epitome of virtue when he actually was a mass murderer. The truth was discovered when eyewitnesses came forward speaking of the atrocities and finding the mass graves of those slaughtered. Continued research into history revealed the truth about Stalin, Lenin, Mao, Pol Pot, and others.

These revelations concerning Stalin and the others are not mere social constructions or the political biases of present-day historians, but form the consensus of scholarly reflection. They are also based on the assumption that we can have a certain access to truth with it comes to the past. And while this is something that Postmodernists are not willing to admit, it is the only sensible approach to understanding history. [UTT 11.5.7]

"Secrets of the World Changers"
with Jeff Myers

PART ONE

I. Living Like Royalty

"God uses ordinary people, with ordinary talents, to put forward into leadership situations so [they] can make an impact on the world for Jesus Christ."

A. The person in the Bible who typifies leadership as it relates to young people is _____Esther_____, who was…

    1. Probably a _____teenager_____.

    2. Put in a position of great responsibility

    3. Responded with creativity and courage

    "For if you remain silent at this time, relief and deliverance for the Jews will arise from another place, but you and your father's family will perish. And who knows but that you have come to royal position for such a time as this?" — Esther 4:14

    "But you are a chosen people, a royal priesthood, a holy nation, a people belonging to God that you may declare the praises of Him who called you out of darkness into His wonderful light." — 1 Peter 2:9

B. You were born to be _____royalty_____.

II. The Foundation of Leadership From a Biblical Standpoint

A. Jesus on leadership: "If anyone wants to be first he must be the very last, and the _____servant_____ of all." — Mark 9:35

B. *Doulos*: One who _____willingly_____ becomes a slave

    "Leadership is a willingness to rise to the bottom." — Dr. Glen Schulz

C. You lead in direct proportion to your willingness to support the weight of your followers.

    "The more responsibility you are willing take for the lives of others, the more of a leader you will be."

D. _____**Leader**_____: A person who views the world from God's perspective, who exercises his or her gifts and talents with excellence and perseverance, and who strategically plans to serve others.

III. Four Aspects of a Breakthrough

A. _____**Strategic vision**_____: Seeing the world as God sees it

B. _____**Strategic mission**_____: Knowing where you fit in God's plan

C. _____**Strategic motivation**_____: Getting the energy to live out God's plan

D. _____**Strategic plan**_____: Organizing your life around God's plan

---

PART TWO

IV. The Big Picture: Developing a Strategic Vision

"The first thing that distinguishes world-changing leaders from everyone else is their vision of the world. They have a stronger sense of how to influence the world through determination and creativity."

"The secret to discovering a sense of vision is learning to see the world as God sees it."

V. Strategic _____**Vision**_____: Seeing the World As God Sees It

A. The lack of vision _____**kills**_____.

"Where there is no vision, the people perish." — Proverbs 29:18

B. Vision-driven people see the world…

1. The way it _____**really**_____ is

…and…

2. The way they want it _____**to be**_____

C. Four characteristics that cause us to lose our vision

1. _____**Relativism**_____: People can't distinguish right from wrong

2. _____**Apathy**_____: People stop caring about others

3. _____**Cowardice**_____: People become too fearful to act on what is right

4. _____**Tyranny**_____: Those in power force their self-serving preferences on others

"In the absence of a biblical morality, a new elite will always come forward to dictate arbitrary absolutes to society." — Francis Schaeffer

5. This vision leads to: _____**Oppression**_____

"When the righteous thrive, the people rejoice; when the wicked rule, the people groan." — Proverbs 28:12

Conclusion

D. Four characteristics of an alternative vision:

    1. _____**Discernment**_____: The ability to distinguish right from wrong and to prefer the right

    2. _____**Conviction**_____: A personal concern about right and wrong for yourself and others

    "See to it that no one takes you captive through hollow and deceptive philosophy." — Colossians 2:8

    3. _____**Courage**_____: Overcoming fear to stand for right and oppose evil

    4. _____**Peace**_____: Those in power rule by objective timeless standards of maintaining freedom with restraint

    5. This vision leads to: _____**Prosperity**_____

    "Misfortune pursues the sinner, but prosperity is the reward of the righteous." — Proverbs 13:21

E. How to get a vision:

    1. _____Notice_____ the problem (Nehemiah)

    2. _____Sense_____ the urgency (Esther)

    3. _____Anticipate_____ involvement (Isaiah)

    4. _____Commit_____ to action (Deborah)

    "In many ways, getting a vision is a skill, and like any skill, it improves with practice. As you improve your ability to get a vision of the world around you, you will improve in your influence in the lives of other people; and as a result, you will move toward becoming a world-changing leader."

PART THREE

VI. Living Like A Winner: Developing a Strategic Mission

"The second thing that distinguishes world-changing leaders from everyone else is their ability to tap into their reservoir of talents and gifts, in order to get more out of every situation and make the most of every opportunity."

VII. Strategic _____Mission_____: Knowing Where You Fit in God's Plan

A. Three crucial facts of Scripture that give us a sense of mission

    1. God _____made_____ you

"For you created my inmost being; you knit me together in my mother's womb. I praise you because I am fearfully and wonderfully made." — Psalm 139:13–14

2. God has _____gifted_____ you to achieve

"There are different kinds of gifts but the same Spirit... Now to each one the manifestation of the Spirit is given for the common good." — 1 Corinthians 12:4–7

3. God _____directs_____ you through your actions

"In his heart a man plans his course, but the Lord determines his steps." — Proverbs 16:9

B. How to develop a mission

1. **Review**_____: Look for clues in your life experiences

2. **Anticipate**_____: Look ahead to determine a course of action

3. **Consult**_____: Get help from the "Solomons" in your life

4. **Enact**_____: Do your best, recognizing that God will steer you

"Your sense of mission does not emerge from other people. It comes from living out the design that God has given to you—that unique ability to do what he specifically has called you to do. And as you live out that sense of mission, you will become a world-changing leader who will make a difference in the world for Jesus Christ."

PART FOUR

VIII. Leadership Fitness: Developing Strategic Motivation

"The third thing that distinguishes world-changing leaders from everyone else is the way they use their energy to accomplish the things that they can accomplish."

IX. Strategic _____Motivation_____: Getting the Energy to Live Out God's Plan

"Perseverance means moving on in spite of great difficulties, taking on the challenges, climbing the mountains of life, and continuing on even in the face of great obstacles."

"We develop a strategy... and then eventually our strategy begins to turn into stress."

A. How to deal with the stresses of life

1. _____**Stress**_____: A condition existing because of strain or deformation

2. _____**Tension**_____: Either of two balancing forces tending to cause strain or deformation

3. Stress is bad, but tension can be good

4. _____**Equilibrium**_____: A state of balance or equality between opposing forces

Conclusion

B. Developing equilibrium

    1. Recognize _____destructive_____ responses [to stress]

    2. Write down what is _____bothering_____ you

    3. Define a _____sunset_____ for each activity

    4. Don't _____sacrifice_____ your basic needs (sleep, food, exercise)

C. Staying motivated

    1. Understand true motivation

        Motivation: "A temporary condition in which individuals direct high levels of concentration and attention toward the competent completion of a task."— Professors Beatty and Payne

    2. A strategy for successful advancement

        i. Plan

        ii. Attack

        iii. Establish

        iv. Regroup (rest)

    3. Other ideas for staying motivated

        i. Challenge yourself regularly

        ii. Study heroes

        iii. Redeem the pockets of time

        iv. Maintain spiritual disciplines

        "The way to stay motivated is to understand the sequence of plan, attack, establish, regroup; and to maintain the basic disciplines of using your time wisely. As you do those kinds of things, you will discover that motivation for most people is not a persistent state of high energy and a positive attitude; but the ability to press on in spite of great difficulties."

PART FIVE

X. Developing a Strategic Plan: Organizing Your Life around God's Plan

"The fourth thing that distinguishes world-changing leaders from everyone else is the way they plan carefully to achieve well-defined goals."

XI. Strategic Plan : Organizing Your Life around God's Plan

A. Learning to redeem the time .

"Be very careful how you live, making the most of every opportunity, because the days are evil." — Ephesians 5:15–16

1. Get a _____planner_____ and use it

2. Plan at the _____beginning_____ of the week

3. Plan based on your _____mission_____ and goals

4. _____Focus_____ on one or two areas each day

B. Learning to set _____goals_____

1. **Record**_____: Write it down

2. **Envision**_____: Imagine the benefits

3. **A**sk_____: Seek help from experts

4. **C**ollect_____: Gain skills and knowledge

5. **H**one_____: Develop a plan of action

PART SIX

XII. As Soon As You Commit to This Process, _____Satan_____ Will Attack You!

Dear Christian Wimp:

Who do you think you are? You'll never pull this off! See enclosed list.
Your adversary, Satan

Reasons why you'll never make it as a leader:
- *You don't have enough clout*
- *No one will pay attention*
- *You'll be too afraid*
- *You're no match for me*

A. **Satan's attack:** "You don't have enough _____clout_____"

  Response: Your weakness is God's _____strength_____

  "Brothers, think of what you were when you were called. Not many of you were wise by human standards; not many were influential... But God chose the foolish things of the world to shame the wise; God chose the weak things of the world to shame the strong... so that no one may boast before him." — 1 Corinthians 1:26–29

B. **Satan's attack:** "No one will pay attention to you. You are too _____young_____"

  Response: Don't be intimidated... set the _____standard_____

  "Don't let anyone look down on you because you are young, but set an example for the believers in speech, conduct, faith, love, and purity." — 1 Timothy 4:12

C. **Satan's attack:** "You'll be _____afraid_____"

  Response: God has given you _____boldness_____

  "For God did not give us a spirit of fear, but a spirit of power, of love, and of self-discipline." — 2 Timothy 1:7

D. **Satan's attack:** "You're no _____match_____ for me"

  Response: _____Victory_____ is inevitable

  "What, then, shall we say in response to this? If God is for us, who can be against us?... In all these things we are more than conquerors through him who loved us." — Romans 8:31, 37

XIII. What Is Worth Living (and Dying) For?

"The sin of our time is the sin that believes in nothing, cares for nothing, seeks to know nothing, interferes with nothing, enjoys nothing, hates nothing, finds purpose in nothing, lives for nothing, and remains alive because there is nothing for which it will die." — Dorothy Sayers

"SECRETS OF THE WORLD CHANGERS"
VIDEO QUESTIONS

Answer the questions below on a separate sheet of paper and be prepared to review your answers in class.

1. What did Jesus say about leadership? What are the characteristics of a Christian leader?

In Mark 9:35 Jesus said that, "if anyone wants to be first he must be the very last, and the servant of all." This description of leadership radically reverses how the world defines a leader. The biblical mandate to leadership is not exercising power over others for personal gain; rather it is obeying God through serving others. Just as our leader Jesus washed the feet of his followers, so must we serve the needs of the world.

[Also discuss Philippians 2:1–8.]

A Christian leader is a person who views the world from God's perspective, who exercises his or her gifts and talents with excellence and perseverance, and who strategically plans to serve others. To view the world through God's perspective one must know his Word and have a biblical worldview. Beyond this, all Christians have been given gifts to exercise in the world. These talents should be developed and employed in an exceptional manner and they should benefit others.

2. What is a strategic vision? What are four characteristics that cause us to lose our vision? What are four characteristics for an alternative vision? How do we get a vision?

Having a strategic vision is to see the world as God sees it.

Currently, there are a number of societal attitudes that, if adopted, can cause us to lose our vision. The first is moral relativism. The ethical attitude of Postmodernism is to privatize morality to either the individual or the community. Moral relativism becomes the root of other problems. The second is apathy. Logically, if there is no universal or transcendent right and wrong, then we can ignore evil and refuse to do good. The third is cowardice. To stand up for right in today's culture is to be intolerant, and so out of fear we opt to do nothing at all. Lastly, the logical outcome of moral relativism is a society where right is decided by those in power. Ultimately this lack of vision leads to oppression.

However, we can develop a Christian vision by adopting some Christian attitudes. The first attitude is discernment. Contrary to the current of the culture at large, people can develop the ability to distinguish between right and wrong and choose to do right. Second, we can and should have conviction—personal concern for others and ourselves. Thirdly, rather than cowardice, we can be courageous and stand up for what is right. Lastly, the logical outcome of moral discernment in society is peace. Ultimately this vision leads to prosperity.

To get a vision, we must:
- Notice the problem
- Sense the urgency
- Anticipate involvement, i.e. plan
- Commit to action

Conclusion

For example, perhaps you live in a city with many homeless and hungry people, or perhaps you live in a town where teen pregnancy is a problem. There are many ethical issues if Christians will first notice them and then be moved by the sense of urgency the problem creates. After recognizing the problem and choosing to be concerned, we can begin to plan our response.

Using the above examples, perhaps you could collect leftover restaurant food in your city and transport it several times a week to a local soup kitchen. Perhaps you could volunteer to tutor a teen mom so that she can graduate college and provide for her family. Lastly, you can put your plan into action.

3. **What is a strategic mission? What are three crucial facts of Scripture that give us a sense of mission? How do we develop a mission?**

Having a strategic mission means to know where you fit in God's plan. Biblically, we can know that God has made you, gifted you, and that he directs you.

To get a mission one must RACE:

- **Review**—look for clues in your life experiences. This is more than just what you are good at. It is most importantly what you enjoy and are passionate about.
- **Anticipate**—look ahead to determine a course of action. Think through the ramifications and long-term implications of a mission. This means researching and planning.
- **Consult**—get help from the "Solomons" in your life. Talk to others that are already in an area of interest. Ask them for advice and mentorship.
- **Enact**—do your best, recognizing that God will steer you. This does not mean that we should sit and wait for God to direct us. Rather, we need to be actively engaged and ready to allow God to direct us.

4. **What is a strategic motivation? How does one stay motivated?**

Having strategic motivation means getting the energy to live out God's plan.

It is important to realize that motivation is not a constant state but rather a temporary condition of high concentration directed toward a goal. Maintaining constant motivation is impossible and trying to achieve such a constant state only leads to stress and burnout. Motivation should follow a pattern: plan, attack, establish, and regroup. The same model is used in war campaigns. First, plan out a battle; then implement the plan. Next, establish yourself and then rest before moving on to the next mission.

Other ways to stay motivated:
- Challenge yourself regularly
- Study heroes
- Redeem the pockets of time
- Maintain spiritual disciplines

5. What is a strategic plan? How do you redeem time? How do you set goals?

Having a strategic plan means organizing your life around God's plan.

To use time effectively, it is prudent to get a planner and use it. This means setting aside time at the beginning of the week to write down daily, weekly, and long-term goals. These goals need to be planned based on your mission. It is also prudent to focus on only one or two areas each day, rather than taking a shotgun approach and shifting focus every few minutes.

To set goals, you must REACH for the prize:
- **Record**—write it down. This will help you organize and prioritize.
- **Envision**—imagine the benefits. This will help give you motivation and a sense of purpose.
- **Ask**—seek help from others. There are number of people who can be resources for your endeavors.
- **Collect**—gain skills and knowledge
- **Hone**—develop a plan of action. It is important to have a map to know where you are going and how you will get there.

GOAL SETTING ACTIVITY

Take some time before the end of the course to allow the students to set some goals. Distribute the "Goal Setting" handout found on the Teacher's CD-ROM in the "Handouts" folder. Students should set at least one goal for each area, remembering that goals must be specific, realistic, and tangible.

FINAL EXAM (180-DAY)
ANSWER KEY

2 points possible per answer

1. D	51. D	101. E
2. B	52. E	102. D
3. C	53. A	103. E
4. C	54. A	104. B
5. C	55. C	105. E
6. D	56. A	106. C
7. D	57. D	107. C
8. C	58. A	108. C
9. B	59. D	109. D
10. D	60. E	110. B
11. C	61. A	111. E
12. D	62. B	112. A
13. D	63. A	113. B
14. D	64. B	114. D
15. E	65. D	115. B
16. D	66. E	116. B
17. E	67. A	117. E
18. B	68. D	118. E
19. D	69. C	119. A
20. E	70. D	120. C
21. C	71. B	121. B
22. E	72. E	122. C
23. E	73. E	123. A
24. E	74. B	124. E
25. A	75. E	125. E
26. E	76. B	126. C
27. E	77. E	127. C
28. C	78. C	128. B
29. B	79. A	129. D
30. C	80. D	130. D
31. E	81. D	131. D
32. D	82. B	132. C
33. E	83. E	133. A
34. A	84. D	134. B
35. E	85. E	135. D
36. C	86. A	136. E
37. C	87. A	137. E
38. B	88. B	138. C
39. A	89. D	139. E
40. E	90. A	140. A
41. C	91. E	141. E
42. B	92. C	142. D
43. C	93. D	143. D
44. A	94. B	144. E
45. D	95. E	145. C
46. E	96. D	146. E
47. C	97. D	147. C
48. B	98. D	148. C
49. D	99. E	149. B
50. C	100. E	150. D

FINAL EXAM (90-DAY)
ANSWER KEY

3 points possible per answer

1.	D	51.	B
2.	B	52.	E
3.	C	53.	C
4.	C	54.	A
5.	C	55.	B
6.	D	56.	E
7.	D	57.	A
8.	C	58.	B
9.	E	59.	D
10.	B	60.	A
11.	D	61.	E
12.	E	62.	C
13.	A	63.	D
14.	E	64.	D
15.	E	65.	D
16.	C	66.	E
17.	B	67.	E
18.	C	68.	E
19.	E	69.	D
20.	D	70.	C
21.	E	71.	C
22.	C	72.	D
23.	C	73.	B
24.	B	74.	E
25.	A	75.	A
26.	E	76.	B
27.	C	77.	D
28.	B	78.	B
29.	C	79.	B
30.	A	80.	E
31.	D	81.	E
32.	C	82.	A
33.	D	83.	C
34.	E	84.	B
35.	A	85.	D
36.	A	86.	D
37.	C	87.	D
38.	A	88.	C
39.	D	89.	A
40.	A	90.	B
41.	D	91.	D
42.	B	92.	E
43.	D	93.	E
44.	E	94.	C
45.	A	95.	E
46.	D	96.	D
47.	C	97.	E
48.	D	98.	C
49.	B	99.	E
50.	E	100.	C

Conclusion

UNDERSTANDING THE TIMES

Fact Sheets

A Summit Ministries Curriculum

Apologetics
Fact Sheet

Key Terms:

Argument from Design: an argument that states that if something exists that is designed, then it must have a designer

Apologetic [from the Greek word *apologia*]: An answer or a reasoned defense*

Apologetics: The field of theology that seeks to provide a reasoned defense of the Christian faith

Kalam Cosmological Argument: A rational reflection of three exhaustive dilemmas regarding the origin of the cosmos: 1) Did the universe have a beginning or has it always existed? 2) Was the beginning caused or uncaused? 3) Was the agent of cause personal or impersonal?

Negative Apologetics: Answers to objections to the Christian faith (defensive)

Positive Apologetics: Supplying reasons for believing the Christian faith (offensive)

Transcendental Argument: A rational comparison of atheism and theism that focuses on the practical outcomes of both worldviews

Key Verses:

Matthew 22:34–40
Acts 17:16ff
Romans 12:1–4

2 Corinthians 10:4–5
Colossians 2

1 Peter 3:13–16
Jude 3

Key Organizations:

American Vision | www.americanvision.com | 770.222.7266 |

Biblical Worldview | www.christianworldview.net |

Christian Answers | www.christiananswers.net |

Christian Apologetics & Research Ministry | www.carm.org |

Christian Research Institute | www.equip.org | 888.700.0274 |

Probe Ministries | www.probe.org | 972.480.0240 |

Tekton Apologetics Ministries | www.tektonics.org |

Stand to Reason | www.str.org | 800.273.2766 |

Summit Ministries | www.summit.org | 719.685.9103 |

---

* Our familiarity with the term apology usually derives from the context of saying we are "sorry" for something we did that was wrong. This is not the original sense of the term. As can be seen from the Greek, an "apologetic" is a reasoned defense of action(s) or belief(s).

KEY PUBLICATIONS:

Areopagus Journal | **Apologetics Resource Center** | www.arcapologetics.org | 205.408.0136 |

Biblical Worldview | **American Vision** | www.americanvision.org |

Christian Research Journal | **Christian Research Institute** | www.equip.org |

First Things | **Institute of Religion and Public Life** | www.firstthings.com |

Southern Baptist Journal of Theology | **Southern Baptist Theological Seminary** | www.sbts.edu |

Summit Journal | **Summit Ministries** | www.summit.org |

KEY SOURCES:
(recommended titles appear in brown)

GENERAL APOLOGETICS

Bahnsen, Greg L. *Always Ready: Directions for Defending the Faith*. Atlanta: American Vision, 1996.

Beckwith, Francis, William Lane Craig, and James Porter Moreland, eds. *To Everyone an Answer: A Case for the Christian Worldview*. Downers Grove, IL: InterVarsity, 2004.

Beisner, E. Calvin. *Answers for Atheists, Agnostics, and Other Thoughtful Skeptics: Dialogs About Christian Faith and Life*. Wheaton, IL: Crossway, 1993.

Carroll, Vincent, and Dave Shiflett. *Christianity on Trial: Arguments against Anti-religious Bigotry*. San Francisco: Encounter Books, 2002.

Copan, Paul. *That's Just Your Interpretation: Responding to Skeptics Who Challenge Your Faith*. Grand Rapids, MI: Baker, 2001.

Corduan, Winfried. *No Doubt About It: The Case for Christianity*. Nashville: Broadman & Holman, 1997.

Evans, C. Stephen. *Pocket Dictionary of Apologetics and Philosophy of Religion*. Downers Grove, IL: InterVarsity, 2002.

Follis, Bryan A. *Truth with Love: The Apologetics of Francis Schaeffer*. Wheaton, IL: Crossway, 2006.

Geisler, Norman L. *Baker Encyclopedia of Christian Apologetics, Baker Reference Library*. Grand Rapids, MI: Baker, 1999.

———. *Christian Apologetics*. Grand Rapids, MI: Baker, 1976.

Geisler, Norman L., and Peter Bocchino. *Unshakable Foundations*. Minneapolis: Bethany, 2001.

Geisler, Norman L., and Ronald M. Brooks. *When Skeptics Ask*. Wheaton, IL: Victor, 1990.

Geisler, Norman L., and Paul K. Hoffman. *Why I Am a Christian: Leading Thinkers Explain Why They Believe*. Grand Rapids, MI: Baker, 2001.

Kreeft, Peter. *Fundamentals of the Faith: Essays in Christian Apologetics*. San Francisco: Ignatius, 1988.

Kreeft, Peter, and Ronald K. Tacelli. *Handbook of Christian Apologetics: Hundreds of Answers to Crucial Questions*. Downers Grove, IL: InterVarsity, 1994.

Lewis, C. S. *Mere Christianity*. San Francisco: HarperSanFrancisco, 2001.

———. *The Pilgrim's Regress: An Allegorical Apology for Christianity, Reason, and Romanticism*. Grand Rapids, MI: Eerdmans, 1992.

McDowell, Josh. *Josh McDowell Answers Five Tough Questions*. Wheaton, IL: Tyndale, 1991.

———. *The New Evidence That Demands a Verdict*. Nashville: Thomas Nelson, 1999.

McDowell, Josh, and Bob Hostetler. *Beyond Belief to Convictions*. Wheaton, IL: Tyndale, 2002.

McGrath, Alister E. *Explaining Your Faith*. Grand Rapids, MI: Baker, 1996.

———. *Intellectuals Don't Need God and Other Modern Myths: Building Bridges to Faith through Apologetics*. Grand Rapids, MI: Zondervan, 1993.

Moreland, James Porter. *Scaling the Secular City: A Defense of Christianity*. Grand Rapids, MI: Baker, 1987.

Fact Sheets

Nash, Ronald H. *Faith and Reason: Searching for a Rational Faith*. Grand Rapids, MI: Baker, 1988.

Noebel, David A. *Understanding the Times: The Collision of Today's Competing Worldviews*. Manitou Springs, CO: Summit Press, 2006.

Plantinga, Alvin. *Warranted Christian Belief*. New York: Oxford University Press, 2000.

Pratt, Richard L. *Every Thought Captive: A Study Manual for the Defense of Christian Truth*. Phillipsburg, NJ: Presbyterian & Reformed, 1979.

Rhodes, Ron. *Answering the Objections of Atheists, Agnostics, and Skeptics*. Eugene, OR: Harvest, 2006.

Samples, Kenneth R. *Without a Doubt: Answering the 20 Toughest Faith Questions*. Grand Rapids, MI: Baker, 2004.

Schaeffer, Francis A. *Death in the City*. Wheaton, IL: Crossway, 2002.

———. *The God Who Is There*. Downers Grove, IL: InterVarsity, 1998.

Strobel, Lee. *The Case for Christ: A Journalist's Personal Investigation of the Evidence for Jesus*. Grand Rapids, MI: Zondervan, 1998.

Wright, N. T. *Simply Christian: Why Christianity Makes Sense*. San Francisco: HarperSanFrancisco, 2006.

Van Til, Cornelius. *The Defense of the Faith*. Philadelphia: Presbyterian & Reformed, 1955.

PROOF OF GOD

Boa, Kenneth, and Robert M. Bowman. *20 Compelling Evidences That God Exists: Discover Why Believing in God Makes So Much Sense*. Tulsa, OK: RiverOak Publishing, 2002.

Geisler, Norman L., and Frank Turek. *I Don't Have Enough Faith to Be an Atheist*. Wheaton, IL: Crossway, 2004.

McGrath, Alister E. *Intellectuals Don't Need God and Other Modern Myths: Building Bridges to Faith through Apologetics*. Grand Rapids, MI: Zondervan, 1993.

Moreland, James Porter. *Scaling the Secular City: A Defense of Christianity*. Grand Rapids, MI: Baker, 1987.

Moreland, James Porter, and Kai Nielsen. *Does God Exist? The Great Debate*. New York: Prometheus, 1993.

Nicholi, Armand M. *The Question of God: C. S. Lewis and Sigmund Freud Debate God, Love, Sex, and the Meaning of Life*. New York: Free Press, 2002.

Plantinga, Alvin. *God and Other Minds: A Study of the Rational Justification of Belief in God*. Ithaca, NY: Cornell University Press, 1990.

———. *God, Freedom, and Evil*. Grand Rapids, MI: Eerdmans, 1977.

PROBLEM OF EVIL/PAIN

Lewis, C. S. *The Problem of Pain*. San Francisco: HarperSanFrancisco, 2001.

Plantinga, Alvin. *God, Freedom, and Evil*. Grand Rapids, MI: Eerdmans, 1977.

Wright, N. T. *Evil and the Justice of God*. Downers Grove, IL: InterVarsity, 2006.

Zacharias, Ravi K. *Deliver Us from Evil: Restoring the Soul in a Disintegrating Culture*. Dallas: Word, 1996.

ART & CULTURE
FACT SHEET

KEY VERSES:

Exodus 35:30–35   Ephesians 5:19
Colossians 3:16   Philippians 4:8

KEY ORGANIZATIONS:

Art and Christianity Enquiry | www.acetrust.org | 020.7374.0600 |

Center for the Study of Popular Culture | www.rightwingwatch.org |

Christians in the Arts Networking | 617.783.5667 |

Christians in the Visual Arts | www.civa.org | 978.867.4124 |

Image | www.imagejournal.org | 206.281.2988 |

KEY PUBLICATIONS:

Books and Culture | **Christianity Today** | www.christianitytoday.com/bc/ |

KEY QUOTES:

"Art worthy of a Christian is defined by skilled human creativity that reflects God's truth or God's beauty."[1]

"Ironically, the ability to say that a work of art can be aesthetically good, but false in the worldview it assumes provides an opportunity for the cultivation of moral capacities that popular culture cannot offer."[2]

"The best way to overcome banality is to demand something better—to seek out, as Paul wrote in Philippians, whatever is noble, right, pure, admirable, and to 'think on these things. Paul is commanding us to discipline ourselves to reflect on excellence. And he doesn't limit that to spiritual things, either. The command applies to everything—the music we listen to, the books and magazines we read, the films we watch."[3]

"Issues of quality and standards have been foolishly abandoned by liberals, who now interpret aesthetics as nothing but a mask for ideology. As a result the far right has gained enormously. What madness is abroad in the land when only neoconservatives will defend the grandeur of art? This does not mean that Christianity can be successfully expressed in every style. Some styles are wholly interwoven with aberrant philosophies (indeed, such styles are often nothing more than philosophical statements, which is why they are so bad aesthetically). Sometimes, Christians follow a particular style uncritically without recognizing the implicit contradictions between their faith and the style they are using to express it. Such incompatibility between form and content results in bad Christian art. (Late Victorian sentimentality, heavy metal nihilism, and pop culture consumerism would not seem to accord with a Biblical sensibility, but such misbegotten hybrids fill the Christian bookstores.)"[4]

[1]. Baldwin, Jr., Summit Ministries Open Forum, July 12, 1994.
[2] enneth A. Myers, *All God's Children and Blue Suede Shoes* (Wheaton, IL: Crossway, 1990), 98.
[3] uck Colson, "Elvis Mania," *Breakpoint with Chuck Colson*, June 1993, 17.
[4] ne Edward Veith, Jr., *State of the Arts: From Bezalel to Mapplethorpe* (Wheaton, IL: Crossway, 1991), 165.

Fact Sheets

KEY SOURCES:

(recommended titles appear in brown)

ART

Brand, Hilary and Adrienne Chaplin. *Art and Soul: Signposts for Christians in the Arts*. Carlisle, CA: Piquant, 2001.

Rookmaker, H. R. *Modern Art and the Death of a Culture*. Westester, IL: Crossway, 1994.

Ryken, Leland. "The Creative Arts," *The Making of a Christian Mind: A Christian World View and the Academic Enterprise*, Arthur Frank Holmes, ed. Downers Grove, IL: InterVarsity, 1985, 105–131.

———. *The Liberated Imagination: Thinking Christianly About the Arts*. Wheaton, IL: H. Shaw, 1989.

———. "The Paradisal Imagination." *Christianity and the Arts 4* (1997): 6–10.

Ryken, Philip Graham. *Art for God's Sake: A Call to Recover the Arts*. Phillipsburg, NJ: P&R Publishers, 2006.

Schaeffer, Francis A. *Art and the Bible*. Downers Grove, IL: InterVarsity, 1973.

Turner, Steve. "Being There: A Vision for Christianity and the Arts." *Trinity Seminary Review 21* (1999): 25–33.

Veith, Gene Edward. "Christianity and Culture: God's Double Sovereignty." *Modern Reformation 6*, no. 1 (1997).

———. "Must Art Be 'Christian' To Be Good." *Christianity Today*, February 1984, 69.

———. "A New Creative Force." *Christianity and the Arts 4* (1997): 37, 39–40.

———. *State of the Arts: From Bezalel to Mapplethorpe*. Wheaton, IL: Crossway, 1991.

CULTURE

Barzun, Jacques. *From Dawn to Decadence: 500 Years of Western Cultural Life*. New York: HarperCollins, 2000.

DeMoss, Robert G. *Learn to Discern*. Grand Rapids, MI: Zondervan, 1997.

Ferguson, Everett. *The Church of Christ: A Biblical Ecclesiology for Today*. Grand Rapids, MI: Eerdmans, 1996.

Hayes, Edward L. and Charles R. Swindoll. *The Church: The Body of Christ in the World of Today*. Nashville: Word, 1999.

Lewis, C. S. *The Abolition of Man*. San Francisco: HarperSanFrancisco, 2001.

Medved, Michael. *Hollywood vs. America: Popular Culture and the War on Traditional Values*. Grand Rapids, MI: Zondervan, 1992.

Myers, Ken. "Is Popular Culture Either?" *Modern Reformation 6*, no. 1 (1997).

Minnery, Tom. *Why You Can't Stay Silent: A Biblical Mandate to Shape Our Culture*. Wheaton, IL: Tyndale, 2001.

Myers, Ken. *All God's Children and Blue Suede Shoes*. Westchester, IL: Crossway, 1989.

Newbigin, Lesslie. *Foolishness to the Greeks: The Gospel and Western Culture*. Grand Rapids, MI: Eerdmans, 1986.

Postman, Neil. *Technopoly: The Surrender of Culture to Technology*. New York: Vintage, 1993.

Rookmaker, H. R. *Modern Art and the Death of a Culture*. Westester, IL: Crossway, 1994.

Schaeffer, Francis A. *A Christian View of Philosophy and Culture*. Westchester, IL: Crossway, 1982.

EDUCATION

Black, Jim Nelson. *Freefall of the American University: How Our Colleges Are Corrupting the Minds and Morals of the Next Generation*. Nashville: WND Books, 2004.

D'Souza, Dinesh. *Illiberal Education: The Politics of Race and Sex on Campus*. New York: Free Press, 1991.

Shortt, Bruce N. *The Harsh Truth About Public Schools*. Vallecito, CA: Chalcedon Foundation, 2004.

Sowell, Thomas. *Inside American Education: The Decline, the Deception, the Dogmas*. New York: Free Press, 1992.

Shapiro, Ben. *Brainwashed: How Universities Indoctrinate America's Youth*. Nashville: WND Books, 2004.

Stormer, John A. *None Dare Call It Education*. Florissant, MO: Liberty Bell Press, 1998.

ENTERTAINMENT

Gabler, Neal. *Live the Movie: How Entertainment Conquered Reality*. New York: Knopf, 1998.

Godawa, Brian. *Hollywood Worldviews: Watching Films with Wisdom and Discernment*. Downers Grove, IL: InterVarsity, 2002.

Postman, Neil. *Amusing Ourselves to Death: Public Discourse in the Age of Show Business*. New York: Viking, 1985.

BIOETHICS & ETHICS
FACT SHEET

KEY TERMS:

ETHICS

Cultural Relativism: The belief that truth and morals are relative to one's culture

Karma: The total effect of one's actions and conduct during each phase of existence, determining his/her destiny

Moral Absolutes: The belief that an absolute ethical standard exists for all individuals regardless of era or culture

Moral Relativism: The ethical belief that morals are relative to the individual

Proletariat Morality: The ethical belief that whatever advances the proletariat and the cause of communism is morally good and whatever hinders the proletariat or communism is morally evil

Utilitarianism: An ethical framework that posits that all action should be directed toward achieving the greatest utility for the greatest number of people (that the end justifies the means)

ABORTION

Law of Biogenesis: Living things reproduce after their own kind

Embryo: An unborn baby from conception to the eighth week of gestation

Fetus: An unborn baby from the eighth week of gestation until birth

BIOETHICS

Bio: Natural and living

Bioethics: Right conduct in the area of biotechnology

Imago Dei: Possessing the image of God

Personhood: The debate in philosophy over what constitutes "being a person"

Viability: The ability to survive on one's own and grow to adulthood

BIOTECHNOLOGY*

Biotechnology: Industrial use of living organisms or the application of technique to living organisms

Artificial Intelligence: An artificial mechanism that can mimic human thinking and independence

Cybernetics: Integration of man and machine

Nanotechnology: Engineering and manufacturing at the molecular level

Stem Cell: Cells in your body that have not been diversified into heart cells, brain cells, etc.

Transgenics: Insertion of DNA of one species into the genetic code of another species

Xenotransplantation: The use of animal tissues, organs, or cells transplanted to or used for contact with human subjects

or additional terms, see www.biotechterms.org

EUTHANASIA	**Active Euthanasia (also known as mercy _killing_):** Occurs when a medical professional deliberately acts to cause the death of a patient

Passive Euthanasia (also known as mercy _dying_): Occurs when a medical professional withdraws extraordinary medical treatment consequently allowing a patient's demise

Voluntary Euthanasia: Occurs when an uncoerced patient chooses to end his or her life

Involuntary Euthanasia: Occurs when a second party makes the decision about whether active or passive measures should be taken to end a patient's life |

KEY FACTS:

ABORTION*	**Statistics:**
- Approximately 126,000 abortions are performed worldwide each day
- Approximately 46 million abortions are performed worldwide each year
- The lifetime average worldwide is about 1 abortion per woman

The Unborn:
- Day 30—heart begins to beat
- Day 40—displays measurable brainwaves
- Day 45—identifiable arms and legs
- Day 70—fingers and genitals appear and the child's face is recognizably human
- The majority of abortions are preformed between the seventh and tenth weeks |
| EUTHANASIA | **Jurisdictions with laws that specifically permit euthanasia:**
- Oregon
- The Netherlands
- Belgium |
| STEM CELL | **Embryonic Stem Cell Research:**
- **K**ills the embryo when extracted
- Provides no scientific achievement

Non-embryonic (Adult) Stem Cell Research:
- Does not kill a human being
- Continues to provide great scientific advancement |

KEY VERSES:

Genesis 1:26–31; 9:6	Proverbs 14:12; 16:25; 24:11–12	1 Corinthians 6:12–20
Exodus 20:13; 21:22–23	Isaiah 5:20–23	Matthew 7:13
Deuteronomy 32:39	Amos 5:15	Romans 1:18–32; 12:9
Psalm 12:8; 139:13–16	Jeremiah 1:5	Hebrews 5:14
Job 42:1–6	Mark 1:41	James 1:27; 2:14–17

*For additional statistics, see The Alan Guttmacher Institute, www.agi-usa.org

Fact Sheets

KEY ORGANIZATIONS:

BIOETHICS	**Center for Bioethics and Human Dignity** | www.cbhd.org | 847.317.8180 |
	Council for Biotechnology Policy | www.waragainsttheweak.com | 888.257.7730 |
	Do No Harm | www.stemcellresearch.org | 202.347.6840 |
ABORTION	**Concerned Women for America** | www.cwfa.org |
	Crisis Pregnancy Centers | www.crisispregnancy.com | 480.446.0500 |
	Eagle Forum | www.eagleforum.org | 618.462.5415 |
	Justice for All | http://jfaweb.org | 316.683.6426 |
	Life Training Institute | http://prolifetraining.com | 719.264.7861 |
	National Right to Life | www.nrlc.org | 202.626.8800 |

KEY QUOTES:

ETHICS

"The fundamental question of ethics is, who makes the rules? God or men? The theistic answer is that God makes them. The humanist answer is that men make them. This distinction between theism and humanism is the fundamental division in moral theory."[1]

"No inherent moral or ethical laws exist, nor are there absolute guiding principles for human society. The universe cares nothing for us and we have no ultimate meaning in life."[2]

"We can rationally discuss and argue with each other about right and wrong without resorting to the claim that ethical judgments are merely subjective or relative and that all such judgments have equal validity. For to claim the latter logically leads one to the bizarre judgment that Mother Teresa is no more and no less virtuous than Adolf Hitler."[3]

"If there is no absolute beyond man's ideas, then there is no final appeal to judge between individuals and groups whose moral judgments conflict. We are merely left with conflicting opinions."[4]

ABORTION

"Many people are very, very concerned with children in India, with the children of Africa where quite a few die of hunger, and so on. Many people are also concerned about all the violence in this great country of the United States. These concerns are very good. But often these same people are not concerned with the millions who are being killed by the deliberate decision of their own mothers. And this is what is the greatest destroyer of peace today—abortion, which brings people to such blindness."[5]

Max Hocutt, "Toward an Ethic of Mutual Accommodation," *Humanist Ethics*, Morris B. Storer, ed. (Buffalo: Prometheus Books, 1980), 137.

William Provine, "Scientists, Face It! Science and Religion are Incompatible," *The Scientist* (September 5, 1988).

Frank Beckwith, "Philosophical Problems with Moral Relativism," *Christian Research Journal* (Fall 1993).

Francis A. Schaeffer, *How Should We Then Live?* (Old Tappan, NJ: Fleming H. Revell, 1976), 145.

Mother Teresa, quoted in Cal Thomas, "Meek Mother Teresa delivers a verbal knockout punch," *Colorado Springs Gazette Telegraph* (February 9, 94).

"'The nurses have to look at the ultrasound picture to gauge how far along the baby is for an abortion, because the larger the pregnancy, the more you get paid. It was very important for us to do that. But the turnover definitely got greater when we started using ultrasound. We lost two nurses—they couldn't take looking at it. Some of the other staff left also.' What about the women having the abortions? Do they see the ultrasound? 'They are never allowed to look at the ultrasound because we knew that if they so much as heard the heartbeat, they wouldn't want to have the abortion.'"[6]

"The fact that restricting access to abortion has tragic side effects does not, in itself, show that the restrictions are unjustified, since murder is wrong regardless of the consequences of prohibiting it; and the appeal to the right to control one's body, which is generally construed as a property right, is at best a rather feeble argument for the permissibility of abortion. Mere ownership does not give me the right to kill innocent people whom I find on my property, and indeed I am apt to be held responsible if such people injure themselves while on my property. It is equally unclear that I have any moral right to expel an innocent person from my property when I know that doing so will result in his death."[7]

"A nurse who had worked in an abortion clinic for less than a year said her most troubling moments came not in the procedure room but afterwards. Many times, she said, women who had just had abortions would lie in the recovery room and cry, 'I've just killed my baby. I've just killed my baby.' 'I don't know what to say to these women,' the nurse told the group. 'Part of me thinks "Maybe they're right."'"[8]

BIOETHICS

"Cloning and the biotech agenda are even worse news for human dignity than abortion. Not only are we taking upon ourselves the godlike prerogative of ending human life as we choose, but we also are attempting to appropriate the prerogative of making human life as we choose."[9]

EUTHANASIA

"It's sad to say, but euthanasia will someday be legalized. There's already a thrust for it legislatively. We shouldn't allow for exceptions because hard cases make bad law. But some doctors are already deciding when the quality of life is over. A lot of it goes on without being prosecuted."[10]

KEY SOURCES/CRITIQUES:
(recommended titles appear in brown)

ETHICS

Bennett, William J. *The Book of Virtues: A Treasury of Great Moral Stories*. New York: Simon & Schuster, 1993.
————. *The Moral Compass: Stories for a Life's Journey*. New York: Simon & Schuster, 1995.
Burke, Thomas J., ed. *The Christian Vision: Man and Morality*. Hillsdale, MI: Hillsdale College Press, 1986.
Chamberlain, Paul. *Can We Be Good without God?* Downers Grove, IL: InterVarsity, 1996.
Davis, John Jefferson. *Evangelical Ethics: Issues Facing the Church Today*. Phillipsburg, NJ: P&R Pub., 2004.
Douma, Jochem. *Responsible Conduct: Principles of Christian Ethics*. Phillipsburg, NJ: P&R Publishers, 2003.
Geisler, Norman L. *Christian Ethics* (Grand Rapids, MI: Baker, 1989.
————. *Ethics: Alternatives and Issues*. Grand Rapids, MI: Zondervan, 1971.
Grenz, Stanley J., and Jay T. Smith. *Pocket Dictionary of Ethics*. Downers Grove, IL: InterVarsity, 2003.
Lewis, C. S. *God in the Dock: Essays on Theology and Ethics*. Grand Rapids, MI: Eerdmans, 1970.

[6] Dr. Joseph Randall, who performed over 32,000 abortions, quoted in David Kupelian and Mark Masters, "Pro-Choice 1991: skeletons in the closet *New Dimensions* (September/October 1991).
[7] Pro-choice philosopher Mary Anne Warren, quoted in Randy Alcorn, *Pro Life Answers to Pro Choice Arguments* (Portland: Multnomah, 1992), 86
[8] Diane M. Gianelli, "Abortion providers share inner conflicts," *American Medical News* (July 12, 1993).
[9] Charles Colson, *Breakpoint Radio Broadcast* (January 2, 2003).
[10] "A matter of life and death," Assemblies of God, USA, at http://pentecostalevangel.ag.org/

Rae, Scott B. *Moral Choices: An Introduction to Ethics.* Grand Rapids, MI: Zondervan, 2000.

Torrance, Alan and Michael Banner, eds. *The Doctrine of God and Theological Ethics.* Edinburgh: T&T Clark, 2005.

Wenham, Gordon J. *Story as Torah: Reading Old Testament Narrative Ethically.* Grand Rapids, MI: Baker, 2004.

Wilkens, Steve. *Beyond Bumper Sticker Ethics: An Introduction to Theories of Right & Wrong.* Downers Grove, IL: InterVarsity, 1995.

ABORTION (CRITIQUE)

Alcorn, Randy C. *Prolife Answers to Prochoice Arguments.* Portland: Multnomah, 1992.

———. *Why Prolife?* Sisters, OR: Multnomah, 2004.

Beckwith, Francis. *Abortion and the Sanctity of Human Life.* Joplin, MO: College Press, 2000.

———. "Abortion, Bioethics, and Personhood: A Philosophical Reflection." *Review of Ethics in a New Millennium. Southern Baptist Journal of Theology 4,* no. 1 (2000): 16–25.

———. *Politically Correct Death: Answering the Arguments for Abortion Rights.* Grand Rapids, MI: Baker, 1993.

———. "Roe V. Wade: Its Logic and Its Legacy." *Southern Baptist Journal of Theology 7,* no. 2 (2003): 4-28.

Beckwith, Francis and Norman L. Geisler. *Matters of Life and Death: Calm Answers to Tough Questions About Abortion and Euthanasia.* Grand Rapids, MI: Baker, 1991.

Brown, Harold O. J. *Death before Birth.* Nashville: Thomas Nelson, 1977.

Farish, Stephen E. "Biblical Principles Touching on the Question of Abortion and the Sanctity of Human Life." *Southern Baptist Journal of Theology 4,* no. 1 (2000): 76–85.

Fournier, Keith A. and William D. Watkins. *In Defense of Life: Taking a Stand against the Culture of Death.* Colorado Springs, CO: NavPress, 1996.

Garton, Jean Staker. *Who Broke the Baby?* Minneapolis: Bethany, 1998.

Gorman, Michael J. *Abortion and the Early Church.* Downers Grove, IL: InterVarsity, 1982.

Grant, George. *Grand Illusions: The Legacy of Planned Parenthood.* Nashville: Cumberland House, 2000.

Hoffmeier, James Karl, ed. *Abortion: A Christian Understanding and Response.* Grand Rapids, MI: Baker, 1987.

Kasun, Jacqueline R. *The War against Population: The Economics and Ideology of World Population Control.* San Francisco: Ignatius, 1999.

Koop, C. Everett and Francis A. Schaeffer. *Whatever Happened to the Human Race?* Westchester, IL: Crossway, 1983.

Koukl, Greg. "Only One Question: Compelling Answers to the Abortion Rights Challenge." *Areopagus Journal 1,* no. 4 (2001): 11–17.

Mitchell, C. Ben. "Persons Beyond Roe V. Wade: The Post-Human Age?" *Southern Baptist Journal of Theology 7,* no. 2 (2003): 68–77.

———. "The Legacy of Roe V. Wade for Bioethics." *Southern Baptist Journal of Theology 7,* no. 2 (2003): 30–39.

Montgomery, John Warwick. *Slaughter of the Innocents: Abortion, Birth Control, and Divorce in Light of Science, Law, and Theology.* Westchester, IL: Cornerstone, 1981.

Moreland, James Porter and Norman L. Geisler. *The Life and Death Debate: Moral Issues of Our Time.* New York: Praeger, 1990.

Weldon, John Ankerberg. "What Does the Bible Teach About Abortion?" *Areopagus Journal 1,* no. 4 (2001): 7–10.

BIOETHICS

Beckwith, Francis and Norman L. Geisler. *Matters of Life and Death: Calm Answers to Tough Questions About Abortion and Euthanasia.* Grand Rapids, MI: Baker, 1991.

Cameron, Nigel M., Scott E. Daniels, and Barbara White, eds. *Bioengagement: Making a Christian Difference through Bioethics Today.* Grand Rapids, MI: Eerdmans, 2000.

Fournier, Keith A. and William D. Watkins. *In Defense of Life: Taking a Stand against the Culture of Death.* Colorado Springs, CO: NavPress, 1996.

Kilner, John Frederic, C. Christopher Hook, and Diane B. Uustal, eds. *Cutting-Edge Bioethics: A Christian Exploration of Technologies and Trends.* Grand Rapids, MI: Eerdmans, 2002.

Koop, C. Everett and Francis A. Schaeffer. *Whatever Happened to the Human Race?* Westchester, IL: Crossway, 1983.

Moreland, James Porter, and Norman L. Geisler. The Life and Death Debate: Moral Issues of Our Time. New York, NY: Praeger, 1990.

CLONING

Annas, G. J. "Why We Should Ban Human Cloning." *New England Journal of Medicine 339*, no. 2 (1998): 122–25.

Kilner, John Frederic and C. Ben Mitchell. *Does God Need Our Help? Cloning, Assisted Suicide, and Other Challenges in Bioethics*. Wheaton, IL: Tyndale, 2003.

Lester, Lane P. and James C. Hefley. *Human Cloning: Playing God or Scientific Progress?* Grand Rapids, MI: Fleming H. Revell, 1998.

Robertson, J. A. "Human Cloning and the Challenge of Regulation." *New England Journal of Medicine 339*, no. 2 (1998): 119–22.

EUTHANASIA (CRITIQUE)

Kilner, John Frederic. *Life on the Line: Ethics, Aging, Ending Patients' Lives, and Allocating Vital Resources*. Grand Rapids, MI: Eerdmans, 1992.

———. *Who Lives? Who Dies? Ethical Criteria in Patient Selection*. New Haven, CT: Yale University Press, 1990.

Kilner, John Frederic, Arlene B. Miller, and Edmund D. Pellegrino, eds. *The Center for Bioethics and Human Dignity Presents Dignity and Dying: A Christian Appraisal*. Grand Rapids, MI: Eerdmans, 1996.

Kilner, John Frederic and C. Ben Mitchell. *Does God Need Our Help? Cloning, Assisted Suicide, and Other Challenges in Bioethics*. Wheaton, IL: Tyndale, 2003.

Kilner, John Frederic, Robert D. Orr, and Judy Allen Shelly, eds. *The Changing Face of Health Care: A Christian Appraisal of Managed Care, Resource Allocation, and Patient-Caregiver Relationships*. Grand Rapids, MI: Eerdmans, 1998.

Orr, Robert D. "The Physician-Assisted Suicide: Is It Ever Justified." *Areopagus Journal 1*, no. 4 (2001): 20–26.

Pankratz, H. Robert C. and Richard M. Welsh. "A Christian Response to Euthanasia, Part 1." *U-TURN 3*, no. 2 (1995).

———. "A Christian Response to Euthanasia, Part 2." *U-TURN 3*, no. 3 (1995).

Stewart, Gary. *Basic Questions on End of Life Decisions*. Grand Rapids, MI: Kregel, 1998.

MORAL ABSOLUTES

Copan, Paul. "'Who Are You to Judge Others?' in Defense of Making Moral Judgments." *Areopagus Journal,* vol. 1, no. 3 (July 2001).

Henry, Carl F. *Christian Personal Ethics*. Grand Rapids, MI: Eerdmans, 1957.

McDowell, Josh and Norman L. Geisler. *Love Is Always Right: A Defense of the One Moral Absolute* (Dallas: Word, 1996).

MORAL RELATIVISM

Beckwith, Francis and Gregory Koukl. *Relativism: Feet Firmly Planted in Mid-Air* (Grand Rapids, MI: Baker, 1998).

Feinberg, John S. and Paul D. Feinberg. *Ethics for a Brave New World*. (Wheaton, IL: Crossway, 1993).

George, Robert P. and John J. Diluilo. *The Clash of Orthodoxies: Law, Religion, and Morality in Crisis*. Wilmington, DE: Intercollegiate Studies Institute, 2001.

Kilpatrick, William. *Why Johnny Can't Tell Right from Wrong*. New York: Simon & Schuster, 1992.

Wiker, Benjamin. *Moral Darwinism: How We Became Hedonists*. Downers Grove, IL: InterVarsity, 2002.

PERSONHOOD

Beckwith, Francis J. "Abortion, Bioethics, and Personhood: A Philosophical Reflection." *Southern Baptist Journal of Theology 4*, no. 1 (2000): 16–25.

Mitchell, C. Ben. "Persons Beyond Roe V. Wade: The Post-Human Age?" *Southern Baptist Journal of Theology 7*, no. 2 (2003): 68–77.

Moreland, J. P. and Scott B. Rae. *Body and Soul: Human Nature and the Crisis in Ethics*. Downers Grove, IL: InterVarsity, 2000.

REPRODUCTION

Kilner, John Frederic, Paige C. Cunningham, and W. David Hager, eds. *The Reproduction Revolution: A Christian Appraisal of Sexuality, Reproductive Technologies, and the Family*. Grand Rapids, MI: Eerdmans, 2000.

Kilner, John Frederic, Rebecca Davis Pentz, and Frank E. Young, eds. *The Center for Bioethics and Human Dignity Presents Genetic Ethics: Do the Ends Justify the Genes?* Grand Rapids, MI: Eerdmans, 1997.

Stewart, Gary. *Basic Questions on Sexuality and Reproductive Technology* Grand Rapids, MI: Kregel 1998.

ROBOTICS AND ARTIFICIAL INTELLIGENCE

Craelius, W. "The Bionic Man: Restoring Mobility." *Science 295*, no. 5557 (2002): 1018–21.

Gomes, L. "No Need to Worry, Your Computer Isn't after Your Job." *Wall Street Journal* (2002).

Vogel, G. "Part Man, Part Computer: Researcher Tests the Limits." *Science 295*, no. 5557 (2002): 1020.

SOCIAL INVOLVEMENT

Grant, George. *Bringing in the Sheaves: Transforming Poverty into Productivity*. (Brentwood, TN: Wolgemuth & Hyatt, 1988.

———. *The Micah Mandate*. Chicago, IL: Moody, 1995.

Henry, Carl F. *Aspects of Christian Social Ethics: The Payton Lectures, 1963*. Grand Rapids, MI: Eerdmans, 1964.

STEM CELL RESEARCH

Barinaga, M. "Fetal Neuron Grafts Pave the Way for Stem Cell Therapies." *Science 287*, no. 5457 (2000): 1421–22.

Perry, D. "Patients' Voices: The Powerful Sound in the Stem Cell Debate." *Science 287*, no. 5457 (2000): 1423.

Regalado, A. ""Supercell" Controversy Sets Off a Scientists' Civil War." *Wall Street Journal* (2002).

Weissman, I. L. "Stem Cells: Scientific, Medical, and Political Issues." *New England Journal of Medicine 346*, no. 20 (2002): 1576–79.

———. "Translating Stem and Progenitor Cell Biology to the Clinic: Barriers and Opportunities." *Science 287*, no. 5457 (2000): 1442–46.

BIOLOGY & SCIENCE
FACT SHEET

KEY TERMS:

Big Bang: A theory of the cosmos' origin; a giant explosion around 14 billion years ago which expanded rapidly, cooled, and coalesced into the universe of today

Cambrian Explosion: The sudden geological appearance of most major groups of animals

Cosmic Evolution: The progression of collective humanity toward an age of higher consciousness

Creationism: the scientific theory that God was directly involved in creating the universe and all living kinds of plants and animals, including mankind

Darwinism: The scientific theory that proposes that gradual changes accumulated over vast periods of time resulting in the evolution of the species

DNA: The storehouse containing all the genetic information necessary for life

Homology: The study of the similarity in structure between different organisms

Icons of Evolution: Distortions of pro-evolution evidence commonly found in textbooks

Intelligent Design: The study of information and design in life and the cosmos

Irreducible Complexity: The philosophical concept that considers the complexity of living organisms—if any part is removed, the system loses function

Macro-evolution: The origin of fundamentally new organisms and plants from other forms of life

Micro-evolution: Small changes within the species of a gene pool

Mutation: Changes in genetic makeup

Natural Selection: The natural process of choosing favorable characteristics and eliminating unfavorable ones through such things as competition, predators, geography, and time

Neo-Darwinism: The theory that new species arise from natural selection acting over vast periods of time on chance genetic mutations in reproductively isolated populations

Second Law of Thermodynamics: A natural law that states that although the total energy in the cosmos remains constant, the amount of energy available to do useful work is always decreasing

Spontaneous Generation: The theory that non-living matter gave rise to living organisms

Punctuated Equilibrium: The theory of evolution that proposes that evolutionary changes occur over a relatively quick period of time, followed by periods of little to no evolutionary change

Teleology: The study of design and purpose in nature

Theistic Evolution: The belief that God works through the natural process of evolution

KEY VERSES:

Genesis 1   Ephesians 5:19   Hebrews 11:3
Mark 10:6   Philippians 4:8

KEY ORGANIZATIONS:

Answers in Genesis | www.answersingenesis.org | 859.727.2222 |

Access Research Network | www.arn.org | 719.633.1772 |

Creation Research Society | www.creationresearch.org | 928.636.1153 |

Discovery Institute | www.discovery.org | 206.292.0401 |

Institute for Creation Research | www.icr.org | 800.337.0375 |

KEY QUOTES:

EVOLUTIONISTS

"Evolution is a fact amply demonstrated by the fossil record and by contemporary molecular biology. Natural selection is a successful theory devised to explain the fact of evolution."[1]

"Man is the result of a purposeless and natural process that did not have him in mind. He was not planned. He is a state of matter, a form of life, a sort of animal, and a species of the Order Primates, akin nearly or remotely to all of life and indeed to all that is material."[2]

"Biology teaches us that the species man was not specially created but is merely, in a long chain of evolutionary changes of forms of life, the last link, made in the likeness not of God but of nothing so much as an ape."[3]

"With me, the horrid doubt always arises whether the convictions of man's mind, which has been developed from the mind of lower animals, are of any value or at all trustworthy. Would any one trust in the convictions of a monkey's mind, if there are any convictions in such a mind?"[4]

CREATIONISTS/ID

"The essential point of creation has nothing to do with the timing or the mechanism the Creator chose to employ, but with the element of design or purpose. In the broadest sense, a 'creationist' is simply a person who believes that the world (and especially mankind) was designed, and exists for a purpose."[5]

"Science is possible only because we live in an ordered universe which complies with simple mathematical laws. The job of the scientist is to study, catalogue and relate the orderliness in nature, not to question its origin. But theologians have long argued that the order in the physical world is evidence for God. If this is true, then science and religion acquire a common purpose in revealing God's work."[6]

[1] ...arl Sagan, *Dragons of Eden* (New York: Random, 1977), 6.
[2] ...eorge Gaylord Simpson, *The Meaning of Evolution* (New Haven, CT: Yale University Press, 1971), 345.
[3] ...urt E. M. Baier, "The Meaning of Life," *Critiques of God*, Peter Angeles, ed. (Buffalo, NY: Prometheus, 1976), 315.
[4] ...harles Darwin quoted in Francis Darwin, ed., *The Life and Letters of Charles Darwin*, Vol. 1 (London: J. Murray, 1888), 316.
[5] ...illip E. Johnson, *Darwin on Trial* (Downers Grove, IL: InterVarsity, 1993), 113.
[6] ...ul Davies, *God and the New Physics* (New York: Simon & Schuster, 1983), 144.

"A science which deals with origin events does not fall within the category of empirical science, which deals with observed regularities in the present. Rather, it is more like a forensic science, which concentrates on unobserved singularities in the past. That is, a science about origins is a singularity science about the past; it differs from a scientific understanding about singularities in the present. A science about the past does not observe the past singularity but must depend on the principle of uniformity (analogy), as historical geology and archaeology do…

Just as a forensic scientist tries to make a plausible reconstruction of an unobserved (and unrepeatable) murder, so the evolutionist and creationist attempt to construct a plausible scenario of the unobserved past singularities of origin. So neither view is operation science. Rather, both are in the domain of origin science…

Some events of origin may have nonnatural primary intelligent causes. But to insist on finding a natural cause where there is evidence for primary intelligent causes is like demanding that a geology class remain at Mount Rushmore until it discovers some natural process of erosion to explain the faces formed on the mountainside."[7]

KEY SOURCES—EVOLUTIONISTS:

ASTRONOMY
Sagan, Carl. *Cosmos*. New York: Random, 2002.

COSMOLOGY
Dawkins, Richard. *The Blind Watchmaker*. New York: Norton, 1996.
Smoot, George and Keay Davidson. *Wrinkles in Time*. New York: W. Morrow, 1993.

DARWINISM
Darwin, Charles. *The Descent of Man and Selection in Relation to Sex*. Princeton: Princeton Univ. Press, 1981.
————. *On the Origin of Species*. Mineola, NY: Dover, 2006.

NEO-DARWINISM
Dawkins, Richard. *The Selfish Gene*. New York: Oxford University Press, 1989.
Sagan, Carl. *The Dragons of Eden*. New York: Random, 1977.

PALEONTOLOGY
Raup, David M. *The Nemesis Affair: A Story of the Death of Dinosaurs and the Ways of Science*. New York: Norton, 1999.
Raup, David M. and Steven M. Stanley. *Principles of Paleontology*. San Francisco: W. H. Freeman, 1978.

PHYSICS
Asimov, Isaac. *Asimov on Physics*. Garden City, NY: Doubleday, 1976.
————. *Understanding Physics*. New York: Walker, 1966.

PUNCTUATED EVOLUTION
Eldredge, Niles. *Reinventing Darwin: The Great Debate at the High Table of Evolutionary Theory*. New York: Wiley, 1995.
————. *Time Frames: The Rethinking of Darwinian Evolution and the Theory of Punctuated Equilibria*. New York: Simon & Schuster, 1985.
————. *Why We Do It: Rethinking Sex and the Selfish Gene*. New York: Norton, 2004.
Gould, Stephen Jay. *The Structure of Evolutionary Theory*. Cambridge, MA: Belknap of Harvard Univ. Press, 2002.

---

[7] Norman L. Geisler and J. Kerby Anderson, *Origin Science: A Proposal for the Creation-Evolution Controversy* (Grand Rapids, MI: Baker, 1987), 14, 25, 30.

Fact Sheets

KEY SOURCES—CREATIONISTS/ID:

(recommended titles appear in brown)

SCIENCE

Davies, P. C. W. *God and the New Physics*. New York: Simon & Schuster, 1983.

Jastrow, Robert. *God and the Astronomers*. New York: Norton, 1992.

Moreland, James Porter. *Christianity and the Nature of Science*. Grand Rapids, MI: Baker, 1989.

Pearcey, Nancy and Charles B. Thaxton. *The Soul of Science: Christian Faith and Natural Philosophy*. Wheaton, IL: Crossway, 1994.

DARWINISM (CRITIQUE)

Bird, Wendell R. *The Origin of Species Revisited*. New York: Philosophical Library, 1989.

Copan, Paul and William Lane Craig. *Creation out of Nothing*. Grand Rapids, MI: Baker, 2004.

Denton, Michael. *Evolution: A Theory in Crisis*. Bethesda, MD: Adler & Adler, 1986.

Gish, Duane T. *Evolution, the Fossils Say No!* San Diego: Creation-Life, 1979.

Johnson, Phillip E. *Darwin on Trial*. Downers Grove, IL: InterVarsity, 1993.

———. *Defeating Darwinism by Opening Minds*. Downers Grove, IL: InterVarsity, 1997.

Lester, Lane P., Raymond G. Bohlin, and V. Elving Anderson. *The Natural Limits to Biological Change*. Dallas: Probe, 1989.

Lubenow, Marvin L. *Bones of Contention: A Creationist Assessment of Human Fossils*. Grand Rapids, MI: Baker, 2004.

Milton, Richard. *Shattering the Myths of Darwinism*. Rochester, VT: Park Street, 1997.

Morris, Henry. *The Long War against God*. Green Forest, AR: Master, 2000.

Simmons, Geoffrey S. *What Darwin Didn't Know*. Eugene, OR: Harvest, 2004.

Taylor, Ian T. *In the Minds of Men: Darwin and the New World Order*. Toronto: TFE, 1984.

Wells, Jonathan. *Icons of Evolution: Science or Myth?* Washington DC: Regnery, 2000.

Wise, Kurt P. *Faith, Form, and Time: What the Bible Teaches and Science Confirms About Creation and the Age of the Universe*. Nashville: Broadman & Holman, 2002.

INTELLIGENT DESIGN

Behe, Michael J. *Darwin's Black Box: The Biochemical Challenge to Evolution*. New York: Free Press, 1996.

Dembski, William A. *The Design Revolution: Answering the Toughest Questions About Intelligent Design*. Downers Grove, IL: InterVarsity, 2004.

———. *Intelligent Design: The Bridge between Science & Theology*. Downers Grove, IL: InterVarsity, 1999.

———. *Mere Creation: Science, Faith and Intelligent Design*. Downers Grove, IL: InterVarsity, 1998.

———. *No Free Lunch: Why Specified Complexity Cannot Be Purchased without Intelligence*. Lanham, MD: Rowman & Littlefield, 2002.

Dembski, William A. and Michael Ruse. *Debating Design: From Darwin to DNA*. New York: Cambridge Univ. Press, 2004.

Johnson, Phillip E. *Defeating Darwinism by Opening Minds*. Downers Grove, IL: InterVarsity, 1997.

McGrath, Alister E. *Dawkins' God: Genes, Memes, and the Meaning of Life*. Malden, MA: Blackwell, 2005.

Moreland, James Porter. *The Creation Hypothesis: Scientific Evidence for an Intelligent Designer*. Downers Grove, IL: InterVarsity, 1994.

Thaxton, Charles B., Walter L. Bradley, and Roger L. Olsen. *The Mystery of Life's Origin*. New York: Philosophical Library, 1984.

NATURALISM (CRITIQUE)

Johnson, Phillip E. *Reason in the Balance: The Case against Naturalism in Science, Law and Education*. Downers Grove, IL: InterVarsity, 1995.

———. *The Wedge of Truth: Splitting the Foundations of Naturalism*. Downers Grove, IL: InterVarsity, 2000.

Fact Sheets

CULTS
FACT SHEET

KEY TERMS:

Cult: A system of religious veneration and devotion directed toward a particular figure or object; a religion

Modalism: The belief that there is only one person in the godhead who appears as three persons: the Father in the Old Testament, the Son in the New Testament, and the Holy Spirit today

Pseudo-Christian Religion: A group of people gathered around an individual (a group of individuals or an organization), who, while claiming to be the true Christian Church and teach true Christianity, actually distort and deny the foundational and distinctive doctrines of the Christian faith

Tri-theism: A belief in three separate gods: Father, Son, and Spirit

Trinity [Trinitarianism]: The belief in one God in three persons: Father, Son, and Spirit

Unitarianism: The belief that the Father is God, the Son is merely a creature, and the Holy Spirit is an impersonal force

---

KEY VERSES:

Psalm 119:105
Proverbs 30:5–6
John 17:17
Romans 5:12ff
2 Corinthians 11:1–15

Galatians 1:6–9; 2:21
Ephesians 2:1ff
Colossians 2:13
1 Timothy 2:5

2 Timothy 3:15–17
Titus 2:11–14; 3:4–8
2 Peter 1:3; 3:15–16
1 John 4:1–6

KEY ORGANIZATIONS:

Christian Research Institute | www.equip.org | 888.700.0274 |

Cult Information Centre | www.cultinformation.org.uk |

Cult FAQ | www.cultfaq.org |

Rick A. Ross Institute | www.rickross.com | 201.434.9234 |

Watchman Fellowship, Inc. | www.watchman.org | 205.833.2858 |

Wellspring | www.wellspringretreat.org | 740.698.6277 |

KEY PUBLICATIONS:

Spiritual Counterfeits Project | **Spiritual Counterfeits Project** | www.scp-inc.org |

KEY QUOTES:

MORMONS

"The Bible is the word of God, written by men. It is basic in Mormon teaching. But the Latter-day Saints recognize that errors have crept into this sacred work because of the manner in which the book has come to us. Moreover, they regard it as not being complete as a guide… Supplementing the Bible, the Latter-day Saints have three other books: the Book of Mormon, the Doctrine and Covenants, and the Pearl of Great Price. These with the Bible constitute the standard works of the church."[1]

"Many men say there is one God; the Father, the Son and the Holy Ghost are only one God. I say that is a strange God anyhow—three in one, and one in three! It is a curious organization… All are to be crammed into one God, according to sectarianism. It would make the biggest God in all the world. He would be a wonderfully big God—he would be a giant or a monster."[2]

"I have always declared God to be a distinct personage, Jesus Christ a separate and distinct personage from God the Father, and that the Holy Ghost was a distinct personage and a Spirit; and these three constitute three distinct personages and three Gods."[3]

"I am going to tell you how God came to be God. We have imagined and supposed that God was God from all eternity. I will refute that idea, and take away the veil, so you may see… he was once a man like us; yea, that God himself, the Father of us all, dwelt on an earth, the same as Jesus Christ himself did; and I will show it from the Bible… Here, then, is eternal life—to know the only wise and true God, and you have got to learn to be Gods yourselves, and to be kings and priest to God, the same as all Gods have done before you."[4]

"The Church of Jesus Christ of Latter-day Saints discounts the notion of Original Sin and its ascribed negative impact on humanity… [W]e believe that we are not born sinners… In other words, we're born good; we learn to sin as we grow older."[5]

"Indeed, we honor and respect Adam and Eve for their wisdom and foresight. Their lives in the Garden of Eden were blissful and pleasant; choosing to leave that behind so they and the entire human family could experience both the triumphs and travails of mortality must not have been easy. But we believe they did choose mortality, and in so doing made it possible for all of us to participate in the Heavenly Father's great, eternal plan."[6]

JEHOVAH'S WITNESSES

"Is [the Bible] too puzzling and complex to be understood? Can the average person understand it? What help is needed for one to grasp the meaning of the Scriptures?… It is obvious that we need help if we are to understand the Bible… [T]he fact is that we cannot understand the Bible on our own. We need help… Jehovah, through his organization, however, has allowed his loyal servants to understand its meaning today… You too can gain this understanding with the assistance of those who are experienced in 'handling the word of the truth aright'… All who want to understand the Bible should appreciate that the 'greatly diversified wisdom of God' can become known only through Jehovah's channel of communication, the faithful and discreet slave [i.e. The Watchtower Bible and Tract Society]."[7]

"Jesus Christ further deserves honor because He is Jehovah's chief angel, or archangel." Footnote 9: "Why do we conclude that Jesus is the archangel Michael… ?"[8]

"In [the] beginning the Word was, and the Word was with God, and the Word was a god."[9]

ordon Bitner Hincklye, *What of the Mormons? A Brief Study of the Church of Jesus Christ of Latter-Day Saints* (Salt Lake City: Church of Jesus rist of Latter-Day Saints), 9, 11.

seph Fielding Smith, *Teachings of the Prophet Joseph Smith* (Salt Lake City: Deseret Book, 1976), 372.

id., 370.

id., 345–46.

ussell M. Ballard, *Our Search for Happiness: An Invitation to Understand the Church of Jesus Christ of the Latter-Day Saints* (Salt Lake City: seret Book, 1993), 87.

id.

ie Watchtower (October 1, 1994), 4 ,6 ,8.

ie Watchtower (February 1, 1991), 17.

hn 1:1 from *The New World Translation of the Holy Scriptures*.

KEY CRITIQUES:

CULTS

Breese, Dave. *The Marks of a Cult: Warning Signs of False Teachings*. Eugene, OR: Harvest, 1998.

Geisler, Norman L. and Ron Rhodes. *When Cultists Ask: A Popular Handbook on Cultic Misinterpretations*. Grand Rapids, MI: Baker, 1997.

Gomes, Alan W. *Unmasking the Cults: Zondervan Guide to Cults & Religious Movements*. Grand Rapids, MI: Zondervan, 1995.

Hexham, Irving. *Pocket Dictionary of New Religious Movements*. Downers Grove, IL: InterVarsity, 2002.

House, H. Wayne. *Charts of Cults, Sects, and Religious Movements*. Grand Rapids, MI: Zondervan, 2000.

Martin, Walter Ralston and Ravi K. Zacharias. *The Kingdom of the Cults*. Minneapolis: Bethany, 2003.

Passantino, Robert, Gretchen Passantino, and Raymond Schafer. *Answers to the Cultist at Your Door*. Eugene, OR: Harvest, 1981.

Rhodes, Ron. *The Challenge of the Cults and New Religions: The Essential Guide to Their History, Their Doctrine, and Our Response*. Grand Rapids, MI: Zondervan, 2001.

Sire, James W. *Scripture Twisting: 20 Ways the Cults Misread the Bible*. Downers Grove, IL: InterVarsity, 1980.

MORMONISM (CRITIQUE)

Abanes, Richard. *Becoming Gods: A Closer Look at 21st Century Mormonism*. Eugene, OR: Harvest, 2004.

Beckwith, Francis, Norman L. Geisler, Ron Rhodes, Phil Roberts, and Jerald and Sandra Tanner. *The Counterfeit Gospel of Mormonism*. Eugene, OR: Harvest, 1998.

Beckwith, Francis, Carl Mosser, and Paul Owen, eds. *The New Mormon Challenge: Responding to the Latest Defenses of a Fast-Growing Movement*. Grand Rapids, MI: Zondervan, 2002.

Blomberg, Craig, and Stephen Edward Robinson. *How Wide the Divide? A Mormon and an Evangelical in Conversation*. Downers Grove, IL: InterVarsity, 1997.

Cowan, Marvin W. *What Every Mormon Should Ask*. Eugene, OR: Harvest, 2000.

Carrigan, Cky John. "The Mormon Mirage." *Southwestern Journal of Theology 46*, no. 2 (2004).

Hinckley, Gordon Bitner. *What of the Mormons? A Brief Study of the Church of Jesus Christ of Latter-Day Saints*. Salt Lake City: Church of Jesus Christ of Latter-Day Saints, 1947.

Holding, James Patrick. *The Mormon Defenders: How Latter-Day Saint Apologists Misinterpret the Bible*. Miami: Tektonics Press, 2001.

McKeever, Bill and Eric Johnson. *Mormonism 101: Examining the Religion of the Latter-Day Saints*. Grand Rapids, MI: Baker, 2000.

Reed, David A. and John R. Farkas. *Mormons: Answered Verse by Verse*. Grand Rapids, MI: Baker, 1992.

Rhodes, Ron. *The 10 Most Important Things You Can Say to a Mormon*. Eugene, OR: Harvest, 2001.

Rhodes, Ron and Marian Bodine. *Reasoning from the Scriptures with the Mormons*. Eugene, OR: Harvest, 1995.

Smith, Joseph Fielding. *Teachings of the Prophet Joseph Smith*. Salt Lake City: Deseret Book, 1976.

JEHOVAH'S WITNESSES (CRITIQUE)

Bowman, Robert M. *Jehovah's Witnesses, Jesus Christ, and the Gospel of John*. Grand Rapids, MI: Baker, 1989.

———. *Understanding Jehovah's Witnesses: Why They Read the Bible the Way They Do*. Grand Rapids, MI: Baker, 1991.

———. *Why You Should Believe in the Trinity: An Answer to Jehovah's Witnesses*. Grand Rapids, MI: Baker, 1989.

Reed, David A. *Answering Jehovah's Witnesses: Subject by Subject*. Grand Rapids, MI: Baker, 1996.

———. *Jehovah's Witnesses: Answered Verse by Verse*. Grand Rapids, MI: Baker, 1986.

Rhodes, Ron. *Reasoning from the Scriptures with the Jehovah's Witnesses*. Eugene, OR: Harvest, 1993.

Fact Sheets

Economics
Fact Sheet

Key Terms:

Capitalism: an economic system based on the peaceful and free exchange of goods and services where all or most of the means of production and distribution (land, factories, railroads, etc) are privately owned and operated for profit

Economic Determinism: The belief that economics (the modes of production and exchange) determines the entire course of history; the social, political, and moral processes of life

Interventionism: Political activity undertaken by a state to influence aspects of economy usually in order to uphold certain moral values

Socialism: An economic system in which the ownership and operation of the means of production and distribution (land, factories, railroads, etc) are controlled by the government. According to Marxism, socialism (i.e. abolition of private property) is the transitional phase between capitalism and communism

Stewardship: The science, art, and skill of responsible and accountable management of resources. Christians believe that God is the ultimate owner of everything and that human beings have been given the responsibility to manage and care for his creation

Universal Enlightened Production: The belief that positive thought creates wealth

Key Facts:

- Christians must act on God's commands to help those who cannot help themselves
- Capitalism is the best strategy for defeating poverty
- Capitalism takes human nature into account

Key Verses:

Exodus 20:15, 17
Proverbs 11:24–26; 16:8;
  17:5; 19:17; 21:13; 22:9,
  28:27; 29:7; 31:8–9
Ecclesiastes 5:19

Acts 4:32-37; 20:35
1 Corinthians 16:2
2 Corinthians 8–9
Philippians 4:12–13

2 Thessalonians 3:7–13
1 Timothy 5-6; 6:6-10, 17–19
James 1:27; 2:14–17
1 John 3:16–18

Key Quotes:

"Christians need to care about the poor: that is one side of Christian social concern. But they also need to become informed about the relevant philosophical, political, and economic issues that ground wise and efficient policies to help the poor. Unfortunately, many Christians act as though the only thing that counts is intention. But when good intentions are not wedded to sound economic theory, good intentions can often result in actions that produce consequences directly opposite to those we planned."[1]

"Just before the collapse of socialism in the Soviet bloc, Lutheran sociologist Peter Berger wrote a marvelous book about the newly industrializing countries of East Asia. These 'little tigers,' or 'little dragons' as they're sometimes called, are part of a capitalist revolution and, as Berger documents, they are defeating poverty at an amazing rate.

‑nald H. Nash, *Poverty and Wealth: The Christian Debate Over Capitalism* (Westchester, IL: Crossway, 1986), 9.

Fact Sheets

He compares them to the Third World nations that have tried socialism for the last three decades and finds that none of the latter have grown, and indeed, that most have moved backward."[2]

"[A]ll men have different gifts, talents, interests, and abilities. Left free, they will exercise those in different ways and will produce different fruits. The only way to arrive at equal fruits is to equalize behavior; and that requires robbing men of liberty, making them slaves."[3]

"If poverty (the lack of money) really were what ails the poor, supplying vast amounts of money surely would alleviate it. But after thirty years of Great Society-style, 'War on Poverty' welfare programs—programs that have transferred (in 1990 dollars) more than $3.6 trillion to the poor—poverty is still winning. We ought to think about that for a minute: In the last thirty years, we gave a million dollars to America's poor nearly four million times over, yet all the while poverty got worse. If the money earmarked for poverty relief in this year's federal budget alone were given to the poor directly, we would have enough funds to raise every man, woman, and child in America above the poverty line and have a cool $60 billion left over to celebrate our victory." Nearly 40 percent of those the U.S. government defines as 'poor' own their own homes—homes that have more living space than that enjoyed by most middle class Europeans. 'Poor' ought to retain its earlier definition: the lack of food, shelter, or clothing. And while we are engaged in the task of redefining, we ought to remind ourselves that the definition of compassion is not increased control of private income by government."[4]

"The century-old question—Does any given 'scheme of help... make demands on men to give themselves to their brethren?'—is still the right one to ask. Each of us needs to ask that question not in the abstract, but personally. We need to ask ourselves: Are we offering not coerced silver, but our lives? If we talk of crisis pregnancies, are we actually willing to provide a home to a pregnant young woman? If we talk of abandoned children, are we actually willing to adopt a child? Most of our twentieth-century schemes, based on having someone else take action, are proven failures. It's time to learn from the warm hearts and hard heads of earlier times, and to bring that understanding into our own lives."[5]

KEY ORGANIZATIONS:

Acton Institute | www.acton.org | 616.454.3080 |

American Enterprise Institute for Public Policy Research | www.aei.org | 202.862.5800 |

Cato Institute | www.cato.org | 202.842.0200 |

Foundation for Economic Education | www.fee.org | 914.591.7230 |

Heritage Foundation | www.heritage.org | 202.546.4400 |

Hoover Institute | www.hoover.org | 650.723.1754 |

Independent Institute | www.independent.org | 510.632.1366 |

Library of Economics and Liberty | www.econlib.org |

Ludwig von Mises Institute | www.mises.org | 334.321.2100 |

Property and Environment Research Center | www.perc.org | 406.587.9591 |

[2] K. E. Grubbs Jr., "A New 'Liberation Theology' for the World: Faith and the Free Market," *Imprimis*, March 1991.
[3] E. Calvin Beisner, *Prosperity and Poverty: The Compassionate Use of Resources in a World of Scarcity* (Westchester, IL: Crossway, 1988), 54.
[4] Michael Bauman, "The Dangerous Samaritans: How We Unintentionally Injure the Poor," *Imprimis 23*, no.1 (1994).
[5] Marvin Olasky, *The Tragedy of American Compassion* (Washington DC: Regnery, 1992), 232–33.

KEY PUBLICATIONS:

Freeman Journal | **Foundation for Economic Education** | www.fee.org | 800.960.4333 |

KEY SOURCES/CRITIQUES:

(recommended titles appear in brown)

ECONOMICS

Carson, Clarence Buford. *Basic Economics*. Wadley, AL: American Textbook Committee, 1988.

Gregg, Samuel. *Economic Thinking for the Theologically Minded*. Lanham, MD: Univ. Press of America, 2001.

Gwartney, James D., Richard Stroup, Dwight R. Lee, and James D. Gwartney. *Common Sense Economics: What Everyone Should Know About Wealth and Prosperity*. New York: St. Martin's, 2005.

Hazlitt, Henry. *Economics in One Lesson*. New Rochelle, NY: Arlington House, 1979.

Heilbroner, Robert L. *The Worldly Philosophers: The Lives, Times, and Ideas of the Great Economic Thinkers*. New York: Simon & Schuster, 1999.

Sowell, Thomas. *Applied Economics: Thinking Beyond Stage One*. New York: Basic, 2004.

———. *Basic Economics: A Common Sense Guide to the Economy*. New York: Basic, 2007.

———. *Marxism: Philosophy and Economics*. New York: Quill, 1985.

CAPITALISM VS. SOCIALISM

Gilder, George F. *Wealth and Poverty*. San Francisco: ICS, 1993.

Griffiths, Brian. *The Creation of Wealth: A Christian's Case for Capitalism*. Downers Grove, IL: InterVarsity, 1984.

Nash, Ronald H. *Poverty and Wealth: The Christian Debate over Capitalism*. Westchester, IL: Crossway, 1986.

Novak, Michael. *The Spirit of Democratic Capitalism*. Lanham, MD: National Book Network, 1991.

Schaeffer, Frankie, ed. *Is Capitalism Christian? Toward a Christian Perspective on Economics*. Westchester, IL: Crossway, 1985.

Soto, Hernando de. *The Mystery of Capital: Why Capitalism Triumphs in the West and Fails Everywhere Else*. New York: Basic, 2000.

PRIVATE PROPERTY

Bethell, Tom. *The Noblest Triumph: Property and Prosperity through the Ages*. New York: St. Martin's, 1998.

INTERVENTIONISM/SOCIALISM (CRITIQUE)

Dalrymple, Theodore. *Life at the Bottom: The Worldview that Makes the Underclass*. Chicago: Ivan R. Dee, 2001.

Gilder, George F. *Wealth and Poverty*. San Francisco: ICS, 1993.

Griffiths, Brian. *The Creation of Wealth: A Christian's Case for Capitalism*. Downers Grove, IL: InterVarsity, 1984.

Hazlitt, Henry. *The Critics of Keynesian Economics*. Lanham, MD: University Press of America, 1983.

———. *The Failure of the New Economics*. Lanham, MD: University Press of America, 1983.

Nash, Ronald H. *Poverty and Wealth: The Christian Debate over Capitalism*. Westchester, IL: Crossway, 1986.

Novak, Michael. *The Spirit of Democratic Capitalism*. Lanham, MD: National Book Network, 1991.

Schaeffer, Franky, ed. *Is Capitalism Christian? Toward a Christian Perspective on Economics*. Westchester, IL: Crossway, 1985.

Soto, Hernando de. *The Mystery of Capital: Why Capitalism Triumphs in the West and Fails Everywhere Else*. New York: Basic, 2000.

STEWARDSHIP

Beisner, E. Calvin and Fieldstead Institute. *Prosperity and Poverty: The Compassionate Use of Resources in a World of Scarcity*. Westchester, IL: Crossway, 1988.

Blomberg, Craig. *Neither Poverty nor Riches: A Biblical Theology of Material Possessions*. Grand Rapids, MI: Eerdmans, 1999.

Fact Sheets

WELFARE (CRITIQUE)

Dalrymple, Theodore. *Life at the Bottom: The Worldview that Makes the Underclass*. Chicago: Ivan R. Dee, 2001.

Grant, George. *Bringing in the Sheaves: Transforming Poverty into Productivity*. Brentwood, TN: Wolgemuth & Hyatt, 1988.

———. *The Dispossessed: Homelessness in America*. Ft. Worth: Dominion Press, 1986.

———. *In the Shadow of Plenty: Biblical Principles of Welfare and Poverty*. Ft. Worth: Dominion Press, 1986.

Nash, Ronald H. *Social Justice and the Christian Church*. Lanham, MD: University Press of America, 1990.

Neuhaus, Richard John. *Doing Well and Doing Good: The Challenge to the Christian Capitalist*. New York: Doubleday, 1992.

———. *Welfare Reformed: A Compassionate Approach*. Phillipsburg, NJ: P&R Publishers, 1994.

Olasky, Marvin N. *The Tragedy of American Compassion*. Wheaton, IL: Crossway, 1992.

HISTORY
FACT SHEET

KEY TERMS:

Creation, Fall, Redemption: The progression of events in God's creation—that all was created good, but mankind rebelled against God and requires divine redemption. Thus, all of creation is sacred and stands under the blessing, judgment, and redeeming purposes of God

Economic Determinism: The belief that economics is the only driving force in history

Evolutionary Godhood: The New Age belief that the divine is the source of evolutionary force and that we are growing toward godhood

Historical Determinism: The Muslim belief that history is not made up of a series of chance happenings; rather, Allah superintends history throughout time, guiding it toward an expression of his will

Historical Evolution: The belief that history is to be understood in terms of unguided evolution but which can now be guided by the ingenuity of mankind

Historical Materialism: The methodological approach to the study of society, economics, and history that looks for the causes of developments and changes in human societies through economic analysis (e.g. social classes, political structures, ideologies, etc.)

Historical Revisionism: The rewriting/editing of the past to serve an ideological purpose
Historicism: The view that past beliefs, morals, and truths should only be understood in relation to the cultural/historical periods in which they arose, not according to any eternal standard of morality and truth

Jihad: An Arabic word that means "striving in the way of God." This striving can take a number of forms, including the daily inner struggle to be a better person or armed struggle fought in defense of Islam

Nihilism: The view that the world, and especially human existence, is without meaning, purpose, comprehensible truth, or essential value

KEY VERSES:

Genesis 3:15   John 1:14   1 Timothy 3:16
Judges 2:10; 21:25   Galatians 4:4

KEY PUBLICATIONS:

Archaeology Odyssey | **Biblical Archaeology Society** | www.bib-arch.org | 800.221.4644 |

Biblical Archaeology Review | **Biblical Archaeology Society** | www.bib-arch.org | 800.221.4644 |

Bible Review | **Biblical Archaeology Society** | www.bib-arch.org | 800.221.4644 |

Christian History | **Christianity Today** | www.christianhistory.net |

Fact Sheets

"Paul regarded the resurrection as an event in history supported by the strongest possible eyewitness testimony, including his own (1 Corinthians 15:5-8). For Paul, the historicity of the resurrection was a necessary condition for the truth of Christianity and the validity of Christian belief."[1]

KEY SOURCES:
(recommended titles appear in brown)

CHURCH HISTORY

Harrison, R. K. *Old Testament Times: A Social, Political, and Cultural Context*. Grand Rapids, MI: Eerdmans, 2005.

Kennedy, D. James and Jerry Newcombe. *What If Jesus Had Never Been Born?* Nashville: Thomas Nelson, 1994.

Noll, Mark A. *Turning Points: Decisive Moments in the History of Christianity*. Grand Rapids, MI: Baker, 2000.

Shelley, Bruce L. *Church History in Plain Language*. Dallas: Word, 1995.

Stark, Rodney. *The Rise of Christianity: How the Obscure, Marginal Jesus Movement Became the Dominant Religious Force in the Western World in a Few Centuries*. San Francisco: HarperSanFrancisco, 1996.

Tenney, Merrill Chapin. *New Testament Times: Understanding the World of the First Century*. Grand Rapids: Eerdmans, 2004.

HISTORICITY OF BIBLE AND CHURCH

Blomberg, Craig. *The Historical Reliability of John's Gospel*. Downers Grove, IL: InterVarsity, 2002.

———. *The Historical Reliability of the Gospels*. Downers Grove, IL: InterVarsity, 1987.

Copan, Paul, ed. *Will the Real Jesus Please Stand Up? A Debate between William Lane Craig and John Dominic Crossan*. Grand Rapids, MI: Baker, 1998.

Craig, William Lane. *Knowing the Truth About the Resurrection: Our Response to the Empty Tomb*. Ann Arbor, MI: Servant, 1988.

Free, Joseph P. and Howard Frederic. *Archaeology and Bible History*. Grand Rapids, MI: Zondervan, 1992.

Geisler, Norman L. *Systematic Theology*. Minneapolis: Bethany, 2002 (Vol. 1, Chapters 25 and 26).

Habermas, Gary R. and Michael R. Licona. *The Case for the Resurrection of Jesus*. Grand Rapids, MI: Kregel, 2004.

Kitchen, K. A. *The Bible in Its World: The Bible and Archaeology Today*. Exeter, RI: Paternoster, 1977.

———. *On the Reliability of the Old Testament*. Grand Rapids, MI: Eerdmans, 2003.

Nash, Ronald H. *The Gospel and the Greeks: Did the New Testament Borrow from Pagan Thought?* Richardson, TX: Probe, 1992.

Thompson, J. A. *The Bible and Archaeology*. Grand Rapids, MI: Eerdmans, 1982.

Wilkins, Michael J. and James Porter Moreland. *Jesus under Fire*. Grand Rapids, MI: Zondervan, 1995.

---

[1] Ronald H. Nash, *Christian Faith and Historical Understanding* (Dallas, TX: Probe, 1984), 112.

HOMOSEXUALITY
FACT SHEET

KEY VERSES:

Genesis 19:1–29	Romans 1:25-32	1 Timothy 1:10
Leviticus 18:22; 20:13	1 Corinthians 6:9–11	

KEY ORGANIZATIONS:

Genesis Counseling | www.genesiscounseling.org | 714.508.6953 |

Desert Stream Ministries | www.desertstream.org | 816.767.1730 |

Exodus International | www.exodusinternational.org | 407.599.6872 |

Love Won Out | www.lovewonout.com | 800.232.6459 |

Family Research Council | www.frc.org | 800.225.4008 |

Focus on the Family | www.fotf.org | 800.232.6459 |

KEY QUOTES:

'It never dawned on these people that my pain was a very real cry to be whole, to be well. A 15-year old crying out for love, and getting instead an empty excuse for healing, empty words that said, 'there are no absolutes,' 'lose your inhibition,' 'experiment with your sexuality.' Think about it… at fifteen, confused and alone, what effect would those words have?… You see, I was one of those children. I was a homosexual. And I am one of the lucky ones… I got out alive."[1]

'But this strategy [of viewing the homosexual struggle as a civil rights issue] is based on two assumptions: that sexuality is equivalent to race in terms of discrimination, and that the full equality of homosexuals can be accomplished by designating gay people as victims. Both are extremely dubious. Unlike blacks three decades ago, gay men and lesbians suffer no discernible communal economic deprivation and already operate at the highest levels of society: in boardrooms, governments, the media, the military, the law and industry."[2] [A pro-homosexual publication]

'As more and more homosexuals come out of hiding, the reality of gay economic and political and education achievement becomes more evident. And as that happens, gay people who insist they are oppressed will increasingly, and not always unfairly, come off as yuppie whiners, 'victims' with $50,000 incomes and vacations in Europe. They may feel they are oppressed, but they will have a harder and harder time convincing the public."[3] [A pro-homosexual publication]

---

ff, "Open Letter from a Survivor," *CFV Report*, Volume 9 (October 1993).

drew Sullivan, "The Politics of Homosexuality," *The New Republic* (May 10, 1993).

nathan Rauch, "Beyond Oppression," *The New Republic* (May 10, 1993).

Fact Sheets

Key Sources/Critiques:

(recommended titles appear in brown)

Homosexuality

Balch, David L., ed. *Homosexuality, Science, and the 'Plain Sense' of Scripture*. Grand Rapids, MI: Eerdmans, 2000.

Haley, Mike. *101 Frequently Asked Questions About Homosexuality*. Eugene, OR: Harvest, 2004.

Bible and Church

Bahnsen, Greg L. *Homosexuality, a Biblical View*. Grand Rapids, MI: Baker, 1978.

Cowan, Steve B. "Abandoning Nature: An Argument against Homosexuality." *Areopagus Journal 1*, no. 4 (2001): 33–36.

Dallas, Joe. *A Strong Delusion: Confronting The "Gay Christian" Movement*. Eugene, OR: Harvest, 1996.

DeYoung, James B. *Homosexuality: Contemporary Claims Examined in Light of the Bible and Other Ancient Literature and Law*. Grand Rapids, MI: Kregel, 2000.

Gagnon, Robert A. J. *The Bible and Homosexual Practice: Texts and Hermeneutics*. Nashville: Abingdon Press, 2001.

Grant, George and Mark Horne. *Unnatural Affections: The Impuritan Ethic of Homosexuality and the Modern Church*. Franklin, TN: Legacy Communications, 1991.

Jones, Stanton L. and Mark A. Yarhouse. *Homosexuality: The Use of Scientific Research in the Church's Moral Debate*. Downers Grove, IL: InterVarsity, 2000.

Mazzalongo, Michael. *Gay Rights or Wrongs: A Christian's Guide to Homosexual Issues and Ministry*. Joplin, MO: College Press, 1995.

White, James R. and Jeffrey D. Niell. *The Same Sex Controversy: Defending and Clarifying the Bible's Message About Homosexuality*. Minneapolis: Bethany, 2002.

Wilder, Terry L. "What the New Testament Does and Does Not Teach About Homosexuality." *Areopagus Journal 1*, no. 4 (2001): 28–32.

Wold, Donald J. *Out of Order: Homosexuality in the Bible and the Ancient Near East*. Grand Rapids, MI: Baker, 1998.

Causes and Counseling

Dallas, Joe. *Desires in Conflict*. Eugene, OR: Harvest, 2003.

Konrad, J. A. *You Don't Have to Be Gay: Hope and Freedom for Males Struggling with Homosexuality or for Those Who Know of Someone Who Is*. Hilo, HI: Pacific, 1992.

Riley, Mona and Brad Sargent. *Unwanted Harvest?* Nashville: Broadman & Holman, 1995.

Wolfe, Christopher, ed. *Same-Sex Matters: The Challenge of Homosexuality*. Dallas: Spence, 2000.

Worthen, Anita and Bob Davies. *Someone I Love Is Gay: How Family and Friends Can Respond*. Downers Grove, IL: InterVarsity, 1996.

Political Action

Burtoft, Larry. *Setting the Record Straight: What Research Really Says About the Social Consequences of Homosexuality*. Colorado Springs, CO: Focus on the Family, 1994.

Grant, George and Mark A. Horne. *Legislating Immorality: The Homosexual Movement Comes out of the Closet*. Chicago: Moody, 1993.

Kennedy, D. James and Jerry Newcombe. *What's Wrong with Same-Sex Marriage?* Wheaton, IL: Crossway, 2004.

Magnuson, Roger J. *Are 'Gay Rights' Right? A Report on Homosexuality and the Law*. St. Paul, MN: The Fund, 1985.

Satinover, Jeffrey. *Homosexuality and the Politics of Truth*. Grand Rapids, MI: Baker, 1996.

Stanton, Glenn T. and Bill Maier. *Marriage on Trial: The Case against Same-Sex Marriage and Parenting*. Downers Grove, IL: InterVarsity, 2004.

Law & Politics
Fact Sheet

KEY TERMS:

LAW

Critical Legal Studies: The deconstruction of law used to discover its subjective meaning and biased intent

Divine Law: Any law that comes directly from the character of God via special revelation

Natural Law: Physical and moral laws revealed in general revelation and built into the structure of the universe (as opposed to the laws imposed by human beings)

Positive Law [or Legal Positivism]: The Humanistic legal school of thought that claims laws are rules made by human beings and that there is no inherent or necessary connection between law and morality

Proletariat Law: A legal system established by state authority that favors the interest of the working people

Shari'ah Law: Islamic law derived from the Qur'an and the Hadith and applied to the public and private lives of Muslims within Islamic states. Shari'ah law governs many aspects of day-to-day life—politics, economics, banking, business, contracts, social issues, etc

Self-law: The New Age legal perspective that maintains that actions are lawful only if honorable to the god within and unlawful if imposed by an outside authority

POLITICS

Anarchy: The complete absence of government and law

Communism: A dream of future utopia brought about by a proletariat revolution and ultimately leading to a classless society in which all property is publicly shared and each person works and is paid according to his or her abilities and needs

Global Islamic States: The vision of many Muslims to bring all nations under Shari'ah law, whether accomplished through peaceful means or jihad

Identity Politics: A political ideology which seeks to advance the interests of particular groups in society which have been perceived to be the victims of social injustice

Justice, Freedom, Order: Principals of human governments instituted by God to protect the innocent, punish the guilty, and preserve the rights of all people against the sinful tendencies of mankind

Leftism: An ideological approach to politics emphasizing the state's role in bringing about social justice, with a special focus on helping the poor or oppressed (due to race, gender, or sexual orientation)

Liberalism: A political tradition emphasizing personal liberties and equality over traditional moral concerns; specific policies include a woman's right to an abortion, promotion of same-sex marriage, equal rights for women, and redistribution of wealth to help the poor

New World Order: The New Age belief that (given each person's evolution toward collective consciousness) humanity will eventually develop the capacity for worldwide self-government

Secular World Government: A non-religious political body that would make, interpret, and enforce a set of laws internationally

Self-government: The New Age political perspective that maintains that each divine individual is evolving the ability to govern him or herself

Social Justice: An ambiguous term used to denote a wide range of meaning—anything from basic social equality (e.g. right to life and liberty) to the equalization of wealth and special rights for minority groups

Statism: A political system in which the concentration of economic controls and planning are placed completely in the hands of a highly centralized government

Theocracy: Any government ruled by a power claiming divine sanction, e.g. ancient Israel and a number of Islamic nations

KEY VERSES:

Deuteronomy 2:37–38;
  4:5–6; 5; 6
Psalms 1–2; 11:11; 14:43;
  19:7–9; 119; 29:2

Zechariah 8:16
Jeremiah 27:5–9, 12
Daniel 2:20-21

Romans 13:1-10
1 Timothy 1:8–11; 2:1
1 Peter 2:13–14

KEY ORGANIZATIONS:

American Center for Law and Justice | www.aclj.org | 800.296.4529 |

American Family Association | www.afa.net |

American Vision | www.americanvision.org | 770.222.7266 |

Eagle Forum | www.eagleforum.org | 618.462.5415 |

Family Research Council | www.frc.org | 800.225.4008 |

Heritage Foundation | www.heritage.org | 202.546.4400 |

The Leadership Institute | www.leadershipinstitute.org | 703.247.2000 |

The Rutherford Institute | www.rutherford.org | 434.978.3888|

Justice Fellowship | www.pfm.org | 877.478.0100 |

KEY PUBLICATIONS:

Citizen Magazine | **Focus on the Family** | www.family.org | 800.232.6459 |

World Magazine | www.worldmag.com | 800.951.6397 |

Human Events | www.humanevents.org | 800.787.7557 |

KEY QUOTES:

"We are a religious people whose institutions presuppose a supreme being."[1]

"To cut off Law from its ethical sources is to strike a terrible blow at the rule of law."[2]

"Government policies of accommodation, acknowledgment, and support for religion are an accepted part of our political and cultural heritage...Any approach less sensitive to our heritage would border on latent hostility toward religion."[3]

"[The] Establishment Clause permits government some latitude in recognizing and accommodating the central role religion plays in our society."[4]

"Why have law and order deteriorated so rapidly in the United States? Simply because for many years it has been commonly taught that life is a random, accidental phenomenon with no meaning except the purely materialistic one. Laws are merely a matter of human expediency. Since humans are allegedly accidents, so are their laws."[5]

"If man cannot know, according to a higher law, what is just or right in a given situation, he cannot protest and criticize legitimately any particular course of action as unjust."[6]

"God has called the Church to serve. And through service He grants us favor with the people. This is a fundamental principle of dominion in the Bible: dominion through service."[7]

"[C]hristians have an important role to play in the organization that most people think of as 'government'—the state. Indeed, believers have a Biblical obligation to be involved in civic affairs, since that sphere, no less than the private realm, is subject to God's rule and requires a generous dose of Christian 'salt.'"[8]

"If while evangelizing we abandon the sociopolitical realm to its own devices, we shall fortify the misimpression that the public order falls wholly outside the command and will of God, that Christianity deals with private concerns only; and we shall conceal the fact that government exists by God's will as His servant for the sake of justice and order."[9]

"Christians realize that man's fallen nature has severe implications for every aspect of his life, including the political realm. The American system of checks and balances, therefore, is embraced by Christians in their political theory because it is a genuine attempt to curtail man's sinful tendencies not only among the private citizens but also among their governors. A Christian worldview is also indispensable for guaranteeing basic human rights for individuals. Because the Christian believes man is created in the image of God, he believes that each individual has value."[10]

"One of the most startling commentaries on this century is the fact that millions more have died at the hands of their own governments than in wars with other nations—all to preserve someone's power."[11]

stice William O. Douglas, Zorach v. Clausen, 343 U.S., 313 (1952).

ssell Kirk, "The Christian Postulates of English & American Law," *Journal of Christian Jurisprudence* (Tulsa: Oral Roberts Univ., 1980), 66.

stice Anthony M. Kennedy, County of Allegheny v. ACLU, 492 U.S., 657 (1989).

d.

E. Wilder Smith, *The Creation of Life* (Costa Mesa, CA: TWFT Publishers, 1970), ix.

n W. Whitehead, *The Second American Revolution* (Westchester, IL: Crossway, 1982), 88.

orge Grant, *The Changing of the Guard: Biblical Principles for Political Action* (Ft. Worth: Dominion Press, 1987), 126.

ug Bandow, *Beyond Good Intentions: A Biblical View of Politics* (Westchester, IL: Crossway, 1988), 148.

rl F. H. Henry, *Twilight of a Great Civilization* (Westchester, IL: Crossway, 1988), 20.

vid A. Noebel, *Understanding the Times: The Religious Worldviews of Our Day and the Search for Truth* (Manitou Springs, CO: Summit Press,), 624–625.

uck Colson, *Kingdoms in Conflict* (Grand Rapids, MI: Zondervan, 1987), 270.

Fact Sheets

KEY CHRISTIAN SOURCES/CRITIQUES:

(recommended titles appear in brown)

LAW

Bastiat, Frédéric, *The Law*. Irvington-on-Hudson, NY: Foundation for Economic Education, 1998.

Bork, Robert H. *The Tempting of America: The Political Seduction of the Law*. New York: Free Press, 1990.

McConnell, Michael W. "The Origins and Historical Understanding of Free Exercise of Religion," *Harvard Law Review*, Vol. 103, no. 1410 (1990).

Titus, Herbert W. *God, Man, and Law: The Biblical Principles*. Oak Brook, IL: Institute in Basic Life Principles, 1994.

VanGemeren, Willem. *The Law, the Gospel, and the Modern Christian*. Grand Rapids, MI: Zondervan, 1993.

Wright, Christopher J. H. *An Eye for an Eye: The Place of Old Testament Ethics Today*. Downers Grove, IL: InterVarsity, 1983.

POLITICS

Amos, Gary T. *Defending the Declaration: How the Bible and Christianity Influenced the Writing of the Declaration of Independence*. Brentwood, TN: Wolgemuth & Hyatt, 1989.

Bandow, Doug and Fieldstead Institute. *Beyond Good Intentions: A Biblical View of Politics*. Westchester, IL: Crossway, 1988.

Bauman, Michael and David W. Hall, eds. *God and Caesar*. Camp Hill, PA: Christian Publications, 1994.

Burke, Thomas J. and Lissa Roche. *Man and State: Religion, Society, and the Constitution*. Hillsdale, MI: Hillsdale College Press, 1988.

Colson, Charles W. and Ellen Santilli Vaughn. *Kingdoms in Conflict*. New York: W. Morrow, 1987.

Doner, Colonel V. *The Samaritan Strategy: A New Agenda for Christian Activism*. Brentwood, TN: Wolgemuth & Hyatt, 1988.

Eidsmoe, John. *God and Caesar: Biblical Faith and Political Action*. Westchester, IL: Crossway, 1984.

Evans, M. Stanton. *The Theme Is Freedom: Religion, Politics, and the American Tradition*. Washington DC: Regnery, 1994.

Grant, George. *The Changing of the Guard: The Vital Role Christians Must Play in America's Unfolding Political and Cultural Drama*. Nashville: Broadman & Holman, 1995.

Hall, David W. *Savior or Servant: Putting Government in Its Place*. Oak Ridge, TN: Kuyper Institute, 1996.

Hart, Benjamin. *Faith and Freedom: The Christian Roots of American Liberty*. Dallas: Lewis & Stanley, 1988.

Neuhaus, Richard John. *The Naked Public Square: Religion and Democracy in America*. Grand Rapids, MI: Eerdmans, 1984.

Rushdoony, Rousas John. *Politics of Guilt and Pity*. Vallecito, CA: Ross House, 1995.

Schlossberg, Herbert. *Idols for Destruction: Christian Faith and Its Confrontation with American Society*. Washington DC: Regnery, 1990.

Smith, Gary Scott, ed. *God and Politics: Four Views on the Reformation of Civil Government*. Phillipsburg, NJ: Presbyterian & Reformed, 1989.

ABORTION

Beckwith, Francis. *Politically Correct Death: Answering the Arguments for Abortion Rights*. Grand Rapids, MI: Baker, 1993.

Beckwith, Francis J. "Roe V. Wade: Its Logic and Its Legacy." *Southern Baptist Theological Journal* 7, no. 2 (Summer 2003): 4–28.

Fournier, Keith A. and William D. Watkins. *In Defense of Life: Taking a Stand against the Culture of Death*. Colorado Springs, CO: NavPress, 1996.

Grant, George. *Grand Illusions: The Legacy of Planned Parenthood*. Nashville: Cumberland House, 2000.

Kasun, Jacqueline R. *The War against Population: The Economics and Ideology of World Population Control*. San Francisco: Ignatius, 1999.

Fact Sheets

CHURCH AND STATE

Cord, Robert L. *Separation of Church and State: Historical Fact and Current Fiction*. Grand Rapids, MI: Baker, 1988.

Eidsmoe, John. *Christianity and the Constitution: The Faith of Our Founding Fathers*. Grand Rapids, MI: Baker, 1987.

Whitehead, John W. *The Second American Revolution*. Elgin, IL: D. C. Cook, 1982.

HOMOSEXUALITY

Burtoft, Larry. *Setting the Record Straight: What Research Really Says About the Social Consequences of Homosexuality*. Colorado Springs, CO: Focus on the Family, 1994.

Grant, George and Mark A. Horne. *Legislating Immorality: The Homosexual Movement Comes out of the Closet*. Chicago: Moody, 1993.

Kennedy, D. James and Jerry Newcombe. *What's Wrong with Same-Sex Marriage?* Wheaton, IL: Crossway, 2004.

Magnuson, Roger J. *Are 'Gay Rights' Right? A Report on Homosexuality and the Law*. St. Paul: The Fund, 1985.

Satinover, Jeffrey. *Homosexuality and the Politics of Truth*. Grand Rapids, MI: Baker, 1996.

Stanton, Glenn T. and Bill Maier. *Marriage on Trial: The Case against Same-Sex Marriage and Parenting*. Downers Grove, IL: InterVarsity, 2004.

LEADERSHIP
FACT SHEET

KEY ORGANIZATIONS:
Growing Leaders | www.growingleaders.com | 678.367.4187 |

Injoy | www.injoy.com | 800.333.6506 |

Myers Institute | www.myersinstitute.org | 423.570.1000 |

The Leadership Institute | www.leadershipinstitute.org | 800.827.5323 |

Passing the Baton International | www.passingthebaton.org | 423.570.1000 |

Summit Ministries | www.summit.org | 719.685.9103 |

KEY PUBLICATIONS:
Discipleship Journal | **NavPress** | www.navpress.com/dj | 800.366.7788 |

Student Leader | **American Student Government Association** | www.asgaonline.com | 352.373.6907 |

KEY QUOTES:
"Now Faithful play the Man, speak for thy God: Fear not the wicked's malice, nor their rod: Speak boldly man, the Truth is on thy side; Die for it, and to Life in triumph ride."[1]

"A ship in the harbor is safe, but that is not what ships are for."[2]

"You never conquer a mountain. Mountains can't be conquered; you conquer yourself—your hopes, your fears."[3]

"Champions know that success is inevitable; that there is no such thing as failure, only feedback."[4]

"The quality of a man's life is in direct proportion to his commitment to excellence."[5]

"Our plans miscarry because they have no aim. When a man does not know what harbor he is making for, no wind is the right wind."[6]

---

[1] John Bunyan
[2] John A. Shedd
[3] Jim Whitaker (first American to reach the summit of Mount Everest)
[4] Michael J. Gelb
[5] Vince Lombardi
[6] Seneca

"I studied the lives of great men and famous women, and I found that the men and women who got to the top were those who did the jobs they had in hand, with everything they had of energy and enthusiasm."[7]

"Life, like war, is a series of mistakes, and he is not the best Christian nor the best general who makes the fewest false steps. Poor mediocrity may secure that; but he is the best who wins the most splendid victories by the retrieval of mistakes. Forget mistakes: organize victory out of mistakes."[8]

"But when I said that nothing had been done I erred in one important matter. We had definitely committed ourselves and were halfway out of our ruts. We had put down our passage money—booked a sailing to Bombay. This may sound too simple, but is great in consequence. Until one is committed, there is hesitancy, the chance to draw back, always ineffectiveness. Concerning all acts of initiative (and creation), there is one elementary truth the ignorance of which kills countless ideas and splendid plans: that the moment one definitely commits oneself, then Providence moves too. A whole stream of events issues from the decision, raising in one's favor all manner of unforeseen incidents, meetings and material assistance, which no man could have dreamt would have come his way." Leadership is not so much the exercise of power itself as the empowerment of others."[9]

KEY SOURCES:
(recommended titles appear in brown)

Boice, James Montgomery. *Ordinary Men Called by God: A Study of Abraham, Moses, and David*. Grand Rapids, MI: Kregel, 1998.

Borthwick, Paul. *Leading the Way: Leadership Is Not Just for Super Christians*. Colorado Springs, CO: Navpress, 1989.

Castle, Tony. *Lives of Famous Christians: A Biographical Dictionary*. Ann Arbor, MI: Servant Books, 1988.

Cole, Edwin Louis. *Courage: Winning Life's Toughest Battles*. Southlake, TX: Watercolor, 2002.

Cowart, John W. *People Whose Faith Got Them into Trouble: Stories of Costly Discipleship*. Downers Grove, IL: InterVarsity, 1990.

De Pree, Max. *Leadership Is an Art*. New York: Currency, 2004.

Engstrom, Theodore Wilhelm. *The Making of a Christian Leader*. Grand Rapids, MI: Zondervan, 1976.

Fisher, Roger, Alan Sharp, and John Richardson. *Getting It Done: How to Lead When You're Not in Charge*. New York: Harper, 1998.

Foxe, John. *Foxe's Book of Martyrs*. Nashville: Thomas Nelson, 2000.

Hyde, Douglas Arnold. *Dedication and Leadership: Learning from the Communists*. Notre Dame, IN: University of Notre Dame Press, 1966.

Johnston, Ray. *Developing Student Leaders: How to Motivate, Select, Train, Empower Your Kids to Make a Difference*. Grand Rapids, MI: Zondervan, 1992.

Kouzes, James M. and Barry Z. Posner. *The Leadership Challenge: How to Keep Getting Extraordinary Things Done in Organizations*. San Francisco: Jossey-Bass, 1995.

Mattson, Ralph. *Visions of Grandeur: Leadership That Creates Positive Change*. Chicago: Moody, 1994.

Sanders, J. Oswald. *Spiritual Leadership*. Chicago: Moody, 1994.

Stanley, Andy. *The Next Generation Leader: 5 Essentials for Those Who Will Shape the Future*. Sisters, OR: Multnomah, 2003.

Stanley, Paul D. and J. Robert Clinton. *Connecting: The Mentoring Relationships You Need to Succeed in Life*. Colorado Springs, CO: NavPress, 1992.

Wilkins, Michael J. *Following the Master: Discipleship in the Steps of Jesus*. Grand Rapids, MI: Zondervan, 1992.

esident Harry Truman
. H. Murray
arren Bennis

Fact Sheets

Philosophy & Logic
Fact Sheet

Key Terms:

LOGIC

Deductive Reasoning: The process of reasoning that starts with an accepted rule and generalizes it to a specific situation in order to reach a conclusion; the conclusion is absolutely certain (e.g. if 5+4 = 9 and 6+3 = 9, then 5+4 = 6+3)

Fallacy: An error in either inductive or deductive reasoning

Inductive Reasoning: The process of reasoning that starts with a general principle and moves toward a rule in order to draw a conclusion; the conclusion is not "absolutely certain" (e.g. a court trial)

Logic [from the Greek *logos*]: The study of reasoning

The Principle of Excluded Middle: A is not non-A (e.g. white is not non-white)

The Principle of Identity: A is A (e.g. white is white)

The Principle of Non-contradiction: A thing cannot be both A and non-A at the same time and in the same sense (e.g. a color cannot be both white and blue)

PHILOSOPHY

Anti-realism: The belief that reality is subjectively constructed by human thought

Correspondence Theory of Truth: The belief that a statement is true if it corresponds to the facts of reality

Cosmology: The study of the structure, origin, and design of the universe

Deconstruction: A theory of literary criticism that seeks to expose the hidden assumptions and prejudices of the author of any written text, emphasizing the underlying racist, sexist, homophobic, or bourgeois bias of authors from the Western philosophic tradition

Dialectical Materialism: The belief that in everything there is a thesis (the way things are) and an antithesis (an opposition to the way things are), which must inevitably clash. The result of the struggle and merging that comes from the clash is the synthesis, which becomes the new thesis. This new thesis will eventually attract another antithesis, and produce a new synthesis

Epistemology: The study of knowledge

Metaphysics: The study of ultimate reality

Mind/Body Problem: The study of the relationship of the mind (e.g. mental events, mental functions, mental properties, and consciousness) to the physical body

Naturalism [or Materialism]: The philosophical belief that reality is composed solely of matter and that all phenomena can be explained in terms of natural causes e.g., law of gravity

Non-naturalism: The belief that everything is a part of God. The things that we can see and feel are only a manifestation of spirit, and all matter will melt away when universal consciousness is achieved

Ontology: The study of existence and being

Realism: The belief that what one encounters in the world exists independently of human thought

Supernaturalism: The belief that reality is more than nature; that a transcendent agent intervenes in the course of natural law

KEY VERSES:

Genesis 1:1
Deuteronomy 6:5
Matthew 22:37
John 1:1

Romans 12:2–3
1 Corinthians 1:18–2:16
2 Corinthians 10:5
Colossians 1:17

Colossians 2:3–8
2 Timothy 3:16
Revelation 19:13

KEY ORGANIZATIONS:

Fallacy Files | www.fallacyfiles.org |

Internet Encyclopedia of Philosophy | www.iep.utm.edu |

Logical Fallacies | www.logicalfallacies.info |

Stanford Encyclopedia of Philosophy | http://plato.stanford.edu |

KEY PUBLICATIONS:

Philosophia Christi | **Evangelical Philosophical Society** | www.epsociety.org |

KEY QUOTES:

"A little philosophy inclineth man's mind to atheism, but depth in philosophy bringeth men's minds about to religion."[1]

"5% think, 10% think they think, 85% would rather die than think."[2]

"Arguments, like men, are often pretenders."[3]

"For we let our young men and women go out unarmed in a day when armor was never so necessary. By teaching them to read, we have left them at the mercy of the printed word. By the invention of the film and the radio, we have made certain that no aversion to reading shall secure them from the incessant battery of words, words, words. They do not know what the words mean; they do not know how to ward them off or blunt their edge or fling them back; they are a prey to words in their emotions instead of being the masters of them in their intellects… We have lost the tools of learning, and in their absence can only make a botched and piecemeal job of it."[4]

gh G.Dick, ed., *Select Writings of Francis Bacon* (New York: Random, 1955), 44.
onymous
to
rothy Sayers, speech at Oxford, 1947, quoted in Roy Maynard, "Trivium Pursuit," *World* (October 8, 1994).

KEY SOURCES:
(recommended titles appear in brown)

LOGIC

Bluedorn, Nathaniel. *The Fallacy Detective: Thirty-Six Lessons on How to Recognize Bad Reasoning*. Muscatine, IA: Christian Logic, 2003.

Bluedorn, Nathaniel and Hans Bluedorn. *The Thinking Toolbox: Thirty-Five Lessons That Will Build Your Reasoning Skills*. Muscatine, IA: Christian Logic, 2005.

Capaldi, Nicholas. *How to Win Every Argument*. New York: MJF, 1999.

Copi, Irving M. and Carl Cohen. *Introduction to Logic*. Upper Saddle River, NJ: Prentice Hall, 2005.

Engel, S. Morris. *With Good Reason: An Introduction to Informal Fallacies*. Boston: St. Martin's, 2000.

Geisler, Norman L. and Ron Brooks. *Come, Let Us Reason: An Introduction to Logical Thinking*. Grand Rapids, MI: Baker, 1990.

Schick, Theodore and Lewis Vaughn. *How to Think About Weird Things*. Boston: McGraw-Hill, 2005.

Walton, Douglas N. *Informal Logic: A Handbook for Critical Argumentation*. New York: Cambridge Univ. Press, 1989.

PHILOSOPHY

DeWeese, Garrett J. and J. P. Moreland. *Philosophy Made Slightly Less Difficult*. Downers Grove, IL: InterVarsity, 2005.

Gaarder, Jostein. *Sophie's World*. New York: Farrar, Straus & Giroux, 1994.

Geisler, Norman L. and Paul D. Feinberg. *Introduction to Philosophy: A Christian Perspective*. Grand Rapids, MI: Baker, 1980.

Moreland, J. P. *Love Your God with all Your Mind*. Colorado Springs, CO: NavPress, 1997.

———. *Scaling the Secular City: A Defense of Christianity*. Grand Rapids, MI: Baker, 1987.

Moreland, J. P. and William Lane Craig. *Philosophical Foundations for a Christian Worldview*. Downers Grove, IL: InterVarsity, 2003.

Nash, Ronald H. *Life's Ultimate Questions: An Introduction to Philosophy*. Grand Rapids, MI: Zondervan, 1999.

———. *Worldviews in Conflict: Choosing Christianity in a World of Ideas*. Grand Rapids, MI: Zondervan, 1992.

Pearcey, Nancy. *Total Truth: Liberating Christianity from Its Cultural Captivity*. Wheaton, IL: Crossway, 2004.

Plantinga, Alvin. *Warranted Christian Belief*. New York: Oxford University Press, 2000.

Schaeffer, Francis A. *A Christian View of Philosophy and Culture*. Westchester, IL: Crossway, 1982.

CHRISTIAN MIND

Blamires, Harry. *The Christian Mind: How Should a Christian Think?* Ann Arbor, MI: Vine, 2004.

———. *The Post-Christian Mind: Exposing Its Destructive Agenda*. Ann Arbor, MI: Vine, 1999.

———. *Recovering the Christian Mind: Meeting the Challenge of Secularism*. Downers Grove, IL: InterVarsity, 1988.

Boice, James Montgomery. *Mind Renewal in a Mindless Age: Preparing to Think and Act Biblically*. Grand Rapids MI: Baker, 1993.

Lewis, C. S. *Mere Christianity*. San Francisco: HarperSanFrancisco, 2001.

Moreland, J. P. *Kingdom Triangle: Recover the Christian Mind, Renovate the Soul, Restore the Spirit's Power*. Grand Rapids, MI: Zondervan, 2006.

———. *Love Your God with All Your Mind*. Colorado Springs, CO: NavPress, 1997.

Moreland, J. P. and William Lane Craig. *Philosophical Foundations for a Christian Worldview*. Downers Grove, IL: InterVarsity, 2003.

Noebel, David A. *Understanding the Times: The Collision of Today's Competing Worldviews*. Manitou Springs, CO: Summit Press, 2006.

Pearcey, Nancy. *Total Truth: Liberating Christianity from Its Cultural Captivity*. Wheaton, IL: Crossway, 2004.

Plantinga, Alvin. *Warranted Christian Belief*. New York: Oxford University Press, 2000.

Sire, James W. *Discipleship of the Mind: Learning to Love God in the Ways We Think*. Downers Grove, IL: InterVarsity, 1990.

———. *Habits of the Mind: Intellectual Life as a Christian Calling*. Downers Grove, IL: InterVarsity, 2000.

Fact Sheets

Summit Ministries © 2009 — 3 of

PSYCHOLOGY
FACT SHEET

KEY TERMS:

Higher Consciousness: The ever-increasing awareness of one's spiritual essence and the underlying spiritual nature in all things

Psychological Dualism (Mind/Body): The belief that the mind and the body exist as separate entities, i.e. the mind is not mere matter

Psychological Monism: The belief that the mind and the body exist as part of the same entity, i.e. the mind is a part of the material body

Self-actualization: The highest level of a person's potential and the ultimate goal of Maslow's "hierarchy of needs" (a theory contending that as humans meet their basic needs, they seek to satisfy successively higher needs)

Socially-constructed Selves: The belief that one's identity is constantly changing as a result of ever-changing social factors

Traditional Behaviorism: A branch of psychology which asserts that human behavior can be reduced into terms of principles that do not require consideration of unobservable mental events, such as ideas, emotions, and a mind, i.e. a form of materialism which claims that all human behavior is the result of materialistic processes and not the free will of the mind

---

KEY VERSES:
Luke 1:46–47
Titus 2:13

KEY ORGANIZATIONS:
Focus on the Family | www.fotf.org | 800.232.6459 |

KEY QUOTES:
"He breathed into his nostrils the breath of life and man became a living soul." — Genesis 2:7

KEY CHRISTIAN SOURCES:
(recommended titles appear in brown)

DUALISM

Moreland, J. P. and Scott B. Rae. *Body & Soul: Human Nature & the Crisis in Ethics*. Downers Grove, IL: InterVarsity, 2000.

HOMOSEXUALITY (CAUSES AND COUNSELING)
Dallas, Joe. *Desires in Conflict*. Eugene, OR: Harvest, 2003.

Konrad, J. A. *You Don't Have to Be Gay: Hope and Freedom for Males Struggling with Homosexuality or for Those Who Know of Someone Who Is*. Hilo, HI: Pacific, 1992.

Fact Sheets

Riley, Mona and Brad Sargent. *Unwanted Harvest?* Nashville: Broadman & Holman, 1995.

Wolfe, Christopher, ed. *Same-Sex Matters: The Challenge of Homosexuality*. Dallas: Spence, 2000.

Worthen, Anita and Bob Davies. *Someone I Love Is Gay: How Family and Friends Can Respond*. Downers Grove, IL: InterVarsity, 1996.

Secular Psychology (critique)

Justman, Stewart. *Fool's Paradise: The Unreal World of Pop Psychology*. Chicago: Ivan R. Dee, 2005.

Kilpatrick, William. *The Emperor's New Clothes*. Westchester, IL: Crossway, 1985.

———. *Psychological Seduction: The Failure of Modern Psychology*. Ridgefield, CT: Roger A. McCaffrey, 1983.

Milton, Joyce. *The Road to Malpsychia: Humanistic Psychology and Our Discontents*. San Francisco: Encounter Books, 2002.

Vitz, Paul C. *Faith of the Fatherless: The Psychology of Atheism*. Dallas: Spence, 1999.

———. *Psychology as Religion: The Cult of Self-Worship*. Grand Rapids, MI: Eerdmans, 1994.

RADICAL ENVIRONMENTALISM
FACT SHEET

KEY TERMS:

Animal Rights: A form of Radical Environmentalism which places non-human species on par with human beings both intrinsically and morally

Deep Ecology: A form of Radical Environmentalism that places an intrinsic value on all nature. This position leads to an ecocentric system of environmental ethics instead of an anthrocentric (people centered) or theocentric (God centered) system

Eco-terrorism: Acts of violence, sabotage, vandalism, property damage, or intimidation committed against individuals and companies in the name of environmentalism

Environmentalism: A broad term that connotes concern and stresses the need for the protection and preservation of the environment. Environmentalists usually operate through peaceful methods of social action (e.g. political lobbying, public awareness campaigns, etc.)

Green Party: A political party with radical environmentalist leanings. Founded in Hobart, Australia in 1972; since that time it has gained, to varying degrees, popularity throughout the world

Radical Environmentalism: An extreme form of environmentalism that views humanity as a mere animal and a plague upon nature and the environment. Radical environmentalists often resort to non-traditional forms of activism (e.g. eco-terrorism)

KEY VERSES:

Genesis 1; 3:17–19; 9:2–3   Romans 8:18–23   Hebrews 1:3
Psalms 8:4–8; 115:16   Colossians 1:17   2 Peter 2:12

KEY ORGANIZATIONS:

Capital Research Center | www.greenwatch.org | 202.483.6900 |

CO$_2$ Science | www.co2science.org | 480.966.3719 |

Competitive Enterprise Institute | http://cei.org | 202.331.1010 |

Enviro Truth | www.envirotruth.org | 202.543.4110 |

Friends of Science Society | www.friendsofscience.org |

Global Warming | www.globalwarming.org |

Heritage Foundation | www.heritage.org | 202.546.4400 |

Cornwall Alliance for the Stewardship of Creation | www.stewards.net | 703.569.4653 |

Junk Science | www.junkscience.com |

Property and Environment Research Center | www.perc.org | 406.587.9591 |

Fact Sheets!

KEY QUOTES:

"Human beings inhabit no more than 3 percent of the land surface of the earth. What's more, the amount of habitable land is not limited. Singapore was once marshland. Much of Holland was once under water… To put the matter in perspective, if the world's 5.4 billion people were put in Jacksonville, Florida, each person would have four square feet to stand in. In Texas each person would have at least fourteen hundred square feet, the area of a good-sized two-bedroom apartment."[1]

"The advocates of government family planning have their own set of justification, thinly disguised to avoid arousing resistance to population control. Sex education, for instance, will overcome 'ignorance' and 'fears and anxieties', and the adolescent pregnancy programs will in turn 'reduce teenage pregnancy and prevent abortion.' Not reported in the headlines, but frankly admitted in the programs, is the truth: the limitation of population. Equally absent from the news are the results of the government programs—no improvement in the psychological or physical health of the young and no reduction in pregnancy or abortion. Nor, ironically, is there any proof that they have reduced fertility. What the programs have achieved, and to a frightening degree, is the power and influence of the clique advocating government family planning, which it well understands is an essential intermediate step toward comprehensive population control."[2]

[Regarding old growth forests, atmospheric CO_2, and the "Greenhouse Effect":]
"Mature trees, like all living things, metabolize more slowly as they grow old. A forest of young, vigorously growing trees will remove five to seven tons more CO_2 per acre than old growth. There are plenty of good reasons to preserve old growth forests, but redressing the CO_2 balance is not one of them. If we were really interested (as we should be) in reducing atmospheric CO_2, we should be vigorously pursuing reforestation and the planting of trees and shrubs, including in urban areas, where local impacts on the atmosphere are greatest.

"Reforestation has been going on through enlightened forestry practices on private lands by timber companies and as a result of changes in agricultural and land use. In the United States, the average annual wood growth is now more than three times what it was in 1920, and the growing stock has increased 18 percent from 1952 to 1977. Forests in America continue to increase in size, even while supplying a substantial fraction of the world's timber needs."[3]

KEY PROPONENTS:

- Lester Brown (President of *The World Watch Institute*)
- Paul Ehrlich
- David Foreman (founder of *Earth First!*)
- Al Gore (former U.S. Vice President)
- Les Knight (founder of *Voluntary Human Extinction Movement*)
- Arne Naess (Norwegian philosopher of ecology)
- Peter Singer (Princeton University)

KEY PROPONENT SOURCES:

ANIMAL RIGHTS

Singer, Peter. *Animal Liberation: A New Ethics for Our Treatment of Animals*. New York: Random, 1975.
———. *In Defense of Animals: The Second Wave*. Malden, MA: Blackwell, 2006.

---

[1] Sheldon L. Richman, "Much Ado About Nothing: Population Growth as Promise, Not Problem," *The World & I*, vol. 8, no. 6 (1993): 374–75.
[2] Jacqueline Kasun, *The War Against Population: The Economics and Ideology of Population Control* (San Francisco: Ignatius, 1988), 206.
[3] Dixy Lee Ray with Lou Guzzo, *Trashing the Planet* (New York: HarperCollins, 1990), 36.

Fact Sheets

ECOLOGY

Brown, Lester Russell. *Plan B 2.0: Rescuing a Planet under Stress and a Civilization in Trouble*. New York: W.W. Norton, 2006.

Brown, Lester Russell and Earth Policy Institute. *Eco-Economy: Building an Economy for the Earth*. New York: W.W. Norton, 2001. Brown, Lester Russell and Worldwatch Institute. *State of the World 2001: A Worldwatch Institute Report on Progress toward a Sustainable Society*. London: Earthscan, 2001.

Brown, Lester Russell, Janet Larsen, Bernie Fischlowitz-Roberts, and Earth Policy Institute. *The Earth Policy Reader*. New York: W.W. Norton, 2002.

Gore, Albert. *Earth in the Balance: Ecology and the Human Spirit*. Boston: Houghton Mifflin, 2000.

Næss, Arne and David Rothenberg. *Ecology, Community, and Lifestyle: Outline of an Ecosophy*. New York: Cambridge University Press, 1989.

POPULATION CONTROL

Ehrlich, Paul R. and Anne H. Ehrlich. *The Population Explosion*. New York: Simon & Schuster, 1990.

KEY SOURCES/CRITIQUES:

(recommended titles appear in brown)

Avery, Dennis T. *Saving the Planet with Pesticides and Plastic: The Environmental Triumph of High-Yield Farming*. Indianapolis: Hudson Institute, 2000.

Bailey, Ronald. *Earth Report 2000: Revisiting the True State of the Planet*. New York: McGraw Hill, 2000.

Bast, Joseph L., Peter Jensen Hill, and Richard Rue. *Eco-Sanity: A Common-Sense Guide to Environmentalism*. Lanham, MD: Madison Books, 1994.

Beisner, E. Calvin. *Prospects for Growth: A Biblical View of Population, Resources, and the Future*. Westchester, IL: Crossway, 1990.

———. *Where Garden Meets Wilderness: Evangelical Entry into the Environmental Debate*. Grand Rapids, MI: Eerdmans, 1997.

Kasun, Jacqueline R. *The War against Population: The Economics and Ideology of World Population Control*. San Francisco: Ignatius, 1999.

Kaufman, Wallace. *No Turning Back: Dismantling the Fantasies of Environmental Thinking*. New York: Basic, 1994.

Lomborg, Bjørn. *The Skeptical Environmentalist: Measuring the Real State of the World*. New York: Cambridge University Press, 2001.

Ray, Dixy Lee and Louis R. Guzzo. *Environmental Overkill: Whatever Happened to Common Sense?* Washington DC: Regnery, 1993.

———. *Trashing the Planet: How Science Can Help Us Deal with Acid Rain, Depletion of the Ozone, and Nuclear Waste (among Other Things)*. Washington DC: Regnery, 1990.

Rubin, Charles T. *The Green Crusade: Rethinking the Roots of Environmentalism*. New York: Free Press, 1994.

Sanera, Michael and Jane S. Shaw. *Facts, Not Fear: Teaching Children About the Environment*. Washington DC: Regnery, 1999.

Simon, Julian Lincoln, ed. *The State of Humanity*. Cambridge, MA: Cato Institute, 1995.

Young, Richard A. *Healing the Earth: A Theocentric Perspective on Environmental Problems and Their Solutions*. Nashville: Broadman & Holman, 1994.

Scriptural Reliability
Fact Sheet

Key Terms:

Critical Methodology: Various methods of examining the Bible with the aim of discovering its "genuineness"

Documentary Hypothesis: A hypothesis derived from criticism which asserts that the Pentateuch is a compilation of various sources usually identified as J.E.P.D.—Yahwist author, Elohist author, Deuteronomist author, and Priestly author

Form Criticism: The means of study and investigation of a biblical writing's structural form. The goal is to discover the "pre-historical" oral and written traditions that gave rise to the text

Redaction Criticism: The study and investigation of a biblical writing to discern how a text has been "edited." The goal is to discover what the ancient writer actually wrote as opposed to what has been handed down to us

Source Criticism: The study and investigation of biblical writings according to their sources of origin

Textual Criticism: The means of study and investigation of biblical writings used to discover the "original wording." The goal is to discover what the ancient writer actually wrote as opposed to what has been handed down to us

The Quest for the Historical Jesus: A movement within secular Christian scholarship that is seeking to discover the "true historical Jesus." Those that are part of this quest assume that Jesus was neither the Son the God nor a performer of miracles.

Key Verses:

Psalm 14:1; 199:89
Isaiah 40:8
Matthew 5:18; 24:35
Mark 13:31

Luke 1:1–4; 16:17; 21:33
Acts 1:1-3; 2:32
1 Corinthians 15:1–9
2 Timothy 3:16

Hebrews 11:6
1 John 1:1-3
Revelation 22:18–19

Key Organizations:

Biblical Archaeology Society | www.bib-arch.org | 800.221.4644 |

Key Publications:

Archaeology Odyssey | **Biblical Archaeology Society** | www.bib-arch.org | 800.221.4644 |

Biblical Archaeology Review | **Biblical Archaeology Society** | www.bib-arch.org | 800.221.4644 |

Bible Review | **Biblical Archaeology Society** | www.bib-arch.org | 800.221.4644 |

Key Quotes:

"The earliest preachers of the gospel knew the value of...first-hand testimony, and appealed to it time and again. 'We are witnesses of these things,' was their constant and confident assertion. And it can have been by no means so easy as some writers think to invent words and deeds of Jesus in those early years, when so many of His disciples were about, who could remember what had and had not happened…

"And it was not only friendly eyewitnesses that the early preachers had to reckon with; there were others less well disposed who were also conversant with the main facts of the ministry and death of Jesus. The disciples could not afford to risk inaccuracies (not to speak of willful manipulation of the facts), which would at once be exposed by those who would be only too glad to do so. On the contrary, one of the strong points in the original apostolic preaching is the confident appeal to the knowledge of the hearers; they not only said, 'We are witnesses of these things,' but also, 'As you yourselves also know' [Acts 2:22]. Had there been any tendency to depart from the facts in any material respect, the possible presence of hostile witnesses in the audience would have served as a further corrective."[1]

"There is no body of ancient literature in the world which enjoys such a wealth of good textual attestation as the New Testament."[2]

"There is, I imagine, no body of literature in the world that has been exposed to the stringent analytical study that the four gospels have sustained for the past 200 years. This is not something to be regretted: it is something to be accepted with satisfaction. Scholars today who treat the gospels as credible historical documents do so in the full light of this analytical study, not by closing their minds to it."[3]

"Skepticism toward the reliability of Scripture seems to survive in many academic circles despite the repeated collapse of critical theories. One still finds a disposition to trust secular writers whose credentials in providing historical testimony are often less adequate than those of the biblical writers. Not long ago many scholars rejected the historicity of the patriarchal accounts, denied that writing existed in Moses' day, and ascribed the Gospels and Epistles to second-century writers. But higher criticism has sustained some spectacular and even stunning reverses, mainly through the findings of archaeology. No longer is it held that the glories of King Solomon's era are literary fabrication, that 'Yahweh,' the redemptive God of the Hebrews, was unknown before the eighth-century prophets, or that Ezra's representations about the Babylonian captivity are fictional. Archaeologists have located the long-lost copper mines of Solomon's time. Tablets discovered at Ebla near Aleppo confirm that names similar to those of the patriarchs were common among people who lived in Ebla shortly before the events recorded in the later chapters of Genesis took place."[4]

KEY SOURCES:

(recommended titles appear in brown)

CANONIZATION, INSPIRATION, AND INERRANCY

Bruce, F. F. *The Books and the Parchments*. Westwood, NJ: Revell, 1963.

———. *The Canon of Scripture*. Downers Grove, IL: InterVarsity, 1988.

———. *The New Testament Documents: Are They Reliable?* Grand Rapids, MI: Eerdmans, 1981.

Carson, D. A. and John D. Woodbridge, eds. *Hermeneutics, Authority, and Canon*. Grand Rapids, MI: Academie, 1986.

Comfort, Philip Wesley, ed. *The Origin of the Bible*. Wheaton, IL: Tyndale, 2003.

Geisler, Norman L., ed. *Inerrancy*. Grand Rapids, MI: Zondervan, 1980.

Warfield, Benjamin and Samuel G. Craig. *The Inspiration and Authority of the Bible*. Philadelphia: Presbyterian & Reformed, 1948.

HISTORICITY OF CHRISTIAN WORLDVIEW

Blomberg, Craig. *The Historical Reliability of John's Gospel*. Downers Grove, IL: InterVarsity, 2002.

———. *The Historical Reliability of the Gospels*. Downers Grove, IL: InterVarsity, 1987.

F. F. Bruce, *Are the New Testament Documents Reliable?* (Grand Rapids, MI: Eerdmans, 1960), 45–46.

F. F. Bruce, *The Books and the Parchments* (Westwood, NJ: Revell, 1963), 178.

Craig Blomberg, *The Historical Reliability of the Gospels* (Downers Grove, IL: InterVarsity, 1987), ix.

Carl F. H. Henry, "The Authority of the Bible," *The Origin of the Bible*, Philip Wesley Comfort, ed. (Wheaton, IL: Tyndale, 1992), 17.

Fact Sheets

Copan, Paul, ed. *Will the Real Jesus Please Stand Up? A Debate between William Lane Craig and John Dominic Crossan*. Grand Rapids, MI: Baker, 1998.

Craig, William Lane. *Knowing the Truth About the Resurrection: Our Response to the Empty Tomb*. Ann Arbor, MI: Servant, 1988.

Free, Joseph P. and Howard Frederic. *Archaeology and Bible History*. Grand Rapids, MI: Zondervan, 1992.

Geisler, Norman L. *Systematic Theology*. Minneapolis: Bethany, 2002 (Vol. 1, Chapters 25 and 26).

Habermas, Gary R. and Michael R. Licona. *The Case for the Resurrection of Jesus*. Grand Rapids, MI: Kregel, 2004.

Kitchen, K. A. *The Bible in Its World: The Bible and Archaeology Today*. Exeter, RI: Paternoster, 1977.

———. *On the Reliability of the Old Testament*. Grand Rapids, MI: Eerdmans, 2003.

Nash, Ronald H. *The Gospel and the Greeks: Did the New Testament Borrow from Pagan Thought?* Richardson, TX: Probe, 1992.

Thompson, J. A. *The Bible and Archaeology*. Grand Rapids, MI: Eerdmans, 1982.

Wilkins, Michael J. and J. P. Moreland. *Jesus under Fire*. Grand Rapids, MI: Zondervan, 1995.

TEXTUAL CONSISTENCY

Archer, Gleason Leonard. *Encyclopedia of Bible Difficulties*. Grand Rapids, MI: Zondervan, 1982.

Kaiser, Walter C. *Hard Sayings of the Bible*. Downers Grove, IL: InterVarsity, 1996.

Geisler, Norman L. and Thomas A. Howe. *When Critics Ask: A Popular Handbook on Bible Difficulties*. Wheaton, IL: Victor, 1992.

Hayley, John W. *Alleged Discrepancies of the Bible*. New Kensington, PA: Whitaker House, 2004.

Sociology
Fact Sheet

KEY TERMS:

Classless Society: The Marxists vision of a future society free from class antagonism, which will purportedly be brought about by the establishment of communism and the demise of oppressive capitalism

Family, Church, State: The Christian belief that society is divided into three God-ordained institutions

Feminism: A broad term that connotes concern and stresses equality between the sexes

Non-traditional Family: A number of alternatives to traditional marriage including modified open marriage, triads, cooperatives, collectives, urban communes, extended intimates, swinging, group marriage, same-sex marriage, part-time marriage, etc.

Polygamy, Mosque, Islamic State: The Islamic belief that society is composed of three institutions: family (which can be polygamous), Mosque, and State

Polymorphous Sexualities: The belief that individuals can exist in more than one gender form—based upon one's sexual identity and preference—(including gay, bi-sexual, lesbian, transgendered, transsexual, etc.)

Radical Feminism: An extreme form of feminism that rejects any inherent differences between the sexes. Radical feminism seeks to challenge all traditional gender standards. Radical feminists often belittle other women who have chosen the occupation of wife and/or mother. They also generally promote promiscuity, lesbianism, abortion, and state-run child care

Sexual Egalitarianism: The belief that all sexual practices—which are based on preference and sexual identity (or polymorphous sexualities) and not physical characteristics—are equal

KEY VERSES:	**FAMILY**	**MEN**
CHILDREN	Psalm 33:10–11;103:9	Psalm 112
Exodus 20:12	Proverbs 11:11; 14:43; 29	Luke 12:39
Proverbs 1:8; 6:20; 17:17	Daniel 2:20-21	Ephesians 5:25–33; 6:4
Ephesians 6:1–3	Romans 13:1–7	Colossians 3:19
Colossians 3:20	1 Timothy 2:1	1 Timothy 3:1–8; 5:8
	1 Peter 2:13–14	Titus 1:7-9; 2:6–8
CHURCH	**MARRIAGE**	**WOMEN**
Matthew 18:15–20	Genesis 1:26–27; 2:18–25	Proverbs 13:4–5; 31:10–31
Acts 20:28	Malachi 2:14–16	Ephesians 5:22–24
1 Corinthians 5:9-13;	1 Corinthians 11:11	Colossians 3:18
11:17–26; 12:4–31	Hebrews 13:4	1 Timothy 5:10–14
Ephesians: 3:6–10; 5:21–24		Titus 1:3–5
Colossians 1:13–20		1 Peter 3:4

Key Organizations:

American Family Association | www.afa.net |

Concerned Women for America | www.cwfa.org | 202.488.7000 |

Eagle Forum | www.eagleforum.org | 618.462.5415 |

Family Research Council | www.frc.org | 800.225.4008 |

Focus on the Family | www.fotf.org | 800.232.6459 |

Promise Keepers | www.promisekeepers.org | 866.776.6473 |

Key Quotes:

"For this reason a man will leave his father and mother and be united to his wife, and the two will become one flesh."— Ephesians 5:31

"The Christian worldview is intimately familiar with the experience of emptiness, with the despair and impotence that radical feminists—like all of us—seek to escape. We call this experience the human condition. Christians know the dark night of the soul, but we also know that self-glorifying rage will only plunge us deeper into the abyss."[1]

"Feminists are becoming difficult to identify, not because they do not exist, but because their philosophy has been integrated into mainstream society so thoroughly. The philosophy is almost unidentifiable as feminist, for it is virtually indistinguishable from mainstream."[2]

"Feminism freed men, not women...feminism gave men all the financial and personal advantages over women. The truth is, a woman can't live the true feminist life unless she denies her child-bearing biology. The reality of feminism is a lot of frenzied and overworked women dropping kids off at day-care centers. Women should get educations so they can be brainy in the way they raise their children. Women and men are not equal, they are different. The economy might even improve if women came home, opening up jobs for unemployed men, who could then support a wife and children, the way it was, pre-feminism."[3]

Key Sources:

(recommended titles appear in brown)

CHURCH

Bonhoeffer, Dietrich and John W. Doberstein. *Life Together*. San Francisco: HarperSanFrancisco, 1993.

Clapp, Rodney. *A Peculiar People: The Church as Culture in a Post-Christian Society*. Downers Grove, IL: InterVarsity, 1996.

Ferguson, Everett. *The Church of Christ: A Biblical Ecclesiology for Today*. Grand Rapids, MI: Eerdmans, 1996.

Hayes, Edward L., Charles R. Swindoll, and Roy B. Zuck. *The Church: The Body of Christ in the World of Today*. Nashville: Word, 1999.

Minnery, Tom. *Why You Can't Stay Silent: A Biblical Mandate to Shape Our Culture*. Wheaton, IL: Tyndale, 2001.

Nouwen, Henri J. M. *My Sister, My Brother: Life Together in Christ*. Iamsville, MD: Word Among Us Press, 2005.

---

[1] Katherine Kersten, "How the Feminist Establishment Hurts Women," *Christianity Today* (June 20, 1994).
[2] Mary A. Kassian, *The Feminist Gospel* (Westchester, IL: Crossway, 1922), 251.
[3] Kay Ebeling, "The Failure of Feminism," *Newsweek* (November 19, 1990).

Fact Sheets

Roberts, Wes and Glenn Marshall. *Reclaiming God's Original Intent for the Church*. Colorado Springs, CO: NavPress, 2004.

Stark, Rodney. *The Rise of Christianity: How the Obscure, Marginal Jesus Movement Became the Dominant Religious Force in the Western World in a Few Centuries*. San Francisco: HarperSanFrancisco, 1997.

Family

Allender, Dan B. and Tremper Longman. *Intimate Allies*. Wheaton, IL: Tyndale, 1995.

Andrews, Robert. *The Family: God's Weapon for Victory*. Mukilteo, WA: Winepress, 2002.

Crabb, Lawrence J. *The Marriage Builder: A Blueprint for Couples and Counselors*. Grand Rapids, MI: Zondervan, 1992.

Dobson, James C. and Gary Lee Bauer. *Children at Risk: The Battle for the Hearts and Minds of Our Kids*. Dallas: Word, 1990.

Elliot, Elisabeth. *Passion and Purity: Learning to Bring Your Love Life under Christ's Control*. Grand Rapids, MI: Fleming H. Revell, 2002.

Gairdner, William D. *The War against the Family*. Toronto: Stoddart, 1992.

Gilder, George F. *Men and Marriage*. Gretna, LA: Pelican, 1986.

Pride, Mary. *All the Way Home: Power for Your Family to Be Its Best*. Westchester, IL: Crossway, 1989.

Schlafly, Phyllis, ed. *Who Will Rock the Cradle? The Battle for Control of Child Care in America*. Dallas: Word, 1989.

Thoburn, Robert. *The Children Trap: Biblical Principles for Education*. Nashville: Thomas Nelson, 1986.

Thomas, Gary. *Sacred Marriage: What If God Designed Marriage to Make Us Holy More Than to Make Us Happy?* Grand Rapids, MI: Zondervan, 2000.

State

Bauman, Michael and David W. Hall. *God and Caesar*. Camp Hill, PA: Christian Publications, 1994.

Burke, Thomas J. and Lissa Roche. *Man and State: Religion, Society, and the Constitution*. Hillsdale, MI: Hillsdale College Press, 1988.

Eidsmoe, John. *God and Caesar: Biblical Faith and Political Action*. Westchester, IL: Crossway, 1984.

Hall, David W. *Savior or Servant? Putting Government in Its Place*. Oak Ridge, TN: Kuyper Institute, 1996.

Smith, Gary Scott. *God and Politics: Four Views on the Reformation of Civil Government*. Phillipsburg, NJ: Presbyterian & Reformed, 1989.

Radical Feminism

Blotnick, Sully. *Otherwise Engaged: The Private Lives of Successful Career Women*. New York: Facts on File, 1985.

Browne, Kingsley. *Biology at Work: Rethinking Sexual Equality*. New Brunswick, NJ: Rutgers Univ. Press, 2002.

Farrell, Warren. *The Myth of Male Power: Why Men Are the Disposable Sex*. New York: Berkley, 2001.

Graglia, F. Carolyn. *Domestic Tranquility: A Brief against Feminism*. Dallas: Spence, 1998.

Levin, Michael E. *Feminism and Freedom*. New Brunswick, NJ: Transaction, 1987.

Mitchell, Brian. *Weak Link: The Feminization of the American Military*. Washington DC: Regnery, 1989.

Rhoads, Steven E. *Taking Sex Differences Seriously*. San Francisco: Encounter Books, 2004.

Sayers, Dorothy L. *Are Women Human?* Grand Rapids, MI: Eerdmans, 2005.

Schlafly, Phyllis. *Feminist Fantasies*. Dallas: Spence, 2003.

Sommers, Christina Hoff. *The War against Boys: How Misguided Feminism Is Harming Our Young Men*. New York: Simon & Schuster, 2000.

———. *Who Stole Feminism? How Women Have Betrayed Women*. New York: Simon & Schuster, 1994.

Tooley, James. *The Miseducation of Women*. Chicago: Ivan R. Dee, 2003.

THEOLOGY
FACT SHEET

KEY TERMS:

THEOLOGY

Atheism: The denial of the existence of a supernatural God

Death of God Theology: A movement which flourished in the 1960s and 1970s, essentially promoting the idea that religion did not need to invoke "God" in the area of theology

General Revelation: God's communication—through nature and conscience—regarding his existence

Neo-orthodoxy: reacting to liberalization in theology, this movement stressed 1) the primacy of revelation while downplaying natural theology and human reason and 2) the near total transcendence and incomprehensibility of God.

Panentheism: the view that God is immanent, yet still transcendent, within the universe

Pantheism: The belief that god is everything and everything is god

Post-conservative Christianity [or Emergent Church]: a relatively new movement of Christians who are incorporating elements of postmodernism into their theology

Religious Pluralism: The belief that one should be tolerant of all religious beliefs since no one religion can be true

Special Revelation: God's specific communication—through the Bible and Jesus Christ—about salvation and himself

Theism: The belief in the existence of a supernatural God

Trinitarian Theism: The belief in one god who exists as three separate persons—Father, Son, and Spirit

HERMENEUTICS

Biblical Criticism: The study and investigation of biblical writings in order to understand the circumstances, background, history, language, authorship, and audience of the text

Exegesis: Extracting the author's original meaning from a text

Hermeneutics: The science of biblical interpretation used to discover the accurate meaning of a given text

Isogesis: Reading a personal bias into the text

RELIGIOUS PLURALISM

Inclusivism: The general sense that Jesus Christ is somehow superior to other religious figures and that salvation is somehow based upon his person and work

Particularism [also, negatively, Exclusivism]: The historical Christian view that the Bible is God's Word and that the person and work of Jesus Christ is the only means of salvation

Pluralism: The view that Christianity and Christ are not unique or superior to other religions or religions figures. Salvation can be found through means other than Jesus Christ.

Restrictivism: The view that only those who hear and respond to the Gospel of Jesus Christ will be saved [all restrictivists are particularists, but not necessarily vice-versa]

Universalism: The belief that everyone (or virtually everyone) will find salvation after death

Fact Sheets

KEY VERSES:

Genesis 1:1	Mark 1:12–13; 12:40	1 Timothy 1:17; 6:16
Proverbs 10:28; 29:1	Luke 4:1–13; 20:47	2 Timothy 3:16–17
Ecclesiastes 7:29	John 3:36; 5:29; 6:33; 14:6	Hebrews 4:12
Matthew 4:1–11; 9:6;	Acts 4:12	1 John 5:12
23:14; 24:46	Colossians 2:9	Revelation 13:3; 14:11

KEY ORGANIZATIONS:

Evangelical Theological Society | www.etsjets.org | 502.897.4387 |

National Association of Evangelicals | http://nae.net | 202.489.1011 |

KEY PUBLICATIONS:

JETS | **Evangelical Theological Society** | www.etsjets.org | 502.897.4387 |

KEY PLURALISM FACTS:

- Sixty-four percent of Americans believe, "Christians, Jews, Buddhists, Muslims and all others pray to the same God, even though they use different names for that God."[1]
- Sixty-four percent of Americans agree with the statement, "All religions are equally good."[2]
- Sixty-two percent of those surveyed agreed that, "It does not matter what religious faith you follow because all faiths reach similar lessons about life."[3]
- Fifty percent of all teenagers and 30 percent of born-again teens agree, "It does not matter what religious faith you follow because all faiths teach similar lessons."[4]
- Fifty-five percent of all teenagers and 36 percent of born-again teenagers believe, "Muslims, Buddhists, Christians, Jews, and all other people pray to the same God, even though they use different names for their God."[5]

KEY QUOTES:

"Even the most tolerant pluralist has difficulties with the aspect of Hinduism which justifies the inequalities of Indian society by its insistence upon a fixed social order, or forcibly burning alive a widow on her late husband's funeral pyre."[6]

"The apostles asserted that Christ alone is the truth in the midst of a world that is more religiously diverse than any we have known in the West until recently."[7]

"'Why should I go to church,' someone once said to me, 'when I have no religious needs?' I had the audacity to reply, 'Because Christianity's true… The needs religion fills are relevant to an assessment of its truth… but were it merely a matter of finding religion to be helpful, then a religious commitment would not be essentially different from a personal preference. We would rightly say that just as some people prefer chocolate to other flavors of ice cream, some people prefer to be Christian than something else or nothing at all merely as a matter of taste. But when

George Barna, *What Americans Believe* (Ventura, CA: Regal Books, 1991), 210–12.
Religion in America, 1996 (Princeton: Princeton Religion Research Center, 1996), 74.
George Barna, *Absolute Confusion* (Ventura, CA: Regal Books, 1994), 207.
George Barna, *Generation Next: What You Should Know About Today's Youth* (Ventura, CA: Regal Books, 1995), 79, 103.
Ibid., 76, 103.
Alister McGrath, *A Passion for Truth: The Intellectual Coherence of Evangelism.* (Downers Grove, IL: InterVarsity, 1996), 190.
David Wells, *No Place for Truth Or Whatever Happened to Evangelical Theology?* (Grand Rapids, MI: Eerdmans, 1993), 104.

something is said to be true, we have a very different situation, especially when it is said of religion. Christianity, as well as other religious claims, are so serious and so demanding personally that adherence to them cannot be properly described as merely a matter of personal taste.'"[8]

"If you had gone to Buddha and asked him, 'Are you the son of Brahma?' he would have said, 'My son, you are still in the vale of illusion.' If you had gone to Socrates and asked, 'Are you the son of Zeus?' he would have laughed at you. If you had gone to Mohammed and asked, 'Are you the son of Allah?' he would first have rent his clothes and then cut your head off. If you had asked Confucius, 'Are you Heaven?' I think he would have probably replied, 'Remarks which are not in accordance with nature are in bad taste.' The idea of a great moral teacher saying what Christ said is out of the question. In my opinion, the only person who can say that sort of thing is either God or a complete lunatic suffering from that form of delusion which undermines the whole mind of man.'"[9]

KEY PROPONENTS:

- John Hick (professor of theology at University of Birmingham, vice-president of the British Society for the Philosophy of Religion, and vice-president of The World Congress of Faiths)
- Wilfred Cantwell Smith (Dalhousie University at Halifax, deceased)
- S. Wesley Ariarajah (Drew University School of Theology)

KEY PROPONENT SOURCES:

Ariarajah, S. Wesley. *The Bible and People of Other Faiths*. Geneva: World Council of Churches, 1985.

————. *Not without My Neighbour: Issues in Interfaith Relations*. Geneva: World Council of Churches, 1999.

Hick, John. *A Christian Theology of Religions: The Rainbow of Faiths*. Louisville, KY: Westminster/John Knox Press, 1995.

————. *God Has Many Names*. Philadelphia: Westminster Press, 1982.

————. *The Metaphor of God Incarnate: Christology in a Pluralistic Age*. Louisville, KY: Westminster/John Knox Press, 2006.

Hick, John and Paul F. Knitter. *The Myth of Christian Uniqueness: Toward a Pluralistic Theology of Religions*. Maryknoll, NY: Orbis, 1987.

Smith, Wilfred Cantwell. *The Meaning and End of Religion*. Minneapolis: Fortress Press, 1991.

————. *Towards a World Theology: Faith and the Comparative History of Religion*. Maryknoll, NY: Orbis, 1989.

Whaling, Frank and Wilfred Cantwell Smith. *The World's Religious Traditions: Current Perspectives in Religious Studies*. New York: Crossroad, 1984.

KEY CHRISTIAN SOURCES/CRITIQUES:

(recommended titles appear in brown)

ATHEISM (CRITIQUE)

Geisler, Norman L. and Frank Turek. *I Don't Have Enough Faith to Be an Atheist*. Wheaton, IL: Crossway, 2004.

McGrath, Alister. *The Twilight of Atheism: The Rise & Fall of Disbelief in the Modern World*. New York: Doubleday, 2004.

Moreland, J. P. and Kai Nielsen. *Does God Exist? The Great Debate*. New York: Prometheus Books, 1993.

Nicholi, Armand M. *The Question of God: C. S. Lewis and Sigmund Freud Debate God, Love, Sex, and the Meaning of Life*. New York: Free Press, 2002.

Plantinga, Alvin. *God and Other Minds: A Study of the Rational Justification of Belief in God*. Ithaca, NY: Cornell University Press, 1990.

Zacharias, Ravi. *A Shattered Visage: The Real Face of Atheism*. Brentwood, TN: Wolgemuth & Hyatt, 1990.

[8] Diogenes Allen, *Christian Belief in a Postmodern World* (Louisville, KY: Westminster/John Knox Press, 1989), 1.
[9] C. S. Lewis, *God in the Dock: Essays on Theology and Ethics* (Grand Rapids, MI: Eerdmans, 1970), 157–58.

BIBLE DOCTRINE

Erickson, Millard J. *Christian Theology*. Grand Rapids, MI: Baker, 1998.

Geisler, Norman L. *Systematic Theology*. Minneapolis: Bethany, 2002.

Grudem, Wayne A. *Bible Doctrine: Essential Teachings of the Christian Faith*. Grand Rapids, MI: Zondervan, 1999.

———. *Christian Beliefs: Twenty Basics Every Christian Should Know*. Grand Rapids, MI: Zondervan, 2005.

———. *Systematic Theology: An Introduction to Biblical Doctrine*. Grand Rapids, MI: Zondervan, 1994.

Henry, Carl F. H. *God, Revelation, and Authority*. 6 vols. Wheaton, IL: Crossway, 1999.

Plantinga, Cornelius. *Engaging God's World: A Christian Vision of Faith, Learning, and Living*. Grand Rapids, MI: Eerdmans, 2002.

HERMENEUTICS

Carson, D. A. *Exegetical Fallacies*. Grand Rapids, MI: Baker, 1996.

Cowan, Steven B. "Scripture Interprets Scripture: The Role of Theology in Biblical Interpretation." *Areopagus Journal 6*, no. 1 (2006): 22–28.

Fee, Gordon D. and Douglas K. Stuart. *How to Read the Bible Book by Book: A Guided Tour*. Grand Rapids, MI: Zondervan, 2002.

———. *How to Read the Bible for All Its Worth*. Grand Rapids, MI: Zondervan, 2003.

Grenz, Stanley J., David Guretzki, and Cherith Fee Nordling. *Pocket Dictionary of Theological Terms*. Downers Grove, IL: InterVarsity, 1999.

LaHaye, Tim. *How to Study the Bible for Yourself*. Eugene, OR: Harvest, 1998.

Lemke, Steven W. "Good Hermeneutics: Rightly Dividing the Word of God." *Areopagus Journal 6*, no. 1 (2006): 7–13.

Patzia, Arthur G. and Anthony J. Petrotta. *Pocket Dictionary of Biblical Studies*. Downers Grove, IL: InterVarsity, 2002.

Peterson, Eugene H. *Eat This Book: A Conversation in the Art of Spiritual Reading*. Grand Rapids, MI: Eerdmans, 2006.

Russell, Walt. *Playing with Fire: How the Bible Ignites Change in Your Soul*. Colorado Springs, CO: NavPress, 2000.

Sire, James W. *Scripture Twisting: 20 Ways the Cults Misread the Bible*. Downers Grove, IL: InterVarsity, 1980.

Snyder, Jason. "Getting the Whole Story: The Importance of Context in Biblical Interpretation." *Areopagus Journal 6*, no. 1 (2006): 14–18.

Sproul, R. C. *Knowing Scripture*. Downers Grove, IL: InterVarsity, 1977.

PANTHEISM (CRITIQUE)

Clark, David K. and Norman L. Geisler. *Apologetics in the New Age: A Christian Critique of Pantheism*. Grand Rapids, MI: Baker, 1990.

Groothuis, Douglas. *Unmasking the New Age*. Downers Grove, IL: InterVarsity, 1986.

RELIGIOUS PLURALISM (GENERAL)

Adler, Mortimer Jerome. *Truth in Religion: The Plurality of Religions and the Unity of Truth*. New York: Macmillan, 1990.

Carson, D. A. "The Challenges of Contemporary Pluralism." *Southern Baptist Journal of Theology 1*, no. 2 (1997): 4–37.

———. *The Gagging of God: Christianity Confronts Pluralism*. Grand Rapids, MI: Zondervan, 1996.

Cowan, Steven B. "Do All Religions Lead to God?" *Areopagus Journal 1*, no. 3 (2001): 7–12.

Detzler, Wayne A. "Evangelism and the Peril of Pluralism." *Christian Apologetics Journal 4*, no. 2 (2005): 45–62.

Geisler, Norman L. "Religious Pluralism: A Christian Response." *Christian Apologetics Journal 4*, no. 2 (2005): 1–28.

Groothuis, Douglas. *Are All Religions One?* Downers Grove, IL: InterVarsity, 1999.

Leffel, Jim and Dennis McCallum. "Postmodern Impact: Religion." *The Death of Truth*, Dennis McCallum, ed. Minneapolis: Bethany, 1996, 200-214.

Hexham, Irving. *Pocket Dictionary of New Religious Movements*. Downers Grove, IL: InterVarsity, 2002.

Hux, Clete. "What About Those Who Have Never Heard?" *Areopagus Journal 1*, no. 3 (2001): 22–25.

Nash, Ronald. "Can Someone Be Saved by Jesus without Faith in Jesus?" *Areopagus Journal 1*, no. 3 (2001): 13–20.

———. *Is Jesus the Only Savior?* Grand Rapids, MI: Zondervan, 1994.

Netland, Harold. *Dissonant Voices: Religious Pluralism and the Quest for Truth.* Grand Rapids, MI: Eerdmans, 1991.

———. *Encountering Religious Pluralism: The Challenge to Christian Faith and Mission.* Downers Grove, IL: InterVarsity, 2001.

Newbigin, Lesslie. "Confessing Christ in a Multicultural Society." *Evangelical Review of Theology 22*, no. 3 (1998): 264–73.

Phillips, Gary. "Religious Pluralism in a Postmodern World." *The Challenge of Postmodernism: An Evangelical Engagement*, David S. Dockery, ed. Grand Rapids, MI: Baker, 2001, 131-143.

Ryken, Philip Graham. *Is Jesus the Only Way?* Wheaton, IL: Crossway, 1999.

Veith, Gene Edward. "Spirituality without Truth." *Postmodern Times: A Christian Guide to Contemporary Thought and Culture.* Wheaton, IL: Crossway, 1994, 192–207.

Stackhouse, John Gordon. *No Other Gods before Me: Evangelicals and the Challenge of World Religions.* Grand Rapids, MI: Baker, 2001.

COMPARATIVE RELIGIONS

Anderson, J. N. D. *Christianity and World Religions: The Challenge of Pluralism.* Downers Grove, IL: InterVarsity, 1984.

Clarke, Andrew D. and Bruce W. Winter. *One God, one Lord: Christianity in a World of Religious Pluralism.* Grand Rapids, MI: Baker, 1992.

Corduan, Winfried. *Neighboring Faiths: A Christian Introduction to World Religions.* Downers Grove, IL: InterVarsity, 1998.

———. *A Tapestry of Faiths: The Common Threads between Christianity and World Religions.* Downers Grove, IL: InterVarsity, 2002.

Fernando, Ajith. *Sharing the Truth in Love: How to Relate to People of Other Faiths.* Grand Rapids, MI: Discovery House, 2001.

Partridge, Christopher H. and Douglas R. Groothuis. *Dictionary of Contemporary Religion in the Western World.* Downers Grove, IL: InterVarsity, 2002.

Van Voorst, Robert E. *Anthology of World Scriptures.* Belmont, CA: Wadsworth, 2005.

HELL AND SALVATION

Crockett, William V. and Stanley N. Gundry, eds. *Four Views on Hell.* Grand Rapids, MI: Zondervan, 1992.

Crockett, William V. and James G. Sigountos. *Through No Fault of Their Own: The Fate of Those Who Have Never Heard.* Grand Rapids, MI: Baker, 1991.

Erickson, Millard J. *How Shall They Be Saved: The Destiny of Those Who Do Not Hear of Jesus.* Grand Rapids, MI: Baker, 1996.

Nash, Ronald H. *Is Jesus the Only Savior?* Grand Rapids, MI: Zondervan, 1994.

Okholm, Dennis L., Timothy R. Phillips, and Stanley N. Gundry, eds. *Four Views on Salvation in a Pluralistic World.* Grand Rapids, MI: Zondervan, 1996.

Stott, John R. W. *The Cross of Christ.* Downers Grove, IL: InterVarsity, 2006.

Tiessen, Terrance L. *Who Can Be Saved: Reassessing Salvation in Christ and World Religions.* Downers Grove, IL: InterVarsity, 2004.

WORLDVIEW
FACT SHEET

KEY VERSES:

Proverbs 3:5–6   Romans 12:1–2   Colossians 1:15ff; 2:1–8

Acts 17:16 ff   2 Corinthians 10:4–5

KEY ORGANIZATIONS:

American Vision | www.americanvision.com | 770.222.7266 |

Christian Research Institute | www.equip.org | 888.700.0274 |

Probe Ministries | www.probe.org | 972.480.0240 |

Stand to Reason | www.str.org | 800.273.2766 |

Summit Ministries | www.summit.org | 719.685.9103 |

KEY PUBLICATIONS:

Areopagus Journal | **Apologetics Resource Center** | www.arcapologetics.org | 205.408.0136 |

Biblical Worldview | **American Vision** | www.americanvision.org | 770.222.7266 |

Christian Research Journal | **Christian Research Institute** | www.equip.org | 888.700.0274 |

First Things | **Institute of Religion and Public Life** | www.firstthings.com | 212.627.1985 |

Imprimis | **Hillsdale College** | www.hillsdale.edu/news/imprimis.asp | 517.437.7341 |

Southern Baptist Journal of Theology | **Southern Baptist Theological Seminary** | www.sbts.edu |

Summit Journal | **Summit Ministries** | www.summit.org | 719.685.9103 |

KEY QUOTES:

"A worldview is, first of all, an explanation and interpretation of the world and second, an application of this view to life. In simpler terms, our worldview is a view of the world and a view for the world."[1]

"The term worldview refers to any ideology, philosophy, theology, movement, or religion that provides an overarching approach to understanding God and the world. Specifically, a worldview should contain a particular perspective regarding each of the following ten disciplines: theology, philosophy, ethics, biology, psychology, sociology, law, politics, economics, and history."[2]

William E. Brown and W. Gary Phillips, *Making Sense of Your World: A Biblical Worldview* (Salem, WI: Sheffield Publishers, 1996), 29.

David A. Noebel, *Understanding the Times* (Eugene, OR: Harvest, 1991), 8.

"A world view is a way one views the whole world. And since people have vastly different views of the world, depending on the perspective from which they view the world, it is clear that one's world view makes a world of difference. A world view is a way of viewing or interpreting all of reality. It is an interpretive framework through which or by which one makes sense out of the data of life and the world."[3]

"So what is a world view? Essentially this: A world view is a set of presuppositions (assumptions which may be true, partially true or entirely false) which we hold (consciously or subconsciously, consistently or inconsistently) about the basic make-up of our world."[4]

"A worldview is not the same thing as a formal philosophy; otherwise, it would be only for professional philosophers. Even ordinary people have a set of convictions about how reality functions and how they should live. Because we are made in God's image, we all seek to make sense of life. Some convictions are conscious, while others are unconscious, but together they form a more or less consistent picture of reality."[5]

KEY SOURCES:
(recommended titles appear in brown)

Baldwin, J. F. *The Deadliest Monster: A Christian Introduction to Worldviews*. New Braunfels, TX: Fisherman, 2001.

Breese, Dave. *Seven Men Who Rule the World from the Grave*. Chicago, IL: Moody, 1990.

Burnett, David. *Clash of Worlds*. Nashville: Oliver Nelson, 1992.

Carson, D. A. *The Gagging of God: Christianity Confronts Pluralism*. Grand Rapids, MI: Zondervan, 1996.

Colson, Charles W. and Nancy Pearcey. *How Now Shall We Live?* Wheaton, IL: Tyndale, 1999.

Eckman, James P. *The Truth about Worldviews: A Biblical Understanding of Worldview Alternatives*. Wheaton, IL: Crossway, 2004.

Geisler, Norman L. *False Gods of Our Time*. Eugene, OR: Harvest, 1985.

Geisler, Norman L. and William D. Watkins. *Worlds Apart: A Handbook on World Views*. Grand Rapids, MI: Baker, 1989.

Guinness, Os and John Seel. *No God but God*. Chicago, IL: Moody, 1992.

Hoffecker, W. Andrew and Gary Scott Smith. *Building a Christian World View*. Phillipsburg, NJ: Presbyterian & Reformed, 1986.

Lewis, C. S. *The Pilgrim's Regress: An Allegorical Apology for Christianity, Reason, and Romanticism*. Grand Rapids, MI: Eerdmans, 1992.

Moreland, J. P. and William Lane Craig. *Philosophical Foundations for a Christian Worldview*. Downers Grove, IL: InterVarsity, 2003.

Nash, Ronald. *Worldviews in Conflict: Choosing Christianity in a World of Ideas*. Grand Rapids, MI: Zondervan, 1992.

Naugle, David K. *Worldview: The History of a Concept*. Grand Rapids, MI: Eerdmans, 2002.

Noebel, David A. *Understanding the Times: The Collision of Today's Competing Worldviews*. Manitou Springs, CO: Summit Press, 2006.

Olasky, Marvin N. and Joel Belz. *Whirled Views: Tracking Today's Culture Storms*. Wheaton, IL: Crossway, 1997.

Pearcey, Nancy. *Total Truth: Liberating Christianity from Its Cultural Captivity*. Wheaton, IL: Crossway, 2004.

Raeper, William and Linda Edwards. *A Brief Guide to Ideas*. Grand Rapids, MI: Zondervan, 2000.

Schaeffer, Francis A. *How Should We Then Live? The Rise and Decline of Western Thought and Culture*. Wheaton, IL: Crossway, 1983.

———. *Naming the Elephant: Worldview as a Concept*. Downers Grove, IL: InterVarsity, 2004.

Sire, James W. *The Universe Next Door: A Basic Worldview Catalog*. Downers Grove, IL: InterVarsity, 2004.

Sproul, R. C. *The Consequences of Ideas: Understanding the Concepts That Shaped Our World*. Wheaton, IL: Crossway, 2000.

---

[3] Norman L. Geisler and William D. Watkins, *Worlds Apart: A Handbook on Worldviews* (Grand Rapids, MI: Baker, 1989), 11.

[4] James W. Sire, *The Universe Next Door: A Basic Worldview Catalog* (Downers Grove, IL: InterVarsity, 1988), 17.

[5] Nancy Pearcey, *Total Truth* (Wheaton, IL: Crossway, 2004), 23.

Fact Sheets

WORLDVIEW: CHRISTIANITY
FACT SHEET

KEY VERSES:

1 Chronicles 12:32	1 Corinthians 2:16; 9:19–23	Colossians 2
Matthew 22:34–40	2 Corinthians 10:4–5	Philippians 2:5
Acts 17:16ff	Ephesians 4:22–24	1 Peter 1:13–16
Romans 12:1–2		

KEY ORGANIZATIONS:

American Vision | www.americanvision.com | 770.222.7266 |

Barna Research Group | www.barna.org | 805.639.0000 |

Biblical Worldview | www.christianworldview.net |

Centurions Program | www.breakpoint.org/resources/centurions | 877.478.0100 |

Christian Research Institute | www.equip.org | 888.700.0274 |

Nehemiah Institute | www.nehemiahinstitute.com | 800.948.3101 |

Probe Ministries | www.probe.org | 972.480.0240 |

Stand to Reason | www.str.org | 800.273.2766 |

Summit Ministries | www.summit.org | 719.685.9103 |

Veritas Forum | www.veritas.org | 617.491.2055 |

KEY QUOTES:

"I now believe that the balance of reasoned considerations tells heavily in favour of the religious, even of the Christian view of the world."[1]

"The Christian belief system, which the Christian knows to be grounded in divine revelation, is relevant to all of life."[2]

"The basic problem of the Christians in this country in the last eighty years or so, in regard to society and in regard to government, is that they have seen things in bits and pieces instead of totals."[3]

E. M. Joad, *Recovery of Belief* (London: Faber & Faber, 1955), 22.
arl F. H. Henry, *Toward a Recovery of Christian Belief* (Westchester, IL: Crossway, 1990), 113.
ancis A. Schaeffer, *A Christian Manifesto* (Westchester, IL: Crossway, 1981), 17.

KEY SOURCES:
(recommended titles appear in brown)

CHRISTIAN WORLDVIEW (DEVELOPMENT)

Colson, Charles W. and Ellen Santilli Vaughn. *Against the Night: Living in the New Dark Ages*. Ann Arbor, MI: Vine, 1989.

DeMar, Gary. *Thinking Straight in a Crooked World*. Asheville, NC: American Vision, 2001.

Henry, Carl F. H. *The Christian Mindset in a Secular Society: Promoting Evangelical Renewal and National Righteousness*. Portland, OR: Multnomah, 1984.

Kennedy, D. James and Jerry Newcombe. *Lord of All: Developing a Christian World-and-Life View*. Wheaton, IL: Crossway, 2005.

Lewis, C. S. *Mere Christianity*. San Francisco: HarperSanFrancisco, 2001.

MacArthur, John, Richard Mayhue, and John A. Hughes, eds. *Think Biblically! Recovering a Christian Worldview*. Wheaton, IL: Crossway, 2003.

Noebel, David A. *Understanding the Times: The Collision of Today's Competing Worldviews*. Manitou Springs, CO: Summit Press, 2006.

Orr, James. *The Christian View of God and the World*. Grand Rapids, MI: Kregel, 1989.

Pearcey, Nancy. *Total Truth: Liberating Christianity from Its Cultural Captivity*. Wheaton, IL: Crossway, 2004.

Phillips, W. Gary and William E. Brown. *Making Sense of Your World: From a Biblical Viewpoint*. Chicago, IL: Moody, 1991.

Schaeffer, Francis A. *A Christian Manifesto*. Westchester, IL: Crossway, 1981.

———. *The Complete Works of Francis A. Schaeffer*. 5 vols. Westchester, IL: Crossway, 1982.

Walsh, Brian J. and J. Richard Middleton. *The Transforming Vision: Shaping a Christian World View*. Downers Grove, IL: InterVarsity, 1984.

Wright, N. T. *Simply Christian: Why Christianity Makes Sense*. San Francisco: HarperSanFrancisco, 2006.

BIBLE SURVEY

Arnold, Bill T. and Bryan Beyer. *Encountering the Old Testament: A Christian Survey*. Grand Rapids, MI: Baker, 1999.

Carson, D. A. and Douglas J. Moo. *An Introduction to the New Testament*. Grand Rapids, MI: Zondervan, 2005.

Dillard, Raymond B. and Tremper Longman. *An Introduction to the Old Testament*. Grand Rapids, MI: Zondervan, 1994.

Elwell, Walter A. and Robert W. Yarbrough. *Encountering the New Testament: A Historical and Theological Survey*. Grand Rapids, MI: Baker, 2005.

Wright, N. T. *The Resurrection of the Son of God*. Minneapolis: Fortress Press, 2003.

WORLDVIEW: COSMIC HUMANISM
FACT SHEET

KEY VERSES:

Genesis 1:1, 27
Psalm 115
John 1:1–3; 14:6

Acts 4:10–12
Romans 2:23
2 Corinthians 11:3–4, 13–15

Colossians 1:15–20; 2
Hebrews 9:27
1 John 1:7–10

KEY ORGANIZATIONS:

Christian Research Institute | www.equip.org | 888.700.0274 |

Spiritual Counterfeits Project | www.scp-inc.org | 510.540.0300 |

Summit Ministries | www.summit.org | 719.685.9103 |

Watchman Fellowship, Inc. | www.watchman.org | 205.833.2858 |

KEY QUOTES:

"The New Age movement… is an extremely large, loosely structured network of organizations and individuals bound together by common values (based in mysticism and monism—the world view that 'all is one') and a common vision (a coming 'new age' of peace and mass enlightenment, the 'Age of Aquarius')." [A]ll New Agers believe that 'all is one'—everything that exists consists of one and the same essence or reality. A second assumption is that this Ultimate Reality is neither dead matter nor unconscious energy. It is Being, Awareness, and Bliss (which is to say, a Hindu conception of God as an impersonal, infinite consciousness and force). The first two assumptions imply two more: all that is, is God (which is pantheism); and man, a part of 'all that is,' is likewise divine."[1]

All that is can form itself into individual droplets of consciousness. Because you are part of all that is, you have literally always been, yet there was the instant when that individual energy current that is you was formed. Consider that the ocean is God. It has always been. Now reach in and grab a cup full of water. In that instant, the cup becomes individual, but it has always been, has it not? This is the case with your soul. There was an instant when you became a cup of energy, but it was of an immortal original Being. You have always been because what it is that you are is God, or Divine Intelligence, but God takes individual forms… As that little form grows in power, in selfhood, in its own consciousness of self, it becomes larger and more Godlike. Then it becomes God."[2]

"There are two fundamental problems with the doctrine of theological monism. First, it is not really theology. We have always known that the universe exists; to simply change its name from 'universe' to 'God' is a meaningless tautology and does not answer the real questions of the origin and purpose of the world or the nature of God. Second, the 'God' of monism is fatally flawed. Since he (or 'it,' which is more accurate) is of one essence with creation and consciousness, God is thus the origin of the imperfection and evil in our world; the foulest deeds and thoughts of humanity literally become attributes of God."[3]

---

iot Miller, *A Crash Course on the New Age Movement* (Grand Rapids, MI: Baker, 1989), 15–16.
ry Zukav (a New Ager), *The Seat of the Soul* (New York: Fireside, 1989), 185–86.
ark C. Albrecht, *Reincarnation: A Christian Critique of a New Age Doctrine* (Downers Grove, IL: InterVarsity, 1982), 106.

KEY PROPONENT SOURCES:

Blavatsky, H. P. *The Secret Doctrine: The Synthesis of Science, Religion, and Philosophy*. Pasadena, CA: Theosophical University Press, 1977.

Campbell, Joseph and Bill D. Moyers. *The Power of Myth*. New York: Doubleday, 1988.

Capra, Fritjof. *The Tao of Physics: An Exploration of the Parallels between Modern Physics and Eastern Mysticism*. Boston, MA: Shambhala, 2000.

Castaneda, Carlos. *The Teachings of Don Juan: A Yaqui Way of Knowledge*. Berkeley, CA: Univ. of California Press, 1998.

Chopra, Deepak. *Ageless Body, Timeless Mind: The Quantum Alternative to Growing Old*. New York: Harmony, 1993.

Ferguson, Marilyn. *The Aquarian Conspiracy: Personal and Social Transformation in the 1980s*. New York: St. Martin's Press, 1980.

Fox, Matthew. *The Coming of the Cosmic Christ: The Healing of Mother Earth and the Birth of a Global Renaissance*. San Francisco: Harper & Row, 1988.

Gawain, Shakti. *Creative Visualization: Use the Power of Your Imagination to Create What You Want in Your Life*. Navato, CA: New World Library, 2002.

MacLaine, Shirley. *Out on a Limb*. New York: Bantam, 1983.

Muller, Robert. *New Genesis: Shaping a Global Spirituality*. Garden City, NY: Doubleday, 1982.

Peck, M. Scott. *The Road Less Traveled: A New Psychology of Love, Traditional Values, and Spiritual Growth*. New York: Simon & Schuster, 2002.

Pirsig, Robert M. *Zen and the Art of Motorcycle Maintenance*. New York: W. Morrow, 1999.

Prophet, Mark and Elizabeth Clare Prophet. *The Lost Teachings of Jesus*. Livingston, MT: Summit Univ. Press, 1986.

Spangler, David. *Emergence: The Rebirth of the Sacred*. New York: Dell, 1984.

KEY CHRISTIAN SOURCES/CRITIQUES:

(recommended titles appear in brown)

Albrecht, Mark. *Reincarnation, a Christian Appraisal*. Downers Grove, IL: InterVarsity, 1982.

Alnor, William M. *Ufos in the New Age: Extraterrestrial Messages and the Truth of Scripture*. Grand Rapids, MI: Baker, 1992.

Ankerberg, John, John Weldon, and Craig Branch. *Thieves of Innocence*. Eugene, OR: Harvest, 1993.

Clark, David K. and Norman L. Geisler. *Apologetics in the New Age: A Christian Critique of Pantheism*. Grand Rapids, MI: Baker, 1990.

Groothuis, Douglas. *Confronting the New Age: How to Resist a Growing Religious Movement*. Downers Grove, IL: InterVarsity, 1988.

————. *Deceived by the Light*. Eugene, OR: Harvest, 1995.

————. *Unmasking the New Age*. Downers Grove, IL: InterVarsity, 1986.

Halverson, Dean C. *Crystal Clear: Understanding and Reaching New Agers*. Colorado Springs, CO: NavPress, 1990.

Mangalwadi, Vishal. *When the New Age Gets Old: Looking for a Greater Spirituality*. Downers Grove, IL: InterVarsity, 1992.

Melton, J. Gordon, Jerome Clark, and A. Kelly Aidan. *New Age Encyclopedia*. Detroit, MI: Gale Research, 1990.

Miller, Elliot. *A Crash Course on the New Age Movement: Describing and Evaluating a Growing Social Force*. Grand Rapids, MI: Baker, 1989.

Noebel, David A. *Understanding the Times: The Collision of Today's Competing Worldviews*. Manitou Springs, CO: Summit Press, 2006.

Sire, James W. *Shirley MacLaine and the New Age Movement*. Downers Grove, IL: InterVarsity, 1988.

Rhodes, Ron. *The Counterfeit Christ of the New Age Movement*. Grand Rapids, MI: Baker, 1990.

Tucker, Ruth. *Another Gospel: Alternative Religions and the New Age Movement*. Grand Rapids, MI: Zondervan, 1989.

WORLDVIEW: ISLAM
FACT SHEET

KEY TERMS:

God: Allah

Islam: Submission to Allah

Muslim: One submitted to Allah

Muhammad: Ultimate and final prophet of Allah

Qur'an: Word of Allah

KEY FACTS:

STATS	• About 1/5th of the world's population is Muslim • Approximately three-quarters of Muslims are non-Arabs • About 5 million live in North America
DATES	• 570 AD — Muhammad is born • 610 AD — Muhammad receives his first visions • 622 AD — Muhammad flees to Medina (this event, known as the Hijira, initiates the Muslim calendar) • 630 AD — Muslims conquer Mecca • 632 AD — Muhammad dies • 636–640 AD — The early conquests of Damascus, Jerusalem, Egypt, and Persia • 650 AD — The canon of the Qur'an established
PILLARS	• The confession of faith: "There is no God but Allah, and Muhammad is his prophet" • Prayers five times a day, facing Mecca • Almsgiving (about 1/40th of income and holdings), primarily for the poor • Fasting during the month of Ramadan • Pilgrimage to Mecca
BELIEFS	• Monotheism • Prophets • Holy books • Angels and jinn • Judgment day • Muslims reject the Trinity • Muslims deny the deity and sonship of Jesus Christ • Muslims deny that Jesus died upon the cross, thus also denying his resurrection • Muslims assert that the Bible is untrustworthy, though the Qur'an is flawless • Muslims face a day of judgment based on good and bad works

KEY PROPONENT SOURCES:

Ahmad, Khurshic, ed. *Islam: Its Meaning and Message.* Leichester, UK: The Islamic Foundation, 1999.

Rahman, Fazlur. *Islam.* Chicago: University of Chicago Press, 1979.

Tabbarah, Afif and Rohi Baalbaki. *The Spirit of Islam: Doctrine and Teachings.* Beirut: Dar El-Ilm Lilmalayin, 1988.

Fact Sheets

KEY CHRISTIAN SOURCES/CRITIQUES:

(recommended titles appear in brown)

ISLAM (GENERAL)	Anderson, Norman. *Islam in the Modern World: A Christian Perspective*. Leicester, UK: APOLLOS/InterVarsity, 1990. Geisler, Norman L. and Abdul Saleeb. *Answering Islam: The Crescent in the Light of the Cross*. Grand Rapids, MI: Baker, 1993. Noebel, David A. *Understanding the Times: The Collision of Today's Competing Worldviews*. Manitou Springs, CO: Summit Press, 2006. Robinson, Stuart. *Mosques and Miracles*. Upper Mt. Gravalt, AU: City Harvest, 2004. Saal, William J. *Reaching Muslims for Christ*. Chicago, IL: Moody, 1991. Schmidt, Alvin J. *Failure of Islam, Triumph of the West*. Boston: Regina Orthodox Press, 2004. Shorrosh, Anis A. *Islam Revealed: A Christian Arab's View of Islam*. Nashville: Thomas Nelson, 1988. St. Clair-Tisdall, W. *Christian Reply to Muslim Objections*. Villach, Austria: Light of Life, 1980. Woodberry, J. Dudley, ed. *Muslims and Christians on the Emmaus Road*. Monrovia, CA: MARC, 1989.
HISTORY	Lewis, Bernard. *What Went Wrong? Western Impact and Middle Eastern Response*. New York: Oxford University Press, 2002. Trifkovic, Serge. *The Sword of the Prophet, Islam: History, Theology, Impact on the World*. Boston, MA: Regina Orthodox Press, 2002. Ye'or, Bat. *Islam and Dhimmitude: Where Civilizations Collide*. Teaneck, NJ: Fairleigh Dickinson Univ. Press, 2002.
BELIEFS	Halverson, Dean C. "Islam." *The Compact Guide to World Religions*, Dean C. Halverson, ed. Minneapolis: Bethany, 1996. 103–120. Markham, Ian S., ed. *A World Religions Reader*. Malden, MA: Blackwell, 2000. 301-331. Cragg, Kenneth. *The Call of the Minaret*. New York: Oxford University Press, 1956. Dashti, 'Ali. *23 Years: A Study of the Prophetic Career of Mohammad*. Translated by F. R. C. Bagley. London: George Allen & Unwin, 1985. Hamada, Louis. *Understanding the Arab World*. Nashville: Thomas Nelson, 1990.
RADICAL ISLAM	Bodansky, Yossef. *Bin Laden: The Man Who Declared War on America*. New York: Random, 2001. El Schafi, Abd. *Behind the Veil*. Caney, KS: Pioneer Book Company, 2001. Horowitz, David. *Unholy Alliance: Radical Islam and the American Left*. Washington DC: Regnery, 2004. Jabbour, Nabeel. *The Rumbling Volcano: Islamic Fundamentalism in Egypt*. Pasadena, CA: Mandate Press, 1993. Rashid, Ahmed. *Jihad: The Rise of Militant Islam in Central Asia*. New Haven, CT: Yale Univ. Press, 2002.

Fact Sheets

WORLDVIEW: MARXISM
FACT SHEET

KEY TERMS:

Bourgeois: The social/economic class that owns private property and the means of production

Communism: The Marxist dream of a future utopia in which all resources for production are owned in common by a classless society

Communist Manifesto: The 1848 political tract issued by Karl Marx and Friedrich Engels which outlined the goal and means of achieving of a classless society (i.e. Communism) through a proletarian revolution

Marxism: The ideology of Karl Marx based upon atheism, dialectical materialism, evolution, and socialism

Proletariat: The working or labor class of society

KEY FACTS:

- Current Communist Countries:

World Ranking	Country	Population	Source
#1 (19.62%)	**China**	1,334,620,000	Chinese govt. population counter (Dec. 2009)
#13 (1.26%)	**Vietnam**	85,789,573	2009 census (Apr. 2009)
#47 (0.35%)	**North Korea**[1]	24,051,706	UN estimate (Oct. 2008)
#75 (0.16%)	**Cuba**	11,204,000	UN estimate (Jul. 2009)
#104 (0.093%)	**Laos**	6,320,000	UN estimate (Jul. 2009)

- Current Number of Citizens in Communist Countries (2009): 1.5 billion
- People Killed by Communism: 110,000,000[2]

KEY VERSES:
Exodus 20:15–17   Acts 5:1–4
Psalm 14   Ephesians 4:28

KEY ORGANIZATIONS:
Christian Anti-Communism Crusade | www.schwarzreport.org | 719.685.9103 |

KEY QUOTES:

[Pro-Marxist speaker] "I think I have to give an even broader historical characterization of the moment in which American Marxists find themselves and in which our pedagogical work takes its significance. Lenin said that the two necessary [but not sufficient] preconditions for social revolution are a class-conscious proletariat and a revolutionary intelligentsia. If, as intellectuals, we can necessarily play only a marginal role in the development of the former, the

---

lthough North Korea has removed all communist terms from its constitution and officially declared itself to be a *socialist* state, in practice very
le has changed. Some sources may not classify it as a communist state, however.
tp://www.hawaii.edu/powerkills/NOTE5.HTM

task of creating the latter is clearly our fundamental one. To create a Marxist culture in this country, to make Marxism an unavoidable presence and a distinct, original, and unmistakable voice in American social, cultural, and intellectual life, in short to form a Marxist intelligentsia for the struggles of the future—this seems to me the supreme mission of a Marxist pedagogy and a radical intellectual life today."[3]

"Marx… taught that God was a projection of man's radical alienation: from himself, from his labor, and from a human community cruelly divided by class barriers. Man's salvation, in Marx's view, thus lay within history, in the creation of a mundane utopia… Lenin, in turn, believed that the advent of this radically secular version of the coming kingdom could be dramatically accelerated by revolutionary action… Whereas Marx simply treated religion contemptuously as a source of man's alienation, Lenin hated the church and saw in it a powerful rival for hearts and minds… The communist animus against religion—and especially Christianity—was no accident: It was an essential part of the Marxist-Leninist package. A communism that had a benign view of Christianity was no more possible than a communism that had a benign view of democracy, or of market economies. Something had to give. As things worked out, of course, it was communism that 'gave.' And the delicious irony was that it 'gave' because what generations of communists took to be mere fantasy—the Christian faith of the people of central and eastern Europe—proved more attractive, more resilient, more revolutionary, and more accurate to human experience than the secular doctrine that proclaimed itself the ultimate expression of revolutionary consciousness."[4]

KEY PROPONENTS:

- Frederick Engels (Deceased)
- Frederic R. Jameson (Duke University)
- Frank Lentrichia (Duke University)
- V. I. Lenin (Deceased)
- Karl Marx; (Deceased)
- Herbert Marcuse (Deceased)
- Joseph Stalin (Deceased)

KEY PROPONENT SOURCES:

Marx, Karl. *Das Kapital*. Washington DC: Regnery, 2000.
Marx, Karl and Friedrich Engels. *On Religion*. New York: Schocken, 1964.
Marx, Karl, Friedrich Engels, et. al. *The Communist Manifesto*. New York: Oxford Univ. Press, 1998.
McFadden, Charles Joseph. *The Philosophy of Communism*. New York: Benziger Brothers, 1939.

KEY CHRISTIAN SOURCES/CRITIQUES:

Bauman, Michael and Lissa Roche, eds. *Man and Marxism: Religion and the Communist Retreat*. Hillsdale, MI: Hillsdale College Press, 1991.
Conway, David. *A Farewell to Marx: An Outline and Appraisal of His Theories*. New York: Penguin, 1987.
Courtois, Stéphane. *The Black Book of Communism*. Translated by Jonathan Murphy and Mark Kramer. Cambridge: Harvard Univ. Press, 1999.
McFadden, Charles Joseph. *Christianity Confronts Communism*. Chicago, IL: Franciscan Herald, 1982.
Noebel, David A. *Understanding the Times*. Manitou Springs, CO: Summit Press, 2006.
Schwarz, Frederick Charles. *Beating the Unbeatable Foe*. Washington DC: Regnery, 1996.
———. *You Can Trust the Communists to Be Communists*. Englewood Cliffs, NJ: Prentice-Hall, 1960.
Solzhenitsyn, Aleksandr. *The Mortal Danger: How Misconceptions About Russia Imperil America*. Translated by Michael Nicholson and Alexis Klimoff. New York: Harper & Row, 1980.
Sowell, Thomas. *Marxism: Philosophy and Economics*. New York: Quill, 1985.

[3] Frederic Jameson, in Stephen H. Balch and Herbert I. London, "The Tenured Left," *Commentary* 82:4 (October 1986).
[4] George Weigel, "The Collapse of Communism," *The World & I*, vol. 8 (May 1993), 372–73.

WORLDVIEW: POSTMODERNISM
FACT SHEET

KEY TERMS:

Modernism: A broad and somewhat ambiguous term used to embrace a diverse range of arts, attitudes, philosophies, and cultural moods which emerged following the 18th century Enlightenment. Epistemologically it is characterized by a strong belief in rationalism and science as a well as a strong skepticism in both the supernatural and the authority of religion

Postmodernism: A broad and somewhat ambiguous term used to describe a philosophical and cultural reaction to the convictions of Modernism (which is sometimes equated with Humanism). Postmodernism is the philosophical proposal that reality is ultimately inaccessible by human investigation, that knowledge is a social construction, that truth-claims are political power plays, and that the meaning of words is to be determined by readers not authors. In brief, reality is what individuals or social groups make it to be

Metanarrative: a single overarching objective interpretation or narrative of reality

KEY FACTS:

- Seventy-two percent of Americans agree, "There is no such thing as absolute truth; two people could define truth in totally conflicting ways, but both could still be correct."[1]
- Seventy-one percent of Americans agree, "There are no absolute standards that apply to everybody in all situations."[2]
- Fifty-three percent of those who claim there is no such thing as absolute truth identify themselves as born-again Christians.[3]
- Forty-two percent of those who identify themselves as evangelical Christians agree, "There is no such thing as absolute truth; two people could define truth in totally conflicting ways but both could still be correct."[4]

KEY VERSES:

Joshua 24:14–15
Judges 17:6; 18:21
1 Kings 18:21
Psalm 31:5; 146:5–6

Proverbs 9:10
Isaiah 59:15
Jeremiah 7:28
Malachi 2:6

John 1:17; 3–4; 14:6; 16:13; 18:38
Romans 1:18-32; 2:8–9
2 Timothy 2:15; 3:14–17
2 John 4–6

KEY QUOTES:

POSTMODERNISTS

"For the pragmatist [postmodernist], true sentences are not true because they correspond to reality, and so there is no need to worry what sort of reality, if any, a given sentence corresponds to – no need to worry about what 'makes' it true."[5]

"Truth isn't outside of power, or lacking in power: contrary to a myth whose history and functions would repay further study, truth isn't the reward of free spirits, the child of protracted solitude, nor the privilege of those who have succeeded in liberating themselves. Truth is a thing of this world: it is produced only by virtue of multiple forms of constraint. And it induces regular effects of power. Each society has its regime of truth, its 'general

George Barna, *Virtual America* (Ventura, CA: Regal, 1994), 83, 283.
Ibid., 85, 230.
Ibid., 83.
Ibid.
Richard Rorty, *Consequences of Pragmatism* (Minneapolis: University of Minnesota Press, 1982), xvi.

Fact Sheets

politics' of truth: that is, the types of discourse which it accepts and makes function as true; the mechanisms and instances which enable one to distinguish true from false statements, the means by which each is sanctioned; the techniques and procedures accorded value in the acquisition of truth; the status of those who are charged with saying what counts as true."[6]

CRITIQUE

"There is one thing a professor can be absolutely certain of: almost every student entering the university believes, or says he believes, that truth is relative. If this belief is put to the test, one can count on the students' reaction: They will be uncomprehending. That anyone would regard the proposition as not self-evident astonishes them, as though he were calling into question 2+2=4... Openness—and the relativism that makes it the only plausible stance in the face of various claims to truth and various ways of life and kinds of human beings—is the great insight of our times... The study of history and of culture [according to this view] teaches that all the world was mad in the past; men always thought they were right, and that led to wars, persecutions, slavery, xenophobia, racism, and chauvinism. The point is not to correct the mistakes and really be right; rather it is not to think you are right at all. The students, of course, cannot defend their opinion. It is something with which they have been indoctrinated."[7]

"Ours is an age in which 'conclusions' are arrived at by distributing questionnaires to a cross-section of the population or by holding a microphone before the lips of casually selected passers-by in the street... In the sphere of religious and moral thinking we are rapidly heading for a state of intellectual anarchy in which the difference between truth and falsehood will no longer be recognized. Indeed, it would seem possible that the words true and false will eventually (and logically) be replaced by the words likable and dislikable."[8]

KEY PROPONENTS:

- Walter Truett Anderson
- Walter Brueggemann
- Jacques Derrida
- Stanley Fish
- Michel Foucault
- Jean Francois Lyotard
- J. Richard Middleton
- Richard Rorty
- Brian J. Walsh

KEY PROPONENT SOURCES:

Anderson, Walter Truett, ed. *The Truth About the Truth: De-Confusing and Re-Constructing the Postmodern World.* New York: Putnam, 1995.

————. *Reality Isn't What It Used to Be.* San Francisco: Harper & Row, 1990.

Derrida, Jacques. *Of Grammatology.* Translated by Gayatri Chakravorty Spivak. Baltimore: Johns Hopkins Univ. Press, 1998.

Fish, Stanley Eugene. *Is There a Text in This Class? The Authority of Interpretive Communities.* Cambridge: Harvard Univ. Press, 1980.

Foucault, Michel. *The Archaeology of Knowledge and the Discourse on Language.* New York: Knopf, 1972.

————. *Madness and Civilization: A History of Insanity in the Age of Reason.* Translated by Richard Howard. New York: Vintage, 1973.

————. *The Order of Things: An Archaeology of the Human Sciences.* New York: Vintage, 1994.

[6] Michel Foucault, "Truth and Power," *The Foucault Reader,* Paul Rabinow, ed. (New York: Pantheon, 1984), 72–73.
[7] Allan Bloom, *The Closing of the American Mind* (New York: Simon & Schuster, 1987), 25-26.
[8] Harry Blamires, *The Christian Mind: How Should a Christian Think?* (Ann Arbor, MI: Servant Books, 1963), 107.

Summit Ministries © 2009

Lyotard, Jean François. *The Differend: Phrases in Dispute.* Translated by Georges Van Den Abbeele. Minneapolis: Univ. of Minnesota Press, 1988.

———. *The Postmodern Condition: A Report on Knowledge.* Translated by Brian Massumi and Geoff Bennington. Minneapolis: Univ. of Minnesota Press, 1984.

Nietzsche, Friedrich. *Beyond Good and Evil.* Translated by Helen Zimmern. Mineola, NY: Dover, 1997.

———. *On the Genealogy of Morals.* Translated by Walter Arnold Kaufmann. New York: Vintage, 1989.

Rorty, Richard. *Achieving Our Country: Leftist Thought in Twentieth-Century America.* Cambridge: Harvard Univ. Press, 1998.

———. *Philosophy and Social Hope.* New York: Penguin, 1999.

———. *Philosophy and the Mirror of Nature.* Princeton: Princeton Univ. Press, 1979.

KEY CHRISTIAN SOURCES/CRITIQUES:

(recommended titles appear in brown)

Allen, David L. "Preaching and Postmodernism: An Evangelical Comes to the Dance." *Southern Baptist Journal of Theology 5*, no. 2 (2001): 62–78.

Beckwith, Francis and Gregory Koukl. *Relativism: Feet Firmly Planted in Mid-Air.* Grand Rapids, MI: Baker, 1998.

Cabal, Ted. "An Introduction of Postmodernity: Where Are We, How Did We Get Here, and Can We Get Home?" *Southern Baptist Journal of Theology 5*, no. 2 (2001).

Carson, D. A. *The Gagging of God: Christianity Confronts Pluralism.* Grand Rapids, MI: Zondervan, 1996.

Copan, Paul. *True for You, but Not for Me: Deflating the Slogans That Leave Christians Speechless.* Minneapolis: Bethany, 1998.

Dockery, David S., ed. *The Challenge of Postmodernism: An Evangelical Engagement.* Grand Rapids, MI: Baker, 2001.

Erickson, Millard J. "Foundationalism: Dead or Alive?" *Southern Baptist Journal of Theology 5*, no. 2 (2001): 20–32.

———. *Truth or Consequences: The Promise and Perils of Postmodernism.* Downers Grove, IL: InterVarsity, 2001.

Groothuis, Douglas R. *Truth Decay: Defending Christianity against the Challenges of Postmodernism.* Downers Grove, IL: InterVarsity, 2000.

Lundin, Roger. *The Culture of Interpretation: Christian Faith and the Postmodern World.* Grand Rapids, MI: Eerdmans, 1993.

McCallum, Dennis, ed. *The Death of Truth.* Minneapolis: Bethany, 1996.

Noebel, David A. *Understanding the Times: The Collision of Today's Competing Worldviews.* Manitou Springs, CO: Summit Press, 2006.

Norris, Christopher. *The Truth About Postmodernism.* Cambridge: Blackwell, 1993.

Parker, James. "A Requiem for Postmodernism, Wither Now?" *Southern Baptist Journal of Theology 5*, no. 2 (2001).

Schreiner, Thomas R. "The Perils of Ignoring Postmodernism." *Southern Baptist Journal of Theology 5*, no. 2 (2001): 2–3.

Veith, Gene Edward. *Postmodern Times: A Christian Guide to Contemporary Thought and Culture.* Wheaton, IL: Crossway, 1994.

WORLDVIEW: SECULAR HUMANISM
FACT SHEET

KEY TERMS:

Humanism: The belief that humanity is the highest of all beings and that truth and knowledge thus rest in science and human reason

Humanist Manifesto: The title of three manifestos laying out a secular humanist worldview. They are *Humanist Manifesto I* (1933), *Humanist Manifesto II* (1973), and *Humanist Manifesto III* (2000), although the latter is actually titled *Planetary Humanism*. The central theme of all three is the elaboration of a philosophy and value system that does not include belief in God

KEY VERSES:

Psalm 14:1   Romans 1:21–23   Colossians 2:1–8
Acts 17:16ff   2 Corinthians 10:5

KEY QUOTES:

HUMANISTS	"There is no place in the Humanist worldview for either immortality or God in the valid meanings of those terms. Humanism contends that instead of the gods creating the cosmos, the cosmos, in the individualized form of human beings giving rein to their imagination, created the gods."[1]

"The classroom must and will become an area of conflict between the old and the new—the rotting corpse of Christianity, together with its adjacent evils and misery and the new faith of Humanism, resplendent in its promise of a world in which the never-realized Christian idea of 'Love thy Neighbor' will finally be achieved."[2] |
| **CRITIQUES** | "The ultimate failure of Secular Humanism is in the fact that of its very nature it promises what it cannot fulfill. By encouraging people to put their trust in earthly happiness it programs them for disillusionment. This is in large measure the reason why the history of the modern world has been characterized, intellectually, by philosophies of pessimism like Existentialism and by often-rancorous bitterness over various plans for worldly improvement. In the twentieth century, mass slaughter has been perpetrated not by religious believers in opposition to heresy but by secularists convinced that their plan for a worldly utopia is the only possible one."[3]

"Bertrand Russell, a clear-headed liberal humanist, wrote as follows about what he called 'the night of nothingness': 'There is darkness without and when I die there will be darkness within. There is no splendor, no vastness, anywhere; only triviality for a moment, and then nothing.' That says it all. Whereas for the Christian nothing is finally trivial, for the humanist everything becomes finally trivial, death, as Russell says, producing precisely that effect."[4] |

---

[1] Corliss Lamont, *The Philosophy of Humanism* (New York: Frederick Ungar Publishing, 1982), 145.
[2] John J. Dunphy, "A Religion for a New Age," *The Humanist*, January/February 1983, 26.
[3] James Hitchcock, *What is Secular Humanism? Why Humanism Became Secular and How It Is Changing Our World* (Ann Arbor, MI: Servant Books, 1982), 141.
[4] J. I. Packer and Thomas Howard, *Christianity: The True Humanism* (Waco, TX: Word, 1985), 231–32.

KEY PROPONENT SOURCES:

SECULAR HUMANISM (GENERAL)

Huxley, Aldous. *Brave New World*. New York: Harper & Row, 1989.

Huxley, Julian. *The Humanist Frame*. London: Allen & Unwin, 1961.

Huxley, Julian, Gilbert Murray, and Joseph Houldsworth Oldham. *Humanism*. London: Watts & Co., 1944.

Kurtz, Paul, ed. *The Humanist Alternative: Some Definitions of Humanism*. Buffalo, NY: Prometheus, 1973.

———. *Humanist Manifesto 2000: A Call for a New Planetary Humanism*. Amherst, NY: Prometheus, 2000.

———. *Humanist Manifesto I and II*. Buffalo, NY: Prometheus, 1980.

———. *A Secular Humanist Declaration*. Amherst, NY: Prometheus, 1980.

———. *Skepticism and Humanism: The New Paradigm*. New Brunswick, NJ: Transaction, 2001.

Lamont, Corliss. *Humanism as a Philosophy*. New York: Philosophical Library, 1949.

———. *The Philosophy of Humanism*. Amherst, NY: Humanist, 1996.

Morain, Lloyd and Mary S. Morain. *Humanism as the Next Step*. Amherst, NY: Humanist, 1998.

Skinner, B. F. *Walden Two*. New York: Macmillan, 1976.

SECULAR HUMANISM AS A RELIGION

Dewey, John. *A Common Faith*. New Haven, CT: Yale University Press, 1991.

Huxley, Julian. *Religion without Revelation*. Westport, CT: Greenwood, 1979.

Kurtz, Paul. *Eupraxophy: Living without Religion*. Buffalo, NY: Prometheus, 1989.

Potter, Charles Francis. *Humanism: A New Religion*. New York: Simon & Schuster, 1930.

———. *Humanizing Religion*. New York: Harper, 1933.

Sellars, Roy Wood. *Religion Coming of Age*. New York: Macmillan, 1928.

KEY CHRISTIAN SOURCES/CRITIQUES:

(recommended titles appear in brown)

Geisler, Norman L. *Is Man the Measure? An Evaluation of Contemporary Humanism*. Grand Rapids, MI: Baker, 1983.

Hitchcock, James. *What Is Secular Humanism? Why Humanism Became Secular and How It Is Changing Our World*. Ann Arbor, MI: Servant, 1982.

LaHaye, Tim. *The Battle for the Mind*. Old Tappan, NJ: Revell, 1980.

LaHaye, Tim and David A. Noebel. *Mind Siege: The Battle for Truth in the New Millennium*. Nashville: Word, 2000.

McDowell, Josh and Don Douglas Stewart. *Understanding Secular Religions*. San Bernardino, CA: Campus Crusade, 1982.

Noebel, David A. *Understanding the Times: The Collision of Today's Competing Worldviews*. Manitou Springs, CO: Summit Press, 2006.

Packer, J. I. and Thomas Howard. *Christianity: The True Humanism*. Waco, TX: Word, 1985.